Small Business Bankruptcy Reorganizations

AF703483

Small Business Bankruptcy Reorganizations

By The Honorable
JAMES A. PUSATERI,
KAREN S. KRESSIN,
JAMES J. O'MALLEY
Editors

BeardBooks
Washington, D.C.

Copyright © 1994 by John Wiley and Sons, Inc.
Originally published as a Wiley Law Publication, 1994
Reprinted 2005 by Beard Books, Washington, D.C.

ISBN 1-58798-260-9

Printed in the United States of America

This publication is designed to provide accurate and authoritative information in regard to the subject matter covered. It is sold with the understanding that the publisher is not engaged in rendering legal, accounting, or other professional services. If legal advice or other expert assistance is required, the service of a competent professional person should be sought.

—From a Declaration of Principles adopted jointly by a Committee of the American Bar Association and a Committee of Publishers

All rights reserved. No part of this publication may be reproduced or transmitted in any form, by any means, electronic or mechanical, including photocopy, recording, or any information storage or retrieval system, without permission in writing from the publisher.

PREFACE

Most business bankruptcies are small business bankruptcies. Small businesses face special problems when attempting to reorganize.

The purpose of this book is to guide the practitioner, bankruptcy specialist or not, through the process of reorganization, with special emphasis on small business cases. It addresses the problems of representing either side in a small business bankruptcy. The text provides some theoretical material as background, but it is intended primarily as a practice guide. Also, most of the chapters include forms or sample documents that apply the principles presented in the text.

This book benefits from the collective expertise of more than 20 bankruptcy specialists from a broad variety of backgrounds. The contribution of these authors constitutes the heart of this work. They offer insights from their own considerable experience that will be helpful to any attorney who handles small business bankruptcies.

June 1994

JAMES A. PUSATERI
KAREN S. KRESSIN
JAMES J. O'MALLEY

PREFACE

ACKNOWLEDGMENTS

The editors wish to thank, first and foremost, the authors of the chapters, without whom there would be no book. Special gratitude is due to the authors who introduced us to others who were willing to contribute chapters.

Chapter 6 benefitted from research and early drafting by Andrew S. Miller (then a summer associate), cite checking and proofreading by Silvestre A. Fontes (law clerk), and overall review and helpful comment from Neal D. Colton, attorney at law, all from the author's firm, Dechert Price & Rhoads. **Chapter 23** was made possible by the thoughtful comments and editorial assistance of Henry R. Setser, attorney at law, of Craft Fridkin & Rhyne, Kansas City, Missouri, the valuable research and cite-checking performed by paralegal Sharon I. Pentola, and the wordprocessing and formatting wizardry of the author's secretary, Doris Heinen. **Chapter 5** never would have gone to print without the extraordinary dedication and computer expertise of paralegal Jean Goodall. The research guidance of Fritz Snyder and Mary Burchill of the University of Kansas School of Law Library is also much appreciated. Mike Vetrano, our acquisition editor at Wiley Law Publications, deserves praise and thanks for patiently guiding this project from conception through completion.

The editors also wish to thank the law firms of the authors for the support that made this book possible. There are, of course, spouses, family members, and friends of the authors and editors, too numerous to mention, whose contribution is perhaps the most important of all.

J.A.P.
K.S.K.
J.O'M.

ABOUT THE CONTRIBUTORS

Christine M. Arguello is an Associate Professor of Law at the University of Kansas where she teaches creditors' and debtors' rights, trial advocacy, and contracts. Prior to joining the faculty in the fall of 1991, she was a partner in the law firm of Holland & Hart in Colorado. She is admitted to practice in Colorado and Florida and was in private practice for 11 years as a civil litigator with emphasis on banking litigation, secured transactions, bankruptcy, and debtor/creditor rights. She received her law degree from Harvard University where she was the articles editor of the *Harvard Civil Rights/Civil Liberties Law Review.*

Gary D. Barnes is a partner in the Kansas City office of Husch & Eppenberger. He represents financial institutions in bankruptcy and insolvency matters and serves as special counsel for several area banks. A Chapter 7 panel trustee, he has also served as a court-appointed bankruptcy examiner. He is co-chair of the ABA Task Force on ERISA plans in bankruptcy proceedings and is the chairman of the Ad Hoc Advisory Committee to the United States Bankruptcy Court for the Western District of Missouri. He received a J.D. from the University of Missouri-Kansas City and a B.A. from William Jewell College. He has been district director and counsel to Missouri Congressman Richard Bolling, and law clerk to Dennis J. Stewart, a former Chief Judge of the United States Bankruptcy Court for the Western District of Missouri.

Carl R. Clark is a graduate of Kansas State University (cum laude) and a graduate of the University of Kansas School of Law. He is a partner in the Overland Park, Kansas, firm of Lentz & Clark, P.A. He has been a Chapter 7 panel trustee in the District of Kansas since 1984 and his firm's practice is limited to representation of debtors and creditors in workouts, restructuring, and bankruptcy cases. He is a member of the Bankruptcy and Insolvency Section of the Kansas Bar Association and serves on the Bankruptcy Rules Committee for the District of Kansas Bankruptcy Court.

Mark A. Craige is a shareholder and director of Morrel, West, Saffa, Craige & Hicks, Inc., Tulsa, Oklahoma, where his practice is devoted to insolvency, reorganization, and related areas He received a B.S. in Computer Science and Accounting (with honors) from Southeastern Oklahoma State University and a J.D. from the University of Tulsa. He is certified in business bankruptcy law by the American Bankruptcy Board of Certification. He is active in the American Bankruptcy Institute and the Bankruptcy and Reorganization Section of the Oklahoma Bar Association. He is a frequent lecturer on bankruptcy topics and has published articles on bankruptcy in the Oklahoma Bar Journal. He is past editor of the Oklahoma Bar Association Bankruptcy Section Newsletter.

John J. Cruciani is a graduate of Benedictine College and the University of Missouri-Kansas City School of Law, where he was a member of the Bankruptcy Moot Court Team. He has clerked for the Overland Park, Kansas, law firm of Lentz & Clark, P.A., which limits its practice to bankruptcy and insolvency. He is a member of the American Bar Association and the American Bankruptcy Institute.

Mark A. Goucher is a graduate of the University of Missouri-Columbia School of Law. Following a two-year clerkship with United States Bankruptcy Judge Karen M. See, he associated, and is currently of counsel, with the law firm of Lentz & Clark, P.A., in Overland Park, Kansas. The firm's practice is limited to representation of debtors and creditors in workouts, restructurings, and bankruptcy matters.

Cynthia F. Grimes is a member of Levy & Craig, P.C., in Kansas City, Missouri. She received her B.A. (with highest distinction, Phi Beta Kappa) and J.D. from the University of Kansas. She was associate editor, *Kansas Law Review.* She was previously a law clerk for Judge John E. Rees of the Kansas Court of Appeals and for United States Bankruptcy Judge James A. Pusateri. She has published numerous articles regarding bankruptcy and frequently lectures on bankruptcy and commercial topics. She is admitted to the bar in Kansas and Missouri and practices primarily in the areas of bankruptcy and commercial litigation.

Paul M. Hoffmann is a member of Smith, Gill, Fisher & Butts, P.C., in Kansas City, Missouri, where he represents debtors, creditors, and other parties exclusively in bankruptcy cases and workouts. He received his B.S.B.A., summa cum laude, from the University of Nebraska at Omaha and his J.D. from the University of Michigan. He is a past-president of the Workout Professionals Association, former chairman of the Ad Hoc Advisory Committee for the United States Bankruptcy Court in the Western District of Missouri, and a frequent author and speaker on bankruptcy and workout matters. He also is certified in business bankruptcy law by the American Bankruptcy Board of Certification.

Patricia K. Kelly is a senior litigation attorney for the City of Colorado Springs, where she has represented the city in Chapter 11 airline cases and Chapter 9 municipality cases, among others. Prior to joining the city attorney's office, she was in private practice for three years, representing various parties in cases under all chapters of the Bankruptcy Code. After graduation from the University of Tulsa School of Law, she was law clerk for Mickey D. Wilson, United States Bankruptcy Judge for the Northern District of Oklahoma, and for the late John F. McGrath, Chief United States Bankruptcy Judge for the District of Colorado. She has published numerous articles on bankruptcy and commercial topics, is co-author of the *Trial Handbook for Colorado Lawyers,* and has frequently lectured on bankruptcy matters.

F. Stannard Lentz is a principal of the Overland Park, Kansas, law firm of Lentz & Clark, P.A., which limits its practice to matters relating to bankruptcy and insolvency. He is a graduate of Washburn University Law School and has been involved in bankruptcy and insolvency law practice for over 20 years. He served as a Chapter 7 panel trustee in the Kansas City Kansas Bankruptcy Court between 1974 and 1980. He is a frequent speaker for the Kansas Bar Association and other organizations in the areas of bankruptcy and insolvency. He has appeared in all editions of *Best Lawyers in America.* He is the immediate past president of the Bankruptcy and Insolvency Section of the Kansas Bar Association, and is a member of the American Bankruptcy Institute and the Kansas and Missouri bars.

Joel H. Levitin is a member of the Bankruptcy and Reorganization Group at Dechert Price & Rhoads in Philadelphia and New York, where he counsels and represents a broad range of debtors, creditors, and other parties in bankruptcy and reorganization matters and general commercial litigation. He graduated from Duke University (magna cum laude) and the University of Chicago Law School (with honors) and served as a law clerk to Judge Norma L. Shapiro of the United States District Court for the Eastern District of Pennsylvania. He is Chair of the Young Members Committee of the American Bankruptcy Institute and is an Adjunct Professor at Temple University School of Law, where he teaches a course on Corporate Reorganization in Chapter 11.

John Lewis, Jr., is an associate with the Kansas City, Missouri, law firm of Craft Fridkin & Rhyne. A cum laude graduate of Morehouse College in Atlanta and a graduate of the George Washington University National Law Center in Washington, D.C., he practices in the areas of bankruptcy, insolvency, and commercial law and also serves as a member of the panel of Chapter 7 trustees for the Western District of Missouri. He is a member of the American Bar Association, National Bar Association, American

Bankruptcy Institute, National Association of Bankruptcy Trustees, and the state bars of Missouri, Kansas, and Pennsylvania.

Douglas M. Neeb is a senior associate in the Kansas City law firm of Smith, Gill, Fisher & Butts, P.C. He focuses on representation of parties in workouts, bankruptcy matters, and commercial litigation. He received an A.B. and a J.D. from the University of Missouri-Columbia and is a member of the American Bankruptcy Institute. He has represented parties in bankruptcy cases in Missouri, Kansas, Texas, Arizona, New York, Pennsylvania, California, Florida, Georgia, and Minnesota. He has previously contributed supplemental material for George I. Wallach, *The Law of Sales Under the Uniform Commercial Code.*

Robert E. Nugent is a shareholder in the firm of Morris, Laing, Evans, Brock & Kennedy, Chartered, Wichita and Topeka, Kansas. He represents agricultural and business debtors, banks, and other creditors in insolvency matters, commercial litigation, and real estate cases. He has served as a Chapter 7 trustee. He is co-author with Hon. John K. Pearson and Mary Patricia Hesse of *Drafting Bankruptcy Reorganization Plans, 2d Ed.* (John Wiley & Sons, Inc. 1993). He has also contributed chapters and articles to the *Kansas Bankruptcy Handbook, 2d Ed.* and the Norton Bankruptcy Advisor. He is a frequent speaker to lawyers and bankers an bankruptcy and commercial law topics He received his B.A. from the University of Kansas and his J.D. from the University of Kansas School of Law.

Hon. David A. Scholl is a United States Bankruptcy Judge in the Eastern District of Pennsylvania, sitting in Philadelphia. Prior to his judicial appointment in August 1986, he had been an attorney and administrator in programs providing free legal services to indigent persons in civil matters in Philadelphia, Delaware County, and the Lehigh Valley area of Pennsylvania. He is a graduate of Franklin and Marshall College (Phi Beta Kappa) and Villanova Law School (Order of the Coif). He has authored almost 500 opinions reported in *Bankruptcy Reporter* and hundreds more published only in computer-accessed services since his appointment to the bench.

Mark A. Shaiken is a shareholder of Stinson, Mag & Fizzell, P.C. He practices primarily in bankruptcy and commercial litigation, and has represented creditors and debtors in Missouri, Kansas, New York, Pennsylvania, Virginia, Mississippi, Massachusetts, Texas, Iowa, and Nebraska in retail, commercial, manufacturing, real estate developer, and oil and gas bankruptcies. He has been a lecturer in continuing legal education programs and a variety of commercial law topics. He graduated from Washburn University Law School with a J.D. degree (cum laude) and served as the associate comments editor for the

Washburn Law Review. He also served as law clerk to James A. Pusateri, United States Bankruptcy Judge for the District of Kansas.

Paul D. Sinclair is a shareholder in the Kansas City, Missouri, law firm of Sinclair, Sawyer, Thompson & Haynes, P.C. He practices primarily in the areas of bankruptcy, insolvency, and business commercial litigation. He has been a frequent author and lecturer in the bankruptcy and real estate areas, and in 1989, the Missouri Bar Association gave him the W. Oliver Rasch Award, its highest award for writing. Topics of articles he has published include piercing the corporate veil, new home warranties, nonmarital property division, prejudgment interest, and stays in bankruptcy. He is a graduate of Boston College (magna cum laude) and a graduate of Georgetown University Law Center.

Lloyd C. Swartz is a shareholder of Consumer Bankruptcy Clinic, P.A., Topeka and Wichita, Kansas. He earned a B.S. in economics from Nebraska Wesleyan University and a J.D. from Washburn University Law School. He practices primarily in bankruptcy and insolvency. He served as Chapter 13 standing trustee for the District of Kansas from 1979 to 1990, and also as a Chapter 7 panel trustee during that period. He has published numerous articles and has delivered frequent lectures on bankruptcy topics.

David A. Warfield is a partner in the St. Louis office of Husch & Eppenberger. He practices in the business bankruptcy and insolvency areas, primarily representing debtors and secured creditors. He is a former co-chair of the Bankruptcy Committee of the Business Law Committee of the Bar Association of Metropolitan St. Louis. He has published articles in the *Commercial Law Journal* and *American Bankruptcy Law Journal*. He received his B.S.B.A. and J.D. from Washington University in St. Louis.

Joseph I. Wittman is a graduate of the University of Kansas and Washburn University Law School. He maintains a private practice of law in Topeka, Kansas, and represents both debtors and creditors under all chapters of the Bankruptcy Code. He has practiced bankruptcy law for over 14 years, and has served as a Chapter 7 panel trustee since 1980. He is a member of the Kansas Bar Association. He has served on the board of directors of the National Association of Bankruptcy Trustees for four years, having also served as that organization's treasurer and vice-president. In 1994 he is president of the Topeka Area Bankruptcy Council and president-elect of the National Association of Bankruptcy Trustees.

Cindi S. Woolery is an attorney at Stinson, Mag & Fizzell, P.C., in Kansas City, Missouri, where she practices in the litigation department, primarily in the area of creditors' rights. She graduated cum laude from the University of

Missouri-Columbia School of Law, where she also earned a master of business administration degree. She is a member of the Order of the Coif and was previously managing editor for the *Missouri Law Review.* She also served as law clerk to John R. Gibson of the Eighth Circuit Court of Appeals.

R. Greg Wright is a member of the Carpenter Professional Association, Topeka, Kansas, where he concentrates his representation in the areas of bankruptcy, commercial law, and general practice. He received a B.S. in education from Ohio University, Athens, Ohio. He also holds an M.A. from the Ohio State University, Columbus, Ohio, and an M.B.A. from Ohio University. His J.D. was earned from Washburn University Law School. He has lectured extensively on bankruptcy related topics and has written pieces for the *Washburn Law Journal.* He is admitted to practice in Kansas and Maryland. He is a member of the American, Kansas, and Topeka Bar Associations, and the Topeka Area Bankruptcy Council.

Kathleen V. Yurchak is an associate with Reed Smith Shaw & McClay in its Philadelphia, Pennsylvania, office. She practices primarily in bankruptcy and commercial litigation with a specific concentration in representing secured creditors in workouts and issues relating to lender liability. She has been a lecturer in continuing legal education programs on a variety of issues relating to commercial litigation and lender liability. She graduated from the University of Denver School of Law. She also served as a law clerk to Judge Patricia Ann Clark, United States Bankruptcy Judge for the District of Colorado.

SUMMARY CONTENTS

DETAILED CONTENTS

CHAPTER 1

SMALL BUSINESS BANKRUPTCY FROM THE PRACTITIONER'S PERSPECTIVE

Robert E. Nugent

§ 1.1 Small Business Bankruptcy in General

Except perhaps on Wall Street, representation of small businesses is the backbone of a business lawyer's practice. For the purposes of this book, a small business is virtually any business that is not "Big Business." The focus here is away from the megacompanies whose financial straits make national headlines and instead on the hometown grocery stores, "mom and pop" heating and air conditioning businesses, small manufacturers, agricultural businesses, non-chain motels, dress shops, and office building partnerships that from time to time find themselves in need of protection from creditors and a chance for a fresh start. These enterprises often have only a small number of creditors, and they may own only a single asset. These attributes do not always comport with the vision of the drafters of Chapter 11 of the Bankruptcy Code, and representation of either debtor or creditor in a small business bankruptcy can present special problems.

The small number of creditors in a small case means that committees are less frequently appointed, but there is more potential for lender control. When a major lender is undersecured, it or a small group of unsecured creditors can block the plan, especially if the owners want to retain an interest after bankruptcy. When a business is closely held, there may be problems involving transfers to insiders and guarantees by insiders. Also, reorganization may be hindered by the owner-manager's reluctance to let go of the reins. Counsel for a small business in bankruptcy needs to pay special attention to these aspects.

Small business cases are easier in some respects. More compact case management is possible, and it may be easier to coordinate the activities of company management and counsel. It is easier to negotiate with a small body of creditors. In a small case, the threat of cramdown is more useful for applying pressure on uncooperative creditors. It is easy to protect a senior lender's interest by solidifying the lender's lien position in relation to the junior creditors. A small case might lend itself to fast-track scheduling, and plan prepackaging and prefiling arrangements are easier. Labor and employee problems come up less often.

§ 1.2 Avenues Available to the Small Business in Trouble

Small businesses that are family farms are eligible for relief under Chapter 12. A small business might choose to liquidate under Chapter 7, but that results in the death of the enterprise, hardly an attractive option to the employees and the owner, who rely on the business for their jobs, and the suppliers, customers, and communities, who benefit from the viability of the business. Chapter 13 is available to the limited class of unincorporated proprietorships whose debt fits within certain requirements. See **Chapter 19.** There is, of course, the option of seeking an informal workout with creditors (see **Chapter 18**), but workouts do not always bear fruit. Recently Congress has been considering various proposed amendments for small business bankruptcies (see **Chapter 24**), but until something along those lines is enacted, many small business operators in financial trouble have no choice but to do the best they can to reorganize under Chapter 11 in its current form.

Chapter 11 is available to all forms of businesses: partnerships (see **Chapter 22**), corporations, limited liability companies, and sole proprietorships. Section 109 of the Bankruptcy Code excludes certain business activities, such as stock brokers, banks, and savings and loan associations, from Chapter 11.

The jurisdiction and structure of the bankruptcy courts have been the subject of considerable controversy. Attempts to resolve the issues have resulted in a unique and awkward allocation of authority between the district and bankruptcy courts with which counsel should be familiar. See **Chapter 23.**

§ 1.3 Representing the Insolvent Small Business

Serving as counsel in a small business bankruptcy can be problematic. Long-time company counsel frequently develop a close, personal relationship with managers and owners. Counsel may be called on for input into business decisions and occasionally may be offered the opportunity to participate in the business either through equity, director status, or both. Personal involvement with management and ownership can give rise to a conflict of interest when the business teeters toward insolvency. Also, counsel may be a creditor, possibly having recently received preferential payments for antecedent services, thereby losing the status of disinterested party. Concurrent representation of a debtor company and its principals is common when business is good, but it may not be appropriate in bankruptcy. Furthermore, bankruptcy and workout representation requires cold analytical review of a company's finances and prospects, difficult advice to give to personal friends. See **Chapter 2.**

In a potential bankruptcy, cash for ongoing operations and professional fees is scarce. Prior to filing, counsel should obtain some form of retainer account from the debtor. In doing so, however, counsel should be scrupulous to ensure that the funds paid in are not subject to the liens of other creditors. Similarly, if any accountants or other professionals will be employed, some form of retainer fund should be created for their compensation as well. Even so, court approval may be necessary for withdrawal from the accounts.

§ 1.4 Cash Collateral and Obtaining Credit

Around the time the case is to be filed, the debtor should be in consultation with its lender regarding use of cash collateral. Cash collateral is the cash or its equivalent in which the debtor and another entity have an interest. See **Chapters 3** and **4.**

Debtor-businesses that depend less on the purchase and resale of inventory and more on the conversion of raw goods and labor into receivables, like factories and farms, for example, may not have cash collateral on which to draw for payment of expenses. For these businesses and for resale businesses without much inventory, additional extensions of credit from some lender will be necessary. See **Chapters 6** and **8.** Ideally, the debtor company will have an independent source of working capital on which to draw. In most cases, however, the debtor must look to its ordinary lender or a similar lender for operating advances. These loans should not be made except on court approval. A lender whose cash collateral is to be used and a lender who is to provide postpetition financing both must be adequately protected by the debtor. See **Chapter 5.**

Arrangements for the use of cash collateral and postpetition credit are best made prepetition. This enables the company to go into the case knowing it has some source of cash for materials, payroll, and other expenses. Creditors have the benefit of gaining some oversight of the company's operations as a result of cash collateral or credit negotiations, and, further, lending creditors can keep track of the status of their collateral. See **Chapter 8.** Debtors filing without those prearrangements run the risk of being denied permission to use cash collateral, resulting in an early failure of the case. Creditors who refuse to compromise at the outset run a parallel risk of having an unacceptable cash or credit arrangement forced on them early in the case. Courts, although they generally strive to protect creditors' interests, prefer early in a case to err on the side of preserving a debtor's opportunity to reorganize.

§ 1.5 Stay Relief, Adequate Protection, and Dismissal for Bad Faith

Shortly after filing, the company will grapple with at least two and maybe three first-wave issues common to most bankruptcy cases: motions for stay relief, motions for adequate protection of the creditor's interests, and, possibly, motions for dismissal of the case for bad faith filing. Volumes of cases and reams of scholarship cover each of these topics, but a few words by way of overview are in order.

Section 362 of the Bankruptcy Code is the source of the automatic stay which is at the core of bankruptcy relief. The stay operates as an injunction against all sorts of creditor activity against the debtor and provides the debtor a respite in which to work out its financial woes. The Code recognizes that this respite cannot be unlimited in scope and duration, particularly when the debtor seeks to keep assets that are not necessary to the reorganization, when the debtor fails to protect the creditors' interest in collateral, when the debtor delays unduly, or when the debtor's general conduct is such that bankruptcy protection is inequitable. Stay relief may be granted for cause, or when the debtor lacks equity in the property and the property is not necessary for an effective reorganization. *Cause* includes the lack of adequate protection. See **Chapter 5.**

Because creditors should apply for adequate protection early in the case, the debtor should be prepared either to argue that none is necessary or to offer protection. When the creditor moves for stay relief, § 362(g) places on the creditor the burden of proof that the debtor lacks equity in the property, but gives to the debtor the burden of proof that the protection tendered is adequate. As with cash and credit issues, debtors and creditors are well advised to work these issues out before filing, if at all possible.

A creditor who believes that the debtor has filed its case in bad faith may seek dismissal or conversion to Chapter 7. Examples of possible bad-faith filings are cases so simple they should be resolved in a nonbankruptcy forum, such as single-asset cases in which one or two creditors claim interests in the debtor's only asset, cases filed immediately after the debtor has dismissed another case or defaulted on another Chapter 11 plan, and cases filed on the eve of execution or foreclosure sale. Generally, if the debtor is in court for the first time or the court can conclude that the debtor's effort to reorganize is facially legitimate, dismissal motions will not be favored early in the case. Debtors should be prepared to answer charges of bad faith by demonstrating reasonable possibilities for successfully restructuring the business.

§ 1.6 Maximizing the Estate

The chances of successful reorganization are improved with each extra dollar that is part of the estate and available for the operation of the reorganized business. The debtor in a Chapter 11, in its capacity as debtor-in-possession, a role analogous to the trustee in Chapter 7, has several very important tools for maximizing the estate. The most important are the strong arm and avoiding powers that can render previously encumbered property unencumbered and available for use by the reorganized business. See **Chapter 12.** The sale of unnecessary assets is also an important source of funds for reorganization. See **Chapter 9.** Assumption, rejection, or assignment of executory contracts and unexpired leases under § 365 can have a significant effect on the funds available for reorganization. For example, a lease can be assigned at a profit, or a money-losing contract can be rejected. Creditors and lessors need to be alert to protect themselves in these matters. See **Chapters 7** and **8.**

§ 1.7 Owner's Assets Outside of Bankruptcy

Competing with the interest of the creditors (and the owners) in successful reorganization is the owners' desire to maximize their personal assets in the event the reorganization fails and the business is liquidated. Exemptions are important to debtors for this reason. See **Chapters 20** and **21.**

Once a reorganization has failed and been converted to Chapter 7, there might be an opportunity for the debtor to transfer to the estate income tax liability on gain from sale of low-basis property, thereby escaping what might in some cases be a very burdensome debt. See **Chapter 10.**

Owners of a business may desire to continue in business after consummation of the plan but may propose a plan that does not pay all secured and unsecured claims in full. The absolute priority rule of § 1129(b)(2)(B) may or may not preclude retention of equity interests in such a situation. See **Chapter 16.**

§ 1.8 Importance of Valuation

Issues of valuation come up in many stages of a case. See **Chapter 11.** Secured claims are allowed based on the value of the collateral. If the property securing the claim is worth less than the amount of the total claim, the claim is *undersecured* and § 506(a) says that the value of the secured portion equals the value of the collateral. The balance of the claim is unsecured. When the creditor's collateral is worth more than the claim, the claim is *oversecured* and the creditor is entitled to collect interest, costs, and attorney's fees up to the value of the collateral under § 506(b).

The value of equipment, inventory, and other assets, and also the rate of depreciation, are relevant to issues of adequate protection in motions for relief from stay, motions for use of cash collateral, and motions for approval of postpetition financing. Issues of value are also central to a determination of insolvency, which is an element in various provisions of the Code, including recovery of preferential transfers in § 547.

Valuation is especially important to a small business with limited assets and limited access to cash or credit. Therefore, valuation of the property of the estate is a critical task and should be accomplished early in the case or, if possible, before it is filed. Small business cases may not warrant the administrative burden of multiple appraisers to value collateral of relatively limited worth. If appraisers are employed by the debtor, counsel should remember that they must be approved by the court if they are to be compensated as professionals under 11 U.S.C. §§ 327 and 330.

§ 1.9 Drafting a Plan of Reorganization

Prior to filing its case, a business should have some idea of how a Chapter 11 reorganization will benefit it. Besides making the whole process more efficient, a partially formulated plan is helpful in negotiating cash collateral, credit, and adequate protection issues with creditors. Debtors cannot solicit votes on a proposed plan without an approved disclosure statement, but they can and should seek input from creditors as to what provisions the plan and disclosure statement should include. See **Chapter 14** for some general guidelines on drafting plans.

§ 1.10 Disclosure Statement, Voting, and Confirmation

Before the debtor can solicit acceptance of its plan, the court must approve and the debtor must promulgate a disclosure statement. The statement is a sort of prospectus designed to give the creditors information on which to base their decision about accepting or rejecting the plan. Section 1125 requires that the disclosure statement contain *adequate information,* which is "information sufficient to enable a hypothetical investor typical of holders of claims . . . to make an informed judgment about the plan." The role of the disclosure statement in a small business case is somewhat questionable. Usually the company's creditors are few and have a good idea about the company's past performance and future prospects. Generally, the company's lender or lenders have long before drawn conclusions about whether the company can effectively reorganize and already know how they will vote without benefit of a disclosure statement. Nevertheless, the adequacy of disclosure statements continues to be a ripe area for litigation. See **Chapter 13.**

After a disclosure statement has been approved, the statement, the plan, and the ballots are mailed out to all parties for consideration and voting. After the voting, the court must determine, after notice and a hearing, whether the plan can be confirmed under the standards of § 1129. See **Chapter 15.** The *absolute priority rule,* which requires payment of unsecured claims in full if the owner is to retain any interest in the business, and the *"new value" exception* have generated much recent litigation.

The absolute priority rule is a significant obstacle to confirmation that is particularly difficult for small businesses to overcome. See **Chapter 16.**

§ 1.11 When to File a Plan

The Bankruptcy Code sets no specific deadline for the debtor to file a plan. Rather, the Code provides in § 1122 that the debtor has the exclusive right to file a plan within the first 120 days after commencement of the case and, if the plan is filed within that time, an additional exclusive 60 days in which to obtain confirmation. These times can be extended for cause on motions filed within the periods. Such motions are granted perhaps more often than they should be.

The exclusivity period is a valuable right of the debtor. If the debtor lets the period expire without filing a plan, anybody can file a plan. Plans filed by creditors usually propose liquidation of some or all of the company's assets, especially when the creditor believes that the assets of the company will be wasted while the company pursues reorganization. Bankruptcy Rule 3016(a) provides that once a disclosure statement has been approved, no other party can file a competing plan.

In a small business case, a creditor's plan can be very bad news. When there are only a small number of creditors, each creditor possesses a sizeable share of the unsecured vote. The competing plan is particularly potent when filed by an undersecured creditor with a large outstanding deficiency. Of course, the creditor cannot file such a plan unless the debtor fails to file any plan or to get the necessary extensions of the exclusivity period. Some creditors' counsel try to obtain relief from the automatic stay if the debtor doesn't file a plan within a certain time. And, in appropriate cases, the court can shorten the 120- and 180-day deadlines for cause. This is another reason that it is a good idea to have a plan formulated, or at least in process, when the petition is filed.

§ 1.12 Postconfirmation and Discharge

Once the debtor's plan has been confirmed, unless the court orders otherwise, all of the estate's property vests in the debtor and the court loses jurisdiction over the case unless jurisdiction is reserved in the plan for specific purposes such as determining and allowing claims, recovering improper transfers, and interpreting the plan. Section 1141 provides that confirmation binds the debtor and all creditors and parties in interest to the provisions of the plan and that the property vests in the debtor free and clear of any claims of any creditor. The corporate debtor obtains a discharge at confirmation covering all preconfirmation debts unless the debts are excepted from discharge under 11 U.S.C. § 523. There is no discharge, however, if the plan provides for liquidation of all the property of the estate, the debtor quits doing business after confirmation, and the debtor would be denied a discharge under 11 U.S.C. § 727(a) if the case were a Chapter 7.

The plan cannot generally be modified postconfirmation. Section 1127 provides for postconfirmation modification before substantial consummation of the plan has occurred. *Substantial consummation,* under § 1101(b), occurs when all the property to be transferred under the plan is transferred and distribution has commenced. In other words, once notes or securities have been issued by the debtor or once payments have been made, the plan probably cannot be modified without the consent of all parties. The confirmed plan operates as a contract among all the parties and is enforceable at civil law as such. See **Chapter 17.**

CHAPTER 2

ATTORNEY EMPLOYMENT AND COMPENSATION UNDER THE BANKRUPTCY CODE

Cynthia F. Grimes

§ 2.1 Introduction

"Compensation is the lubricant which makes the bankruptcy machinery work when applied in the proper places and in the proper amount."[1] This chapter explores various facets of attorney compensation in bankruptcy practice.

The legislative history of the Bankruptcy Code provisions governing attorneys and their compensation reflects extensive debate by Congress. Congress perceived abuse under the Bankruptcy Act of 1898[2] by bankruptcy attorneys whose excessive fees depleted the estate to the detriment of the debtor and the creditors. However, Congress did not wish to discourage competent attorneys from bankruptcy practice, so it indicated an intent to ensure that fees received for bankruptcy services were comparable to nonbankruptcy services.[3] The resulting changes, enacted as Bankruptcy Code §§ 327 and 330, mandate court approval of the employment and compensation of an attorney for the trustee or for the debtor-in-possession. By requiring court approval, the Bankruptcy Code strives to strike a balance between the interests of creditors and the interests of bankruptcy lawyers.

COURT APPROVAL OF ATTORNEY EMPLOYMENT

§ 2.2 Employment of Attorneys by the Trustee or Debtor-in-Possession

A central concept of the Bankruptcy Code is that most attorneys whose fees are to be paid from the estate must seek prior court approval of their employment. The penalty

---

[1] *In re* King Resources Co., 651 F.2d 1349, 1352 (10th Cir.), *cert. denied sub nom.* Citibank, N.A. v. Phoenix Resources Co., 454 U.S. 881 (1981).

[2] Ch. 541, 30 Stat. 544 (repealed 1979).

[3] Notes of Committee on the Judiciary, H.R. Rep. No. 595, 95th Cong., 1st Sess. 329–30 (1977).

for failing to do so may be denial of all compensation. This section examines attorney employment issues relating to trustees and debtors-in-possession. Issues relating to creditors' committees and creditors are discussed in **§§ 2.5** and **2.6,** respectively.

Section 327 governs when the attorney for a trustee or debtor-in-possession must file an application for approval of employment. In general, but with certain exceptions, any professional hired by the trustee or the debtor-in-possession must file an application for approval of employment with the court.

Section 327(a) is the principal subsection governing employment of professionals by a trustee or debtor-in-possession. It provides that:

> the trustee, with the court's approval, may employ one or more attorneys, accountants, appraisers, auctioneers, or other professional persons, that do not hold or represent an interest adverse to the estate, and that are disinterested persons, to represent or assist the trustee in carrying out the trustee's duties under this title.

Employment of professionals under § 327(a) should be contrasted with employment of professionals under § 327(b). Subsection (b) applies to in-house professionals. It provides that if the trustee is authorized to operate the debtor's business, and the debtor has regularly employed attorneys or other professionals, the trustee may retain or replace such professionals "if necessary in the operation of such business." Note that this subsection does not require court approval of the employment.

In determining who should file an application for employment under § 327(a), five issues need to be considered:

1. Is the professional being retained by the trustee?
2. Is the professional a *professional person* within the meaning of § 327(a)?
3. Does the professional "hold or represent an interest adverse to the estate"?
4. Is the professional "disinterested"?
5. Is the professional being retained to represent or assist the trustee in carrying out the trustee's duties under the Bankruptcy Code?

Retainer by the trustee. Section 327(a) does not require that lawyers for debtors under Chapter 7 or Chapter 13 file an employment application, because such lawyers are not retained by the trustee. Subsection 327(d) does, however, allow the trustee to act as his own attorney or accountant, if the court finds that to do so "is in the best interest of the estate."

Professional person. "Professional person" is not defined in the Code. The leading case defining who qualifies as a professional is *In re Johns-Manville Corp.*,[4] which established that professionals are those who play an intimate or central role in the reorganization of the estate.[5] In the *Johns-Manville* case, lobbyists were held not to constitute professionals.[6]

---

[4] 60 B.R. 612 (Bankr. S.D.N.Y. 1986).

[5] *Id.* at 620.

[6] *Id.* at 621.

Twin prongs of no adverse interest and disinterestedness. Employment under § 327(a) requires that the professional meet the twin prongs of not holding or representing an adverse interest and being disinterested. Employment under other sections, such as § 327(b) or (e) or § 1103, requires only one of the prongs, absence of adverse interest. These tests are stricter than most states' disciplinary rules governing conflicts of interest. Nonetheless, counsel should remember that even if an attorney meets both tests, the attorney may be subject to disqualification under state law governing conflicts (for example, because a client refuses to waive a conflict or because of the appearance of impropriety). The twin prongs are examined more fully in §§ **2.3** and **2.4.**

Assistance in carrying out the trustee's duties. Although there are few reported decisions discussing the meaning of this language, attorneys should be aware that not every professional retained by the trustee or debtor-in-possession is employed to assist in carrying out the trustee's duties under the Bankruptcy Code and that § 327(a) may have interplay with other Code sections. For example, a management company whose job is to provide management services to the debtor may not constitute a professional under § 327(a), even though the debtor may require court approval to retain or change the management services as a transaction out of the ordinary course of business under § 363 or may be compelled to accept or reject the management contract as an executory contract under § 365. In *In re Florida Airlines, Inc.,*[7] the court held that the president of the Chapter 11 debtor was a professional person whose employment was required to be authorized under § 327(a).[8] By contrast, in *In re Bartley Lindsay Co.,*[9] the court held that ordinary corporate officers and employees are not professional persons, although the management consultants acting as workout consultants were.[10] This case also contains a list of factors to consider in determining when a debtor's officer is also a professional person.

The language of § 327(a) should also be read in conjunction with § 327(e). Section 327(e), the so-called *special counsel exception,* allows the trustee to employ an attorney for a specified special purpose, "other than to represent the trustee in conducting the case." This provision is designed to apply to attorneys who may have represented the debtor prepetition, typically in an ongoing lawsuit of some kind. Attorneys who qualify for this narrow type of employment are not required to meet the disinterested test, in recognition of the fact that they are typically creditors of the estate at the time of the bankruptcy petition.

§ 2.3 —No Adverse Interest Requirement

The phrase "adverse interest" is not defined by the Code. A frequently used definition is found in *In re Roberts,*[11] which provides that to hold an interest adverse to the estate means:

---

7 110 B.R. 570 (M.D. Fla. 1990).

8 *Id.* at 571.

9 120 B.R. 507 (Bankr. D. Minn. 1990), *aff'd,* 137 B.R. 305 (D. Minn. 1991).

10 *Id.* at 511.

11 46 B.R. 815 (Bankr. D. Utah 1985), *modified,* 75 B.R. 402 (D. Utah 1987).

> (1) to possess or assert any economic interest that would tend to lessen the value of the bankruptcy estate or that would create either an actual or potential dispute in which the estate is a rival claimant; or (2) to possess a predisposition [that is ordinarily created by family ties, friendship, and by fiduciary or official responsibilities] under circumstances that render such a [predisposition] a bias against the estate.[12]

To represent an adverse interest means to serve as agent or attorney for any individual or entity holding such an adverse interest.[13]

The adverse interest test of § 327(a) must be read in conjunction with § 327(c). That subsection provides that a person is not disqualified for employment solely because of the person's employment by or representation of a creditor, unless there is an objection by another creditor or the United States Trustee. If there is an objection, the court shall disapprove the employment if there is an actual conflict of interest.

Courts vary widely in applying the adverse interest test, especially as it relates to whether there is an actual or potential conflict with representation of a creditor. At one extreme, any previous or simultaneous representation by the attorney of parties connected with the case may constitute the representation of an adverse interest. In *In re Butterfield, Limited Partnership,*[14] the court found that simultaneous representation of a debtor-limited partnership and a general partner, even on matters unrelated to the bankruptcy, constitutes representation of an adverse interest because of the "potential conflict."[15] The court in *Butterfield* adopted the language of *In re McKinney Ranch Associates*:[16]

> The jaundiced eye and scowling mien that counsel for debtor is required to cast upon everyone in sight will not likely fall upon the party with whom he has a potential conflict: [*sic*] Any potential conflict represents the potential to overlook an asset or defense of the estate. Thus a potential conflict of interest, while it may be ethically proper, is not normally permitted under section 327.[17]

By contrast, many courts apply a flexible approach.[18] In *In re PHM Credit Corp.,*[19] the court noted that bankruptcy courts should not adhere to a hypertechnical position that ignores "the fundamental economics of the realities of the case." In that case, the district court affirmed on appeal a curative order of the bankruptcy court recusing a member of debtor's attorney's law firm, in order that the firm not be "interested."[20]

In many instances of dual representation, such as representation of a partner and the partnership, a shareholder and the corporation, or the parent corporation and a

---

12 *Id.* at 827.

13 *Id.*

14 131 B.R. 67 (Bankr. E.D. Mich. 1990).

15 *Id.* at 69.

16 62 B.R. 249 (Bankr. C.D. Cal. 1986).

17 *In re* Butterfield, Ltd. Partnership, 131 B.R. 67, 69 (Bankr. E.D. Mich. 1990) (*citing In re* McKinney Ranch Assocs., 62 B.R. 249, 254 (Bankr. C.D. Cal. 1986).

18 *See In re* Interco, Inc., 127 B.R. 633, 638 (Bankr. E.D. Mo. 1991) (discussing simultaneous representation by examiner's law firm of examiner and debtor's investment banker; weighing considerations of practicality).

19 110 B.R. 284 (E.D. Mich. 1990).

20 *Id.* at 289.

subsidiary, there is a unity of interest between the two clients being represented "because they have the same objective, namely to rehabilitate the financially strapped debtor."[21] Nonetheless, attorneys should be reluctant to undertake dual representation of clients in situations such as the following:

1. Representation is related to the bankruptcy, such as representation of an individual partner in workout negotiations while representing the debtor partnership[22]
2. There is a need to advise one client about receiving a preferential transfer from the other client[23]
3. There are two clients whose jointly administered estates are creditors of each other[24]
4. Prepetition debt has been transferred from one Chapter 11 estate to another[25]
5. Dual representation would give the attorney improper access to confidential information of both parties.[26]

§ 2.4 —Disinterestedness Requirement

In addition to the requirement that the professional neither hold nor represent an adverse interest, the professional must also be disinterested.

Disinterested person is defined by § 101(14). In general, an *interested* professional includes one who is a creditor, shareholder, insider, or investment banker of the debtor.[27] Section 101(14) also contains a catch-all provision that includes as interested anyone "with an interest materially adverse to the interest of the estate or of any class of creditors or equity security holders, by reason of any direct or indirect relationship to, connection with, or interest in, the debtor or an investment banker . . . , or for any other reason."[28]

Just as in application of the adverse interest test, courts take different approaches in determining who is disinterested. Some courts insist on an absolute rule prohibiting any attorney who is a creditor of the debtor's estate from representing the debtor.[29] Other courts apply the disinterestedness test on a case by case basis.[30]

---

[21] *In re* Maui 14K, Ltd., 133 B.R. 657, 659 (Bankr. D. Haw. 1991). Under the circumstances of that case, however, the attorney was disqualified.

[22] *In re* TMA Assocs., Ltd., 129 B.R. 643 (Bankr. D. Colo. 1991).

[23] *In re* Maui 14K, Ltd., 133 B.R. 657 (Bankr. D. Haw. 1991).

[24] *In re* Professional Dev. Corp., 129 B.R. 522 (Bankr. W.D. Tenn. 1991).

[25] *In re* Green Street, 132 B.R. 460 (Bankr. D. Utah 1991).

[26] *See In re* Interco, Inc., 127 B.R. 633 (Bankr. E.D. Mo. 1991) (none found in that case, however).

[27] 11 U.S.C. § 101(14)(A)–(D).

[28] 11 U.S.C. § 101(14)(E).

[29] *See In re* Pierce, 809 F.2d 1356, 1362 (8th Cir. 1987) (attorney claiming attorney lien). *See also In re* Huntmar Beaumeade I Ltd. Partnership, 127 B.R. 363, 365 (Bankr. E.D. Va. 1991) (an attorney who receives payment from a creditor is always interested).

[30] *See In re* Martin, 817 F.2d 175, 182 (1st Cir. 1987) (discussing secured retainer agreement; not per se invalid). *See also In re* Gilmore, 127 B.R. 406, 409 (Bankr. M.D. Tenn.

An attorney who undertakes to represent a Chapter 11 or 12 debtor should ensure that he is not a creditor on the date of the filing, either by arranging to receive payment or by waiving any past due fees for services, although payment of such fees on the eve of bankruptcy may constitute an avoidable preferential transfer under § 547(b). In addition, § 1107(b) provides that, "[n]otwithstanding § 327(a) [requiring that a professional be disinterested and not hold or represent an adverse interest], a person is not disqualified for employment under section 327 . . . by a debtor in possession solely because of such person's employment by or representation of the debtor before the commencement of the case."

An example of an attorney's being disqualified for previous representation of the debtor is *In re 419 Co.*,[31] in which the debtor's lawyer had represented the debtor in workout for the previous year and possibly received preferential payments. The attorney in that case was found to be an insider and thus subject to a one-year reachback for setting aside preferences under § 547(b)(4)(B).[32]

The disinterested requirement does not apply to attorneys employed on salary by the debtor,[33] attorneys employed for a specified special purpose,[34] and attorneys employed by a creditors' or equity security holders' committee.[35]

§ 2.5 Employment of Attorneys by Creditors' Committees

When a creditors' committee has been appointed under § 1102, the committee may, subject to court approval, and at a meeting at which a majority of the committee's members are present, select and authorize the employment of one or more attorneys or other agents to represent or perform services for the committee.[36] Subsection (b) of § 1103 provides that an attorney may not, while employed by the committee, represent any other entity having an adverse interest in connection with the case. Representation of one or more creditors of the same class as represented by the committee, however, shall not per se constitute the representation of an adverse interest. The professional retained by the committee need not, however, meet the disinterestedness test.

An example of when representation of a creditor may constitute an adverse interest in committee representation is *In re Electro-Optix, U.S.A., Inc.*[37] In that case, a law firm representing a committee was disqualified for failing to disclose that it continued to represent the largest unsecured creditor while representing the committee, and that the creditor had paid the firm a $25,000 advance for representing the committee.

1991) (finding that attorney lien on unencumbered assets of the estate did not disqualify debtor's attorney, and setting forth 10 factors when a security interest taken by attorney is "materially adverse").

31 133 B.R. 867 (Bankr. N.D. Ohio 1991).

32 *Id.* at 869 (denying application for approval of employment).

33 11 U.S.C. § 327(b).

34 *Id.* § 327(e).

35 *Id.* § 1103.

36 11 U.S.C. § 1103(a).

37 130 B.R. 621 (Bankr. S.D. Fla. 1991).

§ 2.6 Employment of Attorneys by Creditors

No sections of the Code require the court to approve the attorney representing a creditor, although in certain instances the court has authority to control the fees that the creditor's lawyer is paid from the estate. See **§ 2.25.** Federal Rule of Bankruptcy Procedure 2019 requires a creditor's lawyer to make certain disclosures concerning his employment when the attorney represents more than one creditor in a Chapter 9 municipality or Chapter 11 reorganization case. The penalty for failing to file the Rule 2019 statement can include barring the lawyer or the entity from being heard in the case.[38]

§ 2.7 Other Limitations on Employment

Section 327(e) prohibits the trustee from employing a person who has served as an examiner[39] in the case. Also, Bankruptcy Rule 5002 prohibits the appointment of a person who is a relative of the bankruptcy judge approving the employment.

HOW TO APPLY FOR APPROVAL OF EMPLOYMENT

§ 2.8 Sufficiency of Application

If the professional person falls within §§ 327(a) or 1103, the professional must obtain court approval of employment. **Sections 2.8** through **2.13** examine issues of sufficiency of the employment application. **Sections 2.9** through **2.11** cover timeliness, notice, and issues of type of retainer and sources of funds. **Sections 2.12** and **2.13** contain a sample application for employment of an attorney and an attorney affidavit.

Bankruptcy Rule 2014 implements §§ 327 and 1103. It provides that the application shall state specific facts showing the necessity of the employment, the name of the person to be employed, the reasons for the selection, the professional services to be rendered, and any proposed arrangement for compensation. In addition, the application must be accompanied by a verified statement of the person to be employed "setting forth the person's *connections* with the debtor, creditors, any other party in interest, their respective attorneys and accountants, the United States Trustee, or any person employed in the office of the United States Trustee" (emphasis added).

The term "connections" is not defined by the Rules or the Code. In deciding when a particular relationship is a connection that should be disclosed, however, attorneys should note that the court's ability to determine disinterestedness or adverse interest hinges on full and candid disclosure.

---

[38] Fed. R. Bankr. P. 2019(b).

[39] *See* 11 U.S.C. § 1104 (appointment of trustee or examiner).

One case exploring the breadth of the word "connections" is *In re Rusty Jones, Inc.*[40] *Rusty Jones* states that there is a remoteness element to the connections that must be disclosed, and it suggests that the fact one owned a hot dog stand with a party in the case 20 years ago is too remote.[41] However, "[w]hat is important are those connections that presently exist or recently existed between the attorney and the parties in interest, and also past connections of business or personal nature that are either related to the bankruptcy proceedings or could reasonably have an effect on the attorney's judgment in the case."[42]

In complying with the Rule 2014 requirement of disclosing connections, cautious counsel should take the following steps:

Check of creditors. The attorney should obtain a complete mailing matrix, or schedules and statements, and check every creditor's name with the firm's list of former and current clients. The attorney should remember to check for parties to executory contracts and unexpired leases, because such entities may not be creditors but parties in interest. In large cases, in which such checking would be unduly burdensome, the attorney should nonetheless disclose in the affidavit that not all creditors have been checked but that there is no connection with the secured creditors, the 20 largest unsecured creditors, the United States Trustee, or any other party taking an active role in the bankruptcy.

Check of entities related to debtor. The attorney should check for relationships that are not as obvious, such as relationships with partners, subsidiaries, shareholders, officers, directors, or employees of the debtor.

Disclosure. The attorney should disclose any such relationship or past representation and should state whether representation is related or unrelated to the bankruptcy and whether the relationship or representation is continuing.

In cases in which the relationship may be significant (such as representation of the primary secured lender), the attorney should disclose the nature of compensation received, including any payments made for services rendered within the year preceding bankruptcy, and the source and timing of the payments.[43]

Affidavit and documentation. After setting forth all connections, the attorney should affirmatively state that he is disinterested and neither holds nor represents an interest adverse to the estate, as the case may be. The affidavit should be accompanied by a copy of any pertinent documents relating to the engagement, including the retainer agreement and any conflict waivers obtained.

---

40 134 B.R. 321 (Bankr. N.D. Ill. 1991).

41 *Id.* at 346.

42 *Id. But cf. In re* Saturley, 131 B.R. 509 (Bankr. D. Me. 1991) (the attorney should comply punctiliously and should "lay bare all dealings, antecedent and anticipated, regarding work 'in contemplation of or in connection with' the case").

43 *See In re* 419 Co., 133 B.R. 867, 869 (Bankr. N.D. Ohio 1991) (any large or unusual payments within the preference period are relevant to the conflicts analysis and therefore warrant scrutiny by the bankruptcy court). *See also* 11 U.S.C. § 329 (requiring debtor's attorney to file statement of compensation paid or agreed to be paid).

Continuous disclosure. The attorney should bear in mind that the duty to disclose is continuing and should be vigilant for connections that may arise during the case, such as the hiring of a new member of the firm who may have represented another party in interest. If a connection is discovered after the filing of the initial Rule 2014 statement, an amended Rule 2014 statement should be filed as soon as possible, and it should state the reason the connection was not disclosed initially.

§ 2.9 Timeliness of Application

Although the Code does not specifically address the timing of the filing of the application for approval of employment, most courts by judicial gloss require that the application be filed substantially contemporaneously with the commencement of services. A late-filed application is commonly called an *application nunc pro tunc,* and courts are split on whether they have the authority to approve a late-filed application (and thus approve compensation sought for the period before employment was approved).

The majority of courts hold that nunc pro tunc approval of employment can be granted only in extraordinary circumstances, and that simple neglect to seek approval in a timely manner is insufficient.[44] Whether the requirement of extraordinary circumstances will be reanalyzed in light of the new, more flexible standard of excusable neglect established in *Pioneer Investment Services v. Brunswick Associates*[45] has yet to be seen.

§ 2.10 Notice of Application

Sections 327(a) and 1103 require court approval of the application for employment but, unlike other Code sections, do not require that such approval be "after notice and hearing."[46] The only Bankruptcy Rule governing notice of the application for approval of employment is Rule 2014(a), which requires service of the application on the United States Trustee[47] and which does not specify a time period for objecting to the application. Many districts establish the time period and method of service by local rule. Nonetheless, it is prudent practice to serve the application on any party mentioned in the application (such as a party with whom one has listed a connection) and on those who will take an active interest in the case, perhaps the principal secured creditor, the 20 largest unsecured creditors, and any committee. Although a

---

[44] *See In re* Land, 943 F.2d 1265, 1268 (10th Cir. 1991); *In re* Offield, 128 B.R. 548 (Bankr. W.D. Mo. 1991) (extraordinary circumstances found).

[45] __U.S.__, 113 S. Ct. 1489, 123 L. Ed. 2d 74 (1993).

[46] "[A]fter notice and hearing" is defined at 11 U.S.C. § 102(1). Code sections using this language include § 362(b)(1).

[47] The U.S. Trustee has a duty to monitor applications under § 327 and to file comments with respect to such applications whenever deemed appropriate. 28 U.S.C. § 586(a)(3)(H).

failure to object to the application for employment does not prevent the court or a party in interest from raising an objection to qualification later on, specifically at the time of the application for compensation, the failure of an affected party to object may constitute mitigating circumstances that weigh in favor of the attorney's being allowed compensation for fees.

§ 2.11 Type of Retainer and Source of Funds

In many cases, the nature of the retainer received may influence the court's determination of whether the professional is disinterested or holds or represents an adverse interest. The source of funds and nature of the retainer may also raise ethical issues peculiar to bankruptcy.

Courts recognize several different types of retainer agreements. A *classic retainer* is a fee arrangement in which the attorney is entitled to the money regardless of whether the attorney actually performs any services for the client.[48] A classic retainer is not property of the estate and, although it must be disclosed in the § 329 statement, the attorney may draw on the retainer without court approval.[49] Such a retainer may be subject to disgorgement as excessive under 11 U.S.C. § 328 and may be subject to court approval as part of a Chapter 11 plan under 11 U.S.C. § 1129(a)(4).

A *security retainer* is the typical arrangement in which the retainer is held by the attorneys to secure payment of fees for future services.[50] A security retainer is property of the estate, and the attorney may not draw on it until the court grants approval. Any unearned amounts must be returned to the estate.[51]

An *advance payment retainer* is one in which the debtor pays in advance for some or all of the services that the attorney is expected to perform.[52] Such a retainer may be subject to disgorgement for any amounts unearned.

A *secured retainer* is established when the attorney receives and holds the client's money as a pledge, in the form of a possessory security interest, that the attorney's fees will be paid when earned.[53] A security retainer is property of the estate.[54] Some courts hold that the impressment of a lien is "wholly impermissible" because it disqualifies the attorney by making the attorney a creditor and thus "interested."[55]

Finally, an *evergreen retainer* is a retainer that is constantly replenished.[56] The bankruptcy court may disapprove the employment of an attorney with an evergreen retainer, because:

---

48 *In re* Viscount Furniture Corp., 133 B.R. 360, 364 (Bankr. N.D. Miss. 1991).

49 *Id.* at 364.

50 *In re* Viscount Furniture Corp., 133 B.R. 360, 364 (Bankr. N.D. Miss. 1991).

51 *Id.* at 365.

52 *Id.*

53 *Id.*

54 *Id.*

55 *In re* Fitzsimmons Trucking, Inc., 124 B.R. 556, 560 (Bankr. D. Minn. 1991) (in Chapter 11 case).

56 *Id.* at 558.

> [a]ttorneys who have the cushion of an evergreen retainer may not be as ready to counsel their client frankly and firmly about the fairness and propriety of continuing in the reorganization mode, because they will not be subject to the same continuing risks as creditors, taxing authorities, and equity holders until the retainer is consumed.[57]

An agreement with the client to "direct pay" the costs and expenses may be a disguised attempt to gain the cushion of a retainer. This method of compensation has also been held unacceptable.[58]

The debtor's attorney must pay attention to the source of the retainer funds. In a single-asset case, if the retainer is derived from rents secured to a mortgagee, the retainer may be the lender's cash collateral under § 363. When the retainer is derived from personal property that is the collateral of the lender, the attorney may be liable for criminal impairment of a security interest. If, on the other hand, the attorney receives the retainer from a shareholder or general partner of the debtor, the attorney may have unwittingly established a connection that will taint him as having an adverse interest.

§ 2.12 Form: Application to Employ Attorneys

FORM 2–1
APPLICATION TO EMPLOY ATTORNEYS

IN THE UNITED STATES BANKRUPTCY COURT
FOR THE DISTRICT OF ___________

In Re:	)	
	)	
BANKRUPTCY CITY,	)	Case No. ____________
	)	
Debtor.	)	
______________________________	)	

APPLICATION BY DEBTORS TO EMPLOY SMITH & WESSON, P.A., AS ATTORNEY FOR DEBTOR

Bankruptcy City (the Debtor) applies to the Court for an Order pursuant to 11 U.S.C. § 327(a) and Fed. R. Bankr. Proc. 2014 authorizing the employment of David Grayhair, of Smith & Wesson, P.A. (S&W), as attorney for Debtor. In support of its Application, Debtor would show the Court:

1. Debtor commenced this case by the filing of a voluntary petition for Chapter 11 relief on January 1, 1994. Debtor has remained in possession of its assets and has operated its business as debtor-in-possession under 11 U.S.C. §§ 1107 and 1108 since the filing date.

---

[57] *Id.* at 559.

[58] *Id.* at 561.

2. Debtor has retained S&W to represent it in carrying out its duties under Title 11.

3. The services S&W would provide include representing Debtor in its Chapter 11 proceedings, preparing and negotiating plans of reorganization, and other services normally rendered on behalf of Chapter 11 debtors.

4. S&W proposes to represent Debtor at its normal hourly rates, as they may be adjusted from time to time. S&W has received a retainer from Debtor in the amount of $30,000. A copy of S&W's employment agreement is attached hereto as Exhibit A.

5. S&W is a disinterested person and neither holds nor represents an interest adverse to the estate in the matters upon which it is to be engaged, as more particularly set forth in the Affidavit of David Grayhair, attached as Exhibit B.

6. S&W commenced representation of Debtor with respect to this bankruptcy proceeding on December 26, 1993 and provided services before the filing date in preparation for and in contemplation of bankruptcy.

7. S&W's employment is in the best interest of the estate.

WHEREFORE, Debtor prays that the Court authorize Debtor to employ the firm of Smith & Wesson, P.A. as attorney for the Debtor; that such employment be effective as of the date of the commencement of the services on December 26, 1993; and for such other and further relief as the Court deems just.

BANKRUPTCY CITY
BY:____________________
TITLE:____________________

and
SMITH & WESSON, P.A.
BY:________________________
ATTORNEY FOR DEBTOR

§ 2.13 Form: Affidavit of Attorney

FORM 2–2
AFFIDAVIT OF ATTORNEY

IN THE UNITED STATES BANKRUPTCY COURT
FOR THE DISTRICT OF ______________

In Re:	)	
	)	
BANKRUPTCY CITY,	)	Case No. ____________

)
Debtor.)
____________________________________)

AFFIDAVIT

STATE OF ____________)
) ss:
COUNTY OF ___________)

DAVID GRAYHAIR, on behalf of the law firm of Smith & Wesson, P.A., of lawful age, being duly sworn, states:

1. I am an attorney of the law firm of Smith & Wesson, P.A., (S&W) named in the accompanying Application.

2. No agreement or understanding exists between S&W and any other person for any division or sharing of compensation which is prohibited by statute.

3. Except as more particularly set out in Paragraph 4 of this Affidavit, S&W neither holds nor represents an interest adverse to the estate in the matters upon which it is to be engaged, and S&W is a disinterested person, and the employment of S&W would be to the best interest of the estate.

4. To the best of my knowledge, S&W has the following connections with the Debtor, its creditors, other parties in interest, their respective attorneys and accountants, the U.S. Trustee, and other persons employed in the office of the U.S. Trustee:

The Debtor:

S&W previously represented the Debtor in restructuring proceedings terminating in March 1992. Thereafter, S&W did not represent Debtor until it again commenced representation in a foreclosure proceeding filed July 1, 1993, in the District Court of [state district], styled as Big Bank v. Bankruptcy City, Case No. [number]. S&W is not a creditor of Debtor because Debtor paid fees to S&W on a timely and monthly basis during the foreclosure.

The Debtor's Creditors

S&W has represented the Debtor's secured creditor, Big Bank, and continues to represent Big Bank in matters unrelated to the Debtor or to this case. Both Debtor and Big Bank have executed written conflict waivers which are attached hereto as Exhibits 1 and 2. In S&W's opinion, S&W's simultaneous representation of Big Bank and Debtor is not an actual conflict of interest.

In addition, S&W previously represented three years earlier Landscape Company on an unrelated tax matter. Landscape Company is an unsecured creditor of Debtor's, holding a claim in the amount of $[claim amount]. S&W does not currently represent Landscape Company.

Other Parties in Interest

S&W has represented and continues to represent Mr. Partner, the general partner of Bankruptcy City, in the foreclosure proceedings above mentioned. In the event S&W's employment is approved, S&W has informed Mr. Partner it can no longer represent him in the foreclosure or other matters related to this bankruptcy. In S&W's opinion, S&W's previous representation of Mr. Partner is not an actual conflict of interest.

Attorneys and Accountants

S&W has no connection with the attorneys or accountants of any of the parties in interest, except that one member of S&W, Julie Jobjumper, recently joined S&W after leaving Big Bad Firm. Big Bad Firm is the attorney of record in this proceeding for Big Bank, although Ms. Jobjumper never personally represented Big Bank or performed any services on its behalf.

The U.S. Trustee

S&W has no connections with the U.S. Trustee or any persons employed in its office, except that another member of S&W, Joe Trustee, is a panel trustee appointed by the U.S. Trustee's office with respect to Chapter 7 cases.

5. I understand that there is a continuing duty to disclose any such adverse interest.

6. I declare under penalty of perjury that the foregoing is true and correct.

Smith & Wesson, P.A.

By:__________________________
David Grayhair

SUBSCRIBED AND SWORN TO before me on this ____ day of ____________, 1994.

____
Notary Public
My Commission Expires:

COURT APPROVAL OF COMPENSATION

§ 2.14 Compensation of Officers of the Estate

Section 330(a) allows a court to award to a trustee, examiner, professional employed under §§ 327 or 1103, or debtor's attorney (1) "reasonable compensation for actual, necessary services" rendered by those entities or by their paraprofessionals; and (2) "reimbursement for actual, necessary expenses." The statute prescribes that reasonable compensation is based on the nature, the extent, and the value of such services, the time spent on such services, and the cost of comparable nonbankruptcy services. Note that although Chapter 7 or 13 debtors' attorneys need not apply for court approval of employment under § 327(a), § 330(a) requires court approval of those attorneys' compensation.

Sections 328, 329, 330, and 331 govern compensation for services and reimbursement of expenses of an attorney or professional person. Sections 328 and 329 limit compensation, and §§ 330 and 331 govern the application process and the timing of the compensation.

§ 2.15 —Reasonableness Standard

Courts have adopted varying approaches to determining whether compensation is reasonable. *In re Hutter Construction Co.*[59] lists seven recognized methods for computing a reasonable fee. One common approach is the *lodestar standard,* under which the court arrives at the number of hours that should reasonably have been spent and multiplies it by a reasonable fee, which on occasion may thereafter be adjusted up or down.[60] Another approach examines and applies reasonableness factors, which include the time and labor required; novelty and difficulty of the question; skill requisite to perform the legal service properly; preclusion of other employment by the attorney due to acceptance of the case; customary fees; whether the fee is fixed or contingent; time limitations imposed by the client or circumstances; amount involved and results obtained; experience, reputation, and ability of the attorney; the "undesirability" of the case; the nature and length of the professional relationship with the client; and awards in similar cases.[61] Perhaps the clearest statement is set forth in *In re Hutter Construction Co.*: "Be honest."[62]

---

[59] 126 B.R. 1005 (Bankr. E.D. Wis. 1991).

[60] *Id.* at 1010.

[61] Johnson v. Georgia Highway Express, Inc., 488 F.2d 714 (5th Cir. 1974).

[62] 126 B.R. 1005, 1021 (Bankr. E.D. Wis. 1991).

§ 2.16 Limitations on Compensation

Section 328(a) allows the trustee or committee, with court approval, to employ professionals under §§ 327 and 1103 "on any reasonable terms and conditions of employment, including on a retainer, on an hourly basis, or on a contingent fee basis." This section must be read in conjunction with § 504, which prohibits the sharing of compensation. The court may allow compensation on terms other than those approved under circumstances set forth in the statute.

Section 328(b) distinguishes between those services rendered by a trustee and those rendered by the trustee's attorney or accountant. Subsection (b) provides that a trustee who serves as his own attorney or accountant may not be compensated as an attorney or accountant for performing the normal trustee duties.[63]

§ 2.17 Penalties for Nondisclosure or Excessive Fees

Anything less than the full measure of disclosure leaves counsel at risk that all compensation may be denied.[64] Under § 328(a), the court is permitted to deny compensation of fees and expenses to a professional if, at any time during employment, the professional (1) was not disinterested or (2) held or represented an adverse interest. Denial of compensation under this section is not mandatory; however, there are numerous cases in which courts have denied substantial amounts of fees or have compelled attorneys to disgorge previous fee or retainer payments as a penalty for nondisclosure, even when the nondisclosure did not harm the estate.[65]

In addition, § 329 provides penalties for failure of debtors' attorneys to file the statement of compensation and for excessive fees. In addition to any application for approval of employment, debtor's attorneys must file a § 329(a) statement of compensation paid or agreed to be paid and the source of the compensation. Bankruptcy Rule 2016(b) requires that the statement be filed within 15 days after the order for relief and also requires the statement to set out in detail any arrangement for sharing of compensation within a firm. Some cases have held that the timely filing of the § 329(a) statement is an absolute prerequisite to receiving compensation and that, as a general rule, the sanction for failing to file the statement should be denial of all compensation, imposition of a fine, or suspension from practice.[66]

Section 328(b) requires that the amount paid to the debtor's attorney be equal to the reasonable value of the services, and it permits the court to order the return of any excessive amounts paid within the year preceding bankruptcy. In *In re Lilliston,*[67] the

---

63 *See In re* SMS, Inc., 15 B.R. 496, 501 (Bankr. D. Kan. 1981) (attorney time for reviewing obviously perfected proof of claim not compensable).

64 *In re* Saturley, 131 B.R. 509, 517 (Bankr. D. Me. 1991).

65 *See In re* Saturley, 131 B.R. 509 (Bankr. D. Me. 1991); *In re* Kendavis Indus. Int'l, Inc., 91 B.R. 742 (Bankr. N.D. Tex. 1988) (ordering 50 percent reduction of over $4 million fee).

66 *See, e.g., In re* Fricker, 131 B.R. 932, 938–39 (Bankr. E.D. Pa. 1991).

67 127 B.R. 119 (Bankr. D. Md. 1991).

court ordered an excessive, unearned, prepetition retainer turned over to the estate. Bankruptcy Rule 2017 contains a procedural mechanism for implementing this section.

§ 2.18 Timing of Compensation

The general rule, set out in § 331, is that a professional may seek compensation for services and reimbursement of expenses only once every 120 days, unless the court orders otherwise. Compensation awarded before the end of the case is known as interim, as opposed to final, compensation. Section 331 does not mandate that interim compensation be awarded, and any award of interim compensation is still subject to the reasonableness requirements of § 330(a). Any amounts allowed on an interim basis are not final and are subject to re-examination at the close of the case.[68]

Some courts may authorize payment of compensation more frequently than every 120 days. In such cases, the applicant typically must file, in addition to the application for approval of employment, an application for interim and ongoing compensation.[69] Such an application should specify the reasons for receiving payment more frequently than every 120 days, such as the size and complexity of the case. The application should also state that the estate includes sufficient unencumbered assets to ensure payment of all administrative expenses. In the event assets are insufficient to pay all administrative expenses, the professional must share pro rata with other claimants of administrative expenses of the same priority and may be forced to disgorge a portion of the payments received.[70] To guard against this, many courts impose a *hold back* or *retainage,* allowing the professional to receive only 70 percent of fees requested, for example, until the end of the case.[71]

Note that the professional is not authorized to receive payment or draw on a prepetition retainer until authorized under either §§ 330 or 331. An attorney who did so was disqualified from employment and thus from all compensation in *In re Doors & More, Inc.*[72]

Even after the case has been closed or dismissed, the court may have authority over the allowance or disallowance of the fees.[73] The professional should ensure that a final fee application is filed before the end of the case.

---

68 *See In re* Taxman Clothing Co., 134 B.R. 286 (N.D. Ill. 1991) (bankruptcy court abused its discretion in failing to re-examine interim awards in ruling on the final application).

69 *See In re* Commercial Consortium, 135 B.R. 120, 124–25 (Bankr. C.D. Cal. 1991) (guidelines for when interim fees are allowed in Chapter 7).

70 *See* 11 U.S.C. §§ 503(b)(1) and 507.

71 *See In re* Wilson Foods Corp., 36 B.R. 317 (Bankr. W.D. Okla. 1984) (no hold-back required when estate solvent).

72 127 B.R. 1001 (Bankr. E.D. Mich. 1991).

73 *In re* Fricker, 131 B.R. 932, 938 (Bankr. E.D. Pa. 1991) (court does have such authority); *In re* Hutter Constr. Co., 126 B.R. 1005, 1013 (Bankr. E.D. Wis. 1991) (examination of fees after confirmation of Chapter 11 plan; not res judicata under § 1141, based on language in plan).

HOW TO APPLY FOR COMPENSATION

§ 2.19 Contents of Employment Application

Bankruptcy Rule 2016 requires that any entity seeking compensation from the estate must file an application setting forth a detailed statement of (1) the services rendered, time expended and expenses incurred, and (2) the amounts requested. In addition, the application must include a statement as to what payments have theretofore been made or promised, the source of the compensation so paid or promised, and whether any agreement or understanding exists concerning sharing the compensation and the particulars thereof, except that details of any agreement for sharing among members of a firm shall not be required.

Subsections (a)(7) and (c)(2) of Rule 2002 govern the requirements of notice of the application for compensation. Subsection (a)(7) specifies 20 days' notice to all creditors and parties in interest of any application for compensation in excess of $500. Subsection (c)(2) requires that the notice of a hearing shall identify the applicant and the amount requested.

§ 2.20 —Documenting Services and Expenses

Rule 2016 requires a detailed statement of the services rendered and expenses incurred. Courts differ in the amount of detail required of attorneys or other professionals in the itemization of the fees. Attorneys are well advised to ascertain and follow any local rules or practices in documenting fees. The following are, however, general guidelines for itemizing services and expenses.

General information. Every entry should contain the date the service was performed (or the expense was incurred); who performed the service; the amount of time expended; and a description of what was done. Attorneys and law clerks working under or with the chief attorney should also comply with the proper billing standards. A well documented fee application is much harder for opposing parties to attack or for the court to reduce. Good examples of detailed entries are found in *In re Cena's Fine Furniture*[74] and *In re Coastal Equities, Inc.*[75]

Calls and conferences. Time entries for conferences and telephone calls should identify the participants and the substance of the communication, such as,

Conference with attorney X re cash collateral motion.

---

[74] 109 B.R. 575, 582 (E.D.N.Y. 1990).

[75] 39 B.R. 304, 311 (Bankr. S.D. Cal. 1984).

All attorneys and paralegals involved in an intraoffice conference should charge the same amount of time for the conference. Such time might, however, be disallowed as duplicative.

Correspondence. Time entries for preparing or reviewing correspondence should identify to whom the correspondence was directed or from whom it had been received and the substance of the communication therein; for example,

> Draft letter to Trustee re amended schedules.
> Review letter from Trustee re amended schedules.

Research. Time entries for research should include a brief description of the nature of the research; for example,

> Research re burden of proof on stay relief motion.

Avoid describing the research in such general terms that it appears that the attorney was only generally familiarizing himself with the subject or researching an abstract legal question. If the attorney does not want to tip off opposing parties as to the nature of the research, there can be a request that the court review the application or those entries in camera.

Review of file. Time entries for reviewing the file should indicate the purpose for which the file was reviewed, for example,

> Review of file re preparation for disclosure statement hearing.

Travel time. Except in unusual circumstances, most courts disallow all or a portion of travel time. Typically, travel time should be billed at one-half the normal hourly rate and should be set forth separately; for example:

> Travel to and from bankruptcy court for stay relief hearing (1/2 rate): 1.0.
> Attend stay relief hearing: 1.0

Minimum billing units. Many courts require that time should be billed in one-tenths of an hour.

Compound entries. The time spent on each specific task must be indicated separately and not lumped together with others, and each activity should be a separate entry. The following entry is an example of an improper compound billing:

> Review letter from debtor's attorney re adequate protection; telephone conference with client re same; telephone conference with debtor's attorney re rejection of offer; dictate letters to client and debtor's attorney re same: .80

Proper billing would be as follows:

Review letter from debtor's attorney re adequate protection offer: .20
Telephone conference with client re adequate protection offer: .20
Telephone conference with debtor's attorney re rejection of offer: .20
Dictate letters to client and debtor's attorney re rejection of adequate protection offer: .20

Clerical or routine tasks. Avoid describing the tasks performed in terms that make it appear the task was nonprofessional, such as "filing, copying, mailing, and proofreading." Use "review and revise" instead of "proofread," for example.

Prepetition time. The description of time spent prepetition should show that the services related to or were rendered in preparation or contemplation of the bankruptcy.

Personal services. The majority view is that personal services are not compensable as an administrative expense of the estate because such services only provide benefit to the debtor. An example would be defending a dischargeability proceeding.[76]

Duplication of effort. Duplication of effort should be avoided. Some courts allow only one attorney to bill for an intraoffice conference, for example. On the other hand, an attorney can argue that some communication between attorneys is not only expected but essential to competent representation.

Preparation of fee application. Courts are split on whether time spent in preparing the fee application is compensable. The majority hold that reasonable time in preparation may be allowed.[77]

Paralegals. The application should show that the paralegal has exercised some independent and informed judgment in what he or she did and how use of the paralegal has saved attorney time. Secretarial or routine tasks, such as opening mail or copying or filing, are not likely to be allowed, even if nonbankruptcy clients pay for such services.[78]

Expenses. Only "actual, necessary expenses" are allowable under § 330(a). Most courts construe this to mean that professionals may not be reimbursed for expenses that are part of the professional's overhead. Such unreimbursable expenses may include, depending on local practice, photocopy, telefax, express mailing, computerized research expenses, and any markup by the firm on the actual cost to the firm of the expenses.

---

76 *See In re* Reed, 890 F.2d 104 (8th Cir. 1989); *contra In re* Deihl, 80 B.R. 1 (Bankr. D. Me. 1987); *In re* Murray, 132 B.R. 808 (Bankr. D. Mass. 1991) (not a per se rule).

77 *E.g.*, Mares v. Credit Bureau, 801 F.2d 1197 (10th Cir. 1986) (under Civil Rights Act).

78 *See In re* Busy Beaver Bldg. Ctrs., Inc., 133 B.R. 753 (Bankr. W.D. Pa. 1992).

Expenses that are typically allowable are long distance telephone calls, travel costs, postage, and extraordinary photocopy costs, such as for mailing the plan and disclosure statement. Expenses must also be documented and not lumped together. The application should itemize how many photocopies were made, at what price, and what was photocopied.

The need for express mailing or delivery service must be shown (for example, that documents were requested by creditor or that there was some reason for using express mail besides the attorney's waiting until the last minute to file something). It might be a good idea to attach representative bills sent to other, nonbankruptcy clients (after having received their consent) to show that the expenses applied for are not part of overhead.

Hourly rates. The rates normally charged in the locale will be the rates generally allowed. In order to justify a higher than normal rate, the applicant must show that he or she possesses expertise not available in the locale. Be aware that although one's hourly rate may be comparable to local rates, it may be subject to reduction if the task performed could and should have been performed by a lower-priced professional.

Consolidated estates. Time should be kept separately for estates that are administratively (but not substantively) consolidated.[79]

Contemporaneous time-keeping. Recordation of fees and expenses should be done contemporaneously with the services performed or the expenses incurred.

§ 2.21 Judicial Review of Fee Application

The majority view is that, even in the absence of an objection, the court still has the independent judicial duty to determine whether the compensation is reasonable.[80] However, there is a small but determined minority that holds that without an objection by a party in interest, the court is without power to reduce the fees requested.[81] These courts believe that it is the duty of the United States Trustee and not the court to review and raise issues with respect to fees.[82] In denying compensation, most appellate courts have ruled that the bankruptcy court must make specific findings supporting the disallowance.[83]

Attorneys who object to another professional's fee application should follow the suggestions in *In re Hutter Construction Co.*[84] and object with specificity. Blanket and general objections might not be considered.

---

[79] *In re* Hutter Constr. Co., 126 B.R. 1005 (Bankr. E.D. Wis. 1991).

[80] *In re* Cascade Oil Co., 126 B.R. 99, 106 (D. Kan. 1991).

[81] *In re* Jensen's Interiors, Inc., 132 B.R. 105 (E.D. Pa. 1991).

[82] *Id.* at 106.

[83] *In re* N & T Assocs., Inc., 134 B.R. 17, 19 (D. Nev. 1991).

[84] 126 B.R. 1005, 1021 (Bankr. E.D. Wis. 1991).

§ 2.22 Form: Application of Attorney for Fees and Expenses

FORM 2–3
APPLICATION FOR FEES AND EXPENSES

IN THE UNITED STATES BANKRUPTCY COURT
FOR THE DISTRICT OF ______

IN RE: BANKRUPTCY CITY,)
)
) Case No.________
)
Debtor.)

FIRST INTERIM APPLICATION OF SMITH & WESSON, P.A.
FOR COMPENSATION OF SERVICES AND REIMBURSEMENT OF EXPENSES
AS ATTORNEY FOR DEBTOR

Smith & Wesson, P.A. (S&W) applies to the Court pursuant to 11 U.S.C. § 330 and Fed. R. Bankr. Proc. 2016 for compensation of services and reimbursement of expenses as attorney for Bankruptcy City (the Debtor). In support of its application, S&W would show the Court:

1. This case was filed as a voluntary petition for Chapter 11 relief on January 1, 1994.

2. S&W filed its Application for Approval of Employment as attorney for the Debtor on January 1, 1994.

3. The Court entered an order approving S&W's employment on February 1, 1994, effective to the date of the commencement of the services on December 26, 1993.

4. On February 1, 1994, the Court entered an order authorizing S&W to be paid 70 percent of its fees and 100 percent of its expenses on a monthly basis, requiring S&W to file monthly notices of its fee statements and requiring S&W to file interim applications for fees every 120 days.

5. S&W has filed the following monthly fee statements:

	70% Fees Amount Paid	100% Expenses Amount Paid	Total Amount Paid
Notice 1			
Notice 2			
Notice 3			

Notice 4
Notice 5

Totals

6. S&W has thus received payments of $[total payments] and has applied that amount against its $30,000 retainer.

7. This is S&W's first interim application. The application is for the period from December 26, 1993 through April 30, 1994. An itemization of the services rendered and expenses incurred for that period is attached as Exhibit A.

8. With respect to this First Interim Application, S&W requests compensation for attorney fees of $[fee amount] and reimbursement of expenses of $[expense amount], for a total of $[total fees and expenses]. After credit for amounts S&W has received on a monthly basis of $[credit amount], the net amount S&W requests is $[net amount].

9. The services performed for the Debtor during that period included preparing for and filing the bankruptcy petition and schedules, negotiating cash collateral with the bank, preparing and filing the plan and disclosure statement, and otherwise assisting the Debtor in carrying out its duties under this title.

10. The attorneys who performed services and their hourly rates are as follows:

David Grayhair, Partner	$[rate]/hour
Junior Achiever, Associate	$[rate]/hour
Trusty Worker, Paralegal	$[rate]/hour
Naivete Smiley, Law Clerk	$[rate]/hour

11. The case has not been converted. As compensation is received by S&W, it will not be shared or divided.

12. Expenses are charged at S&W's actual cost. S&W charges $.20 per page for photocopies, and $.25 per page for telecopies. S&W has also charged actual expenses for travel, postage, and computerized research.

WHEREFORE, S&W requests that the Court issue an order awarding it compensation for fees of $[fee amount] and reimbursement of expenses of $[expense amount], for a total award of $[total amount]; that, after crediting payments made of $[credit amount], the Court authorize S&W to apply the net amount of $[net amount] against the retainer of $30,000; and for such other relief as the Court deems just.

Respectfully Submitted:
SMITH & WESSON, P.A.
BY:______________________
ATTORNEY FOR DEBTOR

PAYMENT ISSUES FOR DEBTORS' AND CREDITORS' ATTORNEYS

§ 2.23 Treatment of Claims for Fees

Compensation and reimbursement awarded under § 330(a) are administrative expenses of the estate under § 503(b)(1). Attorney's fees that were allowed under other sections, § 506(b) for example, or that were for personal services to the debtor are not administrative expenses. Compensation and reimbursement allowed as administrative expenses under § 503(b)(2) are first priority administrative expenses under § 507.

Under § 504(a), a person receiving compensation under § 503(b)(2) or (b)(4) may not share or agree to share compensation. There are certain exceptions: under § 504(b)(1), members of a firm can share compensation, and under subsection (b)(2), attorneys for creditors who jointly file an involuntary petition may share compensation.[85]

§ 2.24 Chapter 11 Compared with Chapters 12 and 13

In a Chapter 11 case, two sections govern payment of allowed fees. Section 1129(a)(4) requires payments made by a debtor or plan proponent in connection with the case to have been approved or be subject to the approval of the court as reasonable. Section 1129(a)(9)(A) provides that first-priority claimants under § 507(a)(1), which includes attorneys awarded compensation as an administrative expense under §§ 330(a) and 503(b)(2), are entitled to payment of their claims in cash on the effective date of the plan, except to the extent that the claimant agrees to a different treatment.

By contrast, both Chapters 12 and 13 contain identical provisions requiring the full payment, in deferred cash payments, of all claims entitled to priority under § 507.[86]

§ 2.25 Other Code Sections Allowing Award of Fees

In certain instances, attorneys whose fees would ordinarily not be subject to the examination powers of the court, such as creditors' attorneys, may be required to submit their fees for approval to the court. Any submission of fees and expenses falling into these categories should comply with the application standards discussed in this chapter.

---

[85] § 502(b)(4) allows as an administrative expense the attorney's fees of a creditor who files an involuntary petition.

[86] 11 U.S.C. §§ 1222(a)(2), 1322(a)(2).

Representation of debtor or debtor-in-possession. Besides § 327, there are three other Code sections under which the court may allow debtors' attorneys' fees. First, in involuntary cases, § 303(i) authorizes the court to award a reasonable attorney's fee against petitioning creditors and in favor of the debtor, if the court dismisses an involuntary petition other than on consent of all petitioners and the debtor, and if the debtor does not waive the right to judgment.[87]

Second, § 362(h) of the automatic stay provisions mandates that the court award damages, including attorneys' fees, to an individual injured by any willful violation of a stay.

Last, § 523(d) requires the court to grant judgment in favor of a debtor for costs and a reasonable attorney's fee if a creditor files a § 523(a)(2) complaint for determination of dischargeability of a consumer debt without substantial justification.[88] The Code does not define "substantial justification." Attorneys can gain some guidance as to its meaning, however, from the Equal Access to Justice Act,[89] which authorizes an award of fees against the United States in favor of a prevailing party unless the position of the government was "substantially justified."[90]

There is a split of authority concerning whether a debtor must plead a request for fees under § 523(d) in its answer to the complaint, or whether a failure to do so waives the right to request fees.[91]

Representation of trustee. In addition to § 327, § 363(n) specifically allows the trustee to recover attorney's fees incurred in avoiding a sale if the sale price was controlled by an agreement among potential bidders.

Representation of creditor or creditor's committee. A secured creditor's attorney's fees included in a financing package under § 364 are subject to court examination because the fees will be paid from the estate.

Under §§ 365(b) and (d), governing executory contracts and unexpired leases, the trustee or debtor-in-possession is required to cure any default before an executory contract or unexpired lease may be assumed. If the contract or lease allows the creditor or landlord to recover attorney's fees incurred in collection activities when the

---

87 *See In re* Leach, 102 B.R. 805, 808 (Bankr. D. Kan. 1989) (§ 303(i)(1) routinely contemplates the award of attorney fees; award may be made regardless of whether the petition was filed in bad faith or found to be frivolous).

88 *See In re* Burns, 894 F.2d 361 (10th Cir. 1990) (consumer debt defined; loan used to invest in stock market was not consumer debt). *See also In re* Dobbins, 120 B.R. 120 (Bankr. W.D. Mo. 1990), *aff'd,* 151 B.R. 509 (W.D. Mo. 1991) (attorney's fees imposed under § 523(d).

89 28 U.S.C. § 2412(d).

90 *See* Pierce v. Underwood, 487 U.S. 552, 108 S. Ct. 2541, 101 L. Ed. 2d 490 (1988) (standard of review is abuse of discretion; *substantially justified* means to be justified in substance or in the main, not justified to a high degree; the action must be justified to a degree that could satisfy a reasonable person, and it must have a reasonable basis in both law and fact).

91 *Compare In re* Bernhardy, 103 B.R. 198 (Bankr. N.D. Ill, 1989) (not required), *with In re* Cokkinias, 28 B.R. 304 (Bankr. D. Mass. 1983) (required to be pled in answer).

contract or lease is in default, and applicable nonbankruptcy law permits the enforcement of an attorney's fee clause, the creditor or landlord can argue that its attorney's fees should be paid as part of curing the default.[92]

Similarly, under § 502(b)(6), a lessor whose lease is terminated may claim attorney's fees as damages when the attorney's fees are provided for in the lease agreement and are allowable under state law, subject to the cap set forth in that section.[93]

Next, § 503(b)(4), governing the allowance of administrative expenses, allows certain creditors to recover their reasonable attorney's and accountant's fees and expenses as an administrative expense. The creditors include those (a) who file an involuntary petition; (b) who recover, with court approval, and for the benefit of the estate, any property transferred or concealed by the debtor; (c) who incur fees and expenses in connection with the prosecution of a criminal offense relating to the case or to the business or property of the debtor; (d) who make a substantial contribution in a case under Chapter 9 or 11; or (e) who are custodians replaced under § 543.[94]

The section most commonly available to secured creditors is § 506(b). To the extent a secured creditor is oversecured, there shall be allowed "any reasonable fees, costs or charges provided for under the agreement under which such claim arose."

Finally, a creditor who is successful in obtaining a determination that its debt is nondischargeable under § 523(a)(2) may request fees as part of the nondischarged debt.[95]

§ 2.26 Non-Code Bases for Award of Fees

Other sections or rules under which attorneys fees may be awarded (and thus examined) include Bankruptcy Rule 1007(k) (cost of preparing lists and schedules); Bankruptcy Rule 9011 (sanctions); 28 U.S.C. § 1927 (liability for excess costs for vexatious multiplication of pleadings); and Federal Rules of Civil Procedure 26(g), 37(d), 16(f), and 56(g) (violation of discovery and other provisions).

---

92 *See In re* Pacific Sea Farms, Inc., 134 B.R. 11, 15 (Bankr. D. Haw. 1991) (court found debtor was obligated to pay postpetition rental claim, including landlord's attorney's fees, incurred in connection with lease; § 365(d)(3) claims are not limited only to rent claims but include all obligations under the terms of the lease).

93 *See In re* McLean Enter., Inc., 105 B.R. 928 (Bankr. W.D. Mo. 1989).

94 *See In re* Lister, 846 F.2d 55 (10th Cir. 1988) (finding no substantial contribution under the circumstances).

95 *See In re* Kroh, 87 B.R. 1004, 1008 (Bankr. W.D. Mo. 1988) (successful creditor in § 523(a)(2)(B) action entitled to attorney's fees in pursuing dischargeability proceeding when note provided for payment of reasonable attorney fees upon collection of debt; no award made, however, because creditor failed to show what constituted reasonable fees). *See also In re* Martin, 761 F.2d 1163, 1168 (6th Cir. 1985) (debt under § 523(a)(2) includes state-approved contractually required attorney fees).

CHAPTER 3

CASH COLLATERAL: THE DEBTOR'S LIFEBLOOD

Christine M. Arguello

§ 3.1 Introduction

The primary purpose of Chapter 11 reorganization is to allow a debtor the opportunity to reorganize its business so that it may continue its operations, that is, continue to provide jobs, to satisfy creditors' claims, and to produce a return for its owners.[1] The primary assumption behind the reorganization provisions of Chapter 11 of the Code is that the assets of the debtor are more valuable if the business is ongoing than if the business were closed down and the assets liquidated.[2]

However, as a practical matter, to continue with its day-to-day operations, the debtor needs to use assets of the business. For example, to continue in business postpetition, a debtor most likely will sell its prepetition inventory. In order to purchase new inventory, pay the postpetition wages of its employees, pay its monthly rent, and so forth, the debtor may need to use the cash generated by the sale of prepetition inventory. Such use is required especially by small businesses, which generally are not able to hold as much money in reserve as do larger companies. With respect to an insolvent business, withholding the ability to use monies generated by the assets of the business is tantamount to withholding life-support systems from a critically ill individual. From the creditor's perspective, however, allowing a debtor to exhaust, without limitation, revenues generated by the sale of assets which are subject to a creditor's lien results in quite a blow to the secured creditor whose only prospect for payment of its debt may be from proceeds of the sales of inventory. On the other hand, because the value of an ongoing business is generally greater than the value of the piecemeal sale of its assets, a creditor must keep in mind that, provided its interest is protected, it is often better to allow a debtor to use monies generated by the business than to force the business to close down.

Therefore, if a debtor and creditor expect to protect their respective interests, it is essential that both understand the dos and don'ts of using monies generated by a business subsequent to the filing of the bankruptcy petition.

§ 3.2 Section 552: Effect of Bankruptcy on Collateral Given as Security

In order for the debtor to reorganize its business, all the debtor's property, even that subject to a creditor's lien, must be included in the estate.[3] To aid the debtor in achieving its fresh start, § 552(a) of the Bankruptcy Code provides that property acquired by the estate after the filing of bankruptcy will not be subject to a creditor's security interest, even if the security agreement contains a provision encompassing after-acquired property:

> Except as provided in subsection (b) of this section, property acquired by the estate or by the debtor after the commencement of the case is not subject to any lien resulting from any security agreement entered into by the debtor before the commencement of the case.[4]

---

[1] H.R. Rep. No. 595, 95th Cong., 1st Sess. 220 (1977), *reprinted in* 1978 U.S.C.C.A.N. 5787.

[2] *Id.*

[3] 11 U.S.C. § 541. United States v. Whiting Pools, Inc., 462 U.S. 198, 103 S. Ct. 2309 (1983).

[4] 11 U.S.C. § 552(a).

The purpose of § 552(a) is to prevent a creditor's prepetition security interest in after-acquired property from attaching to property acquired by the estate after the filing of a bankruptcy petition.[5] For example, a creditor who has a properly perfected security interest in a debtor's inventory of automobiles "whether now existing or hereafter acquired" will not be able to claim a lien on automobiles acquired postpetition.

In other words, the "hereafter acquired" language is no longer effective as against the estate unless the exception of § 552(b) is applicable:

> if the debtor and an entity entered into a security agreement before the commencement of the case and if the security interest created by such security agreement extends to property of the debtor acquired before the commencement of the case and to proceeds, product, offspring, rents, or profits of such property, then such security interest extends to such proceeds, product, offspring, rents, or profits acquired by the estate after the commencement of the case to the extent provided by such security agreement and by applicable nonbankruptcy law, except to any extent that the court, after notice and a hearing and based on the equities of the case, orders otherwise.[6]

But for the existence of § 552(b), a creditor would appear to have no right to claim an interest in the "product, offspring, rents, or profits" generated by its collateral. Section 552(b) protects the postpetition interests of a creditor who has a properly perfected security interest in postpetition property.

§ 3.3 Section 363(c)(1): General Rule Regarding Sale, Lease, or Use of Property of the Estate

Any analysis of the debtor's rights in a Chapter 11 bankruptcy must begin with the general rule that the debtor-in-possession (hereinafter referred to as debtor) has virtually the same rights and powers granted to a trustee by the Bankruptcy Code.[7] Because of the underlying policies of Chapter 11 reorganization, it is no surprise that one of the rights granted to a trustee and, pursuant to § 1107(a), to a debtor by the Code is the right to continue to operate the business after the bankruptcy petition is filed. The pertinent grant of authority for such use, sale, or lease of property is found in § 363(c)(1) of the Code, which provides:

> If the business of the debtor is authorized to be operated under section 721, 1108, 1304, 1203 or 1204 of this title and unless the court orders otherwise, the trustee may enter into transactions, including the sale or lease of property of the estate, in the ordinary course of business, without notice or a hearing, and may use property of the estate in the ordinary course of business without notice or a hearing.

---

[5] *See* H.R. Rep. No. 595, 95th Cong., 1st Sess. 376-77 (1977), *reprinted in* 1978 U.S.C.C.A.N. 5787, 6332-33; S. Rep. No. 989, 95th Cong., 2d Sess. 91 (1978), *reprinted in* 1978 U.S.C.C.A.N. 5787, 5877.

[6] 11 U.S.C. § 552(b).

[7] 11 U.S.C. § 1107(a).

Section 363(c)(1) allows the debtor to use, sell, or lease property of the estate in the ordinary course of business without securing prior court approval.[8] As long as a debtor is acting in accord with either its historically normal course of business or the normal course of business for the industry, it can continue to buy and sell goods, collect receivables, pay its postpetition accounts, pay its employees' postpetition salaries, enter into contracts for the manufacture of new goods, and so forth.

§ 3.4 —Limitations on the Use, Sale, or Lease of Property

The authorization provided by § 363(c)(1) is not without its limitations. First, the express language limits the sale, lease, or use of property of the estate to that which is done in the ordinary course of business. In order to sell, lease, or use property of the estate other than in the ordinary course of business, the debtor must comply with the provisions of § 363(b) which require notice and a hearing.

For a secured creditor, a second and more important limitation is contained in § 363(c)(2), which provides:

> The trustee may not use, sell, or lease cash collateral under paragraph (1) of this subsection unless—
>
> (A) each entity that has an interest in such cash collateral consents; or
>
> (B) the court, after notice and a hearing, authorizes such use, sale, or lease in accordance with the provisions of this section.[9]

Prior to the passage of the Code in 1978, judges routinely issued ex parte orders authorizing debtors to use, sell, or lease property, leaving creditors claiming an interest in such property to fight an uphill battle in the appellate courts to overturn the order.[10] Sections 363 and 552(b) were included in the Code because of concerns that there were very few limits on a debtor's ability to take action, which resulted in dissipation of collateral such as accounts receivable or cash from sales of inventory.[11] Fortunately for creditors with a security interest in property of the debtor, Congress enacted the provisions of § 363 to provide creditors with some due process and just compensation protections. First, § 363(c)(2) limits rights granted in § 363(c)(1), by prohibiting the use of cash collateral, even if such use would be in the ordinary course of business, unless the creditor consents to such use, or the court, after notice and a hearing, authorizes such use.[12]

In addition, Congress imposed an affirmative duty on the debtor to "segregate and account for any cash collateral in [its] possession, custody, or control" as of the date

---

8 *Id.* § 363(c)(1).

9 11 U.S.C. § 363(c)(2).

10 H.R. Rep. No. 595, 95th Cong., 1st Sess. 182 (1977), *reprinted in* 1978 U.S.C.C.A.N. 5787, 6143.

11 *Id.*

12 11 U.S.C. § 363(c)(2).

of the filing of the Chapter 11 petition.[13] At least one court has ruled that the only relief a creditor may obtain under § 363 is to require the debtor to segregate and account for the cash collateral.[14] A creditor seeking return of cash collateral used by a debtor in violation of § 363(c)(2) may not file a motion pursuant to § 363, but rather must file an adversary complaint pursuant to Rule 7001.[15]

Finally, § 363(e) requires that, upon the request of a secured creditor, the "court, with or without a hearing, shall prohibit or condition such use, sale, or lease as is necessary to provide adequate protection of such interest."[16] The adequate protection requirements of the Code are discussed in greater depth in **Chapter 5** (adequate protection in general) and **§ 3.10** (adequate protection under § 363).

There is no question that by enacting § 363(c)(2), Congress made an important distinction between cash collateral and other property of the estate. This, however, raises the question of what cash collateral is.

§ 3.5 Section 363(a): Definition of Cash Collateral

Section 363(a) defines cash collateral as:

> cash, negotiable instruments, documents of title, securities, deposit accounts, or other cash equivalents whenever acquired in which the estate and an entity other than the estate have an interest and includes the proceeds, products, offspring, rents, or profits of property subject to a security interest as provided in section 552(b) of this title, whether existing before or after the commencement of a case under this title.[17]

As the broad language of § 363(a) indicates, virtually anything can be or become cash collateral. Although accounts receivable, inventory, contract rights, and general intangibles are not cash collateral,[18] as soon as these property interests are converted to a monetary equivalent and received by the debtor, they become the cash collateral of the creditor who holds a properly perfected security interest in the underlying collateral.

Generally, a creditor making a claim to cash collateral must be a secured creditor.[19] Without a secured claim in the property claimed as cash collateral, the creditor "holds no greater interest in [cash collateral] than that of any other general [unsecured] creditor."[20] The property would therefore be part of the bankruptcy estate, free of any

---

13 *Id.* § 363(c)(4). *See In re* White Plains Dev. Corp., 136 B.R. 93, 95 (Bankr. S.D.N.Y. 1992).

14 *In re* Realty Southwest Assocs., 140 B.R. 360, 365 (Bankr. S.D.N.Y. 1992).

15 *Id.* Such a request by the creditor is in the nature of an action for reclamation pursuant to 11 U.S.C. § 546(c), which must be instituted by an adversary complaint.

16 11 U.S.C. § 363(e).

17 11 U.S.C. § 363(a).

18 124 Cong. Rec. S17409 (daily ed. Oct. 6, 1978) (statement of Sen. DeConcini).

19 An exception to this general rule is if the creditor, although unsecured, has a right to setoff. See **§ 3.7.**

20 *In re* Kuhn, 11 B.R. 746, 750 (Bankr. S.D. W. Va. 1981).

encumbrances.[21] Thus, the relevant question for a cash collateral issue is whether the creditor has a valid secured interest in the property it claims as cash collateral.

§ 3.6 Law Controlling Creditor's Interest

The Supreme Court, in the landmark case *Butner v. United States,*[22] ruled that "unless some federal interest requires a different result, property interests created and defined by state law are controlling in bankruptcy."[23] Although *Butner* was decided under the former Bankruptcy Act, courts agree that its holding applies to the current Bankruptcy Code.[24]

As one court noted, the problem created by application of state law to this issue is that, to determine whether a protected property interest exists, "there are potentially as many different answers to the . . . question as there are states with different laws on the enforceability of . . . liens."[25]

Of all the possible things that can become cash collateral, two types of property interests will be further discussed. The first type, funds subject to setoff, is expanded upon because it is an exception to the general rule that in order to be cash collateral, the underlying property must be the subject of a security interest or lien. See § **3.7.** The second type, rents and assignment of rents, is discussed in more detail because considering rents as cash collateral has been the most litigated issue in disputes involving cash collateral in recent years. See §§ **3.8** and **3.9.**

§ 3.7 —Funds Subject to Setoff

Subject to certain exceptions,[26] § 553(a) provides that "this title does not affect any right of a creditor to offset a mutual debt owing by such creditor to the

---

21 *See id.* at 749.

22 440 U.S. 48 (1979).

23 *Id.* at 55.

24 *See* Midlantic Nat'l Bank v. Sourlis, 141 B.R. 826, 829 n.1 (D.N.J. 1992) (citing *In re* Village Properties, Ltd., 723 F.2d 441, 445–46 (5th Cir.), *cert. denied sub nom* Wolters Village, Ltd. v. Village Properties, Ltd., 466 U.S. 974, 104 S. Ct. 2350, 80 L. Ed. 2d 823 (1984)).

25 *In re* Stone Ridge Assocs., Ltd. Partnership, 142 B.R. 967, 970 (Bankr. D. Kan. 1992).

26 The setoff provisions of § 553(a) do not apply to (1) a claim that is disallowed other than under § 502(b)(3); (2) a claim that was transferred by an entity other than the debtor to the creditor during the 90 days before the filing of the petition while the debtor was insolvent; (3) a debt incurred for the purpose of obtaining a right of setoff, while the debtor was insolvent and during the 90 days before the filing of the petition; (4) an offset made during the 90 days before the filing of the petition that improves the creditor's position within the 90 days before the filing of the petition. *See* 11 U.S.C. §§ 553(a)(1)–(3) and 553(b)(1). For purposes of § 553, "the debtor is presumed to have been insolvent on and during the 90 days immediately preceding the date of the filing of the petition." *Id.* § 553(c).

debtor . . . against a claim of such creditor against the debtor."[27] Moreover, § 506 provides that a claim that is subject to setoff under § 553 is "a secured claim to the extent of the value of such creditor's interest in the estate's interest in such property, or to the extent of the amount subject to setoff."[28] In other words, even though the right to setoff is not technically a security interest and is expressly excluded from Article 9 of the U.C.C.,[29] a creditor with setoff rights is treated as a secured creditor for purposes of § 363(a). A creditor who both owes a debt to the debtor and holds a claim against the debtor that may be subject to setoff is actually holding cash collateral despite the fact that the underlying debt owed to the creditor is unsecured. For example, assume that a bank has an unsecured loan to a debtor. Generally, this creditor would stand in no better stead than other unsecured creditors. However, if the debtor has an account with the bank, the money in the account is considered to be a debt owed by the bank to the debtor, which may be set off. As such, the money in the account would be cash collateral and subject to the restrictions of § 363(c).

Because of the automatic stay provisions of § 362, the creditor cannot actually perform a setoff of the funds. There is no real consensus regarding whether the creditor's placement of an administrative freeze on the debtor's account violates the automatic stay.[30] However, the debtor is not allowed to use the funds without consent of the creditor or authorization from the court because that use would violate the § 363(c) prohibition on unauthorized use of cash collateral.[31] Either or both parties may, however, make the appropriate motions to end the stalemate, for example, the creditor may move for relief from stay to assert its right to setoff, or the debtor may move for leave to use the cash collateral.[32]

---

27 11 U.S.C. § 553(a).

28 *Id.* § 506(a).

29 *See* U.C.C. § 9-104(i).

30 *Compare* cases ruling that an administrative freeze is the equivalent of a setoff and thus violates the automatic stay: Cusanno v. Fidelity Bank, 29 B.R. 810 (E.D. Pa.), *aff'g In re* Cusanno, 17 B.R. 879 (Bankr. E.D. Pa.); *In re* New York City Shoes, Inc., 78 B.R. 426 (Bankr. E.D. Pa. 1987); *In re* Wildcat Constr. Co., 57 B.R. 981 (Bankr. D. Vt. 1986); *In re* Rio, 55 B.R. 814 (Bankr. M.D. Ala. 1985); *In re* LGH Resources, Inc., 34 B.R. 202 (Bankr. W.D. Tex. 1983); *In re* Executive Assocs., Inc., 24 B.R. 171 (Bankr. S.D. Tex. 1982); *In re* Nelson, 6 B.R. 248 (Bankr. D. Kan. 1980); *with* cases that allow an administrative freeze of the debtor's account: *In re* Edgins, 36 B.R. 480 (Bankr. 9th Cir. 1984); *In re* Stann, 39 B.R. 246 (D. Kan. 1984); Kenney's Franchise Corp. v. Central Fidelity Bank, 22 B.R. 747 (W.D. Va. 1982), *rev'g In re* Kenney's Franchise Corp., 12 B.R. 390 (Bankr. W.D. Va. 1981); *In re* Williams, 61 B.R. 567 (Bankr. N.D. Texas 1986); *In re* Hoffman, 51 B.R. 42 (Bankr. W.D. Ark. 1985); *In re* Gazelle, Inc., 17 B.R. 617 (Bankr. W.D. Wis. 1982); and *In re* Carpenter, 14 B.R. 405 (Bankr. M.D. Tenn. 1981).

31 *In re* Edgins, 36 B.R. 480, 483 (9th Cir. 1984). Moreover, the turnover provisions of § 542 expressly except from turnover a "debt that may be offset under section 553." 11 U.S.C. § 542(b).

32 *In re* Edgins, 36 B.R. at 483.

§ 3.8 —Controversy over Rents

Although rents are included as cash collateral by the express language of § 363(a), the most litigated issue in recent years has been whether a secured creditor with a prepetition assignment of rents can claim the postpetition rents as cash collateral under § 363. The courts all seem to agree with the general proposition that rents from property that is subject to a properly recorded assignment of rents constitute cash collateral if they are subject to a security interest within the meaning of 11 U.S.C. § 552(b). Although the legislative history of § 363(a) indicates that cash collateral was intended to include "rents received from real property before or after the commencement of the case . . . to the extent that they are subject to a lien,"[33] the issue that has caused so much confusion and controversy in the bankruptcy arena is to what extent the postpetition rents are subject to a prepetition security interest.

Some courts hold that, in order for postpetition rents to be cash collateral under the Bankruptcy Code, a mortgagee with a recorded assignment of rents must take some prepetition action, for example, obtain the appointment of a receiver or take possession or control of the rents. In other words, if the assignment of rents is not enforced prepetition, rents collected postpetition are not cash collateral under § 552(b).[34] One jurisdiction has taken this rationale one step further and has indicated that because state law gave the mortgagor complete control of rents until the mortgagee lawfully obtained possession of them, an interest in rents that is not enforced prepetition is subject to the lien avoidance provisions of § 544.[35]

A second line of cases holds that a secured creditor has no right to collect rents without prebankruptcy enforcement, but allows the secured creditor to claim the postbankruptcy rents as cash collateral from the date that the creditor takes affirmative steps to terminate the debtor's use of the rents. However, even among these decisions, there is not a clear majority view regarding what is the appropriate postpetition action that must be taken by the creditor to perfect its interest in the postpetition rents. Some courts have held that in the absence of prepetition enforcement, a creditor can still perfect an interest in postpetition rents by taking the affirmative step of filing notice pursuant to § 546(b),[36] which provides:

---

33 S. Rep. No. 989, 95th Cong., 1st Sess. 55 (1978), *reprinted in* 1978 U.S.C.C.A.N. 5787, 5841.

34 *In re* Stanley Station Assocs., Ltd. Partnership, 139 B.R. 990 (Bankr. D. Kan. 1992); *In re* American Continental Corp., 105 B.R. 564 (Bankr. D. Ariz. 1989); *In re* Multi-Group III, Ltd. Partnership, 99 B.R. 5 (Bankr. D. Ariz. 1989). *But see* Scottsdale Medical Pavilion v. Mutual Benefit Life Ins. Co. in Rehabilitation (*In re* Scottsdale Medical Pavilion), 159 B.R. 295 (Bankr. 9th Cir. 1993) (criticizing court's rationale in *In re* Multi-Group III, Ltd. Partnership).

35 *In re* Stanley Station Assocs., Ltd. Partnership, 139 B.R. 990 (Bankr. D. Kan. 1992). *But see In re* Stone Ridge Assocs., Ltd. Partnership, 142 B.R. 967 (Bankr. D. Kan. 1992) (although citing *In re Stanley Associates* with approval, court indicated that if debtor lacked reasonable likelihood of reorganization, creditor who had not obtained possession of rents prior to bankruptcy filing was entitled to postpetition rents).

36 Virginia Beach Fed. Sav. & Loan Ass'n v. Wood, 97 B.R. 71 (N.D. Okla. 1988), *aff'd,* 901 F.2d 849, 853 (10th Cir. 1990); Saline State Bank v. Mahloch, 834 F.2d 690,

> The rights and powers of a trustee under sections 544, 545 and 549 of this title are subject to any generally applicable law that permits perfection of an interest in property to be effective against an entity that acquires rights in such property before the date of such perfection. If such law requires seizure of such property or commencement of an action to accomplish such perfection, and such property has not been seized or such action has not been commenced before the date of the filing of the petition, such interest in property shall be perfected by notice within the time fixed by such law for such seizure or commencement.[37]

These courts consider the security interest to be perfected as of the prepetition recording date for purposes of § 544[38] but enforceable only with respect to rents after the filing of the notice.

However, other courts have held that unless state law allows for postpetition perfection to relate back to the date of the execution of the assignment or mortgage, § 546(b) does not permit the postpetition perfection of a prepetition rent assignment.[39] These courts argue that Congress did not intend § 546(b) as a vehicle for postpetition perfection of a security interest in rents. Rather, the primary purpose of § 546(b) was "to protect, in spite of the surprise intervention of a bankruptcy petition, those whom state law protects by allowing them to perfect their liens or interests as of an effective date that is earlier than the date of perfection."[40] These courts assert that the lien interests contemplated by § 546(b) are those with delayed perfection rights such as mechanic's and materialmen's liens.[41]

But even these courts are split regarding the ultimate outcome of a creditor's claim. Some hold that in order for an interest in postpetition rents to be recognized,

---

695–96 (8th Cir. 1987); Casbeer v. State Fed. Sav. & Loan Ass'n (*In re* Casbeer), 793 F.2d 1436 (5th Cir. 1986); *In re* Village Properties, Ltd., 723 F.2d 441 (5th Cir.) *cert. denied sub nom.* Wolters Village, Ltd. v. Village Properties, Ltd., 466 U.S. 974 (1984); Home Sav. Ass'n of Kan. City v. Woodstock Assocs. I (*In re* Woodstock Assocs. I), 120 B.R. 436, 447–48 (Bankr. N.D. Ill. 1990); *In re* American Continental Corp., 105 B.R. 564 (Bankr. D. Ariz. 1989); *In re* National Real Estate Ltd. Partnership-II, 104 B.R. 968 (Bankr. E.D. Wis. 1989).

37 11 U.S.C. § 546(b).

38 This prevents an outcome that would allow the trustee or debtor to avoid the creditor's interest in postpetition rents.

39 Midlantic Nat'l Bank v. Sourlis, 141 B.R. 826 (D.N.J. 1992); *In re* Polo Club Apartments Assocs. Ltd. Partnership, 150 B.R. 840 (Bankr. N.D. Ga. 1993); *In re* Princeton Overlook Joint Venture, 143 B.R. 625, 629 n.10 (Bankr. D.N.J. 1992) (applying New Jersey law). *See also In re* Raleigh/Spring Forest Apartment Assocs., 118 B.R. 42, 46 (Bankr. E.D.N.C. 1990) (§ 546(b) inapplicable to assist creditor because seizure not required by state law for perfection of rent assignment); Sears Sav. Bank v. Tucson Indus. Partners (*In re* Tucson Indus. Partners), 129 B.R. 614 (Bankr. 9th Cir. 1991) (applying Arizona law), *vacated as moot,* 990 F.2d 1099 (9th Cir. 1993).

40 H.R. Rep. No. 595, 95th Cong., 1st Sess. 371 (1977), *reprinted in* 1978 U.S.C.C.A.N. 5787, 6327; S. Rep. No. 989, 95th Cong., 2d Sess. 86 (1978), *reprinted in* 1978 U.S.C.C.A.N. 5787, 5872.

41 *In re* Polo Club Apartments Assocs. Ltd. Partnership, 150 B.R. 840 (Bankr. N.D. Ga. 1993); *In re* Multi-Group III Ltd. Partnership, 99 B.R. 5 (Bankr. D. Ariz. 1989). *See also In re* TM Carlton House Partners, Ltd., 91 B.R. 349 (Bankr. E.D. Pa. 1988).

the right to such rents must have existed prior to the filing of the bankruptcy petition, or some affirmative action, other than filing of a § 546(b) notice, is necessary.[42] To hold otherwise would grant an automatic security interest in rents by the mere happenstance of the bankruptcy filing when "state law would deny such an automatic benefit and require the mortgagee to take some affirmative action before his rights are recognized."[43] These courts conclude that the creditor may "ask the bankruptcy court to authorize those actions necessary to enforce the assignment and thereby complete the assignee's entitlement to the rents."[44] In other words, although the automatic stay prohibits any action against property of the estate, in order to be entitled to the cash collateral protections of § 363, a creditor must take some affirmative postpetition action in the bankruptcy court. For example, a creditor can file a motion claiming such rents as cash collateral. Such a motion can include a myriad of requests for relief, such as a demand for adequate protection, a request for a bankruptcy court to order the debtor to sequester and account for rents, or a request that the court restrain or condition the debtor's use of the rents.[45]

Moving further down the spectrum are the cases which, although they recognize that § 546(b) cannot be used to perfect a security interest in rents, hold that a creditor has a perfected security interest in the rents as of the date of proper state-law recordation. These courts are critical of opinions that require some prepetition action to perfect an interest in rents, and argue that such courts mistakenly equate enforcement or entitlement with perfection of the security interest.[46] They admonish that in order to properly analyze the issues presented by claims that rents are cash collateral, the courts must distinguish between perfection and enforcement of a security interest in rents.[47] Because the intent of § 363 of the Bankruptcy Code was to protect the creditor's rights in rents as an interest in property and as a security interest within the meaning of § 552(b), the bottom line for these courts is what action state law requires a creditor to take in order to perfect a security interest in rents.[48] Whether a

---

[42] *In re* Polo Club Apartments Assocs. Ltd. Partnership, 150 B.R. 840, 853 (Bankr. N.D. Ga. 1993).

[43] *Id.*

[44] *In re* Vienna Park Properties, 136 B.R. 43, 53 (S.D.N.Y. 1992) (quoting *In re* Raleigh/Spring Forest Apartments Assocs., 118 B.R. 42, 46 (Bankr. E.D.N.C. 1990)).

[45] ABN Amro Bank N.V. v. Carmania Corp. N.V. (*In re* Carmania Corp. N.V.), 154 B.R. 160 (S.D.N.Y. 1993); *In re* Village Properties, Ltd., 723 F.2d 441 (5th Cir.), *cert. denied sub nom.* Wolters Village, Ltd. v. Village Properties, Ltd., 466 U.S. 974 (1984); *In re* Casbeer, 793 F.2d 1436 (5th Cir. 1986); *In re* Polo Club Apartments Assocs. Ltd. Partnership, 150 B.R. 840 (Bankr. N.D. Ga. 1993). *See also* Bank of Edwardsville v. J.D. Monarch Dev. Co. (*In re* J.D. Monarch Dev. Co.), 153 B.R. 829 (Bankr. S.D. Ill. 1993) (motion for relief from stay to foreclose is not sufficient action to entitle creditor to rents pending completion of foreclosure sale; creditor should have sought abandonment of property).

[46] *In re* Princeton Overlook Joint Venture, 143 B.R. 625, 630 (Bankr. D.N.J. 1992).

[47] *In re* Vienna Park Properties, 136 B.R. 43 (S.D.N.Y. 1992); *In re* Park at Dash Point Ltd. Partnership, 121 B.R. 850 (Bankr. W.D. Wash. 1990); Midlantic Nat'l Bank v. Sourlis, 141 B.R. 826 (D. N.J. 1992).

[48] Sears Sav. Bank v. Tucson Indus. Partners (*In re* Tucson Indus. Partners), 129 B.R. 614 (Bankr. 9th Cir. 1991), *vacated as moot,* 990 F.2d 1099 (9th Cir. 1993); Midlantic Nat'l Bank v. Sourlis, 141 B.R. 826 (D.N.J. 1992).

state requires some further affirmative action to enforce the right to collect the rents is not relevant to the determination of whether rents under an assignment of rents are cash collateral.[49] Creditors with a properly recorded security interest in rents are protected by § 552(b) and can claim postpetition rents as cash collateral under § 363 regardless of whether they took any prepetition[50] or postpetition action to enforce such an assignment.[51] As such, the creditor does not need to rely on § 546(b) to protect its claim to rents as cash collateral.[52] To hold otherwise would discourage workouts between debtors and creditors by forcing creditors to race to the property to take possession of the rents or to race to the state court to foreclose or obtain appointment of a receiver before the debtor can file a bankruptcy petition.[53] This protection also insulates the creditor from claims of subsequent assignees, including claims by the bankruptcy trustee or debtor-in-possession to avoid, pursuant to § 544, the creditor's § 552(b) claim to the postpetition rents.[54]

§ 3.9 —Solution to the Rents Issue

During the spring 1993 term, Senators Heflin and Grassley introduced Senate Bill 540, a bill addressing certain commercial and consumer issues in bankruptcy.[55] In an effort to achieve uniformity among the courts regarding whether rents and hotel revenues are cash collateral, Senate Bill 540 includes amendments to both § 363 and § 552(b) which would clarify that rents and hotel revenues are cash collateral if the lender has a properly recorded security agreement relating to such rents or revenues.

Senate Bill 540, as amended by the Senate Judiciary Committee, proposes to amend § 363(a) by adding, after the word "property," the following language: "and the fees, charges, accounts or other payments for the use or occupancy of rooms and other public facilities in hotels, motels, or other lodging properties."[56] For a detailed discussion of various issues surrounding hotel revenues, see **Chapter 4.** In addition, Senate Bill 540 proposes adding the following paragraph to Bankruptcy Code § 552(b):

---

49 *In re* Park at Dash Point Ltd. Partnership, 121 B.R. 850 (Bankr. W.D. Wash. 1990); Midlantic Nat'l Bank v. Sourlis, 141 B.R. 826 (D.N.J. 1992).

50 *In re* Park at Dash Point Ltd. Partnership, 121 B.R. at 855; *In re* Vienna Park Properties, 136 B.R. at 52.

51 Sears Sav. Bank v. Tucson Indus. Partners (*In re* Tucson Indus. Partners), 129 B.R. 614 (Bankr. 9th Cir. 1991), *vacated as moot,* 990 F.2d 1099 (9th Cir. 1993); Midlantic Nat'l Bank v. Sourlis, 141 B.R. 826 (D.N.J. 1992). *See also* Scottsdale Medical Pavilion v. Mutual Benefit Life Ins. Co. in Rehabilitation (*In re* Scottsdale Medical Pavilion), 159 B.R. 295 (Bankr. 9th Cir. 1993); *In re* Somero, 122 B.R. 634 (Bankr. D. Me. 1991).

52 Midlantic Nat'l Bank v. Sourlis, 141 B.R. 826 (D.N.J. 1992).

53 *Id.*

54 J.H. Streiker & Co. v. SeSide Co., Ltd. (*In re* SeSide Co., Ltd.), 152 B.R. 878, 884 (E.D. Pa. 1993); *In re* Princeton Overlook Joint Venture, 143 B.R. 625 (Bankr. D.N.J. 1992).

55 *See generally* S. 540, 103d Cong., 1st. Sess. (1993).

56 *Id.* § 206(b).

> (2)(A) Except as provided in sections 363, 506(c), 522, 544, 545, 547, and 548, if
>
> (i) the debtor and an entity entered into a security agreement that was duly recorded in the public records before the commencement of the case; and
>
> (ii) the security interest created by the security agreement extends to
>
> (I) property of the debtor acquired before the commencement of the case; and
>
> (II) (aa) to amounts paid as rents of such property; or
>
> (bb) to amounts paid for the use or occupancy of such property (including fees, charges, accounts, or other payments for the use or occupancy of rooms and other public facilities in a property such as a hotel, motel or other lodging),
>
> the security interest extends to such amounts paid to the estate as rents or as fees, charges, accounts, or other payments after the commencement of the case to the extent provided in the security agreement, whether or not the security interest in such rents, or such fees, charges, accounts or other payments is perfected under applicable nonbankruptcy law, except to the extent that the court, after notice and a hearing and based on the equities of the case, orders otherwise.[57]

Finally, in an effort to resolve the § 544 controversy regarding whether a trustee or debtor has the power to avoid a creditor's interest in postpetition rents and revenues, Senate Bill 540 proposes adding the following language to section 552(b):

> (B) If a security interest extends under subparagraph (A) to rents acquired by the estate after the commencement of the case, the security interest in such rents shall be deemed to be perfected for the purpose of section 544(a).[58]

Although the congressional term concluded without passage of the Heflin-Grassley bill, it is expected that it is only a matter of time before Congress will take action to help the courts close this Pandora's box.

§ 3.10 Necessity of Providing Adequate Protection to the Creditor

Assuming that certain property of the debtor is cash collateral, upon the request of a creditor with an interest in cash collateral, the court is required to prohibit or condition the use of that collateral to the extent necessary to provide adequate protection of such interest to the creditor.[59] The concept of adequate protection in bankruptcy is derived from the Fifth Amendment's protection of property interests.[60] Adequate protection is a question of fact because it has as its linch pin the concept of value

---

57 *Id.* § 206.

58 *Id.*

59 11 U.S.C. § 363(e); *In re* Bumper Sales, Inc., 907 F.2d 1430 (4th Cir. 1990).

60 Wright v. Union Cent. Life Ins. Co., 311 U.S. 273, 61 S. Ct. 196, 85 L. Ed. 184 (1940); H.R. Rep. No. 595, 95th Cong., 1st Sess. 338–40 (1977), *reprinted in* 1978 U.S.C.C.A.N. 5787, 6295–96; S. Rep. No. 989, 95th Cong., 2nd Sess. 49 (1978), *reprinted in* 1978 U.S.C.C.A.N. 5787, 5835.

and therefore is determined on a case-by-case basis.[61] "The principle of adequate protection reconciles the competing interests of the debtor . . . and the secured creditor."[62] The debtor is interested in continuing the operations of the business and reorganizing free from the harassment of creditors. The secured creditor, on the other hand, is interested in preventing depletion of volatile collateral which is subject to rapid dissipation.

Despite the § 363(c) prohibition on use of cash collateral, some debtors continue to use cash collateral without the consent of the creditor or authorization from the court. If the creditor does not request adequate protection, the debtor may not have an affirmative duty to provide adequate protection.[63] Moreover, the courts are divided regarding the date from which the creditor is entitled to adequate protection. Some courts indicate that a secured creditor is entitled to adequate protection against deterioration as of the petition date.[64] Other courts, relying on the express language of § 363(e) which provides that "on request" the court "shall prohibit or condition" the use, sale, or lease of the collateral as is necessary to provide adequate protection, hold that a secured creditor is entitled to adequate protection only upon motion and only prospectively from the time such protection is invoked by the creditor.[65] The Eighth Circuit, in the case of *Ahlers v. Norwest Bank,*[66] rationalized that

> the starting date should not be when the petition is filed, but rather when the secured creditor seeks either possession of the collateral or adequate protection . . . . This ruling will prevent a hardship to the debtor caused by an adequate protection motion filed well after the bankruptcy petition has been filed, which could require sizeable "makeup" payments. It is not unreasonable to require the creditor to be vigilant in requesting protection if it wants this protection.[67]

---

61 Martin v. United States (*In re* Martin), 761 F.2d 472, 474 (8th Cir. 1985); *In re* George Ruggiere Chrysler-Plymouth, Inc., 727 F.2d 1017 (11th Cir. 1984); *In re* Bank Hapoalim B.M. v. E.L.I., Ltd., 42 B.R. 376 (N.D. Ill. 1984); Brookfield Prod. Credit Ass'n v. Borron, 36 B.R. 445 (E.D. Mo. 1983), *aff'd,* 738 F.2d 951 (8th Cir. 1984). See **Ch. 11** for a detailed discussion of valuation.

62 *In re* Planned Sys., Inc., 78 B.R. 852, 861 (Bankr. S.D. Ohio 1987).

63 *In re* Kain, 86 B.R. 506 (Bankr. W.D. Mich. 1988).

64 Travelers Life & Annuity Co. v. Ritz-Carlton of D.C., Inc. (In re Ritz-Carlton, Inc.), 98 B.R. 170 (S.D.N.Y. 1989) (involving collateral that was deteriorating in value as a result of tax liens that accrued during the course of the Chapter 11 case). *See also In re* Datair Sys. Corp., 42 B.R. 241, 243 (Bankr. N.D. Ill. 1984); Metropolitan Life Ins. Co. v. Monroe, 17 B.R. 934, 939 (D. Del. 1982).

65 Ahlers v. Norwest Bank, 794 F.2d 388 (8th Cir. 1986), *rev'd on other grounds,* 485 U.S. 197 (1988); *In re* Best Prods. Co., 138 B.R. 155 (Bankr. S.D.N.Y. 1992); *In re* Greives, 81 B.R. 912 (Bankr. N.D. Ind. 1987); *In re* Wilson, 70 B.R. 46 (Bankr. N.D. Ill. 1987); *In re* Adams, 2 B.R. 313 (Bankr. M.D. Fla. 1980); *In re* Advisory Info. & Management Sys., Inc., 50 B.R. 627 (Bankr. M.D. Tenn. 1985); *In re* Briggs Transp. Co., 47 B.R. 6 (Bankr. D. Minn. 1984); *In re* Northeast Chick Servs., 43 B.R. 326 (Bankr. D. Mass. 1984); *In re* Hinckley, 40 B.R. 679 (Bankr. D. Utah 1984).

66 794 F.2d 388 (8th Cir. 1986) *rev'd on other grounds,* 485 U.S. 197 (1988).

67 *Id.* at 395 n.6. *See also In re* Best Prods. Co., 138 B.R. 155 (Bankr. S.D.N.Y. 1992); *In re* Greives, 81 B.R. 912, 965 (Bankr. N.D. Ind. 1987) ("there is imposed on . . . a secured creditor the obligation to be diligent in requesting adequate protection."); *In re*

In short, the bankruptcy court is not authorized to grant retroactive adequate protection.[68]

Therefore, a creditor claiming an interest in cash collateral would be wise to take steps, immediately following the bankruptcy filing, to preclude a debtor from using cash collateral in violation of § 363(c). Even if the creditor is willing to work out a consensual agreement for the use of cash collateral which provides the creditor with adequate protection, such an agreement is not binding on the estate until approved by the bankruptcy court.[69] Therefore, the creditor would be wise to immediately notify the debtor and the court that it does not consent to the debtor's use of its cash collateral and that it demands adequate protection. In addition, the creditor should demand that the debtor comply with its obligation to segregate and account for cash collateral.[70] Both of these steps can be accomplished by filing a motion with the bankruptcy court.[71]

Wilson, 70 B.R. 46, 48 (Bankr. N.D. Ill. 1987) ("requiring adequate protection to cover depreciation from the date that adequate protection is sought holds two benefits which are consistent throughout all such cases. First, the rule does not reward the creditor for inaction. . . . Second, this rule puts the debtor on notice at the time the creditor's motion is filed that at a future point in time the collateral will have to be relinquished or payments will have to be made."); *In re* Adams, 2 B.R. 313, 314 (Bankr. M.D. Fla. 1980) (secured creditor "should not be allowed to sit back and through his inaction compel the unsecured creditors to become insurers of any deficiency that may arise. The risk of decline in value should by placed on the security [sic] creditor himself, who is best able to anticipate the problem and protect his rights."); *In re* Advisory Info. & Management Sys., Inc., 50 B.R. 627, 629–30 (Bankr. M.D. Tenn. 1985) ("The Bankruptcy Code nowhere puts the responsibility on the debtor to initiate consideration of adequate protection of a creditor's noncash collateral."); *In re* Briggs Transp. Co., 47 B.R. 6, 8 (Bankr. D. Minn. 1984) ("Congress intended to put the burden on the creditor to seek relief from the stay or otherwise demand adequate protection in order to receive adequate protection"); *In re* Northeast Chick Servs., 43 B.R. 326, 332 (Bankr. D. Mass. 1984) (§ 363(e) was never "intended as an 'after the fact' method allowing a creditor to obtain the full amount of its [prepetition] secured claim."); *In re* Hinckley, 40 B.R. 679, 681 (Bankr. D. Utah 1984) ("creditors should be encouraged to quickly pursue their available remedies and not sit on their rights while the collateral diminishes in value") (quoting *In re* Adams, 2 B.R. 313 (Bankr. M.D. Fla. 1980)).

68 *In re* Broomall Printing Corp., 131 B.R. 32 (Bankr. D. Md. 1991).

69 *See* New Hampshire Bus. Dev. Corp. v. Cross Baking Co. (*In re* Cross Baking Co.), 818 F.2d 1027 (1st Cir. 1987) (secured lender, who permits debtor to use cash collateral during reorganization without obtaining cash collateral order continuing its lien on postpetition receivables or ensuring that collections of prepetition receivables during reorganization would be segregated, is not entitled to any portion of monies collected in satisfaction of receivables that arose after the filing of a bankruptcy petition). *But see* Travelers Ins. Co. v. American Agcredit Corp. (*In re* Blehm Land & Cattle Co.), 859 F.2d 137 (10th Cir. 1988) (creditor who failed to obtain court approval of adequate protection agreement not precluded from applying for § 507(b) superpriority administrative expense status which would be paid before all other regular administrative claims).

70 11 U.S.C. § 363(c)(4).

71 *See In re* Best Prods. Co., 138 B.R. 155, 158 (Bankr. S.D.N.Y. 1992) ("By making a motion for adequate protection, a secured creditor demonstrates its concern and puts the debtor in a position where it must decide what it should do with collateral. The debtor is

In addition to triggering the protection of § 363(e), a request for adequate protection aids the creditor in another way. If the court-ordered protection later proves inadequate, the creditor is entitled to a priority expense claim under § 507(b).[72] This claim is a *superpriority,* payable ahead of other administrative expense claims, to the extent of the failure of adequate protection.[73] However, at least one court has held that creditors who claim rights to cash collateral are protected only by §§ 507(b) and 363 and may not attain superpriority status solely by virtue of a claim to cash collateral.[74] In other words, in order to be entitled to § 507(b) priority, a creditor must have sought adequate protection from the court, either through an approved stipulation with the debtor or pursuant to a motion for adequate protection, and the court's award of protection must have proven to be inadequate.

Should a creditor object to the use, sale, or lease of cash collateral, a showing by the debtor that the creditor is adequately protected can defeat the objection.[75] In any hearing held under § 363, the debtor has the burden of proof on the issue of adequate protection and the creditor has the burden of proof on the issue of the validity, priority, or extent of its interest in the property.[76]

Although the existence of an equity cushion alone may constitute adequate protection for purposes of imposition of the automatic stay, an equity cushion alone may not suffice as adequate protection for the debtor's use of cash collateral.[77] Beyond this, the only limitations on the form of adequate protection are fairness and

---

given the option to surrender the property to the entity that has made the request, and avoid providing adequate protection, or provide adequate protection to such entity for the debtor's continued use of the collateral").

72 *See In re* Broomall Printing Corp., 131 B.R. 32 (Bankr. D. Md. 1991); Grundy Nat'l Bank v. Rife, 876 F.2d 361 (4th Cir. 1989); *In re* Callister, 15 B.R. 521 (Bankr. D. Utah 1981); *In re* Blackford Farms, Inc., 68 B.R. 639 (Bankr. N.D. Iowa 1986); *In re* James B. Downing & Co., 94 B.R. 515 (Bankr. N.D. Ill. 1988).

73 *In re* Wise Transp., Inc., 148 B.R. 52 (Bankr. N.D. Okla. 1992) (creditor whose protection under § 361 proved inadequate was entitled to superpriority under § 507(b), such claim being inferior only to payment of the Chapter 7 administrative expenses).

74 *In re* AMT Inv. Corp., 53 B.R. 274, 276–77 (Bankr. E.D. Va. 1985).

75 *In re* Earth Lite, 9 B.R. 440 (Bankr. M.D. Fla. 1981) (equity cushion not enough; adequate protection beyond equity cushion required); *In re* Markim, 15 B.R. 56, 59 (Bankr. E.D. Pa. 1981) (80 percent adequate protection satisfactory to prevail over creditor's objection to use of cash collateral); *In re* Marine Optical, Inc., 10 B.R. 893, 894 (Bankr. D. Mass. 1981) (adequate protection defeated objection).

76 11 U.S.C. § 363(o). *But see In re* Raymond, 99 B.R. 819, 820–21 (Bankr. S.D. Ohio 1989) (although ultimate burden of proof is on debtor to show that creditor is adequately protected, creditor must go forward with some evidence that its interest is not adequately protected, e.g., that the value of the property securing its claim declined since the date of the bankruptcy filing).

77 *In re* Epstein, 26 B.R. 354 (Bankr. E.D. Tenn. 1982) (equity cushion together with monthly payments to secured creditor sufficient adequate protection for debtor's use of cash collateral to pay the actual, necessary operating expenses); *In re* Realty Southwest Assocs., 140 B.R. 360, 365 (Bankr. S.D.N.Y. 1992) (creditor adequately protected because of the substantial equity cushion and because debtor was segregating and accounting for all cash collateral).

equity to the estate, the secured creditor, and other creditors. Such protection can consist of as little as the court's conclusion that the creditor and estate will experience a net savings due to the expenditure of cash collateral.[78] These courts rationalize that, by committing a limited portion of cash collateral to operate and maintain the property, the underlying value of the collateral is protected from decline. Therefore, such limited use provides adequate protection under Code § 363(e).[79]

On the other hand, depending on the complexity of the debtor/creditor relationship, adequate protection may be much more intricate. A good example of the various forms of adequate protection can be found in *Sumitomo Trust & Banking Co., Ltd. v. Holly's, Inc. (In re Holly's, Inc.),*[80] which allowed the following as adequate protection:

1. Monthly payments to the creditor in the amount of $20,000, retroactive for four months, with such payments' being first applied to compensate the creditor for any diminution of the property value and any remaining sums then credited to the principal balance of the allowed secured claim.
2. Establishment by the debtor of a separate account into which 3 percent of gross monthly revenues were to be deposited, with such funds' being exclusively utilized, after giving the creditor written notice and a 10-day opportunity to object, to refurbish the hotel property's operating assets as may be necessitated by wear and tear and depreciation.
3. Maintenance by the debtor of not less than $10,400,000 in fire and casualty insurance, with the creditor to be named as loss payee, on its real and personal property tangible assets.
4. In order to protect the creditor against a possible priming of its lien position, establishment of a property tax account into which the debtor would deposit each month a sum equalling one-twelfth of the yearly tax assessment. These

---

[78] *See* Pension Benefit Guar. Corp. v. Sharon Steel Corp. (*In re* Sharon Steel Corp.), 159 B.R. 730 (Bankr. W.D. Pa. 1993) (approving use of 6 percent of cash collateral to pay prepetition wage claims when failure to allow such use would result in more than 6 percent loss in the value of the collateral); *In re* 499 W. Warren St. Assocs., Ltd. Partnership, 142 B.R. 53 (Bankr. N.D.N.Y. 1992) (creditor adequately protected with respect to debtor's use of limited portion of rents solely for the payment of the reasonable and necessary operating expenses of the property when cash flow from collateral is stable and is sufficient to pay current operating expenses and maintenance costs while still providing a surplus for deposit into an escrow account); *In re* Salem Plaza Assocs., 135 B.R. 753 (Bankr. S.D.N.Y. 1992) (limitation of debtor's use of rents to the necessary operating expenses and requirement that all rents received in excess of these expenses be placed in an interest-bearing escrow account provides creditor with adequate protection).

[79] *In re* 499 W. Warren St. Assocs., Ltd. Partnership, 142 B.R. 53 (Bankr. N.D.N.Y. 1992). *See also In re* Salem Plaza Assocs., 135 B.R. 753 (Bankr. S.D.N.Y. 1992) (limited use of rents solely to pay the necessary operating expenses will not diminish the value of creditor's interest in future rents, and will preserve the base that generates the income stream).

[80] 140 B.R. 643 (Bankr. W.D. Mich. 1992) (discussing provisions in a consensual agreement between the debtor and creditor secured by hotel property).

funds were to be used to pay postpetition real and personal property taxes pursuant to court order or pursuant to confirmation of the Chapter 11 plan.

5. Granting to the creditor a replacement lien on its postpetition property coextensive with the creditor's prepetition mortgage and security interest in the hotel property.
6. Requiring the debtor to provide periodic written financial information to the creditor in the form of

   (a) Copies of income deposit slips on a daily basis
   (b) Copies of the hotel property's so-called green sheet and blue sheet on a weekly basis
   (c) Copies of all reports required to be filed with the U.S. Trustee in the partnership's Chapter 11 case
   (d) Copies of all reports required to be filed with the U.S. Trustee in Holly's Chapter 11 case
   (e) Copies of the so-called Summary 90 profit and loss statements respecting the partnership for each accounting period.

7. Granting the creditor the right to employ, at its own expense, an observer or auditor who would have reasonable access to the books, records, and financial information of the partnership and the right to visit and examine the hotel property upon reasonable notice to the debtor.[81]

In summary, adequate protection can take many forms, including, but not limited to, restrictions on how much and on what the cash is spent, segregation and accounting for cash collateral, regular payments to the creditor to pay down the debt, insurance of the property, rights of inspection of the business and its books and records, establishment of postpetition accounts in the creditor's bank, regular reports regarding the operations of the debtor, postpetition security interest in inventory, equipment, accounts, and so forth. See **Chapter 5.**

§ 3.11 Practical Aspects of Cash Collateral Stipulations

As a practical matter, a debtor has little chance of successfully reorganizing its business if it is not given authorization to use cash collateral. Therefore, the first step a debtor's attorney should take is to scrutinize the loan documents and security filings to make sure that the creditor's claim is properly perfected pursuant to state law. This analysis will require that counsel be familiar with the numerous nuances of the state's version of the Uniform Commercial Code. Unless the debtor is fairly certain that it can persuade the bankruptcy judge that the secured creditor either has no valid claim to the cash collateral or that the secured creditor's interest in the cash collateral is adequately protected, the debtor should attempt to negotiate a consensual agreement with the secured creditor which allows the debtor to use cash collateral, subject

---

[81] *Id.* at 705–06.

to certain restrictions and limitations imposed to provide the creditor with adequate protection. Needless to say, an interruption in the debtor's ability to use cash collateral can be fatal. Therefore, debtor's counsel would be well advised to hold such negotiations either prepetition or immediately following the filing of the petition.

The creditor needs to analyze the situation from both a legal and a business perspective. Because § 544 allows the debtor to void any liens unperfected as of the bankruptcy filing, the creditor must review all of its loan documents and ensure that its lien interests are properly documented and perfected under state law. As a legal matter, if the security interests are not properly perfected, in a bankruptcy the creditor can be relegated to the realm of the unsecured. In such a case, the creditor should give serious consideration to a loan workout with the debtor which would forestall the filing of a bankruptcy until the creditor can properly perfect its interests in the debtor's property. From a business perspective, if the benefits of certain concessions made by the debtor outweigh the downside risks of the use of cash collateral, the creditor should be willing to stipulate to the debtor's use of cash collateral. As a practical matter, in order for the creditor to properly analyze the risks of allowing the use of cash collateral, the debtor will have to make full disclosure of its current and projected financial, managerial, and operational status. As with any negotiation situation, the more concessions the debtor is willing to make, the more liberal the creditor will be in allowing use of cash collateral. However, creditor's counsel must take care not to be too greedy in its demands, because the court may refuse to approve the stipulation.

Once the creditor makes the business judgment that it would be better off allowing the debtor at least a limited use of cash collateral, the creditor needs to determine what provisions will provide it with adequate protection. See **§ 3.16** for a sample cash collateral stipulation.

§ 3.12 Procedure for Obtaining Court Approval Conditioned on Adequate Protection

Assuming that the debtor is unable to obtain the creditor's consent to use the cash collateral, the debtor will be unable to use, sell, or lease cash collateral unless "the court, after notice and a hearing, authorizes such use, sale, or lease in accordance with the provisions of this section."[82]

A request for authorization to use cash collateral is considered a contested matter under the Code and must be made in accordance with Bankruptcy Rule 9014.[83] Rule 9014 provides that "relief shall be requested by motion and reasonable notice and opportunity for hearing shall be afforded the party against whom relief is sought." The motion for authority to use cash collateral must include:

1. The amount of cash collateral sought to be used
2. The name and address of each entity having an interest in the cash collateral

---

[82] 11 U.S.C. § 363(c)(2)(A) & (B).

[83] Fed. R. Bankr. P. 4001(b)(1).

3. The name and address of the entity in control or having possession of the collateral
4. The facts demonstrating the need to use the cash collateral
5. The nature of the protection to be provided to those having an interest in the cash collateral.[84]

The debtor must file and serve the motion for authorization to use cash collateral, together with a notice of hearing thereon, on (1) any entity that has an interest in the cash collateral; (2) on any committee appointed under the Code, or, if no committee has been appointed, on the 20 largest unsecured creditors; and (3) on such other entities as the court may direct.[85] The motion is to be filed in the court where the case is pending.[86] Service may be made by any method authorized by Rule 7004.

A final hearing on a motion for authorization to use cash collateral cannot be commenced earlier than 15 days after service of the motion.[87] This 15-day period cannot be shortened by the court.[88] However, if the motion requests, the court may conduct a preliminary hearing, to be "scheduled in accordance with the needs of the debtor,"[89] before the 15-day period expires. In the preliminary hearing, the court may authorize the use of cash collateral "if there is a reasonable likelihood that the trustee will prevail at the final hearing."[90] However, any order issued prior to a final hearing is limited to "that amount of cash collateral as is necessary to avoid immediate and irreparable harm to the estate pending a final hearing."[91] If a preliminary hearing is requested, the motion must also include the amount of cash collateral sought to be used pending final hearing and specify the protection that will be provided to the creditor.[92]

Stipulations between the debtor and a secured creditor claiming an interest in cash collateral are governed by different procedures than contested motions for authorization. A motion for approval of the stipulation for the use of cash collateral "shall be served on any committee appointed under the Code or its authorized agent, or, if no committee has been appointed, on the creditors listed on the list filed pursuant to Rule 1007(d) and on such other entities as the court may direct."[93] The motion is to be accompanied by a copy of the agreement and a notice specifying the time within which objections may be filed (generally within 15 days of the mailing of notice unless otherwise specified by the court).[94] If no objection is filed, the court may approve or disapprove of the agreement without conducting a hearing.[95] If an objection is filed or if the

---

84 *See* Advisory Committee Notes to 1987 Amendments to Fed. R. Bankr. P. 4001.

85 Fed. R. Bankr. P. 4001(b)(1).

86 Fed. R. Bankr. P. 5005(b).

87 Fed. R. Bankr. P. 4001(b)(2).

88 Fed. R. Bankr. P. 9006(c)(2).

89 11 U.S.C. § 363(c)(3).

90 *Id.*; Fed. R. Bankr. P. 4001(b)(2).

91 Fed. R. Bankr. P. 4001(b)(2).

92 *See* Advisory Committee Notes to 1987 Amendments to Fed. R. Bankr. P. 4001.

93 Fed. R. Bankr. P. 4001(c)(1).

94 Fed. R. Bankr. P. 4001(c)(2).

95 Fed. R. Bankr. P. 4001(c)(3).

court determines that a hearing is appropriate, a hearing can be scheduled on no less than five days' notice to the objector, the movant, the parties on whom service is required, and such other entities as the court may direct.[96] Therefore, at least 20 days will elapse before a stipulation for the use of cash collateral is approved under Rule 4001(d). However, if approval of a cash collateral agreement is needed quickly, the debtor and creditor would be well advised either to move for a reduction of the time under Rule 9006(c)(1)(reduction for cause) or use the preliminary hearing procedures of Rule 4001(b)(2).[97]

§ 3.13 Remedies for Violation of Cash Collateral Rules

Despite the fact that the debtor is prohibited by § 363(c)(2) from using cash collateral without court order or the creditor's consent, some debtors, either through ignorance or outright fraud, proceed to use such monies. In some instances, the debtor might be in violation of a court-approved cash collateral stipulation with the creditor which precluded it from taking certain actions.

In response to such violations, most courts do not hesitate to prohibit further use of cash collateral unless adequate protection is provided. However, as one court noted,

> Once cash collateral has been dissipated and spent, court-fashioned sanctions such as retroactive adequate protection, appointment of a Chapter 11 trustee or prohibitions against the further use of cash collateral can be hollow victories for a secured creditor and do not rise to the level of a "remedy."[98]

Therefore, depending on the egregiousness of the debtor's actions, in addition to or in lieu of adequate protection in the forms described in **§§ 3.10** and **3.11,** some courts have imposed additional sanctions, such as:

1. Imposition of personal liability on the manager of the debtor-business for the value of such collateral and the denial of the manager's Chapter 7 discharge pursuant to §§ 523(a)(4) and 727(a)(2) & (7).[99]
2. Ordering that debtor compensate the creditor for its damages and incarcerating the debtor under the court's civil contempt powers when the debtor failed to comply with such order.[100] However, at least one court has ruled that a contempt order is not available "to enforce the Debtor's compliance with the cash collateral provisions of 11 U.S.C. § 363(c)(2) and (4), nor to punish the

---

96 *Id.*

97 Advisory Committee Notes to 1987 Amendments to Fed. R. Bankr. P. 4001(d).

98 *In re* R.H. Williams, 61 B.R. 567, 575 (Bankr. N.D. Tex. 1986) (expressed in context of a dispute regarding a bank's right to setoff).

99 American Sav. & Loan Ass'n v. Weber (*In re* Weber), 99 B.R. 1001 (Bankr. D. Utah 1989). *See also* Impulsora del Territorio Sur, S.A. v. Cecchini (*In re* Cecchini), 780 F.2d 1440 (9th Cir. 1986).

100 *See In re* Spanish River Plaza Realty Co., 155 B.R. 249 (Bankr. S.D. Fla. 1993).

Debtor who has failed to comply with those provisions, absent first the entry of an appropriate injunctive (mandatorily injunctive, or prohibitorily injunctive) order which specifically requires, or forbids, a course of conduct bottomed on those provisions."[101]

3. An award of monetary compensation if there is evidence of the creditor's actual loss.[102]
4. Appointment of a Chapter 11 trustee or an examiner pursuant to § 1104.[103]
5. Conversion of the case to a Chapter 7 pursuant to § 1112.[104]
6. Granting the creditor relief from stay pursuant to § 362(d)(1).
7. Shifting the burden of proof on the issue of tracing proceeds of cash collateral onto the debtor.[105]

§ 3.14 Form: Motion to Prohibit Use of Cash Collateral

FORM 3–1
MOTION TO PROHIBIT USE OF CASH COLLATERAL

UNITED STATES BANKRUPTCY COURT
FOR THE DISTRICT OF _______

In Re:)
)
______________________________) Case No. ______________
)
Debtor.)

MOTION TO PROHIBIT OR LIMIT USE, SALE, LEASE, OR OTHER DISPOSITION OF CASH COLLATERAL PURSUANT TO 11 U.S.C. § 363 AND FOR IMMEDIATE RELIEF OR ADEQUATE PROTECTION PURSUANT TO 11 U.S.C. §§ 362(d), 362(f), AND 363(e).

[Creditor], a secured creditor of the Debtor, by and through its attorneys, [attorney names], hereby moves this Court for an immediate order for the protection of

---

101 Centerre Bank Nat'l Ass'n v. Continental Marine Corp. (*In re* Continental Marine Corp.), 35 B.R. 990, 992 (Bankr. E.D. Mo. 1984).

102 *In re* Etch-Art, Inc., 48 B.R. 143 (Bankr. D.R.I. 1985).

103 *See* Hester v. NCNB Texas Nat'l Bank (*In re* Hester), 899 F.2d 361 (5th Cir. 1990) (refusing to grant a writ of mandamus with respect to an order of the bankruptcy court denying a stay of the appointment of a receiver); *In re* Anchorage Boat Sales, 4 B.R. 635 (Bankr. E.D.N.Y. 1980).

104 *See In re* Hewett, 32 B.R. 605 (Bankr. W.D. Wash. 1983).

105 Freightliner Market Dev. Corp. v. Silver Wheel Freightlines, Inc., 823 F.2d 362, 369 (9th Cir. 1987).

cash collateral; relief from the automatic stay or adequate protection; and to prohibit the use, sale, lease, or other disposition of collateral. In support thereof, [Creditor] states:

1. These motions are made pursuant to 11 U.S.C. §§ 363 and 362.

2. [Debtor] is a debtor and a debtor-in-possession in a Chapter 11 reorganization pursuant to a Petition in Bankruptcy filed on [date].

3. [Creditor] holds a claim for approximately $[amount] as of [date], with per diem interest accruing theron at the rate of $[interest amount], plus costs and reasonable attorney's fees (hereinafter referred to as Indebtedness).

4. [Creditor]'s claim is evidenced and secured as follows:

a. A promissory note dated [date], evidencing a loan in the original principal sum of $[promissory note amount], executed by [party names]. A copy of the promissory note is attached hereto as Exhibit 1.

b. A security agreement dated [security agreement date], executed by [Debtor], granting [Creditor] a security interest in [description of collateral] (hereinafter referred to as Collateral). A copy of the security agreement is attached hereto as Exhibit 2.

c. Two financing statements evidencing [Creditor]'s security interest in the Collateral recorded [date], at [record number] in the records of [county name] County, [state], and recorded [date], at [record number] in the records of the [state] Secretary of State. Copies of these financing statements are attached hereto as Composite Exhibit 3.

5. The collection of the Collateral creates cash collateral which is security for repayment of the debt owed to [Creditor]. By reason of filing the bankruptcy petition, [Creditor] has been stayed from realizing upon its collateral.

6. [Creditor] objects to the Debtor's use of its cash collateral and demands adequate protection pursuant to 11 U.S.C. §§ 361 and 363 of the Bankruptcy Code.

7. [Creditor] believes its security interest is not being adequately protected by [Debtor] as required by the Bankruptcy Code.

8. [Creditor] requests that [Debtor] be prohibited from any use, sale, lease, or other disposition of [Creditor]'s cash collateral, or, in the alternative, for an Order of this Court limiting and conditioning the use, sale, lease, or other disposition of cash collateral and that the Court provide [Creditor] with adequate protection of its interests pursuant to 11 U.S.C. § 363(e).

Wherefore, [Creditor] asks this Court for:

A. An immediate Order directing that proceeds of any sale or other disposition of [Creditor]'s Collateral be deposited to a separate, segregated, Cash Collateral account, and that [Debtor] be prohibited from making any use of the Cash Collateral;

B. After notice and a hearing, direct that [Debtor] be prohibited from any further use, sale, lease, or other disposition of [Creditor]'s Collateral or the proceeds thereof, except as necessary in the ordinary course of business to preserve and protect the value of the Collateral; or, in the alternative, condition and limit such use and order that [Creditor] be provided with adequate protection in the form of: [specify adequate protection]

Respectfully submitted this ____ day of _________, 19__.

[Firm name]

CERTIFICATE OF MAILING

I certify that on the _____ day of _____________, 19___, a copy of the foregoing Motion was mailed, postage prepaid, duly addressed as follows:

____
____
____

____

§ 3.15 Form: Motion to Approve Cash Collateral Stipulation

FORM 3–2
MOTION TO APPROVE CASH COLLATERAL STIPULATION

UNITED STATES BANKRUPTCY COURT
FOR THE DISTRICT OF _______

In Re:	)	
	)	
__________________________,	)	Case No. _______________
	)	
Debtor.	)	

MOTION TO APPROVE STIPULATION FOR USE OF CASH COLLATERAL; MOTION TO SHORTEN NOTICE PROCEDURE AND FOR EXPEDITED HEARING; AND MOTION TO APPROVE FORM AND METHOD OF NOTICE SENT

[Creditor], a secured creditor of the Debtor, by and through its attorneys, [attorney names], hereby files this Motion to Approve Stipulation for Use of Cash Collateral, Motion to Shorten Notice Procedure and for Expedited Hearing, and Motion to Approve Form and Method of Notice. In support of this Motion, [Creditor] states:

1. These Motions are made pursuant to 11 U.S.C. § 102(1) and Bankruptcy Rules 4001 and 9006(c).

2. On [date], Debtor filed its voluntary petition for relief pursuant to Chapter 11, Title 11, United States Code.

3. On [date], [Creditor] filed its [name of pleading objecting to use of cash collateral] which put [Debtor] on notice of [Creditor]'s objection to [Debtor]'s use of its cash collateral.

4. In violation of Section 363(c)(2) of the Bankruptcy Code and despite receipt of [Creditor]'s [name of pleading objecting to use of cash collateral], [Debtor] continued to use the cash collateral to meet its debts without consent of [Creditor] or an Order of this Court authorizing such use.

5. [Creditor] and [Debtor] have entered into a Stipulation for Use of Cash Collateral pursuant to which [Creditor] is consenting to [Debtor]'s use of cash collateral for the limited purpose of meeting its payroll and necessary expenses. A true copy of said Stipulation is attached hereto as Exhibit A.[106]

6. [Debtor] has represented to [Creditor] that in order for [Debtor] to stay in business, it is essential that the payroll for [date] be met; therefore, [Creditor], in the Stipulation, is agreeing to allow [Debtor], prior to an Order approving this Stipulation, to use cash collateral to meet the [date] payroll.

7. [Creditor] hereby files its Motion for Approval of the Stipulation for Use of Cash Collateral. However, in order to avoid any prejudice to [Creditor], a prompt hearing on the Motion to Approve the Stipulation for Use of Cash Collateral is required, because [Debtor] has already used substantial amounts of cash collateral over the objection of [Creditor] and the Stipulation allows for immediate use of cash collateral to meet the [date] payroll. [Debtor]'s next payroll will be due on [date], and [Creditor] cannot agree to [Debtor]'s use of cash collateral to meet the [date] payroll or other expenses until the Court has ruled on the Motion to Approve Stipulation for Use of Cash Collateral.

---

[106] This stipulation appears in § **3.16**.

8. On [date], [Creditor] sent out a [ ] day calendar notice to [Debtor], the U.S. Trustee, and the members of the unsecured creditors' committee, advising them of this Motion to Approve Stipulation for Use of Cash Collateral. A copy of that notice is attached hereto as Exhibit B.[107] It is imperative that a ruling on the Motion to Approve Stipulation for Use of Cash Collateral be entered as soon as possible, and no later than [date].

9. [Creditor] believes that the Notice fairly informs all parties in interest of the intended action and that the [ ] day calendar notice time is adequate under the circumstances. Timely approval of the Motion is in everyone's best interests, because it allows [Debtor] to remain in business while protecting the interests of [Creditor], the sole secured creditor with respect to the [type of collateral].

WHEREFORE, [Creditor] respectfully requests that this Court enter an Order:

1. Approving the shortened notice procedure;

2. Scheduling [date] as the date for the hearing on the Motion to Approve Stipulation for Use of Cash Collateral;

3. Approving the form and content of Exhibit B;

4. For such other and further relief as this Court deems just and proper.

Respectfully submitted this ___ day of _________, 19___.

[Firm Name]

By [Attorney Name]
[Firm address]

CERTIFICATE OF MAILING

I certify that on the _____ day of _________, 19___, a copy of the foregoing Motion was mailed, postage prepaid, duly addressed as follows:

[names and addresses of
parties who must receive
notice]

____

107 This notice appears in § 3.17.

§ 3.16 Form: Stipulation for Use of Cash Collateral

FORM 3–3
STIPULATION FOR USE OF CASH COLLATERAL

UNITED STATES BANKRUPTCY COURT
FOR THE DISTRICT OF _______

In Re:	)	
	)	
___________________________,	)	Bankruptcy No.
	)	Chapter 11
	)	
Debtor.	)	

STIPULATION FOR USE OF CASH COLLATERAL

[Debtor], Debtor (hereinafter [Debtor]) and [Creditor], (hereinafter [Creditor]) hereby stipulate as follows:

1. [Debtor] is a debtor and a debtor-in-possession in a Chapter 11 reorganization pursuant to a Petition in Bankruptcy filed on [date]. [Optional language: for the limited purpose of this stipulation only,] [Debtor] acknowledges and agrees that it owes [Creditor] the outstanding principal of $[principal sum], plus interest, at the rate specified in the note, which is attached hereto as Exhibit 1, costs, and reasonable attorney's fees (hereinafter referred to as Indebtedness). Said amounts are owed jointly and severally by [Debtor] and [joint debtors/guarantors]. [Optional language: for the limited purpose of this stipulation only,] [Debtor] further recognizes and agrees that [Creditor] holds a first priority perfected security interest in all [description of collateral] currently owned by [Debtor] (Collateral).

2. The collection of outstanding prepetition accounts receivable creates cash collateral which is security for repayment of the debt owed to [Creditor]. By reason of filing the bankruptcy petition, [Creditor] has been stayed from realizing upon its collateral and [Creditor] has objected to the use of its cash collateral and demanded adequate protection pursuant to 11 U.S.C. §§ 361 and 363 of the Bankruptcy Code. The parties wish to come to an agreement so [Creditor] can be adequately protected and so that [Debtor] can use the cash collateral as hereinafter specified.

3. The parties agree that, pursuant to the terms and conditions of this Stipulation, [Debtor] shall have a limited right to use that cash collateral in its ongoing reorganization.

4. (a) [Debtor] shall maintain a Cash Collateral Account with [name of bank], into which [Debtor] will deposit 100 percent of all amounts collected on accounts receivable.

(b) [Debtor] shall maintain a Debtor-in-Possession Account (DIP Account) with [name of bank], into which all amounts which [Creditor] agrees to allow [Debtor] to use, as set forth in paragraph 5(h) herein, shall be deposited.

5. [Creditor] consents to use by [Debtor] of such cash collateral in the ordinary course of its business, under the following conditions:

A. All checks or other noncash deposits must be deposited into the Cash Collateral Account a minimum of three working days before [Creditor] is required to disburse any funds therefrom to the Debtor-in-Possession account in accordance with this Stipulation.

B. [Debtor] agrees to use its best efforts to collect all outstanding accounts receivable within a reasonable period of time.

C. On or before the execution of this Stipulation, [Debtor] will provide to [Creditor] its accounts receivables aging report, itemization of all receipts, profit and loss statements and balance sheets, listings of jobs in progress showing the percentage of completion, accounts payable reports, current financial statements certified by a certified public accountant, and a current payroll ledger for its employees. In addition, [individual joint debtors/guarantors] shall provide to [Creditor] complete, signed and dated personal financial statements.

D. On or before [date], [Debtor] will provide to [Creditor] its revised budget and accounts receivable projections for the months of [state months]. By the 15th day of each succeeding month, [Debtor] shall provide [Creditor] with a budget and job projections for the following month, accounts receivable aging report, itemization of all receipts, profit and loss statements and balance sheets, listings of jobs in progress showing the percentage of completion, and accounts payable reports.

E. By Wednesday of each week before payroll is to be met, [Debtor] shall provide [Creditor] with an updated accounting of its collection of accounts receivables, and a schedule of the amounts which [Debtor] requests that [Creditor] transfer from the Cash Collateral Account to the DIP Account, itemizing each amount that is to be paid from the DIP Account. In addition, by Wednesday of each week before payroll is to be met, [Debtor] shall provide [Creditor] with an updated payroll ledger for its employees.

F. [Debtor] will also provide [Creditor] and its counsel with the monthly reports to the U.S. Trustee.

G. [Creditor] shall have access to review all financial books and records of [Debtor].

H. As long as [Debtor] remains in compliance with the terms of this Stipulation, [Creditor] consents to the use by [Debtor] of the monies in the Cash Collateral Account to fund [Debtor]'s payroll and necessary operating expenses, as itemized in Exhibit 2 hereto, with the following exceptions:

(1) No personal draws will be permitted to be taken by [names of Debtor's principals]. For a period of 60 days from the date of this Stipulation, the amount of salary paid to [names of Debtor's principals] will be limited to the amounts left in the Cash Collateral Account after payment of payroll, necessary operating expenses, and payment of the amount due to [Creditor] as specified in subparagraph ii below. Such salary is not to exceed $[amount] gross per month. [names of joint debtor's/guarantors] have agreed and covenanted to make to [Creditor] a payment in the amount of $[amount] within 60 days from the date of this Stipulation to reduce the Indebtedness. In the event that the $[amount] payment is not made within 60 days of the date of this Stipulation, then the amount of salary paid to [names of Debtor's principals] will be limited to [ ]% of the amounts left in the Cash Collateral Account after payment of payroll, necessary operating expenses, and payment of the amount due to [Creditor] as specified in subparagraph ii below. Such salary is not to exceed $[amount] gross per month.

(2) As adequate protection for [Creditor] and in consideration for [Creditor]'s stipulation to [Debtor]'s use of the cash collateral as specified herein, [Debtor] agrees that it will keep current the monthly payment due on its debt to [Creditor], and that 10% of the accounts receivable collected shall be applied to reduce the Indebtedness due to [Creditor].

I. [Debtor] represents that it has paid all required payroll taxes since the filing of the bankruptcy petition. [Debtor] further covenants that it shall continue to pay all required payroll taxes on a timely basis.

J. [Debtor] covenants and agrees that during the term hereof, it will not, without the prior written consent of [Creditor]:

(1) Engage in any transaction which is not in the ordinary course of [Debtor]'s business as previously conducted;

(2) Engage in new or different business activities;

(3) Increase [Debtor]'s investment, whether by purchase, lease, or otherwise, in fixed or capital assets;

(4) Create, assume, or suffer to exist any lien or security interest, including a lien under Section 364(d) of the Bankruptcy Code, in favor of persons other than [Creditor], except:

(a) Liens or security interests existing on the date of commencement of the bankruptcy case;

(b) Liens expressly consented to in writing by [Creditor].

(c) Liens for state or municipal real estate or personal property taxes.

6. [Creditor] retains the right to refuse future use of cash collateral in the event that the financial reports, accountings and budget projections are unacceptable to it.

7. On or before [date], [Debtor] shall provide [Creditor] with a draft of its proposed plan of reorganization, which shall incorporate the essential provisions of this Stipulation.

8. On or before [date], [Debtor] shall file a meaningful plan of reorganization with the Bankruptcy Court, and shall promptly seek confirmation thereof, including the timely filing of its disclosure statement. That plan shall provide for the payment of the debt owed to [Creditor] according to terms acceptable to [Creditor].

9. (a) This Stipulation is intended to provide adequate protection to [Creditor] for [Debtor]'s use of [Creditor]'s cash collateral. In the event that [Creditor] is damaged by the use of its collateral, it will be entitled to a superpriority claim in accordance with 11 U.S.C. § 507(b). In addition, [Debtor] hereby grants [Creditor] a postpetition security interest (Postpetition Security Interest) commencing [date], in all accounts receivable and equipment presently owned or hereafter acquired by [Debtor]. [Debtor] acknowledges that [Creditor] is not currently adequately protected on a liquidated value basis, and [Debtor] agrees that said Postpetition Security Interest provides a means under §§ 361(2) and 363(e) to provide at least some additional protection to [Creditor]. In addition to the Postpetition Security Interest granted herein, [Debtor] shall execute and deliver to [Creditor] contemporaneously with the execution of this Stipulation, security agreements in the form attached hereto as Exhibit A, and sign all necessary financing statements to perfect [Creditor]'s Postpetition Security Interest.

(b) [Creditor] is entitled on its claim from the date of filing of the voluntary petition to all principal and interest provided in the note, plus all costs of this proceeding, including attorney's fees.

10. If [Debtor] fails to comply with any provisions of this Stipulation, fails to make any timely payment as provided for herein, breaches any other terms, conditions, covenant, or representation of this Stipulation, or if a trustee is appointed in the Chapter 11 case or the case is dismissed or converted to Chapter 7, [Creditor] shall, within its discretion, be entitled to immediate relief from the automatic stay, without need for further hearing, and [Debtor] agrees to consent to the granting of immediate relief from stay to [Creditor] pursuant to § 362 of the Bankruptcy Code.

11. [Creditor] expressly reserves unto itself any and all rights it holds against any guarantors or co-makers of the Indebtedness, and in no means intends to alter, waive, or relinquish those rights by any provision contained herein. [Debtor] and [names of joint debtors/guarantors] acknowledge and agree that nothing contained herein constitutes satisfaction, cancellation, or remuneration of the claims of [Creditor], or impairment of its collateral.

12. This Stipulation shall, in any event, terminate upon the payment in full of all debt owed to [Creditor] by [Debtor], including accrued interest thereon and cost and fees incurred herein, or upon confirmation of [Debtor]'s plan of reorganization, whichever occurs first.

13. In the event of any action at law or suit in equity in relation to this Stipulation or in the event that [Creditor] incurs attorney's fees or legal expenses to protect its rights hereunder, [Debtor] will, if [Creditor] prevails in any such action, pay to [Creditor] a reasonable sum for its attorney's fees and legal expenses.

14. It is agreed that this Stipulation as to [Creditor]'s secured claim shall in no way constitute an admission on the part of [Creditor] as to the status of its claims for purposes of accepting or rejecting a plan under Chapter 11, or for any other election which may be made by [Creditor] in the future under the Bankruptcy Code as to secured or unsecured claimant's status as to all or any part of its respective claims.

15. If for any reason any portion of this Agreement is determined to be unenforceable, remaining portions are unaffected and shall remain in full force and effect.

16. This Stipulation sets forth the complete agreement of the parties. It may not be modified, waived, or changed, except by a written instrument signed by the party to be bound thereto.

17. This Stipulation is binding upon the parties and their respective successors and assigns, including but not limited to any successor entity under any plan of reorganization.

18. This Stipulation is subject to, and shall be effective only upon, entry of an Order of Bankruptcy Court authorizing [Debtor] to enter into and perform this Stipulation in its entirety.

[Debtor's attorney]	[Creditor's attorney]
By:	By:

APPROVED BY:

____

[Debtor]

____

[Joint debtor/guarantor]

____

[Joint debtor/guarantor]

§ 3.17 Form: Notice of Motion to Approve Cash Collateral Stipulation

FORM 3–4
NOTICE OF MOTION TO APPROVE STIPULATION

UNITED STATES BANKRUPTCY COURT
FOR THE DISTRICT OF ____________

In re:)
)
__________________________) Case No.
)
Debtor.)

NOTICE OF MOTION TO APPROVE STIPULATION
FOR USE OF CASH COLLATERAL

TO: ALL PARTIES IN INTEREST:

NOTICE IS HEREBY GIVEN that [Creditor] has applied to this Court and is intending to take action as follows:

Please take notice that [Creditor] has filed a Motion to Approve Stipulation for Use of Case Collateral which was entered into between [Debtor] and [Creditor], a creditor which holds a perfected first position security interest in all accounts receivable of [Debtor]. The Stipulation for Use of Cash Collateral allows [Debtor] to use the cash collateral for the limited purpose of meeting its payroll and necessary operating expenses. The Stipulation calls for substantial reporting requirements which are to be met by [Debtor]. The Stipulation further calls for provision of adequate protection to [Creditor] for agreeing to allow [Debtor] to use [Creditor]'s cash collateral to maintain its operations. Adequate protection is provided by means of a postpetition security interest in accounts receivable, monthly payments on the debt to be kept current, and segregation of 10 percent of amounts collected on accounts receivable for application to reduce the amount of indebtedness. A copy of the Stipulation is enclosed.

[Creditor] has also filed a Motion to Shorten Notice Procedure and for Expedited Hearing. Pursuant to 11 U.S.C. §102(1) and Bankruptcy Rules 4001 and 9006(c), [Creditor] has requested that the Court act on the Motion to Approve Stipulation for Use of Cash Collateral on or before [date], in the absence of a request for a hearing by an interested party. Any party that desires a hearing on said application must file its objection and request for hearing no later than [date], and a copy of said request for hearing must be served upon the applicant named below. Should the Court grant [Creditor]'s Motion for Expedited Hearing, the hearing date on any objections will be scheduled for [date], at a time to be determined by the Court. A request for hearing must be filed with the Clerk of the United States Bankruptcy Court, [street address], [city], [state] [zip code].

Respectfully submitted this ____ day of ______________, 19___.

[Firm Name]
By [Attorney Name]
[Firm address]

CERTIFICATE OF MAILING

I certify that on the _____ day of ___________, 19___, a copy of the foregoing Notice, with accompanying motion, was mailed, postage prepaid, duly addressed as follows:

[names and addresses of
parties who must receive
notice]

____

§ 3.18 Form: Order Approving Notice of Motion

FORM 3–5
ORDER APPROVING NOTICE

UNITED STATES BANKRUPTCY COURT
FOR THE DISTRICT OF ____________

In re:)
)
______________________________) Case No. ____________
)
Debtor.)

ORDER

Upon the Motion made by [Creditor], pursuant to 11 U.S.C. §102(1) and Bankruptcy Rules 4001(d) and 9006(c), and after due deliberation,

IT IS HEREBY ORDERED, ADJUDGED, AND DECREED that:

1. This Court hereby approves the form and content of the Notice, a copy of which is attached hereto as Exhibit A; and

2. This Court hereby grants the shortened notice procedure and schedules [date], as the last date upon which an objection to approve Stipulation for Use of Cash Collateral can be filed.

3. If an objection is made to the Motion to Approve Stipulation for Use of Cash Collateral, a hearing on the Motion will be held on [date], at [address of Court], in Courtroom [number]. In the event no objections are filed with the Court on or before [date], the Court will take immediate action on the Motion to Approve Stipulation for Use of Cash Collateral.

DONE AND ORDERED this ______ day of ____________, 19___, in [city], [state].

BY THE COURT:

____
UNITED STATES BANKRUPTCY JUDGE

CHAPTER 4

HOTEL COLLATERAL AND LENDING ISSUES

Cindi S. Woolery

§ 4.1 Introduction

Assume that a lender makes a loan to a shopping center, office complex, or apartment building. The amount of the loan is based in part on the projected revenue stream generated by the property, that is, the rents. The lender secures the debt by taking a security interest in and lien on the real property, personal property, and the rents and revenues generated by the property. The cash flow generated by the property, typically in the form of the rents paid by the tenants of the property, provides both a source of funds for repaying the debt and a form of collateral to secure the debt. Then assume that the shopping center, office complex, or apartment building experiences financial difficulties and files a bankruptcy petition.

If the lender has perfected its security interest under state law, then, under the majority view, the lender's interest in the rents will continue even after the filing of a bankruptcy petition. Accordingly, the lender may be able to limit how the debtor utilizes its revenues and may be entitled to a replacement lien on other property to compensate for the debtor's use of this cash collateral. This protection for the lender may come at a significant cost to the debtor, which may have difficulty implementing an effective reorganization without the unencumbered use of these funds.

The secured lender, however, cannot assume that the result will be the same if funds are advanced to a hotel,[1] rather than to another income-generating property such as a shopping center, office complex, or apartment building. Despite the similarities between the room rates paid by hotel guests and the rents paid by tenants, the treatment of the two revenues in a bankruptcy case is starkly different under the majority view. Thus, the hotel lender may find that it has no right to claim the postpetition revenues as its collateral, and the hotel debtor may find that it has a significant source of postpetition revenues to aid in its reorganization. This chapter discusses the varying views on these issues and the implications for both lenders and debtors. See **Chapter 3** for analysis of these issues in contexts other than hotels.

SECTION 552 OF THE BANKRUPTCY CODE

§ 4.2 Section 552(a)

Section 552(a) of the Bankruptcy Code provides in part that "property acquired by the estate or by the debtor after the commencement of the case is not subject to any lien resulting from any security agreement entered into by the debtor before the commencement of the case."[2] Thus, if the debtor manufactures inventory, plants a crop, or creates an account receivable postpetition, without using proceeds that can be traced to prepetition collateral,[3] then the debtor alone will have the right to the funds generated by the sale of the inventory or crop or the collection of the account receivable.[4] Accordingly, boilerplate language in a security agreement granting an all-encompassing "floating lien" on all after-acquired property of the debtor will generally be of no use to the

---

[1] Throughout this chapter, the term *hotel* includes motels and other establishments providing short-term lodging.

[2] 11 U.S.C. § 552(a).

[3] Unsecured Creditors Comm. v. Marepcon Fin. Corp. (*In re* Bumper Sales), 907 F.2d 1430, 1436–39 (4th Cir. 1990) (if creditor can trace the source of postpetition property to proceeds of prepetition collateral, the security interest may continue).

[4] *See, e.g.*, *In re* Olsen, 87 B.R. 148, 153 (Bankr. D. Colo. 1988) (crops); Bird v. Plains State Bank, 86 B.R. 660, 662 (D. Kan. 1988) (crops); Hugo v. United States *ex rel.* Farmers Home Admin. (*In re* Hugo), 50 B.R. 963, 967 (Bankr. E.D. Mich. 1985) (crops); First Nat'l Bank v. Texas Tri-Collar (*In re* Texas Tri-Collar), 29 B.R. 724, 727 (Bankr. W.D. La. 1983) (accounts receivable); *In re* Kahl Iron Foundry, 21 B.R. 372, 374 (Bankr. E.D. Mich. 1982) (inventory).

creditor upon the debtor's filing a bankruptcy petition.[5] Such a lien will be cut off at the time the bankruptcy petition is filed.[6]

The effect of this termination of postpetition security interests is to aid the debtor's fresh start by enabling the debtor to use its cash flow in its reorganization efforts free and clear of prepetition encumbrances.[7] This allows the debtor to accumulate cash and strengthen its bargaining position in dealing with creditors and postpetition lenders in its bankruptcy case.[8]

§ 4.3 Section 552(b)

Section 552(b) contains important exceptions to the general rule of § 552(a) that prepetition liens do not extend to postpetition property. It sets forth five specific categories of collateral in which prepetition security interests continue postpetition: proceeds, product, offspring, rents, and profits. Section 552(b) provides, in pertinent part, that:

> [I]f the debtor and an entity entered into a security agreement before the commencement of the case and if the security interest created by such security agreement extends to property of the debtor acquired before the commencement of the case and to proceeds, product, offspring, rents, or profits of such property, then such security interest extends to such proceeds, product, offspring, rents or profits acquired by the estate after commencement of the case to the extent provided by such security agreement and by applicable nonbankruptcy law, except to any extent that the court, after notice and a hearing and based on the equities of the case, orders otherwise.

Section 552(b) permits a creditor's prepetition security interest to attach to postpetition property only if:

1. The creditor's prepetition security agreement granted it a security interest in collateral that existed prepetition and also the proceeds, product, offspring, rents, or profits of such collateral,
2. The debtor has acquired property postpetition that, pursuant to applicable state law, is the proceeds, product, offspring, rents, or profits of the creditor's prepetition collateral, and
3. The bankruptcy court does not find that, based on equitable considerations, the creditor's lien should not extend postpetition.[9]

---

5 United States v. Collins (In re Northeast Chick Serv.), 43 B.R. 326, 331 (Bankr. D. Mass. 1984).

6 *Id. See also* First Nat'l Bank v. Texas Tri-Collar (*In re* Texas Tri-Collar), 29 B.R. 724, 727 (Bankr. W.D. La. 1983).

7 *In re* Nielsen, 48 B.R. 274, 276 (D.N.D. 1984).

8 Philip Morris Capital Corp. v. Bering Trader, Inc. (*In re* Bering Trader, Inc.), 944 F.2d 500, 502 (9th Cir. 1991); Investment Hotel Properties v. New W. Fed. Sav. & Loan Ass'n (*In re* Investment Hotel Properties), 109 B.R. 990, 996 (Bankr. D. Colo. 1990).

9 The equities exception is intended to prevent the secured creditor from receiving a windfall based on the debtor's use of assets of the estate to enhance the value of the collateral at issue. 4 Collier on Bankruptcy ¶ 552.02, at 552-11 (1993).

Section 552(b) balances the interest in not overly burdening the debtor with prepetition obligations against the interest in preserving the secured creditor's bargained-for collateral position.[10]

§ 4.4 The Role of State Law

The controversy regarding postpetition property focuses on the meaning of "proceeds, product, offspring, rents or profits" in § 552(b) under state law. These terms are not defined in the Bankruptcy Code. The Supreme Court, in its landmark decision of *Butner v. United States,*[11] ruled that in bankruptcy cases, property interests, including security interests, are created and defined by state law.[12] Congress has also indicated that property rights should be governed by state law, and that § 552 reflects its historical concern that property rights be governed by the applicable state's law, rather than the "mere happenstance" of bankruptcy.[13]

§ 4.5 Section 552 and Real Property Rents

Commercial loans on rent-generating property are often secured by a security interest in, lien on, or assignment of rents from the property. For example, a creditor making a loan for improvements to a shopping center takes an assignment of the rents paid by the tenants of the shopping center to the owner of the shopping center. In the event of default, the creditor can then require that the tenants pay rent directly to the creditor and not to their landlord, the debtor. Unlike the majority view regarding postpetition hotel room receipts (see **§§ 4.6** through **4.9**), the majority view regarding postpetition real estate rents holds that a lien on or assignment of real property rents, if properly perfected and enforceable, continues postpetition.[14]

---

[10] Philip Morris Capital Corp. v. Bering Trader, Inc. (*In re* Bering Trader, Inc.), 944 F.2d 500, 502 (9th Cir. 1991).

[11] 440 U.S. 48 (1979).

[12] *Id.* at 54–55; *see also In re* Majestic Motel Assocs., 131 B.R. 523, 525 (Bankr. D. Me. 1991); Sacramento Mansion v. Sacramento Sav. & Loan Ass'n (*In re* Sacramento Mansion), 117 B.R. 592, 602 (Bankr. D. Colo. 1990); Super 8 Motels v. M. Vickers, Ltd. (*In re* M. Vickers, Ltd.), 111 B.R. 332, 333 (D. Colo. 1990).

[13] Wolters Village, Ltd. v. Village Properties, Ltd. (*In re* Village Properties, Ltd.), 723 F.2d 441, 444 (5th Cir.), *cert. denied,* 466 U.S. 974 (1984); *see also* Butner v. United States, 440 U.S. 48, 55 (1979).

[14] SLC Ltd. V v. Bradford Group W. (*In re* SLC Ltd. V), 152 B.R. 755, 763 (Bankr. D. Utah 1993); *In re* Foxhill Place Ass'n, 119 B.R. 708, 714 (Bankr. W.D. Mo. 1990); *In re* Bethesda Air Rights Ltd. Partnership, 117 B.R. 202, 209 (Bankr. D. Md. 1990); *In re* Centre of Mo. Ltd., 116 B.R. 138, 141 (Bankr. E.D. Mo. 1990); Northwestern Nat'l Life Ins. Co. v. Metro Square (*In re* Metro Square), 106 B.R. 584, 588 (Bankr. D. Minn. 1989); Oliver v. MBank Dallas (*In re* Oliver), 66 B.R. 426, 429 (Bankr. N.D. Tex. 1986).

SECTION 552 AND HOTEL REVENUES

§ 4.6 The Majority View

A typical situation is seen in *In re General Associated Investors Limited Partnership.*[15] The debtor owned and operated a hotel in Arizona. Deerport was a creditor of the debtor and was owed in excess of $66 million. Deerport held a lien on the real property and the rents, issues, and profits of the real property. Deerport also held a lien on certain personal property of the debtor. After commencing a bankruptcy case, the debtor filed an emergency motion to determine its right to use postpetition income from hotel operations. Not surprisingly, Deerport asserted that postpetition revenues remained encumbered by Deerport's lien and security interest.

The court first ruled that the hotel room revenues were personal property, not real property, because: (a) under Arizona law, a hotel guest is a mere licensee with the right to use the hotel premises, as opposed to a tenant with a right to possess the real property; and (b) this conclusion was consistent with the majority view on the nature of hotel room revenues.[16] Because the room revenues were personal property, the court held that perfection of a security interest in such revenues was governed by the Uniform Commercial Code (the UCC). Under the UCC, perfection required the filing a financing statement with the Secretary of State or other designated entity. Deerport's filed financing statement was insufficient to indicate that Deerport held a security interest in accounts or personal property intangibles. Therefore, the court ruled that Deerport did not have a properly perfected security interest in hotel room revenues.[17]

Moreover, the court held that even if Deerport had properly perfected its security interest, § 552(a) terminated any such interest in postpetition revenues.[18] The court expressly rejected cases holding that hotel room revenues were in the nature of real property. The court emphasized that hotel revenues were generated from services provided by the hotel, such as food, beverages, and tennis, and that revenues generated by services cannot be considered rents or profits.[19] Accordingly, the court held that Deerport had no interest in postpetition hotel revenues.

General Associated Investors is consistent with the majority of courts considering this issue. The majority view holds that the debtor has unencumbered access to the postpetition hotel revenues because such funds are not "proceeds, product, offspring, rents or profits" under state law.[20] The analyses of such courts on this issue is set forth in §§ **4.7** through **4.9.**

---

[15] 150 B.R. 756 (Bankr. D. Ariz. 1993).

[16] *Id.* at 759.

[17] *Id.*

[18] *Id.* at 759–60.

[19] *Id.* at 762.

[20] *See, e.g.,* Greyhound Real Estate Fin. Co. v. Official Unsecured Creditors' Comm. (*In re* Northview Corp.), 130 B.R. 543, 548 (Bankr. 9th Cir. 1991); *In re* General Associated Investors Ltd. Partnership, 150 B.R. 756, 762 (Bankr. D. Ariz. 1993); *In re* Thunderbird Inn, 151 B.R. 224, 227 (Bankr. D. Ariz. 1993); *In re* Tri-Growth Centre City, 133 B.R.

§ 4.7 —Rents

Most frequently, creditors have argued that hotel revenues are rents under state law and, therefore, the creditor's security interest in such rents continues postpetition. Hotel lenders often analogize to cases involving shopping center, office building, or apartment complex debtors. Many courts have rejected such arguments, relying on the personal property view of hotel revenues.[21] At least one court has distinguished between the landlord/tenant relationship and the innkeeper/guest relationship.[22] The principal distinction between the two relationships is that a tenant has exclusive possession of the premises against the world, including the property owner, but a hotel guest has only a limited license to use the property and does not acquire an interest in or possession of the property.[23] Furthermore, courts have emphasized that hotel guests do not pay "rent" because they do not make payments under a "lease."[24] Instead, hotel guests have a contract under which they are entitled to a limited right to use the property.[25] Thus, payments from hotel guests resemble payments on a contract or an account.[26] In one case, the court reasoned that the revenues were not rents because the state statute referred to hotel room charges as "rates" and not as "rents."[27] The court also distinguished between landlords and innkeepers on the basis that a "landlord has no lien on his tenant's property for unpaid rent but an innkeeper has a lien for unpaid charges."[28]

524, 526 (Bankr. S.D. Cal. 1991); *In re* Corpus Christi Hotel Partners, 133 B.R. 850, 854 (Bankr. S.D. Tex. 1991); *In re* Majestic Motel Assocs., 131 B.R. 523, 526 (Bankr. D. Me. 1991); *In re* Nendels-Medford Joint Venture, 127 B.R. 658, 669 (Bankr. D. Or. 1991); *In re* Shore Haven Motor Inn, 124 B.R. 617, 618 (Bankr. S.D. Fla. 1991); Airport Inn Assocs. v. Travelers Ins. Co. (*In re* Airport Inn Assocs.), 132 B.R. 951, 960 (Bankr. D. Colo. 1990); Sacramento Mansion v. Sacramento Sav. & Loan Ass'n (*In re* Sacramento Mansion), 117 B.R. 592, 607 (Bankr. D. Colo. 1990); *In re* Oceanview/Virginia Beach Real Estate Assocs., 116 B.R. 57, 59 (Bankr. E.D. Va. 1990); Super 8 Motels v. M. Vickers, Ltd. (*In re* M. Vickers, Ltd.), 111 B.R. 332, 337 (D. Colo. 1990); Investment Hotel Properties v. New W. Fed. Sav. & Loan Ass'n (*In re* Investment Hotel Properties), 109 B.R. 990, 993–94 (Bankr. D. Colo. 1990); Kearney Hotel Partners v. Richardson (*In re* Kearney Hotel Partners), 92 B.R. 95, 102–03 (Bankr. S.D.N.Y. 1988); Victor Sav. & Loan Ass'n v. Grimm (*In re* Greater Atl. & Pac. Inv. Group), 88 B.R. 356, 359–60 (Bankr. N.D. Okla. 1988); *In re* Ashkenazy Enter., 94 B.R. 645, 647 (Bankr. C.D. Cal. 1986).

21 *See, e.g., In re* Tri-Growth Centre City, Ltd., 133 B.R. 524, 526 (Bankr. S.D. Cal. 1991); *In re* Shore Haven Motor Inn, 124 B.R. 617, 618 (Bankr. S.D. Fla. 1991).

22 Investment Hotel Properties v. New W. Fed. Sav. & Loan Ass'n (*In re* Investment Hotel Properties), 109 B.R. 990, 993–94, (Bankr. D. Colo. 1990).

23 Sacramento Mansion v. Sacramento Sav. & Loan Ass'n (*In re* Sacramento Mansion), 117 B.R. 592, 607 (Bankr. D. Colo. 1990).

24 *In re* Nendels-Medford Joint Venture, 127 B.R. 658, 663 (Bankr. D. Or. 1991).

25 *Id.*

26 Victor Sav. & Loan Ass'n v. Grimm (*In re* Greater Atl. & Pac. Inv. Group), 88 B.R. 356, 359 (Bankr. N.D. Okla. 1988).

27 *In re* Ashkenazy Enter., 94 B.R. 645, 647 (Bankr. C.D. Cal. 1986).

28 *Id.*

One court has held that hotel room revenues are analogous to greens fees paid for the use of golf courses, fees for roller and ice skating rinks, race track admissions, and theater and stadium admissions.[29] In such instances, only a limited license is acquired; simultaneously, an account receivable is created and immediately converted into proceeds.[30]

Courts have also emphasized that hotel room revenues are derived from the provision of services, rather than generated from real property. One court recited a litany of services available at the hotels at issue:

> bell service, maid service, linen service, valet parking, security in the parking facilities, 24-hour security guard, message service, mail facilities, safe deposit, check cashing, reservations with affiliated hotels, limousine, newspapers, cable television, stationery and postcards, amenity packages, robes and slippers, wine and fruit baskets, turn-down service, guidebooks, multi-lingual staff, room service, restaurant, sundry and gift shop, laundry and dry cleaning, car rental, meeting rooms, equipment rental.[31]

Hotel revenues are not "rents" derived from the real property itself, but rather are generated in large part by the incidental services that the hotel furnishes to its guests.[32] Based on their source—personal services rather than real property—such courts conclude that the room revenues are personal property.[33]

As any experienced traveler knows, the level of personal services offered by hotels varies greatly, with the extremes being low-budget motels on one end and five-star hotels on the other. One court, however, rejected the possibility that the outcome of the realty versus personalty issue could vary with the level of services offered by the hotel.[34] The lower court had held that the hotel revenues at issue were rents because the hotel did not offer its patrons food and liquor but only access to vending machines, that is, there were limited services involved. This was reversed because reliance on this kind of distinction would have "absurd results."[35] Such a rule would require a creditor to assess the level of services provided by the hotel before making the loan and securing its collateral. If the hotel provided many services other than rooms for guests, the creditor would file under Article 9 of the UCC. If few services were provided, the creditor would record an assignment of rents under the laws governing real property. For those hotels falling somewhere in between, the creditor would face the risk of using the wrong method to perfect its security interest.[36]

---

29 Kearney Hotel Partners v. Richardson (*In re* Kearney Hotel Partners), 92 B.R. 95, 99 (Bankr. S.D.N.Y. 1988).

30 *Id.*

31 *In re* Ashkenazy Enter., 94 B.R. 645, 647 (Bankr. C.D. Cal. 1986).

32 *In re* Majestic Motel Assocs., 131 B.R. 523, 526 (Bankr. D. Maine 1991).

33 *In re* Thunderbird Inn, 151 B.R. 224, 227 (Bankr. D. Ariz. 1993).

34 Super 8 Motels v. M. Vickers, Ltd. (*In re* M. Vickers, Ltd.), 111 B.R. 332, 336–37 (D. Colo. 1990).

35 *Id.* at 337.

36 *Id.*

§ 4.8 —Proceeds

In some cases, creditors have argued that hotel revenues were proceeds of prepetition collateral within the meaning of § 552(b). Courts are split as to the meaning of *proceeds* under § 552(b). Based on the reference to "applicable nonbankruptcy law" in § 552(b), the UCC definition of proceeds is one possibility:[37] "whatever is received upon the sale, exchange, collection or other disposition of collateral or proceeds."[38] Other courts have rejected the UCC definition in favor of a broader definition based on legislative history providing that proceeds covers any property into which property subject to the security interest is converted.[39] One court has held that the UCC definition is too narrow, but emphasized that an overly broad interpretation of proceeds must be avoided: "If proceeds included funds generated from any use of collateral, arguably all post-petition funds would become proceeds. Congress intended to extend a pre-petition lien post-petition when collateral is converted into new property."[40]

§ 4.9 —Profits

Profits of prepetition collateral are another category of property in which the creditor's security interest continues postpetition.[41] Arguments by creditors that they hold a postpetition interest in profits in the hotel revenue context have generally failed because courts have held that "profits" is a term of art which does not generally apply to all business profits.[42] In one case,[43] the creditor argued that its prepetition security interest in profits encompassed hotel room revenues based on the definition of profits in *Black's Law Dictionary:* "The benefit, advantage, or pecuniary gain accruing to the owner or occupant of land from its actual use; as in the familiar phrase 'rents, issues and profits,' or in the expression 'mesne profits.'"[44] The court rejected the creditor's interpretation of profits for several reasons. First, the creditor's view was contrary to case authority. Second, the creditor's broad interpretation of profits would render "proceeds" redundant. Third, because "proceeds" was to be interpreted broadly, according to legislative history, "profits" should be interpreted narrowly. Finally, a broad interpretation of profits would hamper the debtor's fresh start and deprive the debtor of funds for reorganization or to bargain with for postpetition financing.[45]

---

37 Unsecured Creditors Comm. v. Marepcon Fin. Corp. (*In re* Bumper Sales), 907 F.2d 1430, 1437 (4th Cir. 1990).

38 UCC § 9-306(1).

39 Investment Hotel Properties v. New W. Fed. Sav. & Loan Ass'n (*In re* Investment Hotel Properties), 109 B.R. 990, 995 (Bankr. D. Colo. 1990).

40 *In re* Corpus Christi Hotel Partners, 133 B.R. 850, 856 (Bankr. S.D. Tex. 1991).

41 11 U.S.C. § 552(b).

42 *In re* Majestic Motel Assocs., 131 B.R. 523, 525 (Bankr. D. Me. 1991).

43 Investment Hotel Properties v. New W. Fed. Sav. & Loan Ass'n (*In re* Investment Hotel Properties), 109 B.R. 990 (Bankr. D. Colo. 1990).

44 *Id.* at 995; *see* Black's Law Dictionary 1090 (5th ed. 1979).

45 Investment Hotel Properties v. New W. Fed. Sav. & Loan Ass'n, 109 B.R. at 995–96.

§ 4.10 The Minority View

The minority view[46] is exemplified by *In re S.F. Drake Hotel Associates,*[47] in which the creditor's security interest was held to encompass postpetition hotel room revenues. The debtor contended that the room revenues were not "rents" but rather were "accounts." According to the debtor, every time a room was occupied by a new guest postpetition, a new account was created, and because such accounts were not in existence prepetition, § 552(a) prevented the lien from continuing postpetition.[48] The court declined to adopt the debtor's view for multiple reasons. The court reasoned that hotel room revenues are not generated from services alone without real property. Apartment and office buildings also provide services.[49] Moreover, the hotel guest's primary objective is to obtain shelter.[50] The court also rejected the distinction between hotel revenues and rents based on length of occupancy: "Why should the length of the stay—a day, a week, a month, a year—determine the validity of the parties' security agreement?"[51] Finally, the court found no valid basis for depriving the creditor of postpetition revenues in the hotel loan context but not in the context of rental property such as apartment buildings.[52]

The reasoning of *S.F. Drake Hotel Associates* was followed by an Arizona court in *In re Everett Home Town Limited Partnership.*[53] In that case, the debtor sought to pay various operating expenses with the revenues generated postpetition, and the creditor objected on the basis that such revenues were cash collateral.[54] The court acknowledged the many cases which have held that a security interest in hotel revenues is terminated postpetition by § 552(b) but declined to follow the majority view for multiple reasons. First, the court held that hotel revenues were not accounts under the UCC because, among other things, they were not for the payment of goods. Second, the court rejected the reasoning that hotel revenues are primarily service-based. Third, the court held that the majority view applied a definition of "rents" that was too narrow for purposes of § 552(b). Finally, the court indicated that the terms in § 552 should be defined in their general sense rather than by reference to statutory definitions in state law. According to the court, "rents" has a plain meaning which should be followed and which includes payments from hotel/suite occupants.[55]

---

46 For other cases following the minority view, see T-H New Orleans Ltd. Partnership v. Financial Sec. Assurance (*In re* T-H New Orleans Ltd. Partnership), 10 F.3d 1099, 1106 (5th Cir. 1993), *petition for cert. filed,* 62 U.S.L.W. 3642 (Mar. 17, 1994) (No. 93-1466); *In re* Tavern Motor Inn, 80 B.R. 659, 662 (D. Vt. 1987); *In re* Arriens, 25 B.R. 79, 81 (Bankr. D. Or. 1982).

47 131 B.R. 156 (Bankr. N.D. Cal. 1991).

48 *Id.* at 158.

49 *Id.* at 159.

50 *Id.*

51 *Id.* at 160.

52 *Id.*

53 146 B.R. 453 (Bankr. D. Ariz. 1992).

54 *Id.* at 454–55.

55 *Id.* at 457–58.

The court in *Mid-City Hotel Associates v. Prudential Insurance Company (In re Mid-City Hotel Associates)*[56] applied a different approach when it adopted the minority view by holding that hotel revenues were not "rents," but were either "issues," "profits," "revenues," or "income," and thus were subject to the creditor's security interest and lien.[57] The court relied on the definitions of *issues* and *profits* and *revenue* in *Black's Law Dictionary* and the parties' own intentions, which were to grant a security interest in all of the economic fruits of the debtor's physical use of the real property.[58]

Some states have enacted legislation in recent years that expressly provides that funds generated from licenses for the use of property are considered rents under state law.[59] This would presumably include hotel revenues within the statutory definition of rents.

The minority view may gain new favor because of the recent adoption of the proposed draft of the *Restatement (Third) of Property - Security (Mortgages)*.[60] The proposed draft defines *rents* as "the proceeds payable by a lessee, licensee, or other person for the right to possess, use, or occupy the real property of another."[61] Thus, under the proposed *Restatement (Third),* hotel room receipts would fall within the definition of rents. Whether states will adopt this definition and, correspondingly, whether bankruptcy courts will adopt it when interpreting state law for the purposes of § 552 remains to be seen.

The majority view has been subject to criticism from commentators, largely because of the differing results regarding revenues from hotels and other real properties, such as shopping centers, office complexes, and apartment buildings. It is possible that an intermediate approach could develop, requiring the courts to determine whether the hotel's real property or personal property aspects predominate.[62]

Finally, Congress may resolve the issue in the near future. A bill was introduced in the spring 1993 term which proposes to amend §§ 363 and 552(b) to clarify that hotel revenues are cash collateral if the security agreement covering such revenues has been properly recorded.[63]

---

56 114 B.R. 634 (Bankr. D. Minn. 1990).

57 *Id.* at 641.

58 *Id.* at 641–42.

59 *E.g.,* Kan. Stat. Ann. § 58-2343 (Supp. 1991); N.C. Gen. Stat. § 47-20(b)(1) (Supp. 1992); S.C. Code Ann. § 29-3-80 (Supp. 1993).

60 The proposed draft was approved by the American Law Institute meeting on May 12–15, 1992.

61 Restatement (Third) of Property - Security (Mortgages) § 4.2(a) (Tentative Draft No. 2, May 1992).

62 For additional discussion regarding the nature of hotel revenues postpetition, see C. Edwards & J. Murray, *Hotel Room Revenues: Bates Motel Revisited,* 22 Real Est. L.J. 116 (1993); B. Donahue & W. Edwards, *The Heartbreak Hotel Revisited: Hotel Bankruptcy and Suggested Solutions to the Confusion over the Hotel Income/Receipts Issue,* 111 Banking L.J. 25 (1994); R. Freyermuth, *Of Hotel Revenues, Rents, and Formalism in the Bankruptcy Courts: Implications for Reforming Commercial Real Estate Finance,* 40 UCLA L. Rev. 1461 (1993); C. Averch, *The Heartbreak Hotel for Secured Creditors: When Postpetition Revenue from a Hotel Is Not Subject to a Prepetition Security Interest,* 107 Banking L.J. 484 (1990).

63 S. 540, 103d Cong., 1st Sess. § 206 (1993).

MISCELLANEOUS ISSUES

§ 4.11 Perfection of Real and Personal Property Interests

If hotel room revenues are personal property, then the UCC governs; if they are in the nature of real property, then they are excluded from the UCC.[64] Accordingly, the cautious lender should perfect its security interest in and lien on such revenues under both real and personal property laws. This typically involves recording the assignment of rents in the real property records where the land is located and filing a financing statement in the places required by the state's version of the UCC for taking a security interest in accounts.

§ 4.12 Cash Collateral and 11 U.S.C. § 363

Title 11 U.S.C. § 363 governs the debtor's use, sale, or lease of property in bankruptcy and defines cash collateral. *Cash collateral,* in essence, is any cash or cash equivalent, whenever acquired, in which both the debtor and another party both have an interest.[65] The definition specifically includes "proceeds, products, offspring, rents, or profits of property subject to a security interest as provided in Section 552(b)."[66] Accordingly, if the cash at issue falls within the exceptions to postpetition termination of security interests set forth in § 552(b), then the cash is cash collateral.

Section 363(c)(2) forbids debtors from using cash collateral without consent of the creditor who holds an interest in such collateral or court approval. This prohibition is intended to be self-executing and, on its face, places the burden on the debtor to seek permission to use cash collateral, and it does not require the creditor to do anything to protect its interest in cash collateral. As a practical matter, however, the cautious lender should not rely on the debtor to protect the creditor's interest in cash collateral. Rather, the creditor should file a motion to prohibit the debtor's use of cash collateral immediately upon the commencement of the bankruptcy case and not run the risk that such revenues will be dissipated before the issue is decided.

In the event the court follows the minority view on this issue and holds that the creditor has a continuing security interest in postpetition hotel room revenues, the debtor will likely seek permission from either the court or the creditor to use such funds to operate its business. The debtor will probably be permitted to use such funds in its postpetition operations, but the creditor should have an influential voice in determining how such funds are used. For example, the debtor might be required to submit budgets to the creditor for approval and to report on its actual versus projected results. Moreover, in exchange for the debtor's use of postpetition revenues,

---

[64] § 9-104(j) of Article 9 of the UCC excludes transactions intended to create a security interest in real property from the scope of Article 9, which governs secured transactions.

[65] 11 U.S.C. § 363(a).

[66] *Id.*

the creditor might be entitled to a replacement lien on other property or other form of adequate protection.[67] Adequate protection is discussed in detail in **Chapter 5.**

§ 4.13 Burden of Proof

The creditor bears the burden of establishing the existence and extent of its asserted lien on postpetition revenues.[68] Therefore, the creditor should have: (1) evidence of the debt and security interest, such as a note, security agreement, deed of trust or mortgage, or assignment of rents; and (2) evidence of perfection, such as recording in the real property records or filing of a financing statement. The creditor should also be prepared to explain why the cash flow at issue falls within one or more of the five classes of collateral listed in § 552(b), that is, proceeds, product, offspring, rents, or profits. As explained in **§§ 4.7** through **4.10,** this requires an examination of the state law regarding the nature of such types of property.

---

[67] 11 U.S.C. § 361(2) states that adequate protection may be provided by a replacement lien to the extent that the creditor's interest in the collateral is diminishing.

[68] *In re* Thunderbird Inn, 151 B.R. 224, 227 (Bankr. D. Ariz. 1993); Carlson v. W. J. Menefree Constr. Co. (*In re* Grassridge Ind.), 78 B.R. 978, 980 (Bankr. W.D. Mo. 1987).

CHAPTER 5

THE LAW OF RELIEF FROM THE AUTOMATIC STAY

Patricia K. Kelly

§ 5.1 Introduction

The automatic stay, brought to life by the filing of a bankruptcy case, is one of the fundamental protections provided by the bankruptcy laws.[1] In the case of a small business, just as in other businesses, the automatic stay provides the opportunity to assess the extent of liabilities and the value of the assets of the business. This breathing spell from creditors is important because it grants the debtor time to formulate a repayment or reorganization plan or be relieved of the financial pressures that caused the bankruptcy.[2] The stay doesn't protect just the debtor. It also protects the creditors by preventing particular creditors from acting unilaterally in self-interest to obtain payment from the debtor to the detriment of other creditors.[3]

---

[1] H.R. Rep. No. 595, 95th Cong., 1st Sess. 340 (1977), *reprinted in* 1978 U.S.C.C.A.N. 5963, 6296–97.

[2] *Id.*

[3] Association of St. Croix Condominium Owners v. St. Croix Hotel Corp., 682 F.2d 446, 448 (3d Cir. 1982); *see also* Borman v. Raymark Indus., Inc., 946 F.2d 1031 (3d Cir. 1991); Martin-Trigona v. Champion Fed. Sav. & Loan Ass'n, 892 F.2d 575 (7th Cir.

The stay provided by 11 U.S.C. § 362 is "automatic" because it is triggered against all entities upon the filing of a bankruptcy petition, regardless of whether any parties to the proceeding are aware that a petition has been filed.[4] Because the automatic stay serves the interests of both debtors and creditors, it may not be waived and its scope may not be limited.[5] Thus, all actions against a debtor or against property of the bankruptcy estate are automatically stayed unless modified by court order or waived by the statute itself.

A central purpose of the bankruptcy code is to provide a procedure through which honest but unfortunate debtors can reorder their financial affairs, make peace with their creditors, and enjoy new opportunities in life, unhampered by the pressure and discouragement of preexisting debt.[6] Further, neither the size nor the complexity of a debtor's business structure should preclude the availability of a bankruptcy reorganization if such a remedy is desired, required, and possible.[7] Small businesses are entitled to bankruptcy protection for the purpose of reorganization or liquidation.

§ 5.2 What Is Stayed

All provisions governing the automatic stay are set forth in 11 U.S.C. § 362. The scope of the automatic stay is very broad. Basically, the automatic stay stops all actions against a debtor, debtor-in-possession, or property of the estate unless the stay is modified by court order and except for certain exempt actions covered in **§ 5.3.** Among other things, the automatic stay stops judicial and administrative proceedings, enforcement of judgments, and actions to take property, to perfect liens, to collect claims, and to set off debts.[8] These provisions, in essence, stay acts that immediately or potentially threaten to confiscate the debtor's property or require the debtor to act affirmatively to protect its interests.[9]

Due to the broad scope of the automatic stay, the assertion has been made that the automatic stay is unconstitutional. A free speech issue has arisen in situations in which a creditor advertised that a debtor had not been paying its bills.[10] However,

---

1989); *In re* Parr Meadows Racing Ass'n, Inc., 880 F.2d 1540 (2d Cir. 1989), *cert. denied sub nom.* Suffolk County Treasurer v. Barr, 493 U.S. 1058 (1990); Small Business Admin. v. Rinehart, 887 F.2d 165 (8th Cir. 1989).

[4] Maritime Elec. Co. v. United Jersey Bank, 959 F.2d 1194, 1204 (3d Cir. 1991).

[5] *Id.*; Ostano Commerzanstalt v. Telewide Sys., Inc., 790 F.2d 206, 207 (2d Cir. 1986).

[6] Grogan v. Garner, 498 U.S. 279 (1991); Local Loan Co. v. Hunt, 292 U.S. 234, 244 (1934).

[7] *In re* Cardinal Indus., Inc., 109 B.R. 748 (Bankr. S.D. Ohio 1989).

[8] 11 U.S.C. § 362(a)(1)–(8).

[9] Morgan Guar. Trust Co. v. American Sav. & Loan Ass'n, 804 F.2d 1487, 1491 (9th Cir. 1986), *cert. denied,* 482 U.S. 929 (1987).

[10] *In re* Stonegate Sec. Servs., Ltd., 56 B.R. 1014 (N.D. Ill. 1986); *In re* National Serv., 742 F.2d 859 (5th Cir. 1984) (billboard advertisements, "Beware, this company is in bankruptcy" and "Beware, this company does not pay its bills," constitute free speech and are constitutionally protected); *In re* Stonegate Sec. Servs., Ltd., 56 B.R. 1014 (N.D. Ill. 1986) (truck parked outside business premises with sign, "Stonegate Auto

§ 362 cannot prohibit public criticism unless the criticism interferes with the debtor's reorganization or with the functions of the Bankruptcy Court.[11] The protections granted to the debtor by § 362 include protections of the judicial process itself.[12] Section 362 acts as an injunction against interference with the bankruptcy court's jurisdiction over petitioning debtors.[13]

The reach of the automatic stay extends to all acts against the debtor or the debtor's property, to include a refusal or failure to take an action that is intended to coerce the debtor in some manner.[14] The stay is effective upon the filing of the bankruptcy case and lasts for the duration of the bankruptcy proceedings unless there is a modification by the court.[15] Because the stay is self-executing, all parties who have knowledge of the pendency of the bankruptcy case are bound to honor the stay until relief is granted or the stay is otherwise modified.[16] In addition, once notice of a bankruptcy case has been communicated to creditors, directly or indirectly, the burden is placed on the creditors to decide the bounds of permissible conduct against the debtor.[17] Any action taken in violation of the automatic stay is either void or voidable, depending on the circuit.[18] As broad as the automatic stay is, however, it does not extinguish or discharge any debt through its own provisions.[19]

One of the potential pitfalls for a small business bankruptcy is found in the relationship the debtor has with its lender. Often, businesses have loans and daily deposits with the same lending institution. This can create the potential for problems if the lender has reason to believe the business will not continue to pay its debts when due. The typical lender's recourse is to set off the deposits against the outstanding loans.

Alarms does not pay supplier", "Stonegate Auto Alarms does *NOT* pay suppliers" and "Crime does not pay, Stonegate Auto Alarms the same way" is not prohibited by 11 U.S.C. § 362).

11 *In re* Stonegate Sec. Servs., Ltd., 56 B.R. 1014, 1019 (N.D. Ill. 1986).

12 *Id.* at 1019.

13 *Id.*

14 *In re* Lanford, 10 B.R. 132 (Bankr. D. Minn. 1981) (college violated § 362(a)(6) by withholding a transcript for sole purpose of collecting a prepetition, discharged debt).

15 11 U.S.C. § 362(c), (d); Richard v. City of Chicago, 80 B.R. 451 (N.D. Ill. 1987).

16 NLT Computer Servs. Corp. v. Capital Computer Sys., Inc., 755 F.2d 1253, 1258 (6th Cir. 1985).

17 *In re* Skinner, 90 B.R. 470, 480 (D. Utah 1988), *aff'd,* 917 F.2d 444 (10th Cir. 1990).

18 Easley v. Pettibone Mich. Corp., 990 F.2d 905 (6th Cir. 1993). *Easley* compares cases holding that actions taken in violation of the stay are void and without effect (Raymark Indus., Inc. v. Lai, 973 F.2d 1125, 1132 (3d Cir. 1992); *In re* Schwartz, 954 F.2d 569, 574 (9th Cir. 1992); *In re* Calder, 907 F.2d 953, 956 (10th Cir. 1990); *In re* Smith, 876 F.2d 524 (6th Cir. 1989); *In re* 48th St. Steakhouse, Inc., 835 F.2d 427, 431 (2d Cir. 1987), *cert. denied,* 485 U.S. 1035 (1988); Matthews v. Rosene, 739 F.2d 249, 251 (7th Cir. 1984); *In re* Smith Corset Shops, Inc., 696 F.2d 971, 976 (1st Cir. 1982); Borg-Warner Acceptance Corp. v. Hall, 685 F.2d 1306, 1308 (11th Cir. 1982); *In re* Potts, 142 F.2d 883, 890 (6th Cir. 1944), *cert. denied,* 324 U.S. 868 (1945)) with a case holding that actions taken during the pendency of the stay are voidable (Sikes v. Global Marine, 881 F.2d 176, 178 (5th Cir. 1989)).

19 Pennsylvania Dep't of Pub. Welfare v. Davenport, 495 U.S. 552 (1990).

Before bankruptcy, this may be within the lender's rights under particular state laws. Once bankruptcy is filed, however, such action is automatically stayed. In bankruptcy, setoff is considered to occur when a claim is applied against an asset from a different transaction.[20] This right is not absolute and is limited by the automatic stay. A setoff, in bankruptcy, is not to be confused with the right of recoupment. *Recoupment* allows a claim to be applied against a claim arising from the same transaction and is not subject to the automatic stay.[21] It should be noted that the automatic stay does not defeat the right of setoff; the right is merely stayed pending an orderly examination of the debtor's and creditors' rights in the case.[22]

§ 5.3 What Is Not Stayed

Although the scope of the automatic stay is very broad, there are specific statutory exceptions set forth in 11 U.S.C. § 362(b)(1) through (6). For example, the automatic stay does not affect criminal actions against the debtor, collection of alimony, maintenance, and support from property that is not property of the estate, actions by a governmental unit to enforce the unit's police or regulatory power or to notice tax deficiencies, and actions by lessors under a terminated lease of nonresidential real property.[23] Because these statutory exceptions are a derogation of one of the fundamental purposes of the Bankruptcy Code, they are narrowly interpreted to ensure that all creditors are treated fairly and equally.[24]

Criminal proceedings. Criminal actions, although not typical, may be filed when businesses or their responsible parties violate criminal laws, including environmental criminal provisions. Bankruptcy laws are not a haven for criminal offenders. Rather, the laws are designed to give relief from financial overextension. Thus, criminal actions may proceed in spite of a debtor's bankruptcy.[25] The bankruptcy court does have the power to enjoin state criminal proceedings. However, the *abstention doctrine* to prevent such interference was clearly set forth in *Younger v. Harris,*[26] in which the United States Supreme Court held that except in very extraordinary circumstances, state criminal proceedings may be enjoined only if there is a showing of bad faith or harassment.[27] There is another test, less strict, that is sometimes used to determine whether criminal proceedings should continue. This test is known as the *principal motivation test* and focuses on the purpose behind criminal prosecution,

---

20 *In re* Patterson, 967 F.2d 505 (11th Cir. 1992); Small Business Admin. v. Rinehart, 887 F.2d 165 (8th Cir. 1989).

21 *In re* Holford, 896 F.2d 165 (5th Cir. 1990).

22 *In re* Corland Corp., 967 F.2d 1069 (5th Cir. 1992).

23 11 U.S.C. § 362(b)(1)–(6).

24 *In re* Glasply Marine Indus., Inc., 971 F.2d 391 (9th Cir. 1992).

25 11 U.S.C. § 362(b)(1); H.R. Rep. No. 595, 95th Cong., 1st Sess. 342 (1977), *reprinted in* 1978 U.S.C.C.A.N. 5693, 6299. *See also* S. Rep. No. 989, 95th Cong., 2d Sess. 51 (1977), *reprinted in* 1978 U.S.C.C.A.N. 5787.

26 401 U.S. 37 (1971).

27 *Id.* at 53.

that is, whether it is being utilized strictly as a debt collection device or whether it also includes public policy considerations.[28] Of these two tests, the *Younger* test appears more widely used.[29]

Collection of support. The automatic stay does not apply to the collection of alimony, maintenance, or support from property that is not property of the estate.[30] This may be especially important if the business involved is a sole proprietorship and personal assets and business assets overlap. This exception for the collection of alimony, maintenance, or support, however, does not include actions for the modification of such support.[31] In Chapter 13 bankruptcy cases, in particular, this exception has little practical effect because the bankruptcy estate includes postpetition property and wages.[32] Therefore, all alimony and support comes from property of the estate. In that circumstance, relief from stay should be liberally granted to avoid entangling the federal court in family law matters best left to the state court.[33]

Actions by governmental unit. A governmental entity's action or proceeding to enforce its police or regulatory powers is another statutory exception to the automatic stay.[34] This exception can be very important for small businesses because licenses or franchises granted by governmental entities may be the very revenue source on which the business depends. Liquor licenses, massage licenses, utility franchises, and cable franchises fall into this category. This exception to the automatic stay exists even though a regulatory action may conflict with the bankruptcy court's control of estate assets.[35] The exception is not limited in application only to those actions necessary to protect urgent public health or safety in emergency situations.[36] Once a governmental unit determines that a proceeding to enforce its police or regulatory powers is excepted from the automatic stay under § 362(b)(4), the agency is not required to petition for relief prior to going forth with its proceeding.[37]

Claims brought by debtor. A petition in bankruptcy also does not stay claims, including counterclaims, brought by the debtor itself.[38] Thus, if the business has

---

[28] *In re* Alten, 108 B.R. 16 (Bankr. D.R.I. 1989).

[29] *Id.* at 18.

[30] 11 U.S.C. § 362(b)(2).

[31] *In re* Stringer, 847 F.2d 549, 552 (9th Cir. 1988).

[32] Carver v. Carver, 954 F.2d 1573, 1577–78 (11th Cir. 1992), *cert. denied,* __ U.S.__, 113 S. Ct. 496 (1992).

[33] *Id.*

[34] 11 U.S.C. § 362(b)(4).

[35] Eddleman v. United States Dep't of Labor, 923 F.2d 782, 790 (10th Cir. 1991).

[36] Midlantic Nat'l Bank v. New Jersey Dep't of Envtl. Protection, 474 U.S. 494, 503, *reh'g denied,* 475 U.S. 1090 (1986); *In re* Commonwealth Cos., 913 F.2d 518, 521 (8th Cir. 1990); Brock v. Rusco Indus. Inc., 842 F.2d 270, 273 (11th Cir.), *cert. denied,* 488 U.S. 889 (1988).

[37] NLRB v. Edward Cooper Painting, Inc., 804 F.2d 934, 939 (6th Cir. 1986).

[38] Maritime Elec. Co. v. United Jersey Bank, 959 F.2d 1194, 1203–05 (3d Cir. 1991); Brown v. Armstrong, 949 F.2d 1007, 1009–10 (8th Cir. 1991); Martin-Trigona v.

brought suit to collect payments due or has brought a counterclaim in a suit against it, the debtor's actions are not subject to the automatic stay. However, even though the debtor's actions are not stayed, a creditor's actions in the same case may be stayed; all proceedings in a case are not lumped together for the purpose of automatic stay analysis.[39] For instance, in *In re General Associated Investors, Ltd.,*[40] the debtor had initiated a tax appeal and the taxing authority moved to dismiss the appeal. By doing so, the taxing authority was held to be in violation of the automatic stay because it attempted to control estate property without relief from the automatic stay to do so. In contrast, in other circuits, a party defending a suit brought by the debtor has not been held in violation of the automatic stay when a motion to dismiss was filed, even though this resistance may have burdened rights asserted by the debtor.[41]

Further, the stay does not apply to sales or transfers of property initiated by the debtor[42] and does not affect the running of statutory or contractual time periods.[43] The automatic stay also does not prohibit creditors from making legitimate reports to credit agencies that parties have filed for bankruptcy protection.[44] The filing of a lis pendens does not violate the stay if it does not create a lien, even though it alerts prospective buyers to a potential problem and may thereby diminish the value of estate property.[45] Neither does the automatic stay create an affirmative duty to remedy past acts of fraud or bias or harassment as soon as a petition is filed; the stay applies only to acts taken after a petition has been filed.[46] However, the circuits differ in whether a mere possessory interest in land is property of the estate such that actions by a landlord to retake possession violate the automatic stay. Some circuits

---

Champion Fed. Sav. & Loan Ass'n, 892 F.2d 575, 577 (7th Cir. 1989); Carley Capital Group v. Fireman's Fund Ins. Co., 889 F.2d 1126, 1127 (D.C. Cir. 1989); Freeman v. Commissioner, 799 F.2d 1091, 1093 (5th Cir. 1986).

39 Maritime Elec. Co. v. United Jersey Bank, 959 F.2d 1194, 1204 (3d Cir. 1991).

40 159 B.R. 552 (Bankr. D. Ariz. 1993).

41 United States v. Inslaw, Inc., 932 F.2d 1467 (D.C. Cir. 1991); Martin-Trigona v. Champion Fed. Sav. & Loan Ass'n, 892 F.2d 575 (7th Cir. 1989).

42 *In re* Schwartz, 954 F.2d 569, 574 (9th Cir. 1992).

43 Hazen First State Bank v. Speight, 888 F.2d 574 (8th Cir. 1989); *In re* Maanum, 828 F.2d 459 (8th Cir. 1987), *reh'g denied,* 838 F.2d 991 (8th Cir. 1988); *In re* Tynan, 773 F.2d 177 (7th Cir. 1985); *In re* Glenn, 760 F.2d 1428 (6th Cir.), *cert. denied sub nom.* Miller v. First Fed., 474 U.S. 849 (1985); Moody v. Amoco Oil Co., 734 F.2d 1200 (7th Cir.), *cert. denied,* 469 U.S. 982 (1984); Johnson v. First Nat'l Bank, 719 F.2d 270 (8th Cir. 1983), *cert. denied,* 465 U.S. 1012 (1984).

44 Hickson v. Home Fed., 805 F. Supp. 1567, 1573 (N.D. Ga. 1992); *In re* Sechuan City, Inc., 96 B.R. 37, 43 (Bankr. E.D. Pa. 1989).

45 United States v. Inslaw, Inc., 932 F.2d 1467, 1473 (D.C. Cir. 1991), *cert. denied,* __ U.S. __, 112 S. Ct. 913 (1992); *In re* Knightsbridge Dev. Co., 884 F.2d 145, 148 (4th Cir. 1989); *In re* 48th St. Steakhouse, Inc., 835 F.2d 427, 430 (2d Cir. 1987), *cert. denied,* 485 U.S. 1035 (1988).

46 United States v. Inslaw, Inc., 932 F.2d 1467, 1474 (D.C. Cir. 1991), *cert denied,* __ U.S. __, 112 S. Ct. 913 (1992) (creditor's failure to cure prepetition fraud is not a violation of automatic stay; rather, debtor retains legal rights to sue for fraud and contract remedies).

hold that a mere possessory interest triggers the protection of the automatic stay;[47] another circuit takes the opposite approach.[48]

Whether certain nondebtors are protected by the automatic stay depends on which chapter of the Bankruptcy Code the debtor has selected to proceed under. *Nondebtors,* for purposes of this discussion, are individuals or entities that have cosigned, guaranteed, or otherwise have become jointly liable on a debt with the debtor. Chapters 12 and 13 impose a limited stay of actions against individual cosigners of consumer debt;[49] Chapters 7 and 11 do not. Some circuits make an exception to this general rule when there is an identity between the debtor and non-debtor third party such that the debtor is the real party in interest and a judgment might enter against the interests of the debtor.[50] Absent an identity of interests or statutory protection, the automatic stay does not protect nondebtor codefendants, guarantors, officers, or other nondebtor third parties related to debtors from actions brought against them.[51]

§ 5.4 How Long the Stay Lasts

In general, the stay of an act against property of the estate continues until the property is no longer part of the bankruptcy estate.[52] A party-in-interest who desires to pursue a pending action against property of the estate may file a motion for relief from the automatic stay with the bankruptcy court pursuant to 11 U.S.C. § 362(d).[53] If the action stayed is pending litigation, a party-in-interest may move for relief from stay or file a motion for removal pursuant to 28 U.S.C. § 1478.[54] The stay of any other act within the parameters of 11 U.S.C. § 362(a) continues until the bankruptcy case is closed or dismissed, or until a discharge is granted or denied to an individual

---

47 *In re* Atlantic Business & Community Corp., 901 F.2d 325 (3d Cir. 1990); *In re* 48th St. Steakhouse, 835 F.2d 427, 430 (2d Cir. 1987), *cert. denied,* 485 U.S. 1035 (1988).

48 Erickson v. Polk, 921 F.2d 200 (8th Cir. 1990).

49 11 U.S.C. §§ 1201, 1301.

50 *Compare* A.H. Robins Co. v. Piccinin, 788 F.2d 994 (4th Cir.), *cert. denied,* 479 U.S. 876 (1986) (recognizing the co-debtor stay) *with In re* Lockhard, 884 F.2d 1171 (9th Cir. 1989) (declining to recognize the stay).

51 Credit Alliance Corp. v. Williams, 851 F.2d 119 (4th Cir. 1988); Ingersoll-Rand Fin. Corp. v. Miller Mining Co., 817 F.2d 1424, 1427 (9th Cir. 1987); Browning Seed, Inc. v. Bayles, 812 F.2d 999, 1004 (5th Cir. 1987); Otoe County Nat'l Bank v. W&P Trucking, Inc., 754 F.2d 1324 (10th Cir. 1984); Fortier v. Dona Anna Plaza Partners, 747 F.2d 1324 (10th Cir. 1984); Trimec, Inc. v. Zale Corp., 150 B.R. 685 (N.D. Ill. 1993); *In re* CCDC Fin. Corp., 143 B.R. 946 (D. Kan. 1992); *In re* Advanced Ribbons & Office Prods., Inc., 125 B.R. 259 (Bankr. 9th Cir. 1991).

52 11 U.S.C. § 362(c)(1).

53 Browning v. Navarro, 743 F.2d 1069, 1083 (5th Cir. 1984), *reh'g denied,* 830 F.2d 1126 (5th Cir. 1987).

54 *Id.; see In re* Critical Fork Coal Corp., 18 B.R. 422, 424 (Bankr. W.D. Va. 1982) (§ 362(d) motion for relief from automatic stay and § 1478(b) remand are alternative methods of seeking relief from the automatic stay to pursue pending litigation.)

Chapter 7 case or any Chapter 9, 11, 12, or 13 case.[55] In a Chapter 11 case, confirmation of the plan has the dual effect of revesting the debtor with title to its property and discharging the debtor from all dischargeable debts; therefore, the automatic stay ceases after confirmation of the plan.[56]

A party to an executory contract can move to terminate an assumed contract for postassumption default after the plan has been confirmed.[57] Moreover, the stay does not bar an action by a creditor concerning assets transferred to a successor as part of a confirmed plan.[58]

§ 5.5 Violation of the Automatic Stay

An individual injured by any willful violation of the stay is entitled to recover actual damages, including attorney's fees and costs, and may recover punitive damages in specific circumstances.[59] A corporate debtor, however, cannot recover damages for willful violation of the stay pursuant to 11 U.S.C. § 362; its relief is through contempt proceedings.[60] A *willful violation* does not require a specific intent to violate the automatic stay; damages are authorized upon finding that the creditor knew of the automatic stay and the creditor's actions that violated the automatic stay were intentional.[61]

A creditor's good faith belief that it is not violating the automatic stay is not relevant to whether the act was willful or whether compensation must be awarded.[62] Even good faith reliance on advice of counsel is no defense to an action brought to remedy the willful violation of the automatic stay.[63] An additional finding of egregious actions, maliciousness, or bad faith on the part of the offending creditor warrants the further imposition of punitive damages.[64]

Actions seeking damages for violation of the automatic stay may be enforced even after bankruptcy proceedings have been terminated.[65] The only exception to the normal

---

55 11 U.S.C. § 362(c)(2); Olive St. Inv., Inc. v. Howard Sav. Bank, 972 F.2d 214 (8th Cir. 1992); I.C.C. v. Holmes Transp., Inc., 931 F.2d 984 (1st Cir. 1991).

56 *In re* James Wilson Assocs., 965 F.2d 160, 167 (7th Cir. 1992); Department of Air Force v. Caroline Parachute Corp., 907 F.2d 1469, 1474 (4th Cir. 1990).

57 Department of Air Force v. Caroline Parachute Corp., 907 F.2d 1469 (4th Cir. 1990).

58 *In re* Brady Mun. Gas Corp., 936 F.2d 212, 218 (5th Cir. 1991), *cert. denied sub nom.* Sanders v. City of Brady, Texas, __ U.S. __, 112 S. Ct. 657 (1991).

59 11 U.S.C. § 362(h).

60 *In re* Chateaugay Corp., 920 F.2d 183, 187 (2d Cir. 1990).

61 *In re* Landsdale Family Restaurants, Inc., 977 F.2d 826, 829 (3d Cir. 1992); *In re* Bloom, 875 F.2d 224, 227 (9th Cir. 1989) (citing *In re* Inslaw, 83 B.R. 89, 165 (Bankr. D.D.C. 1988)).

62 *In re* Landsdale Family Restaurants, Inc., 977 F.2d 826, 829 (3d Cir. 1992); *In re* Bloom, 875 F.2d 224, 227 (9th Cir. 1989) (citing *In re* Inslaw, 83 B.R. 89, 165 (Bankr. D.D.C. 1988)).

63 *In re* Taylor, 884 F.2d 478, 483 (9th Cir. 1989).

64 *In re* Crysen/Montenay Energy Co., 902 F.2d 1098, 1105 (2d Cir. 1990); United States v. Ketelsen, 880 F.2d 990, 993 (8th Cir. 1989).

65 Price v. Rochford, 947 F.2d 829, 832 (7th Cir. 1991).

rule for impositon of damages against creditors for violation of the automatic stay lies with government creditors. Governments, unlike other creditors, are immune from monetary damages arising from the willful violation of the automatic stay.[66]

§ 5.6 Relief from Stay in General

The automatic stay is not incontestable, and a party-in-interest may request relief from stay for reasons set forth in 11 U.S.C. § 362(d).[67] Section 362(d) states that:

> On request of a party in interest and after notice and a hearing, the court shall grant relief from the stay provided under subsection (a) of this section, such as by terminating, annulling, modifying, or conditioning such stay—
>
> (1) for cause, including the lack of adequate protection of an interest in property of such party in interest; or
>
> (2) with respect to a stay of an act against property under subsection (a) of this section, if—
>
> (A) the debtor does not have equity in such property; and
>
> (B) such property is not necessary to an effective reorganization.

Section 362(d)(1) and (d)(2) are alternative means of obtaining relief.[68]

Only the court may grant relief from stay. Parties may not engage in self-help measures in derogation of the automatic stay.[69] Consensual agreements between parties concerning application of the automatic stay to their cases are permissible, but only pursuant to applicable rules and procedures and only as specifically authorized by court order after appropriate notice and opportunity for hearing.[70] Therefore, although "handshake deals" may have been the customary order of business outside of bankruptcy, a deal between a creditor and debtor is subject to court approval when the business is in bankruptcy.

Sometimes, bankruptcy is filed while a creditor is engaged in a state law-authorized remedial action such as foreclosure. The bankruptcy court has the authority to grant retroactive relief from stay[71] and annul the stay as if it never existed[72] to allow the foreclosure proceeding to continue.

Provisions governing the burden of proof in relief from stay matters are specifically set forth in 11 U.S.C. § 362(g)(1) and (2). In general, the party opposing the motion has the burden of proof on all issues except how much equity the debtor has in property.[73] However, § 362(g) does not contemplate that a creditor will be allowed

---

[66] United States v. Nordic Village, Inc., 503 U.S. __, 112 S. Ct. 1011 (1992); *In re* Pearson, 917 F.2d 1215 (9th Cir. 1990), *cert. denied*, __ U.S. __, 112 S. Ct. 1291 (1992).

[67] Noli v. Commissioner, 860 F.2d 1521 (9th Cir. 1988).

[68] *In re* Wieseler, 934 F.2d 965, 968 (8th Cir. 1991), *reh'g denied* (8th Cir. 1991).

[69] *In re* Fugazy Express, Inc., 982 F.2d 769, 776 (2d Cir. 1992).

[70] *In re* Randall Enters., Inc., 115 B.R. 292, 295 (Bankr. D. Colo. 1990).

[71] *In re* Schwartz, 954 F.2d 569, 572 (9th Cir. 1992); *In re* Albany Partners, Ltd., 749 F.2d 670, 675 (11th Cir. 1984).

[72] Schulz v. Homes Transp., Inc., 149 B.R. 251, 258 (D. Mass. 1993).

[73] 11 U.S.C. § 362(g)(1), (2).

to blindly assert causes of action without bearing the responsibility for some of the burden of production.[74] See **Chapter 8** for examination of relief from stay from the perspective of a creditor with a secured claim.

§ 5.7 Relief from Stay for Cause

Cause has no clear definition and is an intentionally broad and flexible concept to be determined on a case-by-case basis.[75] Some consideration of the balancing of harms is appropriate in determining whether there is cause to warrant modification of the automatic stay. The court must balance the inherent hardships on all parties and base its decision on the degree of hardship and overall goals of the Bankruptcy Code.[76]

Cause other than for "lack of adequate protection" has been found in a variety of situations. The existence of an imminent state court trial involving the same issues may be cause for the bankruptcy court to abstain from those issues. Several factors that should be considered in determining whether to grant relief from stay to allow litigation to continue in another forum include:

1. Whether another court could grant full relief
2. Whether litigation in another court would affect the administration of the bankruptcy case
3. Whether a specialized tribunal has been established to hear the action
4. Whether the other proceeding involves the debtor as a fiduciary
5. Whether the action primarily involves third parties
6. Whether the judgment claim that might arise from the other action is subject to equitable subordination
7. Whether the movant's success in the other proceeding would result in a judicial lien avoidable by the debtor
8. Whether the parties are ready for trial in the other proceeding
9. What effect the stay has on the parties so that any harm can be balanced.[77]

---

[74] *In re* Sonnax Indus., Inc., 907 F.2d 1280, 1285 (2d Cir. 1990); *In re* Holly's, 140 B.R. 643, 683 (Bankr. W.D. Mich. 1992); *see also* **Ch. 8,** which examines relief from stay from the perspective of a creditor with a secured claim.

[75] *In re* Tucson Estates, Inc., 912 F.2d 1162, 1166 (9th Cir. 1990); Pursifull v. Eakin, 814 F.2d 1501, 1506 (10th Cir. 1987).

[76] *In re* Peterson, 116 B.R. 247 (D. Colo. 1990); *In re* Cardinal Indus., Inc., 116 B.R. 964, 983 (Bankr. S.D. Ohio 1990) (quoting *In re* Pelika Mfg. Corp., 66 B.R. 444, 449 (Bankr. N.D. Ill. 1986)).

[77] *In re* Robbins, 964 F.2d 342 (4th Cir. 1992); *In re* Tucson Estates, Inc., 912 F.2d 1162, 1166 (9th Cir. 1990); *In re* Sonnax Indus., Inc., 99 B.R. 591 (D. Vt. 1989), *aff'd,* 907 F.2d 1280 (2d Cir. 1990). See **Ch. 8** for further discussion of pending litigation and also for a sample motion for relief from stay to pursue pending litigation.

Lack of good faith in filing bankruptcy constitutes cause.[78] Cause to grant relief from stay also exists when a spouse wishes to proceed in state court for support modification.[79] When naked legal title to property has become part of a bankruptcy estate but equitable title is held by another party, cause to grant relief from stay has been found.[80]

Sometimes the debtor's failure to comply with requirements of the Code constitute sufficient misconduct to grant relief from the stay. Examples are postpetition mismanagement,[81] transfer of property without court order and out of the ordinary course of business,[82] failure to follow court orders,[83] and misconduct.[84]

Cause has been found when a debtor was significantly in default under a lease and failed to successfully move for its assumption.[85] It has also been found when the debtor failed to pay postpetition taxes, failed to disclose a bank account on the schedules, and failed to notify a creditor of the account.[86] Relief from stay for cause has also been granted when the automatic stay has been used to shield misconduct by the debtor.[87]

§ 5.8 Relief from Stay for Lack of Adequate Protection

Cause can also include the lack of adequate protection of an interest in property.[88] *Adequate protection* is a flexible concept that requires the court to make decisions on a case-by-case basis, after full consideration of the charcteristics peculiar to each proceeding.[89] Adequate protection is a safeguard that is provided to protect the rights of a creditor with a secured claim during the debtor's bankruptcy proceedings. The creditor should be protected to the extent of the value of its secured interest in property, and the creditor cannot make a constitutional claim to more than that.[90] The concept of adequate protection stems from pre-Code case law recognizing the need to avoid impairment of secured property interests of creditors as

---

78 *In re* Little Creek Dev. Co., 779 F.2d 1068, 1071–73 (5th Cir. 1986); *In re* MGN Co., III, 116 B.R. 654 (Bankr. S.D. Ind. 1989). See **Ch. 8** for some detail on specific aspects of bad faith filing.

79 *In re* MacDonald, 755 F.2d 715, 717 (9th Cir. 1985).

80 *In re* Spencer, 115 B.R. 471 (D. Del. 1990).

81 *In re* Holly's, 140 B.R. 643 (Bankr. W.D. Mich. 1992).

82 *In re* Oklahoma P.A.C. First, Ltd. Partnership, 122 B.R. 394 (Bankr. D. Ariz. 1990).

83 *In re* CGR, Ltd., 56 B.R. 305, 307 (Bankr. S.D. Tex. 1985).

84 Farmers & Merchants Bank & Trust v. Trail W., Inc., 28 B.R. 389, 394 (D.S.D. 1983).

85 *In re* Future Growth Enters., Inc., 61 B.R. 469, 472 (Bankr. E.D. Pa. 1986).

86 *In re* McMartin Indus., Inc., 62 B.R. 718, 723 (Bankr. D. Neb. 1986).

87 *In re* Unioil, 54 B.R. 192 (Bankr. D. Colo. 1985).

88 11 U.S.C. § 362(d)(1).

89 *In re* Monroe Park, 17 B.R. 934, 940 (D. Del. 1982); *In re* Southerton Corp., 46 B.R. 391, 397 (D. Pa. 1982).

90 *In re* Briggs Transp. Co., 780 F.2d 1339, 1342 (8th Cir. 1985).

a matter of constitutional law.[91] Under the current Bankruptcy Code, the concept has been refined but has not yet been specifically defined.

The purpose of adequate protection is to ensure that the creditor with a secured claim receives in value essentially what was bargained for.[92] However, Congress did not state how these bargained-for rights were to be valued, nor when this valuation was to occur; those matters were left for determination on a case-by-case basis.[93] It was expected that courts would apply the concept of adequate protection in light of the facts of each case; it was not intended that the courts develop a hard and fast rule to apply in every case.[94] The flexibility in determining method and time of valuation is important to permit the courts to adapt to varying circumstances and changing modes of financing.[95] As a result, it is well settled that a creditor with a secured claim should receive adequate protection during the automatic stay, but any adequate protection determination must necessarily turn on the unique facts presented by each individual case.[96]

The Bankruptcy Code provides three examples of methods of adequate protection. Pursuant to 11 U.S.C. § 361, adequate protection may be provided by periodic cash payments to the extent that the stay results in a decrease in value of secured property.[97] Adequate protection may also be provided by an additional or replacement lien for the extent of decrease in value[98] or by granting the creditor with a secured claim the indubitable equivalent of the party's interest in property.[99] These means of providing adequate protection are not exclusive or exhaustive.[100] Like the determination of cause, methods of adequate protection are left for determination on a case-by-case basis. However, all these methods rely on the value of the protected party's interest in property.

The extent of protection of a party's interest in property was analyzed in *United Savings Association v. Timbers of Inwood Forest Associates, Ltd.*[101] The value of the interest, when applied to creditors with a secured claim, means the value of collateral without taking into account the creditor's right to immediate possession on default.[102]

---

91 Louisville Joint Stock Land Bank v. Radford, 295 U.S. 555 (1935); *In re* Southerton Corp., 46 B.R. 391, 397 (D. Pa. 1982) (citing Wright v. Union Cent. Life Ins. Co., 311 U.S. 273 (1940)).

92 H.R. Rep. No. 595, 95th Cong., 1st Sess. 339, *reprinted in* 1978 U.S.C.C.A.N. 5963, 6295.

93 *Id.* at 339, 1978 U.S.C.C.A.N. at 6295.

94 *Id.*

95 *Id.*

96 *In re* Ahlers, 794 F.2d 388, 395 (8th Cir. 1986), *cert. granted in part sub nom.* Norwest Bank Worthington v. Ahlers, 483 U.S. 1004 (1987), *rev'd on other grounds,* 485 U.S. 197 (1988).

97 11 U.S.C. § 361(1).

98 *Id.* § 361(2).

99 *Id* § 361(3).

100 **Ch. 3** also describes forms of adequate protection.

101 484 U.S. 365 (1988).

102 *Id.*; *In re* Deico Elecs., Inc., 139 B.R. 945 (Bankr. 9th Cir. 1992).

For that reason, an undersecured creditor (one whose collateral is worth less than the outstanding loan balance against it) is not entitled to postpetition interest as compensation for the delay caused by the automatic stay in foreclosing on collateral.[103] Valueless junior secured positions or unsecured deficiency claims are likewise not entitled to adequate protection,[104] although nothing in *Timbers* prevents adequate protection payments to compensate a creditor for the decline in value of a junior undersecured claim.[105] In addition, "indubitable equivalent" in § 361(3) does not require reimbursement for the "use value" of collateral, as it does in the context of a Chapter 11 plan under § 1129.[106]

Typically, adequate protection payments begin when a creditor would have obtained state law remedies had bankruptcy not intervened, and value is determined as of that date.[107] Then, the amount by which collateral depreciates from that valuation is the amount of adequate protection necessary to compensate the creditor for the loss occasioned by the bankruptcy. At that point, no strict rule applies to the amount, frequency, or commencement of payments.[108] Because the Bankruptcy Code sets forth no mandatory parameters for adequate protection, the courts have fashioned numerous examples of adequate protection through their decisions.

Case law had typically considered the equity cushion in property as a factor of adequate protection. An *equity cushion* is the value in property above the amount owed to the creditor with a secured claim that would shield the interest from loss due to the decrease in value of the property during the automatic stay.[109] Case law had almost uniformly held that an equity cushion of 20 percent or more constituted adequate protection for a secured claim, but an equity cushion of less than 11 percent did not constitute adequate protection.[110] When the equity cushion was in the range of 12 to 20 percent, courts tended to look to other factors for the existence of adequate protection.[111]

Courts have now considered and rejected the equity cushion theory based, in part, upon *United Savings Association v. Timbers of Inwood Forest, Ltd.*[112] One reason for the change is that the Supreme Court determined that the aspect of a creditor's interest in property that merits adequate protection is the value of the collateral.[113] Therefore, as long as the value of the property itself is not declining, the creditor would not be entitled to protection of the accruing interest value of the claim.[114] The

---

103 United Sav. Ass'n v. Timbers of Inwood Forest Assoc., Ltd., 484 U.S. 365 (1988).

104 *In re* Lopez-Soto, 764 F.2d 23, 26 (1st Cir. 1985).

105 Ridgemont Apartment Assocs., Ltd. v. Atlanta English Village, Ltd., 110 B.R. 77 (N.D. Ga.), *aff'd,* 890 F.2d 1166 (11th Cir. 1989).

106 United Sav. Ass'n v. Timbers of Inwood Forest Assoc. Ltd., 484 U.S. at 377.

107 *In re* Deico Elecs., Inc., 139 B.R. 945 (Bankr. 9th Cir. 1992).

108 *Id.*

109 *In re* Kost, 102 B.R. 829, 831 (D. Wyo. 1989).

110 *Id.* at 832 (citing *In re* McKillips, 81 B.R. 454, 458 (Bankr. N.D. Ill. 1987)).

111 *Id.*

112 484 U.S. 365 (1988).

113 *In re* James River Assocs., 148 B.R. 790, 796 (E.D. Va. 1992) (citing United Sav. Ass'n v. Timbers of Inwood Forest Assocs., Ltd., 484 U.S. at 372–73).

114 *Id.* at 796 (citing *In re* Lane, 108 B.R. 6 (Bankr. D. Mass. 1989)).

interest in property to be protected is the value of the collateral, not contractual or legal rights such as receiving interest or being permitted to foreclose on default. When an interest in apartment property, for example, is protected with full maintenance, almost complete occupancy, and sufficient cash flow to pay operating expenses, the lender is adequately protected.[115]

A lien on unencumbered future crops may serve as a basis for adequate protection,[116] as may a lien on well proceeds to be drilled in a proven oil field.[117] However, the debtor's visionary plans for development do not adequately protect a lender with a secured claim.[118] Similarly, the use of business trademarks and service marks, without postpetition payments for their use, denies adequate protection to the creditor who owns the marks.[119]

§ 5.9 Relief from Stay for Lack of Equity and Property Not Necessary for Effective Reorganization

Relief can be granted by the court if the debtor does not have equity in the property and the property is not necessary for an effective reorganization.[120] *Equity,* as used in 11 U.S.C. § 362(d)(2), is the difference between the value of the subject property and the liens against it.[121] Because Congress did not dictate a method of determining value, value is to be determined on a case-by-case basis, taking into account the nature of the debtor's business, market conditions, the debtor's prospect for rehabilitation, and the type of collateral.[122] See **Chapter 11** for a discussion of valuation.

Whether or not property is necessary for an effective reorganization depends upon what the effective reorganization might be. There is no effective reorganization plan if there is no reasonable possibility of a successful reorganization within a reasonable time.[123] Debtors must do more than manifest unsubstantiated hopes for a successful reorganization.[124] The longer a case remains on file, the greater the need for the debtor to show feasibility for an effective reorganization.

---

[115] *In re* Marion St. Partnership, 108 B.R. 218 (Bankr. D. Minn. 1989).

[116] *In re* Ahlers, 794 F.2d 388, 398 (8th Cir. 1986), *cert. granted in part sub nom.* Norwest Bank Worthington v. Ahlers, 483 U.S. 1004 (1987), *rev'd on other grounds,* 485 U.S. 197 (1988).

[117] *In re* O'Connor, 808 F.2d 1393 (10th Cir. 1987).

[118] *In re* Ledgemere Land Corp., 125 B.R. 58 (Bankr. D. Mass. 1991).

[119] *In re* B-K of Kan., Inc., 69 B.R. 812 (Bankr. D. Kan. 1987).

[120] 11 U.S.C. § 362(d)(2).

[121] *In re* Sutton, 904 F.2d 327, 329 (5th Cir. 1990), *reh'g denied* (5th Cir. 1991); Stewart v. Gurley, 745 F.2d 1194 (9th Cir. 1984).

[122] *In re* Sutton, 904 F.2d at 330.

[123] United Sav. Ass'n v. Timbers of Inwood Forest Assocs., Ltd., 484 U.S. 365, 371–74 (1988).

[124] *Id.*; *In re* Canal Place Ltd. Partnership, 921 F.2d 569 (5th Cir. 1991); *In re* Anderson, 913 F.2d 530 (8th Cir. 1990); *In re* T-H New Orleans Ltd. Partnership, 148 B.R. 456 (E.D. La. 1992).

CHAPTER 6

POSTPETITION FINANCING

Joel H. Levitin

§ 6.1 Introduction

Most reorganization clients appear on their bankruptcy attorneys' door steps (or in their reception areas) as a result of a stalemate with their lender. They are usually concerned about the imminent exercise of setoff rights or other remedies by the lender or a downward spiral in revenues creating a severe shortage of operating funds, either in the immediate or short-term future. Generally, they have some serious liquidity problem. In other words, financing, or the insufficiency or lack thereof, is often the primary issue that leads a business to seek bankruptcy advice and to consider filing a bankruptcy petition.

Evaluating the ability to finance a Chapter 11 reorganization case is (or should be) one of the most important considerations in determining whether to file such a case, and the financing issue is best addressed before a decision to file a bankruptcy petition is made. A debtor should have an idea of how it plans to emerge from bankruptcy if things go well before it voluntarily enters what can be a hopeless abyss for so many companies. At a minimum, a prospective debtor should have some idea how it will survive in the near future if a petition is filed.

The bankruptcy reorganization process is likely to be successful or advantageous to a debtor only if the debtor continues to function meaningfully during the process. Even though a debtor will be relieved of having to pay most of its prepetition obligations, at least temporarily, it must still make provisions to meet its postpetition obligations on an ongoing basis. Thus, a debtor should consider what will be its source of operating funds to enable it to conduct its business as usual pending a formulation of a long-term business strategy or a restructuring of its outstanding obligations through a plan of reorganization. In addition, it should consider whether it will need an infusion of new capital to enable it to retool its business or fund a plan of reorganization.

Some businesses are able to operate during their bankruptcy cases by using unencumbered funds or by using cash collateral, either with the consent of the creditor that has a security interest in the collateral or by convincing the bankruptcy court that the creditor's interest in the collateral will be adequately protected even if it is used by the debtor.[1] Even so, a debtor might develop a need for financing as its case progresses, and the issue of financing is frequently revisited on numerous occasions during the course of a case.

This chapter explores postpetition financing issues, including relevant statutory provisions and case law (§§ **6.2** through **6.12**); procedure (§ **6.13**); practical aspects

---

[1] *See* 11 U.S.C. § 363 and **Chs. 3–5;** see also **§§ 6.6–6.10** for a discussion of adequate protection in the context of financing.

of seeking credit and obtaining court approval thereof (§§ **6.14** through **6.19**); and various negotiating issues and points (§§ **6.20** through **6.28**). In addition, it includes a sample motion and a sample order in §§ **6.29** and **6.30.**

§ 6.2 Obtaining Credit under 11 U.S.C. § 364

Postpetition lending arrangements are governed by 11 U.S.C. § 364. Unless approved by the bankruptcy court, prepetition lending arrangements, other than unsecured ones in the ordinary course of business (see § **6.3**), essentially become frozen and cannot be used in the same manner after the filing of a bankruptcy petition.

Debtors cannot enforce prepetition lending agreements as executory contracts, through assumption or otherwise, because they fall within the exception for contracts "to make a loan, or extend other debt financing or financial accommodations."[2] However, a minority of courts has permitted the assumption of prepetition secured financing arrangements under 11 U.S.C. § 365(c)(2) with the consent of the lender.[3] Nevertheless, because § 364 will always apply, and § 365 will only apply in certain limited jurisdictions and circumstances, a debtor is well advised to comply with the provisions of § 364 rather than § 365 in obtaining approval of a postpetition financing arrangement, even if the prepetition lender consents to a continuation of financing.

Section 364 of the Bankruptcy Code provides several different credit alternatives, with varying protections to the postpetition lender:

1. Administrative expense priority[4]
2. Administrative expense superpriority,[5] secured by a lien on unencumbered property[6] or secured by a junior lien on encumbered property[7]
3. Secured by a superpriority lien on encumbered property.[8]

Each of these alternatives requires notice and a hearing in the bankruptcy court, except the first alternative, if credit is extended in the "ordinary course of business."[9]

Although all of these alternatives are available in theory, in practice, most debtor-in-possession financing lenders (sometimes referred to as DIP lenders making DIP loans) usually demand the highest level of protection, simply because those options are available under the Bankruptcy Code. Moreover, lenders are permitted to (and usually do) receive benefits and protections under more than one subsection of § 364, for example, superpriority administrative expense and secured status.

---

[2] 11 U.S.C. § 365(c)(2); *see In re* Sun Runner Marine, Inc., 945 F.2d 1089 (9th Cir. 1991).

[3] *See, e.g., In re* Prime, Inc., 8 Bankr. Ct. Dec. (CRR) 389 (Bankr. W.D. Mo. 1981).

[4] 11 U.S.C. § 364(a) & (b).

[5] *Id.* § 364(c)(1).

[6] *Id.* § 364(c)(2).

[7] *Id.* § 364(c)(3).

[8] *Id.* § 364(d).

[9] *Id.* § 364(a).

§ 6.3 Unsecured Loans in and outside the Ordinary Course of Business

Section 364(a) of the Bankruptcy Code permits a debtor to obtain unsecured credit in the ordinary course of its business as an administrative expense on a par with other administrative expenses in a case, without court approval. For an extension of unsecured credit other than in the ordinary course of business to receive administrative expense priority, court approval is necessary.[10]

The kind of credit extended by one business to another prior to the bankruptcy filing is what is generally considered to be "in the ordinary course."[11] The routine purchase of goods on open account is the most common form of ordinary-course credit for most businesses. Other types of credit that might fall within the ordinary-course category have been considered by courts from time to time.[12]

In most instances, even routine trade credit is unlikely to continue to any major extent during the pendency of a Chapter 11 case, especially if the trade creditors have significant prepetition claims outstanding. Trade creditors might be more willing to extend credit, perhaps on shorter than normal terms, if the debtor has supply options. If there are numerous substitute suppliers competing for a debtor's business, the original supplier, even if it has a large prepetition claim, may take a chance in order not to lose future business. One or more of the others may be willing as well.

Although few debtors are in this enviable position, every dollar "borrowed" in this manner directly benefits cash flow, with minimal burden on the debtor. Therefore, as long as no misrepresentations are made as to a debtor's prospects going forward, it never hurts to attempt to continue or to revive such credit. The debtor, however, should recognize that creditors are generally reluctant to permit themselves to be burned twice, and experience will likely suggest to them that the chance of survival of a Chapter 11 debtor is uncertain, at best.

Courts differ on the question of whether granting an administrative expense priority under § 364(a) and (b) requires an additional showing that the credit extended was an "actual, necessary cost[ ] and expense[ ] of preserving the estate," which is normally required for administrative expense status.[13]

Neither § 364(a) nor (b) is likely to cover funding for the entire operation of a business. Even if a debtor had a general unsecured line of credit prior to its bankruptcy filing, almost no lender would permit its continuance postpetition.

---

[10] 11 U.S.C. § 364(b).

[11] *In re* James A. Phillips, Inc., 29 B.R. 391 (S.D.N.Y. 1983) (in the context of § 363).

[12] *See, e.g., In re* Pacesetter Designs, Inc., 114 B.R. 731, 734 (Bankr. D. Colo. 1990) (injured employee's damages prior to conversion to Chapter 7 found to be unsecured debt incurred in ordinary course); *In re* Harrell, 14 Collier Bankr. Cas. 2d (MB) 212 (Bankr. E.D.N.C. 1985) (lease agreement found to be unsecured extension of credit in ordinary course).

[13] 11 U.S.C. § 503(b)(1)(A). *Compare In re* Club Dev. & Management Corp., 27 B.R. 610 (Bankr. 9th Cir. 1982) (identifying that requirement), *with In re* Waterfront Co., 56 B.R. 31 (Bankr. D. Minn. 1985) (not addressing the issue).

§ 6.4 Loans Providing for Superpriority Administrative Expense Status, Liens on Unencumbered Property, and Junior Liens on Encumbered Property

Section 364(c)(1) of the Bankruptcy Code permits a debtor to grant a postpetition lender an administrative expense claim with priority over all other administrative expense claims in the Chapter 11 case. Sections 364(c)(2) and (3) permit a debtor to grant a security interest in unencumbered property or a junior lien on already encumbered property, respectively. Each of these alternatives requires court approval.

There are two general but similar approaches that courts have used to decide whether to approve financing arrangements under § 364(c). First, in *In re The Crouse Group, Inc.*,[14] the court articulated a three-prong standard. Under that standard, a debtor must prove:

1. It was unable to obtain credit without agreeing to provide the requested protections, that is, credit on less onerous terms was unavailable;
2. The proposed credit is necessary to preserve the assets of the debtor's estate; and
3. The terms of the credit arrangement are fair, reasonable, and adequate.[15]

Only the first prong is contained within the terms of § 364, while the second can be inferred from the language of other sections of the Bankruptcy Code describing the requirements for an administrative priority.[16] Presumably, the third prong is subsumed within the *business judgment test* applied by bankruptcy courts in numerous contexts.[17]

In *In re The Crouse Group, Inc.*,[18] the debtor was a contractor and the lender was its bonding company on certain projects that the debtor had not yet completed. The court found that because the debtor had not conducted an exhaustive search for other credit alternatives but had only approached one other lender, it did not meet its burden on the first prong. Moreover, the court held that the financing arrangement had been crafted not to preserve the debtor's estate, but merely to keep the debtor alive long enough for the bonding company to find a replacement contractor. In other words, it was designed mainly for the benefit of the lender (to guarantee itself priority status while replacing the debtor with a new contractor).

In *In re St. Mary Hospital,*[19] the proposed lender to the hospital-debtor was its parent corporation. The parent wanted to close the hospital on short notice, and it

---

14 71 B.R. 544 (Bankr. E.D. Pa. 1987).

15 *Id.* at 546. *See also In re* St. Mary Hosp., 86 B.R. 393 (Bankr. E.D. Pa. 1988).

16 *See* 11 U.S.C. §§ 503(b), 507(b).

17 *See generally In re* Childworld, 142 B.R. 87, 89 (Bankr. S.D.N.Y. 1992) ("[a] debtor may assume or reject an unexpired lease . . . in the exercise of its best business judgment"); *In re* Chipwich, Inc., 54 B.R. 427, 430–31 (Bankr. S.D.N.Y. 1985) ("the debtor's business judgment should not be interfered with, absent a showing of bad faith or abuse of business discretion").

18 71 B.R. 544 (Bankr. E.D. Pa. 1987).

19 86 B.R. 393 (Bankr. E.D. Pa. 1988).

proposed to make a loan to fund payroll. The court looked beyond the form of the transaction, saying, "We believe that we can and should look beyond the Debtor's immediate financial circumstances to determine who is responsible. . . . Here, we are compelled to conclude that the immediate crisis was largely created by [the parent], which is not an outside lender but the puppeteer of a marionette-debtor."[20] The court refused to approve the loan under the fair, reasonable, and adequate prong, based on its conclusion that the parent had created an artificial cash-flow crisis and then devised the loan arrangement so it could obtain priority status for its loan while at the same time manufacturing an excuse to close the hospital. The court referred to the situation as a "tailored emergency."[21]

A second, somewhat less stringent, approach was applied by the court in *In re Ames Department Stores, Inc.*[22] In that case, the court looked to whether the debtor had shown that it had reasonably attempted but failed to secure credit by merely offering administrative expense priority under § 364(b), and whether the proposed financing arrangement met a fairness standard, focusing on whether the purpose of the arrangement was to benefit a particular creditor rather than the estate as a whole:

> [T]he court's discretion under section 364 is to be utilized on grounds that permit reasonable business judgment to be exercised so long as the financing agreement does not contain terms that leverage the bankruptcy process and powers or its purpose is not so much to benefit the estate as it is to benefit a party-in-interest.[23]

The court did not specifically consider whether the credit was necessary to preserve the estate.

§ 6.5 Loans Providing for Equal or Senior Liens on Encumbered Property

Section 364(d) of the Bankruptcy Code authorizes a debtor, with court approval, to grant a proposed lender lien status of equal or senior priority to existing liens. That section provides:

> (1) The court, after notice and a hearing, may authorize the obtaining of credit or the incurring of debt secured by a senior or equal lien on property of the estate that is subject to a lien only if — (A) the trustee is unable to obtain such credit otherwise; and (B) there is adequate protection of the interest of the holder of the lien on the property of the estate on which such senior or equal lien is proposed to be granted.
>
> (2) In any hearing under this subsection, the trustee has the burden of proof on the issue of adequate protection.

Senior priority liens are sometimes referred to as *priming liens* to the extent they displace other liens. The same basic standard as in § 364(c) applies, with one additional

---

[20] *Id.* at 402.

[21] *Id.* at 401.

[22] 115 B.R. 34 (Bankr. S.D.N.Y. 1990).

[23] *Id.* at 40.

requirement: the debtor must prove that the interests of existing lienholders will be "adequately protected" notwithstanding the subordination of the status of the prior lenders' security interests to that of the new lender. **Sections 6.6** through **6.10** examine adequate protection and approaches to it in the postpetition financing context.

§ 6.6 Adequate Protection

The Bankruptcy Code itself does not define what constitutes adequate protection.[24] Section 361 provides three illustrative, but not exhaustive, examples of adequate protection: cash payments, an additional or replacement lien, and such other relief that constitutes the indubitable equivalent of the creditor's interest. Although these examples are often cited by courts deciding cases under § 364(d) and the other sections of the Bankruptcy Code to which they relate, what constitutes adequate protection is less than definitive.

Basically, courts look to see whether granting a new postpetition creditor a senior lien will deprive the superseded or primed, prepetition (or, perhaps, earlier postpetition) creditors of the value of the security interests for which they bargained when they originally agreed to loan money to the debtor. In performing this analysis, courts generally choose to ignore the fact that in addition to the value of the collateral, existing creditors also impliedly bargained for their particular lien priority and, arguably, the continued existence of excess value. As several courts have stated, "[t]he goal of adequate protection is to safeguard the secured creditor from diminution in the value of its interest during the Chapter 11 reorganization."[25] The issue of adequate protection is generally considered to be a question of fact, subject to the clearly erroneous standard on appeal.[26]

In the majority of cases under § 364(d), debtors have attempted to satisfy their adequate protection burden by establishing the existence of an equity cushion. An *equity cushion* is "the value of the property above the amount owed to the creditor with a secured claim, that will shield the interest from loss due to any decrease in the value of the property."[27] Other debtors have made different arguments, some of which have at least in part had an equity cushion component.

In each of the approaches, it is interesting to note the irony involved when a debtor and its proposed DIP lender attempt to convince a court over the objection of the primed lender that its interests are adequately protected, when the proposed lending arrangement is predicated on the fact that the new lender is unwilling to accept anything other than top billing.

---

[24] *See In re* Reading Tube Indus., 72 B.R. 329, 333 (Bankr. E.D. Pa. 1987).

[25] *See In re* 495 Central Park Ave. Corp., 136 B.R. 626, 631 (Bankr. S.D.N.Y. 1992) (citing *In re* Beker Indus. Corp., 58 B.R. 725, 736 (Bankr. S.D.N.Y. 1986), and Bank of New England v. SWL, Inc., 121 B.R. 413, 418 (D. Me. 1990)); *In re* First S. Sav. Ass'n, 820 F.2d 700 (5th Cir. 1987) (quoting *In re* Beker, 58 B.R. at 736).

[26] *See In re* Snowshoe Co., 789 F.2d 1085, 1088 (4th Cir. 1986) (citing Anderson v. Bessemer City, 470 U.S. 564 (1985)).

[27] *In re* Dunes Casino Hotel, 69 B.R. 784, 794 (Bankr. D.N.J. 1986).

§ 6.7 —Equity Cushion Approach

Several courts seem to have accepted that an equity cushion alone can provide a sufficient guarantee of adequate protection in certain circumstances. For example, in *In re Stanley Hotel, Inc.,*[28] the court held that § 361(3) provides the authority for courts to rely on an equity cushion for adequate protection. The court stated, in a conclusory manner, that § 361(3) "requires that creditors receive the indubitable equivalent of their interests, which permits courts to find adequate protection when there is a sufficient equity cushion in the property involved."[29] However, those courts have not always agreed on what constitutes a sufficient equity cushion or on what is the proper method of valuing collateral of a debtor to determine whether an equity cushion in fact exists.[30] Valuation of assets is obviously of critical importance and is discussed in **§ 6.11.**

In the typical equity cushion case, the court considers whether there is enough value in the debtor's collateral above the amount owed to existing secured creditors so that such creditors would still be fully secured if the proposed senior lien were granted. The court determines the amount of all liens on the assets proposed to be further encumbered and balances the existing liens against the total value of the assets to determine if there is enough value left to support a new lien.[31]

If a debtor has an oversecured creditor it proposes to prime, the debtor needs to take into account in its equity cushion analysis the accrual of interest on the outstanding debt as permitted by *In re Timbers of Inwood Forest Associates, Ltd.*[32] The debtor should also anticipate that arguments may be made that the collateral is depreciating in value and the equity cushion is thus eroding.[33]

---

28 15 B.R. 660 (D. Colo. 1981).

29 *Id.* at 664.

30 *See In re* Phoenix Steel Corp., 39 B.R. 218, 224–25 (D. Del. 1984) (discussing valuation methods and problems with such analyses).

31 *See In re* 495 Central Park Ave. Corp., 136 B.R. 626, 631 (Bankr. S.D.N.Y. 1992); *In re* Phoenix Steel Corp., 39 B.R. 218, 232 (D. Del. 1984). For examples of the application of this principle, see Anchor Sav. Bank FSB v. Sky Valley, Inc., 99 B.R. 117 (N.D. Ga. 1989) (debtor obtained approval of $425,000 loan pursuant to § 364(d) over objection of creditor with $2,852,000 secured claim, when property securing the liens was determined to be worth $8.5 million); *In re* Stanley Hotel, Inc. 15 B.R. 660 (D. Colo. 1981) ($700,000 loan approved when debtor proved that total value of liens against assets was $2.5 million after the loan, while value of assets was between $2.6 and $3.5 million); *In re* Dunes Casino Hotel, 69 B.R. 784 (Bankr. D.N.J. 1986) (court found adequate protection and approved proposed loans totaling $700,000 when total debt would be approximately $17.7 million and total collateral was valued at $26 million, even under worst-case scenario).

32 808 F.2d 363 (5th Cir. 1987), *aff'd,* 484 U.S. 365 (1988). *See, e.g., In re* Timber Prods., Inc., 125 B.R. 433 (Bankr. W.D. Pa. 1990) (court declined to approve loan to continue lumber mill in operation long enough to collect accounts receivable because of anticipated erosion in equity cushion as interest on preexisting secured debt would accrue).

33 In a situation in which a loan pursuant to § 364(d) is approved, there might be an issue of whether a primed secured creditor might later be entitled to relief from the automatic stay for lack of adequate protection, as interest on the old and new loans accrues or the collateral declines in value, and whether it affects the analysis if the primed secured lender originally objected to the postpetition financing arrangement.

§ 6.8 —Future Prospects of Business Approach

Debtors attempting to establish adequate protection of existing liens have also argued that with the benefit of the proposed new loan, the debtor will generate additional value in the collateral that will be more than enough to cover all of the lien claims.[34]

That argument seems to be what won the day for the proposed financing in *In re Snowshoe Co.*[35] In that case, the trustee of a ski resort-debtor sought to obtain court approval of a loan to fund operations and argued that the ski area's anticipated profits would be sufficient to protect the debtor's other creditors. The court of appeals upheld the financing arrangement on the basis of the overall financial analyses presented by the trustee and the anticipated equity cushion created thereby.[36]

A primed lien holder has also been held to be adequately protected when the proposed financing was to be used for renovations of an office building in order to attract new tenants because the value of the building would increase.[37] The debtor, however, must be careful to make a sufficiently strong case for its position,[38] and its business plan must also be realistic.[39]

§ 6.9 —Lien Replacement Approach

Another alternative available to debtors who have unencumbered property is to provide a replacement lien on that property in exchange for the proposed subordination of existing liens. In *In re Reading Tube Industries,*[40] the debtor attempted to provide adequate protection by offering a replacement lien on its net current assets. The court stated that "the debtor must prove that the value of the replacement lien is greater [than] or equal to the difference between the value of the bank's liens on debtor's property and the value of the liens after being primed."[41] The court refused to

---

[34] *See, e.g., In re* Timber Prods., Inc., 125 B.R. 433 (Bankr. W.D. Pa. 1990).

[35] 789 F.2d 1085, 1089 (4th Cir. 1986).

[36] *Id.* at 1090.

[37] *In re* 495 Central Park Ave. Corp., 136 B.R. 626 (Bankr. S.D.N.Y. 1992). *Contra In re* Chevy Devco, 78 B.R. 585 (Bankr. C.D. Cal. 1987) (court rejected argument that shopping center renovations would raise market value and protect creditors because it did not believe that debtor's projections of post-renovation value were accurate).

[38] *See In re* First S. Sav. Ass'n, 820 F.2d 700, 713–14 (5th Cir. 1987) (debtor's adequate protection proposal was grounded on business assumptions contained in overall plan of reorganization, the terms of which had not been disclosed to court or tested in accordance with plan confirmation provisions of Bankruptcy Code; therefore, debtor failed to create sufficient record to support its argument).

[39] *See In re* St. Petersburg Hotel Assocs., 44 B.R. 944 (Bankr. M.D. Fla. 1984) (court found that existing secured creditors would receive adequate protection of their interests only if debtor's business plan succeeded, but concluded that plan was overly optimistic and speculative).

[40] 72 B.R. 329 (Bankr. E.D. Pa. 1987).

[41] *Id.* at 333.

approve the loan because the debtor failed to present sufficient evidence of the value of the proposed replacement lien. In that case, only the debtor's chairman, and not independent appraisers or experts, gave valuation testimony.

In *In re Beker Industries Corp.*,[42] in addition to its other arguments, the debtor proposed granting a replacement lien to establish adequate protection of the interests of objecting creditors, along with the prospect that its reorganization would achieve certain economies. The court held that "[a]dequate protection, not absolute protection, is the statutory standard."[43]

§ 6.10 —Holistic Approaches

Certain courts have applied pieces of both the equity cushion and the business prospects approaches (as well as others) in determining whether existing lenders will be adequately protected notwithstanding a new priming loan. As the court stated in *In re Aqua Associates*,[44]

> [w]e believe that, while the presence of an equity cushion should be a relevant factor, it should not be a determinative factor in any "adequate protection" analysis, and particularly one relating to § 364(d)(1)(B). The important question, in determination of whether the protection to a creditor's secured interest is adequate, is whether that interest, whatever it is, is being unjustifiably jeopardized.[45]

The *Aqua* court believed it was necessary (1) to analyze all of the relevant facts, (2) to examine the value of the collateral, (3) to decide the likelihood that the collateral will depreciate over time, (4) to assess the prospects for a successful reorganization, and (5) to evaluate the chances of the debtor's performing in accordance with a proposed plan.[46] The court held that the debtor needed to show not only that other credit was unavailable, but also that obtaining credit on a superpriority basis was a sound decision in its own right.

> Obtaining credit should be permitted not only because it is not available elsewhere, which could suggest the unsoundness of the basis for use of the funds generated by credit, but also because the credit acquired is of significant benefit to the debtor's estate and that the terms of the proposed loan are within the bounds of reason, irrespective of the inability of the debtor to obtain comparable credit elsewhere.[47]

---

[42] 58 B.R. 725 (Bankr. S.D.N.Y. 1986).

[43] *Id.* at 741.

[44] 123 B.R. 192 (Bankr. E.D. Pa. 1991).

[45] *Id.* at 196. Incidentally, the court noted that in calculating an equity cushion, it had to take into account only the equity status of the objecting creditor, not the value of *all* existing secured creditors' interests including those junior in priority to those of the objecting creditor. Obviously, that makes it easier to meet the adequate protection test, but it does not necessarily make sense, especially if the objecting creditor's liens are already subordinated to those of another party.

[46] *Id.* at 196–97.

[47] *Id.* at 196.

The court also said,

> We believe that such a "holistic approach" is particularly pertinent to consideration of a § 364(d) motion, where the potential of the advance of credit to allow the formulation of a successful plan and thereby benefit the debtor's estate, and the interests of all of its creditors, including secured creditors which it attempts to prime, is at issue.[48]

Other cases have also taken a holistic approach, focusing on what is best for the estate or other creditors as opposed to the desires of the creditor proposed to receive priority status.[49]

§ 6.11 Valuation Standards

The Bankruptcy Code provides no guidance on the issue of which valuation standard should be used in determining whether an equity cushion exists to support a finding of adequate protection. The two polar extremes are *forced liquidation value* (at the low end) and *going-concern value* (at the high end). Other alternatives include *orderly liquidation value* and *wholesale value,* which may or may not be applicable with respect to different types of collateral. Courts are all over the board on this issue, and the directions particular courts take depend on the specific facts involved.

In *In re Phoenix Steel Corp.,*[50] the court selected a middle-of-the-road approach by using the mean of liquidation value and going-concern value, concluding that was the fairest solution under the circumstances. "Valuation in a given case depends on that calculation which properly reflects a secured creditor's true state of protection."[51] Based on that valuation, the debtor had $18.4 million of collateral and existing secured liens of $26 million, so the proposed loan could not be approved.

In *In re Beker Industries Corp.,*[52] the court used going-concern values of collateral and approved a proposed priming loan (including other forms of adequate protection)

---

48 *Id.* at 197.

49 *See, e.g., In re* Plabell Rubber Prods., Inc., 137 B.R. 897 (Bankr. N.D. Ohio 1992) (court declined to approve loan, concluding that debtor failed to show that loan would generate an increase in value of collateral sufficient to protect primed creditors' interests; debtor did not support valuation figures it used in its equity cushion argument with adequate proof; debtor failed to show it had credible plan for revitalizing its business; and loan seemed to be structured solely for benefit of lender who was concerned about salvaging its prepetition loans); *In re* Tenney Village Co., 104 B.R. 562, 568 (Bankr. D.N.H. 1989) (proposed financing would have given postpetition lender control over debtor's business during reorganization process because loan documents contained provisions requiring the debtor (1) to hire a new CEO approved by lender; (2) to get lender approval for all improvements; (3) to hire a consulting firm designated by the lender; and (4) to remit proceeds of all asset sales directly to the lender; and allowing the lender to foreclose upon the occurrence of any termination event defined by the lender).

50 39 B.R. 218 (D. Del. 1984).

51 *Id.* at 224.

52 58 B.R. 725, 741–42 (Bankr. S.D.N.Y. 1986).

because the debtor's projections and appraisals were credible, while those of the subordinated secured party were not.

On the other hand, in *In re Tenney Village Co.,*[53] the court was unable to find an equity cushion because it concluded that particular ski resort assets should be valued at liquidation value rather than going-concern value. Its reasoning was that the resort had little chance of staying in operation long enough to sell the business as a going concern.[54] Valuation is discussed in more detail in **Chapter 11.**

§ 6.12 Good Faith

Section 364(e) provides that a lender that acts in good faith and makes loans pursuant to a court order authorize postpetition financing will be protected if that order is later reversed or modified on appeal. That section states:

> The reversal or modification on appeal of an authorization under this section to obtain credit or incur debt, or of a grant under this section of a priority or a lien, does not affect the validity of any debt so incurred, or any priority or lien so granted, to an entity that extended such credit in good faith, whether or not such entity knew of the pendency of the appeal, unless such authorization and the incurring of such debt, or the granting of such priority or lien, were stayed pending appeal.

The Bankruptcy Code does not define good faith. Usually, the focus is on whether the lender has acted for an improper purpose or with knowledge that a particular lending arrangement is illegal.[55]

Most lenders will insist on a specific finding of good faith in an order approving financing, usually rendering appeals moot with respect to already-loaned funds. However, one court recently found that cross-collateralization of prepetition debt with postpetition assets[56] was contrary to the provisions of the Bankruptcy Code and disapproved the cross-collateralization on appeal, even as to credit extended in reliance on the earlier order.[57] Section 364(e) was held not to apply. Other courts have reached a contrary conclusion.[58]

---

53 104 B.R. 562 (Bankr. D.N.H. 1989).

54 *Id.* at 567.

55 *See In re* EDC Holding Co., 676 F.2d 945 (7th Cir. 1982) (court found lack of good faith, concluding that purpose of loan was to discourage union protesters long enough to enable secured creditor to remove liened inventory, with no benefit to other creditors); *In re* Chicago, Milwaukee, St. P. & Pac. R.R. Co., 799 F.2d 317 (7th Cir. 1986), *cert. denied,* 481 U.S. 1068 (1987) (knowledge of illegality precludes finding of good faith).

56 See **§ 6.26.**

57 *See In re* Saybrook Mfg. Co., 963 F.2d 1490 (11th Cir. 1992).

58 *See, e.g., In re* Adams Apple, Inc., 829 F.2d 1484 (9th Cir. 1987) (dismissing as moot appeal of financing order, including cross-collateralization provision, in light of 11 U.S.C. § 364(e), and appellant's failure to obtain a stay of financing order pending appeal).

§ 6.13 Procedures for Obtaining Approval of Credit

Procedurally, motions to obtain credit are governed by Bankruptcy Rule 4001(c). A copy of the proposed loan agreement must be attached to any motion seeking approval of the agreement. In some cases, the proposed order approving the motion constitutes the financing arrangement and there is no separate agreement, in which case the proposed order should be filed along with the motion. It might be a good idea to include a proposed order, even if the order does not constitute the agreement, to permit advance review by interested parties. Inclusion of a proposed order may be required by the local bankruptcy court rules as well.[59] A sample motion and a sample order for postpetition financing are included in §§ **6.29** and **6.30.**

Financing motions and notices of any hearings scheduled thereon must be served on any official committees or, if no official committees have been appointed, on the debtor's 20 largest unsecured creditors, and on such other parties as the court may direct. At a minimum, service should additionally be made on the U.S. Trustee and on any existing secured creditors that might be affected if the requested relief were granted. As with all procedural and other issues, counsel should always review the local rules of the bankruptcy court in which the case is filed to determine if any local customs or practices apply as well.[60]

A final hearing on a financing motion may not be held sooner than 15 days after service of the motion. However, if the debtor requests a more prompt hearing on the motion, the court may authorize credit, but "only to the extent necessary to avoid immediate and irreparable harm to the estate pending a final hearing."[61] Thus, it is common practice in cases in which financing is required immediately to have an interim hearing on a proposed financing arrangement on the day a bankruptcy case is filed or promptly thereafter, followed by a final hearing two to three weeks later.

§ 6.14 Preparing a Debtor to Seek Credit and Obtaining Court Approval

Businesses must approach the postpetition credit issue differently depending on their prepetition financing and collateral situation. Many businesses operate on some form of line of credit from a lending institution, and very often they have pledged all or

---

59 *See, e.g.,* Local R. Bankr. P. 9014.1(b)(1) (E.D. Pa.) ("Each motion shall be accompanied by . . . [a] proposed form of order which, if entered by the court, would grant the relief sought by the motion").

60 *See, e.g.,* Local R. Bankr. P. 9014.1(c)(1) & (f) (E.D. Pa.) (all motions and the notices of hearings thereon must be served on all "interested persons," defined as the movant, the debtor, the U.S. Trustee, any trustee or interim trustee, all official committees, all entities on the clerk's service list, that is, those that filed requests for notice pursuant to Bankruptcy Rule 2002(i), and "[a]ny person whose interest would be directly, materially and adversely affected if the relief requested in the motion were granted and whose interests are not adequately represented by persons on whom service is otherwise required").

61 Fed. R. Bankr. P. 4001(c)(2).

substantially all of their assets to secure those lines of credit. Depending on the type of business, the assets pledged may include some combination of property, plant, equipment, inventory, cash, and accounts receivable, and the proceeds thereof. Many borrowers also keep their cash in an account at the lender's institution or have executed some form of account pledge agreement, permitting the lender to perfect a security interest in the debtor's cash.

In preparing to obtain credit, a proposed debtor should review and analyze its collateral position vis à vis existing secured lenders and have appraisals performed on its assets. In addition, it should prepare certain financial documents. At the same time, it should consider which and how many lenders to approach. **Sections 6.15** through **6.19** address these issues.

§ 6.15 —Evaluation of Available Assets

The first step in analyzing a potential debtor's borrowing options is to evaluate its assets. Does the debtor have any unencumbered collateral? Naturally, the more unencumbered collateral that is available, the more options the debtor will have in obtaining postpetition financing.

Even though a debtor may believe all of its assets are encumbered, it should do judgment, title, lien, and UCC financing statement searches of all of its known assets. If any of its lender's liens are not properly perfected, they will be avoidable in bankruptcy, and the borrowing picture will improve. The debtor should also consider whether any of its less obvious assets, for example, leasehold interests, litigation rights, and so forth, are not covered by liens. Once a bankruptcy petition is filed, new assets, such as proceeds of avoidance actions (see **Chapter 12**), may also come into being. If they are significant, or potentially so, perhaps they could serve as collateral or partial collateral for a new lender.[62]

A prospective debtor should also consider whether there are any assets owned by other parties, such as principals of the debtor, that might be made available. **Section 6.18** discusses potential sources of funding.

§ 6.16 —Obtaining Appraisals

A debtor should have appraisals performed on any assets that it proposes to encumber, both to convince potential lenders that adequate value exists and, later, to convince a court that value in excess of the value of any encumbered portion of the collateral justifies a further encumbrance and provides adequate protection of existing interests. If a debtor believes it could support a going-concern valuation, it may want to hire an investment banker or underwriter to perform that valuation.

However, a debtor needs to be careful with valuation testimony and evidence early in a case, especially when the debtor is not certain at that time what its end-game strategy will be. For example, the same inflated valuation testimony that helps

---

[62] There is at least an argument that recoveries in such actions are covered by prepetition blanket liens on intangibles. See **§ 6.24.**

a debtor obtain credit may hang the debtor when it later attempts to cram down its prepetition secured lender under a plan of reorganization. In certain situations, a commitment to a particular valuation cannot be avoided, but a debtor should realize that by making certain choices, its later options may be limited. Although valuation findings in one context are not necessarily res judicata when it comes time to apply different sections of the Bankruptcy Code, those findings certainly have some probative value.[63]

It is advisable for the attorney representing the debtor, rather than the debtor directly, to retain the appraiser. By doing so, the debtor at least preserves the argument (which may or may not ultimately be successful) that the original appraisal is protected from disclosure in discovery on the basis that it falls within the work product doctrine or is otherwise privileged. This flexibility could become crucial if the debtor does not agree with the result of the appraisal and chooses to retain a different appraiser. As discussed above, valuation may make all of the difference in whether a proposed credit arrangement will be approved by a court, so a debtor may need more than one bite at the apple.

§ 6.17 —Preparation of Financial Documents

The debtor/proposed borrower will need to provide certain financial information to any lender evaluating whether to extend credit. Much of that information will constitute or form the basis of exhibits to or other support for a financing motion.

At a minimum, the debtor will need to provide a current balance sheet and operating statement. It is preferable for these documents to be audited by an independent accountant or other financial advisor, and an audit will likely lend credibility to the numbers if the financial advisor is known to be reputable. It is not unusual for the lending institution to make a recommendation of particular financial advisors, and such recommendations should be taken very seriously.

In addition, a potential lender will need to see an anticipated budget and cash-flow statement. If these items have also been reviewed and sanctioned by a reputable financial professional, they will be more credible as well. Because credibility of a debtor and its numbers are so important for obtaining credit, the assistance of a respected financial advisor is probably well worth any additional cost. Any testimony from a third party, especially regarding business projections, is likely to be taken more seriously than that of an insider.

How far the budget should extend into the future depends on the size and duration of the loan that is requested and the reasonable predictability of the cash flow of the business; six months would seem to be a minimum. Certainly, the term should be sufficient to show repayment in full of the proposed loan, or at a minimum, a stabilization or increase in the value of the collateral package that is proposed. If the debtor typically experiences a seasonal downturn in performance in the short run, it should extend its budget until performance is expected to rebound, and it should provide the lender with historical analyses to show that an upturn is most likely to follow.

If immediate funding is sought, a debtor should prepare an interim budget identifying only expenditures that are "necessary to avoid immediate and irreparable

---

[63] *See In re* Snowshoe Co., 789 F.2d 1085 (4th Cir. 1986).

harm" pending the final financing hearing.[64] That budget should obviously not include any deferable expenditures.

Any budget should take into account the effect that the filing of a bankruptcy petition will have on anticipated cash flow, much of which will depend on the particular business. As discussed in § **6.3,** in most businesses, trade credit is likely to substantially dry up following a filing. Any budget should therefore contemplate cash on delivery and/or cash in advance for most purchases, at least in the early stages of a bankruptcy case. In addition, a debtor's budget should reflect that it will incur increased professional fees (of the debtor and any committees), that it may have to make deposits with its utility companies (perhaps two to three months' worth), that insurance rates may go up on policies sought to be renewed, that worker's compensation claims (and premiums) are likely to go up, and that revenues are likely to go down as customers with alternative sources of supply spread out their purchases, especially in industries in which continuing support from the debtor is important. A debtor should consider other likely effects as well.

§ 6.18 —Sources of Funding

The courts do not seem to require consideration of loans from sources other than traditional financial institutions.[65] However, in addition to banks and other financial institutions, a debtor should always consider whether it might be able to obtain credit (or guaranties) from any of its insiders, particularly equity owners, directors, or officers.[66] Most often, these alternatives will not be available at the point in time when a business is ready to consider bankruptcy, because the parties that control a debtor have probably exhausted their funds or, at a minimum, their interest in pumping any more money into the business. Occasionally, however, the additional available protections discussed in §§ **6.3** through **6.5** may entice a further investment by an insider or other closely interested party.

A debtor should further consider whether there might be potential funding sources among its major suppliers (especially if it is the primary customer for any of them) or its major customers (especially if it is the sole source of supply for any of them). The benefits to and protection of these parties under § 364 are significant if they qualify, so they may be willing to provide credit on better terms than ordinary third parties would. A debtor never knows how willing or even desperate another party will be to support its operations until it asks. One downside to making such inquiries of customers and suppliers prior to a bankruptcy filing is that the debtor may face

---

64 *See* Fed. R. Bankr. P. 4001(c)(2) and § **6.13.**

65 *See In re* Timber Prods., Inc., 125 B.R. 433, 435 (Bankr. W.D. Pa. 1990) (debtor made efforts to obtain financing only from conventional sources, and court ignored fact that debtor had not exhausted potentially feasible means of raising capital through equity financing or joint venture).

66 *See In re* 495 Central Park Ave. Corp., 136 B.R. 626, 631–32 (Bankr. S.D.N.Y. 1992) (superpriority loan from shareholders of debtor did not violate absolute priority rule); *but see In re* The Midwestern Cos., 47 B.R. 16 (Bankr. W.D. Mo. 1984) (court granted administrative claim but refused to grant lien for loan by insider to debtor, because there was uncertainty whether debtor had resources sufficient to cover administrative costs of case).

increased pressure to pay outstanding amounts and still not get any credit. There is also the danger, if only certain parties are consulted, that uninformed parties will later claim that they were prejudicially misled regarding the debtor's financial condition prior to the bankruptcy.

If a debtor has a relationship with an existing secured lender, that lender, knowledgeable about the debtor's affairs, is often the most likely candidate to fund it in Chapter 11. That is especially true if the lender has a lien on substantially all of the debtor's assets and is either significantly oversecured or significantly undersecured. In the former case, the lender will likely fear a priming battle with another lender, which may be a viable threat, and it will be in a comfortable collateral position if the required loan amounts are within the excess collateral value. In the latter case, unless the lender is prepared immediately to accept its loss and seek the liquidation of the business (with all its negative social and other ramifications), it may be willing to "put good money after bad" to attempt to salvage its investment. In a grossly undersecured situation, a debtor should also explore whether there is any possibility that the existing lender would accept a modest reduction in debt in exchange for an immediate pay-off, either because of the lender's fatigue with the situation or its own need for funds. Refinancing of a reduced loan amount may be available.

The in-between cases, especially when opinions as to collateral values differ, are the most complicated and interesting.

A debtor will obviously gain leverage with its existing lender if it raises the issue of priming, but it has to be careful not to push too hard, especially if its actual leverage (that is, its ultimate ability to persuade a court that a priming will leave the existing lender adequately protected) is minimal. In some situations, the threat of priming, even if somewhat remote, may permit a debtor to obtain better terms from its existing lender.

In deciding whether to concentrate its efforts on its prepetition lender, a debtor should also consider whether it may have any lender liability or other claims against that lender. If so, such claims could provide powerful leverage in negotiating with the lender for postpetition terms. See § **6.22.** On the other hand, if the claims are particularly strong, the debtor may want to avoid that lender entirely, because it would certainly require a release in exchange for a funding commitment.

All things being equal, there are advantages to retaining an existing lender. As between traditional lending institutions, it is likely to provide the most favorable terms. Moreover, the known evil is often perceived as more tolerable than the unknown evil. Certainly, getting a new lender up to speed will be costly emotionally, if not also financially.

§ 6.19 —How Many Lenders Must Be Considered

Most courts have recognized that because § 364 does not specify how many alternate lenders a debtor must consider to meet its burden of establishing that it was unable to obtain financing on less onerous terms than those proposed, they have to decide this issue on a case-by-case basis on the totality of the circumstances.[67]

---

[67] *See, e.g., In re* Reading Tube Indus., 72 B.R. 329, 332 (Bankr. E.D. Pa. 1987) ("the statute fails to explicitly provide how extensive the debtor's efforts to obtain credit must be; therefore, the court must make its decisions on a case by case basis").

All courts seem to agree that a debtor does not have a duty to seek credit from every possible lender, but a debtor must have made some effort to explore alternative financing arrangements.[68] The courts seem to require that the debtor make a reasonable effort in good faith to contact as many lenders as possible, given the debtor's circumstances, to show that credit was unavailable on more favorable terms.[69] However, most courts have taken a reasonable, practical approach and have realized that many efforts would be of no avail and are therefore unnecessary.[70] The rulings in certain cases even suggest that a debtor may not even have to prove that the proposed financing terms are better than any alternatives.[71]

In practical terms, because it is generally not difficult to receive rejections from lenders, especially in the condensed time frame in which most businesses address this issue, a debtor should make inquiry of at least three or four potential lenders; more is certainly better. If numerous lenders were approached prior to the consideration of bankruptcy, less of an emphasis needs to be made on specific DIP lenders.[72]

If the borrowing amount is low enough, or if the debtor operates in a remote location, approaching only local banks should be sufficient.[73] If the amount is larger, a debtor should probably also approach national lending institutions specializing in DIP loans.

---

68 *See, e.g., In re* 495 Central Park Ave. Corp., 136 B.R. 626, 630–31 (Bankr. S.D.N.Y. 1992) ("the debtor must make an effort to obtain credit without priming a senior lien"); *In re* Reading Tube Indus., 72 B.R. 329, 332 (Bankr. E.D. Pa. 1987) ("We do, however, require the debtor *to make an effort* to carry the burden established in Section 364(d)"); *In re* Plabell Rubber Prods., Inc., 137 B.R. 897, 899–900 (Bankr. N.D. Ohio 1992) (debtor could not rely on its own evaluation that credit on less onerous terms was unavailable on the basis solely of discussions with lender in immediate geographic area and informal discussion with another bank's manager).

69 *See In re* Snowshoe Co., 789 F.2d 1085, 1088 (4th Cir. 1986) (debtor must demonstrate good faith effort and that other financing was unavailable); *In re* Reading Tube Indus., 72 B.R. 329, 332 (Bankr. E.D. Pa. 1987) (court surveying case law concluded that contacting from one to forty lenders may be sufficient depending on the circumstances, but no contact with even one outside lender was not good enough).

70 *See, e.g., In re* Snowshoe Co., 789 F.2d 1085, 1088 (4th Cir. 1986) (court did not require debtor to waste time contacting more than one or two likely lenders because ski resort was "vulnerable seasonal enterprise" operating under severe time pressure); *In re* Ames Dep't Stores, Inc., 115 B.R. 34, 40 (Bankr. S.D.N.Y. 1990) (four lenders was enough, given that retail department store chain was "vulnerable seasonal enterprise" and also very few lenders had capability of making loans of magnitude required by debtor); *In re* Sky Valley, Inc., 100 B.R. 107, 113 (Bankr. N.D. Ga. 1988) (unattractive nature of lending situation may excuse debtor from making extensive efforts to contact lenders).

71 *See, e.g., In re* Aqua Assocs., 123 B.R. 192 (Bankr. E.D. Pa. 1991) (court approved DIP loan despite fact that one lender offered $50,000 of requested $162,000 at lower interest rate, which would have benefited estate); *In re* Stanley, 15 B.R. 660 (D. Colo. 1981) (approaching two alternative lenders was enough even though one lender was willing to lend $50,000 on unsecured basis; objecting parties did not show that debtor could have obtained all of $70,000 it needed on an unsecured basis as well).

72 *See In re* Beker Indus. Corp., 58 B.R. 725, 735 (Bankr. S.D.N.Y. 1986) (burden met because debtor contacted 35 to 40 potential lenders prepetition in addition to those contacted postpetition).

73 *See In re* Sky Valley, Inc., 100 B.R. 107, 113 (Bankr. N.D. Ga. 1988) (debtor-golf and ski resort located in rural area of Georgia was not required to have contacted lenders not

If a financing arrangement with the debtor's prepetition lender is proposed, the debtor should not be held to a requirement of contacting quite so many alternate lenders. Most courts are likely to recognize that lenders are reluctant to enter into a priming battle with another lender, and the cost associated with such a battle must be taken into account by the debtor in making its business decision. However, if there is any chance that because of the proposed protections or any other reason the court may view the proposed transaction as a "sweetheart deal" favoring the existing lender to the detriment of other parties, a debtor had better be able to show clearly that it made substantial efforts to pursue other potential lenders. In such a circumstance, it would be most desirable to have gotten an offer of financing from an alternative lender on terms less favorable than those proposed.

A debtor should consider developing the testimony of an expert witness (perhaps a financial advisor) that the terms of a proposed financing are reasonable and that better terms are unlikely to be available,[74] although in many cases this luxury may be prohibitively expensive.

§ 6.20 Negotiating Points

DIP lenders usually attempt to impose many onerous conditions on debtors to which they are making loans. In most cases, debtors have little leverage in negotiating these points because they are desperate for funding to continue operations. Therefore, a debtor often finds itself urging the court to approve an onerous arrangement because it is the best package it could negotiate, although it secretly (or not so secretly) hopes that the court will conclude that certain terms should be modified.

If a committee of creditors or equity security holders is formed in a case, it will usually be done before the final hearing on a proposed financing, and typically such a committee seeks to have the most onerous conditions deleted. In the absence of a committee, the office of the U.S. Trustee often participates in the process. It can sometimes be helpful for a debtor actually to point out particularly onerous provisions of the proposed financing agreement to parties-in-interest. Such parties are generally more effective than the debtor in negotiating the modification or removal of onerous provisions because lenders want to avoid a court fight that could result in the modification or deletion of many more provisions.

In many cases, the court itself raises objections to particular provisions. Most courts are aware that the negotiation process leading to a debtor-in-possession financing agreement is weighted against the debtor.[75]

Experienced postpetition lenders recognize that they are likely to have to make concessions both at the interim hearing and at the final hearing. Most often,

---

located in immediate geographic vicinity; contacting three local lenders was deemed sufficient).

[74] *See In re* 495 Central Park Ave. Corp., 136 B.R. 626, 630–31 (Bankr. S.D.N.Y. 1992) (court relied on expert witness testimony that banks would make commercial real estate loans only if given senior lien).

[75] *See In re* FCX, Inc., 54 B.R. 833, 838 (Bankr. E.D.N.C. 1985) (recognizing that debtor is often "acting out of desperation" and may therefore "compromise[ ] the rights of unsecured creditors").

lenders will not walk away from a debtor with whom they have negotiated over minor modifications.

However, if a court unilaterally modifies a lending arrangement in a manner not agreed to by the lender, then the lender cannot be forced to lend money to the debtor. But if a prepetition lender were to abandon a debtor because of an issue the court felt was improper, that lender could be more vulnerable during the course of the bankruptcy case to a comprehensive review of the entire account relationship, including, for example, issues regarding perfection and historical debits and credits.

Discussed in §§ **6.21** through **6.28** are some common and not so common provisions that lenders seek to include and debtors resist in DIP financing arrangements. Certain of them have been called into question from time to time. In most circumstances, courts will defer to a debtor's business judgment on particular terms, unless such terms provide an undue benefit to a creditor at the expense of the estate.[76]

§ 6.21 —Confirmation of Validity, Priority, and Amount of Prepetition Debt and Security Interests

If a debtor is obtaining financing from its existing lender, that lender will almost always require the debtor to confirm how much money was owed prepetition and that the lender's claims and liens are valid and enforceable. It is not unusual, however, for the rights of other parties, such as a creditors' committee or subsequently-appointed trustee, to be preserved to raise challenges to the lender's claims and liens following a thorough investigation, and most courts will not permit a debtor to waive the claims of those other parties. Sometimes, a lender will insist on a deadline by which all parties must challenge the lender's claims or liens.

§ 6.22 —Release of Lender Liability Claims

Almost always, as a part of clauses confirming the validity and priority of claims and liens, an existing lender will require the debtor to affirm that it has no offsets, claims, or counterclaims against the lender. Again, such clauses are typically not binding on other parties, which may have a deadline to raise such claims.

§ 6.23 —Carve-Outs

Many financing arrangements provide a carve-out from the mandated superpriority liens and administrative claims in favor of the DIP lender for the payment of fees for the debtor's professionals (counsel and financial advisors, in some cases) as well as for those of any official committees. It is also common for there to be such a carve-out for quarterly fees owed to the U.S. Trustee under 28 U.S.C. § 1930(a)(6) and for some trustee's fees if the case is converted to one under

---

[76] *See, e.g., In re* Ames Dep't Stores, Inc., 115 B.R. 34, 39 (Bankr. S.D.N.Y. 1990).

Chapter 7. Sometimes, there is a cap put on those fees, and, sometimes, there is an exception to the carve-out for professional fees expended investigating and challenging the secured lender's claims or liens or in bringing claims against the lender.

The carve-out issue was raised in *In re Ames Department Stores, Inc.*,[77] in which the court initially was not prepared to find that a proposed lending arrangement was satisfactory, in part because it did not include a professional fee carve-out, but the arrangement was approved when it was amended to provide a "reasonable" carve-out of $5 million for professional fees, which the court believed would guarantee the debtor the protection of adequate representation in the adversary process.

§ 6.24 —Liens on Avoidance Action Recoveries

Occasionally, as part of a postpetition financing package, a lender will require a lien on the recoveries in any Bankruptcy Code avoidance actions. Avoidance actions are discussed in **Chapter 12.** Some courts have held that such recoveries are already subject to prepetition blanket liens on intangibles, but that is the minority view. More often, such recoveries are considered to be the assets of unsecured creditors, and courts are reluctant to permit the secured lender to make them unavailable to those creditors.

§ 6.25 —Drop Dead and Default Clauses

Very often, postpetition financing arrangements include provisions that if certain events occur, such as a default under the terms of the postpetition loan or the appointment of a trustee, the financing is immediately terminated, and very often the lender is permitted relief from the automatic stay to pursue its remedies, without having to go back to the court. These latter provisions are sometimes referred to as *drop dead clauses.* They have on occasion been enforced by courts,[78] but they are often viewed suspiciously when they are first proposed.[79]

---

77 115 B.R. 34, 40–41 (Bankr. S.D.N.Y. 1990).

78 *Cf.* Kham & Nate's Shoes No. 2, Inc. v. Bank of Whiting, 908 F.2d 1351 (7th Cir. 1990) (court declined to subordinate claims of postpetition lender for refusing to lend additional money to debtor, when such refusal was authorized under court-approved postpetition financing agreement); *In re* Philadelphia Athletic Club, Inc., 17 B.R. 345 (Bankr. E.D. Pa. 1982) (in context of stipulation resolving motion for relief from stay, court permitted lender to proceed with foreclosure upon default of payments, as agreed by lender and debtor, notwithstanding objection of later-appointed trustee).

79 For example, in *In re* Ames Dep't Stores, Inc., 115 B.R. 34, 40–41 (Bankr. S.D.N.Y. 1990), the court initially was not prepared to approve a proposed lending arrangement, in part because it provided that a default would occur if a trustee or examiner was appointed or if the court granted relief from the automatic stay to any other creditor. The financing arrangement was amended to allow the appointment of a trustee or examiner for fraud or mismanagement and to modify the clause that effectively restricted the court's ability to grant other creditors relief from the automatic stay, and the arrangement was approved.

In addition, it is not uncommon for a lender to require a debtor to waive its right to seek future priming lenders unless and until that lender is paid in full on its postpetition loans.

§ 6.26 —Cross-Collateralization

One of the most litigated issues in the postpetition financing area is cross-collateralization, that is, securing prepetition debt (in addition to postpetition debt) by postpetition assets. Certain courts have permitted cross-collateralization,[80] while other courts have held that it is impermissable and contrary to the spirit of the bankruptcy laws.[81]

§ 6.27 —Break-up Fees

Occasionally, a postpetition lender will require a debtor to agree that if it is unsuccessful in obtaining final approval of a proposed financing arrangement, that it will pay some form of break-up or penalty fee to compensate the lender for participating in the process. Although they are not very common, courts have upheld the payment of these fees, if they are not unreasonable.[82]

§ 6.28 —Enhancement Fees

In certain cases, a lender will request that it be paid an enhancement fee or bonus, in addition to the other costs of providing the loan, if the reorganization case is successful. These types of provisions have also been approved by courts,[83] although they are not particularly common.

---

[80] *See, e.g., In re* Adams Apple Inc., 829 F.2d 1484 (9th Cir. 1987); *In re* Ellingsen MacLean Oil Co., 834 F.2d 599 (6th Cir. 1987), *cert. denied*, 488 U.S. 817 (1988).

[81] *See, e.g., In re* Saybrook Mfg. Co., 963 F.2d 1490 (11th Cir. 1992); see also **§ 6.12.**

[82] *See, e.g., In re* Integrated Resources, Inc., 147 B.R. 650 (S.D.N.Y. 1992) (holding that break-up fee agreements are presumptively appropriate under business judgment rule, and will be upheld unless relationship of parties who negotiated fee is tainted by self-dealing or manipulation, fee hampers bidding, or amount of fee is unreasonable in relation to proposed purchase price).

[83] *See, e.g., In re* Defender Drug Stores, Inc., 145 B.R. 312 (Bankr. 9th Cir. 1992) (upholding enhancement fee of 10 percent in excess of postpetition lender's secured claim upon sale of assets, which became possible only as a result of DIP loans).

§ 6.29 Form: Motion for Order Approving Financing Arrangement

FORM 6–1
MOTION FOR ORDER APPROVING FINANCING ARRANGEMENT

[Caption]

MOTION FOR APPROVAL OF DEBTOR-IN-POSSESSION FINANCING ARRANGEMENT

The above-captioned debtors, [Debtors], hereby move this Court, pursuant to 11 U.S.C. §§ 102, 105, 361, 362, 363, and 364, and Bankruptcy Rule 4001, for orders (1) approving a proposed debtor-in-possession financing arrangement on an interim and final basis; (2) authorizing the incurrence of indebtedness thereunder on a super-priority administrative and secured basis, pursuant to 11 U.S.C. § 364(c) and (d); (3) approving the form and manner of notice in connection therewith; and (4) granting such other relief as is appropriate.

Attached to this Motion as Exhibit A and incorporated by reference herein is the DIP financing agreement.

In support of the Motion, the Debtors respectfully represent as follows:

INTRODUCTION

1. The Court has jurisdiction over this matter pursuant to 28 U.S.C. §§ 157 and 1334. Venue of these cases and this motion in this district is proper pursuant to 28 U.S.C. §§ 1408 and 1409. This is a core proceeding pursuant to 28 U.S.C. § 157(b)(2).

2. [Insert description of factual and procedural history of case, including past dealings between Debtors and Lender.]

. . . 22. Debtors' financing needs exceed amounts available solely through the use of cash collateral.

REQUEST FOR RELIEF

23. By this motion, and as set forth more fully below, Debtors request, among other things, that this Court enter orders (1) approving, on an interim basis until a final hearing, a proposed debtor-in-possession financing arrangement with [Lender] as described herein; and (2) approving, after final hearing, such debtor-in-possession financing arrangement.

A. The Proposed Financing Arrangement

24. Debtors have considered several methods of obtaining debtor-in-possession credit on the best terms possible and have concluded, based upon their discussions with potential lenders, that they are unable to obtain unsecured credit allowable as an administrative expense under 11 U.S.C. § 364(b) or solely on the basis of a superpriority or a junior lien under 11 U.S.C. §364(c)(1) or (3). Debtors own no significant unencumbered assets and are accordingly unable to obtain credit on the basis of 11 U.S.C. § 364(c)(2).

25. In addition to [Lender], Debtors had discussions and negotiations (including preparation of term sheets, proposed financing orders, and loan agreements [modify to suit facts]) with [insert actual number] other potential lenders, [names of lenders]. All proposed lenders insisted on the granting of liens on the Debtors' assets senior to the liens of [Lender]. Because [Lender] would not consent to any such priming, any debtor-in-possession financing with other lenders would have led to costly litigation concerning adequate protection of [Lender's] interest in the collateral, during which the future of Debtors would have been in jeopardy.

26. Although Debtors' concern regarding a costly and lengthy priming battle was a significant factor in the Debtors' analysis of its options, it was not the only factor. Debtors continued to consider and negotiate the terms of possible debtor-in-possession financing from [names of lenders] until such negotiations resulted in [Lender's] offer of financing terms that were attractive to Debtors and in the best interests of their estates. Accordingly, Debtors have concluded that the best terms available under the circumstances are those negotiated with [Lender], the current secured lender.

27. Debtors believe that the proposed financing arrangement with [Lender] will enable [Debtors] to continue operating in the ordinary course during the pendency of these cases.

28. The terms of the proposed financing arrangement were negotiated in good faith and at arm's length, and Debtors believe that the terms and conditions are fair and reasonable. Such terms are contained in the DIP Financing Agreement.

29. Under the DIP Financing Agreement, subject to Court approval, Debtors and their customers would continue to remit payments to [Lender] and Debtors would receive new loans from [Lender], and their cash availability would be increased by approximately $[amount] over that which was available under the loan documents [very fact-specific]. Debtors' total borrowings pursuant to the DIP financing agreement will be referred to herein as the DIP loans.

30. The DIP loans would bear interest at a rate equal to [rate] (the base rate). If a default occurs, default interest would accrue at a rate [percent] higher than the base rate.

31. The DIP loans would be terminable by [Lender] on the earliest of [date], the entry of an order confirming a plan of reorganization, or the occurrence of certain events of default as set forth in the Agreement, including without limitation: failure to make payment of principal or interest; failure to observe any provisions of the DIP financing agreement; filing a motion to obtain financing from a party other than [Lender] unless such financing repays Debtors' obligations to [Lender] in full; misrepresentation in any of the loan documents; appointment of a receiver, trustee, or examiner; entry of an order granting relief from or modifying the automatic stay to allow a creditor to enforce a lien on collateral if such enforcement would have a material adverse effect; dismissal of the Chapter 11 cases, or conversion to Chapter 7; and other events described therein [very fact-specific].

32. Debtors have agreed to use the amounts borrowed under the DIP financing agreement to pay the types of operating and reorganization expenses and purchases reflected on the budget to be attached to the proposed interim order.

33. Pursuant to the DIP financing agreement, [Lender] would increase the availability of the letter of credit facility by approximately $[letter of credit amount] or, upon satisfaction of certain availability tests which Debtors do not currently satisfy, by approximately $[amount]. Finally, as set forth in [paragraph number] above, Debtors' cash availability would increase by approximately $[amount]. All such terms are more fully described in the DIP financing agreement [very fact specific].

34. Subject to the authorization of this Court, as adequate protection and security for the DIP loans and the use of the collateral, Debtors have agreed to grant to [Lender], for all amounts advanced under the DIP financing agreement, as well as interest accrued thereon and fees [very fact specific]:

(a) superpriority administrative status, pursuant to 11 U.S.C. § 364(c)(1), subject only to: (1) allowed professional fees and disbursements including, without limitation, those for attorneys, accountants, other advisers to the Debtors incurred by the Debtors whose retention has been authorized by the Court in an amount not to exceed an average of $[fees amount] per month for the fees and expenses of the professionals for the Debtors, or a pro rata amount for any fraction of a month; (2) allowed professional fees and disbursements incurred after the termination of the DIP financing agreement in an amount, in the aggregate, not to exceed $[amount], together with any remaining portion of the monthly allowance of $[monthly allowance] which at such time was unused and $[amount for trustee] for any duly appointed Trustee; and (3) payment of quarterly bankruptcy fees to the United States Trustee pursuant to 28 U.S.C. § 1930(a)(6) (collectively, the priority fees); and

(b) superpriority secured status ahead of any other current or future holders of mortgages, liens, and security interests on such property, subject only to valid, binding, enforceable, and prior-perfected mortgages, liens, and security interests existing in the collateral as of the petition date and subject to [Lender's] preexisting mortgages, liens, and security interests and to the priority fees.

35. Accordingly, the proposed DIP financing agreement with [Lender] would require the granting of a lien pursuant to 11 U.S.C. § 364(d) senior to all liens other than enforceable prior liens existing as of the petition date and other than the liens securing the loans. Debtors believe and therefore assert that all other lien holders, if any, not currently holding such prior liens will be adequately protected by, without limitation, the continued financing available under the DIP financing agreement, the resulting continued operation of Debtors businesses, and the lack of adverse impact upon such lienholders' interests in Debtors' assets.

36. In the DIP financing agreement, Debtors acknowledge the legally binding and enforceable nature of the indebtedness to [Lender] and the validity, enforceability, and perfection of the liens created thereunder, and that neither are subject to offset, defense, claim, counterclaim, or any other diminution.

37. Facility fees in connection with the DIP Financing arrangement are [insert description of all fees and timetable of payment], thus resulting in a net savings to the Debtors of $[amount of savings] compared with the prepetition financing arrangement.

38. Finally, upon default by Debtors, [Lender] may terminate the DIP financing agreement, release operating information, and, upon 5 days' written notice, exercise rights or remedies under the DIP financing agreement or the loan documents such as the right to modify the automatic stay, with the limitations contained therein, and declare all obligations immediately due and payable. [Insert any other significant terms. Terms shown here are examples of some possibilities.]

39. All of these terms are described more fully in the DIP financing agreement.

40. The benefits to Debtors of the proposed DIP financing agreement are numerous. The terms will enable Debtors to operate in Chapter 11 and attempt to effect a successful reorganization, and will provide the only hope of a significant recovery to [Debtors'] suppliers, employees, and other unsecured creditors, as well as to its customers.

41. Debtors, in their sound and prudent business judgment, have concluded that the DIP financing agreement is the best financing opportunity

available to the Debtors, and that its approval is in the best interests of Debtors' estates, because, among other things, it will obviate the need to engage in a difficult, costly, and time-consuming priming battle; it will provide Debtors with sufficient flexibility to operate their businesses in the ordinary course; and it is fair to Debtors' estates and creditors. Accordingly, Debtors respectfully request that the Court promptly approve the DIP financing agreement.

B. Interim Relief

42. Pending final approval of the DIP financing agreement, Debtors further request that this Court authorize Debtors to obtain loans under the DIP Financing Agreement on an interim basis to the extent necessary to avoid immediate and irreparable harm to Debtors' business. It is essential to the continued operation of Debtors' business that Debtors be authorized by this Court to borrow certain funds under the DIP financing agreement immediately. Debtors will not be able to meet their operating obligations in the absence of interim approval of the DIP financing agreement. Such funds are urgently needed to enable Debtors: (1) to maintain and replenish their inventory and supplies and to provide services to their customers; (2) to meet payroll and other current operating expenses; (3) generally, to continue their ongoing operations and generate funds to pay the claims of creditors; and (4) to finance the completion of performance under various contracts.

43. The estimate of Debtors' actual cash needs during the period pending final hearing on the motion will be set forth in the budget to be attached to the proposed interim order.

44. The interim relief requested herein, pending a final hearing, is necessary, appropriate, and fully warranted, and is essential to the rehabilitation and reorganization effort of Debtors.

45. Accordingly, Debtors respectfully request that, pending a final hearing on this motion, the terms and provisions of the DIP financing agreement be implemented on an interim basis.

46. [Lender] has requested and Debtors have agreed to grant to it (subject to Court approval) certain benefits under 11 U.S.C. §§ 364(c) and (d). Assuming that this Court enters an order approving the DIP financing agreement on an interim basis, but the terms of that Agreement are later modified, vacated, stayed, or terminated by subsequent order of this or any other court, Debtors and [Lender] have agreed and request that this Court hold that [Lender] will be secured in accordance with the terms of the DIP financing agreement to the extent of any amounts previously disbursed (or committed through the issuance of a letter or letters of credit) thereunder, all interest thereon, and all costs related thereto.

FORM AND MANNER OF NOTICE AND SERVICE AND SCHEDULING A FINAL HEARING

47. Debtors further request that this Court approve the form and manner of notice with respect to the interim and final hearings.

48. Notice of this motion has been provided to the Office of the United States Trustee, to counsel for [Lender], and to creditors who have requested notice pursuant to Bankruptcy Rule 2002. In light of the exigencies of the situation, the timing of the filing of Debtors' Chapter 11 petitions, Debtors' immediate need for funds, and the interim relief requested, Debtors respectfully submit that no further notice of the interim hearing is required.

49. Debtors propose that a final hearing on this Motion be scheduled within 30 days of the date hereof, and that the Court order that the Debtors provide at least 20 days' notice of the final hearing on the Motion to the Office of the United State Trustee, to counsel to [Lender] and to creditors who have requested notice pursuant to Bankruptcy Rule 2002.

50. Debtors submit that the form and manner of notice described above for the interim and final hearings constitute adequate and proper notice under the circumstances of these cases. Given the breadth and scope of the proposed manner of notice and service, as set forth herein with respect to the final hearing, Debtors further submit that no further notice is required or necessary.

CONCLUSION

WHEREFORE, and for the reasons set forth in the accompanying memorandum of law, which is incorporated by reference herein, Debtors respectfully request that the Court (a) approve the form and manner of notice and service of this motion; (b) scheduled interim and final hearings on this motion; (c) after expedited consideration, enter an interim order approving the DIP financing agreement and authorizing advances thereunder on an interim basis pursuant to it; (d) after a final hearing, enter a final order approving the DIP financing agreement; and (e) grant Debtors such other and further relief as is just and proper under the circumstances.

[Attorney(s) for Debtors]

§ 6.30 Form: Proposed Final Order Approving Financing Arrangement

This form assumes continuation with the prepetition lender.

FORM 6–2
PROPOSED FINAL ORDER APPROVING FINANCING ARRANGEMENT

[Caption]

FINAL ORDER AUTHORIZING DEBTORS TO OBTAIN
POSTPETITION FINANCING

CAME BEFORE THE COURT on [date], the Motion of the above-captioned Debtors seeking the entry of an order authorizing [Debtors] to obtain postpetition secured financing from [Lender] under Section 364(c) and (d) of Title 11 of the United States Code, 11 U.S.C. §§ 101, *et seq.* (the Bankruptcy Code). The Court, having examined the Motion and the exhibits attached thereto, and upon completion of a preliminary hearing and a final hearing as provided under Rule 4001 of the Federal Rules of Bankruptcy Procedure, having heard the arguments of counsel with respect to the immediate financial need of Debtors for continued financing from [Lender] in accordance with the terms of the loan documents, and sufficient and adequate notice of the Motion and hearing with respect thereto having been given, and begin fully advised in the premises, finds as follows:

[Insert findings of fact, including procedural and factual history of case and description of loans and liens.]

. . . 6. A. From time to time prior to the petition date, [Lender] loaned money to Debtors secured by, among other things, security interests and liens upon the following property of Debtors (collectively referred to as the prepetition collateral):

> (i) all receivables, inventory, equipment, proprietary rights, and proceeds, wherever located and whether now existing or hereafter arising or acquired; (ii) all moneys, securities, and other property and the proceeds thereof, now or hereafter held or received by, or in transit to, [Lender] from or for Debtors, whether for safekeeping, pledge, custody, transmission, collection, or otherwise, including, without limitation, all of Debtors' deposit accounts, credits and balances with [Lender], and all claims of Debtors against [Lender] at any time existing; (iii) all of Debtors' deposit accounts with any financial institutions with which Debtors maintain deposits; (iv) all books, records, and other property relating to or referring to any of the foregoing, including, without limitation, all books, records, ledger cards, data processing records, computer software, and other property, and general intangibles at any time evidencing or relating to the receivables, inventory,

equipment, proprietary rights, proceeds, and other property referred to above; and (v) all interest in real property in which Debtors own the fee estate.

All of the foregoing loans, security interests, and liens are more fully described in the original loan documents.

B. The aforesaid loans, security interests, and liens were evidenced by the following agreements, instruments, and documents, among others (collectively called the original loan documents):

[Insert list and description of loan documents.]

C. [Lender's] security interests in and liens upon the prepetition collateral have been properly perfected with respect to each jurisdiction in which any of the prepetition collateral is located, at least as of the date in which a prepetition financing statement and prepetition mortgages were filed in such jurisdiction. During the ninety (90) days preceding the petition date, all of the tangible assets of Debtors were located exclusively in the states in which the prepetition financing statements and prepetition mortgages were filed.

D. As of [date], Debtors were indebted to [Lender] by reason of the aforesaid loans in the principal amount of approximately $[loan amount], plus accrued interest and costs which [Lender] is entitled to recover pursuant to the loan documents (collectively referred to as the prepetition debt).

[Describe interim orders, if any.]

. . . 10. Interest has continued to accrue on the outstanding aggregate net principal balance of the prepetition debt, and the interim postpetition debt at the rate of interest set forth in the loan documents (as hereafter defined).

11. As security and collateral for the repayment of the prepetition debt, Debtors have granted to [Lender] security interests in the prepetition collateral. As security and collateral for the repayment of the postpetition debt (as hereafter defined), Debtors have granted to [Lender] security interests in the prepetition collateral and the postpetition collateral (as hereafter defined). All liens and security interests granted to [Lender] as evidenced by the loan documents (as hereafter defined) are properly perfected, valid, continuing, fully enforceable, and are senior and first in priority to all other liens, security interests, and claims, if any, in and to the collateral subject only to valid, properly perfected, indefeasible liens and security interests placed on the prepetition collateral which have priority over the liens and security interests of [Lender] prior to the petition date as permitted under the original loan documents.

12. An immediate need exists for Debtors to obtain financing to continue operations. Without such financing, Debtors will be irreparably

harmed because they will be unable to operate their businesses and will be unable to service their customers or fulfill their pending contractual commitments in the ordinary course of their businesses.

13. Debtors are unable to obtain unsecured credit allowable under 11 U.S.C. Section 503(b)(1) as an administrative expense pursuant to Section 364(a) or (b) of the Bankruptcy Code in the amount required to finance continued operations.

14. Debtors have proposed that [Lender] provide financing (the DIP facility) to permit the Debtors' continued operations. Debtors and [Lender] have undertaken negotiations regarding such financing, and Debtors have submitted to this Court the proposed terms of the DIP facility for the Court's approval, all as set forth in the loan and security agreement, copies of which are attached to the Motion as Exhibit A. Debtors have attempted to find alternative financing, and the financing proposed by the Debtors from [Lender] constitutes the best available financing under the conditions.

15. [Lender] has indicated a willingness to provide postpetition financing under the loan documents. [Lender] is and will be acting in good faith in extending the credit authorized hereby as required by Section 364(e) of the Bankruptcy Code and is accordingly entitled to the protections set forth in Section 364(e).

16. The relief hereby granted will prevent immediate and irreparable harm to Debtors and will minimize the disruption of Debtors' businesses and operations as going concerns, enable the Debtors to operate their businesses, and is in the best interests of the Debtors, their estates, and their creditors.

17. It appearing to this Court that the subject of this Order is a core proceeding within the meaning of 28 U.S.C. Section 157, and that proper notice has been given on the hearing upon the Motion in accordance with Bankruptcy Rule 4001(c), which notice was adequate in all respects, and good cause having been shown,

Accordingly, it is hereby ordered, adjudged, and decreed that:

(1) The Motion is hereby granted.

(2) Debtors, as debtors-in-possession be, and hereby are, authorized to borrow money, incur indebtedness, repay indebtedness (including any term loan), grant liens and security interests, and perform their obligations in accordance with the terms of this Order and the conditions set forth in the loan documents, which terms are hereby ratified, authorized, and approved in all respects.

(3) This Order shall be deemed to be and shall constitute a loan agreement, a security agreement (under the applicable provisions of the

Uniform Commercial Code), and a mortgage or deed of trust as may be appropriate between Debtors and [Lender] (as lender, secured party, and mortgagee or beneficiary). The terms and conditions of the loan documents are incorporated herein and made a part hereof by this reference and now and hereafter shall be deemed and held to be enforceable by [Lender] against the Debtors and their estates, as if Debtors delivered the same to [Lender].

(4) To secure all indebtedness that may be incurred and owing by Debtors to [Lender] subsequent to the petition date, [Lender] is hereby granted a first, continuing, valid, perfected, and enforceable security interest in and lien upon all property of the Debtors and the Debtors' estates described in the loan documents, subject only to valid, binding, enforceable, and perfected (or perfectible) mortgages, liens, and security interests having priority over the liens and security interests of [Lender] in the collateral existing on the petition date and subject to [Lenders'] preexisting mortgages, liens, and security interests and as otherwise provided herein. Debtors having established the existence of adequate protection in the manner required under Section 364(d) of the Bankruptcy Code, liens and security interests in the collateral are granted pursuant to Section 364(c) and (d) of the Bankruptcy Code and, except as provided in [Paragraph] below and as permitted by the amended agreement, shall be prior and senior to all other liens, claims, encumbrances, and security interests, subject only to the prior liens, claims, encumbrances, and security interests which secure the prepetition debt and all properly perfected and indefeasible security interests senior to those of [Lender] as of the petition date. If it shall be necessary for [Lender], at any time, to exercise its rights and remedies under the loan documents and applicable law in order to effect repayment of the postpetition debt, [Lender] shall have the right to exercise such rights and remedies as to the collateral as [Lender] shall, in its sole discretion, elect, subject to the express provisions of this Order.

(5) The postpetition debt shall have priority in accordance with the provisions of Section 364(c)(1) of the Bankruptcy Code over all administrative expenses of the kind specified in Section 503(b) or 507(b) of the Bankruptcy Code; and, further, no costs or administrative expenses that have been or may be incurred in these Chapter 11 cases, or in any subsequent Chapter 7 cases (including any priority granted under Section 726(b) of the Bankruptcy Code), and no priority claims are or will be prior to or on a parity with the claim of [Lender] against the Debtors arising out of the postpetition debt or with the security interests and liens of [Lender] in and to the prepetition collateral and to the postpetition collateral; provided, however, that the security interests and liens of [Lender] in the collateral as provided under Section 364(d) and [Lender's] priority under Section 364(c)(1) of the Bankruptcy Code shall be subject to the payment of: (i) allowed professional fees and disbursements including, without limitation, those for attorneys, accountants, other advisers to the Debtors incurred by the Debtors (or any of them) whose retention has been authorized by the Court in an amount not to exceed an average of $[fee amounts] per month for the fees and expenses of the professionals for the

Debtors, or a pro rata amount for any fraction of a month (the carve-out amount); it being understood and agreed that in any month in which the carve-out amount is not actually spent or paid by the Debtors for the payment of professional fees and services, the difference between the carve-out amount for that month and the amounts actually spent or paid by the Debtors during that month shall be cumulated and available for subsequent payment of the fees and expenses of the professionals for Debtors; (ii) if the funding term (as hereinafter defined) ends earlier than the effective date of a plan of reorganization in these Chapter 11 cases, then an amount of up to $[amount] of funds for the allowed fees and expenses of the professionals for the Debtors and up to an additional $[trustee fee] to compensate any duly-appointed trustee in these Chapter 11 cases; and (iii) fees of the U.S. Trustee pursuant to 28 U.S.C. § 1930(a); and (b); provided that the foregoing shall not be construed as consent to the allowance of any of the amounts referred to in the preceding clauses (i), (ii), or (iii) and shall not affect the right of Debtors or [Lender] to object to the allowance of any such amounts; and further provided that the foregoing limitations with respect to [Lender's] priority under 364(c)(1) and 364(d) of the Bankruptcy Code shall only be in effect until the end of the funding term except as provided in preceding clause (ii).

(6) If at any time during these Chapter 11 cases any security interest or lien in the collateral or any portion thereof is granted to any other party pursuant to Section 364(d) of the Bankruptcy Code, which security interest or lien is senior to or on a parity with the security interest(s) or lien(s) of [Lender] therein, the proceeds of any loans, advances, accommodations, or other indebtedness secured by such senior or parity security interest or lien shall be applied first to satisfy the indebtedness of the Debtors to [Lender] in such order as [Lender], in its sole discretion, shall elect. [Lender] shall be given at least twenty (20) days' prior notice and an opportunity for a hearing before this Court prior to the Court's granting to any other party any such senior or parity security interest or lien;

[Insert recitation of specific terms of agreement between Debtor and Lender.]

. . . (7) Debtors shall serve a copy of this final order by first class mail on all parties on whom the Motion was previously served on or before [date].

____

UNITED STATES BANKRUPTCY JUDGE

CHAPTER 7

EXECUTORY CONTRACTS AND UNEXPIRED LEASES

Douglas M. Neeb

§ 7.1 Introduction

In every small business bankruptcy, counsel will likely be faced with issues relating to the proper disposition of prepetition contracts or leases to which the debtor-in-possession is a party.[1] Most of these issues are dealt with in 11 U.S.C. § 365.

[1] Throughout this chapter, reference will be made to the debtor. This reference is intended to refer to a postpetition debtor-in-possession as contemplated in §§ 1101(1), 1107(a), and 1108 of the Bankruptcy Code.

Debtor's counsel in a typical small business bankruptcy is likely to face one or more of the following most common types of relationships:

1. The debtor leases the place from which it conducts its business operations
2. The debtor leases some or all of the equipment it uses in its operations
3. The debtor has contractual obligations to purchase inventory or materials for use in its business operations
4. The debtor has contractual obligations to supply the finished product or service which is the subject of its business.

Chapter 11 of the Bankruptcy Code gives a debtor several options with respect to each of these relationships. However, each of these options can only be exercised with approval of the bankruptcy court, upon compliance by the debtor with certain requirements, and this must be done in a timely manner.

The time limitations are particularly important with respect to unexpired leases of nonresidential real property. The debtor must timely act to prevent rejection of the lease as a matter of law. See § **7.7.**

In general, each prepetition relationship of the debtor must be characterized as either an executory obligation (unexpired) or a nonexecutory obligation. If an obligation is determined to be *executory* or unexpired, a debtor generally has the ability to:

1. Assume the relationship
2. Assume the relationship and assign its rights and duties to a nondebtor third party
3. Reject the relationship.

The primary purpose behind the provisions regarding rejection is to allow the debtor the opportunity to relieve the estate from obligations that are burdensome in order to further the debtor's opportunity to recover, and to permit the nondebtor party to have a breach of contract claim against the estate.[2] On the other hand, the primary purpose behind assumption is to allow the debtor, after reasonable time to reflect, to continue its business relationships as if the bankruptcy had not occurred.[3]

This chapter explores the impact of the Bankruptcy Code on each of these issues. In addition, this chapter gives the practitioner a framework for dealing with each of these issues in a time- and cost-efficient manner.

§ 7.2 Executory Contracts Generally

The provisions of the Bankruptcy Code relating to contracts deal only with the relationships of parties to executory contracts. Therefore, the most important initial determination to be made by counsel is whether the relationship is executory or nonexecutory in nature.

---

[2] *In re* Register, 95 B.R. 73 (Bankr. M.D. Tenn.), *aff'd,* 100 B.R. 360 (M.D. Tenn. 1989).

[3] *In re* Airlift Int'l, Inc., 761 F.2d 1503 (11th Cir. 1985).

The legislative history of § 365 states that *executory* is intended to include "contracts on which performance remains due to some extent on both sides."[4] This definition is different from the traditional pre-Code test first enunciated by Professor Vern Countryman which, for a contract to be classified as executory, required a finding that the failure by either party to complete remaining performance would constitute a material breach.[5] The Countryman definition is still adhered to by some courts,[6] but other courts attempt to use a more pragmatic, result-oriented test "consistent with the intent of the Bankruptcy Code."[7]

In one area nearly all courts and commentators agree: a contract that has been validly terminated prior to the filing of the petition can not be an executory contract.[8] Because the contract has been terminated, it does not exist and therefore cannot be assumed by a debtor who only succeeds to the rights held by the prepetition entity.[9] However, for a prepetition termination to effectively cutoff all the debtor's rights, it must be final and not subject to reversal or other reconsideration under applicable state law.[10]

Given these somewhat differing approaches with respect to determining whether a contract is executory, it is prudent for counsel for the debtor or for a nondebtor party to a contract to proceed as if all relationships, with the exception of promissory notes, are executory and therefore subject to the power of the bankruptcy court.[11] This will likely include hard-to-categorize relationships such as partnership agreements (see **Chapter 22**) and land sale contracts.[12]

---

4 S. Rep. No. 989, 95th Cong., 2d Sess. 58 (1978), *reprinted in* 1978 U.S.C.C.A.N. 5787, 5844; H.R. Rep. No. 595, 95th Cong., 1st Sess. 347 (1977), *reprinted in* 1978 U.S.C.C.A.N. 5963, 6303; *In re* Streets & Beard Farm Partnership, 882 F.2d 233 (7th Cir. 1989).

5 V. Countryman, *Executory Contracts in Bankruptcy Part I,* 57 Minn. L. Rev. 439, 460 (1973).

6 *E.g., In re* Terrell, 892 F.2d 469 (6th Cir. 1989); *In re* Maralak, Ltd., 104 B.R. 446 (Bankr. M.D. Fla. 1989); *but see In re* Jolly, 574 F.2d 349, 351 (6th Cir.), *cert. denied,* 439 U.S. 929 (1978); *In re* Martin Bros. Toolmakers, Inc., 796 F.2d 1435, 1439 (11th Cir. 1987).

7 *In re* Sun Runner Marine, Inc., 116 B.R. 712, *vacated in part, aff'd in part,* 945 F.2d 1089 (Bankr. 9th Cir. 1990); *In re* Sundial Asphalt Co., Inc., 147 B.R. 72 (E.D.N.Y. 1992).

8 *In re* Gourmet Serv., Inc., 142 B.R. 216 (Bankr. S.D. Ohio 1992); *In re* Emilio Cavallini, Ltd., 112 B.R. 72 (Bankr. S.D.N.Y. 1990); *In re* Metro Air Northeast, Inc., 131 B.R. 555 (Bankr. W.D.N.Y. 1989).

9 *E.g., In re* Windmill Farms, Inc., 841 F.2d 1467, 1469–71 (9th Cir. 1988).

10 Moody v. Amoco Oil Co., 734 F.2d 1200, 1212 (7th Cir.), *cert. denied,* 469 U.S. 982 (1984); *In re* Mako, Inc., 102 B.R. 814 (Bankr. E.D. Okla. 1988).

11 The Bankruptcy Code provides special treatment for some specific types of executory contracts that are more technical in nature. These include time-share interests (11 U.S.C. § 365(h), (i)), collective bargaining agreements (§ 1113), repurchase agreements (§ 559), aviation equipment (§ 1110), and landlord bankruptcies (§ 365(h)). These special technical contractual relationships are not dealt with in this chapter.

12 *In re* Coffman, 104 B.R. 958 (Bankr. S.D. Ind. 1988).

The prudent practitioner will attempt to identify all executory relationships as early in representation of the putative debtor as possible. By far the best opportunity to compile a list of all relevant relationships is when preparing the debtor's schedules and statement of financial affairs. In fact, careful preparation of these documents, with substantial counsel participation, should identify all areas of concern. Some, like the debtor's lease of the building from which it conducts its business and any equipment leases, will be obvious. Others, such as the debtor's contract with the provider of its security alarm system, may be more difficult to identify. In preparing the schedules and the statement of financial affairs, counsel should seek to understand the nature of every bill the putative debtor has paid in the previous three months. Review of this time period will likely identify all regular ongoing relationships that must be addressed during the Chapter 11 proceedings. In addition, to make sure that all possible relationships have been accounted for, prudent counsel will include broad language governing assumption in the plan of reorganization.[13]

Counsel for nondebtor parties may want to consider a preemptive motion requesting that the court

1. Determine that the contract is not executory or cannot, for other reasons explored later in this chapter (see **§ 7.15**), be assumed by the debtor; or
2. Require the debtor under § 365(d)(2) of the Bankruptcy Code to make its determination with respect to assumption by a date certain.

If choosing to require the debtor to make its assumption decision by a particular date, counsel to the nondebtor party should also seek an order from the bankruptcy court that requires the debtor to keep performance of its postpetition obligations current.

§ 7.3 Unexpired Leases Generally

The definition sections of the Bankruptcy Code do not provide a definition of the term "lease." The Bankruptcy Code provides treatment for three types of unexpired leases:

1. Residential real property
2. Nonresidential real property
3. Others, such as equipment, vehicles, and other personalty.

Although classification of an obligation as a lease when it relates to real property is usually simple, the same cannot necessarily be said for relationships involving non-real property tangibles like equipment.

A number of cases recognize that a relationship the parties call a lease can be reclassified by the Bankruptcy Code for purposes of treatment in bankruptcy proceedings as a financing relationship. Equipment leases are the most common type of lease subject to this reclassification. Some courts frame the issue as whether the

---

[13] Sample assumption clauses are presented in **§ 7.10.**

relationship is one of a "true lease" or a "disguised financing arrangement."[14] In making the determination, courts are required to apply state law.[15] In addition, consideration is given to the intent of the parties, the circumstances surrounding the transactions, and the economic substance of the transaction.[16]

The consequences of classifying a relationship as a financing transaction instead of a lease are significant. A financing transaction may be treated as an unsecured claim if there has not been proper perfection of the security interest. If the court determines that the relationship is a financing relationship rather than a true lease, the provisions of § 365 of the Bankruptcy Code will not govern the continued relationship. Rather, the focus will turn to whether the nondebtor party holds collateral as security for its financing relationship. Of course, if the nondebtor party is unsecured, it is limited to a prepetition unsecured claim for its damages. Even if the nondebtor party is a secured creditor usually requiring the proper filing of a financing statement, the debtor may have important options with respect to that relationship not available under § 365, such as deacceleration and cram down modification of the interest rate or term.

§ 7.4 Postpetition Obligations

Generally speaking, if the debtor continues to receive benefits from an executory contract or unexpired lease, it must pay for the reasonable value of those benefits. If the relationship is to be assumed by the debtor, this requirement is usually subsumed in the "cure" prerequisites for assumption, discussed in **§ 7.13.** When the court permits the debtor to reject a relationship, determining the postpetition obligations becomes more difficult.

It is clear that during the case and prior to deciding whether to assume or reject the relationship, a debtor may continue to insist on performance by the nondebtor party.[17] Nondebtors are required to perform their obligations under an executory contract unless and until it is rejected.[18] In fact, failure of the nondebtor party to continue to perform its contractual obligations may be a violation of the automatic stay provisions of the Bankruptcy Code. Put another way, courts have recognized that they may compel continued performance by the nondebtor party.[19] However, during the time the debtor is allowed to consider its options, the terms of an executory contract are unenforceable against the debtor.[20]

---

14 *In re* Torgerson Co., 114 B.R. 899 (Bankr. S.D. Tex. 1990); *see also* S. Rep. No. 989, 95th Cong., 2d Sess. 64, *reprinted in* 1978 U.S.C.C.A.N. 5787, 5850.

15 H.R. Rep. No. 595, 95th Cong., 1st Sess. 313–14 (1977), *reprinted in* 1978 U.S.C.C.A.N. 5963, 6271.

16 *In re* Chateaugay Corp., 112 B.R. 335 (Bankr. S.D.N.Y. 1989).

17 *In re* Public Serv., 884 F.2d 11 (1st Cir. 1989).

18 *Id.*

19 Data-Link Sys., Inc. v. Whilcomb & Keller Mortgage Co. (*In re* Whitcomb & Keller Mortgage Co.), 715 F.2d 375 (7th Cir. 1983).

20 *In re* University Medical Ctr., 973 F.2d 1065 (3d Cir. 1992); *In re* Providence Television Ltd. Partnership, 113 B.R. 446 (Bankr. N.D. Ill. 1990).

The debtor must compensate the nondebtor party for the benefits it receives while it decides whether to assume or reject the executory contract.[21] The compensation to be paid by the debtor is the reasonable value of the benefits that it receives.[22]

Two issues generate the most debate with respect to the debtor's postpetition obligations on executory contracts to nondebtor third parties: (1) whether the value of the debtor's obligation is to be measured by the contractual provisions between the parties or by market value, and (2) how long the debtor's obligation continues.

§ 7.5 Value of Obligations

If the debtor ultimately obtains court authority to assume the executory contract, it will only be obligated to compensate the nondebtor party according to the terms of the contract. If, on the other hand, the debtor decides to reject the relationship, the issue of postpetition compensation may be the subject of litigation.

There is a rebuttable presumption that the debtor is obligated to pay the contract price. If the contract amount is less than market amount, the estate may be liable as a postpetition administrative expense for an amount greater than the agreed-upon contractual amount.[23] Conversely, if the contract amount is greater than market value, the debtor may be able to pay less than the agreed-upon amount.

In 1984, Congress amended the Bankruptcy Code to provide specific provisions relating to the conduct of the parties to a nonresidential real property lease under which the debtor is the lessee. Previously the lessor would seek payment as an administrative expense under § 503(b)(1)(A). However, this led the courts to consider the actual and necessary value of the debtor's occupation of the property, which may be different from the lease provisions.[24] Under the new provisions of § 365(d)(3), the debtor must perform all of its obligations under the lease which accrue postpetition during the period in which the debtor is deciding whether to assume or reject the lease.[25] These obligations include not only the timely payment of rent which accrues postpetition but also the timely payment of other monetary obligations such as common-area maintenance charges, real property taxes, percentage of utilities, and regular maintenance. These timely payments are to be made by the debtor without the landlord's having to seek an order directing the payments to be made.[26] The debtor's obligations payable under § 365(d)(3) are distinct from a

---

21 *In re* Thompson, 788 F.2d 560 (9th Cir. 1986).

22 *In re* Three Star Telecast, Inc., 73 B.R. 270 (Bankr. D.P.R. 1987).

23 Peoples Gas Sys., Inc. v. Thatcher Glass Corp. (*In re* Thatcher Glass Corp.), 59 B.R. 797 (Bankr. D. Conn. 1986).

24 *In re* Cardinal Export Corp., 30 B.R. 682 (Bankr. E.D.N.Y. 1983).

25 Section 365(d)(3) provides, in relevant part:

> The [debtor-in-possession] shall timely perform all the obligations of the debtor . . . arising from and after the order for relief under any unexpired lease of nonresidential real property, until such lease is assumed or rejected, notwithstanding § 503(b)(1) of this title.

26 *In re* Western Monetary Consultants, 100 B.R. 545, 547 (Bankr. D. Colo. 1989); *In re* Coastal Dry Dock & Repair Corp., 62 B.R. 879, 883 (Bankr. E.D.N.Y. 1986).

debtor's general administrative expense obligations under § 503 and constitute a separate category under the Bankruptcy Code.[27]

Unlike the alternatives applicable to executory contracts, the Bankruptcy Code provides that, in the case of unexpired leases of nonresidential real property, postpetition rent accrues at the lease rate rather than at some market rate determined by the court.[28] However, if after a nonresidential real property lease has been rejected, either by court order or by expiration of the time for assumption, the debtor continues to be a hold-over tenant, the debtor will be obligated to pay the fair market rent for its use of the property.[29]

Most cases hold that rent must be prorated into pre- and postpetition portions for determination of the debtor's obligations under § 365(d)(3).[30] The debtor is only obligated to pay rent for the postpetition, prerejection period. Further, this prorated calculation will govern the obligation regardless of when the lease may require payment.[31] The proration requirement is also likely to apply to monetary obligations other than rent such as real estate taxes, common area maintenance charges and gross revenue rents.[32]

§ 7.6 Duration of Obligations

The second postpetition issue concerns the effective date of a rejection for purposes of determining when the debtor's obligation to pay postpetition administrative expenses terminates. A number of possible dates can be considered. From earliest to latest, these are:

1. When the debtor's intent to reject is made clear to the nondebtor party[33]
2. When the motion to reject is filed by the debtor with the court[34]

---

27 *In re* Child World, Inc. 161 B.R. 571, 575 n.5 (S.D.N.Y. 1993); *In re* Duckwall-Alco Stores, Inc., 150 B.R. 965, 971 n.10 (D. Kan. 1993).

28 *See* 11 U.S.C. § 365(d)(3); *In re* Duckwall-Alco Stores, Inc., 150 B.R. 965, 971 (D. Kan. 1993); *In re* Paul Harris Stores, Inc., 148 B.R. 307, 312 (S.D. Ind. 1992).

29 *See, e.g., In re* Western Monetary Consultants, 100 B.R. 545, 547 (Bankr. D. Colo. 1989) (after 60-day period rent is determined using objective fair and reasonable value of property; however, there is a rebuttable presumption that lease rent is fair and reasonable); *In re* Homeowner's Outlet Mall Exch., Inc., 89 B.R. 965, 969–70 (Bankr. S.D. Fla. 1988).

30 *In re* Ames Dep't Stores, Inc., 150 B.R. 107 (Bankr. S.D.N.Y. 1993); *In re* Revco D.S., Inc., 111 B.R. 626 (Bankr. N.D. Ohio 1989).

31 *In re* Ames Dep't Stores, Inc., 150 B.R. 107 (Bankr. S.D.N.Y. 1993).

32 *In re* Child World, Inc., 161 B.R. 571 (S.D.N.Y. 1993); *In re* RB Furniture, Inc., 141 B.R. 706, 712 (Bankr. C.D. Cal. 1992); *but see In re* Duckwall-Alco Stores, Inc., 150 B.R. 965, 975 (D. Kan. 1993).

33 *In re* Joseph C. Spiess Co., 145 B.R. 497, 507 (Bankr. N.D. Ill. 1992) (date is day lessor is unequivocally notified by debtor that it intends to reject lease).

34 *In re* 1 Potato 2, Inc., 58 B.R. 752 (Bankr. D. Minn. 1986) (date is day debtor files motion to reject lease).

3. When the court approves the debtor's decision to reject[35]
4. When the order entered by the court authorizing rejection is docketed[36]
5. In the case of a lease of nonresidential real property, upon the expiration of 60 days, unless a clear extension has been entered.[37]

Clearly, an executory contract should only be rejected by entry of a court order, the other methods being too etherial to provide certainty. With regard to leases of nonresidential real property, the majority position appears to be that administrative expense obligations are only tolled upon the entry of an order by the court authorizing and approving the debtor's rejection of a lease, unless the 60th day (or such other day as the court has validly extended the deadline) expires during the time between the debtor's filing of a motion to reject and the court hearing on that motion.[38] As a practical matter, this view seems to be correct because until the entry of an order approving the debtor's rejection of its obligations, a lessor is unable to lease the premises again and in fact may be in violation of the automatic stay if it tries to do so.[39]

The Bankruptcy Code does not provide a specific remedy for a landlord in the event the debtor fails to timely perform its postpetition obligations. Options available to the landlord include filing with the court a motion that requests:

1. Relief from the automatic stay to permit the landlord to pursue an unlawful detainer action in state court
2. An order that the debtor immediately vacate the premises
3. Appointment of a Chapter 11 trustee to administer the estate, or
4. Conversion or dismissal of the case.

§ 7.7 Time Limits in General

The debtor has until confirmation of the plan to assume or reject all executory contracts or unexpired leases, except for unexpired leases of nonresidential real property, which are deemed rejected 60 days after commencement of the case unless the court extends the time. See **§ 7.8.** Section 365(d)(2) provides that the debtor-in-possession may assume or reject an executory contract or unexpired lease at any time before the

---

35 *In re* Garfinckels, Inc., 118 B.R. 154 (Bankr. D.D.C. 1990) (date is when court announces approval of debtor's motion to reject).

36 *In re* Revco D.S., Inc., 109 B.R. 264 (Bankr. N.D. Ohio 1989) (date is when order docketed).

37 *In re* Arizona Appetito's Stores, Inc., 893 F.2d 216, 219 (9th Cir. 1990) (when debtor files motion to reject lease within 60 days, lease is deemed rejected at the end of the 60 days, without the need for court approval).

38 *In re* Duckwall-Alco Stores, Inc., 150 B.R. 965 (D. Kan. 1993) (lease was rejected while motion for rejection was pending when bankruptcy court failed to act on motion within 60-day limit).

39 *In re* Hub of Military Circle, Inc. 13 B.R. 288 (Bankr. E.D. Va. 1981).

confirmation of the plan.[40] However, in order to provide for special circumstances, the Bankruptcy Code allows a party to such contract or lease to request that the court enter an order shortening the time and requiring the debtor-in-possession to decide by a specified date whether it will assume or reject the contract or lease.[41]

The thrust of the statutory provision is to allow a Chapter 11 debtor "reasonable time" within which to elect whether to assume or reject an executory contract or unexpired lease.[42] By setting confirmation as a deadline, the Bankruptcy Code gives the debtor maximum flexibility to determine how to restructure its business in a manner that enables it to be successful without further need for financial reorganization. This time allows the debtor an opportunity to evaluate its financial situation and to make a careful and informed judgment as to whether assumption or rejection is best for an effective reorganization.[43] In fact, some courts are hesitant to permit a debtor to assume its executory obligations too early because to do so would burden the estate with administrative priority claims should the Chapter 11 case fail and the obligations then be rejected.[44]

Although the court cannot order the debtor either to assume or reject an executory contract or unexpired lease, the court may, in its discretion, on motion of the non-debtor party or some other party-in-interest, set a date for assumption or rejection.[45] The standard considered by the court is one of what constitutes a "reasonable time," which depends on the circumstances of each case.[46] Factors to be considered by the court include the type of relationship or interest at issue, the balance of the harm to the parties, the good to be achieved for the estate and its creditors, and the safeguards afforded to the parties by the Bankruptcy Code.[47] The court is also likely to consider the complexity of the case as a factor in determining what length of time is reasonable.[48]

This balancing of the competing interests between the debtor and the nondebtor party gives the court significant flexibility to determine whether the debtor should be required to make its determination prior to the end of the case.

---

40 11 U.S.C. § 365(d)(2).

41 11 U.S.C. §365(d)(2); *In re* Hooker Invs., Inc., 145 B.R. 138 (Bankr. S.D.N.Y. 1992); *In re* Braniff, Inc., 118 B.R. 819 (Bankr. M.D. Fla. 1989).

42 *See* Theatre Holding Corp. v. Mauro, 681 F.2d 102, 105 (2d Cir. 1982); *In re* Lionel Corp., 23 B.R. 224, 225 (Bankr. S.D.N.Y. 1982); *In re* Dunes Casino Hotel, 63 B.R. 939, 949 (D.N.J. 1986). *See also* 2 Collier on Bankruptcy ¶ 365.03[1], at 36,566 (15th ed. 1991).

43 *In re* Whitcomb & Keller Mortgage Co., 715 F.2d 375, 379 (7th Cir. 1983).

44 Institutional Creditors of Continental Airlines, Inc. v. Continental Airlines, Inc. (*In re* Continental Airlines, Inc.), 780 F.2d 1223 (5th Cir. 1986); *In re* First S. Sav. Ass'n, 820 F.2d 700 (5th Cir. 1987).

45 11 U.S.C. § 365(d)(2).

46 Theatre Holding Corp. v. Mauro, 681 F.2d 102, 105 (2d Cir. 1982).

47 *In re* Lionel Corp., 23 B.R. 224, 225 (Bankr. S.D.N.Y. 1982) (quoting *In re* Midtown Skating Corp., 3 B.R. 194 (Bankr. S.D.N.Y. 1980)). *See also In re* Grant Broadcasting of Philadelphia, Inc., 71 B.R. 891, 902 (Bankr. E.D. Pa. 1987); *In re* Giant Mkts. Inc., 28 B.R. 335, 336 (Bankr. M.D. Pa. 1983).

48 *In re* GHR Energy Corp., 41 B.R. 668, 676 (Bankr. D. Mass. 1984).

§ 7.8 Time Limits for Nonresidential Real Property Leases

Unexpired leases of nonresidential real property, under which the debtor is the lessee, are deemed rejected 60 days after commencement of the case unless the court extends the time. Section 365(d)(4) of the Bankruptcy Code provides, in relevant part:

> if the [debtor-in-possession] does not assume or reject an unexpired lease of non-residential real property under which the debtor is the lessee within 60 days after the date of the order for relief, or within such additional time as the court, for cause, within such 60 day period, fixes, then such lease is deemed rejected, and the trustee shall immediately surrender such non-residential real property to the lessor.

In the nonresidential real property lease context, unlike all other executory obligations, the burden is on the debtor to move for an extension of time to weigh its options. Several questions with respect to timing are immediately apparent upon reading of the statutory language. These include:

1. Whether the filing of a motion tolls the automatic rejection or whether the debtor must actually receive an order tolling operation of the section
2. Whether subsequent extensions can be obtained by the debtor after the court fixes a new deadline
3. What constitutes cause for an extension required by the Bankruptcy Code.

It is clear from the case law that, at a minimum, the debtor must file its motion for an extension of time on or before the 60th day after commencement of the case.[49] The statutory language certainly implies that the mere filing of a motion for an extension of time prior to the expiration of the 60-day period does not toll the time obligations of the debtor; only the entry of an order by the court can extend the time past the 60-day limitation.[50] However, not all the cases agree that entry of an order is required. It is possible that such an order can properly be entered ex parte.[51]

A number of cases have considered the question of whether a bankruptcy court has the authority to grant a second extension under § 365(d)(4) more than 60 days after the order for relief. Most of the published decisions have concluded that, despite the necessity of straining the language of § 365(d)(4), the bankruptcy court

---

[49] *In re* Southwest Aircraft Serv., Inc., 831 F.2d 848 (9th Cir. 1987); *In re* By-Rite Distribution, Inc., 55 B.R. 740 (D. Utah 1985); *In re* Wedtech Corp., 72 B.R. 464, 468 (Bankr. S.D.N.Y. 1987).

[50] 11 U.S.C. § 365(d)(4); *In re* James Wilson Assocs., 965 F.2d 160 (7th Cir. 1992); *In re* Sonora Convalescent Hosp., Inc., 69 B.R. 134 (Bankr. E.D. Cal. 1986); *In re* House of Emeralds, Inc., 57 B.R. 31 (Bankr. D. Haw. 1985); *In re* House of Deals of Broward, Inc., 67 B.R. 23 (Bankr. E.D.N.Y. 1986).

[51] Chapman Inv. Assocs. v. American Healthcare Management, Inc. (*In re* American Healthcare Management, Inc.), 900 F.2d 827, 830 (5th Cir. 1990).

has the authority to grant multiple extensions.[52] In each of the published opinions the extension was granted prior to the expiration of any previously granted extension. Therefore, these opinions do not reach the question of whether the motion must be both filed and ruled on within the 60-day period.[53]

In considering whether to grant an extension, the court is required to find sufficient cause.[54] Some factors the court will consider are whether the leases are an important asset of the estate, whether the debtor needs the additional time to make an intelligent and informed decision, whether the debtor continues to make required postpetition payments to the lessor, the number of leases involved, the impact on the lessor of deferring the debtor's decision, and the complexity of the case.[55]

As a practical matter, in most small business bankruptcy cases, the debtor will probably know very early on whether it intends to assume or reject a nonresidential lease under which it is the lessee. This is likely to be a lease on the location from which the debtor conducts its manufacturing, retail, or wholesale activity.

§ 7.9 Practice Considerations

The debtor has unique leverage against the nondebtor party to an unexpired lease or executory contract. Creditors may view the continuation of the relationship with the debtor, even if on a reduced economic return, to be preferable to the loss of an ongoing stream of income and a low percentage return on a general unsecured claim. Therefore, the debtor's threat of rejecting a contract or lease may encourage the nondebtor party to renegotiate the economic terms of the agreement. The debtor may then either (1) assume the modified agreement and thereby have the modified terms approved by the bankruptcy court, or (2) reject the old agreement and immediately request authority to enter into the renegotiated relationship.

If the debtor has decided to reject the agreement, it should file a motion at the earliest opportunity, concurrently with the filing of the case, if at all possible, in order to minimize any possible continued postpetition expense burden on the estate caused by continued use of the nonresidential premises. Obtaining an early order from the bankruptcy court authorizing rejection is better than allowing rejection to take place

---

52 Legacy, Ltd. v. Channel Home Ctrs., Inc. (*In re* Channel Home Ctrs., Inc.), 989 F.2d 682, 687 (3d Cir. 1993) (multiple extensions permitted, even though literal reading of words indicates only one extension may be obtained); Chapman Inv. Assocs. v. American Healthcare Management, Inc. (*In re* American Healthcare Management, Inc.), 900 F.2d 827, 830 (5th Cir. 1990); *In re* Victoria Station, Inc., 875 F.2d 1380 (Bankr. 9th Cir. 1989) (cause must arise within 60-day period); *In re* Advanced Elecs., Inc., 108 B.R. 53 (Bankr. M.D. Pa. 1989). *Contra In re* Coastal Indus., Inc., 58 B.R. 48 (Bankr. N.J. 1986) (court must hear, determine, and grant any extension within 60 days of petition for relief).

53 *But see In re* Southwest Aircraft Servs., Inc., 831 F.2d 848 (9th Cir. 1987), *cert. denied,* 487 U.S. 1206 (1988) (initial extension requested prior to the expiration of the 60-day period but not ruled on until after the expiration of the 60-day period).

54 *In re* Muir Training Technologies, Inc., 120 B.R. 154 (Bankr. S.D. Cal. 1990).

55 *In re* Victoria Station, Inc., 88 B.R. 231 (Bankr. 9th Cir. 1988); *In re* Columbus One Parcel Serv., Inc., 138 B.R. 194 (Bankr. S.D. Ohio 1992).

by reason of the expiration of the 60-day period. Not only is there certainty and finality for all interested parties, but the cost to the estate of preparing a motion and any attendant hearing is likely to be less than the costs of continued use of the nonresidential property.

Decisions to assume should also be promptly exercised. If the debtor intends to continue its operations from the same location, there is no reason why a motion to assume its lease of nonresidential real property should not be filed very shortly after commencement of the case. The debtor should be absolutely sure that assumption is the right decision, however, because after a lease is assumed, a later breach will give rise to an administrative expense priority. See **§ 7.17.**

If the debtor cannot decide, prior to the filing of the petition for relief, whether its interests are best served by assumption or rejection, a motion requesting an extension of the 60-day period should be filed. In requesting additional time, counsel should consider requesting that the court extend the time to assume or reject until confirmation of the plan of reorganization unless the court enters a specific order, after notice and hearing, shortening the time. This type of request, if implemented by the court, may effectively reverse the burden and require the nondebtor landlord to take affirmative steps to shorten the time. It is likely that the court will grant such an order, especially if the request is coupled with the debtor's assurance, incorporated into the court order, that it will keep current on all postpetition rent and other payment obligations.

Landlords can also obtain some protection at this stage. First, landlords should insist that any request for an extension of time beyond the 60-day period be granted only on a showing that the debtor will ultimately be able to fulfill the requirements for assumption, most importantly the prompt cure of all past monetary defaults. The landlord should consider a request that the court require the debtor to reserve, escrow, or otherwise set aside the funds necessary to pay these sums. Second, the landlord should insist that the court order the debtor to keep all postpetition obligations current as required in §§ 365(d)(3) and 503(b)(1) of the Bankruptcy Code. The landlord should try to obtain drop dead language (see **Chapter 6**) in any order entered by the court, that is, the landlord should attempt to have the order provide for the automatic rejection of the nonresidential lease and immediate vacation of the premises by the debtor, without any further court action, if the debtor fails to keep its postpetition obligations current. This type of relief may well solve the problem of the Bankruptcy Code's failure, as noted in **§ 7.7,** to provide a specific remedy for a landlord if the debtor fails to timely perform its obligations. Finally, the landlord should be careful to reserve its rights to contest the debtor's request to assume the nonresidential lease and to have a say in the requirements of any such assumption.

In all of these areas, counsel for a landlord should pay very careful attention to the language of any order prepared for the court. It should be noted that even if the landlord is not successful in some or all of these requests, there is merit in taking an active and somewhat adversary role. This may counteract some of the advantage the debtor has in these matters, and the earlier the court is made aware of a landlord's concerns, the earlier it is likely to require the debtor to address them. **Chapter 8** examines these and other creditor strategies in greater detail.

§ 7.10 Sample Plan Provisions Regarding Executory Contracts

It is important that at the conclusion of the case the debtor and its counsel have accounted for each and every relationship of the debtor by having either assumed or rejected each relationship. This is especially important in the context of the Bankruptcy Code's requirement that assumption take place prior to confirmation of the plan. In addition, it is important to ensure that postconfirmation disagreements about the ongoing obligations of the debtor and the nondebtor third party are minimized.

Section 1123(b)(2) of the Bankruptcy Code specifically permits the plan of reorganization to address assumption or rejection of executory contracts or unexpired leases. The language of a plan of reorganization or confirmation order may provide for the:

1. Assumption of all contracts to which the debtor is a party which are not specifically rejected
2. Rejection of all contracts to which the debtor is a party which are not specifically assumed
3. Assumption or rejection of specific relationships
4. Assumption and assignment of specific relationships.

Including this language will require opposing parties to raise their objections to characterization of a contract or lease at the plan confirmation hearing and place the debtor in the best position for minimizing the likelihood of postconfirmation disputes.

Examples of plan language that can be modified to fit specific needs follow:

Alternativc 1

All executory contracts and unexpired leases shall be deemed assumed by the Debtor unless expressly rejected prior to the effective date, subject to a motion by the Debtor to reject filed on or before the effective date. All cure payments which may be required under § 365(b)(1) of the Bankruptcy Code in connection with such assumption shall be made on the effective date. In the event of a dispute regarding the amount of any such cure payments, the ability of the Debtor to provide adequate assurance of future performance, or any other matter relating to such assumption, the Debtor shall make such cure payments in accordance with final orders of the Bankruptcy Court.

Alternative 2

On the effective date, and to the extent permitted by applicable law, all executory contracts (including unexpired leases) of the Debtor will be assumed in accordance with the provisions of §§ 365 and 1123 of the Bankruptcy Code, excluding (a) any and all executory contracts that are the subject of separate motions filed pursuant to § 365 of the Bankruptcy Code by the Debtor prior to the commencement of the hearing on confirmation of the plan; (b) those contracts listed on any "Schedule of Rejected Executory Contracts" filed by the Debtor on or before entry of the confirmation order, all of which contracts shall be rejected pursuant to the provisions of §§ 365 and 1123 of the Bankruptcy Code; and (c) any and all such contracts rejected prior to entry of the confirmation order.

Alternative 3

Except with respect to contracts and leases previously assumed or rejected by the Debtors and approved by the court prior to the confirmation date, all other executory contracts of the Debtors and unexpired leases the Debtors entered into prior to the petition date which are not expressly assumed by the Debtors pursuant to application filed by Debtors on or before the confirmation date or not otherwise specifically treated in this plan or in the confirmation order shall be deemed to have been rejected by the Debtors on the confirmation date.

§ 7.11 Procedural Requirements for Assumption

The Bankruptcy Code makes it clear that in order for an assumption to be effective, it must be the subject of an order.[56] Federal Rule of Bankruptcy Procedure 6006 governs proceedings to assume, reject, or assign executory contracts or unexpired leases other than as part of a plan of reorganization. Rule 6006(a) states that the proceeding is governed by Rule 9014, which in turn directs that relief shall be requested by motion and that affected parties will be given reasonable notice and opportunity for a hearing. Rule 6006(c) requires that a hearing be set.

It has been held that the hearing referred to in Rule 6006(c) is intended to be a summary proceeding and not one involving lengthy discovery or an extended trial.[57] Other courts have held that at the hearing the court is authorized to consider the validity of the contracts before deciding whether to permit the debtor to assume the obligations.[58]

The bankruptcy court is to determine the propriety of a debtor's request to assume or reject an executory contract or unexpired lease by examining the relationships at issue, the surrounding circumstances, and the debtor's business judgment for its decision.[59] In applying the business judgment test to determine whether to permit the relief requested by the debtor, the court must consider the impact on the estate in general, not just the impact on general unsecured creditors.[60] The debtor bears the burden of proof on this issue.[61]

---

56 11 U.S.C. § 365(a).

57 Orion Pictures Corp. v. Showtime Networks, Inc. (*In re* Orion Pictures Corp.), 4 F.3d 1095, 1099 (2d Cir. 1993); *In re* Docktor Pet Ctr., Inc., 144 B.R. 14, 16 (Bankr. D. Mass. 1992).

58 *In re* National Sugar Ref. Co., 21 B.R. 196, 198 (Bankr. S.D.N.Y. 1982).

59 NLRB v. Bildisco & Bildisco, 465 U.S. 513 (1984); Orion Pictures Corp. v. Showtime Networks, Inc. (*In re* Orion Pictures Corp.), 4 F.3d 1095, 1099 (2d Cir. 1993).

60 *In re* Tilco, Inc., 558 F.2d 1369, 1372–73 (10th Cir. 1977); *In re* Sundial Asphalt Co., 147 B.R. 72 (E.D.N.Y. 1992); *In re* TS Indus., Inc., 117 B.R. 682, 685 (Bankr. D. Utah 1990).

61 *In re* Continental Country Club, Inc., 114 B.R. 73 (Bankr. M.D. Fla. 1970).

§ 7.12 Assumption of Obligations Not in Default

The Bankruptcy Code does not require any specific actions by a debtor prior to authorizing assumption of an executory contract or unexpired lease that is not in default.[62] It is important to note that a debtor is not in default on a contract or lease even if the contract or lease purports to define the filing of a bankruptcy petition as one of the nonmonetary defaults. These ipso facto clauses are specifically rendered unenforceable by §§ 365(b)(2) and 365(e)(1).

Upon the debtor's timely motion and a timely determination by the court that the debtor has exercised reasonable business judgment under the circumstances, a debtor is entitled to an order authorizing assumption of a executory contract or unexpired lease.[63] Again, counsel must pay close attention to obtaining the order authorizing assumption prior to the expiration of the 60-day time limit imposed on the assumption of an unexpired lease of nonresidential real property.

§ 7.13 Assumption of Obligations in Default

The provisions of the Bankruptcy Code set forth three criteria a debtor must meet as a prerequisite to its assumption of an obligation on which it is in default.[64] The debtor is required to promptly cure any existing default,[65] promptly compensate the nondebtor party for any actual pecuniary loss that resulted from the debtor's default,[66] and provide adequate assurances that the debtor will be able to satisfy its future performance obligations under the contract or lease at issue.[67] Each of these criteria is usually fact-specific to the individual case or relationship at issue.[68]

The Bankruptcy Code does not provide any direct guidance on how quickly the debtor must act in order to satisfy the "promptness" requirement of the cure and compensation conditions. The courts have looked at the facts and circumstances of each individual case (and even each contract within each case) to determine what is "prompt."[69] Under this fact-specific analysis, some courts have required immediate payment,[70] but another has permitted a cure that took three

---

62 *In re* Currivan's Chapel of the Sunset, 51 B.R. 217 (C.D. Cal. 1985) (if there has been no default, bankruptcy court could not impose conditions on assumption of lease by debtor).

63 NLRB v. Bildisco & Bildisco, 465 U.S. 513, 523, (1984) (refers to "traditional 'business judgment' standard"); *In re* TS Indus., Inc., 117 B.R. 682, 685 (Bankr. D. Utah 1990).

64 11 U.S.C. § 365(b)(1).

65 *Id.* § 365(b)(1)(A).

66 *Id.* § 365(b)(1)(B).

67 *Id.* § 365(b)(1)(C).

68 *In re* Greyhall Resources, Inc., 63 B.R. 382, 386–92 (Bankr. D. Colo. 1986).

69 *In re* Coors of N. Miss., Inc., 27 B.R. 918, 922 (Bankr. N.D. Miss. 1983).

70 *In re* R/P Int'l Technologies, Inc., 57 B.R. 869 (Bankr. S.D. Ohio 1985) ("forthwith" payment of arrearage); *In re* Lafayette Radio Elecs. Corp., 9 B.R. 993 (Bankr. E.D.N.Y. 1981).

years to complete.[71] Some cases hold that under any circumstances the cure must be completed prior to the confirmation of a plan of reorganization.[72] It is clear that the debtor does not necessarily have to tender payment of the default at the time of assumption,[73] nor does the cure necessarily require cash.[74] In order to establish adequate assurances that there will be a prompt cure of all lease defaults, the debtor must provide evidence that is not speculative and is sufficiently substantive for the court to conclude that the nondebtor party will actually receive the appropriate amounts.[75]

The courts have looked to the individual circumstances of each case to determine what types of actual pecuniary loss have resulted from a debtor's prepetition breach. In making the determination, the courts generally use a three-part test that requires the nondebtor party to establish that

1. The expenses were directly or indirectly related to the debtor's default
2. The expenses were necessary to cure the debtor's default, adequately protect the nondebtor party from further damages, or indemnify the nondebtor party against loss, and
3. The expenses were reasonable.[76]

Other courts have added a component that the expenses must be authorized by the lease or contract at issue.[77] Under § 365(b)(1)(B), courts have required debtors to compensate nondebtor parties for reasonable attorney's fees,[78] interest payments,[79] and late charges.[80]

Likewise, the facts and circumstances of each individual case will determine whether a debtor has provided adequate assurances with respect to its ability to perform its future obligations.[81] Certainly the debtor's financial condition and its prospects for reorganization will play a major role in determining what additional

---

71 *In re* Coors of N. Miss., Inc., 27 B.R. 918, 922 (Bankr. N.D. Miss. 1983).

72 *In re* Offices & Servs. of White Plains Plaza, Inc., 58 B.R. 441 (Bankr. S.D.N.Y. 1986).

73 *In re* Mako, 102 B.R. 818 (Bankr. E.D. Okla. 1988).

74 *In re* Carlisle Homes, Inc., 103 B.R. 524 (Bankr. D.N.J. 1988).

75 *In re* World Skating Ctr., Inc., 100 B.R. 147 (Bankr. D. Conn. 1989).

76 *In re* French, 131 B.R. 138 (Bankr. E.D. Mo. 1991); *In re* Westworld Community Healthcare, Inc., 95 B.R. 730 (Bankr. C.D. Cal. 1989).

77 *In re* F&N Acquisition Corp., 152 B.R. 304 (Bankr. W.D. Wash. 1993).

78 *Id. But see In re* Hillsborough Holdings Corp., 126 B.R. 895 (Bankr. M.D. Fla. 1991) (nondebtor party not entitled to payment of attorney's fees because parties' agreement did not so provide); *In re* Joshua Slocum, Ltd., 103 B.R. 601 (Bankr. E.D. Pa. 1989) (Bankruptcy Code does not create statutory right to recover attorney's fees in absence of agreement between parties).

79 *In re* Hillsborough Holdings Corp., 126 B.R. 895 (Bankr. M.D. Fla. 1991). *But see In re* Eagle Bus Mfg., Inc., 148 B.R. 481 (Bankr. S.D. Tex. 1992).

80 *In re* Joshua Slocum, Inc., 103 B.R. 601 (Bankr. E.D. Pa. 1989).

81 The Bankruptcy Code provides specific guidelines for adequate assurances in the context of shopping center leases, which can be applied as guidance in other circumstances. 11 U.S.C. § 365(b)(3). *See In re* Joshua Slocum, Inc., 922 F.2d 1081 (3d Cir. 1990).

actions are necessary to assure that the debtor can meet its financial obligations.[82] Advance payments of rent under a lease may constitute adequate assurances,[83] as will COD terms for a supply contract[84] or the posting of a surety bond.[85] Creative counsel can likely propose an adequate assurance that will satisfy the court so long as the assurance covers any possible exposure the nondebtor party may have for postpetition, preconversion damages should the case be converted to a liquidation proceeding.

§ 7.14 Assignment

Section 365(f) provides that a debtor may assign an executory contract or unexpired lease under certain conditions. Upon the valid assignment by the debtor of an executory contract or unexpired lease, the debtor's future liability on the assigned relationship is relieved.[86]

An assignment may only be made if the debtor has assumed the contract or lease at issue in accordance with the applicable provisions of § 365[87] and the nondebtor party is provided with adequate assurances of the assignee's future performance.[88] Unlike the other future performance provisions, adequate assurances are required regardless of whether there has been a default by the debtor on the contract or lease.[89]

Once an executory contract has been assigned, the assignee must be concerned with whether an appeal and subsequent reversal of the assignment can affect the transfer. Purchasers at sales authorized under § 363(b) and (c) and lenders who extend credit under § 364 receive statutory assurances that a subsequent reversal cannot affect the validity of the transaction,[90] but courts are split on whether an assignment pursuant to § 365 provides the same type of safe harbor to assignees.[91]

---

82 Richmond Leasing v. Capital Bank, 762 F.2d 1303, 1310 (5th Cir. 1985).

83 *In re* Westview 74th St. Drug Corp., 59 B.R. 747 (Bankr. S.D.N.Y. 1986); *In re* Hub of Military Circle, Inc., 19 B.R. 460 (Bankr. E.D. Va. 1982).

84 *In re* Docktor Pet Ctr. Inc., 144 B.R. 14 (Bankr. D. Mass. 1992).

85 *In re* Charrington Worldwide Enter., Inc., 110 B.R. 973 (M.D. Fla. 1990), *remanded* Airlines Reporting v. Charrington, 922 F.2d 847 (11th Cir. 1990).

86 11 U.S.C. § 365(k).

87 11 U.S.C. § 365(f)(2)(A).

88 *Id.* § 365(f)(2)(B).

89 *Id.*

90 11 U.S.C. §§ 363(m), 364(e).

91 *Compare In re* Stadium Management Corp., 895 F.2d 845 (1st Cir. 1990) (§ 363(m) safe harbor applicable to lease assignments), *with In re* Joshua Slocum Ltd., 922 F.2d 1081 (3d Cir. 1990).

§ 7.15 Prohibitions Against Assumption

The Bankruptcy Code has several sections that deal with prohibitions against assumption by a debtor of executory obligations. As was noted in **§ 7.12,** §§ 365(b)(2) and 365(e)(1) render ipso facto clauses unenforceable.[92] The two major categories of executory obligations that the Bankruptcy Code prohibits a debtor from assuming are those that state law prohibits assignment of[93] and those for loans or other financial accommodation.[94]

As with other provisions in the Bankruptcy Code, Congress has not provided a definition of "financial accommodation." In addition, the legislative history that states that the purpose of the section is to prevent a debtor from being able to "require" a nondebtor party to make "new advances of money" is of little assistance.[95]

Some courts have held that the determining factor in whether a contract is a financial accommodation is whether the central purpose is something other than to extend credit or cash to the debtor.[96] Under this analysis, it has been held that a debtor's agreement with a bank for servicing credit card sales is not a financial accommodation contract because the central purpose of the relationship is for the bank to provide services, that is, collect and remit, not make advances.[97] It has also been held that a lease commitment, even though it contains "incidental" financing aspects, is not a financial accommodation contract.[98]

There are cases that hold that a debtor may be able to assume a financial accommodation obligation if the nondebtor party consents to the assumption.[99] However, because the limitation on assumability is for the protection of all creditors of the estate and not just the putative lender, the agreement of the nondebtor lender to the assumption is not, in and of itself, sufficient.[100] A creditor can, however, be estopped from raising the financial accommodation objection.[101]

The largest category of contracts that are unassumable under the state law prohibition are those for "personal services." The literal language of the statute prevents a debtor from assuming a contract if state law would prevent the assignment of the

---

[92] *E.g., In re* Tom Stimus Chrysler-Plymouth, Inc., 134 B.R. 676 (Bankr. M.D. Fla. 1991); *In re* Braniff, Inc., 118 B.R. 819 (Bankr. M.D. Fla. 1989).

[93] 11 U.S.C. § 365(c)(1).

[94] *Id.* § 365(c)(2).

[95] H.R. Rep. No. 595, 95th Cong., 2d Sess. 348, *reprinted in* 1978 U.S.C.C.A.N. 5963, 6304.

[96] *In re* Thomas B. Hamilton Co., 115 B.R. 384, 387 (Bankr. N.D. Ga. 1990); *In re* Farrell, 79 B.R. 300 (Bankr. S.D. Ohio 1987).

[97] *In re* Thomas B. Hamilton Co., 115 B.R. 384, 387 (Bankr. N.D. Ga. 1990).

[98] *In re* Braniff, Inc., 118 B.R. 819, 845 (Bankr. M.D. Fla. 1989).

[99] *E.g., In re* Prime, Inc., 15 B.R. 216 (Bankr. W.D. Mo. 1981).

[100] *In re* Sun Runner Marine, Inc., 945 F.2d 1089 (9th Cir. 1991).

[101] *In re* Easebe Enters., Inc., 900 F.2d 1417 (9th Cir. 1990); *In re* TS Indus., Inc., 117 B.R. 682 (Bankr. D. Utah 1990) (prepetition workout agreement, even though one of financial accommodation, was assumable because it was entered into in anticipation of bankruptcy).

same contract.[102] The determination of whether an executory contract is one for personal services depends on the nature and subject matter of the contract, the surrounding circumstances, and the intention of the parties.[103] The determination is made according to applicable governing principles of state or federal law.[104] The thrust of the provision is to prevent the bankruptcy of an individual with special talents from permitting the debtor to assume and assign the relationship and thereby compel the nondebtor party to pay for and accept performance from someone else.[105] However, the literal reading would even prevent the debtor itself from assuming such a contract.[106]

State and federal statutes prohibiting assignment of specific kinds of contracts have been used to challenge assignability of contracts in bankruptcy cases. Types of contracts that have been challenged include defense department contracts,[107] housing authority servicing contracts,[108] and power supply contracts.[109]

§ 7.16 Partial Assumptions or Rejections

Recently, substantial litigation has occurred over whether a debtor may bifurcate a contract, that is, assume some parts and reject other parts.[110] The general rule is that a debtor may not assume only favorable parts of a contract but must assume the whole

---

[102] 11 U.S.C. § 365(c)(1).

[103] *In re* Fastrax, Inc., 129 B.R. 274 (Bankr. M.D. Fla. 1991).

[104] *In re* Wills Motors, Inc., 133 B.R. 303, *aff'd sub nom.* SAAB Cars USA, Inc. v. Wills Motors, Inc., 134 B.R. 124 (S.D.N.Y. 1991); *In re* Carlisle Homes, Inc., 103 B.R. 524 (Bankr. D.N.J. 1988).

[105] *In re* Ewing, 147 B.R. 970 (Bankr. D.N.M. 1992); *In re* Terrace Apartments, Ltd., 107 B.R. 382 (Bankr. N.D. Ga. 1989).

[106] *In re* West Elecs., Inc., 852 F.2d 79 (3d Cir. 1988); *In re* Carolina Parachute Corp., 108 B.R. 100 (N.D.N.C. 1989), *aff'd in part, vacated in part sub nom.* Department of Air Force v. Carolina Parachute Corp., 907 F.2d 1469 (4th Cir. 1990). *But see In re* Fastrax, Inc., 129 B.R. 274 (Bankr. M.D. Fla. 1991) (section only prevents assignment, not assumption by debtor); *In re* Cardinal Indus., Inc., 116 B.R. 964 (Bankr. S.D. Ohio 1990) (same).

[107] *In re* Carolina Parachute Corp., 108 B.R. 100 (N.D.N.C. 1989), *aff'd in part, vacated in part,* 907 F.2d 1469 (4th Cir. 1990) (Federal Nonassignment Act prohibits assignment and thus assumption).

[108] *In re* Commonwealth Mortgage Co., 149 B.R. 4 (Bankr. D. Mass. 1992) (Connecticut Housing Finance Authority regulations do not constitute "applicable law" preventing assumption).

[109] *In re* Nitec Paper Corp., 43 B.R. 492 (S.D.N.Y. 1984) (Federal Power Act and Niagara Redevelopment Act prevent assumption by debtor).

[110] An outstanding paper on these "cherry-picking" issues was presented by Leslie J. Polt of Smith, Somerville & Case at the October 1993 National Conference of Bankruptcy Judges. Polt, *"Cherry Picking" the Executory Contract,* ABA Section of Business Law, Comm. on Business Bankruptcy, Subcomm. on Executory Contracts (Oct. 20, 1993).

spectrum of duties, rights, obligations, and benefits.[111] However, courts have recognized that it may be possible for a single writing to actually contain more than one contract, each of which may be separately assumed or rejected.[112] Debtors are more frequently attempting to use this developing area of the law to escape arbitration clauses,[113] noncompete clauses,[114] franchise agreement/lease clauses,[115] and purchase contracts.[116]

§ 7.17 Consequences of Assumption

Once the court has entered an order authorizing and directing the debtor to assume an executory contract or unexpired lease, the debtor's obligations under the document become obligations of the estate as if the bankruptcy had never occurred.[117] Once a lease or executory contract has been assumed, the rights of the parties are governed by state law unless there are contrary provisions in the Bankruptcy Code.[118] In other words, any later breach of the relationship by the debtor will create an administrative expense priority.[119] As discussed in **§ 7.13,** if there was a prepetition breach by the debtor of its obligations under an unexpired lease or executory contract, the debtor is obligated to cure that breach as a precondition to assumption of the relationship. In the event that the cure was not cash in full at the time of the assumption, the remaining payments will also be entitled to administrative expense priority.

§ 7.18 Consequences of Rejection

Upon rejecting an executory contract, the debtor is relieved of all of its obligations under the contract.[120] The nondebtor party is entitled to pursue a remedy for breach of the rejected contract as if the breach occurred immediately prior to the filing of the petition.[121] Generally, this permits the nondebtor party to file a general unsecured

---

111 *In re* Royster Co., 137 B.R. 530 (Bankr. M.D. Fla. 1992); *In re* Three Star Telecast, Inc., 93 B.R. 310 (D.P.R. 1988); *In re* Patella Constr. Corp., 114 B.R. 53 (Bankr. D.N.J. 1990).

112 *In re* Holly's, Inc., 140 B.R. 643 (Bankr. W.D. Mich. 1992); *In re* Giesing, 96 B.R. 229 (Bankr. W.D. Mo. 1989).

113 *In re* Chorus Data Sys., Inc., 122 B.R. 845 (Bankr. D.N.H. 1990).

114 *In re* Hirschorn, 156 B.R. 379 (Bankr. E.D.N.Y. 1993).

115 *In re* Harrison, 117 B.R. 570 (Bankr. C.D. Cal. 1990).

116 *In re* Easthampton Sand & Gravel Co., 25 B.R. 193 (Bankr. E.D.N.Y. 1982).

117 *In re* Taylor, 130 B.R. 849 (Bankr. E.D. Ark. 1991); *In re* Airlift Int'l, Inc., 761 F.2d 1503 (11th Cir. 1985).

118 Wainer v. A.J. Equities, Ltd., 984 F.2d 679 (5th Cir. 1993).

119 *Id.;* R&O Elevator Co. v. Harmon, 93 B.R. 667 (D. Minn. 1988).

120 *In re* Don & Lin Trucking Co., 110 B.R. 562 (Bankr. N.D. Ala. 1990).

121 11 U.S.C. § 365(g)(1); *In re* Udell, 149 B.R. 898 (Bankr. N.D. Ind. 1992).

claim for damages which will in turn be accorded pro rata treatment with other general unsecured claims in any distribution of the estate's assets.[122] The amount of the claim will be the amount of damages to which the nondebtor party would have been entitled for breach under applicable state law.[123]

The nondebtor lessor of nonresidential real property is entitled to immediate surrender by the debtor of the property once the lease has been rejected.[124]

In cases involving unexpired leases of nonresidential real property, the Bankruptcy Code caps the amount of unsecured claim available to the nondebtor party as a result of a rejection by the debtor.[125] Under § 365(d)(3) of the Bankruptcy Code, a landlord is entitled to payment of all postpetition rent and, pursuant to § 365(g)(1) upon rejection of the lease, a prepetition breach and a general unsecured claim is created. However, § 502(b)(6) limits the amount of the landlord's general unsecured claim to the amount of the landlord's unpaid prepetition rents plus the greater of (a) the amount of rent for 15 percent of the remaining term of the lease, not to exceed three years, or (b) rent for one year without acceleration. When determining the value of "rent," it is proper to include not only the baseline rent but other monetary obligations of the tenant, such as utilities, insurance, property taxes, and common area maintenance charges.[126]

The proper way to apply these sections is for the landlord to compute its total damages suffered by breach of the lease under state law. In most circumstances, the total damages will equal the present value of the remaining rent minus the present value of the expected fair rental value for the remaining term of the lease. Any amount in this calculation that exceeds the cap established by § 502(b)(6) will be disallowed. Courts are split on whether postpetition payments received by the landlord, whether from the debtor or some third party, should be deducted from the maximum claim allowed under § 502(b)(6).[127]

---

[122] *In re* Statewide Oilfield Constr., Inc., 134 B.R. 399 (Bankr. E.D. Cal. 1991).

[123] *In re* Minges, 602 F.2d 38, 41 (2d Cir. 1979).

[124] 11 U.S.C. § 365(d)(4); *In re* U.S. Fax, Inc., 114 B.R. 70 (E.D. Pa. 1990).

[125] 11 U.S.C. § 502(b)(6).

[126] *In re* William Brittingham, Inc., 39 B.R. 575, 577 (Bankr. D. Del. 1984).

[127] *Compare In re* Conston Corp., 130 B.R. 449 (Bankr. E.D. Pa. 1991) (postpetition rent payments not deductible); *with In re* First Alliance Corp., 126 B.R. 589 (Bankr. S.D. Cal. 1991) (rent payments should be deducted).

CHAPTER 8

CREDITOR STRATEGIES IN SMALL BUSINESS BANKRUPTCIES

David A. Warfield

§ 8.1 Introduction

A creditor's perspective on a bankruptcy case depends entirely upon the type of credit extended to the debtor. An unsecured creditor's perspective is vastly different from that of a creditor with a security interest or lien on the debtor's property. A landlord's perspective is quite different still. This chapter addresses these different perspectives and discusses certain issues that are common to them.

The filing of a bankruptcy petition imposes a stay of most collection actions.[1] For the unsecured creditor, this means that all efforts to collect any indebtedness incurred by the debtor before the filing of a bankruptcy petition must stop immediately upon the filing of the petition. The creditor cannot commence or continue any litigation or offset any mutual obligations. The stay applies regardless of the creditor's knowledge or lack of knowledge of the filing of the case. Any individual injured by willful violation of the automatic stay may recover actual damages, including costs and attorney's fees and punitive damages.[2] Although there are some exceptions to the automatic stay, few if any of them apply to the typical commercial transaction.[3]

UNSECURED CREDITORS

§ 8.2 Doing Business with the Debtor

One of the most difficult questions facing an unsecured creditor in a Chapter 11 reorganization case is whether it should continue to do business with the debtor during the case. Although the day-to-day business of the debtor may appear unchanged, the filing of a bankruptcy petition completely changes the rules governing the debtor-creditor relationship.

A Chapter 11 debtor-in-possession may operate its business in the ordinary course without further order of the bankruptcy court.[4] Unlike in Chapter 7, no trustee is automatically appointed in a Chapter 11 case. The debtor remains in possession of its assets and continues to manage its financial affairs.[5] The same management that

---

1 *See* 11 U.S.C. § 362(a).

2 *See id.* § 362(h).

3 *See generally id.* § 362(b).

4 11 U.S.C. § 363(c)(1).

5 *Id.* §§ 1107, 1108.

presided over the company's descent into bankruptcy will normally preside over its attempts to reorganize. The prebankruptcy creditor may not even know a bankruptcy has been filed until it receives a notice from the bankruptcy court several days after the filing.

When it files a bankruptcy petition, the debtor is prohibited from paying any invoices related to prebankruptcy events, even if the payment under the invoice is not yet due at the time of the filing. Therefore, a creditor that carefully monitors its receivables may still find itself holding an unsecured claim in a bankruptcy case.

The typical knee-jerk reaction to a bankruptcy filing, particularly when the debtor has made repeated unfulfilled promises to pay, is simply to refuse to do business with the debtor after the bankruptcy filing. Although this reaction is undoubtedly the correct one at times, the creditor that simply refuses as a matter of course to do business with a company in bankruptcy is losing business unnecessarily.

The prebankruptcy creditor's most effective method of limiting its exposure to loss at the hands of a customer in bankruptcy is to cut off credit postbankruptcy. Nothing in the Bankruptcy Code prohibits or limits the right of a company doing business with a debtor to insist on cash in advance or cash on delivery for shipments made or services rendered after the filing.

Creditors must take care not to violate the automatic stay when doing business with the debtor during its Chapter 11 case. For example, the author is familiar with a creditor that held a substantial prepetition claim and continued to do business on a cash-in-advance basis with the debtor after the filing of the bankruptcy case. The creditor increased all of the prices it charged to the debtor by a fixed percentage, across-the-board basis on the day after the filing. The debtor thereafter sued the creditor and claimed that the price increase was a hidden attempt to collect the prepetition balance. The creditor was unable to show that it suffered a commensurate increase in the cost of its goods sold at the time it increased its prices, or that it had increased its prices to its nonbankrupt customers at the same time. The bankruptcy court eventually found in favor of the debtor and ordered the creditor to return to the estate the amount collected as a result of the price increase.

If a creditor decides to extend postpetition trade credit to a company in bankruptcy, the Bankruptcy Code offers some affirmative protection for the creditor. Section 364(a) states that the debtor may obtain unsecured credit in the ordinary course of business without order of the court. The party extending the unsecured credit receives a claim entitling it to administrative expense priority. This gives the claimant priority over all prepetition unsecured claims. An administrative expense claim does not give the claimant priority over prepetition secured claims, however.[6]

Although the phrase "administrative expense claim" sounds good, the postpetition creditor with an administrative claim is not necessarily assured of payment. Administrative claims are paid only after all secured claims are paid in full. Therefore, if there are no unencumbered assets in the bankruptcy estate and the value of the estate's assets is less than the amount of the secured claims, there may be no distribution to administrative claimants, including those who extended credit to a debtor-in-possession postpetition. Before extending unsecured trade credit to a Chapter 11 debtor, the creditor should investigate the debtor's balance sheet carefully.

---

[6] *See id.* § 503(b).

Other factors may affect the desirability of doing business with a debtor during its Chapter 11 case. Perhaps the most important challenge facing the Chapter 11 debtor is financing its business during the case. Postpetition financing is discussed at length in **Chapter 6.** A debtor that has promptly obtained the necessary court approval for use of cash collateral and/or for the borrowing of funds postpetition on a secured basis probably represents as good a credit risk for the unsecured supplier as many of its other customers. If the debtor has reached an agreement to finance its operations postpetition, trade vendors are often encouraged to extend trade credit because of the debtor's liquidity.

Many times a secured creditor with a security interest in the debtor's inventory will consent to the creation of a so-called trade lien in favor of the debtor's suppliers. The secured creditor with a lien on inventory consents to the debtor's granting a lien to suppliers on the products they supply. In other words, the supplier receives a lien akin to a purchase money security interest on the goods it sells the debtor.

If used correctly, this approach benefits all parties. The debtor uses the trade credit to alleviate cash flow problems. The secured lender reduces the amount of postpetition credit it must extend because the trade creditors also extend credit. Finally, the trade creditors receive collateral to secure the credit they extend.

In short, unsecured creditors should not simply refuse to do business with a Chapter 11 debtor. Creative legal thought and careful credit management enable the supplier of a debtor in bankruptcy to continue to make money even after the filing.

§ 8.3 Reclamation

One of the most important rights available to an unsecured creditor in a bankruptcy case is the right of reclamation. The reclaiming seller may be able to improve its position vis-à-vis general unsecured creditors if it successfully navigates the labyrinth of rules, under both the Uniform Commercial Code and the Bankruptcy Code, that govern reclamation claims.

Reclamation under the Uniform Commercial Code. The right of reclamation derives from § 2-702 of the Uniform Commercial Code. To meet the UCC's requirements for reclamation: (1) the buyer must receive the goods on credit; (2) the buyer must receive the goods while insolvent; (3) the seller must make demand for the goods "within ten days after receipt" by the buyer, unless the buyer makes a written misrepresentation of solvency within three months prior to delivery; (4) the goods must be identifiable or fungible with other goods of like kind; and (5) the buyer must remain in possession of the goods.

A reclamation demand should include a detailed description of the goods sold.[7] Under the UCC, the demand may be oral, but the Bankruptcy Code requires that the demand be in writing.[8] If the demand is in writing, the date of the dispatch of the demand is controlling so long as the demand was made in a commercially reasonable fashion.[9]

---

[7] *In re* Braniff, Inc., 113 B.R. 745, 752 (Bankr. M.D. Fla. 1990).

[8] 11 U.S.C. § 546(c)(1).

[9] *In re* Marin Motor Oil, Inc., 740 F.2d 220, 229 (3d Cir. 1984).

Reclamation under the Bankruptcy Code. A seller who makes a valid reclamation demand often fares better than one who does not, even if the buyer files bankruptcy. A reclaiming seller is not stayed by the filing of a bankruptcy petition from making a reclamation demand. Section 546(c) of the Bankruptcy Code preserves the UCC right of reclaiming sellers in a bankruptcy case. Section 546(c) does not expand the right of reclamation under the UCC. In fact, the Bankruptcy Code requires more than the UCC. The reclaiming seller in a bankruptcy case must prove each of the elements required by the UCC, plus: (1) that the goods were sold in the ordinary course of the seller's business; and (2) that the reclamation demand was made in writing.

Good-faith purchaser exception. A very significant exception to the right of reclamation under both the UCC and the Bankruptcy Code is the *good faith purchaser exception.* Section 2-702 of the UCC provides that the right of reclamation is subject to the rights of a "buyer in ordinary course or other good faith purchaser." Many courts have held that a lender with a security interest in the buyer's inventory is a good-faith purchaser. Therefore, under the majority rule, as between a reclaiming seller and an inventory financier with a valid security interest, the inventory financier will have a prior claim.[10]

Value of the right of reclamation. The reclaiming seller that satisfies all the technical requirements for asserting a reclamation claim still must assess the value of its reclamation claim. If there is no lien on the debtor's inventory, the reclamation claim has a value equal to the invoice amount of the goods sold. The bankruptcy court must either order the debtor to return the goods or grant the reclaiming seller one of the alternate remedies set forth in § 546(c): (1) a lien on assets of the estate, or (2) an administrative expense claim. These alternate remedies give the court the flexibility to permit the debtor to use the goods in the reorganization effort while preserving the value of the reclaiming seller's claim.[11] The alternate remedies also protect the reclaiming seller if the debtor sells the goods to be reclaimed.[12]

If there are prior liens on the debtor's inventory, the result is less clear. Some courts hold that the existence of a security interest on the debtor's inventory extinguishes the right to reclaim.[13] Other courts grant a reclaiming seller an administrative expense claim equal to the full value of the goods notwithstanding a lien.[14] The Eighth Circuit has taken the position that a reclaiming seller's rights are "subordinate or inferior to" the rights of the lienholder.[15] Under this view, if the lienholder is paid from the goods or their proceeds, the value of the reclamation claim is zero. If, on the other hand, the lienholder's claim is satisfied out of other sources, the reclamation claim has full value. This analysis is impossible until the lienholder's claim is paid or the lien in the inventory is released.

---

[10] *See, e.g., In re* Pester Ref. Co., 964 F.2d 842 (8th Cir. 1992).

[11] *Id.* at 847.

[12] *In re* Griffin Retreading Co., 795 F.2d 676, 679 (8th Cir. 1986).

[13] *See, e.g., In re* Shattuc Cable Corp., 138 B.R. 557 (Bankr. N.D. Ill. 1992).

[14] *See, e.g., In re* Marko Elecs., Inc., 145 B.R. 25 (Bankr. N.D. Ohio 1992).

[15] *In re* Pester Ref. Co., 964 F.2d 842 (8th Cir. 1992).

Notwithstanding the Eighth Circuit's approach, procedures for dealing with reclamation claims are generally developed in the early stages of most bankruptcy cases, particularly larger ones. Although prompt compliance with all reclamation requirements will seldom result in the return of the goods, a savvy creditor will monitor its customers carefully and make reclamation demands promptly. This careful attention to compliance with the reclamation rules will not guarantee payment, but it may improve the creditor's chances of being paid.

§ 8.4 Filing Proofs of Claim

The unsecured creditor bears the practical responsibility to monitor the bankruptcy case and to make certain that its rights to assert a claim in the case are properly preserved. When a debtor files a bankruptcy case, it must submit to the court a list of creditors with mailing addresses. That list of creditors, sometimes referred to as a *matrix,* is used to send notice to creditors of important dates in the case, including the final date on which to file proofs of claim. If the debtor fails to include the creditor on its matrix, a not uncommon occurrence among companies filing bankruptcy, the creditor will never receive notice. Although a creditor without notice may, as a legal matter, be able to assert good arguments that its late proof of claim should be accepted,[16] as a practical matter, its ability to share in a distribution may be impaired.

The need to file a proof of claim depends on the chapter of the Bankruptcy Code under which the debtor filed. In a Chapter 7 case, an unsecured creditor must always file a proof of claim if it hopes to share in the distribution. An official proof of claim form appears in **Figure 8–1.** In a Chapter 11 case, a creditor whose claim is listed by the debtor as undisputed, noncontingent, and liquidated need not file a proof of claim if it agrees with the amount listed by the debtor.[17]

If a creditor files a proof of claim, it should attach as much documentary proof of the claim as is practicable. Any interested party can file an objection to a proof of claim.[18] The claimant, the debtor, and the trustee must receive at least 30 days' notice of the initial setting of a hearing on a claim objection.[19]

§ 8.5 Serving on a Creditors' Committee

In the early stages of a Chapter 11 case, an unsecured creditor may receive an invitation to join the Official Unsecured Creditors' Committee (the committee). Section 1102(a)(1) of the Bankruptcy Code requires the U.S. Trustee to appoint a committee of creditors holding unsecured claims as soon as practicable after the filing of a Chapter 11 case. Ordinarily, the committee consists of creditors willing to serve who

---

16 Pioneer Inv. Serv. Co. v. Brunswick Assocs. Ltd. Partnership, ____ U.S. ____, 113 S. Ct. 1489 (1993).

17 11 U.S.C. § 1111(a).

18 *Id.* § 502(a).

19 Fed. R. Bankr. P. 3007.

Form 10. PROOF OF CLAIM

United States Bankruptcy Court | **PROOF OF CLAIM**

_______________ District of _______________

In re (Name of Debtor) | Case Number

NOTE This form should not be used to make a claim for an administrative expense arising after the commencement of the case A request for payment of an administrative expense may be filed pursuant to 11 U S C § 503

Name of Creditor
(The person or other entity to whom the debtor owes money or property)

☐ Check box if you are aware that anyone else has filed a proof of claim relating to your claim Attach copy or statement giving particulars

Name and Address Where Notices Should Be Sent

☐ Check box if you never received any notices from the bankruptcy court in this case

☐ Check box if this address differs from the address on the envelope sent to you by the court

Telephone No

THIS SPACE IS FOR COURT USE ONLY

ACCOUNT OR OTHER NUMBER BY WHICH CREDITOR IDENTIFIES DEBTOR

Check here if this claim ☐ replaces / ☐ amends } a previously filed claim dated ________

1 BASIS FOR CLAIM
- ☐ Goods sold
- ☐ Services performed
- ☐ Money loaned
- ☐ Personal injury/wrongful death
- ☐ Taxes
- ☐ Other (Describe briefly)

☐ Retiree benefits as defined in 11 U S C § 1114(a)
☐ Wages, salaries, and commissions (Fill out below)
Your social security number ________
Unpaid compensation performed
from ________ (date) to ________ (date)

2. DATE DEBT WAS INCURRED

3 IF COURT JUDGMENT, DATE OBTAINED

4 CLASSIFICATION OF CLAIM Under the Bankruptcy Code all claims are classified as one or more of the following (1) Unsecured nonpriority (2) Unsecured Priority (3) Secured It is possible for part of a claim to be in one category and part in another
CHECK THE APPROPRIATE BOX OR BOXES that best describe your claim and STATE THE AMOUNT OF THE CLAIM AT TIME CASE FILED

☐ SECURED CLAIM $ ________
Attach evidence of perfection of security interest
Brief Description of Collateral
☐ Real estate ☐ Motor Vehicle ☐ Other (Describe briefly)

Amount of arrearage and other charges at time case filed included in secured claim above
if any $ ________

☐ UNSECURED NONPRIORITY CLAIM $ ________
A claim is unsecured if there is no collateral or lien on property of the debtor securing the claim or to the extent that the value of such property is less than the amount of the claim

☐ UNSECURED PRIORITY CLAIM $ ________
Specify the priority of the claim
- ☐ Wages, salaries, or commissions (up to $2000, earned not more than 90 days before filing of the bankruptcy petition or cessation of the debtor's business, whichever is earlier)-11 U S C § 507(a)(3)
- ☐ Contributions to an employee benefit plan-11 U S C § 507(a)(4)
- ☐ Up to $900 of deposits toward purchase, lease, or rental of property or services for personal, family or household use-11 U S C § 507(a)(6)
- ☐ Taxes or penalties of governmental units-11 U S C § 507(a)(7)
- ☐ Other-Specify applicable paragraph of 11 U S C § 507(a) ________

5 TOTAL AMOUNT OF CLAIM AT TIME CASE FILED $ ________ (Unsecured) $ ________ (Secured) $ ________ Priority $ ________ (Total)

☐ Check this box if claim includes charges in addition to the principal amount of the claim Attach itemized statement of all additional charges

6 CREDITS AND SETOFFS The amount of all payments on this claim has been credited and deducted for the purpose of making this proof of claim In filing this claim, claimant has deducted all amounts that claimant owes to debtor

THIS SPACE IS FOR COURT USE ONLY

7 SUPPORTING DOCUMENTS Attach copies of supporting documents, such as promissory notes, purchase orders, invoices, itemized statements of running accounts, contracts, court judgments, or evidence of security interests If the documents are not available, explain If the documents are voluminous, attach a summary

8 TIME-STAMPED COPY To receive an acknowledgment of the filing of your claim, enclose a stamped, self-addressed envelope and copy of this proof of claim

Date	Sign and print the name and title, if any, of the creditor or other person authorized to file this claim (attach copy of power of attorney, if any)

Penalty for Presenting Fraudulent Claim Fine of up to $500 000 or imprisonment for up to 5 years, or both 18 U S C § § 152 and 3571

GRAHAM PIERCE LEGAL PRINTERS • PO BOX 1866 • FAIRVIEW HEIGHTS IL 62208

Figure 8–1. Official proof of claim form. Reprinted with the permission of Graham Pierce Legal Printers, P.O. Box 1866, Fairview Heights, IL 62208.

hold the seven largest unsecured claims against the debtor. In soliciting potential committee members, the U.S. Trustee uses the list of 20 largest unsecured creditors filed by the debtor.

The committee represents the interests of all unsecured creditors. Although individual unsecured creditors have the right to be heard on any issue in the Chapter 11 case,[20] the committee will speak for the entire unsecured creditor body. The Bankruptcy Court ordinarily gives great weight to the committee's position, because even in a small case the debtor may have dozens or perhaps even hundreds of unsecured creditors.

Although it represents the entire unsecured creditor body, it is a rare committee in which divergent interests are not represented. Some members may have reclamation claims; others may not. Some may have exposure on a preference claim and others may not. Some members may continue to do business with the debtor; others may have ceased doing business altogether with the debtor. The courts are split on whether a competitor of the debtor may serve on a committee.[21] Regardless of these individual interests, the committee members have a fiduciary duty to all other unsecured creditors.[22] Although divergent interests are almost inevitably present on any committee, a creditor that has its own agenda is well-advised to stay off a creditors' committee because of the fiduciary duty a committee member owes to all similarly situated creditors.

The committee plays a significant role in the Chapter 11 process. The committee investigates the acts, conduct, assets, liabilities, and financial condition of the debtor, the operation of the debtor's business, and the desirability of continuing the business.[23] The committee consults with the debtor-in-possession (or the trustee, if one has been appointed) regarding all issues concerning administration of the case.[24] The committee also plays a very vital role in formulating a plan of reorganization.[25] Normally, a committee formally supports or opposes a plan proposed by the debtor and makes a recommendation to its constituency on whether to accept or reject the plan. If the debtor loses its exclusive right to file a plan, the committee often prepares and files its own plan.

Service on a creditors' committee can be time-consuming. Although neither the Bankruptcy Code nor the Bankruptcy Rules presently provide that committee members can recoup out-of-pocket expenses incurred in connection with their duties from the estate, the courts normally approve reimbursement of expenses incurred in the performance of committee-related duties.[26] The committee can also hire professionals, such as lawyers and accountants, to assist in the performance of the committee's responsibilities.[27] The professionals are paid from the bankruptcy estate and not directly by the committee members.

---

[20] 11 U.S.C. § 1109(b).

[21] *Compare In re* Plant Specialties, Inc., 59 B.R. 1 (Bankr. W.D. La. 1986) (competitor may serve on creditors' committee) *with In re* Wilson Foods Corp., 31 B.R. 272 (Bankr. W.D. Okla. 1983) (competitor may not serve on creditors' committee).

[22] *In re* First RepublicBank Corp., 95 B.R. 58, 61 (Bankr. N.D. Tex. 1988).

[23] 11 U.S.C. § 1103(c)(2).

[24] *Id.* § 1103(c)(1).

[25] *Id.* § 1103(c)(3).

[26] *In re* George Worthington Co., 921 F.2d 626 (6th Cir. 1990).

[27] 11 U.S.C. § 1103(a).

SECURED CREDITORS

§ 8.6 Secured Creditor's Perspective

The creditor who bargained for and received a lien or security interest on the debtor's property faces special issues in bankruptcy. The appropriate strategy for a secured creditor depends on the facts and circumstances of the case and particularly on the nature of the creditor's collateral. A creditor with a lien on real estate is in a different posture than a creditor with a security interest in inventory and accounts receivable. A creditor with a lien on property that is appreciating is in a quite different position than a creditor with a lien on property that is depreciating.

When a debtor files bankruptcy, a secured creditor should ask itself two questions: (1) what will I do with my collateral if I get it back?, and (2) is the value of my collateral likely to increase or decrease during the pendency of the bankruptcy case? If the collateral is easily salable and the expenses of liquidation are not prohibitive, the secured creditor may wish to seek relief from the automatic stay and foreclose. If the collateral would decline in value if the creditor had to liquidate it on a forced basis, the creditor may wish to work with the debtor to permit it to reorganize or at least sell the business as a going concern. In either event, the creditor should insist that its interest in the debtor's property be adequately protected during the pendency of the case. **Chapter 5** examines adequate protection in detail. Analysis of the secured creditor's collateral position is absolutely crucial to developing the correct bankruptcy strategy.

One of the most common secured creditor strategies in a bankruptcy case is to file a motion for relief from the automatic stay. If the court grants the secured creditor relief from the stay, the creditor and the debtor return to the legal relationship that existed between them before the filing.[28] After the stay has been lifted, the creditor must comply with any applicable nonbankruptcy law in order to foreclose or repossess its collateral.

§ 8.7 Relief from Stay for Cause

The Bankruptcy Code sets forth two separate standards for relief from the stay. The first standard, contained in § 362(d)(1), provides that the bankruptcy court can grant a creditor relief from the automatic stay "for cause, including the lack of adequate protection of an interest in property."

Bad-faith filing. One example of relief from the stay for cause is the so-called bad-faith filing. Courts have granted creditors relief from the stay when the debtor filed the case merely to delay a collection action with no intent or ability to reorganize.[29]

---

[28] *See In re* Kahihikolo, 807 F.2d 1540, 1542 (11th Cir. 1987) (citing *In re* Winslow, 39 B.R. 869, 871 (Bankr. M.D. Ga. 1984)).

[29] *See generally In re* Albany Partners, Ltd., 749 F.2d 670, 674 (11th Cir. 1984); *In re* Little Creek Dev. Co., 779 F.2d 1068, 1071–73 (5th Cir. 1986); *In re* MGN Co. III, 116 B.R. 654 (Bankr. S.D. Ind. 1989).

Many of these cases have arisen in the context of the so-called single asset case, usually a corporation or partnership that owns a single piece of real estate. The courts have often granted the creditor relief from the stay (or, in some cases, dismissal of the entire bankruptcy case) when several of the following factors were present:

1. The debtor owns only one primary asset, which asset is encumbered by a secured creditor's lien
2. The debtor employs an insignificant number of noninsider employees
3. The debtor generates insignificant cash flow
4. The debtor lacks available sources of income to sustain a reorganization plan and/or make adequate protection payments
5. The debtor has few unsecured creditors, with relatively small claims
6. The debtor's primary asset has been posted for foreclosure
7. Bankruptcy offers the only possibility for forestalling loss of the asset.[30]

New debtor. Another ground for relief from the stay for cause is the so-called new debtor syndrome. If property was transferred to a new entity on the eve of foreclosure and the new entity thereafter files bankruptcy, courts have generally granted creditors relief from the automatic stay (or dismissal, see § **8.19**) for cause.[31]

Pending litigation. Courts sometimes rely on the for-cause standard in granting relief from the stay to parties that are involved in litigation with a debtor at the time of filing. This is especially true if the subject matter of the litigation is covered by insurance so that the estate does not suffer any defense costs. Relief from the stay to pursue pending litigation is usually accompanied by a proviso in the order that the relief shall be limited to liquidation of the claim and that the creditor is precluded from executing on any assets of the estate to satisfy the judgment without first obtaining leave of the court.[32] A sample motion for relief to pursue pending litigation appears in § **8.8.**

Lack of adequate protection. The only example of cause explicitly set forth in the statute is lack of adequate protection.[33] Conceptually, adequate protection means that the creditor's interest in the collateral should not deteriorate during the pendency of the case. In other words, a snapshot of the creditor's collateral position is taken as of the date of filing, and the creditor is entitled to maintain that position throughout the case. Adequate protection is an interim remedy designed to protect the creditor while the debtor enjoys the benefits of the automatic stay. When the automatic stay with respect to a particular piece of property is terminated for any reason, the debtor's obligation to provide adequate protection is also terminated. Specific aspects of adequate protection are addressed in **Chapter 5.** A sample motion for relief from stay or adequate protection appears in § **8.8.**

---

30 *In re* Lindbergh Plaza Assoc., L.P., 115 B.R. 202, 206 (Bankr. E.D. Mo. 1990).

31 *See, e.g., In re* Thirtieth Place, 30 B.R. 503 (Bankr. 9th Cir. 1983).

32 *See In re* Curtis, 40 B.R. 795, 802–03 (Bankr. D. Utah 1984).

33 11 U.S.C. § 362(d)(1). See **Ch. 5** for a detailed discussion of the law of relief from the stay to allow litigation to continue in another forum.

§ 8.8 Form: Motion for Relief from Automatic Stay or for Adequate Protection

FORM 8–1
MOTION FOR RELIEF FROM STAY

Comes now [Creditor], by and through its undersigned counsel, and for its Motion for relief from the automatic stay or, in the alternative, for adequate protection states as follows:

I. JURISDICTION

I. This Court has jurisdiction over this matter pursuant to 28 U.S.C. §§ 157 and 1334 and Rule [Rule number] of the Local Rules for the United States District Court for the [ ] District of [ ]. This is a core proceeding pursuant to 28 U.S.C. § 157(b)(2)(G).

II. PARTIES

II. Creditor is a corporation authorized to do business in the state of [state name].

III. [Debtor] filed a voluntary petition for relief under Chapter [chapter number] of the Bankruptcy Code on [date] (the petition date). [Insert name of trustee if one has been appointed.]

III. RELIEF FROM THE AUTOMATIC STAY

IV. On [date], Debtor executed and delivered to Creditor a [name of document] whereby, inter alia, Debtor granted to Creditor a security interest in all of Debtor's right, title, and interest in and to all [describe collateral] and the proceeds thereof (the collateral) to secure all of Debtor's obligations to Creditor under the [agreement]. A true and genuine photocopy of the [agreement] is attached hereto as Exhibit A and incorporated herein by reference.

V. As of the petition date, Debtor was indebted to Creditor under the [agreement] in the amount of approximately $[debt], plus accruing interest, costs, expenses, and fees of collection (the indebtedness).

VI. Creditor's interests in the collateral have been properly perfected by the filing of Uniform Commercial Code financing statements with the offices and in the indexes noted thereon (the filings). True and correct copies of the filings are attached hereto as Exhibit B and incorporated herein by this reference.

VII. As a result of the foregoing, Creditor holds a valid, perfected, first priority lien and security interest in the collateral to secure repayment of the indebtedness.

VIII. Creditor's interests in the collateral are not adequately protected. The Debtor and/or the Trustee do not enjoy equity in the collateral, and the collateral is not necessary for an effective reorganization.

IX. Sufficient factual and legal cause exists for the relief requested herein under either Section 362(d)(1) or (2).

WHEREFORE, Creditor respectfully requests this Court to enter its order:

(a) granting Creditor relief from the automatic stay, thereby allowing Creditor to exercise its rights and remedies as a secured creditor;

(b) directing that the Debtor and/or Trustee surrender immediate possession of the collateral to Creditor;

(c) stating that no part of the costs of this proceeding be charged against Creditor or against the collateral;

(d) authorizing Creditor to apply the proceeds from any sale of the collateral, plus attorney's fees and expenses incurred to the date of such sale, to its claim, and ordering that Creditor's claim be allowed against Debtor in the amount of any deficiencies; and

(e) granting Creditor such other and further relief as may be necessary to protect its interests in the collateral.

IV. ALTERNATIVE REQUEST FOR ADEQUATE PROTECTION

X. Creditor hereby restates and realleges each and every allegation contained in paragraphs 1 through 9 of this Motion and incorporates the same herein by reference.

XI. Pursuant to 11 U.S.C. § 362(d), this Court may refuse to grant Creditor relief from the automatic stay only if Creditor is provided adequate protection that will result in the realization by the Creditor of the indubitable equivalent of the Creditor's interests in the collateral on the petition date.

XII. The Debtor [Trustee] continues to maintain possession of the collateral.

XIII. The collateral is subject to substantial decline in value by the mere passage of time.

XIV. Realization of the indubitable equivalent of Creditor's interests in the collateral requires that this Court order that the Debtor preserve and adequately protect the collateral.

WHEREFORE, in the alternative, Creditor respectfully requests that this Court enter an order providing Creditor with adequate protection sufficient to insure the indubitable equivalent of Creditor's interests in the collateral, which adequate protection shall include, but not be limited to, an order of this Court requiring that

(a) the Debtor and/or Trustee pay to Creditor such amounts and take such other steps as will adequately protect Creditor against the decline in value of the collateral during the pendency of the automatic stay;

(b) the Debtor and\or Trustee shall cooperate and provide assistance to enable Creditor to inspect the collateral and the Debtor's books and records at any time and from to time to time as Creditor shall reasonably elect to ensure compliance with this Court's order; and

(c) if the Debtor and\or Trustee fails to comply with respect to any order of this Court relating to the collateral, Creditor shall immediately have all the rights and remedies granted to it by its [Contract] and such other and further relief as will provide Creditor with the indubitable equivalent of its interests in the collateral.

[Signature]

§ 8.9 Form: Motion for Relief from Stay to Pursue Pending Litigation

FORM 8–2 MOTION FOR RELIEF FROM STAY TO PURSUE PENDING LITIGATION

Comes now [Movant] (Movant), by and through its undersigned counsel, and for its Motion for relief from the automatic stay to pursue pending litigation states as follows:

I. JURISDICTION

I. This Court has jurisdiction over this matter pursuant to 28 U.S.C. §§ 157 and 1334 and Rule [rule number] of the Local Rules for the United States District Court for the ______ District of ________. This is a core proceeding pursuant to 28 U.S.C. § 157(b)(2)(G).

II. PARTIES

II. Movant is a corporation authorized to do business in the state of [state name].

III. [Debtor] (the Debtor) filed a voluntary petition for relief under Chapter [chapter number] of the Bankruptcy Code on [date] (the petition date). [Insert name of trustee if one has been appointed]

III. FACTS

IV. Prior to the petition date, Movant and Debtor were parties to certain litigation styled [caption] pending in the [court information] Court, case no. [case number] (the pending litigation).

V. [Describe the nature of the pending litigation, including the sort of claim being asserted against the debtor, whether the debtor has insurance for the claim, and the status of the lawsuit.]

VI. Courts have traditionally lifted the automatic stay and permitted pending litigation to conclude in other forums. It is often "appropriate to permit proceedings to continue in their place of origin when no great prejudice to the bankruptcy estate would result, in order to leave the parties in their chosen forum and to relieve the bankruptcy court from many duties that may be handled elsewhere." H.R. Rep. No. 595, 95th Cong., 2d Sess. 341 (1978), S. Rep. No. 989, 95th Cong., 2d Sess. 50 (1978), reprinted in 1978 U.S.C.C.A.N. 5836, 6297. The stay should be modified to permit the continuance of a civil suit if no great prejudice to either the estate or the debtor results, and if the hardship to the plaintiff by continuance of the stay outweighs the hardship to the debtor by a modification of the stay. In re Turner, 55 B.R. 498, 502 (Bankr. N.D. Ohio 1985).

VII. In assessing whether the party wishing to receive relief from the automatic stay has met its burden, the courts have examined the following twelve factors:

(a) whether the relief will result in a partial or complete resolution of the issues;

(b) the lack of any connection with or interference with the case;

(c) whether the foreign proceeding involves the debtor as a fiduciary;

(d) whether a specialized tribunal has been established to hear the particular cause of action and that tribunal has the expertise to hear such cases;

(e) whether the debtor's insurance carrier has assumed full financial responsibility for defending the litigation;

(f) whether the action essentially involves third parties and the debtor functions only as a bailee or conduit for the goods or proceeds in question;

(g) whether the litigation in another forum would prejudice the interests of other creditors, the creditors' committee, and other interested parties;

(h) whether the judgment claim arising from the foreign action is subject to equitable subordination under Section 510(c);

(i) the interests of judicial economy and the expeditious and economical determination of litigation for the parties;

(j) whether the foreign proceedings have progressed to the point where the parties are prepared for trial; and

(k) the impact of the stay on the parties and the "balance of hurt."

In re Curtis, 40 B.R. 795, 802–3 (Bankr. D. Utah 1984) (cited in In re CLC of America, Inc., 68 B.R. 512, 513–14 (Bankr. E.D. Mo. 1986)).

VIII. [Analyze the facts and apply them to the law set forth above.]

IX. Movant acknowledges that it will not seek to enforce any judgment against Debtor or its assets without further order of this Court.

WHEREFORE, Movant respectfully requests that this Court enter its order granting relief from the automatic stay so that Movant may proceed against Debtor in the pending litigation, and for such other and further relief as is just and equitable.

[Signature]

§ 8.10 Relief from Stay for Lack of Equity

Section 362(d)(2) provides a second ground for relief from the stay. This section states that the automatic stay should be lifted with respect to property of the estate if: (1) the debtor does not have equity in such property, and (2) such property is not necessary for an effective reorganization. In determining the equity issue, most courts hold that the amounts of all liens on the property should be considered, not just the movant's liens.[34] The burden of proof on the equity issue rests with the movant.[35]

Once the movant shows the debtor lacks equity in the property, the debtor must then establish that the collateral is "necessary to an effective reorganization." The emphasis is on the word "effective." The Supreme Court has said:

---

[34] Stewart v. Gurley, 745 F.2d 1194, 1195 (9th Cir. 1984); *In re* Louden, 69 B.R. 723, 725 (Bankr. E.D. Mo. 1987).

[35] *See* 11 U.S.C. § 362(g).

> this requires . . . not merely a showing that if there is conceivably to be an effective reorganization, the property will be needed for it, but that the property is essential for an effective reorganization *that is in prospect.*[36]

Therefore, relief from stay hearings have become mini-feasibility hearings with testimony about the likelihood of possible reorganizations.

In any hearing for relief from the stay under § 362(d), the valuation testimony is critical. The creditor should be careful about the valuation testimony presented at the relief from stay hearing. The creditor in a relief from stay hearing usually contends that the value of the collateral is as low as possible. If the debtor survives the relief from stay motion, however, and proposes a plan, the creditor contends that the value of the collateral is as high as possible to limit the debtor's ability to write down the amount of the creditor's secured claim.[37] Although § 506(a) of the Bankruptcy Code provides that value for one purpose is not necessarily the same as value for another purpose, the creditor may not be able to contend credibly that the same collateral should be given different values at different stages in the same case. Valuation is discussed in detail in **Chapter 11.**

§ 8.11 Relief from Stay Procedures

To obtain relief from the automatic stay, the creditor must file a motion. A motion for relief from the stay is not governed by the rules governing adversary proceedings; instead, it is governed by Bankruptcy Rule 9014. This rule incorporates most, but not all, of the Federal Rules of Civil Procedure. Service of the motion may be by first class mail.[38] At a minimum, the creditor should serve the debtor, the debtor's counsel, counsel for any official committees appointed in the case, and the Office of the U.S. Trustee.[39]

Section 362(e) of the Bankruptcy Code sets forth certain time requirements. The court must hold at least a preliminary hearing within 30 days of the filing of the motion, and a final hearing must be commenced within 30 days after the conclusion of the preliminary hearing.[40] Some courts forego the preliminary hearing and proceed directly to the final hearing stage. Other courts construe any motion that seeks relief in addition to modification of the automatic stay, such as adequate protection, as constituting the movant's waiver of the 30-day rule. Creditors are well advised to be fully cognizant of local practice in this area before filing a motion.

Section 362(f) of the Bankruptcy Code provides that a creditor may receive relief from the automatic stay on an expedited basis under certain conditions. If the creditor can demonstrate that relief is "necessary to prevent irreparable damage to the interest of an entity in property" and that "such interest will suffer such damage

---

36 United Sav. Ass'n v. Timbers of Inwood Forest Assocs., Ltd., 484 U.S. 365 (1987) (emphasis added). More on the legal rules in this area can be found in **Ch. 5.**

37 11 U.S.C. § 1129(b)(2)(A).

38 Fed. R. Bankr. P. 9014.

39 Fed. R. Bankr. P. 9013.

40 11 U.S.C. § 362(e).

before there is an opportunity for notice and a hearing," the court may grant expedited relief without notice to the debtor.

§ 8.12 Strategies for Creditors in Relief from Stay Litigation

Review of validity and perfection of liens. Before commencing any litigation for relief from the stay with respect to property of the estate, the creditor should be absolutely comfortable with the validity and perfection of its lien or security interest on the debtor's property. Before filing a motion for relief from the stay, the creditor should review carefully all promissory notes, security agreements, mortgages, or deeds of trust to make certain that its lien or security interest is valid under state law. The creditor should also review the perfection of its lien or security interest. If the creditor does have lien validity or perfection problems, the wise course is generally to keep a low profile in the bankruptcy case and hope that the problems are not noticed.

Early request for relief from stay. The creditor should also consider carefully the stage of the case before filing its relief from stay motion. In the typical Chapter 11 case, the creditor's chance for success in lift-stay litigation increases over time. Most courts are willing to give the debtor a chance to reorganize and will be very reluctant to lift the automatic stay in the early stages of the case.

The creditor may nevertheless be well served by filing a relief from stay motion very early in the case. Filing a motion forces the debtor to provide adequate protection to the creditor. Motions for relief from the automatic stay are almost always coupled with alternative requests for adequate protection. A sample motion for relief from the automatic stay or, in the alternative, for adequate protection appears in **§ 8.9.**

Agreed order for adequate protection. The savvy creditor may file a motion for relief from the automatic stay in the early stages of the case, even though the prospects for success are slim, solely in order to arrive at an agreed adequate protection order with the debtor. This agreed order usually provides that the creditor is adequately protected through periodic cash payments, replacement liens, or some other method. Agreed orders of this type also normally provide that the debtor must insure and maintain the collateral.

The most attractive provision for creditors in these types of agreed orders is the so-called drop dead clause. These clauses provide that, upon the debtor's default under the terms of the agreed order, the secured creditor is entitled to relief from the automatic stay on an expedited basis. These sorts of orders are consistent with the typical bankruptcy court's view that a debtor ought to be afforded an opportunity to reorganize so long as it remains current on its postpetition obligations, including its obligations to provide adequate protection to secured creditors.

Protection of cash collateral. A creditor with a security interest in inventory, accounts receivable, or other assets that are typically consumed in the ordinary course of the debtor's business face special problems in a Chapter 11 reorganization case. Because the debtor uses this sort of collateral in the day-to-day operation of its business during the Chapter 11 proceeding, the secured creditor should move promptly, usually within a day or two after filing, to protect its interest.

Collateral of this sort normally constitutes *cash collateral* within the meaning of § 363(a) of the Bankruptcy Code. A debtor may not use cash collateral in which a creditor holds an interest unless the creditor consents to the use or the court enters an order, after notice and a hearing, authorizing such use.[41] The secured creditor with an interest in cash collateral is entitled to adequate protection of its interest in the cash collateral used by the debtor.[42] Adequate protection of this sort of collateral almost always includes a replacement lien on collateral of the same sort generated by the debtor after the date of filing. This is necessary because § 552 of the Bankruptcy Code limits a secured creditor's interest in property acquired by the debtor after commencement of the case, absent a court order to the contrary. Postpetition financing and cash collateral issues are discussed in more detail in **Chapters 6** and **3,** respectively.

NONDEBTOR PARTY TO UNEXPIRED LEASE OR EXECUTORY CONTRACT

§ 8.13 Assumption or Rejection of Unexpired Leases or Executory Contracts

What if one of the parties to an unexpired lease or other executory contract files bankruptcy? Section 365 of the Bankruptcy Code sets forth a number of very detailed rules governing unexpired leases and executory contracts in bankruptcy proceedings. This issue is also discussed at greater length in **Chapter 7.**

Unexpired leases and executory contracts in general. One of the most fundamental rights available to a bankruptcy trustee or debtor-in-possession is the right to reject burdensome unexpired leases and executory contracts. Through this power, the bankruptcy estate can rid itself of unprofitable leases and contracts. The nondebtor party to a rejected lease or contract is limited to asserting a claim for damages against the estate, as set forth below. Although the courts have not been entirely consistent in articulating the applicable standard for assumption or rejection of an unexpired lease or executory contract, the most common standard applied is business judgment.[43]

Time deadlines for rejection or acceptance. The Bankruptcy Code contains strict time deadlines for the acceptance or rejection of an unexpired lease or an executory contract. Refer to **Chapter 7** for a detailed discussion of this issue.

---

[41] *See id.* § 363(c)(2).

[42] *See id.* § 363(e).

[43] *In re* TS Indus., Inc., 117 B.R. 682, 685 (Bankr. D. Utah 1990).

Rejection of lease or contract. If the estate rejects an unexpired lease or an executory contract, the Bankruptcy Code deems a breach of the lease or contract to have occurred immediately before the date of the bankruptcy filing.[44] The effect of the breach is to enable the nondebtor party to assert a claim against the estate under § 502 of the Bankruptcy Code. The nondebtor party must prove the damages were incurred as a result of the breach. The claim for rejection damages is a general unsecured claim. A claim for damages as a result of the rejection of an unexpired lease of real property is severely limited by § 502(b)(6).[45]

Assumption of lease or contract. In order to assume an unexpired lease or executory contract, the trustee or debtor-in-possession must: (1) promptly cure most existing defaults; (2) compensate the nondebtor party for any actual pecuniary loss resulting from such default; and (3) provide adequate assurance of future performance under such contract or lease.[46] Notwithstanding the requirement of prompt cure of defaults, a trustee or debtor-in-possession need not cure any so-called bankruptcy termination default. Many leases and executory contracts contain language that defines the filing of a bankruptcy petition as a default under the underlying document. Section 365(b)(2) renders such so-called ipso facto clauses generally unenforceable in bankruptcy proceedings.

A very important right of the nondebtor party to an unexpired lease or executory contract is the right to insist on adequate assurance of future performance as a condition to assumption of the lease or contract. In determining whether the requirement has been met, the courts look at whether a deposit has been made, at the financial resources of the assignee of the debtor or assignor, and at the past payment record.[47]

§ 8.14 Assignment of Unexpired Leases or Executory Contracts

Another significant right afforded to trustees and debtors-in-possession is the right to assign an executory contract or unexpired lease, even if the underlying contract or lease prohibits or conditions assignment. Many times, one of the most valuable assets available to a bankruptcy estate is a lease or contract at below-market rates. The estate can assign its interest in a below-market lease, for example, to a third party in exchange for a cash payment. So long as the requirements for assumption are met, the estate can assign such a lease or contract to a third party previously unknown to the nondebtor party to the contract or lease. Assignment to the third party relieves the estate of any further liability to the nondebtor party for any breach of such lease or contract that occurs after the date of such assignment.[48]

---

[44] 11 U.S.C. § 365(g).

[45] See **Ch. 7** for a detailed discussion of § 502(b)(6).

[46] 11 U.S.C. § 365(b)(1).

[47] *In re* Westview 74th St. Drug Corp., 59 B.R. 747 (Bankr. S.D.N.Y. 1986).

[48] 11 U.S.C. § 365(k).

§ 8.15 Special Provisions

In recent years, numerous special interest groups have persuaded Congress to enact special rules governing leases and contracts. These special rules are detailed and beyond the scope of this work. Suffice it to say, however, that a party to any of the sorts of leases or contracts described below should consult § 365 to ascertain various additional rules governing such leases or contracts:

1. Leases of real property in shopping centers
2. Leases of real property where the debtor is an affected air carrier
3. Leases or contracts involving timeshare interests in timeshare plans
4. Executory contracts under which the debtor is a licensor of a right to intellectual property
5. Executory contracts involving the commitment to replenish or maintain capital of a insured depository institution.

§ 8.16 Strategies for Nondebtor Party to Unexpired Lease or Executory Contract

Encouraging assumption. In evaluating potential strategies, the nondebtor party to an unexpired lease or executory contract must first examine its economic alternatives. If the nondebtor party cannot re-let the premises or find a substitute party for the contract on terms as favorable as the original lease or contract, that party does not have a great incentive to force a rejection of the lease or contract. The nondebtor party would be better served by working with the estate to see that the lease or contract is eventually assumed. The nondebtor party in these circumstances will merely monitor the proceedings to ensure that its position does not change or deteriorate during the pendency of the case. The nondebtor party to an unexpired lease of nonresidential real property should insist that it continue to receive rent while the estate evaluates whether to assume or reject the lease.

Resisting assumption. If the nondebtor party believes that it can find a substitute tenant for the lease or party for the executory contract, it should be more aggressive. This nondebtor party can file a motion to compel assumption or rejection of the lease or contract. If granted, it forces the estate to make a decision on the lease or contract sooner than it would otherwise have to. A nondebtor party can also resist assumption of the lease or contract on the grounds that the § 365(b)(1) requirements for assumption have not been met. Provisions of the lease or contract not related to rent are often fertile grounds in this regard. If, for example, the debtor committed waste on real property subject to an unexpired lease, the nondebtor party may argue that repair of the waste is a prerequisite to a prompt cure and, therefore, to assumption.

Objecting to assignment. Regardless of the nondebtor party's economic situation, the nondebtor party to a lease or contract that has been assumed and assigned should examine the proposed assignee very carefully. Although the typical assignee has greater financial wherewithal than the debtor, the nondebtor party should look at the assignee's financial health. If it does not appear that the proposed assignee can make the rent payments, the nondebtor party should object. If the proposed assignee is a "shell" corporation with few assets, the nondebtor may wish to insist on the guaranty of a more substantial corporate affiliate as a condition to assumption and assignment. If the nondebtor party would require a deposit from the assignee absent bankruptcy, it should insist on such a deposit as a condition of assignment.[49] If the proposed assignment involves the lease of real property in a shopping center, the lessor should insist that the special requirements for assumption of a shopping center lease are met.[50]

MISCELLANEOUS CREDITOR STRATEGIES

§ 8.17 Strategies for Creditors when Debtor Proposes a Plan of Reorganization

Exclusivity. The debtor enjoys the exclusive right to propose and file a Chapter 11 plan of reorganization for 120 days after entry of the order for relief.[51] If the plan is timely filed, the debtor has another 60 days to obtain confirmation of the plan. The court can shorten or lengthen the debtor's exclusive period to submit a plan for cause.[52] If the debtor loses the exclusive right to file a plan, any party in interest, including a creditor, may file a plan.[53] Creditor plans are briefly discussed in **§ 8.21.**

Exclusivity is a significant bargaining chip. While the debtor enjoys exclusivity it controls the reorganization process. An aggressive creditor will wish to either move to shorten exclusivity[54] or oppose the debtor's efforts to extend exclusivity.[55] The value to the creditor of this strategy is more apparent at the negotiating table than in the courtroom. A debtor without the exclusive right to file a plan is much easier to deal with than one who still enjoys exclusivity because the threat of a creditor's plan, usually to liquidate the debtor, underlies the negotiations.

Disclosure statement. A plan proponent must prepare a disclosure statement to accompany the plan. The disclosure statement is similar to a prospectus in a securities offering. The disclosure statement should provide information that would "enable a hypothetical reasonable investor . . . to make an informed judgment about the plan."[56]

---

[49] 11 U.S.C. § 365(l).

[50] *See id.* § 365(b)(3).

[51] 11 U.S.C. § 1121(b).

[52] *Id.* § 1121(d).

[53] *Id.* § 1121(c).

[54] *See In re* Crescent Beach, Inc., 22 B.R. 155 (Bankr. D. Me. 1982); *In re* Public Serv. Co., 88 B.R. 521 (Bankr. D.N.H. 1988).

[55] *In re* Southwest Oil Co., 84 B.R. 448, 451 (Bankr. W.D. Tex. 1987).

[56] 11 U.S.C. § 1125(a).

Before the debtor, or any other plan proponent, may use a disclosure statement to solicit votes on a plan, the disclosure statement must be approved by the bankruptcy court.[57] In order to start the plan process, the plan proponent must file a proposed disclosure statement with the court. The court sets a hearing to consider the adequacy of the disclosure statement on not less than 25 days' notice to creditors and interested parties.[58] Objections to the proposed disclosure statement may be filed.

Although creditors often object to the disclosure statement, the author believes those objections are usually a waste of time. Most disclosure statement objections are directed to the confirmability of the plan rather than the adequacy of the disclosure statement. Although some courts will withhold approval of a disclosure statement if the plan is clearly unconfirmable,[59] objections that concern the plan are inappropriate at the disclosure statement stage. In a smaller case, most parties know how they are going to vote regardless of the disclosure statement's content. Armed with the knowledge that no one is likely to rely on the disclosure statement in determining how to cast a ballot, savvy debtor's counsel will readily agree to include in the disclosure statement almost anything the creditor requests in its objection to the disclosure statement. In summary, the creditor should carefully consider its ultimate objective before devoting much time to objecting to the proposed disclosure statement.

Objecting to the plan. Once the disclosure statement has been approved, the plan proponent solicits votes on its plan. The plan, disclosure statement, and a ballot will be mailed to all those entitled to vote on the plan.[60] In addition to voting to reject the plan, an unhappy creditor may object to confirmation. An objection to confirmation contends that one or more of the Bankruptcy Code's criteria for confirmation, set forth in § 1129(a), has not been satisfied. A creditor who opposes confirmation of the plan should not only vote to reject the plan but should also file a separate objection to confirmation.

Although § 1129(a) sets out 13 separate criteria for confirmation, creditors should pay particular attention to two of the criteria. The first is the so-called best interest of creditors test set forth in § 1129(a)(7). The test is quite simple: the plan must provide more to each nonassenting creditor than it would receive in a Chapter 7 liquidation. Every Chapter 11 plan will be measured against a hypothetical liquidation under Chapter 7.[61]

The feasibility test contained in § 1129(a)(11) is the second particularly important criterion for confirmation. The statute provides that confirmation of the plan

---

57 11 U.S.C. § 1125(b).

58 Fed. R. Bankr. P. 3017(a).

59 *In re* Spanish Lake Assocs., 92 B.R. 875, 877 (Bankr. E.D. Mo. 1988); *In re* Pecht, 57 B.R. 137 (Bankr. E.D. Va. 1986).

60 Certain creditors may not be entitled to vote on the plan. An unimpaired creditor, that is, one whose claim is completely unaffected by the plan, will be deemed to have accepted the plan. 11 U.S.C. § 1126(f). Similarly, a creditor or other party who receives nothing under the plan is deemed to have rejected the plan. *Id.* § 1126(g).

61 *See* Cieri, Oyer & Birnbryer, *The Long and Winding Road: The Standards to Confirm a Plan of Reorganization under Chapter 11 of the Bankruptcy Code (Part I)*, 3 J. Bankr. L. & Prac. 3, 53–57 (1993).

should not "likely be followed by the liquidation, or the need for further financial reorganization, of the debtor, or any successor to the debtor under the plan."[62] The debtor must demonstrate that the reorganized debtor will be able to make plan payments and otherwise satisfy its obligations under the plan.

Although the burden of showing compliance with § 1129(a) lies with the plan proponent, the objecting creditor should have its own evidence that demonstrates that the plan proponent cannot meet its burden. This will require, at a minimum, valuation and financial testimony.

§ 8.18 —Section 1111(b) Election

Section 1111(b) is probably the single most difficult and most misunderstood section in the entire Bankruptcy Code. An undersecured creditor with a lien on property that is likely to appreciate in value should seriously consider making the § 1111(b) election.

Although a detailed discussion of § 1111(b) is beyond the scope of this work, a brief review of the circumstances that gave rise to passage of § 1111(b) is necessary for even a rudimentary understanding. Section 1111(b) legislatively overruled the decision under the old Bankruptcy Act in *Great National Life Insurance Co. v. Pine Gate Associates, Ltd.*[63] Pine Gate Associates owned an apartment complex. The secured creditor held a claim against Pine Gate secured by a lien on the apartment complex. The creditor's claim was nonrecourse, that is, the creditor did not have recourse against the debtor for any deficiency claim. The apartment complex was worth substantially less than the outstanding indebtedness. Pine Gate filed bankruptcy and proposed a plan in which the creditor was paid cash in an amount equal to the value of the apartment complex. Because the creditor's claim was nonrecourse, Pine Gate's plan did not propose to pay the creditor anything on account of the deficiency. The bankruptcy court confirmed the plan over the vigorous objection of the secured creditor.

The court's holding in *Pine Gate* gave debtors a powerful new weapon. A debtor could file bankruptcy when property values were low, propose a plan that reduced the secured creditor's claim to the value of the collateral, and preserve to itself any future appreciation in the value of the collateral. The debtor could, for example, confirm a plan that "wrote down" the amount of the secured creditor's claim to the value of its collateral. If the collateral appreciated in value in the years after confirmation of the plan, the debtor could sell the property, satisfy the creditor's lien by paying the lower amount, and pocket all the postconfirmation appreciation.

Secured creditors were outraged by the *Pine Gate* decision and lobbied Congress for a change in the law when the Bankruptcy Code was adopted in 1978. Congress included § 1111(b) in direct response to *Pine Gate.*

Section 1111(b) addresses the *Pine Gate* problem in two ways. First, § 1111(b) provides that nonrecourse creditors have recourse after the bankruptcy filing unless the creditor affirmatively elects to the contrary. This means that a nonrecourse

---

[62] 11 U.S.C. § 1129(a)(11).

[63] 2 Bankr. Ct. Dec. (CRR) 1478 (Bankr. N.D. Ga. 1976).

creditor with a claim of $10 million secured by a lien on property worth $6 million has two claims: (1) a secured claim equal to the value of its collateral, or $6 million; and (2) an unsecured claim equal to the deficiency, or $4 million.

Under § 1111(b), the creditor retains an unsecured claim for any deficiency, so the creditor retains great influence on the structure of any plan. The undersecured creditor's deficiency claim is often the largest single unsecured claim, and usually controls the entire unsecured class.[64] If the unsecured class votes to reject the plan, all classes junior to the unsecured creditors, for example, the shareholders or partners of the debtor, may not retain any interest in the debtor.[65] As a practical matter, this means that the debtor must propose a plan that satisfies the undersecured creditors.

Section 1111(b) protects secured creditors in a second way. The creditor can make an election at any time prior to the hearing on the disclosure statement[66] to forego its right to have recourse against the debtor. This means that the creditor will not have an unsecured deficiency claim and will give up much of its leverage in the formulation of the debtor's plan. If the creditor makes the election, however, the creditor retains a secured claim for the full amount of its debt, not just the value of the collateral. This permits the creditor to participate in any appreciation in the value of its collateral after the confirmation of the debtor's plan. Section 1111(b), read in conjunction with § 1129, also mandates that the plan pay to a creditor that elects under § 1111(b) a stream of payments equal at least to the total amount of the claim with a present value equal to at least the value of the collateral at the time of confirmation of the plan.

Although the operation of § 1111(b) can be quite confusing, the general guidelines are quite simple. An oversecured creditor, i.e. a creditor that holds collateral worth more than the amount of its claim, should not concern itself with § 1111(b) at all. An undersecured creditor, i.e., a creditor that holds collateral worth less than the amount of its claim, should seriously consider making the § 1111(b) election only when it seems likely that the collateral held by the creditor will appreciate in value after confirmation of the plan.[67]

§ 8.19 Conversion or Dismissal of Case

In a Chapter 11 reorganization case, the creditor may wish to file a motion to convert the case to one under Chapter 7 or dismiss the case altogether. Section 1112(b) of

---

[64] See **Ch. 15** for a discussion of the rules governing the acceptance or rejection of the plan by a class of creditors. *See also In re* Greystone III Joint Venture, 102 B.R. 560 (Bankr. W.D. Tex.), *aff'd,* 127 B.R. 138 (W.D. Tex. 1990), *rev'd,* 948 F.2d 134 (5th Cir. 1991). Although the bankruptcy court's holding was eventually reversed by the Fifth Circuit, the bankruptcy court's opinion remains one of the most cogent explanations of § 1111(b) and its impact on the plan process.

[65] This is the so-called *absolute priority rule.* See **Ch. 16** for a discussion of the new value exception to the absolute priority rule.

[66] Fed. R. Bankr. P. 3014.

[67] For a more thorough discussion of § 1111(b), See Pusateri, Swartz & Shaiken, *Section 1111(b) of the Bankruptcy Code: How Much Does the Debtor Have to Pay and When Should the Creditor Elect?*, 58 Am. Bankr. L.J. 129 (1984).

the Bankruptcy Code governs the dismissal or conversion of a Chapter 11 case. Section 1112(b)(2) provides that the court:

> may convert a case under [Chapter 11] to a case under Chapter 7. . . or may dismiss a case under [Chapter 11], whichever is in the best interest of creditors and the estate, for cause, including —
>
> (1) continuing loss to or diminution of the estate and absence of a reasonable likelihood of rehabilitation;
>
> (2) inability to effectuate a plan;
>
> (3) unreasonable delay by the debtor that is prejudicial to creditors;
>
> (4) failure to propose a plan under section 1121 . . . within any time fixed by the court;
>
> (5) denial of confirmation of every proposed plan and denial of a request made for additional time for filing another plan or a modification of a plan;
>
> (6) revocation of an order of confirmation under section 1144 . . . and denial of confirmation of another plan or a modified plan under section 1129 . . .;
>
> (7) inability to effectuate substantial consummation of a confirmed plan;
>
> (8) material default by the debtor with respect to a confirmed plan;
>
> (9) termination of a plan by reason of the occurrence of a condition specified in the plan; or
>
> (10) nonpayment of any fees or charges required under chapter 123 of title 28.

The list of grounds for dismissal or conversion in § 1112(b) is not all-inclusive. For example, courts have often dismissed reorganization cases when the case was filed in bad faith. See **§ 8.7,** and **Chapter 17,** on dismissal of a case postconfirmation. Existence of one or more of the grounds does not require the court to dismiss or convert the case; the bankruptcy court retains broad discretion.

The creditor should weigh a number of factors when considering whether to move for dismissal or conversion of a Chapter 11 case. Unless the creditor can demonstrate that the case was filed in bad faith, the court is unlikely to dismiss or convert a Chapter 11 case in its early stages. Absent bad faith, most courts will give the debtor an opportunity to reorganize and will likely not dismiss or convert a case during the debtor's exclusive period to file a plan.

Once the creditor decides to move for the dismissal or conversion of case, the next decision is which of the two forms of relief—dismissal or conversion—the creditor should pursue. Many creditors move for dismissal simply because the automatic stay is no longer in effect if the case is dismissed. In the author's opinion, however, conversion of the case to one under Chapter 7 is normally the better strategy for the creditor.

There are several advantages from the creditor's perspective to converting the case. For example, if the case is converted, lien and preference avoidance causes of action are preserved, that is, the Chapter 7 bankruptcy trustee will have the right to pursue fraudulent conveyances, preferences, and other causes of action. Of course, if the creditor is a potential defendant in such an action, it may prefer to see the case dismissed. If the case is converted, the creditor's ability to examine the debtor under Bankruptcy Rule 2004 is preserved. This can be used to investigate the existence of hidden assets. As mentioned in **§ 8.14,** one of the more valuable assets in many bankruptcy estates is the estate's interest in a below-market value lease; if the case is converted, that asset can be assumed and assigned to a third party and the proceeds of the sale distributed to creditors.

§ 8.20 Appointment of Trustee or Examiner

A creditor in a Chapter 11 case may also move for the appointment of a Chapter 11 trustee or an examiner. Although the debtor normally remains in possession of its assets and may continue to operate its business under Chapter 11, the Bankruptcy Code provides that the court may appoint a trustee to perform most of the functions of a debtor in a Chapter 11 case. If a trustee is appointed in a Chapter 11 case, the debtor no longer is a debtor-in-possession and the day-to-day authority to operate the business rests with the trustee, not the debtor. The debtor is not completely disenfranchised, however. It may still propose a plan and may appear and be heard on any issue in the case.

Section 1104(a) provides that the court may appoint a trustee (1) "for cause, including fraud, dishonesty, incompetence, or gross mismanagement of the affairs of the debtor by current management, either before or after the commencement of the case," or (2) "if such appointment is in the interest of creditors, any equity security holders, and other interests of the estate." The movant must show that cause exists to justify the appointment of a trustee by clear and convincing evidence. There is a strong presumption that the debtor should remain in possession. The mere fact that present management made business mistakes that led to the company's financial distress is not sufficient to justify appointment of a trustee.[68]

The creditor should consider moving for the appointment of a trustee if the current management has demonstrated itself to be particularly dishonest or incompetent and the creditor's best interest is served by maintaining the going concern value of the business. Appointment of a trustee terminates the debtor's exclusive right to propose a plan.[69] If the creditor is convinced that its best hope for recovery is upon a prompt liquidation, the creditor will probably wish to move for conversion or dismissal of the case instead of appointment of a trustee.

The Bankruptcy Code also permits the appointment of an examiner. Section 1104(b) provides that an examiner may be appointed "to conduct such an investigation of the debtor as is appropriate, including an investigation of any allegations of fraud, dishonesty, incompetence, misconduct, mismanagement, or irregularity in the management of the affairs of the debtor of or by current or former management of the debtor." Appointment of an examiner is often the result of a heavily contested motion to appoint a trustee. The examiner normally submits a written report to the parties and to the court concerning the subject matter of the investigation.

---

[68] *See generally In re* St. Louis Globe-Democrat, Inc., 63 B.R. 131, 138 (Bankr. E.D. Mo. 1985) ("It is reasonable to assume that the majority of businesses that arrive in Chapter 11 have exercised a certain degree of incompetence or mismanagement").

[69] *See* 11 U.S.C. § 1121(c)(1).

§ 8.21 Proposing a Creditor's Plan

Creditors often overlook another strategy: filing a creditor's plan. Once the debtor's exclusive right to file a plan has lapsed or been terminated, the creditor is free to file its own plan. Although this strategy is time consuming and expensive, many creditors have used it to achieve favorable results. A creditor's plan is considered in the same fashion as the debtor's plan and is subject to all of the same confirmation requirements. A creditor interested in proposing its own plan should review **Chapters 14** and **15** of this book carefully.

CHAPTER 9

ASSET SALES IN CHAPTER 11 BANKRUPTCY CASES

Honorable David A. Scholl

§ 9.1 General Role of Asset Sales in Reorganization

Most bankruptcy cases feature sales of at least some of the debtor's assets. Indeed, in a Chapter 7 case, the ultimate goal is to sell all of the debtor's assets as quickly as possible. Many small business cases either begin as Chapter 7 cases or end as Chapter 7 cases when reorganization efforts are frustrated. However, most debtors filing Chapter 11 cases intend, though often with false hope, to reorganize under Chapter 11 and survive.

There is an occasional Chapter 11 case that anticipates, from the outset, a liquidation or sale of all of the debtor's assets. Although the Code appears to contemplate these Chapter 11 cases,[1] at least one court has held that cases that intend to feature "liquidating plans" from the outset cannot be maintained under Chapter 11.[2] However, even in a case in which the debtor seeks to avoid complete liquidation, as opposed to contemplating it from the beginning, it is very likely that sales of certain

[1] *See* 11 U.S.C. §§ 1123(a)(5)(B), (D); 1123(b)(4).

[2] *See In re* Lyons Transp. Lines, Inc., 123 B.R. 526, 530–31 (Bankr. W.D. Pa. 1991).

assets will be a part of the reorganization. Downsizing and liquidation of the least profitable aspects of a debtor's business are often necessary to allow the more profitable core of a business to continue to exist and prosper.

§ 9.2 Statutory Framework

The Bankruptcy Code section that specifically authorizes asset sales of property of a debtor's estate is 11 U.S.C. § 363. However, that section also addresses the "use" and "lease" of property, and therefore the provisions relating specifically to sales are included in most, but not all, of the subsections of that section.[3] Many of these subsections[4] address the problems arising in sales of property owned jointly with a spouse or former spouse and are applicable only to cases of individual debtors who have such property.

The most important of the provisions of § 363 relating to sales, for purposes of this chapter, is § 363(b)(1), which, very simply and succinctly, provides that "[t]he trustee, after notice and a hearing, may use, sell, or lease, other than in the ordinary course of business, property of the estate."

One ambiguity arising from the language of § 363(b) is the meaning of the phrase "other than in the ordinary course of business." "Notice and a hearing" is not required if the sale is in the debtor's ordinary course of business, such as a debtor's normal sales to its customers.[5] However, what are referred to in § 363(b) as asset sales are, by definition, not within the ordinary course of a debtor's business. Therefore, any sales of assets by a debtor whose business is other than sales are almost certainly within the scope of § 363(b)(1).[6] Also, a sale of any assets other than a debtor's products, or even a relatively large sale of those products by a debtor-seller of goods, also may be deemed to be within the scope of § 363(b)(1).

§ 9.3 Notice and a Hearing in Bankruptcy Sales

There is good reason for debtor's counsel to approach asset sales cautiously and to read § 363(b)(1) as broadly as possible. If a sale is effected without the requisite notice and a hearing, as noted in **§ 9.6,** the consequences can be disastrous. Not only can the sale be attacked and undone, but also the debtor may be on its way to making a record for the unwanted appointment of a trustee under 11 U.S.C. § 1104(a)(1) or for denial of confirmation of the plan under 11 U.S.C. § 1129(a)(2).[7] The confidence

---

[3] 11 U.S.C. § 363(b), (d), (e), (f), (g), (h), (i), (j), (k), (m), (n).

[4] *E.g.*, § 363(g), (h), (i), (j).

[5] 11 U.S.C. § 363(c)(1). *See In re* Dant & Russell, Inc., 853 F.2d 700, 703–06 (9th Cir. 1988).

[6] *See, e.g., In re* Selgar Realty Corp., 85 B.R. 235, 240–41 (Bankr. E.D.N.Y. 1988) (sale of properties by debtor who was in the business of renting those properties was not in the debtor's ordinary course of business).

[7] *See, e.g., In re* Brookfield Clothes, Inc., 31 B.R. 978, 985 (S.D.N.Y. 1983); and *In re* Sir Julian, Inc., 95 B.R. 851, 852 (Bankr. S.D. Fla. 1989).

of the court in the debtor may be permanently destroyed if the court senses that the debtor tried to sell its assets, particularly to insiders or parties preselected by the debtor, without giving interested parties or the court any prior notice.

On the other hand, if the sale process follows § 363(b)(1), the sale may well be preserved under § 363(m), which provides that "reversal or modification on appeal of an authorization under subsection (b) . . . does not affect the validity of a sale . . . under such authorization to an entity that purchased . . . such property in good faith."[8] Therefore, there is no reason not to provide "notice and a hearing" to all interested parties prior to a sale of assets in any but the clearest instance of a transaction that is in every way both ordinary and in the course of the debtor's business.

The typical motivation for failing to provide "notice and a hearing" to other interested parties of an asset sale is concern over the cost of mailing notice and a necessity of requiring the appearance of the debtor's principals or counsel at a hearing, which can also be costly. These concerns are not usually warranted. A request to limit notice can be made to the court and will nearly always be granted, limiting the mailing costs. Also, the phrase "notice and a hearing" does not contemplate an actual hearing if there is no objection to the motion.[9] Usually no objection will be filed and no actual hearing will be necessary if the sale involves modest assets or is not controversial. As a result, notice should be supplied to interested parties of every asset sale except those most obviously in the ordinary course of business.

§ 9.4 Suggested Procedures to Sell Assets under 11 U.S.C. § 363(b)

Although the use of § 363(b) as opposed to the plan confirmation process for effecting sales of a debtor's property is criticized in §§ **9.5** and **9.6,** this is not to say that § 363(b) should not be utilized when it is appropriate to do so. It can and should be utilized for sale of assets that do not constitute a substantial portion of the debtor's assets, which can in no sense be viewed as a de facto plan of reorganization. Also, there are instances when all or a substantial portion of a debtor's assets will indeed be wasted or subject to substantial depreciation if a sale is delayed until confirmation. Typical scenarios in which such a situation may be found to exist are when a business is suffering great losses as long as it remains in business, requiring immediate action if the business is to remain active and be sold as a going concern. Often, the timing of a sale is driven by an advantage in effecting an immediate sale due to the seasonal nature of a business. These factors are often so apparent and so strong that all of the interested parties agree that a § 363(b) sale should occur, and even the U.S. Trustee, which often opposes all § 363(b) sales of a substantial portion of a debtor's assets, will be reduced to "taking no position" on the matter.

Determining the procedures to be utilized in a sale process should be resolved prior to the sale and often presents a difficult problem. The process should always allow for interested buyers to outbid even a proposed buyer who has entered into a

[8] *See, e.g.,* Willemain v. Kivitz, 764 F.2d 1019, 1023–24 (4th Cir. 1985); and *In re* Gilchrist, 891 F.2d 559, 560–61 (5th Cir. 1990).

[9] 11 U.S.C. § 102(1).

pre-sale Agreement of Sale with the debtor. Often, a proposed buyer insists on a topping fee, break-up fee, right of first refusal, or other prioritized treatment to guard against the prospect that it will be used as a "stalking horse" for other prospective bidders. Whether such fees work to the advantage of the debtor is somewhat controversial, and they should carefully be limited by measuring the actual benefit realized by the debtor from the proposed buyer's actions.[10] However, on other occasions there is no preselected proposed buyer, and the assets are offered for sale in a (hopefully) competitive auction setting.

In either case, it is wise for the debtor to prepare a motion seeking court approval of the procedures to be utilized prior to the sale. This motion can address precisely what is being sold and the status of related matters, such as executory contracts to be assumed or assigned; describe the increments of bidding and other procedures for the sale; describe the finality or nonfinality of the bid process; and, what is often crucially important, establish the deposit to be required and maximum time that can elapse before the sale must be closed. It may be necessary to have prospective bidders meet some financial qualification test before being allowed to participate as well.[11] An example of such a procedural motion is presented in **§ 9.7.** This motion obviously includes many averments that relate to specific issues in the case, which involved a rather large business; however, the motion is comprehensive and may give counsel for a small business some ideas that can be transposed to small business cases.

If a procedural motion is granted[12] and a sale is conducted, a further motion to approve or confirm the sale under § 363(b) is appropriate. That motion should spell out precisely what is to be sold; what other matters, such as assumption and assignment of executory contracts, are involved in the sale process; the precise consideration to be paid, if an offer is already on the table, and any funding or other contingencies attached to that offer; and give prospective buyers one last chance to propose a competing bid, if it has not been provided that the bid submitted at any

---

10 *Compare In re* Integrated Resources, Inc., 147 B.R. 650 (S.D.N.Y. 1992), *with In re* Twenver, Inc., 149 B.R. 954 (Bankr. D. Colo. 1992). *See generally* Markell, *The Case Against Breakup Fees in Bankruptcy,* 66 Am. Bankr. L.J. 349 (1992); Comment, *An Empirical Study and Proposed Bankruptcy Code Section Concerning the Propriety of Bidding Incentives in a Bankruptcy Sale of Assets,* 93 Colum. L. Rev. 720 (1993); *Breakup Fees and Overbid Amounts (Reported Cases),* Bankr. Ct. Dec. A7 (Apr. 30, 1993).

11 This is a delicate and difficult area. On one hand, the debtor-seller has a great incentive to encourage all bidders, particularly those whose presence may run up the bids. On the other hand, the debtor is ill advised to consummate a sale with a buyer whose financial backing is unsure enough that it may not be able to consummate the sale. *See In re* Joshua Slocum, Ltd., 99 B.R. 261 (Bankr. E.D. Pa. 1989), *aff'd,* 914 F.2d 243 (3d Cir. 1990) (prebidding financial qualification hearing is not required).

12 The motion included in **§ 9.7** was denied, not because it was procedurally defective but solely because the debtor's counsel admitted that the debtor did not intend to file any plan, even a liquidating plan, at any time and intended ultimately to have the case dismissed. In the context of the case, the motion was proposed solely to accommodate an accord reached between the proposed buyer of the debtor's assets and a committee of franchisees of the debtor, a purpose found unacceptable.

prior auction or other sale proceeding is deemed final. An example of such a motion is presented in § **9.8.**[13] Although, again, the sample was produced in connection with a large bankruptcy case, it should be helpful in raising pertinent issues and in serving as a checklist for small business practitioners.

§ 9.5 Preconfirmation Asset Sales Contrasted with Asset Sales Conducted Pursuant to Reorganization Plans

One of the most controversial scenarios in which § 363(b) is invoked in business cases is in an action to obtain court permission to conduct preconfirmation sales of all or a substantial portion of a debtor's assets. There is authority for the principle that such sales are de facto plans of reorganization and can be authorized, if at all,[14] only in emergency situations.[15] Some courts have been somewhat more tolerant of such motions, requiring only a showing of a "sound business purpose" as a precondition for allowing the preconfirmation sale of a substantial portion of the debtor's assets.[16] In some jurisdictions, the U.S. Trustee opposes any such motions and requires, at a minimum, that a record be made to establish that all of the necessary criteria for allowance of such a sale are clearly satisfied, that is:

1. That ample notice of the § 363(b) motion was given to all interested parties
2. That adequate consideration is indeed being paid for the assets sold
3. That an emergency situation truly exists
4. That no collusion or side deals with the buyer have been made on behalf of the debtor's insiders in the transaction, or that any other indicia of bad faith are present.[17]

---

13 The motion included in § **9.8** was ultimately granted in *In re* After Six, Inc., 154 B.R. 876 (Bankr. E.D. Pa. 1993). The principal issue was whether this court should approve the debtor's request that a sale to the highest bidder be approved, or whether it should respect the preference of the creditors' committee and certain labor union-entity creditors that a lower bid from a firm promising to provide employment opportunities to the debtor's former union employees should be accepted. The court held that, although the court should have broad flexibility in considering all aspects of competing bids (citing *In re* Financial News Network, Inc., 980 F.2d 165 (2d Cir. 1992)), it was obliged to accept the debtor's choice in light of the court's doubt that the competing offer was "better," even from this broad perspective. *But cf. In re* Broadmoor Place Inv., 994 F.2d 744 (10th Cir. 1993) (bankruptcy court's approval of offer contrary to the debtor's recommendations affirmed).

14 *See, e.g., In re* Braniff Airways, Inc., 700 F.2d 935, 939–40 (5th Cir. 1983); *In re* Sedona San Carlos Dev. Co., 59 B.R. 113, 115 (Bankr. D. Ariz. 1986); *In re* Fremont Battery Co., 73 B.R. 277, 279 (Bankr. N.D. Ohio 1987).

15 *See, e.g., In re* Solar Mfg. Corp., 176 F.2d 493, 494–95 (3d Cir. 1949); *In re* White Motor Credit Corp., 14 B.R. 584, 590–91 (Bankr. N.D. Ohio 1981).

16 *See, e.g.,* Stephens Indus., Inc. v. McClung, 789 F.2d 386, 389–90 (6th Cir. 1986); *In re* Lionel Corp., 722 F.2d 1063, 1069–71 (2d Cir. 1983).

17 These criteria were deemed appropriate in *In re* Delaware & Hudson Ry., 124 B.R. 169, 176 (D. Del. 1991); *In re* Titusville Country Club, Inc., 128 B.R. 396, 399 (Bankr. W.D.

There is authority for the principle that a particularized finding of good faith by the bankruptcy court is necessary before such a sale can be approved.[18] Creditors who are hostile to the debtor's reorganizational efforts can often find or create ample reasons to oppose such sales as violative of some or all of the aforementioned criteria.

It is certainly true that a § 363(b) sale can be the most significant event in a Chapter 11 case, making the plan process itself anti-climactic. It is also true that an asset sale normally should be conducted within the scope of the plan confirmation process. Conducting asset sales outside of the plan confirmation process eliminates the disclosure and voting process which should normally precede court approval of such a significant event in the debtor's case. Therefore, § 363(b) sales of all or a large portion of a debtor's assets should be the exception rather than the rule.

Many practitioners appear to believe that it is preferable to hold a preconfirmation § 363(b) sale precisely to avoid the time and effort that must be devoted to the disclosure and voting process before a sale of all or most of the debtor's assets takes place. The drafting and necessary delays in the full-blown disclosure and voting process definitely slow down a sale transaction. Submission of a plan also requires the debtor to make commitments for the administration of the entire case at the time the asset sale is contemplated.

These concerns are legitimate, but only to a certain extent. The plan and the disclosure statement must eventually be negotiated and drafted. Time must be expended on the disclosure and voting process at some point. Sooner or later, the debtor must focus on a direction for the entire case. Negotiating, drafting, and settling on a planned course for the entire case are better done sooner rather than later on an ad hoc basis and depending solely on the course of future developments. Small business cases rarely encounter numerous problematic contingencies. Also, the Code contemplates that ordinarily the sale process would be included in the plan, rather than the plan's being an aftermath to the main event of an asset sale.[19]

As a practical matter, a judge hearing a preconfirmation § 363(b) motion that contemplates the sale of a substantial portion of the debtor's assets probably will be inclined to deny the motion whenever it is not clear that all of the requirements (ample notice, adequate consideration, good faith, and the presence of a bona fide emergency) have been satisfied. This is particularly true if the debtor has failed to establish that there is an emergency situation requiring an immediate sale.[20] If there is no emergency, there is no reason not to relegate the sale to the plan confirmation process.

Because most objections to a motion for a preconfirmation sale of a substantial portion of the debtor's assets pursuant to § 363(b) are sufficient to create at least some doubt in the mind of the court as to whether the sale should be allowed, the net result of a typical § 363(b) sale scenario is a denial of the motion in almost every

---

Pa. 1991); *In re* Industrial Valley Refrigeration & Air Conditioning Supplies, Inc., 77 B.R. 15, 21 (Bankr. E.D. Pa. 1987). *But see In re* Conroe Forge & Mfg. Corp., 82 B.R. 781, 786 n.3 (Bankr. W.D. Pa. 1988) ("emergency" test of *In re* Solar Mfg. Corp., 176 F.2d 493 (3d Cir. 1949), remains intact).

[18] *In re* Abbotts Dairies of Pa., Inc., 788 F.2d 143, 147–49 (3d Cir. 1986).

[19] 11 U.S.C. § 1123(a)(5)(D).

[20] *See, e.g., In re* Ancor Exploration Co., 30 B.R. 802, 808 (N.D. Okla. 1983).

instance in which there is genuine opposition to it. Even the almost reflex objections of the U.S. Trustee may be sufficient to result in a denial of a § 363(b) motion.

If the motion is denied, the debtor is compelled to either (1) convert the case, or allow it to be converted, to a Chapter 7 case; (2) resort after all to the plan confirmation process to effect the sale; or (3) attempt to negotiate with the objecting parties for a resolution of their objections to the § 363(b) motion. This negotiation often takes very much the same form as the negotiation that precedes confirmation. Bankruptcy judges expect that this negotiation will occur in the context of the confirmation process, but it is not certain that they will be as patient with extended negotiation on a § 363(b) motion.

If a quick asset sale is necessary, a court will usually be more willing to expedite the plan confirmation process than to allow what should be the centerpiece of a plan to be consummated without the debtor's being subjected to any part of the normal plan confirmation process. Similarly, if disputes arise over the asset sale features in a plan, the court is likely to be receptive to a motion to modify the plan and not require creditors to be re-balloted, pursuant to Federal Rule of Bankruptcy Procedure 3019. The court expects that last-minute negotiations to eliminate specific objections of creditors to plan confirmation will take place in the context of the plan confirmation process. These negotiations are, in fact, the substance of the normal give-and-take that accompanies that process.

On the other hand, an attempt to revise the terms of a preconfirmation § 363(b) motion in response to negotiations with objecting parties will often be less successful. If certain sale procedures have been noticed or advertised, the court will be reluctant to change them at the hearing. A whole new motion, notice, and advertisement may be deemed necessary to accommodate negotiated revisions. This procedure may have to be repeated again and again as new objections to revised sale procedures arise.

In the face of such delays, the court is apt to become skeptical about the very element that purportedly rendered this short-cut process necessary in the first place, that is, the emergency requiring faster action than the normal plan confirmation process permits. Observing this delay, the court is likely to become more and more receptive to opposition to the sale process itself by the U.S. Trustee and any other parties, who, for reasons associated with the merits of the sale proposal or not, wish for it not to take place.

§ 9.6 Other Disadvantages of Preconfirmation Asset Sales

Utilizing the plan process is often superior to attempting to obtain approval of a preconfirmation sale under § 363(b) for additional reasons. An argument can be made that troublesome provisions of § 363, such as § 363(k), which requires that a creditor holding security in the asset be given an opportunity to credit bid "at sale under" § 363(b), may not be applicable in the context of a plan confirmation.[21] At the very

---

[21] *See In re* Orfa Corp. of Philadelphia, 22 Bankr. Ct. Dec. (CRR) 427, 429–30, 1991 WL 225985 at *5 (Bankr. E.D. Pa. Oct. 30, 1991).

least, these provisions will be unlikely to prevent, in themselves, the confirmation of a plan. Also, because the confirmation order ordinarily is issued only after acceptance of a plan by the requisite majority in amount and number of creditors eligible to vote, it is easier to defend an appeal from confirmation of a plan than it is to defend an appeal from a § 363(b) order that has side-stepped the confirmation process. The debtor-appellee in an appeal from a confirmation order can argue that allowance of an appeal will frustrate and delay the wishes of the voting creditor body as a whole. The debtor can also proceed to consummate the plan, and this may render any appeal moot.[22] Any attempt by an appellant to stay the effect of the plan may be conditioned on the requirement of the appellant's posting a substantial bond, which may practically be impossible for the appellant to raise or not worth its financial investment to do so.

Another important disadvantage of a § 363(b) sale, as opposed to utilization of the plan confirmation process, is the susceptibility of such sales to attack if the requirements of § 363(b) are not met. *In re Cavalieri*[23] addressed the sticky situation that results when an asset sale is attempted without "notice and a hearing." In that case, the consumer debtor, having erroneously and fortuitously received clear title to a Mercedes Benz automobile, valued at $17,000 on his schedules, immediately "exchanged" the Mercedes with a friend for two vehicles valued at $5,500.[24] Thus, the debtor intentionally failed to fulfill the notice and hearing requirements of 11 U.S.C. § 363(b)(1). As a result, the sale was avoided by the court and the buyer friend was required to return the Mercedes to the debtor's estate.

Unless the asset sold is real property, 11 U.S.C. § 549(c)[25] will not protect even a good-faith purchaser at a sale that fails to comply with § 363(b). A sale conducted in violation of § 363(b) will therefore almost certainly have to be set aside if any interested party who failed to get proper notice of the sale demands it. The parties may have to face the difficult prospect of conducting a second sale and the possibility that the buyer at the first sale will be required to return the assets and compensate the estate for use or damage to the assets. Because the debtor is the party responsible for setting this mistaken course of events into motion by actions violative of the Bankruptcy Code, a court is unlikely to be sympathetic to the debtor's interest in framing an appropriate remedy.

---

22 *See, e.g., In re* Specialty Equip. Cos., 3 F.3d 1043, 1047 (7th Cir. 1993); Miami Center L.P. v. Bank of New York, 838 F.2d 1547, 1555–57 (11th Cir.), *cert. denied,* 488 U.S. 823 (1988); *In re* AOV Indus., Inc., 792 F.2d 1140, 1147–49 (D.C. Cir. 1986).

23 142 B.R. 710 (Bankr. E.D. Pa. 1992).

24 *Id.* at 712.

25 11 U.S.C. § 549(c) provides as follows:

> The trustee may not avoid under subsection (a) of this section a transfer of real property to a good faith purchaser without knowledge of the commencement of the case and for present fair equivalent value unless a copy or notice of the petition was filed, where a transfer of such real property may be recorded to perfect such transfer, before such transfer is so perfected that a bona fide purchaser of such property, against whom applicable law permits such transfer to be perfected, could not acquire an interest and is superior to the interest of such good faith purchaser.

See, e.g., In re Cavalieri, 142 B.R. 710, 718 (Bankr. E.D. Pa. 1992); *In re* McGowan, 19 B.R. 952, 953–54 (Bankr. E.D. Pa. 1982).

Of course, it is assumed that no principled debtor or debtor's counsel would attempt to evade intentionally the § 363(b) notice process in the manner of the *Cavalieri* debtor. What is more common is counsel's making an honest error at some point in the process, typically in failing to provide the requisite notice to one or two entities out of the large number of interested parties. Nonetheless, the end result may be the same. It is very important, therefore, to provide accurate and appropriate notice of the sale to all interested parties because of the extremely adverse consequences that can result from failing to do so.

For example, confronted with an error in dispatch of notice to a single creditor in *In re Fernwood Markets,*[26] the court found that it was obliged, due to the overriding precepts of due process of law, to declare a § 363(b) asset sale voidable as to the improperly-noticed creditor.[27] It is true that, in so doing, the court granted the creditor a less useful remedy than it had requested. The creditor sought to preserve the sale, but also to preserve its lien against the asset proceeds, otherwise satisfied by the sale.[28] The court granted the objecting creditor only the relief of choosing, within a short time-span, whether it wished to have the entire sale invalidated and redone or not.[29] This resolution was not very practical in serving the creditor's interests. The creditor therefore was obliged ultimately to let the sale stand upon receiving a modest settlement remittance, and it withdrew its objections upon payment of a sum less than its claim.

However, a creditor with an agenda to destroy a debtor may well opt to attempt to undo a sale, no matter how impractical the remedy appears. If the party deprived of notice has acted diligently and in good faith, fundamental due process concepts will have to be weighed against the principles of § 363(m), and *Fernwood Markets* indicates that the due process principles will often win this battle.[30]

Certainly, a sale authorized by § 363(b) is much more difficult to attack than a sale that is not court-approved at all. However, a § 363(b) order can itself be more fragile than it appears at first glance, even with § 363(m) to support its preservation on appeal.

On the other hand, a sale of assets that is authorized in the course of confirmation of a Chapter 11 plan is much more difficult to attack. A confirmation order can be revoked "if and only if such order was procured by fraud," and even then only upon request of a party in interest "at any time before 180 days after the date of the entry of the order of confirmation."[31] Therefore, in the context of plan confirmation, an

---

26 73 B.R. 616 (Bankr. E.D. Pa. 1987).

27 *Id.* at 620 (citing Ray v. Norseworthy, 90 U.S. (23 Wall.) 128 (1874)).

28 *Id.* at 621.

29 *Id.* at 621–22.

30 *Id.* at 620. *See also* M.R.R. Traders, Inc. v. Cave Atlantique, Inc., 788 F.2d 816 (1st Cir. 1986); *In re* Gem de Puerto Rico, Inc., 79 B.R. 142, 144 (D.P.R. 1987), *appeal dismissed,* 860 F.2d 1072 (1st Cir. 1988); *In re* Marcus Hook Dev. Park, Inc., 143 B.R. 648, 659–60 (Bankr. W.D. Pa. 1992); *In re* Century Steel, Inc., 56 B.R. 268, 270 (Bankr. M.D. La. 1985); *In re* First Int'l Serv. Corp., 25 B.R. 66, 70–71 (Bankr. D. Conn. 1982). *But see In re* Edwards, 962 F.2d 641 (7th Cir. 1992); *In re* Met-L-Wood Corp., 861 F.2d 1012, 1018 (7th Cir. 1988), *cert. denied sub nom.* Gekas v. Pipin, 490 U.S. 1006 (1989).

31 11 U.S.C. § 1144.

issue such as that raised by the creditor in *Fernwood Markets* would arguably have to be asserted within 180 days from the order approving the sale or not at all. Even a totally unauthorized sale, such as that engineered by the *Cavalieri* debtor, if done in the context of a Chapter 11 plan confirmation process, could not be subject to attack more than 180 days after confirmation.

The practitioner should therefore think first about incorporating a sale of assets into a plan of reorganization rather than moving for court permission to hold a pre-confirmation § 363(b) sale of all or a significant portion of a debtor's assets. Debtor-clients and impatient buyers should be impressed by the certainty and finality of the plan confirmation process as the primary means for accomplishing the liquidation of a debtor's assets in bankruptcy. Resort to a preconfirmation § 363(b) sale should be made only when there really is no alternative, for example, if the assets will be wasted or be vastly depreciated by any delay in a transfer. Even then, a plan should be waiting in the wings to effect the distribution process shortly after the sale.

It is probably impossible to overestimate the significance of the plan confirmation process in a Chapter 11 case. Confirmation should always be the goal. Getting a plan to confirmation quickly should be the preferred means of achieving that goal. The Code contemplates that a plan will embrace all of the significant decisions relating to the debtor's treatment of claims and disposition of assets. The democratic process of voting on the plan is deemed worthy of the strongest sort of protections from later attack under the Code. The first reflex of an advocate committed to this process should therefore be to utilize the plan confirmation process given by the Code, instead of using § 363(b) to accomplish any significant sale of a debtor's assets.

§ 9.7 Sample Motion to Approve Asset Sale

The following motion was filed in a case in the United States Bankruptcy Court for the Eastern District of Pennsylvania and is reprinted with the permission of the attorney who drafted it.

[Caption]

MOTION OF DEBTOR FOR AN ORDER (1) APPROVING THE SALE OF CERTAIN ASSETS, FREE AND CLEAR OF LIENS, CLAIMS, AND ENCUMBRANCES, PURSUANT TO SECTION 363 OF THE BANKRUPTCY CODE, (2) AUTHORIZING ASSUMPTION AND ASSIGNMENT OF CERTAIN EXECUTORY CONTRACTS AND LEASES PURSUANT TO SECTIONS 363 AND 365 OF THE BANKRUPTCY CODE, (3) APPROVING BIDDING PROCEDURES (INCLUDING TOPPING FEE), (4) SCHEDULING AN EXPEDITED HEARING TO CONSIDER THE BIDDING PROCEDURES, AND (5) GRANTING RELATED RELIEF

[Debtor], debtor-in-possession in the above-captioned Chapter 11 case (the "Debtor"), by and through its counsel, hereby moves this Court for an Order

(i) authorizing the Debtor to enter into and perform its obligations under an Agreement to Purchase Assets between it and [Buyer], (ii) authorizing the Debtor to sell essentially all of its assets, free and clear of liens, claims, and encumbrances, pursuant to Section 363 of the Bankruptcy Code, (iii) authorizing the Debtor to assume and assign certain executory contracts and leases pursuant to Section 363 and 365 of the Bankruptcy Code, (iv) approving the Bidding Procedures proposed by the Debtor, including the Topping Fee, (v) scheduling an expedited hearing to consider the Bidding Procedures; and (vi) granting certain related relief, and, in support thereof, the Debtor alleges as follows:

The Parties

1. On May 4, 1993 (the "Petition Date"), an involuntary petition (the "Petition") was filed against [Debtor], under Chapter 7 of Title 11 of the United States Code, 11 U.S.C. § 101, et seq. (the "Bankruptcy Code"). On June 3, 1993, the Involuntary Petition was amended to seek relief under Chapter 11 of the Bankruptcy Code, and the Debtor consented to entry of an Order for Relief.

2. On June 4, 1993, the Court entered an Order approving the Stipulation and granting relief under Chapter 11 of the Bankruptcy Code (the "Order for Relief").

3. Since the date of the entry of the Order for Relief, the Debtor has remained in possession of its assets and is presently operating its business and managing its property as a debtor-in-possession under Sections 1107 and 1108 of the Bankruptcy Code.

4. The Debtor is engaged in the sale of [specialty food] products and related services, both through its company-operated stores and through a nationwide system of franchisees (the "Franchisees"). The Debtor also operates through various joint ventures in the United States and Canada.

5. Contemporaneous with the Petition Date, the Debtor had approximately 280 company stores. As of the date hereof, the Debtor has approximately 67 operating company stores.

[6–10. Description of the Debtor's business.]

Jurisdiction and Venue

11. This Court has jurisdiction over this matter pursuant to 28 U.S.C. § 1334.

12. This Court has venue over this matter under 28 U.S.C. § 1409.

13. This is a core proceeding under 28 U.S.C. § 157(b)(2)(A), (N), and (O).

14. The Debtor seeks relief under Sections 105, 363 and 365 of the Bankruptcy Code and Federal Rules of Bankruptcy Procedure 2002 and 6004.

Background

15. Over the several years immediately prior to the Petition Date, the Debtor had experienced significant operating losses due to general negative economic conditions, overexpansion of company operations, increased competition in the industry, significant increases in personal injury litigation against the Debtor, and various other factors.

16. In February 1992, the Debtor engaged [Agent] to assist it in its efforts to secure a purchaser for the company's assets. In that connection, more than 125 potential purchasers were contacted and provided with informational materials relating to the company's operations.

17. Prior to and since the Petition Date, the Debtor's business has deteriorated, and it continues to deteriorate rapidly, due to lack of cash and liquid assets, the negative publicity associated with the disputes between the Debtor and its Franchisees, and efforts of certain competitors to interfere with and misappropriate the Debtor's relationships with its Franchisees and customers.

18. As of the Petition Date, the Debtor had essentially no operating funds or other assets which were not subject to the liens of its secured lenders.

19. Subsequent to the Petition Date, this Court has approved both interim and final cash collateral orders which severely restrict the operations and expenditures of the Debtor. The funds available to Debtor from its post-petition operations are insufficient, without alternative financing, to support its operations on a meaningful basis.

20. As of the Petition Date, the Debtor was unable to obtain food inventory to supply its operations and the operations of its Franchisees. Through the intervention of [Buyer], the Debtor has regained access to food inventory. By Order, dated June 4, 1993, this Court approved a Food Acquisition Agreement between the Debtor and [Buyer]. Without the credit support and efforts of [Buyer], the Debtor would have no existing operations and the value of its assets would be severely diminished or lost.

21. On or about August 27, 1993, the Debtor filed an Emergency Motion seeking approval of a Stipulation between the Debtor and the [Buyer], providing for debtor-in-possession financing by [Buyer] to the Debtor in an amount up to $250,000 (the "[Buyer] Financing"). Since the Petition Date, the Debtor has been unable to obtain financing from any source other than [Buyer] and/or its affiliates. The indebtedness due to [Buyer] under the [Buyer] Financing is secured by a lien and security interest on all of the assets of the Debtor.

22. Since the Petition Date, the Debtor has been unable to pay its rental obligations under unexpired leases for its centers and other properties, and many of its landlords have filed motions seeking relief from the automatic stay, rejection of the leases, payment of administrative claims, and other leases.

23. The Internal Revenue Service has filed a proof of claim in this case, asserting a priority claim in excess of $98,000,000.

The Bank Debt

24. The Debtor is indebted to a group of lenders including [Bank 1], [Bank 2], [Bank 3] and [Bank 4] (collectively, the "Bank Group"), pursuant to an Amended and Restated Credit Agreement dated October 31, 1991 (the "Credit Agreement") (the "Bank Debt").

25. As of the Petition Date, the Bank Debt was in excess of $44,000,000. As of the date hereof, the Bank Debt is approximately $31,000,000.

26. The Bank Group asserts a perfected, first priority security interest and lien in all or essentially all of the Assets as collateral security for the Bank Debt.

27. On or about July 21, 1993, the Bank Group filed a Motion seeking relief from the automatic stay to permit it to pursue its state law remedies to marshall and sell the Debtor's assets. Among other things, the Bank Group alleged that the Debtor has no equity in its Assets and that the interests of the Bank Group are not adequately protected. The Bank Group's Motion was granted by Court Order dated November 4, 1993.

28. Pursuant to an Agreement dated August 30, 1993 by and between [Buyer] and the Bank Group, the Bank Group has agreed, inter alia, subject to the terms and conditions set forth in that Agreement, to provide forgiveness of the Bank Debt in the amount requested by [Buyer], in connection with a sale of the Debtor's assets under Section 363 of the Bankruptcy Code. Under the Agreement, [Buyer] also has (i) an option to purchase form the Bank Group, upon foreclosure under state law, all of the Debtor's Assets which constitute collateral for the Bank Debt, and (ii) an option to purchase the Bank Debt.

The Purchase Agreement

29. Over the past several months, the Debtor and its counsel and the Bank Group have spent substantial time and effort pursuing avenues to facilitate a successful reorganization. While the Debtor continues to operate its business, it is apparent that without a rapid sale it will be unable to do so. In an effort to find an appropriate purchaser, the Debtor and the Bank Group have met with and spoken to numerous parties.

30. The Debtor, in its business judgment, has determined that the offer submitted by [Buyer] to purchase substantially all of the Debtor's assets provides the maximum realization to the estate and is in the best interest of the estate.

31. After extensive negotiations, the Debtor and [Buyer] entered into an Amended and Restated Agreement to Purchase Assets of [Debtor] dated [date] (the "Purchase Agreement"). A copy of the Purchase Agreement is attached hereto as Exhibit A. The Purchase Agreement provides for the sale to [Buyer] of essentially all of the operating assets of the Debtor, including without limitation: (a) all bank accounts, lock boxes and safe deposit boxes, and the contents thereof; (b) all accounts and other receivables owed to the Debtor and all promissory notes payable to the Debtor, wherever located; (c) all inventories as of the closing date (including sample supplies and products under development), wherever located; (d) all trade names, trademarks, service marks, logos, trade dress, patents and applications therefor and registrations thereof, and all licenses held or granted in connection with any of the foregoing or other intellectual property, together with the goodwill of the Debtor connected with the use thereof; (e) all owned real property (if any), machinery, equipment, vehicles, furniture, furnishings, leasehold improvements, fixtures, signs, and other personal property; (f) certain leases, franchise agreements, commitments, contracts, and warranties (including prepayments and deposits) to which the Debtor is a party, which are identified in Schedule 1.1(f) of the Purchase Agreement, as amended as of the Closing Date (the "Assumed Contracts"); (g) all technical, processing, or marketing information, including recipes, formulae, developments, inventions, know-how processes, ideas, and trade secrets, and documentation thereof and all claims and documentation thereto; (h) all files, customer records, employee records, logo, customer lists, vendor lists, accounting books, records, ledgers and electronic data processing materials; (i) all rights under agreements concerning confidentiality, noncompetition, or the assignment of ideas or inventions; (j) all prepaid expenses, letters of credit and deposits with third parties, customer credit balances, and advances; (k) all permits, licenses, and governmental agreements, waivers, and authorization of Debtor, which [Buyer] elects to assume prior to closing under the Purchase Agreement; (1) all information systems (hardware and software), programs, manuals, and documentation thereof; (m) all stock joint venture interests and other interests in entities and joint ventures, including without limitation [Subsidiary 1], [Subsidiary 2], and [Subsidiary 3], and those interests identified in Schedule 6.1(e)(iv) of the Purchase Agreement (collectively, the "Ownership Interests"); (n) all prepaid network and/or cable television or radio air time and all rights to any television or radio air time or other advertising; (o) all claims Debtor may have against [shareholder names], in whatever capacity (collectively, the "Shareholder Claims"); and (p) all other rights, property, and assets of the Debtor, tangible or intangible, including contingent assets (except as set forth in paragraph 32 below).

32. The following assets are excluded from the proposed sale to [Buyer]: (a) any and all turnover, fraudulent conveyance, and preference claims arising under the Bankruptcy Code, and any similar claim under state law, except as

described in clause (o) of paragraph 31 above; (b) any and all governmental refunds for income taxes previously paid, and (c) any and all of the Debtor's rights, title, or interests under leases, agreements, commitments, contracts, and warranties not included in the Assumed Contracts.

33. The Debtor believes that all of the Assets constitute collateral for the Bank Debt, except for those assets described on Schedule 1.1 of the Purchase Agreement (collectively, the "Non-Collateral Assets").

34. The Purchase Agreement specifically provides that [Buyer] is not assuming any liabilities of the Debtor except those expressly set forth in the Purchase Agreement. [Buyer] is not a successor corporation to the Debtor and is not responsible for any costs, expenses, losses, or liabilities relating to or arising from any claims by third parties.

35. The purchase price (the "Purchase Price") for the Assets under the Purchase Agreement is (a) for Assets other than the Non-Collateral Assets, the amount of (i) $14,000,000 less (ii) the aggregate of all amounts paid, set-off, or applied against obligations of the Debtor to any lender under the Credit agreement on or after April 27, 1993 and prior to the Closing under the purchase agreement, including without limitation those amounts more fully described in Section II.A of the Purchase Agreement, payable through the delivery, at [Buyer]'s option, of cash and/or evidence of the forgiveness of obligations of the Debtor to repay indebtedness to the Bank Group in an amount equal to the Purchase Price; (b) for the Non-Collateral Assets, an amount equal to the book value thereof on the financial records of the Debtor as of the closing under the Purchase Agreement, but not more than $200,000 in the aggregate, payable in cash at the closing, and (c) for the Shareholder Claims shall be $50,000 payable in cash at the closing.

The Bidding Procedures

36. Article XIV of the Purchase Agreement requires the Debtor to include in any notice of hearing relating to the proposed sale of the Assets that competing bids may be considered only if such offer (a) is in writing, (b) exceeds 110% of the purchase price, (c) is not for less than all of the assets, and (d) is accompanied by a deposit of at least $1,000,000. A proposed form of sale procedures (the "Bidding Procedures") is attached hereto as Exhibit B.

37. Section XIV.B of the Purchase Agreement requires the Debtor to pay to [Buyer] a Topping Fee in the amount of $300,000 in the event, and out of the proceeds of, a sale of the assets to any party other than [Buyer].

38. In view of the substantial financial accommodations and other efforts of [Buyer] and its affiliates in connection with this case, without which the Debtor's operations would have ceased and the value of the Assets lost, the Topping Fee and other Bidding Procedures are reasonable and appropriate.

39. The Debtor seeks expedited approval of the Bidding Procedures, including the Topping Fee, as more fully described in Exhibit B attached hereto.

Executory Contracts and Leases

40. Article III of the Purchase Agreement requires the Debtor to assume, and assign to [Buyer], the Assumed Contracts.

41. The Assumed Contracts include, among other contracts, all franchise agreements between the Debtor and its Franchisees identified in Schedule 1.1(f) of the Purchase Agreement, as amended as of the Closing Date (collectively, the "Franchise Agreements").

42. The Franchise Agreements constitute the Debtor's primary asset. Concurrent with Court approval of a sale of the Assets, the Debtor seeks an Order of this Court permitting the Debtor to assume the Franchise Agreements and assign them to the successful bidder, with any cure that is required by Section 365(b) of the Bankruptcy Code to be made only by the Debtor.

43. [Buyer] has the financial ability to perform all obligations under the Assumed Contracts which accrue after the date of assignment.

44. The Debtor believes that it is in the best interests of its estate to assume and assign to Buyer the Assumed Contracts, pursuant to the Purchase Agreement.

The Sale

45. As a result of its discussions and negotiations with [Buyer] and others, the Debtor believes that [Buyer's] offer to purchase the Debtor's assets represents the highest and best offer available to the Debtor.

46. The Debtor believes that there is compelling justification for the transactions contemplated by the Purchase Agreement, and for the approval and prompt consummation of those transactions pursuant to Sections 105, 363, and 365 of the Bankruptcy Code, including the following:

a. the Debtor will realize the substantial consideration either in cash or by way of reduction of the Bank debt and/or the [Buyer] Financing;

b. the going concern value of the Debtor's Assets will be realized, avoiding further deterioration of the value of its Assets due to its severe cash shortage and its inability to obtain adequate financing for continuing operations;

c. the Debtor's estate will avoid much of the substantial administrative expenses (operational, professional, and others) associated with the Debtor's continuing operations;

d. the sale to [Buyer] will substantially eliminate the hardships visited on the Franchisees as a result of the Debtor's limited operations;

e. sale of the assets to [Buyer], a financially viable purchaser, promotes the viability of its franchisee system, the most significant and valuable asset of the Debtor; and

f. sale of the Assets to [Buyer] will permit the business and operations of the Debtor to continue and increase, all to the benefit of future employees, franchisees, and customers of [Buyer].

47. The proposed sale to [Buyer] represents an arms-length transaction for fair and reasonable consideration. [Buyer] is purchasing the Assets as a good faith purchaser and, absent a stay of an Order approving the sale of the Assets to [Buyer], [Buyer] will be entitled to the protection of Section 363(m) of the Bankruptcy Code.

48. In light of the continuing deterioration of the Debtor's assets and its inadequate cash flow, a sale of the Debtor's assets cannot await the confirmation of a plan of reorganization. The delay engendered by the plan negotiation, drafting, solicitation, and confirmation process would likely destroy the Debtor's operations and assets, as well as significantly increase administrative expenses.

49. An immediate sale of the Assets is essential to maximize the value of the Assets and the associated return to the Debtor's estate.

50. The proposed sale to [Buyer] must be approved on or before December 22, 1993 to enable the enterprise to initiate its post-Christmas advertising campaign. Advertising for this critical time period traditionally begins December 26, 1993, and failure to begin this campaign on time will have a serious detrimental effect on the value of the Debtor's operations.

51. Section 363(b) permits a debtor to sell its assets outside of the ordinary course of business.

52. Under governing case law, a debtor acting in good faith is to be given deference with respect to the manner in which it chooses to sell its assets in a liquidating Chapter 11 case.

53. Section 363(f) of the Bankruptcy Code provides that a debtor may sell its property free and clear of any and all liens, claims, encumbrances, and interests of an entity other than the estate if (i) applicable non-bankruptcy law permits sale of such property free and clear of such interest; (ii) such entity consents; (iii) such interest is a lien and the price at which such property is to be sold is greater than the aggregate value of all liens on such property; (iv) such interest is in bona fide dispute; or (v) such entity could be compelled, in a legal or equitable proceeding, to accept a money satisfaction of such interests. The Debtor seeks to sell its Assets

free and clear of all liens, claims, encumbrances, and interests, with any such liens, claims, encumbrances, and interests to attach to the proceeds of such sale to the same extent, priority, and status as existed with respect to the Assets.

54. The Debtor requests that the Court schedule a hearing on December 9, 1993 to consider the Bidding Procedures, and enter an Order on December 9, 1993, in the form attached to this Motion: (a) approving the Sale Procedures attached as Exhibit B to this Motion, including the Topping Fee described therein; (b) scheduling a hearing on or before December 22, 1993 to consider and approve the Purchase Agreement and to authorize the Debtor to consummate the transactions contemplated therein; (c) approving the Notice of Motion attached hereto as Exhibit C; (d) directing the Debtor to serve a copy of the Notice of Motion by regular mail, postage prepaid, on all known creditors and parties-in-interest, not later than December 13, 1993, and requiring the Debtor to publish such Notice of Motion once in The Philadelphia Inquirer and the Wall Street Journal not later than December 15, 1993.

WHEREFORE, the Debtor respectfully requests that the Court (1) enter an Order in the form attached to this Motion approving the Bidding Procedures (including the Topping Fee), scheduling a hearing to consider the proposed sale of the Assets, approving the form of Notice attached as Exhibit C to this Motion, and fixing the manner of service thereof; and (2) enter an Order in the form attached to this Motion approving the sale of the Debtor's Assets, free and clear of liens, claims, encumbrances, and interests, pursuant to Section 363 of the Bankruptcy Code, and the assumption and assignment of the Assumed Contracts pursuant to Section 365 of the Bankruptcy Code; and (3) granting such other and further relief as is appropriate under the circumstances.

[counsel signature]

[date]

§ 9.8 Sample Motion to Approve Asset Sale (Alternate)

This motion was filed in the United States Bankruptcy Court for the Eastern District of Pennsylvania and is reprinted with the permission of the attorney who drafted it.

[Caption]

DEBTORS' MOTION FOR AN ORDER APPROVING THE SALE OF CERTAIN PERSONAL PROPERTY AND INTANGIBLE ASSETS FREE AND CLEAR OF ALL LIENS, CLAIMS, AND ENCUMBRANCES PURSUANT TO 11 U.S.C. § 363; AUTHORIZING THE ASSUMPTION AND ASSIGNMENT OF CERTAIN EXECUTORY CONTRACTS PURSUANT TO 11 U.S.C. § 365; AND GRANTING RELATED RELIEF

The above-captioned debtors and debtors-in-possession (collectively, the "Debtors") hereby move this Court for an order (i) authorizing [Debtor 1] and [Debtor 2] to enter into and perform all of their obligations under an Asset Purchase Agreement dated April 1, 1993 (the "Asset Purchase Agreement," attached hereto as Exhibit A and incorporated by reference herein), with [Buyer]; (ii) authorizing the Debtors to sell certain personal property and intangible assets free and clear of all liens, claims, and encumbrances, pursuant to 11 U.S.C. § 363; (iii) authorizing the assumption and assignment of certain executory contracts pursuant to 11 U.S.C. § 365; and (iv) granting other related relief, and in support thereof respectfully represent as follows:

INTRODUCTION

1. On February 26, 1993 (the "Filing Date"), the Debtors filed with this Court separate, voluntary petitions for relief under Chapter 11 of the Bankruptcy Code. On March 2, 1993, this Court entered an Order directing that these cases be jointly administered and procedurally consolidated pursuant to Bankruptcy Rule 1015(b).

2. The Debtors continue to manage their properties and operate their business as debtors-in-possession pursuant to 11 U.S.C. §§ 1107 and 1108. No trustee or examiner has been appointed in these cases.

3. The Court has jurisdiction over this matter pursuant to 28 U.S.C. §§ 157 and 1334. Venue of these cases and this motion in this District is proper pursuant to 28 U.S.C. §§ 1408 and 1409. This is a core proceeding pursuant to 28 U.S.C. § 157(b)(2).

4. On March 17, 1993, an official committee of unsecured creditors (the "Committee") was appointed, and it selected and retained [Law Firm] (the "Committee Counsel") as its counsel.

5. As of April 1, 1993, [Debtor 1] and [Debtor 2] entered into the Asset Purchase Agreement to sell, subject to Court approval, their intellectual property rights, fixed assets, inventory, advertising materials, customer lists, and certain litigation rights, all as more fully described in the Asset Purchase Agreement and below, to [Buyer]. Among other things, this Motion requests Court approval of the Asset Purchase Agreement and the sale proposed therein.

FACTUAL BACKGROUND

Description of the Debtors' Business

6. Debtor [Holding Company], a Delaware corporation, is a holding company which owns, inter alia, all of the issued and outstanding common stock of [Debtor 1], an operating company. [Debtor 1], a Pennsylvania corporation, maintains its corporate headquarters and operated production facilities in

Philadelphia, Pennsylvania. [Debtor 2], a wholly-owned subsidiary of [Debtor 1], is a Delaware corporation which owns, inter alia, the trademark and name, [debtor's tradename].

7. [Debtor] was a manufacturer of men's [specialty clothing] for the rental and retail markets. As of the Filing Date, [Debtor 1] did business with in excess of 800 trade vendors and had more than 345 employees.

8. [Debtor 1]'s gross billings for the fiscal year ending June 27, 1992, were in excess of $32,000,000. Losses for this period exceeded $11,300,000.

9. Prior to the Filing Date, [Debtor 1] explored numerous reorganization alternatives both inside and outside of Chapter 11 which might have enabled it to survive as a going concern. However, its secured lender concluded that such alternatives would have required additional funding in amounts in excess of what it was willing to provide based on its evaluation of the financial condition and prospects of [Debtor 1].

10. As a result, on the Filing Date, the Debtors discontinued manufacturing operations and have since been attempting to maximize the value of their estates by seeking purchasers of various of their assets and collecting over 2000 accounts receivable totalling approximately $15,000,000.

The Debtors' Obligations

11. [Debtor 1] is obligated on an unsecured basis under various bond indentures in the approximate pre-petition amount of $45,000,000.

12. The pre-petition trade obligations of [Debtor 1] total approximately $1,000,000.

13. The Debtors also have significant other contingent, unliquidated, pre-petition liabilities totalling as much as $10,000,000 to $20,000,000.

14. [Debtor 1]'s primary secured creditor is [Credit Co.], pursuant to a credit agreement dated as of January 25, 1990 (as amended from time to time, including all supporting documentation, the "Pre-Petition Credit Agreement").

15. The aggregate loans, advances, and other such indebtedness, including, without limitation, the principal thereof, interest thereon, and fees, costs, and expenses in connection therewith owed by [Debtor 1] to [Credit Co.] under the Prepetition Credit Agreement and outstanding as of the Filing Date were approximately $4,000,000 (collectively, the "Pre-Petition Indebtedness").

16. Pursuant to various pledge agreements, security agreements, mortgages, guarantees, and other documents, all or substantially all of the Debtors' assets secure the Pre-Petition Indebtedness.

17. Prior to the Filing Date, only limited funds were available to [Debtor 1] under the Pre-Petition Credit Agreement, and [Credit Co.] refused to support [Debtor's] continuing losses.

18. Since the Filing Date, [Credit Co.] has continued as [Debtor 1]'s secured lender pursuant to a Debtor-in-Possession Financing Agreement (the "DIP Financing Agreement"), which has been approved by the Court on an interim basis and which provides funds for the payment of limited expenses of [Debtor 1].

THE ASSET PURCHASE AGREEMENT WITH [BUYER]

The Terms of the Asset Purchase Agreement

19. Both prior to and since the Filing Date, the Debtors have attempted to solicit bids for the purchase of their assets.

20. On April 1, 1993, after weeks of arm's length negotiations which began prior to the Filing Date, and subject to the approval of this Court pursuant to 11 U.S.C. § 363, the Debtors entered into the Asset Purchase Agreement with [Buyer]. Capitalized terms used herein without definition have the same meanings ascribed to them in the Asset Purchase Agreement.

21. The Asset Purchase Agreement, which is subject to the Debtors' right to solicit and receive higher or better offers pursuant to 11 U.S.C. § 363, provides for the sale (the "Asset Sale") to [Buyer] of assets (the "Assets") of the Debtors, including (i) all of the Debtors' intellectual property rights (including patents, trademarks, and license agreements), customer lists, advertising materials, and other intangible assets (the "Intangible Assets"); (ii) [Debtor 1]'s inventory (including finished goods, work-in-process, and raw materials) (the "Personal Property Assets"); (iii) all fixed assets (the "Fixed Assets") of the Debtors, except those set forth in Exhibit 1.3(f) of the Asset Purchase Agreement; and (iv) all rights under the [Lawsuit name] (the "Litigation").

[22. Describes the litigation in the case.]

23. Some of the primary terms of the Asset Purchase Agreement are outlined below.

24. The purchase price for the Assets under the Asset Purchase Agreement is $4 million cash to be paid on the date of the Closing plus an amount that is a function of [Debtor 1]'s cost of its piece goods and finished goods inventory existing several days prior to the date the sale would be approved by the Court (estimated to be approximately $1–1.5 million as of the operative date under the Asset Purchase Agreement), to be paid within 150 days of the Closing (and secured by an irrevocable letter of credit which may be drawn upon unconditionally).

25. The Asset Purchase Agreement provides that the Closing, at which [Debtor 1] must deliver the Assets to [Buyer] free and clear of all liens, encumbrances, and claims of any kind or nature, must occur on or before May 17, 1993.[1] The Debtors believe that the Assets will diminish in value to [Buyer] and to all other prospective bidders if the May 27, 1993 date is missed.

26. The Asset Purchase Agreement provides for certain bidding and notice procedures leading up to an auction sale in open court and provides, inter alia, that any alternative bid must be at least 10% higher than the purchase price proposed in the Asset Purchase Agreement, and that if the Debtors receive a higher or better offer for certain of the Assets, the Court approves a sale of such Assets to a party other than [Buyer], and, among other things, the Asset Purchase Agreement is not terminated, [Buyer] will be entitled to recover its actual, reasonable, out-of-pocket costs and expenses in connection with the Asset Purchase Agreement to a maximum of $150,000. Simultaneously with the filing of this Motion, the Debtors have requested approval of these (and other) particular provisions of the Asset Purchase Agreement by way of a Motion for Approval of (i) Notice and Bidding Procedures for, and (ii) Certain Terms of, a Proposed Sale of Assets under 11 U.S.C. § 363 (the "Notice and Bidding Procedures Motion") and have requested expedited hearing thereon.

27. As part of the bidding procedures, the parties have agreed that bidding on the Assets will be on a bulk as well as individual basis in three indivisible lots as follows: (i) the Intangible Assets and the Litigation, (ii) the Fixed Assets, and (iii) the Inventory.

28. In addition, upon approval of the Notice and Bidding Procedures Motion, the Debtors have agreed to seek a stay of the Injunction until the earlier of the Closing or the termination of the Asset Purchase Agreement.

29. The Debtors will retain their cash, accounts receivable, claims of the estates (other than the Litigation), and other assets not specifically identified above. [Debtor 1] will work diligently to collect its receivables, and the Debtors will investigate and pursue other claims they may have in order to maximize the value of the estates for the benefit of the Debtors' creditors.

Assumption and Assignment of Certain Executory Contracts

30. As part of the Asset Purchase Agreement, [Debtor 1] has agreed to assume and assign to [Buyer] certain Seller Licensor Agreements, as defined and more fully described in the Asset Purchase Agreement and attached as Exhibit 1.1.1.B thereto (collectively, the "Assumed Contracts").

---

[1] The Asset Purchase Agreement fixes such date as May 19, 1993, but the parties have subsequently agreed to the May 27, 1993 date.

31. The Assumed Contracts are in full force and effect, and either (i) there are no pre-petition or post-petition defaults thereunder, or (ii) any such defaults have been cured or will be promptly cured prior to the Closing.

32. [Buyer] has the financial and other wherewithal to perform all remaining obligations (which are believed to be minimal) under the Assumed Contracts or the other parties to the Assumed Contracts have consented or will consent to the assignments proposed herein, so the requirements for adequate assurance by [Buyer] of future performance under the Assumed Contracts are met pursuant to 11 U.S.C. § 365(f).

33. As a result of the assignments proposed herein, and as provided in the Asset Purchase Agreement, [Debtor 1] should be relieved of any continuing obligations under the Assumed Contracts pursuant to 11 U.S.C. § 365(k).

34. [Debtor 1] has properly exercised its business judgment by its decision to assume and assign the Assumed Contracts pursuant to the Asset Purchase Agreement, and there is good and sufficient cause for the granting of the relief requested herein.

Business Judgment of the Debtors

35. After a thorough review of the current strategic position of the Debtors, their current financial condition, their reasonable financial outlook, their current liquidity position, the purchase proposals received, and the Debtors' prospects for reorganization, the Debtors' Boards of Directors, exercising their sound business judgment, have instructed management to proceed with the Asset Sale pursuant to the Asset Purchase Agreement.

36. The Debtors' directors and management have concluded that the Asset Sale pursuant to the Asset Purchase Agreement and the terms thereof will maximize the value of the Debtors' estates for the benefit of their creditors and, therefore, that the Asset Sale is in the best interests of Debtors, their estates, and their creditors.

37. In the absence of such a sale as proposed herein, the Debtors will have no alternative other than a piecemeal, "fire sale" liquidation, which would likely generate a much smaller recovery.

38. The Debtors submit that the purchase price to be paid by [Buyer] and the remaining terms of the Asset Purchase Agreement are fair and reasonable and likely represent (or will lead to) the highest and best recovery for the Debtors.

Good Faith of [Buyer]

39. The terms of the Asset Purchase Agreement have been reached after weeks of arm's length negotiations, with both sides giving and taking on various issues.

40. [Buyer] is completely unrelated to the Debtors, and none of the Debtors' directors, management, or insiders has been offered by, or accepted employment from, [Buyer] in connection with the Asset Purchase Agreement being consummated.

41. The Debtors believe that [Buyer] is proceeding in good faith and, therefore, is entitled to the protection of 11 U.S.C. § 363(m).

Benefits to the Estates of the Asset Sale

42. In addition to maximizing the value of the estates for the benefit of the Debtors' creditors, the Asset Sale will enable the Debtors promptly to file a plan of reorganization. It is anticipated that this plan will address the disposition of the Debtors' remaining assets.

SALE PURSUANT TO 11 U.S.C. § 363

43. The Bankruptcy Code allows a debtor-in-possession, "after notice and a hearing [to] use, sell or lease, other than in the ordinary course of business, property of the estate." 11 U.S.C. § 363(b). In fact, a Chapter 11 debtor may in certain circumstances sell all or substantially all of its assets, or a substantial asset, pursuant to 11 U.S.C. § 363(b) prior to the filing of a plan of reorganization. In re Naron & Wagner Chartered, 88 B.R. 85, 87 (Bankr. D. Md. 1988); see also In re Lionel Corp., 722 F.2d 1063 (2d Cir. 1983); and In re Abbotts Dairies of Pennsylvania, Inc., 788 F.2d 143 (3d Cir. 1986).

44. To meet the standard under 11 U.S.C. § 363, "there must be some articulated business justification for [the sale] . . . Whether the proffered business justification is sufficient depends on the case." In re Continental Airlines, Inc., 708 F. 2d 1223, 1226 (5th Cir. 1986). Accord In re Ionosphere Clubs, Inc. 98 B.R. 174, 175 (Bankr. S.D.N.Y. 1989).

45. The Court in Lionel set forth a nonexclusive list of relevant factors to be considered in evaluating the business justification for a proposed sale outside the ordinary course of business under 11 U.S.C. § 363(b):

a. The proportionate value of the assets to be sold to the estate as a whole;

b. The amount of elapsed time since the filing;

c. The likelihood that a reorganization plan would be proposed and confirmed in the near future;

d. The effect of the proposed disposition on future plans of reorganization;

e. The proceeds to be obtained from the disposition vis-à-vis any appraisals of the property;

f. Whether the disposition is by sale, use, or lease; and

g. Whether the asset is increasing or decreasing in value.

Lionel, 722 F.2d at 1071. See also Continental Air Lines, 780 F.2d at 1226. These factors are not designed as a rigid checklist, but simply give guidance to a court considering a sale under Section 363. Lionel, 722 F.2d at 1071.

46. When the Lionel factors are applied to the facts present in this case, it is clear that there are compelling and sound business purposes for the Debtors to seek approval of the Asset Sale in the context of 11 U.S.C. § 363(b), as opposed to under a plan of reorganization, including the following:

a. It being only six weeks since the Filing Date and less than one month since the formation of the Committee, the Debtors and their creditors have not yet reached agreement on the terms of a plan of reorganization, nor is it likely that such terms will be able to be negotiated in a reasonably short time frame. In addition, [Debtor 1] is only able to generate sufficient cash flow to satisfy limited short-term expenses, and the Debtors are unable to obtain sufficient post-petition financing to resume or maintain operations until a plan of reorganization can be consummated. Thus, the Debtors may not be able to avoid liquidation if they are unable to consummate the asset sale in the context of 11 U.S.C. § 363, as opposed to in a plan of reorganization, and a liquidation sale of the Assets would likely generate substantially less proceeds than the purchase price proposed under the Asset Purchase Agreement.

b. The Debtors' business is seasonal. If [Debtor's tradename] and inventory are not available during the late Spring and Summer seasons for marketing as a quality men's wear label by a manufacturer or distributor able to enjoy the long-term benefit of its efforts, their value will diminish. A reintroduction of [Debtor's tradename] will be more costly six or eight months from now, as distinguished from keeping the name of the marketplace. Further, prompt disposition of [Debtor's tradename] and inventory will permit the purchaser to work with the Debtors' customers to fill in their [Debtor's tradename] lines, which now are incomplete. The Debtors hope that by continuing the [Debtor's tradename] line by a purchaser able to meet customer needs, the customers will be less likely to raise breach of contract claims, if any, in defense of accounts receivable collection efforts, which the Debtors will commence soon. Lastly, the [lawsuit name] is at a unique stage, where the value of resolving the issues arising from the Injunction is at its greatest point before the effect of the Injunction, either to the detriment of the Plaintiffs and other related parties or to the strategic benefit of other potential purchasers of the Assets, is fully quantified.

c. The Agreement requires the Asset Sale to be consummated on or before May 27, 1993. If the Asset Sale is not approved and the Asset Purchase Agreement is terminated, even if the Debtors are not forced to liquidate, there is no guarantee (and, in fact, it is unlikely) that the Assets could ever be sold for a price that would even approximate the purchase price proposed to be paid by [Buyer].

d. The Asset Sale and the proposed notice provisions set forth in the Asset Purchase Agreement and in the Notice and Procedures Motion will provide ample time for scrutiny by parties-in-interest and enable the Debtors and this Court to consider higher or better offers which may be submitted by other parties. Any sale under a plan would likely not be as conducive to competitive bidding and may thus deprive the Debtors of the opportunity to realize the maximum value of the Assets.

e. The price to be paid under the Asset Purchase Agreement for the Assets is fair and reasonable, and the Assets are promptly declining in value.

f. The Assets are only a portion of the total assets of the estates, which total assets include, among other things, significant accounts receivable.

g. [Buyer] has acted in good faith pursuant to 11 U.S.C. § 363(m). [Buyer] is unrelated to the Debtors, and no principals or insiders of the Debtors have entered into any employment agreements with, or received any promises of employment from, [Buyer].

47. The Asset Sale meets all of the requirements of 11 U.S.C. § 363(f) to sell the Assets free and clear of all liens and encumbrances because the only party with a security interest in the Assets, [Credit Co.], will receive either the proceeds or a lien thereon to the extent of the value of its secured claim as of the date assets are to be transferred.

NOTICE OF THIS MOTION AND OF THE PROPOSED SALE

48. The Debtors propose that notice of this Motion and of the proposed sale and the hearing thereon be provided to the Office of the United States Trustee, to [Credit Co.], to [Credit Co.]'s counsel, to any other secured creditors with liens on assets proposed to be sold, to all tax authorities, to all parties of which the Debtors are aware with a specific interest in the Motion (such as parties to the Seller Licensor Agreements subject to assumption and assignment hereunder and to all parties which have expressed an interest in purchasing any of the Debtors' assets since the Filing Date), to the members of the Committee, to Committee Counsel, to counsel to the unofficial committee of bondholders, to the twenty largest unsecured creditors of each of the Debtors, to all parties requesting notice pursuant to Bankruptcy Rule 2002, and to the Debtors' equity security holders. If the notice and bidding procedures proposed in the Notice and Bidding Procedures Motion are approved by this Court, notice will be provided to all

other known creditors of the Debtors and notice of the availability for the sale of the Assets will be widely published.

49. The Debtors respectfully submit that such notice is adequate, proper, and sufficient under the circumstances of these cases to assure that all possible bidders will be aware of the availability of the Assets and to maximize the recovery therefrom.

50. The Debtors respectfully request that a final hearing (the "Final Hearing") on the Asset Sale and the other relief requested in this Motion be held on or before May 14, 1993, to enable the Closing to occur on or before May 27, 1993, as required in the Asset Purchase Agreement.

CONCLUSION

51. The value of [Debtor 1] continues to erode to the detriment of the Debtors' creditors, and the Debtors' assets will soon have little value at all if the Asset Purchase Agreement is not approved and the procedures proposed herein are not implemented immediately.

WHEREFORE, the Debtors respectfully request that this Court enter an order (i) authorizing the Debtors to enter into and perform all of their obligations under the Agreement, (ii) authorizing the Debtors to sell the Assets free and clear of all liens, claims, and encumbrances, pursuant to 11 U.S.C. § 363, (iii) authorizing [Debtor 1] to assume and assign the Assumed Contracts, and (iv) granting such other and further relief as is just and proper.

[counsel signature]

[date]

CHAPTER 10

INCOME TAX IMPLICATIONS OF TRANSFERS OF LOW BASIS PROPERTY IN CHAPTER 7 AND 11 BANKRUPTCY

Joseph I. Wittman

§ 10.1 Introduction

Many individuals or joint owners have property that cannot be disposed of without incurring substantial tax liabilities. Real property with a low tax basis may have appreciated over many years. Personal property may have been depreciated over time on tax returns leaving little or no tax basis. The property may be farmland, manufacturing equipment, an apartment complex, or another type of property.

When property is disposed of, any increase in its value since the time the seller acquired it is regarded by the Internal Revenue Code as income. As such, it is subject to income tax. In the small business context, this type of tax liability may come into play in numerous ways. The following fact situation is an example. Mr. and Mrs. Smith own, among other things, a small commercial building. The building has appreciated greatly in value over the years. They inherited it in 1963 when its value was $10,000. Today the building is worth $100,000. Sale of the building today would subject the Smiths to income tax on the $90,000 increase in value.

The Smiths also own personal property used in their business that originally cost $200,000. On each year's tax return they have taken the allowed depreciation on their equipment. When the class life of the equipment has passed (probably seven years), the entire original cost has been written off. If they sell the property after that for anything at all, say $2,000, income tax will be owed on the $2,000. This is true even though the sale price is far below the original purchase price.

If the Smiths encounter financial difficulty, the property might be foreclosed on by a lender who has taken a mortgage or security interest in the property. If the property is taken away by foreclosure, the former owner still owes the income tax. A deed in lieu of foreclosure has the same result.

Bankruptcy may or may not provide an avenue for the owner to escape income tax on the increase in value of the low basis property. Besides, even if it does, the tax liability does not simply vanish; it is shifted to the estate. This chapter explores the tax and bankruptcy law in this area.

§ 10.2 Basis and Adjusted Basis

An understanding of the concept of basis is necessary to an understanding of the problems of a sale or transfer of low basis property. Any sale or exchange of property for an amount in excess of basis is income to the transferor.[1] The *basis* of property is the cost of the property.[2] The *adjusted basis* of property is the cost adjusted as permitted by the Internal Revenue Code.[3] These adjustments include the cost of improvements, which are added to the basis, and allowed depreciation deductions, which are subtracted from the basis.[4] For instance, if a house was purchased for $50,000, improvements costing $20,000 have been made, and $15,000 of depreciation has been allowed, the basis of the house would be $55,000.

Purchase Price of House	$50,000
Improvements	+20,000
Total Basis	70,000
Less Depreciation	−15,000
Net Adjusted Basis	$55,000

[1] 26 U.S.C. § 1001(a) (1984). Hereinafter, 26 U.S.C., the Internal Revenue Code, will be referred to as I.R.C. *See also* Treas. Reg § 1.1001-1(a).

[2] I.R.C. § 1012.

[3] *Id.* § 1011(a).

[4] I.R.C. § 1012 (1954); I.R.C. § 1016 (1986).

If equipment used in a business was bought for $5,000, and after five years $4,000 of depreciation has been allowed by the Internal Revenue Code, the basis after five years would be $1,000.

Purchase Price of Equipment	$5,000
Less Depreciation	–4,000
Adjusted Basis	$1,000

If the house is sold for $100,000, the gain that is taxed is the difference between the purchase price and its adjusted basis, or $45,000 ($100,000 – $55,000 = $45,000). If the equipment sells for $1,500, the taxable gain on the sale would be $500. ($1,500 – $1,000 = $500). The tax is due on the gain whether the transferor receives cash, release of liability for debt, or other consideration.[5] A sale or exchange is a taxable event that may generate tax liability for the transferor.

Another factor an owner of low basis property must consider in this analysis is debt discharge income. The satisfaction of an obligation or discharge of debt at less than face value creates *debt discharge income* to the transferor.[6] Debt discharge income is excluded from gross income if the discharge occurs in bankruptcy.[7] However, if a bankruptcy is not filed, the debtor will be taxed on the gain from the transfer in satisfaction of debt as well as on the debt discharge income.[8]

In the example in § **10.1,** if the Smiths sell their building, they will have taxable income of $90,000 ($100,000 – $10,000). The taxes due because of the sale might exceed $25,000.[9] If the Smiths are in financial difficulty, however, the situation is even worse. If the building is mortgaged for $120,000, a sale will not retire the debt. If the property is foreclosed or turned over to the creditor by a deed in lieu of foreclosure, they will have debt discharge income of $20,000 ($120,000 – $100,000). The Smiths would be taxed on $110,000.

A sale or exchange of the property outside of bankruptcy is not beneficial for the Smiths. The only alternative may be to file bankruptcy and deal with the property in the bankruptcy to avoid tax consequences.

§ 10.3 Tax Provisions Applicable to Bankruptcy

Section 1398 of the Internal Revenue Code (I.R.C.) is the section that links the I.R.C. to the Bankruptcy Code and provides the opportunity for a debtor to shift income tax liability for the transfer of low basis property to the estate. Section 1398

---

[5] *See* I.R.C. § 1001(b)(1984); Helvering v. Hammel, 311 U.S. 504 (1941).

[6] I.R.C. § 61(a)(12). *See* United States v. Kirby Lumber Co., 284 U.S. 1 (1931).

[7] I.R.C. § 108(a)(1). There are other tax consequences to bankruptcy discharge income, however. See the discussion of net operating losses in § **10.13.**

[8] *See* James I. Shepard, The Trustee's Bankruptcy Tax Manual 31–38 (1992).

[9] This figure assumes a joint tax return with two exemptions, the standard tax deduction, and the 28 percent tax bracket.

applies only to bankruptcy cases filed under Chapter 7 and Chapter 11. It also applies only to debtors who are individuals, not to partnerships or corporations.[10]

Upon commencement of a bankruptcy case under Chapter 7 or Chapter 11, all property of the debtor becomes property of a bankruptcy estate.[11] The bankruptcy estate is a separate taxable entity.[12] Upon filing, the bankruptcy estate succeeds to certain tax attributes of the debtor. One of these attributes is basis.[13]

The aspect of I.R.C. § 1398 that arguably opens the door for the debtor to escape income tax on the gain from a sale is the provision that states that the transfer of property from the debtor to the bankruptcy estate is not a disposition for tax purposes.[14] Likewise, when an estate is terminated, the transfer of property back from the estate to the debtor is not a disposition for tax purposes.[15] No tax liability, therefore, is incurred when the property passes from the debtor to the estate. Because the estate is a separate taxable entity, if the estate sells the property, the estate (not the debtor) owes the tax. If the property is not disposed of by the trustee during the life of the bankruptcy estate, it will revert to the debtor at the close of the case by operation of law,[16] carrying its tax attributes with it.

The debtor has to hope that the property is transferred while it is property of the estate. Conversely, the interest of the estate lies in disposing of the property in such a way that tax liability on the gain is not incurred by the estate. The remainder of this chapter sets out and discusses the legal arguments that can be made on each side of this issue.

§ 10.4 Abandonment Generally

The primary ways the trustee can dispose of property of the estate are sale and abandonment. The Bankruptcy Code provides:

> (a) After notice and a hearing, the trustee may abandon any property of the estate that is burdensome to the estate or that is of inconsequential value and benefit to the estate.
>
> (b) On request of a party in interest and after notice and a hearing, the court may order the trustee to abandon any property of the estate that is burdensome to the estate or that is of inconsequential value and benefit to the estate.
>
> (c) Unless the court orders otherwise, any property scheduled under section 521(1) of this title not otherwise administered at the time of the closing of a case is abandoned to the debtor and administered for purposes of section 350 of this title.

---

10 *See* I.R.C. § 1398(a)(1986). Portions of § 1398 are reprinted in **§ 10.14.**

11 11 U.S.C. § 541(a). In Chapter 11 the debtor fills the role of trustee, in the capacity of debtor-in-possession. *See* 11 U.S.C. §1101(1).

12 *See* I.R.C. § 1398(c).

13 *Id.* § 1398(g)(6).

14 *Id.* § 1398(f)(1).

15 *Id.* § 1398(f)(2).

16 11 U.S.C. § 554(c). *See* 11 U.S.C. § 704.

> (d) Unless the court orders otherwise, property of the estate that is not abandoned under this section and that is not administered in the case remains property of the estate.[17]

Because property passes to and from the bankruptcy estate without tax consequences, abandonment during the case may allow the debtor to trap the tax problems in the estate and emerge from bankruptcy free of the obligation to pay the tax. The trustee, however, has a duty to protect the estate and will be reluctant to allow the estate to incur tax liability.

Bankruptcy Rule 6007 establishes the procedure for abandonment. The trustee may abandon property after proper notice.[18] The trustee, or the debtor-in-possession in a Chapter 11, must give notice of abandonment to all creditors and parties in interest.[19] If no objection is filed, the property is abandoned without court order. This is termed a nonjudicial or administrative proceeding.[20] Only if an objection is filed does this become a judicial proceeding.

As pointed out in *In re Carron,*[21] there is no necessity for court approval of the trustee's notice of abandonment, unless an objection is filed. As a practical matter, notice can be given to creditors, in the notice of § 341 meeting sent out by the bankruptcy clerk, that the trustee may abandon property, giving parties in interest 15 days after the time fixed by the court to object to such abandonment.[22]

A creditor can request abandonment under Bankruptcy Rule 6007(b), by motion with notice to the trustee.[23] This procedure is a judicial proceeding because it is by motion as opposed to being by notice alone. Abandonment to a creditor is discussed in more detail in **§ 10.6.**

All property not administered by the trustee is abandoned to the debtor on the closing of the case. Closing takes place after the trustee has filed and given notice to the debtor and creditors of the final report under 11 U.S.C. § 704 and Bankruptcy Rule 2002(f), and has distributed funds of the estate.[24] Then, according to 11 U.S.C. § 350, the bankruptcy estate is fully administered. **Sections § 10.5** through **§ 10.7** examine specific arguments regarding abandonment and the taxability of gain.

§ 10.5 Abandonment as a Nontaxable Event

It is well settled that the trustee is not obligated to administer burdensome or unprofitable property.[25] The trustee would want to abandon low basis, overencumbered property back to the debtor.

---

17 11 U.S.C. § 554.

18 Fed. R. Bankr. P. 6007(a).

19 *Id.*

20 William L. Norton Jr., 9 Norton Bankruptcy Law & Practice 2d, 365–68 (1993) (editor's comments).

21 50 B.R. 27 (Bankr. N.D. Ga. 1984).

22 Fed. R. Bank. P. 6007(a).

23 Fed. R. Bank. P. 6007(b).

24 11 U.S.C. § 726.

25 Stanolind Oil & Gas Co. v. Logan, 92 F.2d 28, 31 (5th Cir.), *cert. denied,* 302 U.S. 763 (1938). *See In re* Wilson, 94 B.R. 886 (Bankr. E.D. Va. 1989).

The trustee would contend that an abandonment is not a taxable event, arguing that abandonment is the same as if the property never was property of the estate. Justice Cardozo's statement in *Brown v. O'Keefe*[26] supports this position:

> Whatever title or inchoate interest may have passed to the trustee was extinguished by relation as of the filing of the petition when the trustee informed the court that the shares were burdensome assets, and was directed by the court to abandon and disclaim them. In such case "the title stands as if no assignment had been made." A precise analogy is found in the law of gifts and legacies. Acceptance is presumed, but rejection leaves the title by relation as if the gift had not been made.[27]

This reasoning was followed in the Ninth Circuit cases *Wallace v. Lawrence Warehouse Co.*[28] and *Mason v. Commissioner.*[29] *Wallace* states, "The ordinary rule is that, when a trustee abandons property of the bankruptcy, title reverts to the bankrupt, nunc pro tunc, so that he is treated as having owned it continuously."[30] This theory is known as the *relation back* or *deflection* theory.[31] As stated in *In re Cruseturner,*[32] the property "stands as if no bankruptcy had been filed."[33]

Cruseturner, a consolidation of three cases, addresses what happens to nonexempt property before the debtor redeems it. It asked whether nonexempt property revests in the debtor upon release from the estate. *Cruseturner* states that the law under the Bankruptcy Act of 1898 as expressed in the Ninth Circuit case of *Wallace* is equally compelling under the Bankruptcy Code. *Cruseturner* cites applicable legislative history of the Code:

> Abandonment may be to any party with a possessory interest in the property abandoned. In order to aid administration of the case, [11 U.S.C. § 554(c)] deems the court to have authorized abandonment of any property that is scheduled under Section 521(1) and that is not administered before the case is closed. That property is deemed abandoned to the debtor.[34]

The intent of the Bankruptcy Code, therefore, in keeping with the former law, was that right and title to abandoned property revert to the prebankruptcy status.[35] This usually means that the property reverts to the debtor. However, as discussed in **§ 10.6,** abandonment may be to a creditor under 11 U.S.C. § 554(b).

---

26 300 U.S. 598 (1937).

27 *Id.* at 602 (citations omitted).

28 338 F.2d 392 (9th Cir. 1964).

29 646 F.2d 1309 (9th Cir. 1980).

30 338 F.2d 392, 394 n.1 (9th Cir 1964).

31 *See* Nelson, *Taxation of Abandonments in Bankruptcy,* 10 J. Agric. Tax'n & L. 221, 236–39 (1988).

32 8 B.R. 581 (Bankr. D. Utah 1981).

33 *Id.* at 591.

34 *Id.* at 591 (citing H.R. Rep. No. 595, 95th Cong., 1st Sess. 337; S. Rep. No. 989, 95th Cong., 2d Sess. 92 (1978), *reprinted in* 1978 U.S.C.C.A.N. 5878, 6333).

35 *Id.* at 591–92.

This view could be buttressed by § 722, which authorizes the debtor to redeem abandoned property. In order for the debtor to redeem property, the property must have reverted to the debtor's ownership. Otherwise the provision dealing with redemption of abandoned property in § 722 would be meaningless. The trustee could argue that an abandonment of property by the trustee returns the property to the debtor with the same tax attributes it had when the bankruptcy was filed, including liability for income tax on gain because of a foreclosure by the secured creditor.

The tax effect of an abandonment during the case has been examined in a line of cases from the Eighth Circuit.[36] In *In re McGowan,*[37] the bankruptcy court held that an abandonment of property by a trustee during the case is not a sale or exchange that generates a tax problem for the estate.[38] In *McGowan,* the trustee abandoned farm machinery at the request of a secured creditor. The debtor had no equity, and the property was overencumbered. The court decided the case based on its interpretation of "termination of the estate," as used in § 1398 of the Internal Revenue Code.[39]

The court noted that I.R.C. § 1398(f)(2) does not define termination of the estate. It noted that "termination" does not mean "dismissed" because § 1398 does not apply upon a dismissal.[40] The court reasoned that it could have the following meanings: (1) closing of a case after full administration; (2) abandonment or exemption; (3) completion of foreclosure proceedings following modification of the stay; or (4) other meanings. The court concluded that *termination of the estate* includes termination of the estate's interest in the property under § 554(a).[41]

In *In re Bentley,*[42] the circuit court held that a sale of corn by the trustee during the case, with a subsequent abandonment of proceeds, was taxable to the estate.[43] That case involved a sale and then an abandonment, as opposed to *McGowan,* which involved only an abandonment. *Bentley* is distinguishable from *McGowan* on this

---

36 *In re* McGowan, 95 B.R. 104 (Bankr. N.D. Iowa 1988); *In re* Olson, 930 F.2d 6 (8th Cir. 1991), *aff'g per curiam* 121 B.R. 346 (N.D. Iowa 1990), *aff'g* 100 B.R. 458 (Bankr. N.D. Iowa 1989); *In re* Bentley, 79 B.R. 413 (Bankr. S.D. Iowa 1987), *rev'd,* 916 F.2d 431 (8th Cir. 1990).

37 95 B.R. 104 (Bankr. N.D. Iowa 1988).

38 *Id.* at 108.

39 *Id.* at 107. See **§ 10.14** for text of portions of I.R.C. § 1398.

40 *In re* McGowan, 95 B.R. at 107.

41 *Id.*

42 916 F.2d 431 (8th Cir. 1990), *aff'g* 89 U.S. Tax Cas. (CCH) ¶ 9597 (S.D. Iowa 1989), *rev'g* 79 B.R. 413 (Bankr. S.D. Iowa 1987).

43 916 F.2d at 431–32. Note, however, that the bankruptcy court determined that the estate was not liable for taxes on the sale of corn. The court reasoned that the I.R.C. assesses the tax on gross income of the debtor *to which the estate is entitled.* The estate was not entitled to this property, because it was the subject of a lien, so the bankruptcy court found no tax liability. 79 B.R. at 416. The district court reversed the bankruptcy court, finding that because the sale occurred during the bankruptcy, despite the fact the estate received no benefit, the tax flowed to the estate. 89 U.S. Tax Cas. (CCH) ¶ 9597 (S.D. Iowa 1989). The court did indicate, in dicta, that if the trustee abandoned the grain before any sale, the debtor would bear the tax. 89 U.S. Tax Cas. (CCH) ¶ 9597.

point. The court did not discuss termination of the estate, as *McGowan* did. It found that to hold otherwise would impair the debtor's fresh start.[44]

In the third case, *In re Olson,*[45] the Eighth Circuit Court of Appeals agreed with the bankruptcy and district courts and held that abandonment of estate property during the case is not a sale or exchange and not taxable to the estate.[46] At the bankruptcy level, Judge Edmonds, who also had decided *McGowan* two years earlier, relied on I.R.C. § 1398(f)(2) rather than the relation back concept of *Cruseturner.*[47] Judge Edmonds found that an abandonment is a transfer under 11 U.S.C. § 101(50),[48] reasoning that even though it is not a transfer of title, it is a relinquishment of control.[49]

The *Olson* bankruptcy court distinguished the tax cases of *Yarbro v. Commissioner*[50] and *Commissioner v. Tufts,*[51] which involved nonbankruptcy sales of property. It declined to elevate relief from administering burdensome property to the status of a sale or exchange. The court pointed out that the trustee does not receive or bargain for any consideration for relinquishing control, so abandonment was not a sale or exchange. Finally, the court, although indicating that its definition of termination of the estate may have been overbroad in *McGowan,* found no reason why abandonment during the case should be treated any differently from abandonment at the close of a case.[52]

A letter from James J. Keightly, Assistant Chief Counsel to the Internal Revenue Service, to Michael L. Paup, Deputy Assistant Attorney General, Tax Division, Department of Justice, supports the approach taken by the Eighth Circuit.[53] Mr. Keightly indicated that the intent of Congress was not to tax the estate upon abandonment of property under 11 U.S.C. § 554. He stated that § 554 abandonment is "almost indistinguishable from termination of the estate with respect to that property."[54] It is unclear from Mr. Keightly's letter whether the same result would follow from an abandonment under 11 U.S.C. § 554(b) to a secured creditor.

---

44 916 F.2d at 433.

45 930 F.2d 6 (8th Cir. 1991), *aff'g per curiam* 121 B.R. 346 (N.D. Iowa 1990), *aff'g* 100 B.R. 458 (Bankr. N.D. Iowa 1989).

46 *Id.* at 8.

47 100 B.R. at 462–63.

48 That section, now 11 U.S.C. § 101(58), defines *transfer* for purposes of the Bankruptcy Code.

49 100 B.R. at 463.

50 737 F.2d 479 (5th Cir.), *cert. denied,* 469 U.S. 1189 (1984).

51 461 U.S. 300 (1983).

52 *In re* Olson, 100 B.R. at 462–63.

53 Letter from James J. Keightly, Assistant Chief Counsel to the I.R.S., to Richard L. Paup, Deputy Assistant Attorney General, Tax Div., Dep't of Justice (Mar. 14, 1989), *printed in* Madoff, *A Reappearance of the Tax Consequences of Abandonment in Bankruptcy,* 50 Tax Notes 786 n.9 (1991). This letter was in response to the request of the Executive Office of the United States Trustees for the views of the IRS regarding abandonment of property pursuant to 11 U.S.C. § 554.

54 *Id.* This view has been expressed by the Internal Revenue Service in another instance. A private letter ruling has cited *McGowan* for the proposition that "§ 1398(f)(2) also applies to an abandonment of property by the trustee, and therefore the estate does not

§ 10.6 Abandonment to a Creditor

It may or may not be possible to abandon property specifically to a particular secured creditor. The view that it is not possible is supported by *In re Carron.*[55] In that case, Judge William L. Norton, Jr. stated that § 554 abandonment is not intended to determine issues of ownership and possession of property.[56] He explained the interplay of § 554 and Bankruptcy Rule 6007(b) concerning abandonment of property on motion of a secured creditor in these words:

> Besides being vague and imprecise, such a judicial finding of the proper lien holder and creditor entitled to possession is not allowed in an abandonment motion under Bankruptcy Rule 6007(b). The procedure under Rule 6007 does not permit a judicial determination of validity and extent of a lien which procedure is governed by Rule 7001(2) adversary proceeding procedure. Nor can abandonment procedure be used to determine legal possession of the abandoned property. Abandonment of property may not be made to a particular creditor.
>
> * * *
>
> The finding in § 554 and Rule 6007 is only that the property in question has no realizable equity for the Title 11 estates and should be abandoned from the estate. It is abandoned to the debtor and his non-bankruptcy estate and creditors as their interest may be under state law.[57]

A line of cases follows this approach. In *In re Dewsnup,*[58] the court was convinced by the rationale of *Cruseturner* that property abandoned by a trustee stands as if no bankruptcy had been filed.[59] In *In re Perry,*[60] a creditor sought relief from stay to repossess a vehicle. The trustee had filed a no-asset report, abandoning all nonexempt property. The court found the abandonment was to the debtor, not to the creditor.

---

incur a tax liability when the property is abandoned." Priv. Ltr. Rul. 90-17-075 at 2 (Jan. 31, 1990) (*citing In re* McGowan, 95 B.R. 104, 107 (Bankr. N.D. Iowa 1988)), *revoked on other grounds,* Priv. Ltr. Rul. 91-22-042 (Mar. 4, 1991) (sale of homestead out of which debtor had right to claim exemption of $30,000; gain on sale is tax liability of the estate and is an administrative expense under 11 U.S.C. § 503(b); because administrative expense may not impair exempt property under 11 U.S.C. § 522(k), estate must bear the tax). Another private letter ruling has stated that an abandonment during the case back to the debtor is not a sale or other disposition of property. Priv. Ltr. Rul. 92-45-023 at 4 (Nov. 6, 1992).

55 50 B.R. 27, 29–31 (Bankr. N.D. Ga. 1984).

56 *Id.* at 28–29.

57 *Id.*

58 87 B.R. 676 (Bankr. D. Utah 1988), *aff'd on other grounds,* 908 F.2d 588 (10th Cir. 1990), *aff'd sub nom.* Dewsnup v. Timm, ____ U.S. _____, 112 S. Ct. 773 (1992).

59 *Id.* at 681 (citing *In re* Cruseturner, 8 B.R. 581, 590–91 (Bankr. D. Utah 1981)) (relying on Brown v. O'Keefe, 300 U.S. 598 (1937)).

60 29 B.R. 787 (D. Md. 1983), *aff'd sub nom.* Riggs Nat'l Bank v. Perry, 729 F.2d 982 (4th Cir. 1984).

On the other hand, specific abandonment to a secured creditor was allowed in *In re Karl A. Neise, Inc.*[61] In that case, the court decided an adversary proceeding involving a lien contest between competing creditors in overencumbered property. The court ordered the trustee to turn over possession of the assets to the senior lien holder, after determining the lien priorities, because no equity existed for the estate.[62]

In *In re Butler,*[63] the trustee sought to abandon the estate's claim to proceeds from the sale of the debtors' former land by a mortgage broker who purchased the land subject to the debtors' repurchase option. The court found that the trustee was abandoning rights that arose under a compromise agreement by reason of avoidance powers under 11 U.S.C. § 548. The court recognized that legislative history states that property can be abandoned to anyone with a "possessory interest." However, the court expanded this language to include the mortgage broker, who did not have an actual possessory interest in the property.[64]

In *GMAC v. Bell,*[65] the court hinged its decision to approve specific abandonment to GMAC on a clause in the security agreement. The security agreement contained a clause granting the creditor the right to repossession upon filing of bankruptcy. Even though such clauses are not effective under 11 U.S.C. § 541(c)(1), the court held that the clause became effective again upon abandonment by the trustee and the creditor had the primary possessory interest, not the debtor.[66]

In *In re R-B Co.,*[67] a Chapter 11 case, a plan was confirmed giving the debtor the option of abandoning certain encumbered property, and the court held that the debtor could abandon the property specifically to the creditor. The *In re R-B Co.* court cited Judge Norton's rationale from *In re Carron,* but instead ordered the abandonment.[68] The court did not believe that the abandonment transfers title even as part of a confirmed plan. Therefore, the court allowed the abandonment to the creditor, but not in full satisfaction of the claim of the creditor as provided in the plan, even though the creditor did not want the property.

Whether property may be abandoned to a specific creditor is important in the income tax context. Abandonment directly to a creditor is in many ways analogous to a deed in lieu of foreclosure, and deeds in lieu of foreclosure are taxable events.[69] Whenever abandonment to a creditor takes place, therefore, the debtor can make a strong argument that such an abandonment is a taxable transfer just like a foreclosure or deed in lieu of foreclosure.[70] Therefore, the debtor might argue, the estate must bear any income tax liability on the transfer.[71]

---

61 31 B.R. 409 (Bankr. S.D. Fla. 1983).

62 *Id.* at 412.

63 51 B.R. 261 (Bankr. D.D.C. 1984).

64 *Id.* at 265.

65 700 F.2d 1053 (6th Cir. 1983).

66 *Id.* at 1058.

67 59 B.R. 43 (Bankr. W.D. La. 1986).

68 *Id.* at 46.

69 I.R.C. § 61(a)(3); Helvering v. Hammel, 311 U.S. 504 (1941).

70 Rev. Rul. 76-111, 1976-1; C.B. 214–15; Laport v. Commissioner, 671 F.2d 1028 (7th Cir. 1982).

71 *See* Brown v. O'Keefe, 300 U.S. 598 (1937); *In re* Cruseturner, 8 B.R. 581 (Bankr. D. Utah 1981).

§ 10.7 Abandonment as a Taxable Event

The debtor's primary approach must be to convince the court that abandonment, either to the secured creditor or to the debtor, is a taxable transfer. This argument was accepted by the bankruptcy court for the District of Massachusetts in the 1991 case *In re A.J. Lane & Co.*[72] In that case, the court ruled that the trustee's abandonment of property to the debtor prior to the closing of the case was a sale or exchange, taxable to the estate.[73]

A.J. Lane involved three apartment complexes which were valued at $53 million with a tax basis of $12 million. Foreclosure of the properties would generate a gain of $41 million and a tax liability of $3.2 million after use of considerable net operating losses. The net operating losses belonged to the estate, not the debtor. If the debtor were found to be liable for the tax, liability would be approximately $13 million because the net operating losses would not be available to the debtor after the bankruptcy estate was closed.

Two of the apartment complexes were refinanced for sufficient amounts to discharge the debts against the property. A refinancing on the third property was not worked out and the trustee sought to abandon the property on the eve of foreclosure, because even using the net operating losses, substantial tax liability would follow. The property had a basis of $5.1 million and was sold at foreclosure for $25,000, subject to the first mortgage.[74]

The debtor argued that the abandonment of the property would not rid the estate of tax consequences, contending that the abandonment was essentially a sale or exchange. The court agreed. In reaching its decision, it looked at the problem from three perspectives: benefit to the estate, termination of the estate, and fresh start and fairness.[75] In so doing, it provided a useful framework for constructing arguments on both sides of this issue. In most jurisdictions, it is an open question whether abandonment is a taxable event that results in tax liability for the estate. **Sections 10.8** through **10.10** set out some of the arguments each side can make.

It should be noted that two cases since *A.J. Lane* specifically disagree with its holding and find that abandonment of property by the trustee is not a taxable event and does not result in tax liability for the estate. In *In re Terjen,*[76] the court held that an abandonment of property, with proper notice and absent debtor objection, does not create a taxable incident to the estate and the debtor is stuck with the resulting tax consequences. *In re Burpo,*[77] an Eighth Circuit bankruptcy decision, follows the line established by *Olson* and *Bentley.* It recognized that an abandonment of overencumbered property may place the debtor in a precarious tax situation, but the court found that the trustee may abandon burdensome property without any adverse tax consequences to the estate.

---

72 133 B.R. 264 (Bankr. D. Mass. 1991). *See* Wallace, *Is a Midstream Abandonment of Property by a Bankruptcy Trustee Taxable to the Estate,* 77 J. Tax'n 26 (1992), for a detailed discussion of *A.J. Lane.*

73 *Id.* at 274.

74 *Id.* at 266–67.

75 *Id.* at 269–74.

76 154 B.R. 456 (Bankr. E.D. Va. 1993).

77 148 B.R. 918 (Bankr. W.D. Mo. 1993).

§ 10.8 Benefit to the Estate Arguments

In *In re A.J. Lane & Co.,*[78] the trustee sought to abandon overencumbered property that secured a recourse debt. A foreclosure was scheduled for only a few weeks after the bankruptcy court hearing. The court held the abandonment of the third apartment complex was essentially a sale or exchange because a foreclosure of a recourse mortgage is equivalent to a sale.[79] The court followed *Yarbro v. Commissioner,*[80] which involved property that had declined in value and that was secured by a nonrecourse mortgage. The mortgagor abandoned the property to the creditor but did not deed it to the creditor. The creditor foreclosed. The court held the abandonment of real property subject to nonrecourse debt is a sale because there is relief from the debt.[81]

Even though the debt in *A.J. Lane* was recourse, the court stated that the benefit received is the amount of the debt that is discharged, which is the same benefit that flows from the foreclosure of a nonrecourse mortgage.[82] The court saw the abandonment as a sine qua non to the foreclosure. The court determined that the estate received a benefit of the discharge of the secured portion of the debt.[83]

A debtor, therefore, can cite *A.J. Lane* to support a contention that the estate ought to bear the tax liability because it has received the benefit of a discharge of the secured portion of the debt. The *A.J. Lane* court also saw a benefit to the estate in the proposed surrender of the property,[84] and a debtor can make this argument also.

A.J. Lane views the foreclosure as nothing more than a "mechanical process to clear title."[85] A Maryland decision, *In re Rubin,*[86] agrees with the benefit analysis of *A.J. Lane.* Rubin was a general partner in a partnership and guarantor of a real estate loan. Rubin defaulted on the loan. He worked out an agreement whereby the lender would take the property, release its claim against the partnership, and reduce its claim against the estate by some $6 million. Rubin filed bankruptcy to avoid the debt discharge income. The court weighed the respective tax liabilities. If the tax liability rested on the partners, $1 million in tax would result. If the liability fell to the estate, the tax would be $300,000 and the claim against the estate would be reduced by $6 million. The court chose the estate.[87]

The benefit is derived from satisfaction of that part of the debt equal to the fair market value of the property. In *Helvering v. Nebraska Bridge Supply & Lumber Co.,*[88] the debtor received a benefit to the extent of the foreclosure of a non-recourse

---

[78] 133 B.R. 264 (Bankr. D. Mass. 1991).

[79] 133 B.R. at 272.

[80] 737 F.2d 479 (5th Cir.), *cert. denied,* 469 U.S. 1189 (1984).

[81] *Id.* at 485.

[82] *In re* A.J. Lane & Co., 133 B.R. at 270. In *A.J. Lane* the debt was recourse. That fact affects only the amount of the benefit received.

[83] *Id.*

[84] *Id.* at 271.

[85] *Id.* at 270.

[86] 154 B.R. 897 (Bankr. D. Md. 1992).

[87] *Id.* at 902.

[88] 312 U.S. 666 (1941).

tax lien. A deed in lieu of foreclosure in *Laport v. Commissioner*,[89] created the same result: a satisfaction of debt equal to the value of the property.

The trustee can counter these arguments by citing *In re McGowan*[90] and *In re Olson.*[91] In those cases, the court held that debt discharge is not sufficient benefit to warrant placing tax liability on the estate,[92] and neither is the removal of burdensome property from the estate.[93]

§ 10.9 Termination of the Estate Arguments

The *A.J. Lane* court looked closely at the statutory language and decided that the Internal Revenue Code does not include abandonment among the transfers that are not taxable events. A transfer of property from the debtor to the estate is tax free under I.R.C. § 1398(f)(1). A transfer of property from the estate to the debtor upon termination of the estate is tax free as well under § 1398(f)(2). Therefore, the *A.J. Lane* court reasoned, a transfer during the case must be taxable because it does not occur at the termination of the estate.[94] Further support for the court's conclusion came from § 1398(i), which states that the unused tax attributes are transferred back to the debtor upon termination of the estate. The court was unable to reconcile these provisions without concluding that abandonment during the administration of the estate cannot be a termination within the meaning of the Internal Revenue Code. Noting that the debtor succeeds to the unused net operating losses of the estate under I.R.C. § 1398(g), the *A.J. Lane* court reasoned that termination of the estate cannot mean anything except the closing of the case. The court found that it would be unfair to allow the estate to utilize tax attributes during the case and send low basis property back to the debtor just as the debtor is emerging from bankruptcy.[95]

Another argument that termination means the "closing of the estate" is that termination of a probate estate occurs when all assets have been distributed.[96] Similarly, a

---

89 671 F.2d 1028 (7th Cir. 1982).

90 95 B.R. 104 (Bankr. N.D. Iowa 1988).

91 930 F.2d 6 (8th Cir. 1991), *aff'g per curiam* 121 B.R. 346 (N.D. Iowa 1990), *aff'g* 100 B.R. 458 (Bankr. N.D. Iowa 1989).

92 *In re* Olson, 930 F.2d. at 8.

93 *In re* McGowan, 95 B.R. at 108.

94 133 B.R. 264, 270 (Bankr. D. Mass. 1991).

95 *Id.* at 274–75. Proposed I.R.S. regulations effective November 8, 1992 added certain passive activity losses to the list of tax attributes transferred to the estate. The proposed regulations state the transfer of a passive activity loss to the debtor, other than by sale or exchange, prior to termination of the estate is not a disposition for tax purposes. The proposed regulations open the door to an argument that if this tax attribute passes back to the debtor tax free, the others should as well. However, the proposed regulations do not address the *A.J. Lane* issue of whether an abandonment is a sale or exchange. *See* Lipton, *Proposed 1398 Regs. Raise Conflict Between Debtors and Bankruptcy Trustee,* 79 J. Tax'n 12 (1993).

96 Treas. Reg. § 1.641(b)-3(a).

partnership is terminated when business and financial affairs are discontinued and all assets are distributed to the partners at the end of the winding-up period.[97]

The trustee, on the other hand, can cite to *McGowan*[98] and *Olson*[99] to support a contention that termination of the estate includes termination of the estate's interest in the property under 11 U.S.C. § 554(a). Abandonment during the case should be treated the same as abandonment at the close of the case.[100] The trustee can also argue, citing *Olson,* that abandonment, as mere relief from administering burdensome property, is not a sale or exchange that triggers tax liability because the trustee does not receive or bargain for any consideration for relinquishing control.[101]

Additionally, the Bankruptcy Code provides that for state income tax purposes, "Neither gain nor loss shall be recognized on a transfer—other than a sale, of property from the estate to the debtor."[102] Therefore, the argument goes, an abandonment of property during the case should not have different consequences for state and federal income tax purposes.

A trustee can also point to the letter of James J. Keightly as support for the position that the estate should not be taxed upon abandonment of property under 11 U.S.C. § 554. The Keightly letter takes the position that abandonment during the case qualifies as termination of the estate with respect to that property, and I.R.C. § 1398(f)(2) applies.[103]

§ 10.10 Fresh Start and Fairness Arguments

Fresh start is a basic tenet of bankruptcy law, and absent any countervailing policy, fresh start is controlling.[104] Fresh start is the policy behind allowing the debtor to discharge debts and start anew. In *In re A.J. Lane & Co.,*[105] the tax due on foreclosure would have been $3.2 million. Transfer of that tax liability to the debtor clearly would have impaired the debtor's fresh start. The estate could utilize the net operating losses to minimize tax liability. The refinancing on two of the three apartment complexes avoided large gains that otherwise would have been realized.[106] Finally,

---

97 Treas. Reg. § 1.708-1(b)(1)(i). See James I. Shepard, Trustee's Bankruptcy Tax Manual 146–48 (1992), for a general discussion of termination of the estate.

98 95 B.R.104, 107 (Bankr. N.D. Iowa 1988).

99 100 B.R. 458, 462–63 (Bankr. N.D. Iowa 1989).

100 *Id.*

101 See § **10.5;** James I. Shepard, Trustee's Bankruptcy Tax Manual 146 (1992).

102 I.R.C. § 1398(i).

103 Letter from James J. Keightly, Asst. Chief Counsel to the I.R.S., to Richard L. Paup, Deputy Assistant Attorney General, Tax Div., Dep't of Justice (Mar. 14, 1989) (*printed in* Madoff, *A Reappearance of the Tax Consequences of Abandonment in Bankruptcy,* 50 Tax Notes 786 n.9 (1991)).

104 *In re* A.J. Lane & Co., 133 B.R. 264, 274 (Bankr. D. Mass. 1991). *See* Local Loan Co. v. Hunt, 292 U.S. 234 (1934).

105 133 B.R. 264, 274 (Bankr. D. Mass. 1991).

106 *Id.* at 274.

the court used the legislative history of § 346, dealing with transfers as they pertain to state and local taxes, to support its view that unused tax attributes should be used to facilitate the fresh start of the debtor.[107]

Other courts have also used a fresh start analysis to focus on the inability of the debtor to pay tax liability generated by an abandonment. In *In re Laymon,*[108] abandonment was denied because the debtor would have had a $17,000 tax liability on abandonment, and the estate had received $22,000 in postpetition rental income before the trustee decided to abandon the property to secured creditors. In *In re Matson,*[109] assets in the debtor's possession at the start of the case might have been available to pay at least part of the tax on the property at issue if she had not filed bankruptcy. The court found that it would "impair her fresh start [to saddle] her with property which she does not want and which would then be foreclosed upon or turned over to the secured creditors, resulting in a substantial tax liability for her,"[110] when the estate had reaped benefits from the property it had obtained from her. *In re Rubin*[111] also employed a fresh start analysis. In *Rubin* the court found the abandonment produced a $6 million claim reduction at the expense of $300,000 tax liability.[112]

As with the other points already discussed, countervailing arguments can be made by trustees on this point, too. *In re Burpo*[113] recognized the fresh start concept but found it unpersuasive in the face of the potential liability to the estate and trustee if there are insufficient funds to pay the tax liability. In that case, the debtor sought to have the trustee sell highly depreciated, low basis properties that were valued at $1.29 million encumbered by $1.05 million in debt.[114]

The *In re Olson* bankruptcy court decision acknowledged the debtor's fresh start argument, but found it unpersuasive. It pointed to statutory limits to fresh start incorporated into the Bankruptcy Code in § 727 (denial of discharge) and § 523 (exceptions to discharge).[115]

§ 10.11 Effect of Abandonment at Close of Case

Section 1398(f)(2) states that at the termination of the estate, a transfer of assets back to the debtor is not taxable. Pursuant to § 554(c), property that the trustee does not administer is abandoned back to the debtor on the closing of a case. Notice to the debtor and creditors is required pursuant to Bankruptcy Rule 6007(a). Notice is usually given in the summary of the final report of the trustee's intended distribution.

---

107 *Id.*

108 Civ. 6-89-235 (D. Minn. July 21, 1989), *described in* David Tatge, et al., Chapter 7 Bankruptcy Trustee's Manual 328 n.61 (John Wiley & Sons 1993).

109 No. 90-42308-7 (Bankr. D. Kan. Dec. 13, 1991).

110 *Id.* at 3.

111 154 B.R. 897 (Bankr. D. Md. 1992).

112 *Id.* at 902.

113 148 B.R. 918 (Bankr. W.D. Mo. 1993).

114 *Id.* at 920.

115 100 B.R. 458, 464 (Bankr. N.D. Iowa 1989). See James I. Shepard, The Trustee's Bankruptcy Tax Manual 80–82 (1992), for a discussion of liability for unpaid taxes, the countervailing policy to fresh start.

As described in **§ 10.4,** the closing of a case takes place after the trustee has administered all assets and made distributions, and the clerk of the court ministerially closes the case. Any property that is unadministered on closing returns to the debtor. This type of abandonment leaves the debtor with the same tax liabilities the debtor faced on entering the case unless the tax liability has been trapped in the estate by the trustee's actions or inactions.

In *In re Prospero,*[116] the debtor had made payments on and lived in the property, and the trustee did not abandon. The court closed the case with the property unadministered. The court held that § 554(c) contemplates the situation in which property is held in the estate unadministered, although the court indicated this is rare.

§ 10.12 Disposition under 11 U.S.C. § 725

At least one court, in an unpublished opinion, *In re Matson,*[117] has suggested that the way to dispose of overencumbered property may be under § 725 of the Bankruptcy Code. Section 725 provides as follows:

> **Disposition of certain property.** After the commencement of a case under this chapter, but before final distribution of property of the estate under section 726 of this title, the trustee, after notice and a hearing, shall dispose of any property in which an entity other than the estate has an interest, such as a lien, and that has not been disposed of under another section of this title.

The court in *In re Matson* focused on the language "such as a lien" to suggest that the property can be administered by court order to the secured creditors, thus eliminating the need to foreclose the lien. This would be beneficial when the property is overencumbered and has no value to the estate or debtor.[118]

Section 725 is rarely cited and even less understood. Prior to the enactment of the Bankruptcy Code in 1978, this provision did not exist. The legislative history suggests that the section deals with the following types of property:

1. Property subject to a lien
2. Co-owned property
3. Consigned or bailed goods.[119]

The legislative history behind § 725 identifies the purpose:

> This section requires the court to determine the appropriate disposition of property in which the estate and an entity other than the estate have an interest. It would apply, for example, to *property subject to a lien or property co-owned* by the estate and another

[116] 107 B.R. 732 (Bankr. C.D. Cal. 1989).

[117] No. 90-42308-7 (Bankr. D. Kan. Dec. 13, 1991).

[118] *Id.* at 3.

[119] H.R. Rep. No. 595, 95th Cong., 1st Sess. 382–83 (1977); S. Rep. No. 989, 95th Cong., 2d Sess. 96 (1978), *reprinted in* 1978 U.S.C.C.A.N. 5787.

> entity. . . . The *purpose* of the section is to give the court appropriate authority to ensure that collateral or its proceeds is *returned to the proper secured creditor,* that *consigned or bailed goods* are returned to the consignor or bailor and so on. Current law is curiously silent on this point, though case law has grown to fill the void. The section is in lieu of a section that would direct a certain distribution to secured creditors. It gives the court greater flexibility to meet the circumstances, and it is broader, permitting disposition of property subject to a co-ownership interest.[120]

Even if § 725 is available to a trustee to dispose of property that is overencumbered, there remains the question of the tax ramifications of such a disposition. Under the broad reaches of the Internal Revenue Code, if the trustee transfers the property directly to the secured creditor, such a transfer appears to be taxable.[121] No cases have examined whether a disposition under § 725 creates a taxable event.

§ 10.13 Practical Steps to Minimize Tax Impact

The debtor and the trustee each want to minimize or eliminate the impact of income tax from abandonment of property. This section explores various alternatives available to the debtor and to the trustee.

Net operating losses. A *net operating loss* is the excess of allowable deductions over gross income.[122] The Internal Revenue Code allows taxpayers to use net operating loss carryovers to reduce taxes in a later year and to use net operating loss carrybacks to reduce taxes (and get a refund for taxes paid) for a previous year. Generally, net operating losses can be carried back three tax years from the year with the loss and carried forward 15 years.[123] A net operating loss can reduce tax that otherwise would be owed from a sale of the debtor's property. Net operating losses are equally available to individuals and bankruptcy estates. Any unused net operating losses are transferred to the estate upon filing of the case.[124]

A debtor can utilize net operating losses to offset tax liability before filing bankruptcy. Use of net operating losses may eliminate or reduce tax liability that would otherwise follow the debtor into the bankruptcy. Unused net operating losses will be used by the trustee to offset the tax liability of the estate. Any unused net operating losses return to the debtor at the close of the case. However, because § 108 of the Internal Revenue Code excludes the income from discharge of indebtedness from gross income, the debtor must reduce tax attributes to the extent of discharge of indebtedness.[125] The debtor may reduce the basis of depreciable property first, before reducing net operating losses, if that is advantageous.[126]

---

120 *Id.* (emphasis added).

121 Helvering v. Hammel, 311 U.S. 504 (1941).

122 I.R.C. § 172(c).

123 *Id.* § 172(b)(1)(A).

124 *Id.* § 1398(g).

125 *Id.* §§ 108(b)(1) & (2)(A).

126 *Id.* §§ 108(b)(5)(A) & (B).

Estimated tax payments. A second option for the debtor who has substantial tax liability before filing is to make estimated tax payments to the Internal Revenue Service from the sale or disposition of nonexempt property. These prepayments of estimated tax reduce or eliminate the debtor's tax liability. A trustee in a Colorado bankruptcy case tried to recover such payments in *In re Halle*[127] but was unsuccessful. The court found that the debtor had incurred a gain on disposition of property before filing and had made estimated tax payments to the Internal Revenue Service from the disposition of other assets. The court held that the trustee could not reach these tax payments because the debtor had at least a contingent debt to the Internal Revenue Service at the time the estimated payments were made.

Short tax year election. The debtor may elect a short taxable year under I.R.C. § 1398.[128] This provision allows the debtor to have two taxable years within one calendar year. The first ends on the day before filing the bankruptcy. The second begins on the date of filing. This option allows the debtor, not the estate, to utilize net operating losses to reduce tax liability. However, debtors need to be cautious. If net operating losses and payment of estimated taxes do not eliminate the tax liability, the unpaid taxes will be paid by the trustee in the bankruptcy only after the payment of administrative expenses of the Chapter 7.[129] These unpaid taxes are nondischargeable to the debtor.[130]

Manipulation of bankruptcy filing date. The debtor can manipulate the filing date. For instance, if the debtor owns property that has been foreclosed on but is subject to a right of redemption, the debtor would be well-advised to file bankruptcy on the day before the redemption rights expire.

In a state in which foreclosure has two components, a sale and a period of redemption, the debtor maintains rights in the property through the expiration of the redemption period. The tax consequences are triggered when the right of redemption expires.[131] Section 108(b)(2) of the Bankruptcy Code extends this unexpired right by a maximum of 60 days. Therefore, the trustee has as little as 60 days to determine what to do. If abandonment occurs on the 61st day, the tax gets trapped in the estate.[132] Knowledge of applicable foreclosure law as it pertains to the transfer and title of property is advisable.

Chapter 11 to 7 rollover. The way rollover works is, initially the debtor files a Chapter 11 and sells the property during the pendency of the Chapter 11 case, but

---

127 132 B.R. 186 (Bankr. D. Colo. 1991).

128 I.R.C. § 1398(d)(2)(A).

129 11 U.S.C. § 726(b).

130 *Id.* § 523(a)(1)(A).

131 See James I. Shepard, The Trustee's Bankruptcy Tax Manual 54–59 (1992), for a discussion of the concepts dealing with the fixing of the taxable event in foreclosure sale, expiration of right of redemption, or other event. In Kansas, for instance, the debtor's right to foreclose property expires upon the running of the right of redemption, usually six months after sheriff's sale. Kan. Stat. Ann. § 60-2414 (1993).

132 James I. Shepard, Trustee's Bankruptcy Tax Manual 54–59 (1992).

before confirmation of a plan.[133] The secured creditor receives the proceeds from the sale but there is little or no money to pay any taxes from the sale. Subsequently, the case is converted to a Chapter 7. The Chapter 7 trustee must file all necessary tax returns and deal with the payment of the taxes incurred in the Chapter 11.[134]

The taxes from the sale of property in the Chapter 11 are administrative expenses but are subordinate to Chapter 7 administrative expenses.[135] If insufficient funds exist to pay all administrative expenses, the unpaid expenses remain in the Chapter 7.

This tactic is currently used by some debtors. However, the approach has some inherent problems, which have not been addressed in the case law. Because all taxes incurred by debtors-in-possession are administrative claims, how are these claims to be paid, since they must be paid upon the effective date of the plan?[136] Second, can a finding of feasibility be made if the administrative claims cannot be paid in full upon confirmation?[137] Also, a court must not confirm a plan if the principal purpose is tax avoidance.[138] Therefore, good faith may also become an issue.[139]

§ 10.14 Text of I.R.C. § 1398

Sec. 1398. Rules Relating to Individuals' Title 11 Cases.

(a) Cases to Which Section Applies.

Except as provided in subsection (b), this section shall apply to any case under chapter 7 (relating to liquidations) or chapter 11 (relating to reorganizations) of title 11 of the United States Code in which the debtor is an individual.

(b) Exceptions Where Case is Dismissed, Etc.

(1) Section does not apply where case is dismissed. This section shall not apply if the case under chapter 7 or 11 of title 11 of the United States Code is dismissed.

(2) Section does not apply at partnership level. For purposes of subsection (a), a partnership shall not be treated as an individual, but the interest in a partnership of

---

133 Confirmation of a plan vests all of the property back in the debtor. 11 U.S.C. § 1141(b). Therefore the sale/exchange must occur before confirmation. *See* Onsager, *Assigning Tax Liability Between the Bankruptcy Estate and the Individual Debtor,* 75 J. Tax'n 102, 105 (1991).

134 Holywell v. Smith, ___ U.S. ___ 112 S. Ct. 1021 (1992) (Justice Thomas, writing for the majority, held the successor trustee in a conversion from Chapter 11 to a Chapter 7 must file all necessary tax returns for the debtor, including any that were not filed during the previous Chapter 11).

135 11 U.S.C. § 726(b).

136 *Id.* § 1129(a)(9)(A).

137 *Id.*

138 *Id.* § 1129(d); *In re* McDonald, 128 B.R. 161 (Bankr. W.D. Tex. 1991); *In re* Pizza of Haw., Inc., 761 F.2d 1374 (9th Cir. 1985); *In re* Stratford Ass'n, 145 B.R. 689, 697 (Bankr. D. Kan. 1992) (plan should not be confirmed if it is likely to be followed by liquidation; therefore, the plan must be feasible and not promote visionary schemes).

139 11 U.S.C. § 1129(a)(3); 5 Collier on Bankruptcy ¶ 1129.02[a][ii], at 1129 (15th ed. 1993).

a debtor who is an individual shall be taken into account under this section in the same manner as any other interest of the debtor.

(c) Computation and Payment of Tax; Basic Standard Deduction.

(1) Computation and payment of tax. Except as otherwise provided in this section, the taxable income of the estate shall be computed in the same manner as for an individual. The tax shall be computed on such taxable income and shall be paid by the trustee.

(2) Tax rates. The tax on the taxable income of the estate shall be determined under subsection (d) of section 1.

(3) Basic standard deduction. In the case of an estate which does not itemize deductions, the basic standard deduction for the estate for the taxable year shall be the same as for a married individual filing a separate return for such year.

(d) Taxable Year of Debtors.

(1) General rule. Except as provided in paragraph (2), the taxable year of the debtor shall be determined without regard to the case under title 11 of the United States Code to which this section applies.

(2) Election to terminate debtor's year when case commences.

(A) In general. Notwithstanding section 442, the debtor may (without the approval of the Secretary) elect to treat the debtor's taxable year which includes the commencement date as 2 taxable years—

(i) the first of which ends on the day before the commencement date, and

(ii) the second of which begins on the commencement date.

(B) Spouse may join in election. In the case of a married individual (within the meaning of section 7703), the spouse may elect to have the debtor's election under subparagraph (A) also apply to the spouse, but only if the debtor and the spouse file a joint return for the taxable year referred to in subparagraph (A)(i).

(C) No election where debtor has no assets. No election may be made under subparagraph (A) by a debtor who has no assets other than property which the debtor may treat as exempt property under section 522 of title 11 of the United States Code.

(D) Time for making election. An election under subparagraph (A) or (B) may be made only on or before the due date for filing the return for the taxable year referred to in subparagraph (A)(i). Any such election, once made, shall be irrevocable.

(E) Returns. A return shall be made for each of the taxable years specified in subparagraph (A).

(F) Annualization. For purposes of subsections (b), (c) and (d) of section 443, a return filed for either of the taxable years referred to in subparagraph (A) shall be treated as a return made under paragraph (1) of subsection (a) of section 443.

(3) Commencement date defined. For purposes of this subsection, the term "commencement date" means the day on which the case under title 11 of the United States Code to which this section applies commences.

(e) Treatment of Income, Deductions and Credits.

(1) Estate's share of debtor's income. The gross income of the estate for each taxable year shall include the gross income of the debtor to which the estate is entitled under title 11 of the United States Code. The preceding sentence shall not apply to any amount received or accrued by the debtor before the commencement date (as defined in subsection (d)(3)).

(2) Debtor's share of debtor's income. The gross income of the debtor for any taxable year shall not include any item to the extent that such item is included in the gross income of the estate by reason of paragraph (1).

(3) Rule for making determinations with respect to deductions, credits, and employment taxes. Except as otherwise provided in this section, the determination of whether or not any amount paid or incurred by the estate—

(A) is allowable as a deduction or credit under this chapter, or

(B) is wages for purposes of subtitle C,

shall be made as if the amount were paid or incurred by the debtor and as if the debtor were still engaged in the trades and businesses, and in the activities, the debtor was engaged in before the commencement of the case.

(f) Treatment of Transfers Between Debtor and Estate.

(1) Transfer to estate not treated as disposition. A transfer (other than by sale or exchange) of an asset from the debtor to the estate shall not be treated as a disposition for purposes of any provision of this title assigning tax consequences to a disposition, and the estate shall be treated as the debtor would be treated with respect to such asset.

(2) Transfer from estate to debtor not treated as disposition.

In the case of a termination of the estate, a transfer (other than by sale or exchange) of an asset from the estate to the debtor shall not be treated as a disposition for purposes of any provision of this title assigning tax consequences to a disposition, and the debtor shall be treated as the estate would be treated with respect to such asset.

(g) Estate Succeeds to Tax Attributes of Debtor.

The estate shall succeed to and take into account the following items (determined as of the first day of the debtor's taxable year in which the case commences) of the debtor—

(1) Net operating loss carryovers. The net operating loss carryovers determined under section 172.

(2) Charitable contributions carryovers. The carryover of excess charitable contributions determined under section 170(d)(1).

(3) Recovery of tax benefit items. Any amount to which section 111 (relating to recovery of tax benefit items) applies.

(4) Credit carryovers, etc.

The carryover of any credit, and all other items which, but for the commencement of the case, would be required to be taken into account by the debtor with respect to any credit.

(5) Capital loss carryovers. The capital loss carryover determined under section 1212.

(6) Basis, holding period, and character of assets. In the case of any asset acquired (other than by sale or exchange) by the estate from the debtor, the basis, holding period, and character it had in the hands of the debtor.

(7) Method of accounting. The method of accounting used by the debtor.

(8) Other attributes. Other tax attributes of the debtor, to the extent provided in regulations prescribed by the Secretary as necessary or appropriate to carry out the purposes of this section.

* * *

(i) Debtor Succeeds to Tax Attributes of Estate.

In the case of a termination of an estate, the debtor shall succeed to and take into account that items referred to in paragraphs (1), (2), (3), (4), (5), and (6) of subsection (g) in a manner similar to that provided in such paragraphs (but taking into account that the transfer is from the estate to the debtor instead of from the debtor to the estate). In addition, the debtor shall succeed to and take into account the other tax attributes of the estate, to the extent provided in regulations prescribed by the Secretary as necessary or appropriate to carry out the purposes of this section.

[Subsection (j) is omitted.]

CHAPTER 11

VALUATION OF PROPERTY

Paul D. Sinclair

§ 11.1 Valuation Generally

Valuation is a central concept in bankruptcy reorganization and liquidation and pertains to almost every aspect of a case including obtaining credit, lifting the automatic stay, plan confirmation, and avoidance actions.[1]

Valuation may be a double-edged sword. Although it may be attractive for a debtor to give a low value to its assets, thus establishing insolvency in order to recover preferential transfers, that same low value may later make it impossible to confirm a plan of reorganization because it shows that the debtor lacks equity. Likewise, for the secured creditor, a low value showing no equity in connection with a motion to lift the stay can result in the creditor's being hoisted on its own petard at a cram down hearing when it wishes to maximize the amount of its secured claim to force the debtor to repay the maximum amount of principal, interest, and attorney's fees.

---

[1] The purpose of this chapter is not to replace the available treatises, articles, and books on this topic. The reader is particularly directed to 1 Collier on Bankruptcy ¶ 101.32 (15th ed. 1992) on the term *insolvent* and ¶ 506.04[2] on valuation of collateral as part of its discussion of 11 U.S.C. § 506(a). Also, Shannon P. Pratt, Valuing Small Businesses and Professional Practices (1986), and Mr. Pratt's subsequent books on valuation of businesses are collectively considered to be the valuation Bible by many expert witnesses. For many years, another key resource was the work of Robert Morris & Associates, which set out voluminous quantities of statitistical information on businesses, thus giving the experts a comparative basis on which to analyze a specific debtor. With the explosion in computer information in recent years, such statistical information is available on CD-ROM for use by experts. In a sufficiently challenging case, there is no substitute for a review of Shannon Pratt's work in order to comprehend the underlying concepts and questions to be put to experts.

Section 506(a) provides that the value of assets shall be determined in light of the purpose of the valuation and the proposed disposition or use of such property. This is reinforced by the legislative history, which states that a valuation early in the case in a proceeding under §§ 361, 362, or 363 would not be binding on the debtor or creditor at the time of confirmation of the plan. Nevertheless, although the statutory language and legislative history may preclude the use of estoppel when a party changes its position on value, credibility is an omnipresent consideration in any court of law.

This chapter considers two basic types of valuation issues, and it is critical to recognize the distinction between them. The two types are: (1) an overall assessment of the debtor's assets and liabilities, and (2) valuation of a particular asset or group of assets. In connection with a determination of solvency as an element of a preferential transfer action under § 547, for example, the court must make an overall assessment of the debtor's assets and liabilities. By contrast, the resolution of an adequate protection dispute under § 361 or an expanding inventory problem under § 547(c)(5) requires valuation of a particular asset or group of assets. Principles applicable to one type of analysis may not necessarily be applicable to the other.

§ 11.2 Definition of Value and Valuation

Section 101(32) of the Bankruptcy Code sets forth the *balance sheet test* of insolvency: a debtor is insolvent if the sum of its debts is greater than all of its property "at a fair valuation." The definition is different when the debtor is a general partnership, in which case, in addition to the assets of the partnership, the court will consider the excess of the value of each general partner's nonpartnership property.[2] An entity's assets do not include property transferred with intent to hinder, delay, or defraud creditors,[3] but on the other hand, property that is the subject of a preferential transfer must be counted among the debtor's assets when its solvency at the time of such transfer is in issue.[4]

A key concept is the interpretation of the statutory language "fair value." *Fair value* means neither forced sale nor going concern value, but rather the amount of money that the debtor could raise from its property in a short period of time, but not so short as to approximate a forced sale, if the debtor operated in a reasonably prudent and diligent manner, taking into account the payments of its debts.[5] Stated differently, fair value is determined by estimating what the debtor's assets would realize if sold in a prudent manner in current market conditions.[6] *Collier on Bankruptcy* takes this a step further by referring to fair value as a "reasonable estimate of what can be realized from the assets by converting them into, or reducing

---

[2] 11 U.S.C. § 101(32)(B).

[3] *Id.* § 101(32)(A)(i).

[4] *In re* Utrecht Coal Co., 63 F.2d 745 (2d Cir. 1933).

[5] *In re* Tennessee Chem. Co., 143 B.R. 468, 474 (Bankr. E.D. Tenn. 1992); *In re* McLean Indus., 132 B.R. 247, 258 (Bankr. S.D.N.Y. 1991); Jahn v. Reading Body Works, Inc. (*In re* A. Fassnacht & Sons, Inc.), 45 B.R. 209, 217 (Bankr. E.D. Tenn. 1984); *In re* Utility Stationery Stores, 12 B.R. 170 (Bankr. N.D. Ill. 1981).

[6] Cissell v. First Nat'l Bank, 476 F. Supp. 474, 482 (S.D. Ohio 1979).

them to cash, under a carefully guarded if not idealized condition."[7] In the context of preferences, assets must be valued at what they are reasonably worth at the time of the allegedly preferential transfer and not what they turned out to be worth at some time after the bankruptcy intervened.[8]

Balance sheets cannot necessarily be relied on as indicators of value. A balance sheet is merely a mathematical expression of the use or sale value of assets. Also, balance sheet value can be adversely affected by continuing ongoing losses of the failing business or expenses of administration.

CONTEXTS OF VALUATION

§ 11.3 Involuntary Petition

An order for relief under an involuntary petition will be entered under § 303(h) of the Code only if the debtor is not paying its debts as they become due or if a receiver or trustee was appointed to take charge of substantially all of the debtor's property. Thus, the issue is whether the debtor is paying debts as they mature, not whether it is solvent.

Nevertheless, because inability to pay debts is closely linked to the quantum of liabilities in comparison with assets, both the debtor and creditors will almost inevitably end up, if a contested hearing on an involuntary petition takes place, analyzing the debtor's solvency.

§ 11.4 Cash Collateral Orders and Obtaining Credit

At the beginning of many reorganization cases, the debtor-in-possession is confronted with having to obtain, under § 363(c), the court's permission to use cash collateral that is the property of one or more of its secured creditors. See **Chapter 3.** Similarly, if a debtor is unable to obtain operating credit through administrative expense treatment or by new liens on property not otherwise subject to a lien, the court may be requested to authorize a superpriority lien under § 364(d) of the Code. See **Chapter 6.** In either of these instances, it is necessary to determine the value of the secured creditors' existing collateral. If new collateral is to be given, its value must be determined.[9]

---

[7] 1 Collier on Bankruptcy ¶ 101.32[5] (15th ed. 1992).

[8] Cissell v. First Nat'l Bank, 476 F. Supp. 474, 482 (S.D. Ohio 1979).

[9] Valuation of property in the context of obtaining credit was at issue in *In re* Phoenix Steel Corp., 39 B.R. 218 (D. Del. 1984).

§ 11.5 Adequate Protection

Section 362 of the Code protects the debtor with an automatic stay, § 363 provides for the debtor to use encumbered property in the ordinary course of business, and § 364 provides for the debtor to borrow money, but all are limited by the provision in § 361 for adequate protection to the creditor. *Adequate protection* under § 361 may be furnished in three different ways: periodic cash payments, an additional replacement lien on other property, or such other relief as will result in the creditor's receiving the indubitable equivalent of its interest in the collateral.

The question of valuation invariably underlies any issue concerning adequate protection. Sometimes it is necessary to determine what periodic payments may be appropriate when, for example, the property is depreciating at a relatively fixed rate. An example of a depreciating asset of this type is a delivery truck.[10]

§ 11.6 Lift of Automatic Stay

Under 11 U.S.C. § 362(d)(2), the stay may be lifted for actions against property if the debtor does not have any equity and the property is not necessary for an effective reorganization.[11] See **Chapter 5.** From the valuation standpoint, in determining whether equity exists, all liens on the property must be considered rather than simply the lien of the moving creditor.[12]

§ 11.7 Determination of Secured Claims

Section 506(a) of the Bankruptcy Code provides that a creditor is secured to the extent of the value of its lien and unsecured to the extent that its collateral is worth less than the amount of its claim. It goes on to state that value "shall be determined in light of the purpose of the valuation and of the proposed disposition or use of such

---

10 Valuation used to be an issue in cases involving the now rejected notion of equity cushion. *See In re* Alyucan Interstate Corp., 12 B.R. 803, 810 n.14 (Bankr. D. Utah 1981). *Alyucan* and subsequent cases, however, decisively rejected the equity cushion analysis. The rationale for this is that § 361 does not speak in terms of preserving the equity cushion but rather in terms of compensating the secured creditor for any decrease in the value of its interest in property. 12 B.R. at 811. Thus, instances could arise in which the secured creditor is undersecured and thus there is no equity cushion. Unless the value of the collateral is decreasing, the creditor is not entitled to adequate protection payments. United Sav. Ass'n v. Timbers of Inwood Forest Assocs., Ltd., 484 U.S. 365 (1988).

11 Two cases presenting a thoughtful valuation analysis in the context of the lift of the automatic stay are *In re* Monica Road Assocs., 147 B.R. 385 (Bankr. E.D. Va. 1992) (undeveloped ground), and *In re* Ascher, 146 B.R. 764 (Bankr. N.D. Ill. 1992) (commercial laundry).

12 Stewart v. Gurley, 745 F.2d 1194 (9th Cir. 1984); *In re* Eisentrager, 102 B.R. 181, 182 (Bankr. W.D. Mo. 1989); *In re* Faires, 34 B.R. 549, 551 (Bankr. W.D. Wash. 1983).

property."[13] The determination of value of a secured claim in one aspect of a bankruptcy proceeding is not necessarily res judicata in other aspects of the proceeding.[14]

Bankruptcy Rule 3012, on valuation of security, provides that the court may determine the value of a claim secured by a lien on the property in which the estate has an interest on the motion of any party in interest. The courts, however, generally will not act on such a motion unless a proof of claim has been filed.[15] In connection with such a motion, the valuation is a contested matter governed by Bankruptcy Rule 9014, while validity, priority, or extent of a lien is an adversary proceeding governed by Part VII of the Bankruptcy Rules.[16]

§ 11.8 Plan Confirmation

Valuation of property is critical at the plan confirmation stage, especially when there is a question about whether a debtor's proposed cram down of a plan of reorganization is fair and equitable.[17]

As part of the confirmation of a plan of reorganization and a cram down of a secured creditor who is retaining its lien and receiving payments, the court must of necessity under § 1129(b)(2)(A)(i) value the rate of interest to be paid and the proposed principal reduction of the debt to determine whether the deferred cash payments total the allowed amount of the claim as of the effective date of the plan.[18] Although not the same as putting a dollar figure on a tangible asset, comparing interest rates and principal amortization rates with the increase or decrease in the value of the collateral and possible effects over the life of the plan is clearly a matter of valuation.

§ 11.9 Avoiding Powers

Probably the single most widely litigated valuation question is the determination of solvency at the time of an allegedly avoidable transfer. Insolvency is an element of voidable preference under § 547(b)(3) and fraudulent transfer under

[13] *In re* Datair Sys. Corp., 42 B.R. 241, 243–44 (Bankr. N.D. Ill. 1984).

[14] *In re* Fairchild, 31 B.R. 789, 795 (Bankr. S.D. Ohio 1983).

[15] *In re* Dembo, 126 B.R. 195, 200 (Bankr. E.D. Pa. 1991); *In re* Hotel Assocs., Inc., 1 Collier Bankr. Cas. 2d (MB) 819 (Bankr. E.D. Pa. 1980).

[16] Examples of cases in which the court made a valuation determination under § 506(a) are *In re* Savannah Gardens-Oaktree, 146 B.R. 306 (Bankr. S.D. Ga. 1992), and *In re* Usury, 106 B.R. 759 (Bankr. M.D. Ga. 1989).

[17] Cases dealing with valuation in the cram down context include *In re* Future Energy Corp., 83 B.R. 470 (Bankr. S.D. Ohio 1988), and *In re* Sandy Ridge Dev. Corp., 881 F.2d 1346 (5th Cir. 1989).

[18] The benchmark for almost 60 years in this area has been *In re* Murel Holding Corp., 75 F.2d 941 (2d Cir. 1935), which held that a 10-year moratorium on the repayment of principal failed to constitute indubitable equivalence permitting cram down. *See also In re* Briscoe Enters., 994 F.2d 1160 (5th Cir. 1993).

§ 548(a)(2)(B)(i), so valuation of the business as a whole is important in these avoidance actions.[19]

In determining whether a company is insolvent at the time of a preferential transfer, the court need not be exact in its value as to the extent of the insolvency.[20]

FACTORS AFFECTING VALUATION

§ 11.10 Retail and Wholesale Value

Valuation in the bankruptcy context frequently involves determining what sort of value is the correct value in given situations. Examples of types of value are retail value, wholesale value, liquidation value, going-concern value, intrinsic value, and actual value. These categories may sometimes need to be further analyzed. For example, the proper question may well be, "wholesale value to whom?" How to label the value allocated is frequently the most crucial question in the litigation process. Resolving that question often decides the case. In *In re Taxman Clothing Co.,*[21] the question was whether the clothing in a modest retail store should be fixed at retail value (the price sold to customers), wholesale value (the price paid by the debtor), or liquidation value (46 percent of the original wholesale cost). The court decided that inventory in the circumstances of that case should be valued at the debtor's purchase price.

Furniture and fixtures in a retail store, on the other hand, are purchased by the debtor at retail from a supplier and then used in the debtor's business. Thus, on a going-concern basis, although the inventory is properly valued at a wholesale cost, the furnishings and equipment must be valued at a fairly depreciated retail cost. Of course, if the debtor were actually on its death bed, the appropriate measure of value would be liquidation value, which is frequently in the range of 40 to 60 percent of wholesale cost.

§ 11.11 Entity Being Valued

Another question in valuation is which entity is being evaluated. For example, in some instances, the court may value a parent and subsidiary together.[22] In other instances such consolidation may be refused.[23]

---

[19] Cases dealing with valuation issues in the voidable transfer context include *In re* Taxman Clothing Co., 905 F.2d 166 (7th Cir. 1990); *In re* Energy Coop., Inc., 109 B.R. 822 (N.D. Ill. 1989); and *In re* Ebbler Furniture & Appliances, Inc., 804 F.2d 87 (7th Cir. 1986).

[20] *In re* Tennessee Chem. Co., 143 B.R. 468, 479 (Bankr. E.D. Tenn. 1992).

[21] 905 F.2d 166 (7th Cir. 1990).

[22] Cissell v. First Nat'l Bank, 476 F. Supp. 474 (S.D. Ohio 1979).

[23] *In re* Total Technical Servs., Inc., 150 B.R. 893, 900 (Bankr. D. Del. 1993).

§ 11.12 Time of Valuation

In connection with a preferential transfer, the solvency of the debtor is to be determined at the time of the transfer, not at the time the petition was filed.[24] Moreover, the debtor's assets have to be valued at the time of the transfer and not at what the assets turned out to be worth at some time after the bankruptcy intervened.[25] Sometimes the solvency of the company as of the end of a reporting period, such as the end of a particular fiscal year or month, must be established. Then adjustments are made as a result of profit and loss during the time between the reporting period and the actual time of the transfer. In *In re Coated Sales, Inc.*,[26] this methodology was referred to as an adjustment for "the roll forward period." In other instances, if insolvency can be shown in a prior period with no intervening financial changes that would have improved the debtor's condition, the insolvency may be considered established.[27] In another case, a 57-day gap between the relevant date and the time a financial statement was available was deemed to be acceptable when there was no material change in the debtor's financial condition.[28]

§ 11.13 Going-Concern and Liquidation Value

Normally a business must be valued as a going concern.[29] Liquidation value, on the other hand, is appropriate if the business is "on its death bed."[30] However, caution should be taken not to consider a business property "dead" merely because hindsight reveals that the debtor was traveling on the road to financial ruin.[31]

The rationale behind the preference for going concern as the correct market value is that because the property was assembled for the conduct of a business and is fit for such use, it should be given that use. The additional increment of value reflects in part not only the business' earning power, but the ready availability of customer lists, established supply lines, and other attributes making it possible for a purchaser to step in and immediately commence operations.[32] This is particularly so when as part of its plan, the debtor will retain the assets and use them as part of its reorganization.[33]

---

24 *In re* Parker Steel Co., 149 B.R. 834, 844 (Bankr. N.D. Ohio 1992).

25 *In re* Coated Sales, Inc., 144 B.R. 663, 668 (Bankr. S.D.N.Y. 1992); Cissel v. First Nat'l Bank, 476 F. Supp. 474, 484 (S.D. Ohio 1979).

26 144 B.R. 663, 678–79 (Bankr. S.D.N.Y. 1992).

27 *In re* Total Technical Servs., Inc., 150 B.R. 893, 899 (Bankr. D. Del. 1993).

28 *In re* McLean Indus.,132 B.R. 247, 258–59 (Bankr. S.D.N.Y. 1991).

29 *In re* Bellanca Aircraft Corp., 56 B.R. 339, 386 (Bankr. D. Minn. 1985), *aff'd in part, remanded in part,* 850 F.2d 1275 (8th Cir. 1988).

30 *In re* Taxman Clothing Co., 905 F.2d 166, 170 (7th Cir. 1990).

31 *Id.* at 170. *See* 1 Collier on Bankruptcy ¶ 56.04, at 506-27-28 (15th ed. 1992).

32 *In re* Bellanca Aircraft Corp., 56 B.R. 339, 386 (Bankr. D. Minn. 1985), *aff'd in part, remanded in part,* 850 F.2d 1275 (8th Cir. 1988).

33 *In re* Savannah Gardens-Oaktree, 146 B.R. 306, 309–10 (Bankr. S.D. Ga. 1992). In *In re* Bellanca Aircraft Corp., 56 B.R. 339, 387–88 (Bankr. D. Minn. 1985), *aff'd in part, remanded in part,* 850 F.2d 1275 (8th Cir. 1988), a preference case, the court concluded

It has been held that although normally the going-concern value is appropriate, to treat a dead company as a going concern would be misleading and would fictionalize the company's true financial condition.[34] For a going-concern valuation, however, the business does not have to be a thriving concern and to be "dead" it must be "wholly inoperative, defunct or dead on its feet."[35]

In *In re Coated Sales, Inc.,*[36] the court made a careful analysis and determined that going-concern value could not be used in the case. The court said that it was not relying on hindsight, which would be improper, but rather on the fact that it was inescapable that the debtor was beyond normal "serious financial trouble" and was in a state of financial ruin, and that a massive fraud in fact had been committed. In this context, the court held, no going-concern value would be considered.[37] In a much smaller case involving a car wash, *In re Davis,*[38] despite the serious financial difficulties of the debtor, the court refused to use a liquidation value and instead found that going-concern value was appropriate. The cash equity the debtor needed to raise to stay alive was very modest. The court found that the debtor did not lose hope or cease his intent to continue operations until very late in the game, and thus the going-concern value was applicable.[39]

Going-concern value applies only to the property needed to operate the business. In *In re Tennessee Chemical Co.,*[40] part of the debtor's plant with a book value of $20 million was sold for $500,000 after the bankruptcy. The court found that the sale was actually a sale at the going-concern value, because it was sold as an operating unit, but thus only a part of the business was considered to be a going concern and therefore it had a greatly reduced value.[41]

When the testimony supporting competing values such as going-concern and liquidation value is fairly well balanced, rather than selecting one or the other, the court sometimes simply splits the difference between the two values.[42]

---

that under either going-concern or liquidation values, a lower value had to be used because by the time of the transfers, the debtor was no longer a viable operating entity. In *Savannah Gardens,* by contrast, the debtor was proposing what the court thought was an acceptable form of reorganization and the going-concern value was utilized. In fact, in the battle between the debtor's and creditor's experts, the court determined that the debtor's appraiser assumed continuing operations, while the creditor's appraiser assumed an immediate sale. 146 B.R. at 309.

34 *In re* Art Shirt Ltd., 93 B.R. 333, 341 (E.D. Pa. 1988).

35 *Id.* at 341. *Art Shirt Ltd.* was a preference action, and the court found that due to a substantial ERISA withdrawal liability, the court had to consider this a "dead concern, and no going concern value could be applicable." *Id.* In reaching this conclusion, the bankruptcy court relied in part on the testimony of an accountant that in an accounting sense the business was not a going concern. *Id.* at n.8.

36 144 B.R. 663 (Bankr. S.D.N.Y. 1992).

37 *Id.* at 668.

38 120 B.R. 823 (Bankr. W.D. Pa. 1990).

39 *Id.* at 826.

40 143 B.R. 468 (Bankr. E.D. Tenn. 1992).

41 *Id.* at 476.

42 *See, e.g., In re* Phoenix Steel Corp., 39 B.R. 218, 226–27 (D. Del. 1984); *In re* Coated Sales, Inc., 144 B.R. 663, 677 (Bankr. S.D.N.Y. 1992); *In re* Damron, 8 B.R. 323 (Bankr. S.D. Ohio 1980).

§ 11.14 Adjusted Book Value

Rather than using completely independent values, the court may sometimes accept the value of the company shown on the books. Theoretically, this is original cost less applicable depreciation. Such a value was accepted in connection with a car wash in *In re Davis.*[43] However, in that case, the car wash was only acquired in 1985 and the bankruptcy occurred two years later; therefore, not much depreciation was applicable.

By contrast, in *In re Tennessee Chemical Co.,*[44] the court rejected that approach. It said that although cost less depreciation may be the correct book value under generally accepted accounting principles, it does not necessarily reflect fair value. In *Tennessee Chemical,* the business had been acquired in 1982 or 1983, and the applicable balance sheet reflected cost less depreciation in April 1989. The court said that cost minus depreciation for five to six years does not automatically equal market value or any other measure of fair value.[45]

Book value is not inadmissible evidence of fair market value.[46] However, because generally accepted accounting principles (GAAP) are not synonymous with any specific valuation policy, a GAAP balance sheet, which does not indicate how the debtor's assets were valued, may be deemed to have no probatave weight at all.[47] Asset values carried on a balance sheet, even if derived in accordance with GAAP, do not necessarily reflect fair value.[48] Also, strictly requiring courts to apply GAAP would make accountants and the board that promulgates GAAP the arbiters of insolvency questions. Under the Code, judges are to make such decisions.[49] Although GAAP determinations are relevant, they are not controlling.[50]

The argument that the bankruptcy schedules must be treated as market value because the schedules are supposed to list market value[51] has also been rejected.[52] In valuing a business, courts may also take into account the fact that the existence of a Chapter 11 proceeding itself causes a drop in value.[53]

§ 11.15 Market Value Approach

Because value is approached on a case-by-case basis, each case is necessarily unique unto itself. In the real estate context, (see **§ 11.21**), the court considers: (1) the

---

43 120 B.R. 823, 826 (Bankr. W.D. Pa. 1990).

44 143 B.R. 468 (Bankr. E.D. Tenn. 1992).

45 *Id.* at 471.

46 Inter-state Nat'l Bank v. Luther, 221 F.2d 382, 391 (10th Cir. 1955).

47 *In re* F&S Cent. Mfg. Corp., 53 B.R. 842, 849 (Bankr. E.D.N.Y. 1985). *See also In re* Sierra Steel, Inc., 96 B.R. 275, 278 (Bankr. 9th Cir. 1989); Porter v. Yukon Nat'l Bank, 866 F.2d 355 (10th Cir. 1989).

48 *In re* Simco Mechanical, 151 B.R. 978, 982 (Bankr. S.D. Fla. 1993).

49 *In re* Parker Steel Co., 149 B.R. 834, 835 (Bankr. N.D. Ohio 1992).

50 *Id.*

51 Fed. R. Bankr. P. 1007; Official Bankruptcy Form 6.

52 *In re* Tennessee Chem. Co., 143 B.R. 468, 471 (Bankr. E.D. Tenn. 1992).

53 *Id.* at 478.

income approach, (2) the market value approach, and (3) the replacement cost approach.

In connection with the market value approach, factors other than the total cost of a comparable property may be considered. For example, in *In re Savannah Gardens-Oaktree,*[54] the court considered not merely the gross sales price of comparable properties, but the further factors of the number of units in each property, the year built, the price as a multiple of the gross income, the price per square foot, and the price per unit. The court particularly discounted the creditors' appraiser's exaggerated downward adjustment of the gross income multiplier used to discredit the debtor's position.[55]

§ 11.16 Income Approach

The income approach takes the net operating income (NOI) after all expenses, with a reserve for depreciation (the capital cost of maintaining the premises), and then divides that figure by a reasonable rate of return expected in the marketplace based upon comparable properties. In the *Savannah Gardens* case,[56] the creditors' appraiser stated that the rate of capitalization for comparable properties ranged between 6.5 and 12.17 percent. In other words, the net operating income for each property ranged between 6.5 and 12.17 percent of the purchase price of each comparable apartment complex. The court then went a step further and added a capitalization rate based on a mortgage/equity method. Using that method, the court assumed that a portion of the purchase price of the complex would be financed, that the debtor would pay interest on the purchase loan, and thus the capitalization rate should be blended with the loan rate for the property. This resulted in a capitalization rate for the particular complex in that case of 11.99 percent.

§ 11.17 Depreciated Replacement Cost

In some instances, it may be possible to replace the assets in question more cheaply than they can be purchased in the marketplace. In such a situation, the replacement cost may well be relevant. However, in a troubled industry, the value of the tangible assets is frequently far exceeded by the replacement cost. This may be the result of extensive overbuilding. In *In re SM 104 Ltd.*,[57] the question was whether to consider the replacement cost of an office building in a substantially overbuilt market. Neither the debtor's nor creditor's appraisers gave much weight to the replacement value. As the court said, if some disaster destroyed the debtor's building, given the excess of available office space in south Florida, it would be fruitless to rebuild the property. Instead, a rational investor might well pocket the insurance proceeds and sell the ground for some other use. Thus, the depreciated replacement cost was rejected.

---

[54] 146 B.R. 306 (Bankr. S.D. Ga. 1992).

[55] *Id.* at 311.

[56] 146 B.R. 306 (Bankr. S.D. Ga. 1992).

[57] 160 B.R. 202 (Bankr. S.D. Fla. 1993).

Similarly, in *In re Energy Co-operative, Inc.*,[58] the market for refineries such as the one owned by the debtor, which had a book value of $161 million, was totally nonexistent. It seemed that this refinery could not be given away. There was simply tremendous overcapacity in the refinery business. The court concluded that although discounted replacement cost may sometimes be a significant consideration in the value of an asset, this was not one of those circumstances.[59]

§ 11.18 Reduction for Costs of Sale

A question frequently presented to courts is whether the fair value of an asset must be reduced by the costs of sale or liquidation of that asset. The argument is frequently advanced by those favoring an interpretation of "the value of such creditor's interest in the estate's interest in such property" in § 506(a) to mean the value of the collateral to the creditor who would be liquidating it. On the other hand, it is argued that such an interpretation renders the last sentence surplusage when it says that the value shall be determined "in light of the purpose of the valuation and the proposed disposition or use of such property." That has been interpreted to mean that if the debtor retains the property, then there are no liquidation or other sale costs that should be considered. Consequently, the amount to be paid to the secured creditor in its stream of payments must be based upon the full fair value without reduction for costs of sale.[60] In *In re Beacon Hill Apartments, Ltd.*,[61] the court took this one step further. A secured creditor had an equity cushion in the collateral, and the court found that because the mortgage provided that the costs of sale were to be paid by the debtor, the fair value to be paid over to the creditor at the sale was not to be reduced by the expenses of liquidation.

§ 11.19 Presumptions and Burden of Proof

In connection with the confirmation of a plan of reorganization, it is the plan proponent who must request confirmation pursuant to § 1129(b) and who has the actual burden of establishing that a secured creditor will receive value at least equal to that of the secured creditor's interest in the property.[62] In that regard, for a cram down under § 1129(b), the burden of proof is by a preponderance of the evidence.[63] In connection with insolvency under § 547(b) the debtor has the ultimate burden of

58 109 B.R. 822 (N.D. Ill. 1989).

59 *Id.* at 828.

60 *In re* Balbus, 933 F.2d 246, 251–52 (4th Cir. 1991); *In re* Usury, 106 B.R. 759, 761–62 (Bankr. M.D. Ga. 1989); *In re* Huff, 159 B.R. 262, 263–64 (Bankr. W.D. Mo. 1993).

61 118 B.R. 148, 152–53 (N.D. Ga. 1990).

62 *In re* Rusty Jones, Inc., 110 B.R. 362 (Bankr. N.D. Ill. 1990); *In re* San Felipe & Boss, Ltd., 115 B.R. 526 (S.D. Tex. 1990); *In re* Crowthers McCall Pattern, Inc., 24 Collier Bankr. Cas. 2d (MB) 611 (Bankr. S.D.N.Y. 1990).

63 *In re* Briscoe Enters., 994 F.2d 1160, 1165 (5th Cir. 1993).

proof on insolvency but, at least during the 90-day period, there is a presumption of insolvency. This means that the defendant has the burden of going forward with evidence to rebut that presumption.[64] Federal Rule of Evidence 301 defines the meaning of that presumption such that although the defendant has the burden of going forward, the ultimate burden of proof does not shift and still remains on the trustee or debtor.[65] While the introduction of the debtor's schedules showing solvency may be sufficient to rebut the presumption of insolvency,[66] the schedules alone may not carry the day because they may not reflect actual market conditions with respect to a reasonable sale of the debtor's property.[67]

§ 11.20 Methods of Evidence

The basic evidence on valuation may include the debtor's schedules and financial statements, but it is obvious that in a great many cases it is impossible to dispense with expert testimony. Two cases cited in this chapter, *In re Savannah Gardens-Oaktree*[68] and *In re SM 104, Ltd.,*[69] contain examples of why the court may choose to find one appraiser more credible than another. These include an improper use of comparable properties, unrealistic capitalization rates, a failure to accurately adjust the solvency determination to the date of the alleged preference, and reliance without explanation on out-of-town comparables.

One warning in this context—particularly applicable to non-real estate appraisals—is that an appraiser should not rely heavily on balance sheets derived in accordance with generally accepted accounting principles and accounting principles derived from the Internal Revenue Code. These may not comport with reality. For example, in *In re Simco Mechanical, Inc.,*[70] although the trustee's appraiser had long known the accountant for the debtor, he never made any attempt to contact that accountant.[71] An appraiser not only needs the written information but also should make all possible efforts to contact those who have an ongoing working knowledge of the debtor's operation. In another case,[72] the court discounted an appraiser's testimony concerning the fair market value of real estate because the appraiser owned comparable property located nearby, and it was thus a possible conflict of interest for that appraiser because as an owner he may wish to maximize the value of the property.[73]

---

64 11 U.S.C. § 547(f).

65 *In re* Pembroke Dev. Corp., 122 B.R. 610, 611 (Bankr. S.D. Fla. 1991); *In re* Bellanca Aircraft Corp., 56 B.R. 339, 384 (Bankr. D. Minn. 1985), *aff'd in part, remanded in part,* 850 F.2d 1275 (8th Cir. 1988).

66 *In re* Koubourlis, 869 F.2d 1319, 1322 (9th Cir. 1989).

67 *In re* Pembroke Dev. Corp., 122 B.R. 610, 612 (Bankr. S.D. Fla. 1991).

68 146 B.R. 306 (Bankr. S.D. Ga. 1992).

69 160 B.R. 202 (Bankr. S.D. Fla. 1993).

70 151 B.R. 978 (Bankr. S.D. Fla. 1993).

71 *Id.* at 982.

72 *In re* SM 104, Ltd., 160 B.R. 202 (Bankr. S.D. Fla. 1993).

73 *Id.* at 213.

The actual testimony is governed by Rules 701 through 704 of the Federal Rules of Evidence.[74] One question that arises is whether the owner can testify as to the owner's opinion of value. Generally, a landowner (or a principal corporate officer of a corporation owning land) may give that opinion. Furthermore, the landowner should be allowed to testify concerning comparable properties if the owner has actual knowledge of the statistics of comparable sales, as opposed to mere offers or asking prices.[75]

SPECIFIC ASSET CATEGORIES

§ 11.21 Real Estate

The methodolgies for establishing value for real estate are discussed in §§ **11.15** through **11.17.** Some representative cases discussing various types of real estate valuations are *In re Monica Road Associates,*[76] *In re Stockbridge Properties I, Ltd.,*[77] *In re SM 104, Ltd.,*[78] and *In re Savannah Gardens-Oaktree.*[79]

In real estate valuations, there are a number of crucial concepts, including comparative capitalization rates, the combination of capitalization rates considering both a mortgage and equity investment, a stabilized value for the property (if the property is still being rented), and discounted cash flows until the property achieves a stabilized value. Particularly with respect to the cases involving raw land, an appropriate discount factor must be taken into account when other nearby parcels of raw land are available for sale. This is sometimes referred to as an *absorption rate consideration,* reflecting the period of time before land will in fact be developed. The discount factor considered in connection with the absorption rate is a critical component in discounting the present value of raw land.

§ 11.22 Accounts Receivable

Accounts receivable must be discounted for a variety of factors related to both collectability and delay in collection. In *In re Total Technical Services, Inc.,*[80] a portion of the receivables amounting to $182,000 were owing for a period ranging from three months to over a year.[81] As a consequence, the court discounted the total receivables by a factor of $65,000, resulting in an approximate value of $3,600,000.

---

[74] *See also* B. Russell, Bankruptcy Evidence Manual 390–409 (1993).

[75] United States v. 10,031.98 Acres of Land, 850 F.2d 634, 639 (10th Cir. 1988).

[76] 147 B.R. 385 (Bankr. E.D. Va. 1992) (raw land).

[77] 141 B.R. 469 (Bankr. N.D. Ga. 1992) (raw land).

[78] 160 B.R. 202 (Bankr. S.D. Fla. 1993) (office building).

[79] 146 B.R. 306 (Bankr. S.D. Ga. 1992) (apartment complex).

[80] 150 B.R. 893 (Bankr. D. Del. 1993).

[81] *Id.* at 902.

§ 11.23 Inventory

Inventories are to be valued with appropriate regard for the age and condition of the stock, the season of the year, and the general state of the trade. In *In re Total Technical Services, Inc.*,[82] inventory was valued at cost despite the fact that it consisted of spare parts, many of which had already been used for repairs by this service company. The return of the old spare parts to the inventory without a reduction in value of the inventory required that the dollar amount of the inventory had to be substantially reduced. In *In re Taxman Clothing Co.*,[83] a preference case, the court determined that the value of a retail clothing store's inventory for the purposes of the solvency determination was to be based on the actual wholesale cost to the debtor rather than a liquidation value, which would have been a 46 percent discount from the wholesale cost.[84] This was based on a going-concern valuation of the retail store even though it was operating under doubtful circumstances.[85]

§ 11.24 Plant and Equipment

Plant and equipment likewise must be valued based on actual market conditions and not simply on what the financial statements may show. The most dramatic example of this was *In re Energy Co-operative, Inc.*,[86] in which a refinery with a $161 million book value in fact had no value because of a tremendous over-capacity in the industry.[87] In *In re Ascher*,[88] the court considered the valuation of a commercial laundry. The court valued the laundry based on an income approach, which included not merely an analysis of a 25 percent expected return on equity of a prospective investor, but also based on 45 percent of the purchase price's being borrowed and a 12 percent interest rate.

In *In re David Jones Builder, Inc.*,[89] the court considered a variety of adjustments in connection with determining the solvency of a commercial contractor. In that context, the court accepted a reduction in the book value of construction equipment, vehicles, and office furnishings and equipment by 30 percent to reduce it to the actual fair market value of the personal property.[90] In *In re Coated Sales, Inc.*,[91] another preference action, the debtor wrote down the office furniture and fixtures by $115,000 and leasehold improvements by $33,000. The court accepted the write-down.[92] Last, in *In re*

---

[82] 150 B.R. 893, 901 (Bankr. D. Del. 1993).

[83] 905 F.2d 166 (7th Cir. 1990).

[84] *Id.* at 168–171.

[85] *Id.* at 171.

[86] 109 B.R. 822 (N.D. Ill. 1989).

[87] *Id.* at 830.

[88] 146 B.R. 764 (Bankr. N.D. Ill. 1992).

[89] 129 B.R. 682 (Bankr. S.D. Fla. 1991).

[90] *Id.* at 691.

[91] 144 B.R. 663 (Bankr. S.D.N.Y. 1992).

[92] *Id.* at 677.

Tennessee Chemical Co.,[93] again a preferential transfer case, the court accepted a write-down of a plant from a book value of $20 million to $500,000 based on an actual sales price of the plant after the filing of the bankruptcy proceeding.[94]

§ 11.25 Motor Vehicles

As a general matter, the courts have accepted valuations of automobiles at wholesale.[95] In this regard, substantial reliance is placed upon the last sentence of § 506(a), which states that the value is to be determined in light of the purpose of the valuation and proposed disposition. If the creditor (such as a bank) is not in the business of selling automobiles, wholesale value represents what the creditor will get by the customary means of disposition.[96] In *In re Johnson,*[97] the court stated that value would be set at the amount the creditor would expect to receive if the vehicle were repossessed and sold in a commercially reasonable manner. The court further stated that there are "no hard and fast rules" to valuation, although whether the vehicle is essential or simply incidental to the plan will be considered in choosing between replacement (retail) and wholesale value. The vehicle at issue had been repossessed and placed for sale on the creditor's lot at the time of filing, and the creditor testified he would receive no less than $5,500 for it. The court used this figure to value the vehicle and, citing *In re Coby,*[98] did not deduct sales costs or commissions from the projected sales price. However, *Coby* actually holds just the opposite, expressly stating that costs of liquidation should be deducted in determining value.[99]

Several recent cases have used retail value for automobiles, finding that wholesale value is inappropriate if the vehicle is not being liquidated and sold.[100] These cases particularly focus on the language of § 506(a) that valuation is determined in light of the purpose of the valuation and the proposed disposition or use of the property.[101] When the debtor will retain the vehicle, valuation based on liquidation ignores the fact that no sale is contemplated. The purpose of the valuation is to determine the amount the creditor will be paid for the debtor's continued use and possession of the vehicle.[102] The retail value is generally determined by reference to the NADA *Bluebook.*[103] Two courts that applied the wholesale value also stated that a retail, or

---

93 143 B.R. 468 (Bankr. E.D. Tenn. 1992).

94 *Id.* at 476–79.

95 *In re* Mitchell, 954 F.2d 557 (9th Cir. 1992).

96 *In re* Owens, 120 B.R. 487 (Bankr. E.D. Ark. 1990).

97 117 B.R. 577 (Bankr. D. Idaho 1990).

98 109 B.R. 963 (Bankr. D. Nev. 1990).

99 109 B.R. at 964–65.

100 *In re* Johnson, 145 B.R. 108 (Bankr. S.D. Ga. 1992) (citing *In re* Reynolds, 17 B.R. 489 (Bankr. N.D. Ga. 1981)).

101 *In re* Green, 151 B.R. 501 (Bankr. D. Minn. 1993).

102 *Id.* at 506.

103 *In re* Arnette, 156 B.R. 366 (Bankr. D. Conn. 1993); *In re* Green, 151 B.R. 501 (Bankr. D. Minn. 1993); *In re* Reynolds, 17 B.R. 489 (Bankr. N.D. Ga. 1981).

replacement cost, might be appropriate if the vehicle were essential to effectuation of the debtor's plan of reorganization or used as part of a going concern with good reorganization prospects.[104]

At least two courts have used the average of NADA wholesale and retail to value automobiles. In *In re Stauffer,*[105] the court reasoned that wholesale ignores the creditor's risks under a Chapter 13 plan and retail causes the debtor to pay more than the creditor would receive in an immediate sale. The average value is most equitable.[106] Both of these cases gave consideration to the specific condition of the car to make adjustments to the average value.

§ 11.26 Net Operating Loss Carrybacks

As a general matter, when a debtor's fortunes have suffered a quick reversal, in the three years prior to the bankruptcy it may have paid federal income taxes. If it paid taxes, it may be eligible for a net operating loss carryback, thus earning a substantial tax refund. However, that refund may not be applicable if the shareholders were the customers of the debtor and purchased products from the debtor at what may be an arguably favorable price. In such circumstances, the net operating loss carryback may not be available, and thus there should be no reduction.[107]

§ 11.27 Securities

As a general rule, stock, bonds, and other securities have a readily ascertainable price in a normally active market and should be valued at the applicable quotations for the pertinent date. If, however, it is an unlisted security or one for which there is no regular market, the actual determination of value may be more difficult. For example, in *In re Future Energy Corp.,*[108] the plan of reorganization proposed transferring to secured creditors unlisted common stock. Because the secured creditors would be forced to give up cash collateral, the court found that the proposed transfer of unlisted stock could not be considered the indubitable equivalent and therefore the plan could not be confirmed. The evidence was that there had been a great fluctuation in the price of the stock in the six months preceding the confirmation hearing, the stock was thinly traded, and prospective stockholders might experience difficulty in selling their shares due to illiquidity. The court did not determine the value but simply rejected the plan.[109] By contrast, in *In re Tennessee Chemical Co.,*[110] a case

---

104 *In re* Mitchell, 954 F.2d 557 (9th Cir. 1992); *In re* Malody, 102 B.R. 745 (Bankr. 9th Cir. 1989).

105 141 B.R. 612 (Bankr. N.D. Ohio 1992).

106 *Id.* at 614; *In re* Chapman, 135 B.R. 11 (Bankr. M.D. Pa. 1990).

107 *In re* Energy Co-op., Inc., 109 B.R. 822, 831 (N.D. Ill. 1989).

108 83 B.R. 470 (Bankr. S.D. Ohio 1988).

109 *Id.* at 494–96.

110 143 B.R. 468 (Bankr. E.D. Tenn. 1992).

involving an allegedly preferential transfer, the trustee appeared to have received a bona fide offer for unlisted stock in the amount of $1,750,000. Under a fair valuation standard, the court must consider what the stock could have been sold for in a reasonably short period of time. The value of an asset must be reduced if there is no present market value. However, the trustee did have an offer at that amount, and the court determined that, for its purposes, the stock would be valued at $1,750,000.[111]

§ 11.28 Licenses, Permits, and Other Intangibles

Generally, property to be included as an asset in a determination of value would include choses-in-action, contract rights, patent rights, copyrights, and trademarks, licenses, franchises, and permits under state and federal regulatory statutes.[112] However, in connection with licenses, such as the license to manufacture the products of another company, if those licenses require a consent to assignment, the court may value those licenses at zero.[113]

§ 11.29 Contingent Assets

It makes no difference whether a debtor has a contingent asset or a contingent liability; that asset or liability must be reduced to its present or expected value before it can be determined whether the firm's assets exceed its liabilities.[114] In *In re Plihal,*[115] the court valued the contingent right of a debtor to receive rent from land and added that into the debtor's assets as part of the determination of solvency. By contrast, in *Porter v. Yukon National Bank,*[116] the court refused to consider placing any value on notes of a company called "Delaware Energy Shares" supposedly in the amount of $5,760,000. The value of this asset was disputed in the testimony, with the creditors' experts discounting the value because the note was a product of a merger, and it was unclear as to whether the condition for payment of the note under the merger agreement had been met.[117]

---

111 *Id.* at 474.

112 1 Collier on Bankruptcy ¶ 101.32, at 101–96 (15th ed. 1992).

113 *In re* Bellanca Aircraft Corp., 56 B.R. 339, 387–88 (Bankr. D. Minn. 1985), *aff'd in part, remanded in part,* 850 F.2d 1275 (8th Cir. 1988).

114 *In re* Xonics Photochemical, Inc., 841 F.2d 198, 200 (7th Cir. 1988).

115 97 B.R. 554 (Bankr. D. Neb. 1989).

116 866 F.2d 355 (10th Cir. 1989).

117 *Id.* at 358–59.

§ 11.30 Capitalized Expenses and Good Will

As a general proposition, good will may be included as a element of going-concern value.[118] However, when the income approach is used to value an asset, and thus the ability of the asset to produce income is considered, good will should not be a separate additional item. Good will is rather a balance sheet item, sometimes entered on the books at the time of acquisition of a company to reflect this going-concern value.

Similarly, at the commencement of a business or with the addition of new operations, under the Internal Revenue Code the cost of setting up a new operation may have to be capitalized. Thus, in adjusting the book value, courts may consider whether to continue to carry these capitalized items. In *In re Coated Sales, Inc.*,[119] in considering a solvency determination in connection with an allegedly preferential transfer, the court eliminated from the assets good will carried on the books of the debtor's subsidiaries. As pointed out by the court, good will represents not only the favorable consideration shown by the public but it is the ability of a business to generate income in excess of normal rates. Because at the time of the preferential transfer none of the subsidiaries was operating at a profit, the good will had to be written off.[120] Similarly, the company had capitalized costs of setting up a computerized inventory system that had been terminated. This amount also had to be written off.[121]

In *In re Davis,*[122] intangible organizational costs that were not readily convertible to cash were eliminated from the company's balance sheet to determine solvency.

§ 11.31 Value of Equity for Cram Down

In order for there to be a cram down of unsecured debt under § 1129(b), the new equity holders must make a capital investment that exceeds the value of the stock retained. Whether the new value exception in fact exists is beyond the scope of this chapter. (See **Chapter 16**). If new value is to be considered,[123] however, the court is required to compare the shareholder's retained interest with the new capital investment to determine whether the new investment equals or exceeds the retained interest in the corporation.[124]

The appropriate standard for valuing a company undergoing reorganization was articulated by the Supreme Court in *Consolidated Rock Products Co. v. DuBois.*[125]

---

[118] *In re* Bellanca Aircraft Corp., 56 B.R. 386 (Bankr. D. Minn. 1985) (citing Woodward v. White Satin Mills Corp., 42 F.2d 987 (8th Cir. 1930)).

[119] 144 B.R. 663 (Bankr. S.D.N.Y. 1992).

[120] *Id.* at 672.

[121] *Id.* at 675.

[122] 120 B.R. 823, 826 (Bankr. W.D. Pa. 1990).

[123] *See* Bonner Mall Partnership v. U.S. Bancorp Mortgage Co. (*In re* Bonner Mall Partnership), 2 F.3d 899 (9th Cir. 1993), *cert. granted,* ___ U.S. ___, 126 L. Ed. 2d 648, *removed from argument calendar,* ___ U.S. ___, 114 S. Ct 1367 (1994).

[124] *In re* Future Energy Corp., 83 B.R. 470, 499 (Bankr. S.D. Ohio 1988); *In re* Sawmill Hydraulics, Inc., 72 B.R. 454, 458 (Bankr. C.D. Ill. 1987).

[125] 312 U.S. 510 (1941).

The Court pointed out that earning capacity is the essential criterion to be determined. This requires consideration of not only the sum of the values based on physical factors and assigned to the separate units of the property but also the earning capability as well.

In *Sawmill Hydraulics, Inc.,*[126] the court denied a confirmation because inadequate evidence was presented to the court for determining the value of the retained interest. Because it was the debtor's burden to prove value and it failed to do so, the plan could not be confirmed.[127]

In *In re Future Energy Corp.,*[128] testimony was adduced on this point, but the court found it inconclusive. This was based on (1) the debtor's failure to offer the past earnings record, (2) no analysis of factors that might influence future income, (3) no testimony on market conditions in the debtor's industry, and (4) no testimony on the planned future business activities of the debtor. In addition, the court was given no basis for the projected future income of the debtor, nor was there an analysis of the postconfirmation debt structure. Given these considerations, confirmation was denied.

SPECIFIC LIABILITY CATEGORIES

§ 11.32 Environmental Liabilities

In valuing a company's solvency, all factors must be considered. In *In re Coated Sales, Inc.,*[129] the court discounted the company's value because of a contaminated landfill site.

§ 11.33 Deferred Taxes

When a company slides into bankruptcy, it may well be carrying on its balance sheet deferred income taxes. Because those taxes may never be paid, it may be appropriate in a given instance to eliminate the deferred income taxes from the liabilities of the debtor.[130]

---

126 72 B.R. 454 (Bankr. C.D. Ill. 1987).

127 *Id.* at 458.

128 83 B.R. 470, 501–02 (Bankr. S.D. Ohio 1988).

129 144 B.R. 663, 670–72 (Bankr. S.D.N.Y. 1992).

130 *In re* Sierra Steel, Inc., 96 B.R. 275, 278 (Bankr. 9th Cir. 1989); *In re* S.N. Brown Elec. Corp., 136 B.R. 598, 600–01 (Bankr. D. Mass. 1992); *In re* Tennessee Chem. Co., 143 B.R. 468, 473 (Bankr. E.D. Tenn. 1992).

§ 11.34 ERISA Withdrawal Liability

The elimination of deferred income taxes may reduce the company's liability, but an unfunded pension liability may substantially increase a debtor's liabilities.[131] Because applicable accounting standards may allow a defined pension benefit plan to be amortized over a number of years, the balance sheet in *In re Tennessee Chemical Co.,*[132] showed a pension debt of $6.3 million. However, this accounting method assumes that the business will continue as a going concern. If that going-concern value is inapplicable, as the court found in *Tennessee Chemical,* the total liability, in this instance $16.9 million, had to be included as a liability of the company.

§ 11.35 Contingent Liabilities and Pending Litigation

Under § 502(c), the court must estimate the value of any contingent or unliquidated claim, the fixing or liquidation of which would unduly delay the closing of the case. In *Bittner v. Borne Chemical Co.,*[133] a leading case in this area, the court valued a tortious interference claim at zero because it was uncertain that the claimants would succeed. In so ruling, the court prevented creditors from exercising excessive control over the reorganization when ultimately they may have had no claim.[134]

In *In re Farley,*[135] the court declined to value the creditor's tort claims at zero as in *Bittner* because the state court had already denied the debtor's summary judgment motion on the claim and the case was scheduled for jury trial. The claim was valued at the stipulated amount of damages discounted by the chance that the debtor would not be found liable. Thus, a 25 percent chance of recovering on a $5 million claim resulted in a value of $1.25 million.

In *In re Nova Real Estate Investment Trust,*[136] a contingent claim involving multiple parties and multiple issues, the court estimated the value of a creditor's unliquidated claim based on a percentage (in this case, one-seventh) of the loss of all creditors on a fidelity bond covering losses to the debtor.

In *In re Lane,*[137] the court valued a misrepresentation claim against the debtor. The debtor claimed the loss was on the order of $100,000 and the creditor claimed $5 million, but the court set its value at $550,000.

In *In re Federal Press Co.,*[138] finding that the resolution of a products liability claim for negligence in manufacturing a press would unduly delay administration of

---

[131] *In re* Art Shirt Ltd., 93 B.R. 333, 339 (E.D. Pa. 1988); *In re* Tennessee Chem. Co., 143 B.R. 468, 473–74 (Bankr. E.D. Tenn. 1992).

[132] 143 B.R. at 473–74.

[133] 691 F.2d 134 (3d Cir. 1982); *see also In re* Brints Cotton Mktg., Inc., 737 F.2d 1338 (5th Cir. 1984).

[134] Bittner v. Borne Chem. Co., 691 F.2d at 137; *see also In re* Corey, 892 F.2d 829 (9th Cir. 1989).

[135] 146 B.R. 748 (Bankr. N.D. Ill. 1992).

[136] 23 B.R. 62 (Bankr. E.D. Va. 1982).

[137] 68 B.R. 609 (Bankr. D. Haw. 1986).

[138] 116 B.R. 650 (Bankr. N.D. Ind. 1989).

the bankruptcy, the court estimated the probable value of the claim at $950,000, based on the national average verdict for the amputation of multiple fingers with the same range of lost wages and medical expenses claimed, as listed in the *Personal Injury Valuation Handbook.*

Contingent claims may well include the liabilities of a debtor as a surety, guarantor, or endorser. In *In re Fox,*[139] the court held that a creditor's claim against the debtor on its guaranty of a third party's obligation was contingent on the third party's not paying. To estimate the claim, the court had to take into account the ability of the primary obligor to pay.[140] This required an analysis of the primary obligor's assets and liabilities. The court in *Fox* did not consider a coguarantor or payments made by it in evaluating the claim because the debtor's obligation was in no way conditioned on the default of the second guarantor. The court did not specifically value the claim.

In the case of a guaranty by a third party of a debt owed by the debtor, § 502(e) applies. In *In re Erin Food Services, Inc.,*[141] the court stated, without explanation, that the guarantor held a contingent claim equal to the value of the collateral pledged to secure its nonrecourse personal guaranty. Under § 502(e), however, the claim of the guarantor is allowed only to the extent that it becomes fixed by making payments to the creditor on the debt.[142]

In *In re Davis,*[143] the court considered whether liability for future rent was a contingent liability. It found that based on its going-concern valuation, the debtor had no obligation as of the date of transfer for the rent due for the remainder of the term. The court thus refused to accelerate the debt.[144]

§ 11.36 Convertible or Preferred Stock

In *In re Tennessee Chemical Co.,*[145] the court considered whether to include in the debtor's liabilities the redemption price of redeemable preferred stock. The stock provided for mandatory redemption, as well as for the payment of dividends and interest on the unpaid dividends. This made the redemption price look like a debt, and the accountants who audited the financial statements reached the same or a similar conclusion. Nevertheless, the plaintiff trustee in this preferential transfer action did not attempt to prove the effect of state law on the stockholder's rights, and thus the court refused to count the redemption price as a debt.[146]

---

139 64 B.R. 148 (Bankr. N.D. Ohio 1986).

140 *Id.* at 153.

141 980 F.2d 792 (1st Cir. 1992).

142 *In re* Early & Daniel Indus., Inc., 104 B.R. 963, 965 (Bankr. S.D. Ind. 1989), *In re* LaBonte, 13 B.R. 887 (Bankr. D. Kan. 1981).

143 120 B.R. 823 (Bankr. W.D. Pa. 1990).

144 *Id.* at 826.

145 143 B.R. 468 (Bankr. E.D. Tenn. 1992).

146 *Id.* at 473.

§ 11.37 Valuation Issue Checklists

No single checklist of documents or request for information can comprehensibly take into consideration the particular features of each debtor or items to be valued. The checklists in §§ **11.38** through **11.41,** however, list documents to request for a valuation, information to request for a valuation, and typical adjustments that are made in the process of valuation to a debtor's balance sheets and income statements. Although not all items will apply to every small business bankruptcy, the items serve as a reminder of possible areas to investigate.

§ 11.38 —Checklist of Documents to Request Regarding Valuation

_____ 1. Bankruptcy Schedules and Statement of Affairs

_____ 2. Audited and unaudited financial statements (last six years)

_____ 3. Monthly financial statements (last two years)

_____ 4. Federal tax returns (last three years), including all schedules and attachments

_____ 5. Articles of Incorporation, Bylaws, and Minutes (last three years)

_____ 6. Filings with Securities and Exchange Commission and State Securities Commissions (last three years)

_____ 7. If available, auditor's management letter (last six years)

_____ 8. Contracts

- _____ (a) Purchasing
- _____ (b) Sales
- _____ (c) Franchise agreements
- _____ (d) Dealer/Distributor agreements
- _____ (e) Management/Sales employment agreements, including covenants against competition
- _____ (f) Collective bargaining agreements
- _____ (g) Marketing/Advertising materials for all major products or services
- _____ (h) Pending litigation materials, including attorney opinion letters sent to auditors (last three years)

_____ 9. General insurance package, including fidelity coverage, errors and omissions coverage, and directors' and officers' liability coverage

_____ 10. Health insurance plan and monthly billings (last twelve months)

_____ 11. Pension plan documents, including agreement and fund statement (last three years)

_____ 12. Resumes of officers and directors

_____ 13. Organizational chart (last three years)

_____ 14. Stock transfer agreements

_____ 15. Periodic billings from all lenders (last twelve months)
_____ 16. Security agreement, financing statements, mortgages, and deeds of trust
_____ 17. Real and personal property tax billings (last two years)
_____ 18. Check registers (last six months)
_____ 19. Leases with tenants and landlords
_____ 20. Equipment leases, with all schedules
_____ 21. Closing statements on all properties sold or acquired in last twelve months (major items or if developer, for example, all properties sold)
_____ 22. Environmental reports and studies for all properties
_____ 23. Appraisals of properties owned
_____ 24. Summary/detail of last four physical inventories

§ 11.39 —Checklist of Schedules to Request Regarding Valuation

_____ 1. Ten largest suppliers
_____ 2. Breakdown of sales by period
_____ 3. Breakdown of inventory levels at end of each period
_____ 4. Breakdown of dollar volume of product sales to major industries
_____ 5. Breakdown of dollar volume of product sales by geographical area, including export sales
_____ 6. Breakdown of sales and profits by product line or division
_____ 7. Ten largest customers
_____ 8. Principal competition
_____ 9. Total annual property rents
_____ 10. Total annual equipment rents
_____ 11. Major historical capital expenditures
_____ 12. Directors
_____ 13. Management/officers and key personnel (including persons responsible for banking relations, lending relations, inventory control, accounts receivable, and accounts payable)
_____ 14. Description of family relationship among directors, officers, and key personnel
_____ 15. Compensation of all officers, managers, directors, and key personnel
_____ 16. Insider relationships between management/directors and customers, suppliers, accountants, or attorneys
_____ 17. Stockholders, along with a list of insider relationships with management, directors, customers, suppliers, accountants, or attorneys
_____ 18. Analysis of aging of receivables
_____ 19. Analysis of aging of payables

_____ 20. Experience on receivables sold or pledged
_____ 21. Detail of current borrowings
_____ 22. Current and funded debt
_____ 23. Itemization, description, and value of all intangibles or contingent assets
_____ 24. Itemization, description, and amount of unliquidated, contested, or contingent liabilities

§ 11.40 —Checklist of Adjustments to Balance Sheet

_____ Cash
_____ Compensating balances
_____ Stocks, bonds, and other securities
_____ Deposits
_____ Accounts receivable
_____ Inventory
    _____ Book to actual physical inventory
    _____ FIFO versus LIFO
    _____ Write-down and write-off policies
    _____ Tax effect, if valuing stock
_____ Prepaid expenses
_____ Other current assets
_____ Real estate
_____ Furniture, fixtures, equipment, and leasehold improvements
    _____ Replacement or reproduction cost
    _____ Used replacement cost
    _____ Depreciated replacement cost
    _____ Liquidation value
_____ Intangible assets
    _____ Leaseholds
    _____ Patents and copyrights
    _____ Net operating loss carrybacks, and possible tax refunds
_____ Liabilities
    _____ Interest-bearing debt
    _____ Deferred taxes
    _____ Preferred stock
_____ Contingent or off-balance sheet assets and liabilities
    _____ Product liability
    _____ Lawsuits
    _____ Regulatory compliance

- _____ Environmental liabilities
- _____ Past service liability
- _____ Employment agreements
- _____ Unrecorded obligations
- _____ Liens

§ 11.41 —Checklist of Adjustments to Income Statement

- _____ Compensation to owners
- _____ Amortization
- _____ Depreciation
- _____ Cost of goods sold
    - _____ Adjustments for companies using LIFO accounting
    - _____ Unconventional practices
- _____ Occupancy costs
    - _____ Rent or leased premises
    - _____ Owner-occupied premises
- _____ Nonrecurring items
    - _____ Business interruptions
    - _____ Insurance proceeds
    - _____ Lawsuit settlements
    - _____ Gains or losses on disposal of assets
    - _____ Discontinued operations
    - _____ Payments on employment contracts and covenants not to compete
    - _____ Abnormal market conditions
- _____ Unrecognized costs
    - _____ Accrued expenses
    - _____ Bad debts
    - _____ Insured liabilities
    - _____ Insurable liabilities
- _____ Imminent changes
- _____ Nonoperating income and expenses
- _____ Adjustments for taxes

CHAPTER 12

AVOIDING POWERS: SPECIAL BANKRUPTCY RIGHTS TO ATTACK CLAIMS OR LIENS AND RECOVER TRANSFERS

Paul M. Hoffmann

§ 12.1 Introduction

The Bankruptcy Code contains many provisions that can be used to materially modify the claims and liens that otherwise could be asserted by certain creditors. The primary Bankruptcy Code provisions of this nature are 11 U.S.C. §§ 510, 544, 545, 547, 548, and 553. This chapter explains these provisions generally, highlights many leading cases, and discusses the applications of several of the provisions to small business bankruptcy cases. A related topic, avoidance of liens on exempt property under § 522(f), is discussed in **Chapter 20.**

Small businesses are likely to face many of the issues discussed in this chapter, particularly issues regarding transactions with insiders. Prudent counsel should carefully identify all transfers to and from insiders and evaluate them under the principles discussed here. Of all the issues facing small business owners, those that create potential personal liability often create the greatest concerns. Moreover, counsel who fails to identify or anticipate these issues often has a very unhappy client.

SUBORDINATION

§ 12.2 Subordination in General

Section 510 of the Bankruptcy Code identifies the circumstances under which any claim (secured, priority under § 507, or unsecured) may be subordinated to other claims. Subordination is not the same as disallowance. *Disallowance* relieves the debtor of any obligation on the claim, whereas *subordination* only changes the priority of a claim relative to other claims. In general, subordination is most likely to be pursued by a trustee lacking sufficient funds to pay all creditors in full. Additionally, subordination can adversely affect security interests; subordination of a secured claim to the level of a general unsecured claim may result in distribution of the proceeds of the previously secured creditor's collateral pro rata among all general unsecured creditors. The previously secured creditor loses the ability to foreclose on its collateral and take all the proceeds for itself.

§ 12.3 Contractual Subordination

Section 510(a) of the Bankruptcy Code acknowledges the enforceability of contracts between or among creditors which subordinate claims. Why this is expressed in the Bankruptcy Code is not clear, except that it codifies case law under the former Bankruptcy Act and eliminates any question about the enforceability of these contracts. However, the legislative history of § 510 notes that these contract rights can be waived as part of a plan of reorganization.[1]

In addition, the scope of subordination contracts is not well settled. For example, it is not clear that the beneficiary of a subordination contract may go so far as to cast votes to accept or reject a plan for the subordinated creditor.[2] Nor is it clear whether a subordination agreement held by or for the benefit of more than one senior lender is enforceable if the majority of, but not all, creditors required under § 1126 vote to modify the subordination agreement.[3]

§ 12.4 Securities Claims

Section 510(b) of the Bankruptcy Code expresses a legislative policy that claims for rescission of security purchases must be treated no better than the security itself.

---

[1] H.R. Rep. No. 595, 95th Cong., 1st Sess. 359 (1977), *reprinted in* 1978 U.S.C.C.A.N. 5787; S. Rep. No. 989, 95th Cong., 2d Sess. 74 (1978), *reprinted in* 1978 U.S.C.C.A.N. 5963.

[2] *In re* National Gypsum Co., No. 390-37213-SAF/11 (Bankr. N.D. Tex. July 8, 1992) (discussed in S. Mayerson, *When Bondholders' Votes Upset a Plan,* Nat'l L.J. 29–33 (June 14, 1993).

[3] Note, *The Outer Fringes of Chapter 11: Nonconsenting Senior Lenders' Rights Under Subordination Agreements in Bankruptcy,* 91 Mich. L. Rev. 281 (1992).

Thus, a security holder cannot convert an equity interest to an unsecured claim by alleging fraud in the purchase of the security. However, this provision does not require subordination of a claim for breach of a security purchase agreement.[4] Note that *security* is defined in § 101(49) to include notes, bonds, and debentures, but not debt for goods sold or services delivered. Prudent counsel should not assume that § 510(b) is limited to stocks or partnership interests.

§ 12.5 Equitable Subordination

Section 510(c) of the Bankruptcy Code articulates the broad rule that a bankruptcy court may subordinate a claim "under principles of equitable subordination." The legislative history of this provision expressly incorporated existing case law and left further development of this provision to the courts.[5]

The doctrine of equitable subordination is traceable to the United States Supreme Court case *Pepper v. Litton,*[6] in which an insider's claim for unpaid wages was disallowed (as opposed to subordinated) under the general equity powers of the bankruptcy court. In so holding, the Supreme Court stated that the bankruptcy court's powers "have been invoked to the end that fraud will not prevail, that substance will not give way to form, that technical considerations will not prevent substantial justice from being done."[7] The Supreme Court went on to note that insiders' dealings with bankrupt companies are subject to "rigorous scrutiny" and that the insider bears the burden of proving good faith and "inherent fairness."[8]

The case law that has developed under § 510(c) after enactment of the Bankruptcy Code provides substantial guidance and limitation in pursuing equitable subordination. In general, as noted in *Pepper,* courts first examine whether the creditor in question was an insider of the debtor under § 101 of the Bankruptcy Code. If so, then the insider's claim is subject to "rigorous scrutiny."

The exact contours of this requirement are not clear, but it appears to primarily influence the burden of proof. On one hand, insider claims are not automatically subordinated under § 510(c); the other elements discussed below must be proven. On the other hand, once the debtor or trustee provides a "substantial basis" to support an allegation of "impropriety," then the burden of proof essentially shifts to the creditor in question to prove good faith and the fairness of the claim in question.[9] This should be distinguished from non-insider claims for which the debtor or trustee must prove grounds for equitable subordination by a preponderance of evidence.

For either insider or non-insider claims, the following three requirements must be satisfied before a claim can be equitably subordinated:

---

4 *In re* Wyeth Co., 134 B.R. 920 (Bankr. W.D. Mo. 1991).

5 124 Cong. Rec. H11,095 (daily ed. Sept. 28, 1978); 124 Cong. Rec. S17,412 (daily ed. Oct. 6, 1978).

6 308 U.S. 295 (1939).

7 *Id.* at 304–05.

8 *Id.* at 306.

9 Wilson v. Huffman (*In re* Missionary Baptist Found. of Am., Inc.), 712 F.2d 206 (5th Cir. 1983).

1. The creditor whose claim is to be subordinated must have engaged in some type of inequitable conduct
2. The misconduct must have injured creditors of the debtor or conferred an unfair advantage on the creditor
3. Equitable subordination must be consistent with the principles of the Bankruptcy Code.[10]

Reported cases under § 510(c) appear to grant equitable subordination under circumstances falling into two broad fact patterns. The first category is claims of insiders who advance funds to a troubled debtor as secured or unsecured loans instead of capital contributions while at the same time misleading trade creditors and others into extending credit in circumstances where the credit is not likely to be repaid.[11] The other category is claims of outside secured lenders who exercise control over the debtor to the point that the secured claims become paid or preferred over trade and other creditors who are misled, directly or indirectly, by the outside creditor into extending additional credit.[12] Note, however, that reported cases subordinating non-insider creditor claims are rare.[13]

§ 12.6 Subordination of Punitive Claims

One fairly recent development that should be closely watched is the subordination of tax penalty claims without any allegation or proof of inequitable conduct by the taxing authority.[14] In essence, these cases hold that tax penalties should be subordinated

---

[10] Sloan v. Zions First Nat'l Bank (*In re* Castletons, Inc.), 990 F.2d 551 (10th Cir. 1993); First Nat'l Bank v. Rafoth (*In re* Baker & Getty Fin. Serv., Inc.), 974 F.2d 712 (6th Cir. 1992); Capitol Bank & Trust Co. v. 604 Columbus Ave. Realty Trust (*In re* 604 Columbus Ave. Realty Trust), 968 F.2d 1332 (1st Cir. 1992); Triple E Corp. v. Holmes (*In re* ASI Reactivation, Inc.), 934 F.2d 1315 (4th Cir. 1991); Spacek v. Thomen (*In re* Universal Farming Indus.), 873 F.2d 1334 (9th Cir. 1989); Bergquist v. Anderson-Greenwood Aviation Corp. (*In re* Bellanca Aircraft Corp.), 850 F.2d 1275 (8th Cir. 1988); Estes v. N&D Properties, Inc. (*In re* N&D Properties, Inc.), 799 F.2d 726 (11th Cir. 1986); *In re* Mobile Steel, 563 F.2d 692 (5th Cir. 1977).

[11] *E.g.,* Summit Coffee Co. v. Herby's Foods, Inc. (*In re* Herby's Foods, Inc.), 2 F.3d 128 (5th Cir. 1993); Stoumbos v. Kiliminik, 988 F.2d 949 (9th Cir. 1993); Fabricators, Inc. v. Technical Fabricators, Inc. (*In re* Fabricators, Inc.), 926 F.2d 1458 (5th Cir. 1991).

[12] *E.g.,* Capitol Bank & Trust Co. v. 604 Columbus Ave. Realty Trust (*In re* 604 Columbus Ave. Realty Trust), 968 F.2d 1332 (1st Cir. 1992).

[13] *E.g.,* Sloan v. Zions First Nat'l Bank (*In re* Castletons, Inc.), 990 F.2d 551 (10th Cir. 1993); First Nat'l Bank v. Rafoth (*In re* Baker & Getty Fin. Serv., Inc.), 974 F.2d 712 (6th Cir. 1992); Kham & Nate's Shoes No. 2, Inc. v. First Bank of Whiting, 908 F.2d 1351 (7th Cir. 1990); Spacek v. Thomen (*In re* Universal Farming Indus.), 873 F.2d 1334 (9th Cir. 1989).

[14] Burden v. United States, 917 F.2d 115 (3d Cir. 1990); Schultz Broadway Inn v. United States, 912 F.2d 230 (8th Cir. 1990); *In re* Virtual Network Serv. Corp., 902 F.2d 1246 (7th Cir. 1990). *Contra* United States v. Mansfield Tire & Rubber Co. (*In re* Mansfield Tire & Rubber Co.), 942 F.2d 1055 (6th Cir. 1991).

below general unsecured claims, but above equity claims, because tax penalties are intended to punish the insiders (usually equity holders) who directed the debtor not to pay the taxes, and the penalty should not dilute the distribution otherwise available to innocent trade and other creditors. This reasoning could be extended to other claims constituting a penalty, such as punitive damage claims and fines.[15] It is an open question whether this reasoning also could be extended to other analogous claims for nonpecuniary losses, such as some forms of prepayment charges, late charges, and tort damages for pain and suffering.

STRONG ARM POWERS

§ 12.7 Strong Arm Powers in General

Absent a bankruptcy filing, relevant state law generally gives judgment creditors, bona fide purchasers of real estate, and other specific creditors various rights to attack or supersede various claims or liens asserted against a debtor. For example, § 9-301 of the Uniform Commercial Code allows a judgment creditor to assert priority over an unperfected security interest. In addition, most states have fraudulent conveyance laws (that differ from § 548, discussed in §§ **12.23** through **12.27**) for the benefit of certain creditors in certain situations.

Section 544 of the Bankruptcy Code essentially allows the debtor-in-possession or trustee to assert these state law claims. Thus, for example, § 544 has been successfully used to challenge the scope of a security interest,[16] a fraudulent conveyance under state law,[17] an unperfected stock pledge,[18] a defective water/sewer lien,[19] a lease that was a disguised security interest without a filed financing statement,[20] a financing statement in a debtor's trade name instead of the debtor's legal name,[21] and an unrecorded deed.[22] In addition, § 544 has been successfully asserted to set aside a stock redemption that was invalid under state law,[23] and to block efforts by a junior secured creditor to marshall assets to the detriment of unsecured creditors.[24]

---

15 *E.g., In re* Channel One Communications, Inc., 125 B.R. 234 (Bankr. E.D. Mo. 1991).

16 *In re* Newman, 993 F.2d 90 (5th Cir. 1993); *In re* Seaway Express Corp., 912 F.2d 1125 (9th Cir. 1990); *In re* Missionary Baptist Found. of Am., Inc., 796 F.2d 752 (5th Cir. 1986).

17 *In re* Green, 986 F.2d 145 (6th Cir. 1993); *In re* Agricultural Research & Technology Group, Inc., 916 F.2d 528 (9th Cir. 1990); Joe T. Dehmer Distrib., Inc. v. Temple, 826 F.2d 1463 (5th Cir. 1987).

18 *In re* Hill, 981 F.2d 1474 (5th Cir. 1993).

19 McLean v. City of Phila., Water Revenue Bureau, 891 F.2d 474 (3d Cir. 1989).

20 *In re* Merritt Dredging Co., 839 F.2d 203 (4th Cir. 1988); *In re* Pacific Express, Inc., 780 F.2d 1482 (9th Cir. 1986).

21 Pearson v. Salina Office Coffee House, Inc., 831 F.2d 1531 (10th Cir. 1987).

22 *In re* Washburn & Roberts, Inc., 795 F.2d 870 (9th Cir. 1986).

23 Lippi v. City Bank, 955 F.2d 599 (9th Cir. 1992).

24 *In re* Center Wholesale, Inc., 759 F.2d 1440 (9th Cir. 1985).

Note, however, that § 544 avoiding powers differ from nonbankruptcy laws permitting the attack of claims and liens in two ways. First, any recovery under § 544 generally will be for the benefit of all creditors in the bankruptcy case, not just those creditors who would have had standing under relevant state law absent the bankruptcy case. Second, any claim asserted by the debtor-in-possession or trustee under § 544(a) (but not § 544(b)) are based on the rights of a hypothetical creditor under state law and thus are not subject to any particular defenses that might be available against an actual creditor who otherwise could have asserted the state law claim. For example, § 9-401(2) of the Uniform Commercial Code generally does not allow a creditor with actual knowledge of a misfiled financing statement to assert priority over an otherwise perfected security interest. However, a debtor-in-possession or a trustee in bankruptcy as a hypothetical creditor cannot be deemed to have actual knowledge of such facts.

At the same time, a debtor-in-possession or trustee in bankruptcy generally is deemed to have constructive knowledge of facts which a reasonable inquiry would have disclosed. Thus, for example, a trustee cannot avoid an unrecorded real estate deed if the grantee openly occupies the property in question and relevant state law would have prevented any possible purchaser or other creditor from avoiding the deed under these circumstances.[25] One court even went so far as to hold that an involuntary petition against the debtor, by itself, is enough constructive notice to defeat a trustee's use of § 544.[26] On the other hand, another court held, applying Vermont law, that a mortgage missing one of two witness signatures did not give constructive notice of the mortgage.[27]

Prudent counsel in any bankruptcy case should carefully review all liens (tax liens, mortgages, security interests, judgment liens, mechanic's liens, reclamation claims, and so forth) to be certain they were properly perfected under relevant state law. If not, they probably can be avoided under § 544. Counsel also should investigate whether any transfer of real estate is avoidable for failure to properly record a deed. Finally, counsel should investigate whether any transfer by the debtor prior to bankruptcy is recoverable under the relevant state bulk sale or fraudulent conveyance statute (which generally has a statute of limitations longer than the one-year period under § 548).

§ 12.8 Alter Ego and Constructive Trust Claims

Although § 544 broadly permits a debtor-in-possession or trustee to assert creditors' rights to avoid transfers by a debtor, courts are split on allowing a debtor-in-possession or trustee to pursue claims as a creditor against third parties, most notably alter

---

[25] *In re* Weisman, 5 F.3d 417 (9th Cir. 1993).

[26] Briggs v. Kent (*In re* Professional Inv. Properties of Am.), 955 F.2d 623 (9th Cir. 1992).

[27] Stern v. Continental Assurance Co. (*In re* Ryan), 851 F.2d 502 (1st Cir. 1988). *Cf. In re* Casbeer, 793 F.2d 1436 (5th Cir. 1986); *In re* New Concept Realty & Dev., Inc., 753 F.2d 804 (9th Cir. 1985).

ego and breach of fiduciary duty claims.[28] *Alter ego claims* involve the rights of creditors under state law to pierce the debtor's corporate existence to pursue claims against shareholders or other related entities for claims against the debtor. *Breach of fiduciary duty claims* are an emerging concept under various states' laws to pursue directors or other insiders for authorizing actions by an insolvent debtor that damage creditors, such as directing the debtor to make a fraudulent transfer. In addition, courts are split on allowing a defendant to assert a constructive trust claim under § 541(d) as a defense to assertion of a claim under § 544. Some courts allow creditors with unperfected liens to impose a "constructive trust" on what otherwise would have been their collateral, and then hold that § 541(d) allows the constructive trust to be enforced despite § 544.[29]

STATUTORY LIENS

§ 12.9 Statutory Liens in General

Section 545 of the Bankruptcy Code essentially is intended to prevent states and other governmental units from enforcing statutes which alter the priorities and rights created under the Bankruptcy Code. At the same time, § 545 also establishes a public policy of extending the bona fide purchaser powers of a trustee in bankruptcy to

---

[28] *See* St. Paul Fire & Marine Ins. Co. v. Pepsico, Inc., 884 F.2d 688 (2d Cir. 1989); Ashland Oil, Inc. v. Arnett, 875 F.2d 1271 (7th Cir. 1989); Gibraltar Sav. v. LD Brinkman Corp., 860 F.2d 1275 (5th Cir. 1988), *cert. denied,* 490 U.S. 1091 (1989); Williams v. California 1st Bank, 859 F.2d 664 (9th Cir. 1988); Steyr-Daimler-Puch of Am. Corp. v. Pappas, 852 F.2d 132 (4th Cir. 1988); Koch Ref. v. Farmers Union Cent. Exch., Inc., 831 F.2d 1339 (7th Cir. 1987), *cert. denied,* 108 U.S. 1077 (1988); Chicago Florsheim Shoe Co. v. Cluett, Peabody & Co., 826 F.2d 725 (7th Cir. 1987); S.I. Acquisition, Inc. v. Eastway Delivery Serv. (*In re* S.I. Acquisition, Inc.), 817 F.2d 1142 (5th Cir. 1987); Mixon v. Anderson (*In re* Ozark Restaurant Equip. Co.), 816 F.2d 1222 (8th Cir.), *cert denied,* 484 U.S. 848 (1987); American Nat'l Bank v. MortgageAmerica Corp. (*In re* MortgageAmerica Corp.), 714 F.2d 1266 (5th Cir. 1983); Green v. Bate Records, Inc. (*In re* 10th Ave. Record Distribs., Inc.), 97 B.R. 163 (S.D.N.Y. 1989); Fisher, Hecht & Fisher v. D.H. Overmyer Telecasting Co. (*In re* D.H. Overmyer Telecasting Co.), 56 B.R. 657 (Bankr. N.D. Ohio 1986). *See generally* Hull, *A Void in Avoidance Powers? The Bankruptcy Trustee's Inability to Assert Damages Claims on Behalf of Creditors Against Third Parties,* 46 U. Miami L. Rev. 263 (1991).

[29] National Bank of Alaska, N.A. v. Erickson (*In re* Seaway Express Corp.), 912 F.2d 1125 (9th Cir. 1990); Sanyo Elec., Inc. v. Howard's Appliance Corp. (*In re* Howard's Appliance Corp.), 874 F.2d 88 (2d Cir. 1989); Chbat v. Tleel (*In re* Tleel), 876 F.2d 769 (9th Cir. 1989); Belisle v. Plunkett, 876 F.2d 512 (7th Cir. 1989); City Nat'l Bank v. General Coffee Corp., 828 F.2d 699 (11th Cir. 1987); Vineyard v. McKenzie (*In re* Quality Holsteen Leasing), 752 F.2d 1009 (5th Cir. 1985). *See generally* Cuevas, *Bankruptcy Code Section 544(a) and Constructive Trusts: The Trustee's Strong Arm Powers Should Prevail,* 21 Seton Hall L. Rev. 678 (1991).

personal property in the context of statutory liens.[30] For most small business, § 545 will be important to avoid federal and state tax liens, landlord liens, and various specific statutory liens.

§ 12.10 Definition of Statutory Lien

Section 101(53) of the Bankruptcy Code defines a statutory lien as a:

> lien arising solely by force of a statute on specified circumstances or conditions, or lien of distress for rent, whether or not statutory, but does not include security interest or judicial lien, whether or not such interest or lien is provided by or is dependent on a statute and whether or not such interest or lien is made fully effective by statute.

Judicial Lien is defined in § 101(36) as a "lien obtained by a judgment, levy, sequestration, or other legal or equitable process or proceeding." And the word *lien* is defined in § 101(37) as a "charge against or interest in property to secure payment of a debt or performance of an obligation."

Examples of statutory liens include mechanic liens,[31] warehousemen's liens,[32] tax liens, and attorney's liens.[33] Examples of liens that are *not* statutory liens include common law pledges,[34] consensual real estate encumbrances,[35] and judicial liens.[36]

Note that consensual liens are not statutory liens under § 101(53), even though they may otherwise arise by statute. Thus, for example, a landlord who otherwise is automatically entitled to a statutory lien for rent (which is avoidable under § 545) may sidestep § 545 by creating the same lien by contract in the lease agreement.[37] Accordingly, any mechanic or materialman on a construction project, any landlord, any warehouseman, and any other party who ordinarily enters a contract with a debtor should not rely on statutory liens alone, but should instead seriously consider obtaining a consensual lien as part of the contract.

One should not assume that failure to observe the formalities in obtaining or enforcing the statutory lien renders the lien invalid or avoidable. For example, one

---

30 As discussed in **§ 12.7** above, § 544 grants a trustee in bankruptcy the power to avoid any interest in real estate that could be avoided by a bona fide purchaser. Thus, for example, a trustee in bankruptcy can avoid an unrecorded deed on real estate as if the trustee were a bona fide purchaser who purchased the real estate without notice of the unrecorded deed. Section 544 does not extend to personal property, however, because such an extension might destroy certain security interests in instruments, documents, securities, and chattel paper under §§ 9-308 and 9-309 of the Uniform Commercial Code.

31 *In re* APC Constr., Inc., 112 B.R. 89 (Bankr. D. Vt. 1990), *aff'd,* 132 B.R. 690 (D. Vt. 1991).

32 *In re* Zaisan, Inc., 80 B.R. 832 (Bankr. S.D. Tex. 1987).

33 *In re* Electronic Metal Products, Inc., 916 F.2d 1502 (10th Cir. 1990).

34 *In re* Vescovo, 125 B.R. 468 (Bankr. W.D. Tex. 1990).

35 *In re* Practical Inv. Corp., 95 B.R. 935 (Bankr. E.D. Va. 1989).

36 *In re* Ressler, 61 B.R. 403 (E.D. Tenn. 1986).

37 Dallas v. S.A.G., Inc., 836 F.2d 1307 (11th Cir. 1988).

court has held that a materialman lien creditor fraudulently induced into surrendering possession of goods otherwise subject to a possessory statutory lien still has an enforceable lien in bankruptcy.[38] Another court has held that failure to prosecute a lawsuit to enforce a mechanic's lien does not extinguish the lien in a bankruptcy case; it just eliminates the right to foreclose the lien.[39]

§ 12.11 Ipso Facto Liens

Section 545(1) allows a trustee to avoid a statutory lien that essentially becomes effective when a debtor is insolvent or commits what used to be known under the Bankruptcy Act as an "act of bankruptcy". This provision is intended to prevent states from altering the priorities under the Bankruptcy Code. This provision has been interpreted broadly and has even been held to apply to a statute that created a lien on any "voluntary transfer of property in reduction or satisfaction of indebtedness."[40]

The legislative history of § 545 also says that a trustee in bankruptcy may avoid a lien under this section even if the lien has been enforced by sale before commencement of the case.[41] However, this statement may be too broad. It probably would be more accurate to say that enforcement of an avoidable statutory lien under § 545 may be set aside as a preference under § 547 so long as the other requirements of § 547 are met.[42]

§ 12.12 Bona Fide Purchaser Status

Probably the most powerful feature of § 545 is the trustee's ability to avoid a statutory lien that, under relevant law, is subject to the rights of a bona fide purchaser. This feature overlaps § 544(a)(3) in the area of real estate, but stands alone in the area of personal property. Note, however, that this provision of § 545 is subject to the powers of the statutory lienholder (such as a mechanic's lien creditor) under § 546(b) to perfect a statutory lien after commencement of a bankruptcy case if such delayed perfection relates back to a period prior to the commencement of a bankruptcy case.

When determining whether relevant law gives a bona fide purchaser any priority over a statutory lien, a careful distinction must be drawn between a bona fide purchaser and other persons who may be protected under relevant law. For example, one case held that a statutory lien subject to the rights of a "buyer in the ordinary course of business" is not avoidable under § 545(2) because a buyer in the ordinary

---

38 *In re* Garland Corp., 6 B.R. 452 (Bankr. D. Mass. 1988).

39 *In re* Paul Potts Builders, Inc., 608 F.2d 1279 (9th Cir. 1979).

40 *In re* Knights Athletic Goods, Inc., 128 B.R. 679 (Bankr. D. Kan. 1991).

41 H. Rep. No. 595, 95th Cong., 1st Sess. 371 (1977); *reprinted in* 1978 U.S.C.C.A.N. 5963.

42 11 U.S.C. § 547(c)(6). *In re* Nucorp Energy, Inc., 902 F.2d 729 (9th Cir. 1990); *In re* Lewis, 70 B.R. 699 (Bankr. D. Kan. 1987).

course of business is more than just a bona fide purchaser—it is a bona fide purchaser who also purchases from a debtor in the business of selling goods of that kind.[43] This was so even though the debtor in question was in the business of selling the goods in question.

Probably the most important application of § 545(2) is against federal and state tax liens. Any federal tax lien not perfected by filing a notice of tax lien is avoidable under § 545(2) because the Internal Revenue Code states that such a lien is not enforceable against a bona fide purchaser.[44] Moreover, any federal tax lien for which a notice of tax lien has been properly filed is still subject to the rights of a bona fide purchaser under the Internal Revenue Code and thus is avoidable under § 545(2) in the case of certain kinds of personal property: motor vehicles, cash, securities, and possibly inventory.[45] State tax liens may be subject to similar exceptions. In this regard, also note that § 724(b) of the Bankruptcy Code subordinates tax liens to priority claims under § 507(a)(1)–(6) in Chapter 7 cases, and this provision may apply in Chapter 11 cases via § 1129(a)(7).

§ 12.13 "Secret" Liens

Section 545 does not allow a trustee in bankruptcy to avoid statutory liens that arise automatically under specified circumstances without means of providing notice to creditors or other parties. Examples of such statutory liens include producers' liens on products delivered for processing, suppliers' "trust" claims against food brokers under the Perishable Agricultural Commodities Act, and various environmental lien laws that create first priority liens against real estate determined to be contaminated, regardless of any prior perfected liens. Challenges to such "secret" liens have been uniformally rejected.[46] However, a tension continues to exist in this area.[47]

PREFERENCES

§ 12.14 Preferences in General

Section 547 of the Bankruptcy Code is primarily used to avoid and recover payments and other transfers of property on unsecured past due obligations made within 90 days before the bankruptcy case was filed. To the extent the transfer is avoided and

43 *In re* Woods Farmers Co-op Elevator Co., 946 F.2d 1411 (8th Cir. 1991).

44 26 U.S.C. §6323(a).

45 26 U.S.C. § 6323(b)(1), (2), and (3).

46 *In re* Loretto Winery, Ltd., 898 F.2d 715 (9th Cir. 1990); *In re* Martin Exploration Co., 731 F.2d 1210 (5th Cir. 1984); and *In re* Tape City, U.S.A., Inc., 677 F.2d 401 (5th Cir. 1982).

47 *E.g.*, *In re* Loretto Winery, Ltd., 898 F.2d 715, 725 (dissenting opinion); Epling, *Environmental Liens in Bankruptcy*, 44 Bus. Law. 85 (1988).

recovered, the creditor will be able to assert an unsecured claim in the bankruptcy case.[48] However, this usually results in the creditor's only getting back a small fraction of the amount originally recovered.

Section 547 ostensibly serves two general policies: (1) to deter unusual action by either the debtor or its creditors during, and thus hastening, the debtor's slide into bankruptcy, and (2) to equalize distributions to unsecured creditors by forcing unsecured creditors who have inappropriately extracted payments prior to the debtor's filing bankruptcy to disgorge their recovery and split everything pro rata with other unsecured creditors.[49] The preference provisions probably accomplish little in the way of deterrence because creditors rarely know (and a debtor rarely realizes) that the debtor, in fact, will file bankruptcy within 90 days, and, furthermore, most creditors, even if they knew of the impending bankruptcy filing, would prefer the risk of having to disgorge cash in hand to the near certainty of receiving no payment at all. Equalization of creditors' recovery is only satisfied in a very general sense because (1) preferences are not always pursued, (2) preference law is not applied consistently, and (3) the recovery of preferences, in this author's experience, rarely makes a material difference in the percentage recovery to creditors in a given case. Practitioners, therefore, will find it virtually impossible to justify the preference laws to a creditor/client being sued for recovery of a preference.

§ 12.15 Prima Facie Case

The elements of a preference are specified in § 547(b), which states: a trustee may avoid any (1) transfer, (2) of the debtor's property, (3) to or for the benefit of a creditor, (4) for or on account of an antecedent debt, (5) made while the debtor was insolvent, (6) within 90 days before the petition was filed (or up to one year for an insider), and (7) that enables such creditor to receive more than it would have received if the debtor was liquidated under Chapter 7.

Section 547(f) creates a rebuttable presumption that the debtor was insolvent during the 90 days before the filing of bankruptcy. The date of a transfer is determined under the rather technical rules of § 547(e). In this regard, the Supreme Court has held that a check is transferred under § 547(b) on the date it clears the bank, although a different date (such as the date the check is delivered to the creditor) may be the transfer date for the purpose of the defenses in § 547(c).[50] Also, courts are split on whether § 547(e)(2) creates a 10-day limit on perfection of a lien after the transfer in question.[51] This problem arises mostly in those states that permit a creditor up to 20 days to file a financing statement perfecting a purchase money security interest with priority over any prior recorded financing statement. On its face, § 547(e) deems such a financing statement filed more than 10 days after the closing

---

[48] 11 U.S.C. § 502(h).

[49] H.R. Rep. No. 595, 95th Cong., 1st Sess. 177–78 (1977); *reprinted in* 1978 U.S.C.C.A.N. 5963.

[50] Barnhill v. Johnson, 112 S. Ct. 1386 (1992).

[51] GMAC v. Busenlahner (*In re* Busenlahner), 918 F.2d 928 (11th Cir. 1990).

to create a lien on such date to secure an antecedent claim (when the loan was closed), thus exposing the lien to possible avoidance as a preference. Finally, note that late payment of trust fund taxes, for example, employee withholding taxes, are not preferences,[52] although late payment of other tax claims may be preferences.[53] In practice, the existence of the § 547(b) elements is usually clear; defendants often stipulate to the prima facie case and focus instead upon establishing one or more defenses.

§ 12.16 Major Defenses

The defenses to assertion of a preference claim are set forth in § 547(c). A complete discussion of all these defenses is beyond the scope of this chapter.[54] The primary defenses are discussed in §§ **12.17** through **12.20.**

§ 12.17 —Contemporaneous Exchange

Under § 547(c)(1), a transfer that is a contemporaneous exchange is not voidable. The contemporaneous exchange defense in § 547(c)(1) is a corollary to the antecedent debt requirement in § 547(b)(2). The classic example of a contemporaneous exchange is a check given in return for goods received (as long as the check is deposited and clears the bank in the ordinary course of business). To be a contemporaneous exchange, a transfer must satisfy both a subjective test and an objective test. The subjective requirement is that the debtor and defendant intended the transaction to be a contemporaneous exchange.[55] The objective requirement is that the transaction in fact was a substantially contemporaneous exchange.[56] Moreover, the transfer must be for "new value," which is defined in § 547(a)(2) to essentially cover new goods or services received by the debtor at the time of the transfer.

---

52 Begier v. Internal Revenue Service, 496 U.S. 53 (1990).

53 124 Cong. Rec. H11,097 (daily ed. Sept. 28, 1978); 124 Cong. Rec. S17,414 (daily ed. Oct. 6, 1978).

54 Over 250 circuit court of appeals opinions after 1980 cite § 547, and over half of these cases are dated after 1989. A good article discussing all § 547 defenses is Bloom, Goreleck, & MacKenzie, *Exceptions to Bankruptcy Preferences: Countryman Updated,* 47 Bus. Law. 529 (1992), which builds on a leading article by Harvard Law School's Professor Vern Countryman, *The Concept of a Voidable Preference in Bankruptcy,* 38 Vand. L. Rev. 713 (1985).

55 11 U.S.C. § 547(c)(1)(A). *See* National City Bank v. Hotchkiss, 231 U.S. 50 (1913) (lien given in the afternoon after bank discovered financial problems with the borrower, to secure loan that had been made in the morning, was a transfer for an antecedent debt).

56 11 U.S.C. § 547(c)(1)(B). *See* Dean v. Davis, 242 U.S. 438 (1917) (mortgage recorded one week after loan was funded was substantially contemporaneous, hence not a transfer for an antecedent debt).

§ 12.18 —Ordinary Course of Business

The ordinary course of business defense in § 547(c)(2) is not defined with any specificity or consistency among courts. In essence, this defense is intended to protect transfers in the ordinary course of business between the debtor and defendant because such transfers are not the result of any pressure from the defendant tending to hasten the debtor's slide into bankruptcy. See the discussion of policy in **§ 12.14.** However, this defense tends to go against the other policy, ensuring equality of distributions. As a result, courts are widely split over the relevant standards and, more importantly, the application of those standards to a particular set of facts.[57]

This defense also has subjective and objective aspects, much like the contemporaneous exchange defense discussed in **§ 12.17.** The defendant bears the burden of proving that the transfer in question was ordinary under the historical relationship between the parties (subjective), as well as "ordinary" in the common relationships between others in the shoes of the debtor and defendant (objective).[58] Note that, although § 547(c)(2) originally limited this defense to transfers made less than 45 days after the debt was incurred, the 45-day rule was deleted by Congress in 1984 amendments, and a recent Supreme Court decision has extended § 547(c)(2) to long-term debt as well as short-term debt.[59]

Assuming there is nothing out of the ordinary surrounding the transfer in question (such as the use of a certified check instead of a regular business check, the use of overnight mail instead of regular mail, or the creditor's refusal to ship until a past due invoice is paid), the inquiry generally boils down to comparing the number of days the alleged preference was late against the number of days the debtor historically has been late in making payments. If the former is larger than the latter, then the alleged preference probably will not be protected under the ordinary course of business defense.[60]

§ 12.19 —Subsequent New Value

The *subsequent new value defense* under § 547(c)(6) essentially gives the creditor/defendant a credit for any new value extended after the alleged preference occurred. For example, a creditor that ships new goods on credit after getting an alleged preference is entitled to deduct against the alleged preference the amount of the invoice for the subsequent shipment. At bottom, this defense focuses on the net effect to the debtor's estate of the preferential transfers and subsequent advances; the

---

[57] *See* Tabb, *Rethinking Preferences,* 43 S.C. L. Rev., 981 (1992).

[58] Jones v. United Sav. & Loan Ass'n, 9 F.3d 680 (8th Cir. 1993); *In re* Tolona Pizza Prod. Corp., 2 F.3d 1029 (7th Cir. 1993); Logan v. Basic Distrib. Corp. (*In re* Fred Hawes Org., Inc.), 957 F.2d 239 (6th Cir. 1992); WJM, Inc. v. Massachusetts Dep't of Pub. Welfare, 840 F.2d 996 (1st Cir. 1988). *Compare* J.P. Fufe, Inc. v. Bradco Supply Corp., 891 F.2d 66 (3d Cir. 1989); Marathon Oil Co. v. Flatau (*In re* Craig Oil Co.), 785 F.2d 1563 (11th Cir. 1986).

[59] Union Bank v. Wolas, ___ U.S. ___, 112 S. Ct. 527 (1991).

[60] *E.g.*, Lovett v. St. Johnsburg Trucking, 931 F.2d 494 (8th Cir. 1991).

creditor/defendant is subject to preference liability only if and to the extent that the net effect of these transfers was a decrease in the debtor's estate.[61]

However, unlike the net result rule of the former Bankruptcy Act, this defense does not simply net out the payments and new value between a debtor and defendant during the preference period. Only new value extended after an alleged preference can be credited, and only up to the amount of the alleged preference.[62] Thus, for example, an initial preference of $100, a subsequent new value advance of $200, and a subsequent preference of $100 still leaves the defendant exposed for the full $100 amount of the last preference.

§ 12.20 —Earmarking

In addition to the seven § 547(c) statutory defenses to a preference, one common law defense also should be noted. This common law defense is known as *earmarking*. Under this theory, a transfer to a creditor of property acquired on unsecured credit from a third party for this purpose is not a preference because the third party is intentionally substituted as an unsecured creditor in place of the would-be defendant.[63] The classic example is an unsecured bank loan for the specific purpose of making the otherwise preferential payment. Note, however, that this is a very narrow defense; any discretion the debtor has to use the funds to pay other debts destroys the defense.[64] Thus, for example, a draw by a debtor on an unsecured or undersecured line of credit does not satisfy this defense, even though one creditor is merely substituted for another.

§ 12.21 Insider Guaranties

The Fifth, Sixth, Seventh, Ninth, and Tenth Circuits have interpreted §§ 547 and 550 to, in essence, extend the 90-day preference period to the one-year period applicable to insiders if the transferee has a guaranty from, or other recourse against, an insider of the debtor.[65] The theory is that (1) the payment to the non-insider creditor is a

---

[61] *E.g.*, Kroh Bros. Dev. Co. v. Continental Constr. Eng'g, Inc., 930 F.2d 648 (8th Cir. 1991).

[62] *In re* Wadsworth, Inc., 711 F.2d 122 (9th Cir. 1983). *Contra In re* Meredith Manor, Inc., 902 F.2d 257 (4th Cir. 1990).

[63] National Bank of Newport v. National Herkimer County Bank, 225 U.S. 178 (1912); Grubb v. General Contract Purchase Corp., 94 F.2d 70 (2d Cir. 1938).

[64] McCuskey v. National Bank of Waterloo (*In re* Bohlen Enter.), 859 F.2d 561 (8th Cir. 1988).

[65] Levit v. Ingersoll Rand Fin. Corp. (*In re* V.N. Deprizio Constr.), 874 F.2d 1186 (7th Cir. 1989); *In re* Sufolla, Inc., 2 F.3d 977 (9th Cir. 1993); Southmark Corp. v. Southmark Personal Storage, Inc. (*In re* Southmark Corp.), 993 F.2d 117 (5th Cir. 1993); Ray v. City Bank & Trust Co. (*In re* C-L Cartage Co.), 899 F.2d 1490 (6th Cir. 1990); Manufacturers Hanover Leasing Corp. v. Lowrey (*In re* Robinson Bros. Drilling, Inc.), 892 F.2d 850 (10th Cir. 1989).

preference to the debtor's insider because it reduces the insider's contingent claim against the debtor that would have arisen if the insider had made the same payment to the non-insider, and (2) the preference can be recovered from the non-insider as the initial transferee under § 550. This theory has been hotly contested by non-insider defendants (typically banks) and may be barred by legislation now pending in Congress.[66]

Courts outside of these circuits are divided on this issue.[67] Even those courts that follow this theory allow the non-insider defendant to assert its own defenses under § 547(c). Moreover, at least one court has held that this liability can be avoided by the insider's waiving any contingent claim against the debtor.[68] However, one commentator has suggested that such a waiver may create a fraudulent conveyance claim against the non-insider under § 548.[69]

One circuit has also held that no liability attaches to the non-insider if the insider received no "quantifiable monetary advantage" from the transfer.[70] In that case, the insider's guaranty was limited to about $19.35 million, the total debt to the outside creditor was about $62 million, and the alleged preferential transfers were for about $2 million. The transfers did not reduce the guarantor's liability to the outside creditor, hence the requirement in § 547(b) that the transfer be "to or for the benefit of" the insider was not satisfied. This reasoning might be extended to prevent recovery from a non-insider if the insider never would have paid the non-insider to create the insider's claim against the debtor in the first place (that is, the insider got no "quantifiable monetary advantage" from reduction of a guaranty liability that the insider could not pay anyway).

---

66 S. 540, § 214, 103d Cong., 2d Sess. (1994).

67 For authority in support of the *Deprizio* result, *see, e.g.*, Tidwell v. Amsouth Bank, N.A. (*In re* Cavalier Homes, Inc.), 102 B.R. 878 (M.D. Ga. 1989); *In re* Installation Servs., 101 B.R. 282 (Bankr. N.D. Ala. 1989); Coastal Petroleum Corp. v. Union Bank & Trust Co. (*In re* Coastal Petroleum Corp.), 91 B.R. 35 (Bankr. N.D. Ohio 1988); First State Bank v. W.E. Tucker Oil Co. (*In re* W.E. Tucker Oil Co.), 64 B.R. 183 (W.D. Ark. 1986); Mixon v. Mid-Continent Sys. (*In re* Big Tree Transp., Inc.), 41 B.R. 16 (Bankr. W.D. Ark. 1983). For contrary authority, *see, e.g.*, T.B. Westex Foods, Inc. v. Alaska Continental Bank (*In re* T.B. Westex Foods, Inc.), 96 B.R. 77 (Bankr. W.D. Tex. 1989); *In re* Aerco Metals, Inc., 60 B.R. 77 (Bankr. N.D. Tex. 1985); *In re* Mercon Indus., 37 B.R. 549 (Bankr. E.D. Pa. 1984); Schmitt v. Equibank (*In re* R.A. Beck Builder, Inc.), 34 B.R. 888 (Bankr. W.D. Pa. 1983); Backhus v. Central Trust Co., N.A. (*In re* Duccilli Formal Wear, Inc.) 8 Bankr. Ct. Dec. (CRR) 1180 (Bankr. S.D. Ohio 1982); Bakst v. Schilling (*In re* Cove Patio Corp.), 19 B.R. 843 (Bankr. S.D. Fla. 1982).

68 *In re* Fastrans, Inc., 142 B.R. 241 (Bankr. E.D. Tenn. 1992).

69 Borowitz, *Waiving Subrogation Rights and Conjuring Up Demons in Response to Deprizio,* 45 Bus. Law. 2151 (1990).

70 Travelers Ins. Co. v. Cambridge Meridian Group, Inc. (*In re* Erin Food Serv., Inc.), 980 F.2d 792 (1st Cir. 1992).

§ 12.22 Practice Tips for Preferences

Prudent counsel should identify any possible preferences as soon as possible. This is required by question 13 in the Statement of Financial Affairs filed by all debtors (Official Bankruptcy Form No. 8, for debtors engaged in business), but often is answered inaccurately or incompletely. At a minimum, counsel should get a copy of all checks written in the 90 days before the debtor filed bankruptcy and compare them to all invoices for those checks. This task should not be overly burdensome in most small business cases, particularly if the check ledger references invoice numbers. If any check was sent after the due date of its invoice, then it is probably a prima facie preference. A more complete investigation should follow to determine subsequent new value and ascertain the debtor's history of payments to the creditor to see if the payment, although late, was nonetheless in the ordinary course of business.

Prudent counsel next should assess whether to pursue the preference claims before or after confirmation of a plan of reorganization. In general, preference claims are pursued after confirmation of a plan because other issues usually are more important. This also avoids creating general unhappiness among creditors who are still deciding whether to extend credit after the case is filed, and who will be asked to vote on any proposed plan of reorganization. Note, however, that failure to adequately reserve the right to pursue preferences in a plan of reorganization may preclude later pursuit of preferences. See § **12.34.**

FRAUDULENT TRANSFERS

§ 12.23 Fraudulent Transfers in General

Section 548 of the Bankruptcy Code allows a debtor-in-possession or a trustee to recover fraudulent transfers. This remedy is in addition to any relevant state laws regarding fraudulent transfers, which are available in bankruptcy under § 544. See § **12.7.** There are many reported cases under this provision,[71] with the most notable cases relating to foreclosure sales and failed leveraged buyouts, discussed in §§ **12.25** and **12.26,** respectively.

§ 12.24 Prima Facie Case

Section 548 establishes two alternative grounds for avoiding a fraudulent transfer. Section 548(a)(1) is subjective, based on the debtor's intent to "hinder, delay or defraud" creditors. This provision has its roots in the Statute of Elizabeth in England

---

[71] Over 132 circuit court of appeals opinions after 1980 cite § 548, and over half of these cases are after 1989.

in 1570.[72] Courts have developed rules of circumstantial evidence, known as *badges of fraud,* useful in establishing this subjective intent:

1. The transfer was to an insider
2. The debtor retained possession or control of the property transferred after the transfer
3. The transfer was not disclosed or was concealed
4. Before the transfer was made, the debtor had been sued or threatened with suit
5. The transfer was of substantially all of the debtor's nonexempt assets
6. The value of the consideration received by the debtor was not reasonably equivalent to the value of the asset transferred
7. The debtor was insolvent when, or became insolvent shortly after, the transfer was made
8. The transfer occurred shortly before or after a substantial debt was incurred.[73]

Section 548(a)(2), more commonly used, is objective, based on the debtor's (1) receiving "less than a reasonably equivalent value" in exchange for the transfer (although this does not apply to any transfers with the general partner of a partnership), plus (2) being or becoming "insolvent," or left with "unreasonably small capital," or liable on debts "beyond the debtor's ability to pay as such debts matured." No proof of the debtor's subjective intent is necessary under this provision. Thus, for example, perfectly innocent charitable contributions or gifts by an insolvent debtor may be recovered under this provision.

Note that a preference under § 547 cannot be a fraudulent transfer under § 548, because satisfying or securing an antecedent debt is defined as *value* under § 548(d)(2).[74] In addition, in contrast to § 547(f), no presumption of insolvency exists under § 548. Last, any good-faith transferee will be credited with the amount of value for the transfer under § 548(c).

On its face, § 548 appears to apply only to transfers within one year before the filing of the bankruptcy case. However, in the related contexts of denial of discharge under § 727(a)(2) (regarding transfers of property with intent to hinder, delay, or defraud creditors within one year before a debtor files bankruptcy) and state statutes of limitation, various courts have developed a theory of *concealment* which may enable a debtor-in-possession or trustee to reach and avoid transfers that occurred more than a year before the debtor filed bankruptcy.[75]

---

[72] H.R. Rep. No. 595, 95th Cong., 1st Sess. 375 (1977), *reprinted in* 1978 U.S.C.C.A.N. 5963; S. Rep. No. 989, 95th Cong., 2d Sess. 89–90 (1977), *reprinted in* 1978 U.S.C.C.A.N. 5787.

[73] *See* Uniform Fraudulent Transfer Act, § 4(b). *See also In re* Brantz, 106 B.R. 62 (Bankr. E.D. Pa. 1989); *In re* Pinto Trucking Serv., Inc., 93 B.R. 379 (Bankr. E.D. Pa. 1988); and *In re* BGNX, Inc., 75 B.R. 44 (Bankr. S.D. Fla. 1987).

[74] This overrules Dean v. Davis, 242 U.S. 438 (1917).

[75] *E.g., In re* Oliver, 819 F.2d 550 (5th Cir. 1987); *In re* Espino, 48 B.R. 232 (Bankr. S.D. Fla. 1985), *aff'd,* 806 F.2d 1001 (11th Cir. 1986). *Compare* Collins v. Environmental Sys. Co., No. 92-3519, 1993 WL 302863 (8th Cir. 1993).

§ 12.25 Foreclosure Sales

Three distinct lines of authority have developed in the circuit courts regarding the application of § 548(a)(2) to foreclosure sales. Under the line of cases following *Durrett v. Washington National Insurance Co.,*[76] a foreclosure sale generally is considered a fraudulent transfer if the debtor receives less than 70 percent of the fair market value of the foreclosed property. Although this is not the precise holding in *Durrett,* many attorneys and courts now use the 70 percent rule as a general guideline. Under the line of cases following *In re Madrid,*[77] a noncollusive foreclosure sale conducted in accordance with relevant state law is presumed to involve reasonably equivalent value regardless of the amount bid. Under the line of cases following *In re Bundles,*[78] the court assesses various factors, including but not limited to the *Durrett* and *Madrid* factors. The Supreme Court has granted certiorari and heard oral argument in a case that may resolve this split among the circuits.[79]

§ 12.26 Leveraged Buyouts

Many recent reported cases address the application of § 548 in the context of leveraged buyouts.[80] In general, these cases involve an acquired company's pledging all of its assets to secure a loan to an acquiring company, which uses the proceeds to buy the stock of the acquired company from its shareholders. In essence, the acquired company has distributed the value of its assets to its shareholders without maintaining an adequate reserve for existing creditors. Viewed in this context, the result in these cases is not surprising.

However, several significant aspects of the § 548 analysis have been developed under these cases. First, courts routinely ignore the form of a transaction and focus on its substance. Thus, for example, a transaction structured as a loan to the acquired corporation with the proceeds paid as dividends to the shareholders does not insulate

---

[76] 621 F.2d 201 (5th Cir. 1980).

[77] 21 B.R. 424 (Bankr. 9th Cir. 1982), *aff'd on other grounds,* 725 F.2d 1197 (9th Cir. 1982), *cert. denied,* 469 U.S. 833 (1984).

[78] 856 F.2d 815 (7th Cir. 1988).

[79] BFP v. Imperial Sav. & Loan Ass'n (*In re* BFP), 974 F.2d 1144 (9th Cir. 1992), *cert. granted,* 124 L. Ed. 2d 635 (1993).

[80] *E.g.,* Crowthers McCall Pattern, Inc. v. Lewis, 129 B.R. 992 (S.D.N.Y. 1991); C-T of Va. Inc. v. Euroshoe Assoc., 762 F. Supp. 675 (W.D. Va. 1991), *aff'd,* 953 F.2d 637 (4th Cir. 1992); Moody v. Security Pac. Business Credit, Inc., 971 F.2d 1056 (3d Cir. 1992); Mellon Bank, N.A. v. Metro Communications, Inc., 945 F.2d 635 (3d Cir. 1991); Kupetz v. Continental Ill. Nat'l Bank & Trust Co., 77 B.R. 754 (C.D. Cal. 1981), *aff'd sub nom.* Kupetz v. Wolf, 845 F.2d 842 (9th Cir. 1988); Weiboldt Stores, Inc. v. Schottenstein, 845 F.2d 842 (9th Cir. 1988); *In re* Ohio Corrugating Co., 70 B.R. 920 (Bankr. N.D. Ohio 1987); United States v. Gleneagles Inv. Co., 565 F. Supp. 556 (M.D. Pa. 1983), *aff'd sub nom.* United States v. Tabor Court Realty Corp., 803 F.2d 1288 (3d Cir. 1986).

the lender from attack, even though the lender can argue that the debtor received reasonably equivalent value in the form of the loan proceeds.[81]

Second, courts exercise broad discretion in fashioning a remedy for an allegedly fraudulent conveyance. Thus, for example, the court in one case not only avoided the liens to the lender but also subordinated the lender's claims to all other unsecured claims.[82] In another case, the court imposed a constructive trust on the assets of a transferee who received the proceeds of the transaction.[83]

Third, courts appear to be developing a body of case law regarding "unreasonably small capital" and "debts . . . beyond the debtor's ability to pay" to establish insolvency under § 548. In essence, the cases appear to fall back on traditional tort concepts of foreseeability and proximate cause. If the subsequent bankruptcy of the borrower was foreseeable and was proximately caused by the fraudulent conveyance, then the courts following this approach consider the borrower to have become insolvent as a result of the fraudulent conveyance.[84]

§ 12.27 Guaranties

Incurring obligations without receiving reasonably equivalent value can be a fraudulent transfer as much as conveying assets. This is particularly important in guaranties by affiliated corporations. If the guaranty is *upstream* (by a subsidiary for the benefit of a parent company) or *cross-stream* (by a sister company for the benefit of another sister company under common ownership), courts generally consider the guaranty to be unenforceable as an obligation incurred without receipt of reasonably equivalent value, if the guarantor-debtor was insolvent when the guaranty was executed.[85]

If the guaranty is *downstream* (by an individual shareholder or parent company for the benefit of a subsidiary), courts generally consider the guaranty enforceable because the value of the parent company's or shareholder's stock in the subsidiary generally increases in proportionately to the amount of the guaranty.[86] However, even this is not true if the subsidiary is insolvent at the time the guaranty is issued (so that the debtor/parent company's investment in the subsidiary creates no proportionately increased value in the parent company's stock in the subsidiary) and the guaranty does not make the subsidiary solvent.[87]

---

[81] *E.g.*, Moody v. Security Pac. Credit, Inc., 127 B.R. 958 (W.D. Pa. 1991); Yoder v. T.E.L. Leasing, Inc. (*In re* Suburban Motor Freight, Inc.), 124 B.R. 984 (Bankr. S.D. Ohio 1990).

[82] *In re* O'Day Corp., 126 B.R. 370 (Bankr. D. Mass 1991).

[83] Voest-Alpine Trading USA Corp. v. Vantage Steel Corp., 919 F.2d 206 (3d Cir. 1990).

[84] *Compare In re* O'Day Corp., 126 B.R. 370 (Bankr. D. Mass. 1991), *with* Mellon Bank, N.A. v. Metro Communications, Inc., 945 F.2d 635 (3d Cir. 1991).

[85] *See In re* C-T of Va., Inc., 124 B.R. 700 (W.D. Va. 1990); *In re* Chicago, Mo. & W. Ry., 124 B.R. 769 (Bankr. N.D. Ill. 1991).

[86] *See In re* W.T. Grant Co., 699 F.2d 599 (2d Cir. 1983), *cert. denied,* 464 U.S. 822 (1983); *In re* Metro Communications, Inc., 95 B.R. 921 (Bankr. W.D. Pa.), *amended,* 135 B.R. 17 (Bankr. W.D. Pa. 1989).

[87] *In re* Rodriguez, 895 F.2d 725 (11th Cir. 1990); Commerce Bank of K.C., N.A. v. Achtenberg, No. 90-0950-CV-W-6, 1993 WL 476510 (W.D. Mo. Nov. 10, 1993).

The need to assess the real economic burden created by a guaranty colors all of the cases in this area. The court has to factor in the amount of the guaranty, the likelihood that the guaranty will be asserted against the debtor, and the availability of reimbursement from any third parties for any payments on the guaranty.[88] Needless to say, a court may, on the basis of subsequent developments, disagree with the way the parties characterized the transaction at the time the guaranty was given.

SETOFF

§ 12.28 Setoff in General

Section 553 of the Bankruptcy Code follows historical tradition and practical reality in allowing a creditor to offset mutual prepetition obligations with the debtor regardless of the preference provisions of § 547 or the rules for equitable subordination under § 510. Setoff, however, is subject to three important exceptions. First, the creditor cannot make the offset after the debtor files bankruptcy until relief from the automatic stay has been granted. This creates significant problems for creditors (primarily banks) when debtors attempt to collect their claims against the creditor, for example, by withdrawing cash from a bank before the creditor gets relief from the automatic stay. Many courts allow the creditor to place an administrative freeze on payment of the debtor's claim against the creditor so long as the creditor promptly seeks relief from the automatic stay.[89]

Second, the creditor's offset rights cannot be exercised if the debtor provides adequate protection to the creditor for its offset rights, for example, by granting the creditor a lien on other unencumbered property in lieu of the creditor's debt to the debtor. In general, a debtor will seek to prevent an offset if the debtor intends to continue doing business with that creditor, or if the debtor needs the credit extended by the creditor (such as a letter of credit from a bank), to maintain a relationship with customers or suppliers. In effect, § 363 allows a debtor to treat a creditor with offset rights the same as a secured creditor with a lien on collateral.[90]

Last, a creditor may not manipulate its offset rights during the 90 days before the debtor files bankruptcy to enhance its recovery on a claim against the debtor. Thus, § 553(a)(2) prohibits a creditor from offsetting a claim acquired from another creditor after the case is filed or during the 90 days before the case is filed. Similarly,

---

88 Butler Aviation Int'l, Inc. v. Whyte (*In re* Fairchild Aircraft Corp.), 6 F.3d 1119 (5th Cir. 1993); *In re* Xonics Photochemical, Inc., 841 F.2d 198 (7th Cir. 1988); Rubin v. Manufacturers Hanover Trust Co., 661 F.2d 979 (2d Cir. 1981).

89 *E.g., In re* Edgins, 36 B.R. 480 (Bankr. 9th Cir. 1984); *In re* Learn, 95 B.R. 495 (Bankr. N.D. Ohio 1989); *In re* Craddock-Terry Shoe Corp., 91 B.R. 392 (Bankr. W.D. Va. 1988); *In re* Wilde, 85 B.R. 147 (Bankr. D.N.M. 1988); *In re* Bass Mechanical Contractors, Inc., 84 B.R. 1009 (Bankr. W.D. Ark. 1988); *In re* Crispell, 73 B.R. 375 (Bankr. E.D. Mo. 1987); *In re* New York City Shoes, Inc., 78 B.R. 426 (Bankr. E.D. Pa. 1987); *In re* Williams, 61 B.R. 567 (Bankr. N.D. Tex. 1986).

90 *See* 11 U.S.C. § 506(a) (regarding determination of secured status).

§ 553(a)(3) prohibits a creditor from incurring a debt to the debtor during those 90 days "for the purpose of obtaining a right of setoff," and § 553(b) prohibits a creditor from offsetting mutual debts to the extent of any "improvement in position" during the 90-day period regardless of the creditor's intent or acquisition of other creditor claims.

Section 553 does not apply to situations involving both prepetition and postpetition obligations. Thus, a creditor cannot offset a postpetition obligation to a debtor against a prepetition claim against the debtor. This seems to go against the plain language of § 553. The reasoning, however, is that the postpetition debtor is considered a debtor-in-possession, which is a separate legal entity, so there is no mutuality between the parties,[91] even though the economic effect of this situation is the same as offsetting mutual prepetition obligations. This is because the debtor's prepetition claim against the creditor becomes a postpetition asset of the debtor-in-possession which the creditor gets to offset under § 553.

§ 12.29 Recoupment Distinguished

Setoff must be carefully distinguished from recoupment. *Recoupment* is limited to mutual prepetition obligations arising out of the same transaction, whereas *setoff* also includes mutual prepetition obligations arising out of separate transactions. None of the limitations described in **§ 12.28** applies to recoupment, which is essentially an adjustment to arrive at the amount actually owed the debtor under the relevant contract. Examples of recoupment include Medicare payment adjustments to a hospital in bankruptcy,[92] offsetting arbitration awards,[93] overpayment on goods against subsequent purchases,[94] claims for damaged or defective goods against the unpaid purchase price,[95] unearned commissions,[96] security deposits[97] and deductions under a construction contract for a contractor in bankruptcy.[98]

---

91 Cooper-Jarret, Inc. v. Central Transp., Inc., 726 F.2d 93 (3d Cir. 1984); Ram Constr. Co. v. American States Ins. Co., 749 F.2d 1049 (3d Cir. 1984).

92 *In re* Yonkers Hamilton Sanitarium, Inc., 34 B.R. 385 (S.D. N.Y. 1983).

93 *In re* Davidovich, 901 F.2d 1533 (10th Cir. 1990).

94 *In re* B&L Oil Co., 782 F.2d 155 (10th Cir. 1986); *In re* Midwest Serv. & Supply Co., 44 B.R. 262 (D. Utah 1983).

95 *In re* Rooster, Inc., 127 B.R. 560 (Bankr. E.D. Pa. 1991).

96 *In re* Vaughter, 109 B.R. 229 (Bankr. W.D. Tex. 1989).

97 *In re* Public Serv. Co., 107 B.R. 441 (Bankr. D.N.H. 1989).

98 Newberry Elec., Inc. v. MCI Constructors, Inc. (*In re* Newberry Corp.), 145 B.R. 998 (Bankr. 9th Cir. 1992); *In re* A-1 Hydro Mechanics Corp., 92 B.R. 451 (Bankr. D. Haw. 1988); *In re* Alpco, Inc., 62 B.R. 184 (Bankr. S.D. Ohio 1986).

GENERAL RULES

§ 12.30 Who Can Sue

The plain language of the Code sections discussed in this chapter authorize a trustee to pursue these remedies. A debtor-in-possession also can exercise these powers of a trustee pursuant to § 1107 of the Bankruptcy Code. Most courts also recognize that an unsecured creditors' committee may obtain an order authorizing exercise of these powers, but only after demonstrating that the debtor-in-possession or trustee has unjustifiably failed or refused to pursue these powers, or has a conflict of interest.[99] Note that a lender with a lien on general intangibles does not have a lien on a debtor-in-possession's rights to pursue these remedies.[100]

§ 12.31 Who Can Be Sued

Section 550(a) of the Bankruptcy Code specifies that any transferee in the chain of title to an asset may be sued, as well as any "entity for whose benefit such transfer was made." However, § 550(b) of the Bankruptcy Code protects any innocent transferee, that is, a transferee who takes for value, in good faith, and without knowledge of the avoidability of the prior transfer, or any subsequent good-faith transferee after the initial transferee.

One difficult question in this area is whether a trustee or debtor-in-possession may sue a governmental entity, for example, to recover a preference. State and federal governmental units enjoy sovereign immunity from legal action in bankruptcy or otherwise, unless the immunity is clearly waived.[101] Section 106 expressly eliminates governmental immunity in certain circumstances. Under § 106(a), if a governmental unit has filed a proof of claim, the governmental unit is deemed to have waived sovereign immunity with respect to any claim by the estate "that arose out of the same transaction or occurrence."[102] Section 106(b) provides "[t]here shall be offset against an allowed claim or interest of a governmental unit any claim against such governmental unit that is property of the estate." Also, regardless of whether the governmental unit has filed a claim, § 106(c) waives sovereign immunity to the

---

[99] *In re* Xonics Photochemical, Inc., 841 F.2d 198 (7th Cir. 1988) (dicta); *In re* STN Enters., 779 F.2d 901 (2d Cir. 1985); *In re* Allegheny Int'l, Inc., 93 B.R. 903 (Bankr. W.D. Pa. 1988); *In re* Philadelphia Light Supply Co., 39 B.R. 51 (Bankr. E.D. Pa. 1984); *In re* Jermoo's, Inc., 38 B.R. 197 (Bankr. W.D. Wis. 1984).

[100] *In re* Tek-Aids Indus., Inc., 145 B.R. 253 (Bankr. N.D. Ill. 1992); *In re* Sun Island Foods, 125 B.R. 615 (Bankr. D. Haw. 1991); *In re* Integrated Testing Prods. Corp., 69 B.R. 901 (D.N.J. 1987).

[101] *See* James W. Moore et al., 2A Moore's Federal Practice ¶ 8.17[2] (2d ed. 1985); *In re* Professional Sales Corp., 56 B.R. 753 (N.D. Ill. 1985).

[102] *In re* Puhlman Constr. Indus., 27 Collier Bankr. Cas. 2d (MB) 707 (Bankr. N.D. Ill. 1992) (claim for unpaid taxes).

extent of a debtor's obtaining injunctive or declaratory relief, but not monetary damages.[103] Thus, for example, a governmental unit is always subject to the automatic stay[104] but cannot be sued for violating the automatic stay under § 362(h) unless it has filed a proof of claim.[105]

§ 12.32 What Can Be Recovered

Essentially, three remedies are available in avoidance actions: (1) nullification of the transfer, (2) preservation of the avoided transfer for the benefit of the estate, and (3) recovery of a money judgment, if appropriate, against the transferee. Nullification is a form of declaratory relief by the bankruptcy court in which the transfer in question is declared null and void (that is, avoided). This may be the only relief necessary if, for example, the only issue is the validity of a lien against the debtor.

Preservation of the avoided transfer occurs automatically under § 551. In essence, preservation precludes a junior lien from benefiting from avoidance of a superior lien. Thus, for example, avoidance as a fraudulent conveyance of a first mortgage for $30,000 on a piece of real estate worth $50,000 which is subject to a second mortgage for $40,000 will allow the debtor to sell the property for $50,000, keep the first $30,000 for the benefit of all creditors pro rata, and distribute the $20,000 balance to the junior mortgagee. This way, the junior creditor's lien does not become a first lien by virtue of the avoidance, with the junior creditor's collecting $40,000 and the estate's only getting the last $10,000.

If appropriate, § 550(a) of the Bankruptcy Code specifies that the debtor-in-possession or trustee can recover either the property transferred or the value of such property. Section 550(c) states that a debtor-in-possession or trustee is entitled to only a single satisfaction. Section 550(d) allows a good-faith transferee to have a lien on the recovered property to secure the lesser of the costs of any improvements to the transferred property or any increase in the value of the property from the improvements.

§ 12.33 Statute of Limitations

Section 546(a) of the Bankruptcy Code requires that an action under §§ 544, 547, 548, or 553 of the Bankruptcy Code be commenced by the earlier of (1) two years after appointment of the trustee, or (2) closing or dismissal of the case. In addition, § 550(e) requires that an action for recovery of property or its value under § 550 be commenced before the earlier of (1) one year after avoidance of the transfer in

---

103 Hoffman v. Connecticut Dep't of Income Maintenance, 492 U.S. 96 (1989); United States v. Nordic Village, Inc., ___ U.S. ___, 112 S. Ct. 1011 (1992).

104 *In re* Pearson, 917 F.2d 1215 (9th Cir. 1990); United States v. McPeck, 910 F.2d 509 (8th Cir. 1990).

105 Small Business Admin. v. Rinehart, 887 F.2d 165 (8th Cir. 1989); *In re* James, 120 B.R. 802 (E.D. Pa. 1990), *aff'd,* 940 F.2d 46 (3d Cir. 1991). *Contra In re* Everet, 127 B.R. 781 (Bankr. E.D.N.C. 1991).

question, or (2) closing or dismissal of the case. This latter provision rarely is an issue because recovery under § 550 typically is combined with avoidance actions under §§ 544, 547, 548, or 553.

Courts are split on whether § 546(a) applies to debtors-in-possession.[106] Courts are also split on whether § 546(a) starts over after conversion of a case.[107] Prudent counsel should conservatively assume that § 546 applies from the date the bankruptcy case is filed and either get their actions filed within two years or get an order extending the deadline.

Note that § 546 does not apply to any other causes of action available to a debtor-in-possession or trustee, for example, a breach of contract or tort lawsuit. Instead, § 108(a) specifies that any such action must be commenced before the later of (1) the end of the otherwise applicable nonbankruptcy limitations period, or (2) two years after the order for relief,[108] which is not necessarily the same date as the date of appointment of a trustee. Note also that § 546 does not apply to any defensive use of the avoidance powers, such as a trustee's seeking denial of a claim under § 502(d).[109]

§ 12.34 Res Judicata

Debtors often defer the filing of avoidance actions, lender liability actions, and other lawsuits until after confirmation of a plan of reorganization. Plans of reorganization commonly contain a generic reservation of rights to assert avoidance actions and other claims. Recent cases have held that debtor attempts to assert lender liability and other claims against secured creditors after confirmation of a plan that otherwise specifically addresses the treatment of the secured creditor's claim are barred by res judicata.[110] The language of these opinions also might be used to preclude assertion of any avoidance action that is not clearly reserved in the plan of reorganization and confirmation order.

---

106 Holding that § 546(a) applies to debtor-in-possession: *In re* Software Centre Int'l, Inc., 994 F.2d 682 (9th Cir. 1993); Zilkha Energy Co. v. Leighton, 920 F.2d 1520 (10th Cir. 1990); Sparmal Enters., Inc. v. Moffit Realty Corp., 126 B.R. 559 (S.D. Ind. 1991). Holding that it does not: *In re* Century Brass Prod., Inc., 127 B.R. 720 (Bankr. D. Conn. 1991); *In re* Korvettes, Inc., 67 B.R. 730 (Bankr. S.D.N.Y. 1986).

107 Holding that § 546(a) does not start over: *In re* Eye Contact, Inc., 97 B.R. 990 (Bankr. W.D. Wis. 1989); *In re* Grambling, 85 B.R. 675 (Bankr. D. Conn. 1988). Holding that it does: *In re* Wood, 113 B.R. 253 (S.D. Miss. 1990); *In re* Moody, 77 B.R. 566 (S.D. Tex. 1987), *aff'd,* 862 F.2d 1194 (5th Cir. 1989).

108 *See* 11 U.S.C. §§ 301, 302, 303.

109 *In re* Octagon Roofing, 156 B.R. 214 (Bankr. N.D. Ill. 1993); *In re* Minichello, 120 B.R. 17 (Bankr. N.D. Pa. 1990); *In re* Mid Atl. Fund, Inc., 60 B.R. 604 (Bankr. S.D.N.Y. 1986).

110 *In re* Heritage Hotel Partnership I, 160 B.R. 374 (Bankr. 9th Cir. 1993); Sanders Confectionery Prod., Inc. v. Heller Fin., Inc., 973 F.2d 474 (6th Cir. 1992), *cert. denied,* ___ U.S. ___, 113 S. Ct. 1046 (1993); Eubanks v. FDIC, 977 F.2d 166 (5th Cir. 1992); *In re* Chattanooga Wholesale Antiques, Inc., 930 F.2d 458 (6th Cir. 1991); Sure-Snap Corp. v. State Street Bank & Trust Co., 948 F.2d 869 (2d Cir. 1991); *In re* Howe, 913 F.2d 1138 (5th Cir. 1990).

§ 12.35 Checklist for Identifying Voidable Liens and Transfers

This checklist is for debtors-in-possession and trustees to use when reviewing the facts of a bankruptcy case. It flags fact patterns that might give rise to an avoidance action. References to the Bankruptcy Code and the sections of this chapter are provided.

AVOIDABLE TRANSFER CHECKLIST

____ 1. Has any creditor contractually agreed to subordination of a claim? 11 U.S.C. § 510(a); **§ 12.3.**

____ 2. Is there a claim for "rescission" of a security purchase? 11 U.S.C. § 510(b); **§ 12.4.** Note: § 101 defines a *security* to include notes and bonds.

____ 3. Has an insider advanced funds to debtor in the form of a loan instead of capital contribution while misleading creditors into extending credit under circumstances where credit is not likely to be repaid? 11 U.S.C. § 510(c); **§ 12.5.**

____ 4. Has an outside lender exercised control over debtor so that its claims are paid before those of other creditors who have been misled, directly or indirectly, by the secured creditor into extending additional credit? 11 U.S.C. § 510(c); **§ 12.5.**

____ 5. Has a creditor engaged in any other type of inequitable conduct that has injured other creditors or conferred an unfair advantage on itself? 11 U.S.C. § 510(c); **§ 12.5.**

____ 6. Is there a claim that is punitive or nonpecuniary in nature? 11 U.S.C. § 510(c); **§ 12.6.**

  ____ Tax penalties
  ____ Fines
  ____ Punitive damages
  ____ Prepayment penalties
  ____ Late charges
  ____ Pain and suffering
  ____ Other

____ 7. Is a security interest improperly perfected under state law? 11 U.S.C. § 544; **§ 12.7.**

  ____ Tax liens
  ____ Mortgages
  ____ Security interests
  ____ Judgment liens
  ____ Mechanic's liens
  ____ Reclamation claims
  ____ Leases that are in fact unperfected security interests
  ____ Other liens

____ 8. Is a real estate transfer deed unrecorded or improperly recorded under state law? 11 U.S.C. § 544; § **12.7.**

____ 9. Does a creditor have an alter ego or breach of fiduciary duty claim against a third party? 11 U.S.C. § 544; § **12.8.**

____ 10. Has there been a bulk sale subject to avoidance under state law? 11 U.S.C. § 544; § **12.7.**

____ 11. Is there a statutory lien avoidable under 11 U.S.C. § 545? 11 U.S.C. § 545; §§ **12.9–12.13.**

____ 12. Has there been a transfer to a creditor within 90 days before filing vulnerable to attack as a preference? 11 U.S.C. § 547(b); §§ **12.15–12.20.**

- ____ Payments on past due unsecured debts
- ____ Contemporaneous exchange
- ____ Subsequent new value
- ____ Ordinary course of business
  - ____ Timing of invoices/payments
  - ____ Method of payment
  - ____ Creditor pressure for payment

____ 13. Has there been a transfer to or for the benefit of an insider creditor within one year of filing vulnerable to attack as a preference? 11 U.S.C. §§ **12.15–12.21.**

____ 14. Has there been a transfer under circumstances that indicate that debtor intended to hinder, delay, or defraud a creditor? 11 U.S.C. § 548(a)(1); § **12.24.**

- ____ Transfer to insider within one year
- ____ Debtor retained control over property transferred
- ____ Concealed transfer
- ____ Transfer after debtor was sued or threatened with suit
- ____ Transfer of all or substantially all of debtor's nonexempt assets
- ____ Transfer for less than reasonably equivalent value
- ____ Transfer made when or shortly before debtor became insolvent or undercapitalized in business
- ____ Transfer made shortly before or after substantial debt incurred

____ 15. Has there been a transfer for less than reasonably equivalent value when debtor was or became insolvent, unreasonably undercapitalized, or liable on debts beyond debtor's ability to pay? 11 U.S.C. § 548(a)(2); § **12.24.**

____ 16. Has there been a transfer vulnerable under state fraudulent transfer laws, which might have longer statutes of limitations than 11 U.S.C. § 548? 11 U.S.C. § 544; §§ **12.7, 12.23.**

____ 17. Does any theory of concealment in conjunction with state law extend the statute of limitations beyond that of 11 U.S.C. § 548? § **12.24.**

____ 18. Has there been a foreclosure sale for less than reasonably equivalent value? 11 U.S.C. § 548; **§ 12.25.**

____ 19. Has a corporate debtor pledged its assets to borrow money to pay to shareholders? 11 U.S.C. § 548; **§ 12.26.**

____ 20. Has an insolvent corporation given a guaranty for the benefit of a parent, subsidiary, or sister corporation? 11 U.S.C. § 548; **§ 12.27.**

____ 21. Has a creditor manipulated its setoff rights within 90 days of filing? 11 U.S.C. § 553; **§ 12.28.**

____ 22. Is there a lien against exempt property? 11 U.S.C. § 522(f); **Chapter 20.**

CHAPTER 13

DISCLOSURE STATEMENT STRATEGIES FOR DEBTORS AND CREDITORS

Mark A. Craige

§ 13.1 Introduction

The purpose of a disclosure statement is to provide information to creditors to enable them to decide how to vote on the plan. Title 11 U.S.C. § 1125 governs disclosure statements.

In the typical small business case, the primary purpose of the disclosure statement is to comply with the statutory requirement that there be one. The Bankruptcy Code clearly states that some type of document must be submitted to and approved by the court as complying with the statutory requirements. The requisite disclosure statement does not necessarily have to be an independent document apart from the plan. For example, in a case in which the assets are to be sold at a public auction for cash and the cash is to be distributed, the debtor in bankruptcy might be able to get court approval of one document that both describes the method of liquidation and embodies the plan without needing a separate disclosure statement. However, most cases require two documents, a disclosure statement and the plan of reorganization.

In some districts, courts have adopted a fast-track "Chapter 11(a)," wherein the disclosure statement is given provisional approval without a hearing, and any objections to the document are heard at the time of confirmation of the plan. The provisional approval is given by the court after it reviews the document and finds that it meets a basic minimum standard. This is the approach taken by the small business bankruptcy amendment passed by the Senate in April 1994. See **Chapter 24.**

This author has had an experience that suggests that the creditors in the average small business case do not make much actual use of the disclosure statement. In the district involved, the local rules provide that, upon approval of the disclosure statement, the court clerk will mail to persons listed on the matrix the order approving disclosure statement, setting confirmation hearing and fixing deadlines for voting and objections, along with a blank ballot. At the same time, the plan proponent is directed to mail the plan and disclosure statement to the names on the matrix list. The effect of this rule is that creditors receive a one-page order and a blank ballot before they receive the plan and disclosure statement. On one particular occasion, four ballots were returned before the plan and disclosure statement reached the creditors. The tally was three "for" and one "against." Needless to say, those creditors made absolutely no use of the disclosure statement because they voted before they saw it. It's like voting for a political party without knowing who the candidates are.

Regardless of any lack of attention paid to disclosure statements, they still must be filed. Some creditors actually do use the document and, more importantly, the law requires the filing of disclosure statements.

§ 13.2 Drafting Disclosure Statements

The leading case setting out the minimum requirements for disclosure statements is *In re Malek.*[1] The local bankruptcy rules of the Eastern District of Oklahoma, and

---

[1] 35 B.R. 443 (Bankr. E.D. Mich. 1983).

possibly other districts as well, have adopted the *Malek* elements as minimum requirements for disclosure statements. The pertinent part of these rules is set forth in § **13.22.**

In general, the disclosure statement should describe the nature of the business, the circumstances that drove the business into bankruptcy, and the intentions of the owners insofar as reorganization is concerned. All disclosure statements should include certain items. If each is included, there should be no problem getting the disclosure statement approved. Each case, however, is different. Therefore, each disclosure statement must be tailored to meet the facts and circumstances of the particular case.

The essential parts of a disclosure statement are:

1. Introduction
2. Summary of the plan
3. Definitions
4. Voting
5. Detailed description of the classification and treatment of creditors' claims by class
6. History of the debtor prior to filing
7. Postpetition operations
8. Financial analysis
9. Disclosure of insiders
10. Postconfirmation management personnel and compensation
11. Liquidation analysis
12. Pending and contemplated litigation
13. Significant factors affecting the plan
14. Tax impact

Sample disclosure statements are presented in §§ **13.20** and **13.21.**

§ 13.3 —Preliminary Sections

Introduction. The introduction orients the reader to the overall purpose of the disclosure statement. It is also a good place to set forth the legal standard for approval contained in 11 U.S.C. § 1125.

Summary of plan. This section of the disclosure statement should present an overall outline of the plan. The treatment of each general class should be discussed. The general classes of claims are:

1. Administrative[2]
2. Priority[3]

---

[2] 11 U.S.C. § 503.

[3] *Id.* § 507.

3. Secured[4]

4. Unsecured[5]

5. Interest holders.[6]

For example, priority tax claims must be paid in full. Therefore, the disclosure statement should describe them as such and state whether they will be paid over a term or in cash. If they are to be paid over a term, the disclosure statement should specify the term, which cannot be longer than six years from the date of assessment, and whether or not interest will be paid.[7]

Definitions. It is important to set out the general definitions of various terms used in the plan and disclosure statement. This is a good place to set out the interest rate to be used in the plan, under "Plan Rate of Interest." Terms used in the disclosure statement must be consistent with the plan itself. This section must be carefully thought through, because the terms used should be defined precisely to fit the needs of the particular situation. It is a good idea to begin a list of terms to be used and then build on it as the disclosure statement and plan are drafted. Once the two basic documents have been prepared, the attorney should review them to determine if various items can be standardized with a defined term.

When analyzing a disclosure statement, an attorney for a creditor must be very careful of all defined terms. If a term is defined in the definition section, that definition will control, not the common usage of the term. If a definition differs from the common definition, the creditor's attorney must be careful to keep it in mind when analyzing the substantive provisions of the plan.

Voting. A discussion of the voting procedure is necessary in order to inform unrepresented creditors of the voting process. The sample disclosure statements presented in §§ **13.20** and **13.21** have voting sections that are standard form and used in many disclosure statements. The voting process is controlled by 11 U.S.C. § 1129, and thus there is little leeway for changing the substance of this portion of the disclosure statement. It is not possible to change the voting procedure unless Congress enacts new legislation. Therefore, the voting section can be drafted to the attorney's satisfaction and then stored in word processing to be inserted as a standard part of any disclosure statement.

§ 13.4 —Description of Classification and Treatment of Claims

This portion of the disclosure statement is really a restatement of the provisions of the plan that specify how various classes of claims are to be paid. As a practical matter,

---

[4] *Id.* § 1129(b)(2)(A).

[5] *Id.* § 1129(b)(2)(B).

[6] *Id.* § 1129(b)(2)(C).

[7] *Id.* § 1129(a)(9)(C).

the plan should be drafted first, setting forth with specificity the classification and treatment of the various creditors. Once this portion of the plan document has been satisfactorily drafted, a word processor can be used to copy and paste it onto the disclosure statement. Thoroughness is important in the creditor treatment section so the court can evaluate it independently, without reference to the plan. One of the key issues in any reorganization is the feasibility of the plan, pursuant to § 1129(a)(9). In order to assess feasibility, those evaluating the plan must know how much money will be required on a periodic basis, usually monthly, to repay the creditors and the amount of money that will realistically be available to fund the repayment. Consequently, the treatment of each class, including the payments to each class, must be made clear in order for the creditors and the court to assess the feasibility issue.

Another issue in many small business cases is voting by class. Sometimes there are unusual classifications, such as separate classes for deficiency and trade claims. The classification of creditors must be set out in detail. It is a good idea to discuss in the disclosure statement the basis for anything out-of-the-ordinary in order to prepare for the battle that is bound to come at the confirmation hearing.

§ 13.5 —History of the Debtor

This section should be a narrative discussion of the activities of the business prior to its seeking relief under Chapter 11. This section can consist of a page or two, or more if the debtor and debtor's attorney fancy themselves writers. It is important to be completely honest in the presentation of the facts. Obviously, the debtor possesses much more information about the facts leading up to the insolvency than the attorney. Counsel can begin by asking the client to write a story about how the business got started and then what went right and what went wrong along the way.

Following a basic outline in documenting the history of the business is helpful. The narrative should begin by describing the basic business, that is, whether it is manufacturing, retailing, service, or something else. Next, it should detail the unique aspects of the particular business, including the product, the market, and the competition. It should discuss the management as it has grown and changed. Finally, it should state the reason or reasons why the debtor found it necessary to seek relief by filing bankruptcy. For example, was the debtor being sued by creditors? Was a sheriff's sale imminent? Were taxing authorities threatening seizure of assets?

§ 13.6 —Postpetition Operations

If the operation of the business has been altered significantly, this section should narrate in detail the changes, and explain why the changes occurred. If the management team has been replaced, the section should describe the new managers and relate why a new team was hired in place of the previous personnel. On the other hand, the operational aspect of the business may not have been altered significantly and, if that is the case, there should be a discussion as to why there have been no changes.

Of course, in many cases management is powerless to prevent the chain of events that leads to the filing. The unrelenting rain in the Midwest in 1993 which drove thousands from their homes and businesses, the riots in Los Angeles, the series of disasters in California, including forest fires, mudslides, and earthquakes, freezing temperatures that ruin crops at the peak of the growing season, not to mention the domino effect that such occurrences have on businesses not directly touched by the whims of nature—these are all natural calamities that interrupt business operations and could not have been prevented by even the best-trained and most devoted management team. Discuss what management has done postpetition in response to the events and how the operation will overcome the impact of the disaster.

Debtors-in-possession are required to file monthly operating reports that detail the financial results of each month's business from the time the case was filed until the plan is confirmed.[8] Although such reports are public record, it is a good idea to summarize them. An easy format is to put the categories on a spreadsheet and have a separate column for each month.

§ 13.7 —Financial Analysis

This is a crucial section. In it the disclosure statement must discuss the financial aspects of the plan. Essentially, the debtor needs to demonstrate that the business has sufficient cash flow to fund the plan of reorganization. First, it should discuss the cash requirements of the plan. How much money will be needed? When will money be needed? For what duration of time will certain amounts of money be needed?

Second, the disclosure statement should show the origin of the money. Attaching several cash flow projections is a good idea. The courts usually require an analysis of cash flow for a number of years postconfirmation. The debtor's accountant should be asked to prepare the projections once the cash requirements have been determined for the creditor classes and incorporate them into the cash flow statements. Generally, cash flows are done on computerized spreadsheets. These software packages enable the user to prepare various cash flow scenarios using different assumptions.

The basis for the cash flow projections should be discussed. The assumed percentage of increase in revenue and expenses, if any, should be disclosed, and the document should recite why the increases are expected to occur. Often, this is the weakest part of the debtor's case. It is essential for the attorney to spend time with the debtor, the accountant, and any economic experts familiar with the case to assure the best financial projection. This is the time to decide what evidence to put on at the confirmation hearing to establish feasibility.

It is a good idea to develop an overall business plan as the end product of the joint efforts of the various experts and management. Then, the business plan should be incorporated into the disclosure statement as a part of the financial analysis of the reorganization plan. It should be kept in mind that a Chapter 11 plan is a restructuring of the debts of a business.

---

[8] 11 U.S.C. §§ 1107(a), 1106 (a)(1), 704(8).

An in-depth discussion of all aspects of financing should be given. If this portion of the disclosure statement is done well, feasibility disputes will be minimized.

Creditors are generally skeptical about whether or not the debtor will be able to pay their claims. This section provides an opportunity to convince creditors to give the debtor a chance to pay its debts. On the other hand, from the creditor's perspective, this section calls for careful scrutiny. The creditor who has serious questions regarding the debtor's ability to make payments according to the plan should engage a financial expert to review this portion of the disclosure statement and make an independent determination as to whether or not the debtor's financial projections are credible. If the financial expert determines that the financial projections are not realistic, the expert will be able to advise the creditor of the problems. If something of major significance has been omitted that should have been included in the disclosure statement, an objection to the disclosure statement may be appropriate. However, most of the time, objections are based on opinions rather than on facts, and the financial experts of the plan proponent and the plan opponent may have varying ideas about things like the percentage of increase in expenses versus revenue, the need for capital expenditures in a given fiscal year, the amount of compensation necessary to retain the executive management team, and whether particular items of expense or revenue are realistic. Items like these should be reserved for the feasibility battle at confirmation. The disclosure statement should consider issues like the expiration of a patent, the need for major capital expenditures, such as clean-up of an environmental hazard, or the failure to adequately fund a pension plan. In the event major items such as these have been omitted, they are more than likely intentional omissions. If defeat of the plan is the objective, then filing an objection that exposes an intentional, or at least grossly negligent, omission of a significant factor will demonstrate to the court that the plan proponent's honesty and integrity are questionable at best. That demonstration may determine whether confirmation is approved or disapproved if the confirmation litigation is a close call.

§ 13.8 —Disclosure of Insiders

Insider dealings are commonplace in small businesses. The disclosure statement should discuss them fully. It should explain the relationship between the corporate officers, directors, and shareholders. The same set of people usually hold several of these corporate positions. Many times it is mom and pop, sons and daughters who own and operate small businesses. The disclosure statement should discuss the family employees, what they are paid, and why.

A full disclosure of insider transactions, discussed openly and honestly in this section, can help the debtor regain a creditor's trust. Creditors often suspect that debtors in bankruptcy are busy feathering their own nests at the expense of the creditors. If questionable insider transactions have occurred, the debtor should discuss them in detail and set forth in the disclosure statement the reasons why such transactions are going to stop and the steps being taken to prevent any recurrence. It is much better to hit this issue head-on than to have one of the creditors surprise the court and the other creditors. If the estate has claims against insiders, there is the danger that a trustee will be appointed. This is particularly true if an attempt is made to conceal, or at least ignore, transactions of this type.

One question that usually arises in this area is whether or not the debtor-in-possession intends to sue one of the principals in the company, who many times is a close relative or business associate of the current management. A good way to deal with this is to describe the possible claims and put them into a trust for the unsecured creditors to deal with postconfirmation. This allows the creditors some measure of comfort that the claims will be dealt with fairly by an independent trustee and, at the same time, will permit the main objective of a confirmed plan to be accomplished. Needless to say, the debtor's attorney should plan to spend a good portion of time preparing this section because it is a sensitive area, particularly in the small business case.

From the creditor's perspective, however, if the debtor has skimmed over the insider issue, the creditor and its attorney should call the debtor's hand and require it to reveal the transactions. If the debtor tries to avoid the issue, the creditor should include proposed language in the objection and ask the court to require that the proposed language be inserted in the disclosure statement verbatim.

§ 13.9 —Postconfirmation Management Personnel and Compensation

This issue is related somewhat to the insider transactions issue. The disclosure statement needs to explain thoroughly who is going to run the company and how much they are going to be paid. Any restrictions on increasing compensation should be detailed. Conversely, if no increases in compensation will be made for the duration of the reorganization, the disclosure statement should say, "Any increases in compensation of postconfirmation management will be governed by the prevailing market conditions and the profitability of the company," or words to that effect. Market and cash flow always affect compensation of management.

§ 13.10 —Liquidation Analysis

A specific requirement for the confirmation of any plan, liquidation analysis is extremely significant. The debtor needs to demonstrate that, as of the effective date of the plan, creditors will be paid at least what they would get from a Chapter 7 liquidation. The comparison date is usually the date of confirmation of the plan, but it can be defined as some other reasonable date.

The analysis must not be calculated as of the filing of the case. It must take into account any postpetition lending or cash collateral orders and the accompanying liens that usually go with such orders. The drafter needs to ask whether all of the assets of the estate were encumbered postpetition and, if so, how much is owed on the post-petition debt and whether it will consume the assets of the estate that were unencumbered as of the petition date.

The liquidation analysis must take into account the cost of liquidation under Chapter 7. The statutory trustee fees and allowable expenses pursuant to 11 U.S.C.

§ 330 should be included. Additionally, calculation of the amount that would remain for unsecured claims should take into account payments to administrative, priority, and secured creditors. Usually, there is very little, if anything, left for the unsecured claims in a Chapter 7 liquidation. Values and expenses must be estimated fairly. If it is necessary to have the assets of the estate appraised for valuation purposes under 11 U.S.C. § 506, the appraiser can be asked to calculate a liquidation value. This liquidation appraisal can be included in the disclosure statement. If there are unencumbered assets, it may be necessary to have them appraised and include their fair market value in the disclosure statement because they will be central to confirmation. In reality, the debtor must treat the unsecured class of creditors better than a Chapter 7 trustee would treat them if the debtor is to persuade them to vote for the plan. There is no reason for unsecured creditors to vote for the plan if the appointment of a Chapter 7 trustee would improve their chances of payment.

Creditors will be interested in having an appraisal, with the appraiser's valuing the assets under both liquidation and going-concern scenarios. Going-concern value, if there is in fact a going concern, is used in the determination of the value of secured claims. Liquidation value must be known in order to evaluate whether the plan gives the creditors all of the payments to which they are entitled. If the proffered disclosure statement does not demonstrate that creditors are in fact receiving at least the funds to which they are entitled, the creditors have a valid confirmation objection. However, many times the issues will distill down to a battle of appraisers regarding the value of certain assets and the projected costs of the hypothetical Chapter 7. If a plan proponent is inept enough to disclose that the plan does not meet this requirement, is there a valid objection to the disclosure statement? Because the disclosure statement is an information document, and if the information contained is correct, perhaps no objection to the disclosure statement should be filed. On the other hand, if the plan is so flawed that it does not meet the liquidation test, then perhaps an objection to the disclosure statement pointing this out may prevent an unnecessary expense to the estate by preventing the balloting of a plan which, on its face, can never be confirmed. Each case must rise and fall on its own facts and circumstances. The impact on the client as well as the estate and the other creditors should be considered, then it should be decided when to raise the issue to best accomplish the client's objectives.

The drafter of a disclosure statement must make sure that it contains the proper information to inform the creditors on the liquidation value issue. This is perhaps most important when there are competing plans. Creditors naturally favor the plan that pays them the most money in the least amount of time and with the least amount of risk involved. Creditors should carefully analyze the debtor's assertion that nothing would be received in a Chapter 7 case. Although it is often true that unsecured creditors receive nothing, it is not always the case.

§ 13.11 —Pending and Contemplated Litigation

It is important to discuss all litigation concerning the business. There are two categories: *pending litigation* concerns cases pending as of the filing of the plan, and *contemplated litigation* concerns cases the reorganized entity intends to file after the plan is confirmed.

Many pending cases, such as foreclosures and debt collection matters, will be resolved by the confirmation of the plan. Other cases, such as those in which the debtor is the plaintiff seeking damages, will be continued. Whatever the status is to be, cases should be discussed briefly and their intended disposition explained.

Cases that will be filed after the plan is confirmed generally are transfer avoidance cases under 11 U.S.C. §§ 544, 547, 548, and 550. It is essential that the plan reserve jurisdiction to the court to hear these matters and that they be specifically preserved postconfirmation. The disclosure statement should advise all parties of known or contemplated claims that are likely to be filed. After all, the purpose of the disclosure statement is to provide sufficient information to allow a party to cast a knowledgeable vote for or against the plan. A party who is going to be sued after the plan is confirmed needs to know that the debtor intends to sue.

In discussing any litigation, the plan drafter should set out the theory of recovery and the operative facts as objectively as possible. It is necessary to make some sort of disclosure about the amount of money or property the debtor believes would be recovered. The drafter should be as fair as possible in this regard, because the other creditors will want to know the benefit to be obtained from a successful suit, while the party being sued will want the amount of possible damages to be understated. Counsel should always disclaim any opinion about litigation in the disclosure statement just as in a letter to a client about a contemplated case.

§ 13.12 —External Factors

This provision needs to be drafted on a case-by-case basis. Various types of businesses are affected by different factors. The debtor should be able to tell counsel what factors affect the business in question.

Market factors affect all businesses. The disclosure statement should discuss the market environment within which the particular debtor operates. For example, weather, war, population changes, governmental regulation of prices, international competition, and the effect of tariffs and duties may affect the business. Other concerns might be supply of raw materials, fluctuation of interest rates, and other factors. If the debtor is an international company, the stability of the government of the foreign country is a factor, so the disclosure statement should address the effect of a change in the foreign government or nationalization of the debtor's assets by the foreign government.

Creditors should look for omission of some really significant matter. For example, the physical manufacturing plant might need major renovation in the future, or there might be some environmental problem that does not, as of the time of the confirmation, represent a fixed liability but could represent a liability in the future. If there is truly a major circumstance that could affect the plan's success, the drafter should make sure it is in the disclosure statement. This is where some discovery may be needed. It may be necessary to convene a Rule 2004 examination to elicit such matters.

§ 13.13 —Tax Impact Analysis

Tax impact analysis may require either debtor's or creditor's counsel to consult a tax expert. Important considerations are the effect of discharge on net operating loss carryovers, the effect of increased taxes on the net cash flow stream available to service the plan payments, tax consequences to creditors in a "debt-for-equity swap plan," and the effect on equity holders of the elimination of their equity interest in order to comply with the absolute priority rule. **Chapter 10** explores some tax consequences of bankruptcy in more detail. The best advice is to have someone with tax expertise review the plan and give guidance on the plan's tax impact on all of the parties in the case. Debtors should get such an opinion in writing and attach it as an exhibit to the disclosure statement. Creditors should compare their own analysis to the one done by the plan proponent. If there is a substantial difference, they should object and ask that the plan proponent be compelled to also include the creditor's analysis in the disclosure statement.

§ 13.14 Notice of Hearing

Proper notice must be given of the hearing to approve the disclosure statement. Bankruptcy Rule 3017(a) requires that there be 25 days' notice of the hearing on the disclosure statement. This is one time limit that cannot be shortened. The disclosure statement should not be circulated to the parties until after it has been approved. However, most courts use an order, such as those in **§§ 13.15** through **13.18,** to notice the hearing and advise the parties where they can get a copy of the proposed disclosure statement if they wish to analyze it before determining whether they have objections. The debtor should not send the proposed disclosure statement to the creditors when filing it because the debtor will be required to send the court-approved disclosure statement to the names on the matrix even if that duplicates mailing of a preapproved disclosure statement. Also, mailing the proposed plan and the disclosure statement before court approval could be considered improper solicitation of the creditors for approval of the plan. Section 1125(b) permits the solicitation of binding acceptances of a plan only after the approval of the disclosure statement. Mailing the disclosure statement to the creditors before it is approved could taint the entire plan.

§ 13.15 —Form: Order Requiring Debtor to Notice Disclosure Statement

FORM 13–1
ORDER REQUIRING DEBTORS TO NOTICE DISCLOSURE STATEMENT

CAPTION

ORDER REQUIRING DEBTORS TO NOTICE DISCLOSURE STATEMENT

NOW, on this [date], a Disclosure Statement having been filed by the debtors on [filing date];

IT IS HEREBY ORDERED that the Debtors, by [mailing date] shall cause to be mailed to all creditors listed and those not listed but filing claims herein, all equity security holders, and other parties in interest, a copy of the Notice attached hereto as Exhibit A, and to mail a copy of the Disclosure Statement to those required by Bankruptcy Rule 3017(a).

IT IS FURTHER ORDERED that the Debtors, upon mailing of said Notice and Disclosure Statement, shall file with the Clerk of the Bankruptcy Court a Certificate of Mailing listing the names and addresses of those parties to whom a Notice and Disclosure Statement was mailed.

____

U.S. BANKRUPTCY JUDGE

EXHIBIT A

NOTICE TO CREDITORS AND OTHER PARTIES IN INTEREST

NOTICE IS HEREBY GIVEN THAT THE DEBTOR-IN-POSSESSION HAS FILED A DISCLOSURE STATEMENT.

NOTICE IS FURTHER GIVEN that a complaint objecting to the discharge under Section 727 must be filed not later than the first date set for hearing on confirmation.

The Honorable [Bankruptcy Judge], has directed that all creditors be noticed concerning this Disclosure Statement.

YOU ARE FURTHER NOTIFIED that all creditors have until [objection date] to file a written objection thereto. If no objection to the Disclosure Statement is filed, the Disclosure Statement may be approved, after review by the Court, without hearing.

If an objection is filed, an evidentiary hearing will be held before the Court at [address] on [hearing date].

Creditors who wish a copy of the Disclosure Statement must request one in writing from [party].

YOU ARE FURTHER NOTIFIED that because of the length of time between distribution of the disclosure statement and hearing date, the Court will expect counsel for the Debtor(s), in a case where objections to a Disclosure Statement are made, to communicate with the objecting creditors and attempt to comply with appropriate objections by filing an amended disclosure statement. The amendment, if any, should be filed and circulated as the Court requires in a timely fashion so that objection to it may be made prior to the scheduled hearing date. Failure of counsel for the Debtor(s) to communicate with creditors and to make timely amendments, if appropriate, may result in dismissal.

DATED

____
U.S. BANKRUPTCY JUDGE

§ 13.16 Form: Order and Notice of Hearing on Disclosure Statement

FORM 13–2
ORDER AND NOTICE OF HEARING ON DISCLOSURE STATEMENT

ORDER AND NOTICE OF HEARING ON DISCLOSURE STATEMENT

TO THE CREDITORS AND OTHER PARTIES IN INTEREST:

A Plan and Disclosure Statement under Chapter 11 of the Bankruptcy Code was filed on [filing date], by [Debtor], the debtor-in-possession.

IT IS ORDERED AND NOTICE IS HEREBY GIVEN THAT:

The hearing to consider approval of the Disclosure Statement will be on the [date] of [month], 199[ ], at [time] o'clock [A./P.]M., at the United States Bankruptcy Court for the [District], [address].

The last date to file and serve written objections to the Disclosure Statement is on [objection date].

The United States Trustee shall file a Response to the Debtor's Disclosure Statement filed [filing date] within fifteen (15) days from the entry of this Order.

Requests for copies of the Plan and Disclosure Statement should be directed to:

[Attorney name and address]

[Dated]

____
U.S. BANKRUPTCY JUDGE

§ 13.17 —Form: Order to Notice Reorganization Plan

FORM 13–3
ORDER REQUIRING DEBTORS TO NOTICE
PLAN OF REORGANIZATION

CAPTION

ORDER REQUIRING DEBTORS TO NOTICE PLAN OF REORGANIZATION

NOW, on this [date] day of [month], the debtors' Disclosure Statement having been filed on [filing date],

IT IS HEREBY ORDERED that the debtor, on or before [mailing date] shall cause to be mailed to all creditors listed herein and those not listed but filing claims, all equity security holders, the U.S. Trustee, and other parties in interest, a copy of the final Disclosure Statement, a copy of the final Plan of Reorganization, a copy of the Order and Notice approving the Disclosure Statement, and fixing times for filing acceptances or rejections to the plan, objections to confirmation, administrative claims, a time for hearing on confirmation and Ballot.

IT IS FURTHER ORDERED that the Debtors, upon mailing of said final Disclosure Statement and Plan, Order, Notice, and Ballot, shall file with the Clerk of the Bankruptcy Court a Certificate of Mailing listing the names and addresses of those parties to whom the Disclosure Statement, Plan, Order, Notice, and Ballot was mailed.

____
U.S. BANKRUPTCY JUDGE

§ 13.18 —Form: Order and Notice of Reorganization Plan Hearing

FORM 13–4
ORDER AND NOTICE OF
REORGANIZATION PLAN HEARING

CAPTION

ORDER COMBINED WITH NOTICE OF
(1) APPROVAL OF THE DISCLOSURE STATEMENT
(2) FIXING A TIME FOR FILING ACCEPTANCES OR REJECTIONS OF THE PLAN
(3) FIXING A TIME FOR FILING OBJECTIONS TO CONFIRMATION
(4) FIXING A TIME FOR FILING ADMINISTRATIVE CLAIMS

(5) FIXING A TIME FOR FILING OBJECTIONS TO DISCHARGE
(6) FIXING A TIME FOR HEARING ON CONFIRMATION

A Disclosure Statement was filed by the Debtor on [filing date].

The Court finds that the Disclosure Statement contains adequate information as required by 11 U.S.C. 1125;

IT IS THEREFORE ORDERED AND NOTICE IS HEREBY GIVEN THAT:

(1) The Disclosure Statement as filed, amended, and/or modified by the Debtor is approved.

(2) [Acceptance/rejection date] is fixed as the last date for acceptance or rejection of the enclosed Plan of Reorganization. All acceptances or rejections must be filed in writing with the Clerk of the Bankruptcy Court [court address] by said date. A copy of the ballot shall be supplied to the plan proponent at [proponent address].

(3) [Objection date] is fixed as the last day for filing objections to the confirmation of the Plan. The objections, in writing, must be filed with the Clerk of the Bankruptcy Court by said date and served in accordance with Federal Rules of Bankruptcy Procedure 3020(b)(1).

(4) [Claims date] is fixed as the last day for filing administrative claims. The claims, in writing, must be filed with the Clerk of the Bankruptcy Court by that date.

(5) [Objection to discharge date] is fixed as the last day for filing complaints objecting to the discharge under Section 727 of the Code. The complaints must be filed with the Clerk of the Bankruptcy Court by that date.

(6) A hearing for consideration of confirmation of the Plan of Reorganization will be held on [date, time] in the United States Bankruptcy Court [court address].

There shall be mailed to all creditors and other parties in interest a copy of this Order and Notice, a copy of the final Disclosure Statement, a copy of the final Plan of Reorganization and appropriate forms for acceptance or rejection of the Plan.

DATED

____
U.S. BANKRUPTCY JUDGE

§ 13.19 Resolution of Objections to Disclosure Statements

The primary rule regarding litigation of disclosure statements is, "Don't!" Disputes over disclosure statements should be resolved by negotiation rather than by litigation. Trials over disclosure statements in small business cases should be avoided if possible. If a trial is necessary, it will most likely be a legal argument over the sufficiency of what has been done or attempted to be done in order to satisfy the particular creditor's objections. Only on rare occasions should it be necessary to put on witnesses and introduce documentary evidence. The best approach is not to litigate it at all.

From the debtor's perspective, the best method for resolving any objections to the disclosure statement is to inquire of the objecting party what precisely the objecting party believes is lacking in the proffered document. If there is merit to the objection, the debtor should put the requested element in. A good approach is to write a letter asking counsel for the objecting party to provide specific language to include and, unless it is totally inappropriate, include it.

Generally, if the objecting party is objecting for the purpose of being obstructionist, the debtor will get responses such as "It needs more detail," or "There should be a fuller discussion" of some particular matter. This type of response is difficult to deal with, because the party is really saying that it does not like anything the debtor is doing and is not going to agree to anything within reason. To deal with this type of party, the attorney should ask the party in writing to specify the additional information it desires and then make an effort to satisfy the party before filing an amendment to the disclosure statement. If the party is still not satisfied, it probably never will be. In such a case, it is necessary to let the court resolve the dispute.

The other types of objections most commonly encountered are in fact objections to the plan itself, not the disclosure statement. These objections refer to classification of claims, treatment of particular classes of claims, feasibility, the absolute priority rule, and other such matters. The issue in the approval of the disclosure statement concerns the information it contains, not the substance of the plan. It is important to focus on the task at hand, which is to get the disclosure statement approved so that the case can move on to the issues in the plan. Most of the time, a suggestion to objecting counsel that the confirmation issues be tried at the confirmation stage will put things in perspective. Debtor's counsel should make the same point to the judge. Most judges prefer to save the real issues for confirmation and will rule on the objections accordingly.

Creditors' attorneys should focus on the issues. They should analyze the document to see what additional information the average creditor needs to know about the debtor. Counsel should file objections but be prepared to provide the debtor with specific language and items. Putting the proposed language in the body of the objection itself is the most effective method. Counsel should refrain from objecting to the plan in the context of the disclosure statement. Confirmation objections should be saved for objections to the plan. Issues such as feasibility, classification of claims, treatment of particular creditors' claims, violations of the absolute priority rule, and like matters are not grounds for denial of approval of the disclosure statement. They will be more effective if saved for the appropriate time.

There is, however, an exception to this general rule. It has been held that "A disclosure statement will not be approved where . . . it describes a plan which is fatally flawed and thus incapable of confirmation.'[9] If it is the goal of the creditor to defeat the entire reorganization effort as fast as possible, and the creditor is fairly certain the plan is fatally flawed, then it will be worthwhile to raise the objections demonstrating the fact that the plan is already dead, even though the debtor does not know it yet.

Unless the plan is fatally flawed, creditors need to bear in mind that the denial of approval of a disclosure statement is not going to win the case if conversion or dismissal is the creditor's objective. In fact, objecting will further delay litigation of the real issues surrounding the plan. Because delay generally is detrimental to a creditor, it is best to go on to the issue of confirmation rather than to spend time litigating the disclosure statement.

Feasibility of the plan is usually a major issue. The plan proponent should therefore have some type of cash flow analysis that will demonstrate the feasibility of the plan. If the plan proponent's own numbers show lack of feasibility, a creditor certainly does not want to help out by showing the proponent the error of its ways before the confirmation hearing. However, most of the time the plan proponent will present some type of cash flow analysis demonstrating that the plan will work. If the creditor's analysis differs from the analysis offered by the plan proponent, argument at the disclosure statement hearing about feasibility should be avoided, but an objection to the analysis should be made. The creditor should show the court its own cash flow analysis. A creditor can and should request that the plan proponent be ordered to include the creditor's perspective along with the proponent's so that all creditors will have the benefit of both cash flow analyses when making their decisions. Creditors should be aware that the other classes of creditors may vote in favor of the plan anyway and should plan the overall litigation strategy carefully before objecting, in order to ensure that the creditor's alternative analysis is used to the best advantage.

When an objection to a disclosure statement is sustained, it usually is not necessary to have another hearing if the remedy is to add something to the disclosure statement. Because the actual document is not circulated to all of the parties until after it has been approved, there is generally no due process problem with amending it at the hearing and approving it at the same time. This prevents an additional delay in getting to the confirmation hearing.

Whether representing the plan proponent or an opponent in the disclosure statement process, counsel should focus on the real issue. In other words, if the disclosure statement tells everyone concerned what they should know about the plan, or comes close, then the parties ought to get on with the main issue of plan confirmation. If the disclosure statement is clearly deficient, the parties should try to resolve the matter by some type of agreement to include additional information and avoid actual litigation on the disclosure statement. Delays confound the system and generally do not benefit anyone involved, neither debtor, creditor, committee, nor trustee. If this attitude is taken by all sides, unnecessary delays can be avoided, and the case can be propelled on to the real issues.

---

[9] *In re* 266 Washington Assocs., 141 B.R. 275 (Bankr. E.D.N.Y. 1992). *See also In re* Eastern Me. Elec. Coop., Inc., 125 B.R. 329 (Bankr. D. Me. 1991); *In re* Valrico Square Ltd. Partnership, 113 B.R. 794, 796 (Bankr. S.D. Fla. 1990) ("Soliciting votes and seeking court approval on a clearly fruitless venture is a waste of the time of the Court and the parties"); *In re* Pecht, 53 B.R. 768 (Bankr. E.D. Va. 1985); *In re* Kehn Ranch, Inc., 41 B.R. 832 (Bankr. D.S.D. 1984).

§ 13.20 Sample Disclosure Statement for Reorganization of Oil Company

IN THE UNITED STATES BANKRUPTCY COURT FOR THE
DISTRICT OF KANSAS

IN RE:	)	
WILSON, JAMES P.	)	Case No.
d/b/a WILSON OIL COMPANY,	)	Chapter 11
Debtor.	)	

AMENDED
DISCLOSURE STATEMENT

I. INTRODUCTION

A. Purpose of this Disclosure Statement

On March 19, 1992, James P. Wilson, d/b/a WILSON OIL COMPANY the Debtor-in-Possession, filed his Petition for Relief under Chapter 11 of the United States Bankruptcy Code (the Code) in the United States Bankruptcy Court for the District of Kansas (the Court). On May 4th 1992, the Debtor filed his Plan. Before the Plan can be approved by the Court and before solicitations for acceptance of the Plan can be sought, the Debtor is required to submit to the holders of claims or interests in the estate a Disclosure Statement containing adequate information concerning the Plan. Adequate information means information of a kind, and in sufficient detail, as far as is reasonably practicable in light of the nature and history of Debtor's operation and the condition of its books and records that would enable a hypothetical, reasonable investor typical of holders of claims or interests of the relevant Classes to make an informed judgment about the Plan. The sole purpose and use of this Disclosure Statement is to furnish the holders of Claims and interests adequate information pertaining to the Plan.

II. DEFINITIONS

The following definitions apply to the Plan and this Disclosure Statement exclusively. Any terms used by the Plan defined by 11 U.S.C. § 101 shall mean the same as defined by such section unless otherwise provided herein.

1. Allowed Claim: An allowed claim is any claim of any creditor listed on the mailing matrix filed by the Debtor, and as amended by the Debtor, in this case. Allowed Claims shall be allowed in the amount set forth in the Debtor's schedules unless provided otherwise in this Plan. If a claim is listed as UNKNOWN, it shall be assigned a value

		of zero. Allowed Claims are also those claims of creditors who have timely filed Proofs of Claim. In the event of a difference between the claim scheduled by the Debtor and the Proof of Claim, the Proof of Claim filed by a creditor shall control unless the same is objected to by the Debtor.
3.	Claims Bar Date:	The calendar date by which those having claims for payment from the Debtor must file a proof of claim. Claims not filed by this date will be treated as scheduled in the schedules filed by the Debtor. The Court has determined the 17th day of July, 1992 to be the deadline for the filing of Claims.
4.	Confirmation:	A judicial determination by the Court at the confirmation hearing to be set in the future that the Plan complies with the requirements of 11 U.S.C. § 1129 and is therefore determined to be a confirmed Plan as that term is defined by the Bankruptcy Code.
5.	Debtor:	JAMES P. WILSON, d/b/a WILSON OIL COMPANY, an individual.
6.	Disclosure Statement:	This document and any amendments or modifications thereto filed by the Debtor, and ultimately approved by this Court pursuant to 11 U.S.C. § 1125.
7.	Effective Date:	Ten days after the date of the docketing of a final Order confirming the Plan.
8.	Monthly Payment Due Date:	The twenty-fifth day of the first full month following the effective date of the Plan.
9.	The Plan:	The Plan is the document and any amendments or modifications thereto filed by the Debtor as the Plan of reorganization.
10.	Plan Rate of Interest:	The interest rate for the Plan shall be 10 percent per annum simple interest computed based on the outstanding principal

		balance of the claim as of the effective date of the Plan.
11.	Secured Claim:	A claim that has some security interest, mortgage, or other lien upon property of the estate and is a secured claim to the extent of the value of the property so securing such claim pursuant to 11 U.S.C. § 506.
12.	Unsecured Claim:	Any claim that is not a secured claim.

III. SUMMARY OF THE PLAN

The following summary describes the general approach of the Plan. There are many provisions in the Plan which are not covered in this summary. The Plan should be read carefully to understand all aspects of the Plan.

Essentially, the Plan contains the following elements:

1. Claims in Class 1 are administrative expenses. Administrative expenses include all professional fees including attorney's and accountant's fees and allowed expenses of the foregoing which have accrued from the Petition date and which can be expected to accrue prior to confirmation. Class 1 claims will be paid in full in cash at confirmation or as soon as an Order allowing such claims is entered.

2. Payment in full of all tax priority claims in deferred cash payments with interest at the Plan Rate.

3. Payment of allowed secured claims in full in deferred cash payments over a commercially reasonable time with sufficient interest thereon to provide for the payment of the present value of the respective claims.

4. Provision for allowed unsecured claims to be treated in one class. Each unsecured claim will be paid, in cash, the amount of the claim over a term of ten years without interest to be amortized on a straight-line basis.

5. Interest holders shall retain their prepetition interest.

A COPY OF THE PLAN IS ENCLOSED WITH THIS DISCLOSURE STATEMENT AND IS ON FILE WITH THE CLERK OF THE COURT. YOU ARE ENCOURAGED TO READ IT THOROUGHLY.

IV. VOTING

Before the Plan can be confirmed by the Court, it must be submitted to the creditors and interest holders who must be provided with an opportunity to vote on whether to accept or reject the Plan. In order for the Plan to be accepted by creditors, a majority in number and a two-thirds majority in amount of allowed claims voting of each impaired class of creditors and a two-thirds majority in amount of the class of interest holders must vote to accept the Plan. Each category of claims is grouped into a class, i.e., Class 1, Administrative; Class 2, Priority; etc. This designation is for ease of organization of this document. Within each Class are various Sub-Classes. Each Sub-Class shall be treated as a separate class of claims for all purposes.

All creditors' claims will be deemed allowed for the purpose of voting on the Plan in the amount as shown on the schedules, or in the amount of a timely filed proof of claim, whichever is greater, unless an order is entered by the Court determining or estimating the amount of a creditor's claim prior to confirmation, in which case the claim will be treated for voting according to such order. Under the Plan, approval is required from at least one class of creditors, inasmuch as all creditors hereunder are impaired to some extent. If at least one class of claims accepts the Plan, then the Court may confirm the Plan notwithstanding the failure of such class to accept the Plan if the Court determines the Plan complies with U.S.C. § 1129(b) with respect to such class.

A creditor may vote to accept or reject the Plan by completing and mailing the ballot to Samuels & Johnson, attorneys for the Debtor, 9th Floor, Towne Plaza West, 5 East 31st Street, Tulsa, Oklahoma 74135. The ballot will be provided to all creditors by the attorneys for the Debtor. The Court will fix a date as the last date by which ballots must be received. No vote received after such time will be counted. The attorneys for the Debtor will count the ballots and file them with the Court on or before the date set for hearing on the confirmation of the plan, which is described hereafter.

Whether or not a creditor or interest holder votes on the Plan, such person will be bound by the terms and treatment set forth in the Plan if the Plan is accepted by other requisite majorities of creditors and interest holders and is confirmed by the Court. Allowance of a claim for voting purposes and disallowance of any claim for voting purposes does not necessarily mean that all or a portion of the claim will be allowed or disallowed for distribution purposes. Creditors who do not vote on the Plan shall be deemed to have accepted the Plan.

The Court will set a hearing on the confirmation of the Plan. At the hearing on the confirmation of the Plan, the Court will determine whether the Plan meets the requirements of § 1129 of the Code, which requires that the Plan and the Debtor comply with Chapter 11 of the Code, that the Plan is prepared in good faith and is not otherwise prohibited by law. All payments for services or costs and expenses by the Debtor or a person acquiring property under the Plan must be disclosed to the Court and found reasonable.

If there is no dissenting class, the test for confirmation is whether the Plan is in the best interests of the creditors and interest holders and is feasible. If there is a dissenting class, the Plan may nevertheless be confirmed if the Court finds that all other requirements of § 1129 are met except the requirement for acceptance by each class, and that the Plan does not unfairly discriminate and is fair and equitable respecting each class of impaired and dissenting creditors or interest holders.

All creditors, interest holders, and parties in interest will receive a notice of the deadline for voting, ballot, return envelope, notice of the time and place of the confirmation hearing, and such other information and instructions as the Court may order.

V. ANALYSIS AND TREATMENT OF CLAIMS

Following is a designation of all classes of claims and interest in the estate. Each sub-class shall constitute a separate class for voting purposes.

ALL CREDITORS UNDER THIS PLAN ARE IMPAIRED.

CLASS 1: Administrative Claims

Class 1 - Allowed Claims arising under 11 U.S.C. § 507(a)(1), (3), (5) and (6) of the Code. This Class includes the claim of the Debtor's attorneys for attorney's fees, which constitute an administrative priority claim. Any fees paid to attorneys must be approved in advance by the Court. It is anticipated at the present time that the attorneys will file an application for final compensation in this case in an amount not to exceed $15,000.00. The attorneys were paid prepetition retainers in the amount of $7,500.00, thus providing for potential claims in this Class in the amount of $7,500.00.

The attorneys for the Debtor will file an application for final compensation subsequent to the confirmation of this Plan. Property of the estate shall not revest in the Debtor until such time as the attorney's fee issue has been finally determined and all allowed claims paid.

CLASS 2: Includes all priority claims entitled to priority under 11 U.S.C. § 507(a)(7).

Class 2(a) Includes property taxes in the amount of $8,557.08 as set forth in the Debtor's amended Schedule E. The Debtor will pay these claims in full with interest at the Plan Rate over a term of 5 years. Payments will begin on the Monthly Plan Payment Due Date in the amount of $182.00 per month.

Class 2(b) Includes claims of the United States of America for the tax years 1990 and 1991. The returns for these years are under preparation but not yet filed. The Debtor has net operating loss carryforward of $128,279.00 plus tax losses for 1990. It is not anticipated there will be any tax payable for either year. If any tax is payable, it will be paid at the time of the filing of the return. Historically, the Debtor has only been required to pay self-employment tax of not more than $1,000.00. Therefore, this class will be paid in full upon the filing of the return and it is not anticipated the liability will exceed $1,000.00 for either year.

CLASS 3: Includes all secured claims.

Class 3(a) Includes the Secured Claim of Bank of Kildare, Kildare, Kansas (BoK), in the amount of $179,042.00. This claim is fully secured by a properly perfected first in priority mortgage in the real property, and certain oil and gas leases of the Debtor. The allowed Secured Claim of BoK will be paid in full over a term of 10 years with interest at the Plan Rate. The payments shall be made monthly on Monthly Plan Payment Due Date and shall be $2,366.00 per month.

Class 3(b) Includes the Secured Claim of Chrysler Credit Corp. (CCC), in the amount of $6,125.00, having as collateral a properly perfected security interest in the Debtor's 1990 Dodge Ram 50 pickup truck. The allowed Secured Claim of CCC will be paid over a period of 60 months with interest thereon at the Plan rate. The payment shall be $130.00 per month, payable on the Monthly Payment Due Date.

Class 3(c) Includes the Secured Claim of Ford Motor Credit Corp. (FMC), which is a claim secured by a lien on a 1989 Mustang. The allowed Secured Claim of FMC will be paid over a period of 60 months with interest thereon at the Plan rate. Payments shall be paid monthly in payments of $200.00 per month, payable on the Monthly Payment Due Date.

Class 3(d) Includes the Secured Claim of General Motors Acceptance Corp. (GMAC) in the amount of $20,829.00, which is secured by a lien on the Debtor's 1990 Chevrolet one-ton truck. The allowed Secured Claim of GMAC will be paid in full. The Debtor shall sell the vehicle securing this claim pursuant to 11 U.S.C. § 363 free and clear of all liens and encumbrances. The lien of GMAC shall attach to the proceeds, which shall be delivered to GMAC within 10 days of the sale. The sale shall be completed within 30 days of the Effective Date of the Plan. In the event the vehicle sale does not produce enough funds to pay this claim in full, the Debtor will make up the difference in cash from the income of the operations.

Class 3(e) Includes the Secured Claim of Independent Motorcycles (IMC), in the amount of $1,500.00 which is secured by a lien on the Debtor's 1990 Yamaha Big Bear four-wheeler. The Allowed Secured Claim of IMC will be paid over a period of 12 months with interest thereon at the Plan rate. Payment shall be paid made within one year of the Effective Date of the Plan.

Class 3(f) Includes the Secured Claim of VNFSC, in the amount of $18,803.57, which is secured by a lien on the Debtor's 1990 Chevrolet one ton truck. The allowed Secured Claim of VNFSC will be paid over a period of 60 months with interest thereon at the Plan rate. Payments shall be paid monthly in payments of $400.00 per month, payable on the Monthly Payment Due Date.

Class 3(g) Includes the Secured Claim of Porter State Bank (PSB), in the amount of $287.00, which is secured by a lien on the Debtor's Panasonic copier. The Allowed Secured Claim of PSB will be paid over a period of 12 months with interest thereon at the Plan rate. Payment shall be paid made within one year of the Effective Date of the Plan.

Class 3(h) Includes the Secured Claims of Old Prairie Pump & Supply (OPPS), in the amount of $11,718.44; Wharton Drilling Tool & Supply (WDTS), in the amount of $12,868.00; and Cosgrove Oil Well Services (COWS), in the amount of $22,023.66, which are secured by mechanic's liens on the Debtor's oil and gas leases. The allowed Secured Claims in this class will be paid in full over a period of 72 months with interest thereon at the Plan rate. Payments shall be paid monthly in payments in the following amounts per month, payable on the Monthly Payment Due Date: 1.) OPPS, $217.00; 2.) WDTS, $238.00; 3.) COWS, $408.00. The total payments to this class are $863.00 per month.

CLASS 4 Unsecured claims

Class 4 Includes all Unsecured Claims as set forth on the Debtor's Chapter 11 Schedule F. All allowed claims within this class shall be paid in full in cash over a term of 10 years without interest. Payments shall be payable on the Monthly Plan Payment Due Date. The Debtor's Schedule F has $82,387.20 in claims in this class. The payment to this class will be $686.56 per month.

CLASS 5 Interest holders

Class 5 Class 5 includes the interest of James P. Wilson in the nature of the ownership of all nonexempt assets of the estate. The interest holder shall retain his prepetition interests. This includes the Debtor, as holder of 100% of the ownership of the assets retained.

VI. HISTORY OF DEBTOR PRIOR TO FILING

The Debtor started in the oil business as a roughneck, roustabout, and pumper for Drexel Oil Co. in the mid 1970s after completing a college degree. Later, he moved to a position with Allegheny Petroleum.

Mr. Wilson purchased 7 leases from Rod Harrison for $200,000.00 in April 1985. The leases purchased were the Jocque, Ross, Crabtree, Brighton, Ingraham, Westerbrook, and Snowdon. Initially, these leases produced 7 barrels per day. However, a program of water flooding and drilling additional wells resulted in a significant increase in the production. Wells in this area will produce at a greater rate initially during the "flush" period, then decline to a flat production curve.

These wells "flushed" 50 barrels per day and are now flat at 30 barrels per day. With the additional wells, the overall production is 35 to 40 barrels per day.

The Bank of Kildare (BoK) furnished the financing to purchase some of the wells in operation as well as the commercial building where the office and shop are located. The Debtor believes the BoK is oversecured; however, BoK demanded additional collateral in the early part of 1992. The Debtor was unable to post the additional collateral and therefore faced a default call on the notes. This circumstance precipitated the filing of this case.

VII. CURRENT OPERATION

The current operation includes the daily management of 38 producing oil wells which produce a combined total of 35 to 40 barrels of oil per day. The production curve on all producing wells is either flat or increasing. The Debtor is essentially the only full time employee. The Debtor owns 100% of the working interest of all leases. All leases are 1/8th royalty interest to the landowner. Various contractors are engaged on an as-needed basis.

The following is a lease-by-lease breakdown of the operation.

A. Wells

This is an 80-acre lease with 6 producing wells and 2 injection wells. The production curve is increasing and is currently at 7 barrels per day. This is a water flood secondary recovery and a vacuum system. These wells were drilled in the early 1980's. Attached as Exhibit E is a cash flow statement for this lease.

B. Grayson

This is an 80-acre lease with 5 producing wells and 3 injection wells. The production curve is increasing and is currently at 7 barrels per day. This is a water flood secondary recovery and a vacuum system. The source of the water flood and the vacuum system is located on the adjacent Smith lease. These wells were drilled in the early 1980s. This lease has additional drilling sites for 10 wells.

There are two existing wells with potential for production; however, the effect of the water flood on these has yet to be fully evaluated. It is believed there is potential for at least one of these wells to be placed into production. Attached as Exhibit F is a cash flow statement for this lease.

C. Snowdon

This is a water flood secondary recovery involving 80 acres in Woodson County, KS. There are 15 producing wells and 10 injection wells on this lease. There are 15 additional drilling sites with 6 already pressured by the present injection wells. There were 4 wells in operation at the time the Debtor purchased this lease making 2 barrels per day total. The remaining wells were drilled by the Debtor beginning in 1987. The production on these wells is flat at 15 barrels per day. The productive life of these wells is projected by the Debtor to be another 20 years. There are wells adjacent to this lease which have been in production since the early 1960s. Attached as Exhibit G is a cash flow statement for this lease.

D. Ingraham

This is a 240-acre lease with 8 producing wells and 6 injection wells. The production curve is flat and is currently at 9 barrels per day. This is a water flood secondary recovery and a vacuum system. These current producing wells were drilled in the early 1980s. There are sites for an additional 15 wells. There are 7 temporarily abandoned wells on this lease. Attached as Exhibit H is a cash flow statement for this lease.

E. King

This is a 40-acre lease with 9 wells and 4 injection wells. However, only 2 of the wells are in production. The production on this lease is 1/2 barrel per day. This was to be a water flood secondary recovery; however, the secondary recovery was not successful. These current producing wells were drilled in the early 1980s. Attached as Exhibit I is a cash flow statement for this lease.

F. Westerbrook

This lease has 70 acres with 2 producing wells making 1 barrel per day and sites for an additional 25 wells. There is proven production on all adjacent properties. The adjacent Snowdon lease demonstrates this lease has very good potential for a water flood. These wells were drilled in the early 1980s. The production curve is flat on this lease. There is potential for 35 barrels per day in full utilization. Attached as Exhibit J is a cash flow statement for this lease.

G. Crabtree

This 80-acre lease is not in production, and all equipment, except for the tank batteries, has been removed. There are 11 wells which could be produced at approximately 1 barrel per day. These wells have been temporarily abandoned. If the market price for crude oil reaches $25.00 per barrel, this well can be operated at a positive cash flow. Attached as Exhibit K is a cash flow statement for this lease.

H. Brighton

This 40-acre lease is not in production, and all equipment, except for the tank batteries, has been removed. There are 2 wells which could be produced at approximately 1 barrel per day. These wells have been temporarily abandoned. If the market price for crude oil reaches $25.00 per barrel, this well can be operated at a positive cash flow. Attached as Exhibit L is a cash flow statement for this lease.

I. Russell

This 160-acre lease is not in production, and all equipment is still in place. There is 1 well which could be produced at approximately 1 barrel per day. This well has been temporarily abandoned. If the market price for crude oil reaches $23.00 per barrel, this well can be operated at a positive cash flow. This well requires propane to operate due to the lack of electrical power. Attached as Exhibit M is a cash flow statement for this lease.

Attached is a cash flow statement of the current operation, designated Exhibit A.

The Debtor also has a program for drilling additional wells to maintain the existing production. The additional wells will increase the production by one barrel per year. The Debtor's proposed operations are set forth on the attached Exhibit B.

IX. FINANCIAL ANALYSIS

In order to intelligently analyze the economic feasibility of this Plan, one must first determine the amount of cash needed to fund the Plan. The attached Exhibit C is a summary of the cash requirements for the Plan on a yearly basis and demonstrates that the maximum cash required on an annual basis to fund this Plan in year one is $67,223.00, which includes one-time expenditures of $9,287.00. In the remaining years, the cash requirements decrease to $4,828.00 monthly or $57,936.00 annually in years two through five; $3,916.00 monthly or $46,992.00 annually in year six; and $3,053.00 monthly or $36,636.00 annually in years seven through ten.

An analysis of the projected income has been prepared and is attached as Exhibit D. The assumptions for the projection are set forth on the Exhibit. Exhibit D is a conservative estimate in that it assumes the high rate of increase in expenses, an annual increase of production from new drilling of 1 barrel per year, and no increase in the price of oil. Even under these very conservative estimates, the Plan will pay all debts in full, maintain a cash reserve to fund the additional drilling program, and provide a cushion against cash short falls.

The market price for oil is projected at $18.25 per barrel. The $14.50 figure used is the net to the Debtor after royalties are paid. This projected price was the price of oil to the time of the filing of the original Disclosure Statement. As of the filing of this amended Disclosure Statement, the price received by the Debtor had risen to $16.23 per barrel.

Exhibits E through M provide a lease-by-lease breakdown of income and expenses. The numbers on these particular exhibits are based on an average of the last six months of operations. If one totals the expenses on the individual lease analysis exhibits and compares them to the projected expenses, the actual expenses are at least 10 percent less than those projected, which adds additional cushion to the projected income totals.

X. COMPARISON OF THE PLAN TO CHAPTER 7 CASE

All secured creditors would receive the value of their collateral or the collateral itself if the estate of the Debtor were liquidated under Chapter 7. As provided by the various Classes of this Plan, each secured creditor is receiving at least the present value of its particular item of collateral by virtue of the stream of deferred cash payments and the imposition of the plan rate of interest, plus the retention of the lien on their collateral. As such, each secured creditor is receiving not less than would be received if the case were liquidated under a Chapter 7.

If the Debtor were liquidated at confirmation, the unsecured creditors would be paid some distribution. However, the Debtor believes that in a liquidation sale, the wells would not be operated efficiently, resulting in a sale of the operation not as a going concern. Under such conditions, it is likely the unsecured creditors would not be paid in full.

Unsecured creditors of the Debtor are treated within Class 4 of this Plan. This Class provides for payment in full to the unsecured class. Therefore, the value of property to be distributed to holders of allowed unsecured claims is not less than would be paid if the estate were liquidated under Chapter 7 as of confirmation. In fact, under this Plan, creditors will receive substantially more than would be distributed under Chapter 7. Debtor therefore alleges it is in the best interest of all unsecured creditors to vote for the confirmation of this Plan.

XI. INSIDER TRANSACTIONS

Debtor intends to continue as the operator of the business. Additionally, the Debtor's wife works in the operation. They are paid wages only after the operating costs and Plan payments are completed. There is no discrimination in favor of relatives of the Debtor.

The Plan makes provision for the acquisition of a small operating loan from the Debtor's father. The Plan provides for such financing pursuant to 11 U.S.C. § 364. The terms of the loan are in accordance with ordinary terms and provide for interest at the Plan Rate.

Other than the transactions described above, there are no other insider transactions in these cases.

XIII. LITIGATION

There was no pending litigation at the time of the filing of this case. No litigation is contemplated postpetition.

XIV. SIGNIFICANT FACTORS AFFECTING THE PLAN

Market price of crude oil. The current price being received by the Debtor is $18.25 per barrel. The current market trend is for an increase to $22.00 per barrel by the middle of the summer. However, the market for oil is a volatile market. The Debtor cannot accurately predict the market in the future. In the event the price of oil goes down significantly, it will adversely affect the feasibility of this Plan.

Production from the wells. The production from the wells in the geographical region is fairly predictable when the production curve is flat. As set forth above, almost all of the wells of the Debtor are in this status. However, it is impossible to guarantee the future of any oil well.

Equipment failures. The operation of a water flood is dependent on the water injection plant continuing in operation. The failure of the equipment can be occasioned by weather, mechanical failure, failure of electrical supply, and general wear and tear on the equipment. In the event of a catastrophic failure of an injection system, the production of the wells will be significantly diminished. Production lost cannot be regained; however, the injection system can be repaired and put back into operation. This increases the cost of operation and adversely affects the net income available for the funding of this Plan.

XV. TAX IMPACT

Each creditor is encouraged to have a tax analysis done independently to determine the impact of the Plan on each particular creditor's individual tax picture.

To the extent they have previously written off as a bad debt their claims against the Debtor, creditors who receive cash from this Plan will recognize ordinary income. However, the recognition of income would be no more than would have originally occurred had the particular claim been paid as originally agreed.

The Plan will not result in the recognition of gain or income to the Debtor and should not have any adverse tax impact upon the reorganized Debtor. The Debtor has $128,279.00 in loss carryforward. Thus, the Debtor's operations will be essentially tax free for the next five years. It is difficult to predict the tax picture beyond this term because, as everyone knows, the tax laws will likely change substantially between now and the end of a five-year period. The cash-flow analysis set forth in Exhibit D to this Disclosure Statement includes a year-by-year analysis of the income tax impact on the income stream of the Debtor.

XVI. REQUIRED DISCLOSURES

No payments of the kind described in § 1129(a)(4)(A) of the Code are contemplated or provided by the Plan.

No arrangements exist between the Debtor and his counsel pertaining to the retention of counsel to implement the Plan, other than the retention of Debtor's counsel by the Debtor.

Respectfully submitted,

Attorneys for Debtor-in-Possession

ADDENDUM TO AMENDED DISCLOSURE STATEMENT

As of June 16, 1992, the King, Crabtree, Brighton, and Russell leases are not in production. There are no expenses and no income.

This supercedes the information in Debtor's Amended Disclosure Statement to which this Addendum is attached.

____

James P. Wilson

EXHIBIT A

JAMES P. WILSON — Cash Collateral Hearing

WILSON INCOME AND EXPENSE STATEMENT

Income

Lease Name	Average Production
Grayson	6 barrels
Wells	6 barrels
Snowdon	17 1/2 barrels
Ingraham	10 barrels
Westerbrook	1/2 barrel

Total 40 barrels at $14.00 net per barrel
$560.00 per day x 30 = $16,800.00 per month

Production Expenses

Electric	4,000.00	
Chemical	100.00	
Equipment	733.00	(GMAC loan)
Winch Truck	553.00	(Viola National Bank)
Fuel	1,000.00	
Insurance	50.00	
Contract labor	2,000.00	

Miscellaneous	1,000.00	
Subtotal		9,436.00
Office Building Expenses		
Bank payment	500.00	
Telephone	150.00	
Electric	150.00	
Building Insurance	100.00	
Subtotal		900.00
Living Expenses	1,800.00	
		1,800.00
Total Expenses		12,136.00

Income	16,800.00	
Expenses	–12,136.00	
	4,664.00	Available for debt service

EXHIBIT B

PROPOSED PLAN OF OPERATION

Wilson Oil Company has several leases, with their production curves from flat to an upward trend. The leases that are flat, i.e., Snowdon and Ingraham, have just flattened out and would be expected to remain flat for an extended period of time. The above mentioned leases are producing a combined 23 BOPD creating $122,061 gross income at today's price of $18.00. The leases have a combined 30 drilling locations left, so with the additional locations and the existing wells, these leases curves would stay flat with the opportunity to increase production at any time. A well can be drilled and completed on these properties for a little over $7500.00. These wells have a tendency to flush for quite a while, so for an investment of $7500.00 we expect a return of 6 BOPD average over 6 months, which creates $15,372.00 gross profit and $7,872.00 net profit on top of settling down to a barrel to a barrel-and-one-half added production.

We intend to keep the production for these leases at least at their present production. If the price declines, we will drill more wells to create quantity to achieve the same gross amount. If the price goes up substantially, we would also drill more wells to take advantage of the increase.

The Wells and the Grayson are two leases that are together geographically. These leases' curves are in an upward trend. There are new floods and wells are still responding. At present, the combined gross income is $63,510.00 annually. We are in the process as this is being written of putting on 3 wells on the Grayson. The first is making a steady 1 BOPD, which creates another $5,292.50 annually. We expect the other 2 wells to do the same, which would create a combined $15,871.50 annually. There are also 15 to 20 drilling locations left on these two leases. Drilling a well would average $7,100.00 with an expected return of 5 BOPD average for the first 5 months, creating $11,056.25 gross profit and a net profit of $3,956.25, at the same time settling down to 1 BOPD, which would add $5,292.50 profit per well drilled per year. There is a lot of life in these two leases. The curve has not flattened out, and when it does we can project a drilled well per year to keep it on the rise.

The Westerbrook is a lease that has proven worth because the Snowdon, located south of the Westerbrook, has proven that the Westerbrook will water flood. The curve is flat with a gross annual income of approximately $3,000.00 created by two wells. There is no drive to the formation and to create this would take an increase in the price of oil. There are approximately 30 drilling locations on the lease. The water flooded average production in the area is 1.16 BOPD per well. This times 30 locations equals 35 BOPD. At $20 oil, this will create a gross annual income of $205,677.49.

The Crabtree and the Brighton are stripped at the present time. They will generate 3 BOPD together, creating a gross profit of $17,629.50 at $20 oil.

In closing, at the present the leases are generating approximately $200,000. With 10 wells drilled over the next 5 years, this would create another $60,000 per year. Many traders are predicting $20 posted price which would be a dramatic difference of another $64,000, creating $250,000 to $300,000 annually. With expansion of the Westerbrook and the locations drilled of the above mentioned leases, it is plausible to project a $500,000 annual gross profit.

EXHIBIT C

Monthly cash requirements:

class	3 (a) Bank of Kildare	$2,366.00
	3 (b) Chrysler Credit Corp.	130.00
	3 (c) Ford Motor Credit	200.00
	3 (f) VNFSC	400.00
	3 (h) OPPS, WDTS & COWS	863.00
	3 Unsecured creditors	687.00
	Total	4,646.00

Payments due within one year of Effective Date.

Class 1	est $7,500.00
3(d)	Due on sale of vehicle.

3(e)		1,500.00
3(g)		287.00
	Total	9,287.00

Summary of cash requirements over life of Plan

Year	Monthly	Annually	
1	4,646.00	65,039.00	incl. 9,287.00 nonrecurring
2–5	4,646.00	55,752.00	
6	3,916.00	46,992.00	
7–10	3,053.00	36,636.00	

EXHIBIT E

WELLS

Electric	$ 860.00
Chemical	$ 30.00
Fuel	$ 197.00
Insurance	$ 10.00
Contract Labor	$ 446.50
Parts	$ 75.00
Miscellaneous	$ 250.00
Total	$1,868.50

7.5 BOPD x $16.00 x 30.42 days = $3,650.40
−1,868.50
$1,781.90

EXHIBIT F

GRAYSON

Electric	$306.00
Chemical	$ 30.00
Fuel	$197.00
Insurance	$ 10.00
Contract Labor	$398.00
Parts	$175.00
Miscellaneous	$250.00
Total	$1,366.00

6 BOPD x $16.00 x 30.42 days = $2,920.32
− 1,366.00
$1,554.32

EXHIBIT D

Assumptions			
Current Price of Oil per Barrel	$14.50	Annual Increase in Expenses	10.0%
Annual Increase in Oil Price	2.5%	Loss Carry Forward	($128,279.00)
Annual Increae in Production	0.5 BPD	Effective Tax Rate	30.00%

Income	Monthly	Year 1	Year 2	Year 3	Year 4	Year 5	Year 6	Year 7	Year 8	Year 9	Year 10
	17,641.67	211,700.00	219,704.91	227,977.75	236,526.91	245,361.05	254,489.06	263,920.13	273,663.69	283,729.48	294,127.52
Production Expenses											
Electric	4,000.00	48,000.00	52,800.00	58,080.00	63,888.00	70,276.80	77,304.48	85,034.93	93,538.42	102,892.26	113,181.49
Chemical	100.00	1,200.00	1,320.00	1,452.00	1,597.20	1,756.92	1,932.61	2,125.87	2,338.46	2,572.31	2,829.54
Fuel	1,000.00	12,000.00	13,200.00	14,520.00	15,972.00	17,569.20	19,326.12	21,258.73	23,384.61	25,723.07	28,295.37
Insurance	50.00	600.00	660.00	726.00	798.60	878.46	966.31	1,062.94	1,169.23	1,286.15	1,414.77
Contract Labor	2,000.00	24,000.00	26,400.00	29,040.00	31,944.00	35,138.40	38,652.24	42,517.46	46,769.21	51,446.13	56,590.74
Miscellaneous	1,000.00	12,000.00	13,200.00	14,520.00	15,972.00	17,569.20	19,326.12	21,258.73	23,384.61	25,723.07	28,295.37
Subtotal	8,150.00	97,800.00	107,580.00	118,338.00	130,171.80	143,188.98	157,507.88	173,258.67	190,584.53	209,642.99	230,607.28
Office Building Expenses											
Telephone	150.00	1,800.00	1,980.00	2,178.00	2,395.80	2,635.38	2,898.92	3,188.81	3,507.69	3,858.46	4,244.31
Electric	150.00	1,800.00	1,980.00	2,178.00	2,395.80	2,635.38	2,898.92	3,188.81	3,507.69	3,858.46	4,244.31
Building Insurance	100.00	1,200.00	1,320.00	1,452.00	1,597.20	1,756.92	1,932.61	2,125.87	2,338.46	2,572.31	2,829.54
Subtotal	400.00	4,800.00	5,280.00	5,808.00	6,388.80	7,027.68	7,730.45	8,503.49	9,353.84	10,289.23	11,318.15
Living Expenses	1,800.00	21,600.00	23,760.00	26,136.00	28,749.60	31,624.56	34,787.02	38,265.72	42,092.29	46,301.52	50,931.67
Total Expenses	10,350.00	124,200.00	136,620.00	150,282.00	165,310.20	181,841.22	200,025.34	220,027.88	242,030.66	266,233.73	292,857.10
Net Income	7,291.67	87,500.00	83,084.91	77,695.75	71,216.71	63,519.83	54,463.72	43,892.25	31,633.03	17,495.75	1,270.42
Plan Payments	5,768.00	69,223.00	58,176.00	58,176.00	58,176.00	58,176.00	46,992.00	36,636.00	36,636.00	36,636.00	36,636.00
Annual Income Tax	2,187.50	26,250.00	24,925.47	23,308.72	21,365.01	19,055.95	16,339.12	13,167.68	9,489.91	5,248.73	381.13
Cummulative Income Tax		(102,029.00)	(77,103.53)	(53,794.80)	(32,429.79)	(13,373.84)	2,965.27	16,132.95	25,622.86	30,871.58	31,252.71
Cash Reserve		18,277.00	43,185.91	62,705.65	75,746.36	81,090.19	101,935.76	96,024.33	81,531.45	57,142.48	21,395.77

EXHIBIT G

SNOWDON

Electric	$ 677.39
Chemical	$ 30.00
Fuel	$ 197.00
Insurance	$ 10.00
Contract Labor	$1,689.00
Parts	$ 350.00
Miscellaneous	$ 250.00
Total	$3,203.39

15.5 BOPD x $16.00 x 30.42 days = $7,544.16
−3,203.39
$4,340.77

EXHIBIT H

INGRAHAM

Electric	$870.00
Chemical	
Fuel	$197.00
Insurance	$ 10.00
Contract Labor	$314.36
Parts	$ 43.50
Miscellaneous	$250.00
Total	$1,684.86

7.5 BOPD x $16.00 x 30.42 days = $3,650.40
−1,684.86
$1,965.55

EXHIBIT J

WESTERBROOK

Electric	$ 55.00
Chemical	
Fuel	$197.00
Insurance	$ 10.00
Contract Labor	$100.00
Miscellaneous	
Total	$362.00

.5 BOPD x $16.00 x 30.42 days = $243.36
−362.00
−$118.64

§ 13.21 Sample Disclosure Statement for Reorganization of Motel

IN THE UNITED STATES BANKRUPTCY COURT FOR THE
NORTHERN DISTRICT OF OKLAHOMA

IN RE:	)	
	)	Case No.
WELCOME HOME, INC.	)	Chapter 11
d/b/a Windsor Inn,	)	
	)	
Debtor.	)	

DISCLOSURE STATEMENT

I. INTRODUCTION

A. Purpose of this Disclosure Statement

On July 8th, 1992, Welcome Home, Inc., an Oklahoma Corporation, d/b/a Windsor Inn (Debtor), the Debtor-in-Possession, filed its Petition for Relief under Chapter 11 of the United States Bankruptcy Code (the Code) in the United States Bankruptcy Court for the Northern District of Oklahoma (the Court). On December 30, 1992, the Debtor filed its Plan. Before the Plan can be approved by the Court and before solicitations for acceptance of the Plan can be sought, the Debtor is required to submit to the holders of claims or interest in the estate a Disclosure Statement containing adequate information concerning the Plan. Adequate information means information of a kind, and in sufficient detail, as far as is reasonably practicable in light of the nature and history of Debtor's operation and the condition of its books and records, that would enable a hypothetical, reasonable investor typical of holders of claims or interests of the relevant Classes to make an informed judgment about the Plan. The sole purpose and use of this Disclosure Statement is to furnish the holders of claims and interests adequate information pertaining to the Plan.

II. DEFINITIONS

The following definitions apply to the Plan and this Disclosure Statement exclusively. Any terms used by the Plan defined by 11 U.S.C. § 101 shall mean the same as defined by such section unless otherwise provided herein.

1.	**Allowed Claim:**	An allowed claim is any claim of any creditor listed on the mailing matrix filed by the Debtor, and as amended by the Debtor, in this case. Allowed Claims shall be allowed in the amount set forth in the Debtor's schedules unless provided otherwise in this Plan. If a claim is listed as UNKNOWN, it shall be assigned a value of zero. Allowed Claims are also those claims of creditors who have timely filed Proofs of Claim. In the event of a difference between the claim scheduled by the Debtor and the Proof of Claim, the Proof of Claim filed by a creditor shall control unless the same is objected to by the Debtor. In the event a claim is to be objected to, the procedure shall be controlled by the terms of the Plan.
2.	**Claims Bar Date:**	The calendar date set by the Court as the last day for persons desiring to file a claim to do so. Disputed and Unliquidated Claims and Claims scheduled as UNKNOWN not filed by this date will not be paid any money. Other scheduled claims will be deemed allowed as scheduled if no claim is filed by this date.
3.	**Confirmation:**	A judicial determination by the Court at the confirmation hearing to be set in the future that this Plan complies with the requirements of 11 U.S.C. § 1129 and is therefore determined to be a confirmed Plan as that term is defined by the Bankruptcy Code.
4.	**Debtor:**	WELCOME HOME, INC., d/b/a Windsor Inn, an Oklahoma corporation.
5.	**Disclosure Statement:**	This document and any amendments or modifications thereto filed by the Debtor, and ultimately approved by this Court pursuant to 11 U.S.C. § 1125.
6.	**Effective Date:**	Ten days after the date of the docketing of a final Order confirming this Plan.
7.	**Monthly Payment Due Date:**	The twenty-fifth day of the first full month following the effective date of this Plan.

8.	**The Plan:**	The document and any amendments or modifications thereto filed by the Debtor as the Plan of reorganization.
9.	**Plan Rate of Interest:**	The interest rate for this Plan shall be 9 percent per annum simple interest computed based on the outstanding principal balance of the claim as of the effective date of the Plan.
10.	**Secured Claim:**	A claim that has some security interest, mortgage, or other lien upon property of the estate and is a secured claim to the extent of the value of the property so securing such claim pursuant to 11 U.S.C. § 506.
11.	**Unsecured Claim:**	Any claim that is not a secured claim.

III. SUMMARY OF THE PLAN

The following summary describes the general approach of the Plan. There are many provisions in the Plan which are not covered in this summary. The Plan should be read carefully to understand all aspects of the Plan.

Essentially the Plan contains the following elements:

1. Claims in Class 1 are administrative expenses. Administrative expenses include all professional fees, including attorney's and accountant's fees and allowed expenses of the foregoing, which have accrued from the Petition date and which can be expected to accrue prior to confirmation. Class 1 claims will be paid in full in cash at confirmation or as soon as an Order allowing such claims is entered.

2. Payment in full of all tax priority claims in deferred cash payments with interest at the Plan Rate.

3. Payment of allowed secured claims in full in deferred cash payments over a commercially reasonable time with sufficient interest thereon to provide for the payment of the present value of the respective claims.

4. Provision for allowed unsecured claims to be paid in full.

5. Interest holders shall retain their prepetition interests.

A COPY OF THE PLAN IS ENCLOSED WITH THIS DISCLOSURE STATEMENT AND IS ON FILE WITH THE CLERK OF THE COURT. YOU ARE ENCOURAGED TO READ IT THOROUGHLY.

IV. VOTING

Before the Plan can be confirmed by the Court, it must be submitted to the creditors and interest holders, who must be provided with an opportunity to vote on whether to accept or reject the Plan. In order for the Plan to be accepted by creditors, a majority in number and a two-thirds majority in amount of allowed claims voting of each impaired class of creditors and a two-thirds majority in amount of the class of interest holders must vote to accept the Plan. Each category of claims is grouped into a class, i.e., Class 1, Administrative; Class 2, Priority; etc. This designation is for ease of organization of this document. Within each Class are various Sub-Classes. Each Sub-Class shall be treated as a separate class of claims for all purposes.

All creditors' claims will be deemed allowed for the purpose of voting on the Plan in the amount as shown on the schedules, or in the amount of a timely filed proof of claim, whichever is greater, unless an order is entered by the Court determining or estimating the amount of a creditor's claim prior to confirmation, in which case the claim will be treated for voting according to such order. The presumption for voting shall not prejudice any party's rights to object to a claim as provided for in the Plan. Under the Plan, approval is required from at least one class of creditors, inasmuch as all creditors hereunder are impaired to some extent. If at least one class accepts the Plan, then the Plan may be confirmed notwithstanding the rejection of any other class because all classes are being paid in full under the Plan.

A creditor may vote to accept or reject the Plan by completing and mailing the ballot to Samuels & Johnson, attorneys for the Debtor, 9th Floor, Towne Plaza West, 5 East 31st Street, Tulsa, Oklahoma 74135. The ballot will be provided to all creditors by the attorneys for the Debtor. The Court will fix a date as the last date by which ballots must be received. No vote received after such time will be counted. The attorneys for the Debtor will count the ballots and file them with the Court on or before the date set for hearing on the confirmation of the plan, which is described hereafter.

Whether or not a creditor or interest holder votes on the Plan, such person will be bound by the terms and treatment set forth in the Plan if the Plan is accepted by other requisite majorities of creditors and interest holders and is confirmed by the Court. Allowance of a claim for voting purposes and disallowance of any claim for voting purposes does not necessarily mean that all or a portion of the claim will be allowed or disallowed for distribution purposes. Creditors who do not vote on the Plan shall be deemed to have accepted the Plan.

The Court will set a hearing on the confirmation of the Plan. At the hearing on the confirmation of the Plan, the Court will determine whether the Plan meets the requirements of § 1129 of the Code, which requires that the Plan and the Debtor comply with Chapter 11 of the Code, that the Plan is prepared in good faith and not otherwise prohibited by law. All payments for services or costs and expenses by the Debtor or a person acquiring property under the Plan must be disclosed to the Court and found reasonable.

If there is no dissenting class, the test for confirmation is whether the Plan is in the best interests of the creditors and interest holders and is feasible. If there is a dissenting class, the Plan may nevertheless be confirmed if the Court finds that all other requirements of § 1129 are met except the requirement for acceptance by each class, and that the Plan does not unfairly discriminate and is fair and equitable respecting each class of impaired and dissenting creditors or interest holders.

All creditors, interest holders, and parties in interest will receive a notice of the deadline for voting, ballot, return envelope, notice of the time and place of the confirmation hearing, and such other information and instructions as the Court may order.

ANY PARTY IN INTEREST WHO FAILS TO VOTE WILL BE BOUND BY THIS PLAN IF THE NECESSARY CONFIRMATION REQUIREMENTS ARE OTHERWISE MET. FAILURE TO VOTE AND/OR OBJECT TO THIS PLAN MAY BE DEEMED AN ACCEPTANCE OF THE PLAN.

V. ANALYSIS AND TREATMENT OF CLAIMS

Following is a designation of all classes of claims and interest in the estate. Each sub-class shall constitute a separate class for voting purposes.

ALL CREDITORS UNDER THIS PLAN ARE IMPAIRED.

Class 1: Administrative Claims

Class 1 - Allowed Claims arising under 11 U.S.C. § 507(a)(1), (3), (5) and (6) of the Code. This Class includes the claim of the Debtor's attorney for attorney's fees, which constitutes an administrative priority claim. Any fees paid to attorneys must be approved in advance by the Court. It is anticipated at the present time that the attorneys will file an application for final compensation in this case in an amount not to exceed $15,000.00. The attorneys were paid postpetition retainers in the amount of $5,000.00, thus providing for potential claims in this Class in the amount of $10,000.00.

The attorneys for the Debtor will file an application for final compensation subsequent to the confirmation of this Plan. Except as otherwise provided for in the Plan, property of the estate shall not revest in the Debtors until such time as the attorney's fee issue has been finally determined and all allowed claims paid.

CLASS 2: All priority claims.

Includes all priory claims entitled to priority under 11 U.S.C. § 507(a)(7).

Class 2(a) Includes lodging taxes in the amount of $365.47 as set forth in the Debtor's Schedule E. The Debtor will pay this claim in full in cash within 10 days of confirmation. The payment to this class is $365.47.

CLASS 2(b) Includes claims of the United States of America for the unpaid withholding taxes in the amount of $7,321.81. This class will be paid in full in deferred cash payments over a term of 5 years with interest at the Plan rate. The payments to this class will be $152.00 per month and shall be payable on the Monthly Plan Payment Due Date. Payments shall be first applied to the § 941 tax liability commonly referred to as the Trust Fund Portion. The payments hereunder shall constitute voluntary payments. The designation of the allocation provided for herein is necessary to protect the interest of the estate in having current management's potential personal liability retired first in order to allow for continuity of management.

CLASS 2(c) Includes the claim of the Oklahoma Tax Commission for sales tax in the amount of $23,460.44. This class will be paid in full in deferred cash payments over a term of 5 years with interest at the Plan rate. The payments to this class will be $487.00 per month and shall be payable on the Monthly Play Payment Due Date.

CLASS 3: Secured claims.

Class 3(a) Includes the Secured Claim of Friends Bank of Ogalalla (FBO), in the amount of $507,492.23. This claim is fully secured by a properly perfected first-in-priority mortgage in the real property of the Debtor. The allowed Secured Claim of FBO will be paid in full over a term of 15 years with interest at the Plan Rate. The payments shall be made monthly on Monthly Plan Payment Due Date and shall be $5,147.00 per month.

Class 3(b) Includes the Secured Claim of Petroleum Bank (PB), in the amount of $45,073.12, having as collateral a second mortgage on the real property of Debtor. This claim also has a promissory note as collateral. Additionally, this claim has a guarantor, Mr. Lewiston, who is believed to have paid off the note at the demand of PB and is presently the holder of the note. The allowed Secured Claim of PB, or its assignee, shall be paid in full over a period of 10 years with interest at the Plan Rate. The payment shall be $571.00 per month, payable on the Monthly Plan Payment Due Date. The additional collateral for this claim, a promissory note payable by an unrelated third party, will be enforced and all payments collected shall be paid on the principal balance of the claim. Payments hereunder shall continue until the claim is paid in full.

Class 3(c) Includes the Secured Claim of Jenny Ellis, which is scheduled as Judson Corporation (JE), in the amount of $42,000.00, which is a claim secured by security interest in the Debtor's old telephone system. The allowed Secured Claim of JE will be paid in full. The collateral securing this claim shall be returned to JE. Additionally, the Debtor disputes the validity of this claim and will file an objection to any proof of claim filed. In the event the Court ultimately allows JE a claim, it will be paid in full in deferred cash payments over a term of 7 years with interest at the Plan Rate. Assuming the claim is fully allowed as scheduled, the payments shall be in the amount of $643.00 per month, payable on the Monthly Plan Payment Due Date. The payments to this class shall not begin until such time as the claim is determined by a final order of this Court. At the time of the filing of this Plan, no proof of claim had been filed by JE. If no proof of claim is timely filed, there will be no payments to this class other than the return of the collateral securing this class. However, the Debtor will escrow an amount sufficient to make each payment that would be due as if the claim were allowed on the date of confirmation. Upon the entry of a final order allowing JE a claim, all funds in the escrow account will be paid to JE and the remaining payments made until such time as the claim is paid in full.

CLASS 4: Unsecured claims

CLASS 4 Includes all Unsecured Claims as set forth on the Debtor's Chapter 11 Schedule F totalling $7,215.00. All allowed claims within this class shall be paid in full in cash over a term of 24 months with interest at the Plan Rate. Payments shall be payable on the Monthly Plan Payment Due Date. The Debtor's Schedule F has $7,215.72 in claims in this class. The payment to this class will be $330.00 per month.

CLASS 5: Interest Holders

Class 5 Class 5 includes the interest of Mary E. Dawes, the sole shareholder of the corporation. The interest holder shall retain her prepetition interest.

VI. HISTORY OF DEBTOR PRIOR TO FILING

The Debtor purchased the existing motel facility in 1990. The sale was arranged by Anderson Enterprises, through its president, Nelson Yates. Yates operated the motel and was the sole executive in charge of operations. In August 1991, present management became concerned with the propriety of the daily operations. After investigation, it was determined Yates was not paying the bills of the corporation, including the payroll taxes, as they came due, but was misappropriating the funds. In addition, the existing second mortgage to Petroleum Bank was executed without proper corporate authorization and the proceeds were misappropriated by Yates. In November 1992, Yates was relieved of his position and the current management began operations.

There was also litigation in this Court between Welcome Home, Inc. and the Debtor concerning the right to operate the facility. The Debtor prevailed in that case and has operated the facility to the present time.

Due to Yates' failure to make the payments to the Friends Bank of Ogalalla, the secured loan became in default and a foreclosure was filed. The Debtor attempted to negotiate an arrangement to catch up the 6 payments in arrears, but to no avail. The Bank sought the appointment of a receiver, which resulted in the filing of this case.

VII. CURRENT OPERATION

The current operation consists of a 40-room motel located in Bartlesville, Oklahoma. It was constructed in 1982 and seems to have an excellent reputation in the community. The occupancy levels are consistently good, and the average monthly room revenue is consistent at $25,000.00. Even though Phillips Petroleum, the largest industry in the city, which is its world headquarters, has had some recent reductions in employment, room revenues have remained consistent. The typical guests include doctors associated with the local hospital, business people in town associated with the Phillips companies, and state employees.

IX. FINANCIAL ANALYSIS

In order to intelligently analyze the economic feasibility of this Plan, one must first determine the amount of cash needed to fund the Plan. The attached Exhibit A is a summary of the cash requirements for the Plan on a yearly basis. It demonstrates that the maximum cash required on an annual basis to fund this Plan in year one is $98,325.47, which includes one-time expenditures of $10,365.47. In the remaining years, the cash requirements decrease to $7,330.00 monthly or $87,960.00 annually in years two through three; $7,000.00 monthly or $84,000.00 annually in years four and five; $6,361.00 monthly or $76,332.00 annually in years six through seven; $5,718.00 monthly or $68,616.00 annually in years eight through ten; and $5,147.00 monthly or $61,764.00 annually in years eleven through fifteen.

Attached as Exhibit B is a five-year cash flow projection. The first page is a month-by-month projection for 1993 and the second page is an annual projection for 1993 through 1997. The expenses are projected to increase at the annual rate of 3.5 percent, and the income is projected to increase at an annual rate of 6.5 percent. The net cash available for debt service is $118,036.45 in the first year and increases each year thereafter. This provides a margin of 20 percent in year one and a greater margin each year thereafter. This demonstrates the economic feasibility of this plan. The Debtor believes it will be able to make required payments under the Plan and that there will not be a need for any further reorganization or liquidation.

X. COMPARISON OF THE PLAN TO CHAPTER 7 CASE

All secured creditors would receive the value of their collateral or the collateral itself if the estate of the Debtor was liquidated under Chapter 7. As provided by the various Classes of this Plan, each secured creditor is receiving at least the present value of its particular item of collateral or the amount of its claim, whichever is less, by virtue of the stream of deferred cash payments and the imposition of the plan rate of interest, plus the retention of the lien on its collateral. As such, each secured creditor is receiving not less than would be received if the case were liquidated under a Chapter 7.

If the Debtor were liquidated at confirmation, the unsecured creditors would be paid some distribution. However, the Debtor believes that in a liquidation sale, the hotel would not be operated efficiently, if at all, resulting in a sale of the operation not as a going concern. Under such conditions, it is likely the unsecured creditors would not be paid in full.

Unsecured creditors of the Debtor are treated within Class 4 of this Plan. This Class provides for payment in full of the unsecured class. Therefore, the value of property to be distributed to holders of allowed unsecured claims is not less than would be paid if the estate were liquidated under Chapter 7 as of confirmation. In fact, under this Plan, creditors will receive substantially more than would be distributed under Chapter 7. Debtor therefore alleges it is in the best interest of all unsecured creditors to vote for the confirmation of this Plan.

XI. INSIDER TRANSACTIONS

Debtor intends to continue to employ as the operator of the business all current management. The class 5 equity holder, Mary E. Dawes, is paid compensation only after all operating expenses and Plan payments are funded.

Other than the transactions described above, there are no other insider transactions in these cases.

XII. LITIGATION

1. Friends Bank of Ogalalla vs. Welcome Home, Inc. This was an action by the secured creditor, FBO, to foreclose its mortgage. The confirmation of this Plan will result in the dismissal of this action as moot. No further litigation is contemplated in this case.

2. Welcome Home, Inc. vs. Davidson. This matter concerns the enforcement of a promissory note which is collateral on the secured class 3(b) claim of Petroleum Bank, or its assignee. The Debtor may assist in the collection of this matter because all payments on this note go to reduce the liability of the Debtor on its obligation to this class 3(b).

3. Welcome Home, Inc. vs. Nelson Yates. The Debtor is investigating the viability of a cause of action against Mr. Yates for various matters including breach of fiduciary, conversion, and fraud. It has not been determined if Mr. Yates can respond to any damages that might be recovered and therefore, the economic wisdom of this action is as yet undetermined. All proceeds from this action, if any are recovered, will be used to retire outstanding claims against the estate in accordance with the priority of the then outstanding claims.

XIII. SIGNIFICANT FACTORS AFFECTING THE PLAN

There are various market factors that may adversely affect the viability of this Plan over which the Debtor has no control and which may not be predicted with any degree of certainty. Such factors include natural disaster causing physical damage to the property. To protect against this risk, the Debtor has hazard insurance, but the extent of such events may exceed the available coverage.

The Phillips companies are a major economic force in the Bartlesville community. In the event this company moves or suffers a significant downturn, it would adversely affect the cash flow of the Debtor.

Tourism is a source of business for the Debtor. In the event energy costs increase dramatically, there would be a decrease in tourism and at the same time an increase in the operating costs of the Debtor beyond those projected. Such an event would adversely affect the cash flow.

XIV. TAX IMPACT

Each creditor is encouraged to have a tax analysis done independently to determine the impact of the Plan on each particular creditor's individual tax picture.

To the extent they have previously written off as a bad debt their claims against the Debtor, creditors who receive cash from this Plan will recognize ordinary income. However, the recognition of income would be no more than would have originally occurred had the particular claim been paid as originally agreed.

The confirmation of this Plan will not adversely affect the Debtor's tax posture. Because the Plan proposes to pay all claims in full, any loss carryforward will be retained by the Debtor.

XV. REQUIRED DISCLOSURES

No payments of the kind described in § 1129(a)(4)(A) of the Code are contemplated or provided by the Plan.

No arrangements exist between the Debtor and its counsel pertaining to the retention of counsel to implement the Plan, other than the retention of Debtor's counsel by the Debtor.

Respectfully submitted,

Attorneys for Debtor-in-Possession

EXHIBIT A

Monthly cash requirements:

class 2 (b) Withholding Taxes	$ 152.00
2 (c) Okla. Tax Comm.	487.00
3 (a) Friends Bank	5,147.00
3 (b) Petroleum Bank	571.00
3 (c) Ellis	643.00
4 Unsecured creditors	330.00
Total	7,330.00

Payments due within one year of Effective Date

Class 1	est $10,000.00
2 (a)	365.47
Total	10,365.47

Summary of cash requirements over life of Plan

Year	Monthly	Annually	
1	7,330.00	98,325.47	incl. 10,365.47 non-recurring
2–3	7,330.00	87,960.00	
4–5	7,000.00	84,000.00	
6–7	6,361.00	76,332.00	
8–10	5,718.00	68,616.00	
11–15	5,147.00	61,764.00	

EXHIBIT B

CASE: WELCOME HOME, INC.
CHAPTER 11 Mary Dawes, Pres.
FILED 7/8/92

CASH FLOW PROJECTION - 5 YEARS

	1993	1994	1995	1996	1997
ROOM REVENUE	317674.97	338323.84	360314.89	383735.36	408678.16
TELEPHONE REVENUE	6436.24	6854.60	7300.14	7774.65	8280.01
LAUNDRY REVENUE	681.25	725.53	772.69	822.92	876.41
VENDING REVENUE	400.57	426.61	454.34	483.87	515.32
MISCELLANEOUS REVENUE	659.77	702.66	748.33	796.97	848.77
TOTAL REVENUES	325852.80	347033.23	369590.39	393613.77	419198.66
SALARY - OFFICERS					
SALARY - ADMIN	19045.85	19712.45	20402.39	21116.47	21855.55
WAGES - CLERICAL	38009.05	39339.36	40716.24	42141.31	43616.25
WAGES - MAIDS	19805.12	20498.30	21215.74	21958.29	22726.83
WAGES - MAINT	3129.38	3238.91	3352.27	3469.60	3591.04
TEMP HELP	610.44	631.81	653.92	676.81	700.50
FICA TAX - EMPLOYERS	6119.21	6333.38	6555.05	6784.48	7021.94
FUTA TAX	610.44	631.81	653.92	676.81	700.50
SUTA TAX	1640.02	1697.42	1756.83	1818.32	1881.96
EMPLOYEE BENEFITS	122.09	126.36	130.78	135.36	140.10
ACCOUNTING & LEGAL	6104.44	6318.09	6539.23	6768.10	7004.98
AUTO EXPENSE	610.44	631.81	653.92	676.81	700.50
ADVERTISING	311.45	322.35	333.63	345.31	357.39
BANK CHARGES	1220.89	1263.62	1307.85	1353.62	1401.00
CREDIT CARD DISCOUNTS	6898.02	7139.45	7389.33	7647.95	7915.63
COMM & TRAVEL BUR	122.09	126.36	130.78	135.36	140.10
DUES & SUBSCRIPTIONS	366.27	379.09	392.35	406.09	420.30
EQUIPMENT RENTAL	3446.69	3567.32	3692.18	3821.40	3955.15
INSURANCE - GENERAL	9603.38	9939.50	10287.38	10647.44	11020.10
INSURANCE - OFFICERS'S	1939.50	2007.38	2077.64	2150.36	2225.62
LICENSE & TAXES	1416.60	1466.18	1517.49	1570.61	1625.58
REAL ESTATE TAXES	5684.70	5883.66	6089.59	6302.73	6523.32
LINEN & LAUNDRY	1654.06	1711.95	1771.87	1833.88	1898.07
MISCELLANEOUS EXPENSE	122.09	126.36	130.78	135.36	140.10
OFFICE SUPPLIES	1220.89	1263.62	1307.85	1353.62	1401.00
POSTAGE	1526.11	1579.52	1634.81	1692.03	1751.25
REPAIR	10377.55	10740.76	11116.69	11505.77	11908.47
OKLA TOURISM TAXES	366.27	379.09	392.35	406.09	420.30
SUPPPLIES - MOTEL	17163.73	17764.46	18386.22	19029.73	19695.77
CONTINENTAL BREAKFAST	3651.68	3779.48	3911.77	4048.68	4190.38
TELEPHONE	13479.21	13950.98	14439.27	14944.64	15467.71
TRAVEL EXPENSE	5217.59	5400.20	5589.21	5784.83	5987.30
TRAVEL MEALS	655.62	678.56	702.31	726.89	752.34
UTILITIES - GAS/ELECTR	22427.22	23212.17	24024.60	24865.46	25735.75
UTILITIES - WATER	3138.29	3248.13	3361.82	3479.48	3601.26
TOTAL EXPENSES	207816.35	215089.92	222618.07	230409.70	238474.04
NET	118036.45	131943.31	146972.33	163204.07	180724.63

EXHIBIT B (*Continued*)

CASE: WELCOME HOME, INC.
CHAPTER 11 Mary Dawes, Pres.
FILED 7/8/92

CASH FLOW PROJECTION - 1993

ROOM REVENUE	21832.79	28067.22	27120.66	26766.40	28281.34	32252.50	32010.85	23518.22	25645.62	26702.29	22738.54	22738.54	317674.97
TELEPHONE REVENUE	1079.40	662.07	641.03	760.78	443.43	167.53	188.33	304.10	435.00	335.37	708.60	708.60	6434.24
LAUNDRY REVENUE	63.00	9.14	203.18	109.62	19.43	55.13	3.78	6.51		24.68	93.39	93.39	681.25
VENDING REVENUE	3.15	18.56			81.27	31.02	50.86	45.18	64.00	69.85	18.34	18.34	400.57
MISCELLANEOUS REVENUE	117.84	41.06	89.73	147.16	34.65	69.34	104.78	11.33	17.05	9.25	8.79	8.79	659.77
TOTAL REVENUES	23096.18	28798.05	28054.60	27783.96	28860.12	32575.52	32358.60	23887.34	26161.67	27141.44	23567.66	23567.66	325852.80
SALARY - OFFICERS													
SALARY - ADMIN	1560.00	1564.89	1569.79	1574.70	1579.63	1584.58	1589.54	1594.52	1599.52	1604.53	1609.55	1614.59	19045.85
WAGES - CLERICAL	3113.23	3122.98	3132.76	3142.57	3152.41	3162.29	3172.19	3182.13	3192.09	3202.09	3212.12	3222.18	38009.05
WAGES - MAIDS	1622.19	1627.27	1632.37	1637.48	1642.61	1647.75	1652.91	1658.09	1663.28	1668.49	1673.72	1678.96	19805.12
WAGES - MAINT	256.32	257.12	257.93	258.74	259.55	260.36	261.17	261.99	262.81	263.64	264.46	265.29	3129.38
TEMP HELP	50.00	50.16	50.31	50.47	50.63	50.79	50.95	51.11	51.27	51.43	51.59	51.75	610.44
FICA TAX - EMPLOYERS	501.21	502.78	504.35	505.93	507.52	509.11	510.70	512.30	513.91	515.52	517.13	518,75	6119.21
FUTA TAX	50.00	50.16	50.31	50.47	50.63	50.79	50.95	51.11	51.27	51.43	51.59	51.75	610.44
SUTA TAX	134.33	134.75	135.17	135.60	136.02	136.45	136.87	137.30	137.73	138.16	138.60	139.03	1640.02
EMPLOYEE BENEFITS	10.00	10.03	10.06	10.09	10.13	10.16	10.19	10.22	10.25	10.29	10.32	10.35	122.09
ACCOUNTING & LEGAL	500.00	501.57	503.14	504.71	506.29	507.88	509.47	511.07	512.67	514.27	515.88	517.50	6104.44
AUTO EXPENSE	50.00	50.16	50.31	50.47	50.63	50.79	50.95	51.11	51.27	51.43	51.59	51.75	610.44
ADVERTISING	25.51	25.59	25.67	25.75	25.83	25.91	25.99	26.07	26.16	26.24	26.32	26.40	311.45
BANK CHARGES	100.00	100.31	100.63	100.94	101.26	101.58	101.89	102.21	102.53	102.85	103.18	103.50	1220.89
CREDIT CARD DISCOUNTS	565.00	566.77	568.54	570.33	572.11	573.90	575.70	577.50	579.31	581.13	582.95	564.77	6898.02
COMM & TRAVEL BUR	10.00	10.03	10.06	10.09	10.13	10.16	10.19	10.22	10.25	10.29	10.32	10.35	122.09
DUES & SUBSCRIPTIONS	30.00	30.09	30.19	30.28	30.38	30.47	30.57	30.66	30.76	30.86	30.95	31.05	366.27
EQUIPMENT RENTAL	282.31	283.19	284.08	284.97	285.86	286.76	287.66	288.56	289.46	290.37	291.28	292.19	3446.69
INSURANCE - GENERAL	786.59	789.05	791.52	794.00	796.49	798.98	801.49	804.00	806.52	809.04	811.58	814.12	9603.38
INSURANCE - OFFICERS'S	158.86	159.36	159.86	160.36	160.86	161.36	161.87	162.38	162.88	163.39	163.91	164.42	1939.50
LICENSE & TAXES	116.03	116.39	116.76	117.12	117.49	117.86	118.23	118.60	118.97	119.34	119.72	120.09	1416.60
REAL ESTATE TAXES	465.62	467.08	468.54	470.01	471.48	472.96	474.44	475.92	477.41	478.91	480.41	481.91	5684.70
LINEN & LAUNDRY	135.48	135.90	136.33	136.76	137.19	137.61	138.05	138.48	138.91	139.35	139.78	140.22	1654.06
MISCELLANEOUS EXPENSE	10.00	10.03	10.06	10.09	10.13	10.16	10.19	10.22	10.25	10.29	10.32	10.35	122.09
OFFICE SUPPLIES	100.00	100.31	100.63	100.94	101.26	101.58	101.89	102.21	102.53	102.85	103.18	103.50	1220.89
POSTAGE	125.00	125.39	125.78	126.18	126.57	126.97	127.37	127.77	128.17	128.57	128.97	129.37	1526.11
REPAIR	850.00	852.66	855.33	858.01	860.70	863.39	866.10	868.81	871.53	874.26	877.00	879.75	10377.55
WLA TOURISM TAXES	30.700	30.09	30.19	30.28	30.38	30.47	30.57	30.66	30.76	30.86	30.95	31.05	366.27
SUPPPLIES - HOTEL	1405.84	1410.24	1414.66	1419.09	1423.53	1427.99	1432.47	1436.95	1441.45	1445.97	1450.50	1455.04	17163.73
CONTINENTAL BREAKFAST	299.10	300.04	300.98	301.92	302.86	303.81	304.76	305.72	306.68	307.64	308.60	309.57	3651.68
TELEPHONE	1104.05	1107.51	1110.98	1114.46	1117.95	1121.45	1124.96	1128.48	1132.02	1135.56	1139.12	1142.69	13479.21
TRAVEL EXPENSE	427.36	428.70	430.04	431.39	432.74	434.09	435.45	436.82	438.19	439.56	440.93	442.32	5217.59
TRAVEL MEALS	53.70	53.87	54.04	54.21	54.38	54.55	54.72	54.89	55.06	55.23	55.41	55.58	655.62
UTILITIES - GAS/ELECTR	1836.96	1842.71	1848.48	1854.27	1860.08	1865.91	1871.75	1877.61	1883.49	1889.39	1895.31	1901.25	22427.22
UTILITIES - WATER	257.05	257.86	258.66	259.47	260.29	261.10	261.92	262.74	263.56	264.39	265.21	266.05	3138.29
TOTAL EXPENSES	17021.74	17075.05	17128.53	17182.17	17235.98	17289.97	17344.12	17398.44	17452.93	17507.59	17562.42	17617.42	207816.35
NET	6074.44	11723.00	10926.07	10601.79	11624.14	15285.55	15014.48	6488.90	8708.74	9633.85	6005.24	5950.24	118036.45

§ 13.22 Example of Local Rules Regarding Minimum Content Requirements for Disclosure Statements

This excerpt from Amended Rules of the United States Bankruptcy Court for the Eastern District of Oklahoma (July 1, 1989) was taken from *In re Malek.*[10]

Rule III.C.2. Minimum Content Requirements - The Disclosure Statement formulated pursuant to Sec. 1125 filed pursuant to B.R. 3016(c) and subject to Court approval in accordance with B.R. 3017, should be constructed to sell the proposed Plan of Reorganization to affected creditors. As such, each Disclosure Statement filed with the Court must meet the following minimum requirements of disclosure before approval will be considered:

[10] 35 B.R. 443 (Bankr. E.D. Mich. 1983).

(a) Description of business - The debtor must furnish information describing the nature of the business being reorganized under Chapter 11. This analysis must include the competitive conditions in the industry and the debtor's role in that industry. He must disclose whether or not he is dependent upon one or more customers or clients. Where the debtor is a licensed professional whose income is derived from providing services that are billed on an hourly rate, the debtor must provide information giving the creditor a good faith estimate of the number of clients, the anticipated services, the hourly rate, and the anticipated annual billings that will provide the source of his income. The Chapter 11 debtor should provide a description of the service to be rendered, location of principal and branch offices, employee staff and payroll and salaries of officers and directors. Any special property interests, such as patents, trademarks, licenses, or franchises should be disclosed and described.

(b) History of the Debtor - The Chapter 11 debtor should describe, in detail, his activities before filing, including the reasons for filing the Chapter 11. This history should be provided in a neutral, objective and noninflammatory manner. Litigation issues are to be described in an objective professional tone, free of any mischaracterization of the issues to be resolved in such litigation. Where possible, the debtor should provide an evaluation of the probable success of any litigation and its effect on the debtor's business or his plans for reorganization under Chapter 11.

(c) Financial Information - The debtor must provide a prepetition statement of assets and liabilities together with a profit and loss analysis. The debtor must also provide financial information sufficient to inform the creditors of all liens, encumbrances, security interests, loans or other financial obligations which may impair the debtor or his assets.

(d) Description of the Plan - The Plan of Reorganization must be described in sufficient detail to give the creditors enough information to determine how their rights will be affected.

(e) How the Plan is to be executed.

(f) Liquidation Analysis.

(g) Management to be retained and the compensation of the personnel retained.

(h) Projection of Operations - The debtor should provide the projection of operations subsequent to confirmation so that the Court may determine the feasibility of the Plan. The debtor must provide sufficient financial information to determine if the projections for operations subsequent to confirmation are feasible. The debtor is required to make a full, clear and complete disclosure of all underlying assumptions. If the Plan assumes an increase in income, the basis for this assumption must be set forth. If the future operationscontain a risk of loss of income or anticipated financial instability, the factors that may cause a loss or diminution of income should be set forth.

(i) Litigation - All pending or contemplated litigation of whatever nature must be described fully, completely and in detail. Trial dates, where known, must be disclosed. Appeals, filed or contemplated, must be disclosed. The Disclosure Statement must include a professional evaluation of the probable success of any pending or contemplated litigation.

(j) Transactions with Insiders - The Disclosure Statement must describe fully, completely and in detail all transactions with insiders. If there are no such transactions, debtor must so state.

(k) Tax Consequences - The Disclosure Statement must reveal the probable tax consequences if the Chapter 11 Plan is confirmed. If there are no tax consequences, the Disclosure Statement must contain an affirmative statement of that fact.

CHAPTER 14

DRAFTING BANKRUPTCY REORGANIZATION PLANS

Robert E. Nugent

§ 14.1 Introduction

Drafting a bankruptcy plan of reorganization requires an understanding of the statutory requirements of the Bankruptcy Code and a certain amount of creativity of counsel. In general, the plan is a contract between the debtor and the creditors. It defines the manner in which the debtor will honor its obligations once they are recast by bankruptcy. Detailed discussion of this topic is beyond the scope of this chapter,[1] but a general introduction to the basic principles is in order.

[1] For a more complete discussion of plan drafting, see John K. Pearson, Robert E. Nugent, & Mary Patricia Hesse, Drafting Bankruptcy Reorganization Plans (2d ed., John Wiley & Sons 1993).

§ 14.2 Statutory Requirements

Title 11 U.S.C. § 1123(a) sets out certain matters that must be addressed in a plan. Claims must be classified into separate classes,[2] and each claim within a class should be treated similarly unless the holder of a claim agrees to less favorable treatment.[3] The plan must specify which claims are impaired and which are not impaired.[4] An *impaired claim* is one that is not paid according to the original contract between the parties.[5] Treatment of each impaired class must be set out in the plan.[6]

The plan must provide adequate means for plan implementation, such as:

1. Retention by the debtor of all or any part of the property of the estate
2. Transfer of all or part of the property of the estate to other entities
3. Merger or consolidation of the debtor with another entity
4. Sale of all or any part of the property of the estate, subject to or free of any liens
5. Distribution of all or any part of the property of the estate among those having an interest in the property
6. Satisfaction or modification of any lien
7. Cancellation or modification of any indenture
8. Curing or waiving of any default
9. Extension of any maturity date
10. Change in interest rate or any other term of outstanding securities
11. Amendment of the debtor's charter
12. Issuance of securities of the debtor, or of any entity to which property of the estate has been transferred or which has merged with the debtor, for cash, for property, for existing securities, or in exchange for claims or interests, or for any other appropriate purpose.[7]

In addition, a plan may:

1. Impair or leave unimpaired any class of claims
2. Provide for assumption, rejection, or assignment of executory contracts or unexpired leases of the debtor (see **Chapters 7** and **8**)
3. Provide for settlement or adjustment or retention and enforcement, of any claims belonging to the debtor
4. Provide for sale of some or all of the assets of the debtor (see **Chapter 9**)
5. Include any other provision not inconsistent with the Bankruptcy Code.[8]

---

[2] 11 U.S.C. § 1123(a)(1).

[3] *Id.* § 1123(a)(4).

[4] *See id.* § 1123(a)(2)&(3).

[5] *See id.* § 1124(1).

[6] *Id.* § 1123(a)(3).

[7] 11 U.S.C. § 1123(a)(5).

[8] *Id.* § 1123(b).

§ 14.3 Treatment of Secured Claims

Secured claims are generally classified by including each secured creditor in its own class. The provisions made for secured creditors are largely dictated by the confirmation standards contained in 11 U.S.C. § 1129(b)(1) and (2). That subsection outlines *cram down,* the conditions under which a plan may be confirmed without the acceptance of all impaired classes. The plan may adjust the amount that the debtor must pay to a secured creditor to reflect the value of the creditor's security, but to be eligible for cram down, the plan must not discriminate unfairly and must be fair and equitable.[9] Secured claims that are impaired are nonetheless fairly and equitably treated if they are treated in one of three ways under § 1129(b)(2)(A). First, the debtor may repay an amount equal to the value of the secured creditor's interest in the collateral in deferred payments over a period of time and at a rate of interest that will assure that the payments have a present value equal to the present value of the property.[10] Second, the debtor may provide for the liquidation and turnover of proceeds of the assets to the creditor.[11] Third, the debtor may provide for the creditor to realize the indubitable equivalent of its claim, perhaps by surrender of the assets securing it.[12]

§ 14.4 Hypothetical Case

The following simple example involves the mythical debtor, XYZ Corp. When its case is filed, XYZ Corp. holds inventory worth $100,000 and machinery and equipment worth $250,000. It is indebted to Last National Bank in the amount of $500,000, secured by all of those assets. XYZ owes trade debt of $75,000 to various vendors. The corporation has had a prepetition appraisal of its assets done and wishes to base its plan on these values.

XYZ chooses to employ the repayment option, which is the one most frequently used by debtors. To fulfill the requirements of 11 U.S.C. § 1129(b)(2)(A)(i), XYZ Corp.'s analysis should proceed through the following steps.

1. Determination of secured status. Section 506 limits the extent of a secured claim to the value of the collateral securing it. Last National Bank is therefore secured to the extent of $350,000 ($100,000 inventory + $250,000 machinery).
2. Choice of payment scheme. XYZ Corp.'s equipment will last at least another 10 years. Its inventory, however, is likely to turn over many times during that period. Although the express language of § 1129(b)(2)(A)(i) might permit all of this debt to be rolled together and treated as one long-term obligation, 11 U.S.C. § 1129(b)(1) requires that the treatment be fair and equitable. Fairness

---

[9] 11 U.S.C. § 1129(b)(1).

[10] *Id.* § 1129(b)(2)(A)(i). Sample plans utilizing this option are presented in §§ **14.9** & **14.10.**

[11] *Id.* § 1129(b)(2)(A)(ii). A sample plan is presented in § **14.11.**

[12] *Id.* § 1129(b)(2)(A)(iii).

might preclude a 10-year inventory loan period. XYZ Corp. should consider proposing a short-term revolving inventory note and a 10-year machinery and equipment note.

3. Choice of interest or discount rate. The stream of payments must have a present value equal to the value of the collateral itself, so a rate of interest must be factored in. The rate to be applied is frequently the subject of litigation, but many courts prefer to charge reorganizing debtors the "market rate."[13] This requires debtors and creditors to determine either by agreement or through litigation what the market rate for a similar loan to a similar borrower might be. This also entails convincing the court that there is a market for reorganization loans.[14]

§ 14.5 Sample Plan Provision for a Secured Claim

The following is a sample plan provision for Last National Bank's secured claim.

The secured claim of Last National Bank, secured by inventory and machinery and equipment shall be paid as follows:

(1) Inventory: Bank's claim shall be allowed in the amount of $100,000, secured by the inventory of XYZ Corp. and all subsequently acquired inventory. The claim shall be repaid as follows. XYZ shall give Bank a note for $100,000, which shall be due and payable within one year of the effective date of the plan and which shall bear interest at the rate of 8.0 percent per annum. Principal and interest shall be payable by the application of 50 percent of the monthly collections of receivables by XYZ to the balance of said note. Bank may, in its discretion and as XYZ may request, advance additional funds up to $100,000 to XYZ. Bank shall retain its lien on the inventory and proceeds thereof.

(2) Machinery and Equipment: Bank's claim as it is secured by machinery and equipment, having a value of $250,000, shall be repaid as follows. XYZ shall pay said amount over ten years, bearing interest at 8.0 percent, in quarterly payments of $9,138.94, the first being due and payable 90 days after the effective date of the plan and payable every 90 days thereafter until paid in full. Bank shall retain its lien on machinery and equipment and the proceeds, products, and replacements thereof.

§ 14.6 Treatment of Unsecured Claims

Once the hypothetical XYZ Corp. (see **§ 14.4**) has settled on a treatment of Last National Bank's secured claims, it must consider the treatment to be given unsecured claims. XYZ has $75,000 of unsecured trade debt, and the Last National Bank has a

---

[13] *See* Hardzog v. Federal Land Bank, 901 F.2d 858 (10th Cir. 1990).

[14] *In re* Stratford Ass'n, 145 B.R. 689 (Bankr. D. Kan. 1992).

deficiency claim of $150,000 because it is undersecured. The treatment of the bank's secured claim passes muster under the Code, but XYZ is not out of the woods yet.

Section 1129(a)(7)(B) requires that each claimant receive on account of its claim not less than it would receive in a Chapter 7 case. This is the *liquidation* or *best interests of the creditor test.* It requires that a hypothetical Chapter 7 analysis be run to ascertain how much unsecured creditors would receive after liquidation and deductions for payment of secured and priority claims and administrative expenses. This amount is generally substantially less than full payment. For instance, the unsecured creditors of XYZ Corp. would likely receive nothing in the event of liquidation under Chapter 7.

Although minimal or no payment to unsecured creditors would satisfy § 1129(a)(7)(B), a debtor that proposes to pay so little would likely run afoul of the absolute priority rule of § 1129(b)(2)(B). That rule requires that a plan provide for each unsecured claimant to receive property equal to the amount of its claim if the holder of any junior claim or interest is to receive or retain any property. The absolute priority rule gives unsecured creditors a cudgel to use against debtors. If the unsecured creditors are offered less than full payment, they can object to retention of the business by its owners. Case law suggests that injection of new value into the business by the owners may justify an exception to the absolute priority rule, but the new value must be in "money or money's worth," ruling out noncash contributions.[15] This topic is discussed at length in **Chapter 16.**

A debtor, therefore, must offer unsecured creditors a treatment it can afford but which is also attractive to the unsecured creditors. Each creditor can vote, but the vote's weight depends on the amount of the claim. Section 1126 provides that a class of claims accepts a plan when more than 50 percent in number and two-thirds in amount of claims voting accept the plan. Therefore, a shade over a third of the claim dollars, voting to reject, can doom a plan to failure.

In the hypothetical of **§ 14.4,** the bank's unsecured deficiency claim is classified and treated with the general trade claims. This means that the bank has absolute veto power over the plan because it will vote $150,000 to the trade creditors' $75,000. Some consideration could be given to segregating the bank's deficiency claim into another class, but the prevailing view is that absent special circumstances, there is no basis for discrimination between the unsecured deficiency claim of an undersecured secured creditor and other unsecured claims. See **Chapter 15.**

This problem is particularly likely to arise in small Chapter 11 cases, in which one or two secured creditors can control the unsecured class and wield a veto power over the plan. If the debtor is in a jurisdiction that disfavors separate classification of deficiency claims, aggressive negotiation of a compromise plan or even litigation may be necessary to obtain confirmation.

---

[15] Case v. Los Angeles Lumber Prods. Co., 308 U.S. 106 (1939) (first statement of new value exception); Ahlers v. Norwest Bank Worthington, 485 U.S. 197 (1988) (questioning existence of exception); Bonner Mall Partnership v. U.S. Bancorp Mortgage Co. (*In re* Bonner Mall Partnership), 2 F.3d 899 (9th Cir. 1993), *cert. granted,* ___ U.S. ___, 126 L. Ed. 2d 648 (1994) (exception survived enactment of Code).

§ 14.7 Sample Plan Provisions for Unsecured Claims

The following are suggested provisions that can be used in XYZ's plan for its unsecured creditors.

(1) Unsecured claim of Last National Bank: The remaining $150,000 of Bank's claims shall be allowed as unsecured and paid as a general unsecured claim.

(2) General unsecured claims: General unsecured claims shall be paid as follows: 5 percent of each allowed general unsecured claim will be paid on Jan. 1, 1995, another 5 percent will be paid on Jan. 1, 1996, and another 5 percent will be paid on Jan. 1, 1997, for a total of 15 percent, without interest.

§ 14.8 Sample Plans

Three sample plans of reorganization which illustrate repayment of claims (§§ **14.9** and **14.10**), the liquidation of claims (§ **14.11**), and various other claim treatments follow. The names have been changed to protect the insolvent.

§ 14.9 —Sample Plan of Reorganization with Repayment of Claims

IN THE UNITED STATES BANKRUPTCY COURT
FOR THE DISTRICT OF [STATE]

In re:	)	
	)	
HENRY'S, INC.	)	Case No. __________
	)	Chapter 11
Debtor	)	
______________________________	)	

DEBTOR'S PLAN OF REORGANIZATION
[DATED]

Henry's, Inc., Debtor-in-Possession (Henry's), hereby submits as proponent its Plan of Reorganization.

ARTICLE 1
SUMMARY OF THE PLAN

The Plan of Reorganization provides for continued operations under existing management. Future expenses of operation will be reduced by cost-cutting measures, as described more fully in the Disclosure Statement. Administrative expenses, priority tax claims, the secured claims of Kiowa State Bank & Trust Company (KSB&T) and Office Supply, Inc. will be paid in full as hereinafter described. All unsecured creditors will receive installment payments totalling 40 percent of allowed claims. A more detailed discussion of this Plan of Reorganization is set forth in the Debtor's Disclosure Statement dated September 16, 1992.

ARTICLE 2
DEFINITIONS

Section 2.1. Certain Defined Terms. The following terms (whether or not underscored) when used in this Plan shall, except when the context otherwise requires, have the following meanings (such definitions to be equally applicable to the singular and plural forms thereof):

Administrative claim: An administrative expense that is entitled to priority pursuant to § 507(a)(1) of the Code and allowed under § 503 of the Code.

Allowance date: The date as of which an order of the court allowing a claim in this case has become final and nonappealable and no appeal therefrom is pending.

Allowed claim: The amount of a claim (1) a proof of which is filed within the time fixed by the Bankruptcy Court, or (2) that has appeared, or hereafter appears, in the schedules filed by the Debtor under § 521(1) of the Code, except a claim that is scheduled as disputed, contingent, or unliquidated as to amount and, in each case, to which no objection to the allowance thereof has been filed within any applicable period fixed by the court, or as to which the allowance date has occurred. Allowed claim shall not include any administrative claim.

Code: The Bankruptcy Reform Act of 1978, Pub. L. No. 95-598, 11 U.S.C. §§ 101 et seq., as amended.

Confirmation date: The date of the entry of an order of the Bankruptcy Court confirming the Plan.

Court: The United States Bankruptcy Court for the District of [state], including the United States Bankruptcy Judge sitting in this case.

Creditor: Any creditor holding a claim in Classes 1 through 3.

Debtor: Henry's, Inc., referred to as Henry's.

Effective date: The date on which the order of the Bankruptcy Court confirming the Plan has become final and nonappealable and no appeal therefrom is pending, or at such earlier date on or after the confirmation date as the Debtor elects.

Filing date: August 10, 1992.

Plan: This Debtor's Plan of Reorganization, as it may be modified in accordance with Article 10.

Priority tax claim: An allowed claim entitled to priority pursuant to § 507(a)(7) of the Code.

Term of the Plan: A period beginning on the effective date and terminating on the date all payments required by the Plan have been completed.

Walnut Retail Store: Retail facilities located at [address], [city], [state], under a lease with W. A. Smith, Jr. and H. R. Smith.

Warehouse facility: Warehouse located at [address], [city], [state], leased from Limited Investments.

West Street retail store: Retail facilities located at [address], [city], [state], under a lease with Tom Rose and Heather Rose.

Section 2.2. Other Defined Terms. Terms for which meanings are provided in the Code and in the Rules of Bankruptcy Procedure shall, unless otherwise defined herein or the context otherwise requires, have such meanings when used herein.

Section 2.3. Cross-References, Etc. References in this Plan to any Section or Article are, unless otherwise specified, to such Section or Article of this Plan. The words "hereof," "herein," "hereunder," and similar terms shall refer to this Plan and not to any particular Section or provisions of this Plan.

Section 2.4. Headings. The various headings of this Plan are inserted for convenience only and shall not affect the meaning or interpretation of this Plan or any provision hereof.

ARTICLE 3
CLASSIFICATION OF CLAIMS

Administrative claims and priority tax claims are not otherwise classified under the terms of the Plan and are treated in accordance with the terms of Article 4 hereof.

Class 1: Fully secured claim of Kiowa State Bank & Trust Company.

Class 2: Fully secured claim of Office Supply, Inc.

Class 3: All unsecured claims.

ARTICLE 4
PROVISION FOR PAYMENT OF ADMINISTRATIVE CLAIMS, EXPENSES AND CERTAIN PRIORITY CLAIMS

Section 4.1. Administrative Claims: Administrative claims, including fees due under 28 U.S.C. § 1930, shall, if not previously paid in full, be paid by the Debtor on the effective date, except that:

(a) any professional employed at the expense of the bankruptcy estate that may be entitled to an allowance of fees and expenses shall be paid in a time and in an amount determined by the court; and

(b) administrative expenses incurred by the Debtor during the pendency of the reorganization case and prior to the effective date, which are payable in the ordinary course of business after the effective date, shall be paid by the Debtor in the ordinary course of business after the effective date.

Any holder of an administrative claim may agree in writing to a less favorable treatment.

Section 4.2. Priority Tax Claims. The Debtor is current on all income taxes, withholding taxes, sales taxes, and ad valorem taxes, and shall remain current from and after the effective date.

ARTICLE 5
TREATMENT OF CLASSES NOT IMPAIRED UNDER THE PLAN

Section 5.1. Class 2—Secured Claim of Office Supply, Inc.: The Debtor is in possession of photocopiers under lease with Office Supply, Inc., which represent secured transactions. The Debtor is current under these leases, and this Plan shall not alter the legal, equitable, and contractual rights of said creditor.

ARTICLE 6
TREATMENT OF CLASSES IMPAIRED UNDER THE PLAN

Classes 1 and 3 are impaired under the Plan.

Section 6.1. Class 1 - Kiowa State Bank & Trust Company: The secured claim of Kiowa State Bank & Trust Company in the amount of $99,983.55, together with a) interest thereon at the KSB&T base rate plus 1.75 percent per annum (current effective rate—8.75 percent), and b) attorney fees and expenses of KSB&T as allowed by the court shall be paid in full as follows: accrued interest through the effective date and allowed attorney fees and expenses shall be paid from the life insurance loan proceeds account established pursuant to the cash collateral order entered on [date], with the remaining balance of said account applied in reduction of the principal indebtedness. The remaining principal balance, together with the interest rate above specified, shall be amortized and paid with monthly installments of principal and interest over the four years following the effective date, with the first payment due on the first day of the month following the effective date. (The initial amortization shall be calculated with level payments of principal and interest, using the contract rate of interest on the effective date. Upon a change in the applicable interest rate, the remaining indebtedness shall be similarly reamortized over the remaining term of the four-year period, with the monthly payment amounts adjusted accordingly.)

The following instruments executed by Henry's in favor of KSB&T:

> Promissory note of April 15, 1992; security agreement dated March 16, 1989; life insurance assignments of March 14, 1989 and March 16, 1989; loan agreement dated April 15, 1992; guaranty of Bertrand Henry dated March 16, 1989, together with two related security agreements of even date therewith; and all UCC financing statements of record (Loan Documents);

shall remain effective after the effective date, with the following exceptions:

a) Payment schedule shall be as specified above;

b) Events of default entitling KSB&T to accelerate remaining indebtedness shall be limited to: 1) failure to timely make a payment specified above within 15 days of the due date; 2) failure to maintain a total of accounts less than 90 days and inventory at cost with totals exceeding one and one-half (1 1/2) times outstanding indebtedness due KSB&T; 3) the failure to cure, after 30 days' notice of default, any material requirement of the Loan Documents, as modified herein;

c) The negative covenants specified in Article IV of the Loan Agreement dated April 15, 1992, except for subparts H and J, are deleted;

d) The requirement in Article III, Section C of the Loan Agreement of April 15, 1992 requiring an accountant's review of Henry's annual financial statement is deleted;

e) The provisions of this Plan shall control over any inconsistent provisions of the Loan Documents.

Without limiting the generality of the foregoing, KSB&T shall retain its lien on all the Debtor's accounts receivable, inventory, furnishings, furniture and equipment, and the collateral assignment of certain life insurance policies on Bertrand Henry and Robert Henry.

Section 6.2. Class 3 - Unsecured Claims: All allowed unsecured claims not separately classified shall be paid as follows: 5 percent of each allowed claim shall be paid on December 31, 1992, 15 percent on December 31, 1993, and 20 percent on December 31, 1994.

ARTICLE 7
IMPLEMENTATION OF PLAN

Henry's shall continue business operations and pay creditors pursuant to the terms of this Plan. Cost-cutting measures to make these creditor payments feasible will be implemented, as more fully described in the Disclosure Statement. On the effective date, all assets of the bankruptcy estate of Henry's shall vest in Henry's, subject to any valid lien, security interest, mortgage, or other interest in property provided for in the Plan.

ARTICLE 8
TREATMENT OF INTEREST HOLDERS

All equity owners in Henry's shall retain their interests, but no dividends shall be paid to said shareholders during the term of the Plan.

ARTICLE 9
EXECUTORY CONTRACTS AND UNEXPIRED LEASES

Henry's hereby assumes the following executory contracts and unexpired leases:

A. Lessor — W. A. Smith, Jr., and H. R. Smith
Property Leased — Retail location located at [address], [city], [state]

B. Lessor — Tom Rose and Heather Rose
Property Leased — Retail store located at [address], [city], [state]

C. Lessor — Limited Investments
Property Leased — Warehouse facility located at [address], [city], [state]

D. Annual bulk space retail advertising contract with the Daily Journal Publishing Company, Inc., which provides for reduced advertising rates.

E. Advertising contract with Baby Bell Yellow Pages.

F. Group health and dental insurance contract with Health Plus, Inc.

G. Group disability and life insurance contract with North Star Corporation.

Leases with Hickory Mall Associates Limited Partnership and Western Management, Inc. were terminated prepetition, and claims with respect to said leases, if any, are included in Class 3.

Henry's has a lease with Nicholas Saint covering nonresidential real property located at [address] and a sublease thereof to Pinto Development Center, Inc.

The deadline to assume or reject these leases is October 8, 1992; Henry's will file a motion on or before said deadline to assume or reject these leases.

ARTICLE 10
MISCELLANEOUS PROVISIONS

Section 10.1. Retention of Jurisdiction: After the effective date, the court shall retain jurisdiction for the following purposes only:

A. To rule on the allowance of claims and to hear any objections thereto;

B. To conclude any adversary proceedings or contested matters pending upon the effective date;

C. To allow and approve or disapprove the payment of any administrative expenses not previously allowed;

D. To determine and resolve questions concerning the existence of defaults under the Plan;

E. To modify the Plan pursuant to § 1127(b) of the Code;

F. To correct any defect, to cure any omission, or to reconcile any inconsistency in the Plan or Order of Confirmation, as may be necessary to carry out the purposes and intent of the Plan; and

G. To issue any order necessary to carry out the terms of the Plan.

Section 10.2. Adversary Proceedings: Henry's reserves the right to begin or continue any adversary proceedings or contested matters permitted under the Code and the applicable Federal Rules of Bankruptcy Procedure.

Section 10.3. Modification of Plan: Henry's may submit modifications of the Plan to the court at any time prior to confirmation pursuant to § 1127 of the Code.

Section 10.4. Default: If any payment required under this Plan is not paid on or before the date specified herein, Henry's shall have thirty (30) days to make said payment before being deemed in default.

Section 10.5. Charter Amendment: Henry's shall amend its charter to provide a provision prohibiting the issuance of nonvoting equity securities, and providing the appropriate distribution of voting powers among all classes of securities possessing voting powers.

ARTICLE 11
DISCHARGE OF DEBTOR

Except as otherwise expressly provided in the Plan, on the effective date the Debtor and all property of the bankruptcy estate shall be discharged and released from any and all claims, debts, or encumbrances that arose before the confirmation date. The discharge and release provided will have the effect set forth in the Bankruptcy Code.

Dated this 18th day of September, 1992.

[Attorney signature]

§ 14.10 —Sample Plan of Reorganization with Repayment of Claims (Alternate Form)

IN THE UNITED STATES BANKRUPTCY COURT
FOR THE DISTRICT OF [STATE]

In re:	)	
	)	
AGRI COOP	)	Case No. __________
	)	Chapter 11
Debtor	)	
____________________	)	

DEBTOR'S PLAN OF REORGANIZATION
DATED JANUARY 31, 1992

Agri Coop, Debtor-in-Possession (Coop), hereby submits as proponent its Plan of Reorganization.

ARTICLE 1
SUMMARY OF THE PLAN

The Plan of Reorganization provides for continued coop operations under existing management. Administrative expenses and priority tax claims will be paid in full. Deferred grain contracts will be paid on the effective date of the Plan. Obligations to holders of certificates of indebtedness will be paid in full, at fixed interest rates, over a three (3) year period beginning December 1, 1992. The secured claim of First Bank will be paid in full at a fixed interest rate, over a period of approximately twenty (20) years. The secured claims of Farm Credit Leasing Services Corp. and Equipment & Financing Inc. will be unimpaired by the Plan. All unsecured claims not separately classified, including the unsecured claim of Farmland Industries, Inc., will be paid in full, plus interest, over six (6) years beginning September 1, 1992. Prepetition patron credits on account due to overpayments and prepayments will be honored in regular business transactions. All executory contracts and unexpired leases will be assumed. A more detailed discussion of this Plan of Reorganization is set forth in the Debtor's Disclosure Statement dated January 31, 1992.

ARTICLE 2
DEFINITIONS

Section 2.1. Certain Defined Terms. The following terms (whether or not underscored) when used in this Plan shall, except when the context otherwise requires, have the following meanings (such definitions to be equally applicable to the singular and plural forms thereof):

Administrative claim: An administrative expense that is entitled to priority pursuant to § 507(a)(1) of the Code and allowed under § 503 of the Code.

Allowance date: The date as of which an order of the court allowing a claim in this case has become final and nonappealable and no appeal therefrom is pending.

Allowed claim: The amount of a claim (1) a proof of which is filed within the time fixed by the Bankruptcy Court, or (2) that has appeared, or hereafter appears, in the schedules filed by the Debtor under § 521(1) of the Code, except a claim that is scheduled as disputed, contingent, or unliquidated as to amount and, in each case, to which no objection to the allowance thereof has been filed within any applicable period fixed by the Court, or as to which the allowance date has occurred. Allowed claim shall not include any administrative claim.

Code: The Bankruptcy Reform Act of 1978, Pub. L. No. 95-598, 11 U.S.C. §§ 101-1330, as amended.

Confirmation date: The date of the entry of an order of the Bankruptcy Court confirming the Plan.

Court: The United States Bankruptcy Court for the District of [state], including the United States bankruptcy judge sitting in this case.

Creditor: Any creditor holding a claim in Classes 1 through 7.

Debtor: Agri Coop, as referred to as the Coop.

Eagleton facilities: The improved real property located in [county], [state], as described on Schedule A filed with the court on January 2, 1992, including the elevator/office, grain loading facility, fertilizer plant, and service station.

Effective date: The date on which the order of the Bankruptcy Court confirming the Plan has become final and nonappealable and no appeal therefrom is pending, or at such earlier date on or after the confirmation date as the Debtor elects.

Filing date: December 18, 1991.

Middle City facilities: The improved real property located in [county], [state], as described on Schedule B filed with the court on January 2, 1992, including the elevator/office, fertilizer plant, hardware/lumber store, and service station.

Plan: This Debtor's Plan of Reorganization, as it may be modified in accordance with Article X.

Priority tax claim. An allowed claim entitled to priority pursuant to § 507(a)(7) of the Code.

Term of the Plan: A period beginning on the effective date and terminating on the date all payments required by the Plan have been completed.

Section 2.2. Other Defined Terms. Terms for which meanings are provided in the Code and in the Rules of Bankruptcy Procedure shall, unless otherwise defined herein or the context otherwise requires, have such meanings when used herein.

Section 2.3. Cross References, Etc. References in this Plan to any Section or Article are, unless otherwise specified, to such Section or Article of this Plan. The words "hereof," "herein," "hereunder," and similar terms shall refer to this Plan and not to any particular section or provisions of this Plan.

Section 2.4. Headings. The various headings of this Plan are inserted for convenience only and shall not affect the meaning or interpretation of this Plan or any provision hereof.

ARTICLE 3
CLASSIFICATION OF CLAIMS

Administrative claims and priority tax claims are not otherwise classified under the terms of this Plan and are treated in accordance with the terms of Article 4 hereof.

Class 1: Unpaid sellers under deferred grain contracts.

Class 2: Holders of certificates of indebtedness.

Class 3: Patrons with prepetition credits on account due to overpayments and prepurchases.

Class 4: The fully secured claim of First Bank.

Class 5: The fully secured claim of Farm Credit Leasing Services Corp., assignee of Farmland Industries Corp.

Class 6: The fully secured claim of Equipment & Financing Inc.

Class 7: All unsecured claims not separately classified, including the claim of Farmland Industries, Inc.

ARTICLE 4
PROVISION FOR PAYMENT OF ADMINISTRATIVE CLAIMS, EXPENSES, AND CERTAIN PRIORITY CLAIMS

Section 4.1. Administrative Claims: Administrative claims, including fees due under 28 U.S.C. § 1930, shall, if not previously paid in full, be paid by the Debtor on the effective date, except that:

(a) any professional employed at the expense of the bankruptcy estate that may be entitled to an allowance of fees and expenses shall be paid in a time and in an amount determined by the Court; and

(b) administrative expenses incurred by the Debtor during the pendency of the reorganization case and prior to the effective date which are payable in the ordinary course of business after the effective date shall be paid by the Debtor in the ordinary course of business after the effective date.

Any holder of an administrative claim may agree in writing to a less favorable treatment.

Section 4.2. Priority Tax Claims. Ad valorem taxes on the real and personal property owned by the Debtor shall be paid in full on the date due or the effective date, whichever is later.

ARTICLE 5
TREATMENT OF CLASSES NOT IMPAIRED UNDER THE PLAN

Section 5.1. Class 1 - Deferred Grain Contracts: The unpaid balances on outstanding deferred grain contracts, together with interest from the contract date at the rate of six-and-one-half percent (6 1/2%) per annum, shall be paid in full on the effective date. Any holder of a claim under Class 1 may agree in writing to receive payment at dates later than specified above.

Section 5.2. Class 3: Prepetition credits on account due to overpayments and prepurchases shall be honored in regular business transactions.

Section 5.3. Classes 5 and 6: The legal, equitable, and contractual rights to which the Class 5 and 6 creditors are entitled shall remain unaltered, with any postpetition payment defaults cured on the effective date.

ARTICLE 6
TREATMENT OF CLASSES IMPAIRED UNDER THE PLAN

Classes 2, 4, and 7 are impaired under the Plan.

Section 6.1. Class 2 - Certificates of Indebtedness: The principal amounts of all certificates of indebtedness shall be paid in full, together with interest thereon at the rate of seven-and-one-half percent (7 1/2%) per annum from March 1, 1991, to April 30, 1991, interest from May 1, 1991, to the effective date at the rate of seven percent (7%) per annum, and interest thereafter at the rate of six-and-one-half percent (6 1/2%) per annum, amortized with level semi-annual payments over three (3) years, commencing on December 1, 1992, and continuing thereafter each June 1 and December 1, until the obligations are paid in full.

Section 6. 2. Class 4 - First Bank: The secured claim of First Bank in the principal amount of $2,436,018.48, together with interest thereon at the national variable rate plus one-and-one-half percent (1 1/2%) per annum on the sum of $1,204,821.00 until the effective date, interest at the rate established by First Bank according to law for term viable loans on the sum of $1,231,197.48 until the effective date, and reasonable attorney's fees and expenses of First Bank as allowed by the court shall be paid in full as follows: accrued interest through the effective date shall be paid on the effective date; allowed attorney's fees shall be paid on the allowance date or effective date, whichever is later; the remaining principal balance, together with interest thereon at the rate of six-and-one-half percent (6 1/2%) per annum, shall be paid with monthly installments of $8,333.33 plus accrued interest commencing on May 1, 1992, and on the first day of each month thereafter, with the monthly principal installments to increase to $10,833.33 on September 1, 1998, until the indebtedness is paid in full. First Bank shall retain its lien on all of the Coop's improved real property, inventory, equipment, vehicles, accounts receivable, and general intangibles; provided, however, that First Bank's lien on inventory shall be subordinate to purchase money security interests as specified in Article 7 below. First Bank stock owned by the Coop shall reduce the foregoing payment obligation pursuant to First Bank rules and regulations.

Section 6.3. Class 7 - Unsecured Claims. All allowed unsecured claims, not separately classified, including the claim of Farmland Industries, Inc., shall be paid in full. Such claims, together with interest thereon at the rate of six-and-one-half percent (6 1/2%) per annum from and after the effective date, shall be amortized with level monthly payments over a six (6) year period, commencing on September 1, 1992, and continuing on the first day of each month thereafter, until the indebtedness is paid in full.

ARTICLE 7
IMPLEMENTATION OF PLAN

The Coop shall continue business operations and pay creditors pursuant to the terms of this Plan. Arrangements with one or more suppliers will be set up to purchase inventory on short term credit; pursuant to [statute], such suppliers will be given a security interest in said inventory, with priority over the lien of First Bank. Additionally, the Coop will not offer deferred grain contracts to its customers in the future unless those contracts are guaranteed by a letter of credit obtained by the Coop. More complete descriptions of the implementation and means of completing the Plan are set out in the Disclosure Statement.

On the effective date, all assets of the bankruptcy estate of the Coop shall vest in the Coop subject to any valid lien, security interest, mortgage, or other interest in property provided for in the Plan.

ARTICLE 8
TREATMENT OF INTEREST HOLDERS

All equity owners in the Coop shall retain their interests, which shall be unimpaired under the Plan.

ARTICLE 9
EXECUTORY CONTRACTS AND UNEXPIRED LEASES

The Debtor hereby assumes all executory contracts and unexpired leases, except as otherwise expressly provided herein. Without limiting the generality of the foregoing, the following executory contracts and unexpired leases are expressly assumed:

A. Track lease with Burlington Northern Railroad;

B. Operating lease agreement with Agri Limited Partnership;

C. Input finance program contract with the Cooperative Finance Association Inc.;

D. Grain merchandising agreement with Continental-COF Company;

E. Uniform grain storage agreement with Commodity Credit Corporation; and

F. Lease of service station to Ron Ellison.

ARTICLE 10
MISCELLANEOUS PROVISIONS

Section 10.1. Retention of Jurisdiction: After the effective date, the court shall retain jurisdiction for the following purposes only:

A. To rule on the allowance of claims and to hear any objections thereto;

B. To conclude any adversary proceedings or contested matters pending upon the effective date;

C. To allow and approve or disapprove the payment of any administrative expenses not previously allowed;

D. To determine and resolve questions concerning the existence of defaults under the Plan;

E. To modify the Plan pursuant to § 1127(b) of the Code;

F. To correct any defect, to cure any omission, or to reconcile any inconsistency in the Plan or Order of Confirmation, as may be necessary to carry out the purposes and intent of the Plan; and

G. To issue any order necessary to carry out the terms of the Plan.

Section 10.2. Adversary Proceedings: The Coop reserves the right to begin or continue any adversary proceedings or contested matters permitted under the Code and the applicable Federal Rules of Bankruptcy Procedure.

Section 10.3. Modification of Plan: The Coop may submit modifications of the Plan to the court at any time prior to confirmation pursuant to § 1127 of the Code.

Section 10.4. Default: If any payment required under this Plan is not paid on or before the date specified herein, the Coop shall have thirty (30) days to make said payment before being deemed in default.

Section 10.5. Charter Amendment: The Coop shall amend its charter to provide a provision prohibiting the issuance of nonvoting equity securities, and providing the appropriate distribution of voting powers among all classes of securities possessing voting powers.

Section 10.6. Federal Warehouse License: The Coop's warehouse license issued by the U.S. Department of Agriculture and the corresponding warehouse bond shall vest with the Coop, as reorganized, on the effective date.

ARTICLE 11
DISCHARGE OF DEBTOR

Except as otherwise expressly provided in the Plan, on the effective date the Debtor and all property of the bankruptcy estate shall be discharged and released from any and all claims, debts, or encumbrances that arose before the confirmation date. The discharge and release provided will have the effect set forth in the Bankruptcy Code.

Dated this 31st day of January, 1992.

[Attorney signature]

§ 14.11 —Sample Plan of Reorganization with Liquidation of Assets

UNITED STATES BANKRUPTCY COURT
FOR THE DISTRICT OF [STATE]

In re:	)	
	)	
STEVEN H. JONES	)	Case No. ___________
SUSAN J. JONES	)	
	)	
Debtors	)	
______________________________	)	

STEVEN H. JONES AND SUSAN J. JONES'S FIRST AMENDED PLAN OF REORGANIZATION DATED JUNE 21, 1993

ARTICLE 1
Summary of Plan

Debtors Steven H. Jones and Susan J. Jones [Debtors] hereby propose their first amended Plan of Reorganization dated June 21, 1993 (Plan). Under this Plan, certain of the Jones's nonexempt assets will be marshalled, transferred to a liquidating trust, and liquidated for the benefit of those creditors which have security interest in the assets and general creditors. All other nonexempt assets will be retained in the estate, which will remain open postconfirmation subject to other terms of the Plan. All proceeds remaining, if any, after the payment of allowed secured, administrative, and priority claims will be paid pro rata to unsecured creditors. Debtors have real estate, partnership interests, stock in a close corporation, bank holding company stock, and possibly other assets which can be liquidated.

ARTICLE 2
Definitions

As used in this Plan and Disclosure Statement, the following terms shall have the respective meanings set forth below, and, unless the context requires otherwise, such meaning shall be equally applicable to the singular and plural forms of the terms defined. Unless otherwise defined, the terms used in this Plan shall have the same meaning ascribed thereto in the Bankruptcy Code and the Bankruptcy Rules. The following definitions of terms shall also apply to these terms as utilized in the Disclosure Statement.

2.1 Administrative claim: Any claim for payment of any cost or expense of administration of the Chapter 11 case is entitled to priority in accordance with §§ 503(b) and 507(a)(1) of the Bankruptcy Code, including, without limitation, any actual and necessary expenses of preserving the Debtor's estate and operating the business from and after the petition date to and including the confirmation date (other than such claims or portions thereof which, by their express terms are not due or payable by the distribution date) and all allowances of compensation and reimbursement approved by the court in accordance with the bankruptcy code, and any fees or charges assessed against the Debtors' estate under Chapter 123 of Title 28, United States Code.

2.2 Allowed claim: Any claim (a) based on an application of a professional person to the extent such application is approved by final order; (b) allowed under this Plan; or (c) proof of which was either timely and properly filed, deemed filed under applicable law or by reason of an order of the Court, or, if no proof of claim was filed or order entered, which has been or hereafter is listed by the Debtors on their schedules filed under § 521(1) of the Bankruptcy Code as liquidated in an amount and not disputed or contingent, provided that a timely filed proof of claim shall supersede any scheduling of such claim, and, in either case, a claim as to which: (i) no objection to the allowance thereof has been timely filed on or before the distribution date or such other applicable period of limitation fixed by the Bankruptcy Code or by an order of the Court; or (ii) any objection has been withdrawn pursuant to the provisions of this Plan or has been overruled by a final order of the Court.

2.3 Allowed priority claim: All or that portion of any priority claim which is or has become an allowed claim.

2.4 Assets: All personal and real property of the Debtors, whether tangible or intangible, of the Debtors' estate, as defined in § 541 of the Bankruptcy Code, as of the effective date, including without limitation the property set forth in the Disclosure Statement.

2.5 Ballot date: The date set by the Court as the last date for timely submission of a ballot accepting or rejecting this Plan.

2.6 Bankruptcy Code: The Bankruptcy Reform Act of 1978, as amended, and as applicable to the Chapter 11 case, § 101 et seq. Title 11, United States Code.

2.7 Bankruptcy Rules: The rules of procedure applicable to cases or proceedings pending before the Court, now existing or as hereafter amended.

2.8 Business day: Any day on which banks are open to carry on their ordinary commercial banking business in [city], [state].

2.9 Cash: Cash or cash equivalents.

2.10 Causes of action: All accounts, contract rights, general intangibles, and all rights, claims, and causes of action of any kind, whether legal or equitable, of the Debtors, for affirmative recovery of cash or other property of the estate (whether such causes are the subject of presently pending lawsuits, adversary proceedings or appeals, or otherwise) existing before the effective date, including such that have accrued or may thereafter accrue relating to those matters that have occurred on or prior to the effective date.

2.11 Chapter 11 case: The Chapter 11 case commenced by the Debtors on September 17, 1992.

2.12 Class: Any group of holders of claims or interests as specified in Article III of this Plan.

2.13 Collateral: Property in which the Debtors have an interest that secured, in whole or in part, payment of a claim.

2.14 Confirmation date: The date of entry of the Confirmation Order in accordance with the provisions of the Bankruptcy Code, provided, however, that if on motion the Confirmation Order or consummation of the Plan is stayed pending appeal, then the confirmation date shall be the date of entry of the Final Order vacating such stay or the date on which such stay expires or is no longer in effect.

2.15 Confirmation order: Order of the Court confirming the Plan and approving the transactions contemplated herein.

2.16 Contested claim: Any claim or interest that has been scheduled by the Debtors as contingent, unliquidated, or disputed, or with respect to which an objection has been interposed in accordance with the Bankruptcy Code, Bankruptcy Rules, this Plan, or orders of the Court.

2.17 Court: The United States Bankruptcy Court for the District of [state], or such other Court as may have jurisdiction of the Chapter 11 case.

2.18 Creditor: Any entity that is the holder of a claim or an interest, including but not limited to: (a) a claim that arose on or before the petition date; (b) an interest that arose on or before the record date; (c) a claim against the Debtors' estate of any kind specified in §§ 502(g), 502(h), or 502(i) of the Bankruptcy Code; or (d) an administrative claim.

2.19 Creditor's committee: The committee of four creditors established at the first meeting of creditors conducted on October 23, 1992, and consisting of: [names of committee members].

2.20 Debtors: Steven H. Jones and Susan J. Jones.

2.21 Disclosure Statement: The written Disclosure Statement in respect to this Plan approved by the court pursuant to § 1125 of the Bankruptcy Code.

2.22 Estate liabilities: Amounts required herein to be paid on account of allowed claims and interest, costs, and expenses of administering the estate in completing this Plan.

2.23 F.D.I.C.: The Federal Deposit Insurance Corporation.

2.24 Fee application: An application of a professional person under §§ 330, 331, or 503 of the Bankruptcy Code for allowance of compensation and reimbursement of expenses in the Chapter 11 case.

2.25 Final order: An order or a judgment that has not been reversed, stayed, modified, or amended, and as to which (a) the time to appeal or seek review, reargument, or rehearing has expired, and as to which no appeal or petition for certiorari, review, or rehearing is pending; or (b) if appeal, review, reargument, rehearing, or certiorari of the order has been sought, the order has been affirmed or the request for review, reargument, rehearing, or certiorari has been denied and a time to seek a further appeal, review, reargument, rehearing, or certiorari has expired, as a result of which such order shall have become final and nonappealable in accordance with applicable law.

2.26 Impaired: When used with respect to any claim, interest or class, it has the same meaning as that contained in § 1124 of the Bankruptcy Code.

2.27 Liquidating Trust: The Steven H. Jones and Susan J. Jones Liquidating Trust to be established upon confirmation of the Plan for the purpose of marshalling and liquidating the nonexempt assets of Steven H. Jones and Susan J. Jones and ratable distribution of the proceeds of same to those creditors holding allowed unsecured claims, after appropriate deduction for administrative expenses.

2.28 Liquidating trustee: The trustee or the co-trustees of the Liquidating Trust who will be named at confirmation, his, her, or their successors and assigns.

2.29 Plan: The Plan of Liquidation proposed by the Debtors, either in its present form or as it may be amended or modified.

2.29A Postconfirmation Debtors: The Debtors immediately after the confirmation date.

2.29B Postconfirmation estate: The estate remaining open upon and after the confirmation date for a period of two years thereafter for the purpose of retaining certain nonexempt property of the estate.

2.30 Proceeds: Proceeds realized from the operation, sale, liquidation, settlement, prosecution, or other disposition, as applicable, of the assets.

2.31 Professional person: Any entity retained or to be compensated pursuant to §§ 326, 327, 328, 330, 331, 503(b), or 1103 of the Bankruptcy Code.

2.32 RTC: The Resolution Trust Corporation.

2.33 Secured claim: A claim of a creditor arising on or before the petition date to the extent (a) secured by a lien on collateral that is not void or avoidable under applicable state and federal law, including the Bankruptcy Code, or (b) subject to setoff under § 553 of the Bankruptcy Code, in each case to the extent of the value of said creditor's interest in the Debtors' interest in the property or the amount of the setoff, as applicable; provided, however, that nothing herein shall prohibit a secured creditor from making the election provided in § 1111(b)(2) of the Bankruptcy Code.

2.34 Secured creditor: Any creditor that is the holder of a secured claim.

2.35 Tax claim: Any claim that is entitled to priority in payment under § 507(a)(7) of the Bankruptcy Code.

2.36 Undetermined claim: A claim that is: (a) a contested claim; (b) a claim arising through rejection of executory contracts or unexpired leases pursuant to this Plan; (c) an undetermined administrative claim in respect of an application of a professional person; or (d) a claim that is unliquidated or contingent.

2.37 Unsecured claim: An unsecured claim against the Debtors that is not entitled to priority pursuant to the Bankruptcy Code.

2.38 Unsecured creditor: Any creditor that is the holder of an unsecured claim.

ARTICLE 3
Classification of Claims

The claims are classified as set forth below. Administrative claims and priority claims are treated in accordance with the terms of Article IV hereto and, because they are not voting claims, are not classified below.

3.1 Class One: Secured claim of First Cooperative Bank & Trust Company ($300,000.00):

3.1.1 Secured claim of First Cooperative Bank & Trust Company: The secured claim of First Cooperative Bank & Trust Company (FCB), as amended on or about May 27, 1993 in the amount of $379,527, is secured by an assignment of Steven H. Jones' partnership interest in Shawnee Associates, a [state] general partnership which owns Shawnee Shopping Center. FCB values the interest at $70,000. Debtors have agreed with FCB that FCB's security interest is perfected. Although FCB maintains other claims against partnerships of which Steven H. Jones is a general partner, this is the only portion of FCB's claim which results directly from a note by Steven H. Jones to FCB. All of FCB's other claims, including the unsecured portion of this claim ($309,527), will be treated as a single unsecured claim.

3.1.2 Treatment of claim: Steven H. Jones' partnership interest in Shawnee Associates will remain in the postconfirmation estate. At FCB's option, FCB may immediately realize upon said asset or, in the alternative, FCB may receive the proceeds of said asset if Shawnee is sold. FCB shall therefore receive the indubitable equivalent of its secured claim. The balance of FCB's claims, arising out of partnership obligations, shall be treated as unsecured.

3.1.3 Impairment: FCB is impaired.

3.2 Class Two: Secured claim of Resolution Trust Corporation as successor to Santa Fe Savings & Loan Association ($35,976.55 and $38,926.58): Debtors understand that Santa Fe Savings & Loan Association is currently under the supervision of the Resolution Trust Corporation.

3.2.1 Secured claim of RTC: The secured claim of RTC is secured by first mortgages upon the following described real estate, to wit:

[legal description] (the Grandview property)

[legal description] (the Kessler property)

in the amounts of $35,769.55 and $38,926.58 respectively. The mortgages are not cross-collateralized. The properties are two duplexes rented by Susan J. Jones to residential tenants.

The Grandview property is jointly held by Steven H. Jones and Susan J. Jones. The Kessler property is held by Steven H. Jones. Both properties are operated by Susan J. Jones. Debtors believe that these properties have value well in excess of $74,723.13 (the sum of the claims) and that RTC is oversecured. Both loans are current.

3.2.2 Treatment of claim: RTC's claims will be paid as follows:

Debtors have listed the duplexes for sale, and RTC's liens thereon will be paid upon the closing of these sales. At confirmation, the duplexes will be transferred to the Liquidating Trust. While awaiting sale, RTC will be paid regular monthly payments according to the terms of its notes and real estate mortgages. The Debtors' postpetition agreement to pay RTC monthly payments as adequate protection of its interest in the estate's interest in the properties will be continued in full force and effect pending the sale of the properties as against the liquidating trustee. Debtors will, in all other respects, abide by the terms and covenants of the notes and real estate mortgages.

3.2.3 Retention of lien: RTC will retain its real estate mortgages upon the duplexes and its assignments of rent contained within those mortgages.

3.2.4 Impairment: RTC is unimpaired.

3.3 Class Three: Secured claim of Bart Switzer ($464,833.00):

3.3.1 Secured claim of Bart Switzer: The claim of Bart Switzer (Switzer) comprises two promissory notes, one dated September 11, 1989 in the amount of $304,608.00 with accrued interest (the 1989 note) and the other dated June 28, 1991 in the amount of $160,225.00 (the 1991 note). The 1989 note is an obligation of Blue Ridge Associates, a [state] general partnership, consisting of Steven H. Jones and Susan J. Jones, which was dissolved before the Chapter 11 Case. The 1991 note is an obligation of Steven H. Jones.

3.3.2 Treatment of claim: The 1989 note is secured by an assignment of Steven H. Jones and Susan J. Jones' interest in Blue Ridge Associates, a [state] general partnership, which held a 27% interest in A Associates, a 19% interest in B Associates, and a 19% interest in C Associates. The last three named partnerships are all [state] general partnerships which hold raw land for development. Switzer has agreed that, effective upon confirmation, he will release his security interest in these partnership interests. The interests will be conveyed to the Liquidating Trust at confirmation and liquidated thereby.

The 1991 note is secured by a valid and perfected security interest in Steven H. Jones' 8% partnership interest in the Park Apartments, a [state] general partnership, and Steven H. Jones' stock option agreement on 7,000 shares of Tech-Tran Corp., pursuant to a certain agreement dated February 5, 1991 between Edward M. Evans, Bart Switzer, and Steven H. Jones. Claimant states in his

Proof of Claim No. 33 that the property described has a value of not more than $80,000.

3.3.4 Disposition of collateral: Debtors' interest in Park Associates Partnership and the Tech-Tran option will be retained in the Post-Confirmation Estate and Switzer will retain his lien thereon. Switzer may, at his option, realize upon the interests. In the event Switzer realizes upon these assets and a surplus of funds remains after payment in full of this portion of his allowed secured claim, Switzer will account to the Liquidating Trust for same.

3.3.5 Impairment. Switzer's claim is impaired.

3.4 Class Four: Secured claim of Federal Deposit Insurance Corporation as successor of Northern State Bank ($221,750.00 approximate):

3.4.1 Secured claim of Federal Deposit Insurance Corporation (FDIC): The secured claim of FDIC is based upon a promissory note given by Steven H. Jones to Northern State Bank (Northern) in payment of certain guaranty obligations of Jones' arising out of deficiencies on the Old Hotel project and the Waterview North project in which Steven H. Jones was a general partner. The claim is secured by Jones' interest in Waterview Shops, although it is unclear that the security interest is properly perfected. FDIC is undersecured. FDIC's other claims are against partnership of which Steven H. Jones is a general partner, those being Terrace Mobile Home Park Partnership and Village Associates. Those claims will be treated as unsecured.

3.4.2 Treatment of claim: FDIC's secured claim will be paid as follows:

Steven H. Jones will retain the estate's interest in Waterview Shops at confirmation, subject to FDIC's lien. The balance of FDIC's claim will be treated as unsecured. If it is determined that the asset can be conveyed to the Liquidating Trust and liquidated and that the proceeds thereof will be sufficient to pay FDIC's lien as well as any income tax incurred by the estate upon its conveyance, the asset will be conveyed to the Liquidating Trust and sold. If it appears that the conveyance of the shops to the Liquidating Trust will have no adverse tax consequences, the asset may also be conveyed to the Trust for liquidation. If the proceeds of the liquidation are insufficient to pay FDIC's claim in full, the balance of the claim will be treated as unsecured.

3.4.3 Impairment: FDIC's claim is impaired.

3.5 Class Five: General unsecured claims

3.5.1 Description of class: The class of general unsecured claims shall consist of the following: (a) unsecured claims against the Debtors or either of them; (b) obligations of partnership of which Steven H. Jones or Susan J. Jones, or both of them, are partners and for which they may be personally liable;

(c) obligations of Steven H. Jones and/or Susan J. Jones to partnerships or the partners of partnerships on account of unpaid cash calls or other liquidated obligations; and (d) other proven claims against Steven H. Jones and/or Susan J. Jones arising prior to confirmation.

3.5.2 Treatment of claim: The Class Five general unsecured creditors shall receive payment in respect of their proven liquidated claims in the following manner:

(a) Upon confirmation, the following nonexempt assets of the Debtors' will be conveyed to the Liquidating Trust to be held in trust and liquidated for the benefit of the Class Five creditors and any secured creditors which claim liens or security interests in and to any of the assets so conveyed:

All Debtors' interest in Dominion Banqueshares Limited (the bank stock)		
All Debtors' interest in A Associates	)	collectively
All Debtors' interest in B Associates	)	the bare land
All Debtors' interest in C Associates	)	interests
All Debtors' interest in Northgate Ventures	)	
All Debtors' interest in the Grandview and Kessler Duplexes		

(b) The balance of Debtors' nonexempt assets will be retained in the estate, which will remain open postconfirmation for a period not exceeding two years after the confirmation date.

(c) A Liquidating Trust shall be established, as set forth in Article 5 below. Debtors intend that a separate Liquidating Trust be established, which trust will be a separate taxable entity and which trust shall, from the proceeds of the liquidation of its assets, first pay administrative claims, the trust's administrative expenses and costs, and then the claims of the unsecured creditors, as allowed herein.

(d) If the Trust does not net on the sale of the bank stock and other assets sufficient funds to pay administrative expenses in the estimated amount of $200,000 ($150,000 professional fees and $50,000 other administrative claims) and a dividend of 20 percent of the total allowed unsecured claims, Debtors shall retain all of their nonexempt property other than the property transferred to the Liquidating Trust under subsection (a) of ¶3.5.2 within the postconfirmation estate and not transfer it to the Liquidating Trust at confirmation, subject to certain provisions below. Any property remaining in the postconfirmation estate at the end of two years next succeeding the confirmation date shall be deemed abandoned to the Debtors. Debtors may, at their option, cause the postconfirmation estate to withdraw from any partnership in which they are partners and which partnership interest remains in the postconfirmation estate. Provided, however, that Debtors may only withdraw from partnerships such that the estate does not sustain taxable income upon the transfer of partnership interests in excess of that which can be absorbed by the estate's tax attributes and long-term loss. Alternatively, the nondebtor partners of any partnership in which the Debtors claim an interest and which interest is in the postconfirmation estate may elect to walk-down the Debtors' interest, held in the postconfirmation estate, under the terms of their partnership agreements. The partners shall be relieved from the automatic stay for that purpose. At the end of the two-year period, any remaining partnership interests (or other assets) from which Debtors have not withdrawn or have not been walked down shall be deemed abandoned to the postconfirmation Debtors, subject only to the provisions below and to any valid, preexisting liens.

(e) If, after the Liquidating Trust sells the bank stock and any other of its assets, sufficient funds have been generated to pay all administrative claims in full and a dividend to the unsecured creditors of 20 percent of the allowed unsecured claims, Debtors may cause the postconfirmation estate to convey to the Liquidating Trust for liquidation properties retained in the estate, provided that the extent of such conveyances does not generate taxable income to the estate or Trust, the tax upon which exceeds the Trust's then-existing cash surplus (considering accrued trust expenses) after payment of all administrative claims and the 20 percent dividend described above.

(f) If the Debtors should receive either proceeds of or distributions from any partnership interests remaining in the postconfirmation estate, the same shall promptly be conveyed to the Liquidating Trust.

(g) Debtors may also elect to abandon properties out of the postconfirmation estate prior to the end of the two-year period after the confirmation date.

3.5.4 Impairment: The Class of general unsecured creditors' claims is impaired.

ARTICLE 4
Payment of Administrative Claims and Expenses and Certain Priority Claims

4.1 Administrative claims: There are three types of administrative claims. They will be paid as described below.

4.1.1 Professional fees and expenses; costs: The claim of Debtors' counsel, Debtors' accountants, Chapter 11 fees owed due to the Executive Office of the United States Trustee, court costs, and other expenses shall be paid in full in cash out of the first proceeds generated by the Liquidating Trust. These administrative claims shall amount to approximately $150,000 cash.

4.1.2 Partners' Section 503(b) Claims: Various partners have filed claims for reimbursement of capital payments made into the partnership postpetition for the purpose of preserving assets to the estate. These claims will be allowed in an amount not to exceed $50,000 in the aggregate. The parties entitled to such payments are [names]. These parties have agreed to subordinate their claims to the payment of professional fees.

4.1.3 Administrative claims for taxes: Administrative claims for taxes of the estate will be assumed in rem and paid by the Liquidating Trust to the extent that there are insufficient estate assets to pay such taxes, it being understood that, pursuant to ¶3.5.3(e) there will be no estate taxes generated in excess of the Trust's then-existing cash surplus.

4.2 Acceptance and payment by the Liquidating Trust of administrative claims: The Liquidating Trust will, on the confirmation date, accept the administrative claims for payment from the proceeds of the liquidation. Any holder of an administrative claim may agree in writing to be paid from the proceeds of the Liquidating Trust. Any holder of such claim shall be deemed to have agreed to this treatment by accepting the Plan or by the holder's silence.

4.3 Deposit claims: Priority claims include the claims of tenants having paid security deposits on the Kessler and Grandview properties. These will be repaid in the ordinary course of business.

4.4 Election regarding passive activity loss: The Debtors and the estate elect that Debtors' passive activity losses and credits and I.R.C. § 465 losses shall become a part of the estate's tax attributes along with all of the Debtors' other carryforward tax attributes in accordance with Treas. Reg. §§ 1398-1 and 1398-2 and § 1398 of the Internal Revenue Code.

ARTICLE 5
Means of Execution of this Plan and Distribution of Proceeds

5.1 Liquidating Trust: A liquidating trust known as the Jones Liquidating Trust (Liquidating Trust or Trust) shall, upon the confirmation date, be created for the benefit of the creditors. The Liquidating Trust shall liquidate and distribute the proceeds of the estate assets transferred to the Trust pro rata among those unsecured creditors with proven claims, after paying administrative claims, the Trust's expenses and costs, to include state and federal income taxes incurred by the Trust, as well as other expenses. To the extent estate assets subject to proven liens of record are sold, the proceeds of those assets shall first be paid to the holders of those liens, then as set forth above. The liquidating trust shall be established according to the terms of the Trust, which is attached hereto and made a part hereof marked Exhibit A.

The court shall retain jurisdiction over the Liquidating Trust while it is administering assets and paying claims. Upon the settling of estate assets on the Trustee, the Debtors shall cease to be debtors-in-possession of those assets and shall have no powers with respect to the liquidation of the assets in the Trust. The property of the Liquidating Trust shall not include (a) any assets which are not proceeds, products, offspring, rents, or profits of property of the estate, or

(b) any assets which the postconfirmation Debtors acquire after confirmation. The liquidating trustee shall make distributions of all asset proceeds, after making deductions for the payment of liens covering particular assets sold, to the holders of administrative claims in full, and, thereafter, to the allowed claims of unsecured creditors, pro rata. The property of the Liquidating Trust shall be liable for the payment of administrative and priority tax claims incurred by the estate during preconfirmation administration and resulting from the vesting of its property in the Liquidating Trust.

5.2 Debtors' cooperation: Debtors shall cooperate with the liquidating trustee in the marshalling of trust assets, the liquidation of assets, and such other activities as liquidating trustee shall deem appropriate. The Debtors shall execute any and all necessary documents and fully cooperate in effectuating the transfer and sale of all personal and real property.

5.3 Liquidation: The activities of the Liquidating Trust shall be conducted in a manner reasonably calculated under the then-existing circumstances to maximize the proceeds of any liquidation to timely fund and make payment to the creditors of Steven H. Jones and Susan J. Jones.

5.4 Trustee selection: The Debtors or any other party in interest may propose a liquidating trustee to the court. With the advice of the Debtors and with the advice and consent of the creditors' committee, the court shall appoint a liquidating trustee or its successors and condition its powers in accordance with the Liquidating Trust.

ARTICLE 6
The Postconfirmation Debtors and the Postconfirmation Estate

6.1 The Postconfirmation Debtors: Upon confirmation, the estate created when this case was commenced shall remain open. The Debtors shall remain debtors-in-possession as to any property remaining in the estate and not transferred to the Liquidating Trust. Debtors shall have the duty of administering such property while it remains in the estate. If the Debtors receive any distributions from or proceeds of any estate property, they will promptly remit such funds, net of any income taxes accruing as a result of distribution or disposition of the properties in question, to the Trust. The Debtors shall, as further set forth in paragraph 15.2, retain as their sole and separate property, distinct from the postconfirmation estate, any property they accumulate postconfirmation (including postconfirmation income for personal services rendered by them or either of them) to the extent such property is not a proceed or product of estate property. The postconfirmation Debtors' reporting duties under the Code and Rules shall be limited to the property of the postconfirmation estate. The Debtors shall be responsible for seeing that tax returns for the postconfirmation estate are filed.

6.2 The Postconfirmation estate: The postconfirmation estate shall consist of all nonexempt property contained in the estate at the confirmation date except that property which is conveyed to the Liquidating Trust upon confirmation or from time to time thereafter. The postconfirmation estate shall retain all tax attributes of the prepetition Debtors including but not limited to tax loss carryforwards and passive activity losses under Internal Revenue Code § 465. The postconfirmation estate shall be a continuation of the estate and shall remain an entity distinct and separate from the postconfirmation Debtors.

ARTICLE 7
Assumption and Rejection of Executory Contracts

7.1 Debtors have concluded that the partnership agreements under which Steven H. Jones and Susan J. Jones are general partners are executory. Debtors do not intend to assume these contracts. Debtors are empowered to sell or convey their interests in the partnerships without assuming the contracts per se. All of said contracts are accordingly rejected. All other executory contracts and unexpired leases of the Debtors are rejected as well, except for the shareholders' agreement for Dominion Banqueshares, Inc. and collateral documents, as well as any other contracts described upon a list to be filed with the court on or before the confirmation date.

ARTICLE 8
Preservation of Claims for Benefit of Liquidating Trust

8.1 The estate may have claims for avoidance of preferences, fraudulent transfers, fraudulent conveyances, and other claims. Any such claims, known or unknown, discovered or undiscovered, arising before or after the commencement of this case, and otherwise available to Debtors, shall be preserved for the benefit of and vested in the Liquidating Trust upon confirmation of the Plan.

ARTICLE 9
Reservation of Cram Down Rights

9.1 Debtors expressly reserve the right pursuant to § 1129(b) of the Bankruptcy Code to request the court to confirm this Plan if all the applicable requirements of § 1129(a) of the Bankruptcy Code have been met other than those of § 1129(a)(8).

ARTICLE 10
Modification of Plan

10.1 Amendments prior to confirmation date: Modifications or amendments to this Plan may be proposed in writing by Debtors or creditors at any time before the confirmation date, provided that this Plan, as modified, meets the requirements of the Bankruptcy Code.

10.2 Amendments after confirmation date: This Plan may be modified by Debtors at any time after the confirmation date and before its substantial consummation, provided that this Plan, as modified, meets the requirements of the Bankruptcy Code and the court, after notice and hearing, confirms this Plan, as modified.

10.3 Effect on claims: A holder of a claim that has accepted or rejected this Plan shall be deemed to have accepted or rejected, as the case may be, this Plan, as modified, unless, within the time fixed by the court, such holder changes its previous acceptance or rejection.

ARTICLE 11
Retention of Jurisdiction

11.1 Purposes: Notwithstanding entry of the confirmation order, the court shall retain jurisdiction over the Chapter 11 case for the following purposes:

(a) to determine any and all objections to the allowance of claims or interests, both before and after the confirmation date, including any objections to the classification of any claim or interest;

(b) to determine any and all fee applications and other applications for other fees and expenses authorized to be paid or reimbursed in accordance with the Bankruptcy Code;

(c) to determine any and all pending applications for the assumption or rejection of executory contracts or for the rejection or assumption and assignment, as the case may be, of unexpired leases to which any debtor is a party or with respect to which it may be liable; to hear and determine any actions to void or terminate unexpired contracts or leases; and to hear and determine and, if need be, to liquidate any and all claims arising therefrom;

(d) to hear and determine any and all actions initiated by the Debtors, their counsel, or the liquidating trustee or its counsel, whether by motion, complaint, or otherwise;

(e) to determine any and all applications, motions, adversary proceedings, and contested or litigated matters, whether pending before the Court on the confirmation date or filed or instituted after the confirmation date, including without limitation proceedings to recover voidable or avoidable transfers under the Bankruptcy Code or other applicable law;

(f) to modify this Plan, the Disclosure Statement, or any document created in connection with this Plan, including the indenture creating the Liquidating Trust, or remedy any defect or omission, or reconcile any inconsistency in any order of the Court, this Plan, the Disclosure Statement, or any document created in connection with this Plan, in such manner as may be necessary to carry out the purposes and effects of this Plan to the extent authorized by the Bankruptcy Code;

(g) to ensure that the distribution is accomplished in accordance with the provisions of this Plan;

(h) to allow, disallow, determine, liquidate, or estimate any claim or interest, and to enter or enforce any order requiring the filing of any such claim of interest before a particular date;

(i) to enter such orders as may be necessary to consummate, implement, and effectuate the operative provisions of this Plan and all documents and agreements provided for herein or therein or executed pursuant hereto or thereto, including without limitation entering appropriate orders to protect the Debtors from creditor action, and including without limitation taking any and all necessary actions to further the ends of the Liquidating Trust;

(j) to hear any other matter not inconsistent with Chapter 11 of the Bankruptcy Code;

(k) to enter and implement such orders as may be appropriate in the event the confirmation order is for any reason stayed, reversed, revoked, or vacated;

(l) to determine other matters as may arise in connection with this Plan, the Disclosure Statement, or the confirmation order;

(m) to enter a final decree closing the Chapter 11 case.

11.2 Exclusive Jurisdiction: The court shall have exclusive jurisdiction to resolve all controversies, suits, and disputes that may arise in connection with the interpretation, enforcement, consummation, implementation, or administration of this Plan and the Disclosure Statement, and all entities shall be enjoined from commencing any legal or equitable action or proceeding with respect to such matters in any other court, or administrative or regulatory body.

11.3 Abstention: If the Court abstains from exercising jurisdiction or is otherwise without jurisdiction over any matter arising out of the Chapter 11 case, including the matters set forth in Article VIII hereof, this Article XI shall have no effect upon and shall not control, prohibit, or limit the exercise of jurisdiction by any other court having competent jurisdiction with respect to such matter.

11.4 Application to Liquidating Trust: The court shall also retain jurisdiction over the Liquidating Trust and shall be available to make any and all determinations as set forth in 11.1(a) through (m) above. The estate shall remain open and the Court's jurisdiction in this case shall not terminate until the last act of the liquidating trustee has been completed and the liquidating trustee has made its final report and request for discharge to this court.

ARTICLE 12
Resolution of Undetermined Claims

12.1 Procedure: Within 45 days after the entry of the confirmation order, unless such date is extended by order of the Court after notice and hearing, from the date the confirmation order becomes final, the Debtors shall file with the court objections to claims and interests and shall serve a copy of each such objection upon the holder of the claim or interest to which such objection pertains unless otherwise ordered by the Court. The Debtors shall litigate to judgment, settle, or withdraw objections to contested claims.

12.2 Allowance of claims: At the time, and to the extent, that an undetermined claim becomes an allowed claim, such allowed claim shall be entitled to all distributions from the fund applicable to such claim or interest. Such distributions shall be made in the manner provided for by this Plan and the terms of any final order of the court with respect to such claim or interest.

12.3 Rights of creditors: Unless and until an undetermined claim becomes an allowed claim, no creditor holding such a claim shall have any claim against the distribution held or reserved by the trustee with respect to such claim.

12.4 Reserve for disputed claims: Debtors contemplate filing objections to certain of the claims filed by creditors in this case. The trustee will, while such objections are pending, segregate from the proceeds of Liquidating Trust property such a proportion of the proceeds as he or she deems necessary for the payment of disputed claims when and if they are allowed. The segregated proportion shall not exceed twenty (20) percent of the aggregate face amount of the claims objected to.

ARTICLE 13
General Provisions

13.1 Certain rights unaffected: This Plan shall not affect or impair any rights or obligations which the Debtors' creditors may have among themselves as to their respective claims or the relative priority or subordination thereof.

13.2 Headings: The article and section headings used in this Plan are inserted for convenience and reference only and neither constitute a part of this Plan nor in any manner affect the terms, provisions, or interpretations of this Plan.

13.3 Severability: Should any term or provision in this Plan be determined to be unenforceable, such determination shall in no way limit or affect the enforceability and operative effect of any other term or provision of this Plan.

13.4 Governing law: Except to the extent that the Bankruptcy Code is applicable, the rights and obligations arising under this Plan and any documents, agreements, and instruments executed in connection with this Plan (except to the extent such documents, agreements, and instruments designate otherwise) shall be governed by and construed and enforced in accordance with the laws of the state of [state name].

13.5 Successors and assigns: The rights and obligations of any entity named or referred to in this Plan shall be binding upon and shall inure to the benefit of the successors and assigns of such entity.

13.6 Discharge: Upon confirmation, Debtors shall be discharged from the balance of their obligations that are dischargeable under § 1141 as more fully specified in Article XVI.

13.7 Environmental claims: The Debtors are not aware of any liabilities, claims, or obligations due and owing to the Environmental Protection Agency, to the [state] Department of Health and Environment, or to any appropriate agencies in the state of [name] or any other state in which the Debtors have operated. Unless any such claims by any of the above and foregoing agencies or governmental organizations have been filed on or before the bar date and subsequently allowed, such entities shall be barred from participation in the distribution of any dividends in this proceeding.

13.8 Priority wage claims: Debtors set forth that all salaries due and owing as of the date of filing (if any) have been paid. Unless and in accordance with the provisions of the bar date established by the court (January 15, 1993), a claim has been timely filed and subsequently allowed for accrued vacation time, sick leave, severance pay, or bonus due prepetition or postpetition to any of the Debtors' employees or agents, no payment will be allowed.

ARTICLE 14
Vesting of Property of Estate; Liquidating Trust Establishment

14.1 Vesting of property of estate in Trust: Upon confirmation, all nonexempt assets of the estate enumerated in ¶3.5.2 shall directly vest in the Liquidating Trust, established pursuant to Article 5 of this Plan, for the benefit of the creditors. The postconfirmation estate shall retain the balance of Debtors' nonexempt property, and the postconfirmation Debtors shall retain all of their exempt property.

ARTICLE 15
Other Materials

15.1 The attention of holders of claims is directed to the Disclosure Statement approved by the Court in connection with this Plan.

ARTICLE 16
Effect of Confirmation as to Discharge; Property Acquired by Debtors Postconfirmation

16.1 Discharge: Steven H. Jones and Susan J. Jones shall, upon confirmation, be discharged from any debt arising before the confirmation date and any debt of a kind specified in §§ 502(g), 502(h), or 502(i) of the Bankruptcy Code whether or not (a) a proof of claim based upon the debt is filed or deemed filed under § 501 of the Bankruptcy Code; (b) such a claim is allowed under § 502 of the Bankruptcy Code; or (c) the holder of such claim has accepted the Plan.

16.2 Property acquired by Debtors postconfirmation: On the confirmation date, Debtors shall cease to be debtors-in-possession of any property conveyed to the Liquidating Trust. As set forth in Article VI, the postconfirmation estate will retain all nonexempt property not conveyed to the Liquidating Trust upon confirmation or thereafter. Any property Debtors may acquire after that date (including income from personal service), so long as the same is not proceeds, products, offspring, rents, or profits of property of the estate as described in § 541(a)(6), shall be free and clear of any claim against the Debtors incurred prior to the confirmation date and shall not be property of the Liquidating Trust or accountable to said Trust.

[Debtors' signatures]
[Attorney Signature]

EXHIBIT A

JONES LIQUIDATING TRUST

THIS LIQUIDATING TRUST is made effective the _______ day of _________, 199__, pursuant to Steven H. Jones and Susan J. Jones' First Amended Plan of Reorganization dated June 21, 1993 (the Plan), if and as amended, and pursuant to the order of the United States Bankruptcy Court for the District of [state], [location] (the court), dated the __ day of ____________, 199__, confirming the Plan, and is accepted by ___________________, as trustee (the trustee), upon the terms and conditions contained herein.

WITNESSETH:

WHEREAS, Steven H. Jones and Susan J. Jones (the Debtors) filed their voluntary petition for reorganization under Chapter 11 of the Bankruptcy Code in the United State Bankruptcy Court for the District of [state], [location], on September 17, 1992;

WHEREAS, the Debtors' Disclosure Statement and Plan provide for the creation of a Liquidating Trust to liquidate certain nonexempt assets of the Debtors and distribute the proceeds from such liquidation to creditors, all pursuant to the Disclosure Statement, the Plan, and the terms and conditions contained herein;

WHEREAS, the Court has confirmed the Plan establishing this Liquidating Trust and ordered the transfer of certain remaining assets from the Debtors' bankruptcy estate direct to this Liquidating Trust; and

WHEREAS, the Court retains jurisdiction over the Debtors' bankruptcy estate and over this Liquidating Trust for the purpose of ensuring that the Plan is implemented as confirmed and to resolve any issues involving this Liquidating Trust which are raised by the trustee, the Debtors, a creditor, or other party;

NOW, THEREFORE, for and in consideration of the premises and the covenants herein to be performed, and the acceptance of the Liquidating Trust by trustee, the terms and conditions of the Liquidating Trust are as follows:

ARTICLE I
DEFINITIONS

1.1 Trustee. When used herein, "trustee" shall mean and refer to that person or entity, whether one or more, who is at the time serving as trustee of the Liquidating Trust created herein.

1.2 Name of Liquidating Trust. The Liquidating Trust established hereby shall be known as the Jones Liquidating Trust.

1.3 Uniform Trustees' Powers Act. When used herein, "Uniform Trustees' Powers Act" shall mean and refer to that uniform act as adopted by the state of [name], in its present form and as amended from time to time.

1.4 Revised Uniform Principal and Income Act. When used herein, "Revised Uniform Principal and Income Act" shall mean and refer to that uniform act as adopted by the state of [name], in its present form and as amended from time to time.

1.5 Titles. Titles of items and subitems in the provisions of this Liquidating Trust are for convenience only and shall not be relied upon in construing or interpreting any provisions hereof.

1.6 Other. All definitions as set forth in the Plan are incorporated in this Liquidating Trust as if fully set forth herein.

ARTICLE II
TRANSFERS TO LIQUIDATING TRUST

2.1 Transfer of assets to Liquidating Trust. Concurrently herewith, the Debtor's bankruptcy estate, pursuant to the Disclosure Statement, the Plan, and the order of the Court confirming the Plan, has transferred to and vested in the Liquidating Trust certain nonexempt assets of the Debtors' bankruptcy estate, the receipt of which is hereby acknowledged by trustee. Trustee shall liquidate the assets and distribute the proceeds to the creditors, all upon the terms and conditions hereinafter set forth.

2.2 Description of assets. The assets transferred to and vested in the Liquidating Trust shall include but not be limited to the following:

(a) All causes of action, rights, claims, demands against any third parties, investors, individuals, or insiders with respect to any entities Debtors own or have an interest in or can assert in any fashion, whether prepetition or postpetition, including but not limited to actions under §§ 544–550 of the Bankruptcy Code, to recover assets on behalf of the bankruptcy estate and the benefit of the creditors;

(b) The Debtors' interest in Dominion Banqueshares Limited (the bank stock), A Associates, B Associates, C Associates, Northgate Ventures, and the Grandview and Kessler duplexes;

2.3 Additional documents. Debtors shall execute any and all documents and fully cooperate in effectuating the transfer and vesting of title of all personal and real property of Debtors' bankruptcy estate to and in the liquidating trust.

2.4 Retained jurisdiction. The court shall retain jurisdiction over the Debtors' bankruptcy estate and over this Liquidating Trust for the purpose of insuring that the Plan is implemented as confirmed, to resolve any issues involving this Liquidating Trust, and to assist and pass upon the liquidating trustee's efforts to liquidate the assets.

ARTICLE III
TERMINATION OF LIQUIDATING TRUST

3.1 Termination of Liquidating Trust. This Liquidating Trust shall terminate upon the earlier of (a) five (5) years from the date of the Court's order confirming the Plan, or (b) the date when all of the trust assets of the Liquidating Trust have been converted to cash and all costs, expenses, taxes, obligations, and liabilities incurred by trustee in administering or in any manner connected with this Liquidating Trust (the administrative expenses) have been fully paid and discharged and all remaining trust assets of the Liquidating Trust have been distributed to creditors.

3.2 Final report and accounting. Upon the termination of the Liquidating Trust, trustee shall file with the court a final report and accounting setting forth all the receipts and disbursements of the Liquidating Trust from its creation.

3.3 Discharge of trustee. Upon termination of the Liquidating Trust and the approval by the Court of trustee's final report and accounting, trustee shall be discharged by the Court form the duties of trustee and shall be released form further liability for all matters associated with the Liquidating Trust.

ARTICLE IV
DISTRIBUTIONS FROM LIQUIDATING TRUST

4.1 Liquidation of trust assets. Trustee shall use its best efforts and judgment to liquidate and convert to cash all of the trust assets. The timing of sales of trust assets and the consideration received therefor shall be determined by trustee, taking into account the need for a timely liquidation of the trust assets but balanced against obtaining the maximum amount of funds for distribution to creditors. The sale of the stock in Dominion Banqueshares Limited shall be subject to Court approval. Trustee shall make continuing efforts to dispose of and liquidate the trust assets, make timely distributions to creditors, and not unduly prolong the duration of this Liquidating Trust.

4.2 Allowed secured claims. To the extent trust assets subject to allowed secured claims are sold by trustee, the proceeds from the sales of those trust assets shall first be paid to those creditors who have allowed secured claims, but only to the extent such creditors' allowed secured claims cover the specific trust assets sold. Any remaining proceeds after the payment of allowed secured claims shall be distributed as provided below.

4.3 Administrative claims and trust expenses. After the payment of allowed secured claims as provided above, the remaining proceeds from the sales of trust assets shall be used for the payment of administrative claims, including tax liability, pursuant to the terms of the Plan. The administrative claims shall be a charge against the trust assets and shall be paid prior to a distribution to creditors under Section 4.4, or, alternatively, trustee shall reserve such funds prior to making a distribution to creditors under Section 4.4 to allow for the later payment of such items. The Liquidating Trust assumes in rem the tax liability to the extent provided by the Plan which, after use by the estate of its tax attributes including Debtors' passive activity losses and credits and I.R.C. § 465 losses, may constitute an administrative claim. After deductions for payment of allowed secured claims, and before deductions for payment of administrative claims, the liquidating trustee may utilize proceeds of trust assets for the payment of the Trust's administrative expenses and costs.

4.4 Allowed unsecured claims. After the payment of the amounts identified in Sections 4.2 and 4.3, trustee shall distribute all remaining proceeds and trust assets to the creditors. Any such distribution shall be made pro rata among the creditors with allowed unsecured claims based upon the amount of each creditor's unsecured claim. The time and manner of any and all such distributions shall be determined by trustee based upon available funds and the closeness in time of the last distribution.

4.5 No reversion to Debtors. In no event shall any of the trust assets of this Liquidating Trust ever revert to or become distributed to Debtors.

ARTICLE V
POWERS OF TRUSTEE

5.1 Powers conferred by Uniform Trustees' Powers Act. The trustee of the Liquidating Trust established hereunder is hereby granted all of the powers, privileges, and immunities conferred upon trustees by the Uniform Trustees' Powers Act, and shall be governed by the provisions of that Act, except as any of those provisions may be specifically limited herein or any of those provisions may be in direct conflict with the provisions hereof. Other powers conferred upon trustee herein, except to the extent that any of them may specifically limit or be in direct conflict with powers conferred by said Act, shall be deemed not to be in limitation or restriction of the powers conferred by said Act, but shall be construed as conferring additional powers and as enlargements of such powers. In dealing with trustee, third persons shall be protected and shall not be bound to inquire into the powers of trustee or to assure themselves of the proper application of trust assets paid or delivered to trustee, all in accordance with the protection afforded to third persons under said Act. More specifically, in no case shall any party dealing with trustee in any manner whatsoever in relation to the trust assets, including but not limited to any party to whom trust assets shall be conveyed or contracted to be sold by trustee, (a) be obligated to see to the application of any money or proceeds borrowed or advanced on said trust assets, (b) be obligated to see that the provisions of the Plan or the terms of this Liquidating Trust have been complied with, (c) be obligated or privileged to inquire into the necessity or expediency of any act of trustee, or (d) to inquire into any other limitation or restriction of the power and authority of trustee. As to any party dealing with trustee in any manner whatsoever in relation to the trust assets, the power of trustee to act or otherwise deal with said assets shall be absolute, provided, however, that the trustee's sale of the stock in Dominion Banqueshares Limited shall be subject to court approval.

5.2 Miscellaneous trustee powers. Trustee shall have the power and authority to perform the following acts:

(a) Perfect and secure trustee's right, title, and interest to the assets comprising the trust estate;

(b) Reduce all of the trust assets to trustee's possession and hold the same;

(c) Sell and convert the trust assets to cash and distribute the net proceeds as specified herein;

(d) Manage and protect the trust assets and distribute the net proceeds, as specified herein;

(e) Grant options to purchase, contract to sell, and sell the trust assets or any part or parts thereof for such purchase price, whether in cash or otherwise, and on such terms as trustee deems appropriate;

(f) Exchange and re-exchange the trust assets or any part or parts thereof for other real or personal property;

(g) Release, convey, or assign any right, title, or interest in or to the trust assets;

(h) Pay and discharge any costs, expenses, trustee's fees, or obligations deemed necessary to preserve the trust assets or any part thereof or to preserve this Liquidating Trust;

(i) Purchase insurance to protect from liability the trust assets, trustee, or any creditor;

(j) Deposit trust funds, draw checks, and make disbursements of trust funds;

(k) Employ and have such attorney, accountants, engineers, agents, tax specialists, real estate professionals, bank specialists, and any other assistants as may be deemed necessary by trustee;

(l) File all state and federal tax returns of whatever kind due on behalf of the Liquidating Trust or in regard to its operation, and pay any and all tax, interest, and penalty due thereon;

(m) Employ real estate brokers, salesmen, managers, or other persons necessary to operate and manage the real estate and other properties subject to this Liquidating Trust;

(n) Borrow money on either an unsecured basis or by pledging as security all or a portion of the trust assets;

(o) Issue certificates of indebtedness secured by the Trust assets;

(p) Exercise any and all powers granted to trustee by any agreements or by common law or any statute which serves to increase the extent of the powers granted to trustee hereunder;

(r) Take any action required or permitted by the Plan or by any order of the court;

(s) Engage in and carry on any business or undertaking and enter into any partnership with any person, firm, corporation, or any trustee under any other trust;

(t) Join in any Plan of Reorganization or readjustment of any individual, corporation, partnership, or other entity, or take any other action necessary to protect the trust assets;

(u) Negotiate, renegotiate, and enter into contracts and execute obligations, negotiable and nonnegotiable;

(v) Vote shares of stock in person or by proxy, with or without power of substitution;

(w) Alone or with others form, reorganize, or extend the life of any corporation or other entity and exercise or perform any and all rights, privileges, and powers herein to the holder of any stock, securities, or other evidence of ownership comprising at any time a part of the trust assets;

(x) Institute and defend causes of action;

(y) Settle, compromise, or adjust by arbitration or otherwise any disputes or controversies in favor of or against the Liquidating Trust;

(z) Waive or release rights of any kind;

(aa) Appoint, remove, and act through agents, managers, and employees, and confer upon them such power and authority as may be necessary or advisable;

(bb) Have instituted on behalf of the Liquidating Trust all claims or causes of actions which could be brought by a trustee or debtor-in-possession under the Bankruptcy Code, and prosecute or defend all appeals on behalf of Debtors; and

(cc) In general, without in any manner limiting any of the foregoing, deal with the trust assets or any part or parts thereof in all other ways as would be lawful for any person owning the same to deal therewith, whether similar to or different from the ways above specified, at any time or times hereafter.

5.3 Voting trusts. With reference to any securities held by trustee, trustee shall have full right, power, and authority to participate in and enter into voting trusts as trustee may deem advisable.

5.4 Investments. Trustee shall have full right, power, and authority to invest and reinvest any and all funds coming into its hands as a part of the Trust assets, so long as such funds are invested in accordance with 11 U.S.C. § 345 relating to the money of estates.

5.5 Nominees. Trustee shall have full right, power, and authority to hold any asset of the Liquidating Trust in the name of nominees (who may be Trustee, individually, or any other person or persons or corporations or companies selected by Trustee) or in other form without disclosure of the trust relationship, and with respect to third persons dealing with any such nominee, Trustee shall be fully liable for and bound by any act of such nominee in connection with the asset so held.

5.6 Rules of accounting. In the administration of the Liquidating Trust created hereunder, all receipts and expenditures shall be allocated between and charged to principal and income in accordance with the provisions of the Revised Uniform Principal and Income Act, except that the provisions of the Revised Uniform Principal and Income Act relating to unproductive property shall not apply.

5.7 Accounting and waiver of bond. Trustee shall keep an accounting of receipts and disbursements, which shall be open for inspection by the creditors at all reasonable times, and trustee shall otherwise keep the creditors generally informed in the matter of the Liquidating Trust. Any trustee hereunder shall be permitted to serve without the necessity of giving bond, unless the Court shall otherwise require.

5.8 Limitations on powers of trustee. Notwithstanding anything contained in this Liquidating Trust to the contrary, trustee shall not:

(a) Lend money to Debtors or any partnership, corporation or organization in which Debtors have an interest;

(b) Otherwise deal with Debtors or any partnership or corporation or other entity or organization in which Debtors have an interest except as contemplated by the Plan;

(c) Be required to surrender any assets of the trust estate upon being tendered substitute assets in exchange therefor, regardless of the relative values of the assets involved;

(d) Enter into any transaction or involvement with the Debtors which would cause this Liquidating Trust to be considered a "grantor trust" under the provisions of §§ 671–678 of the Internal Revenue Code of 1986, as amended.

ARTICLE VI
TRUSTEE

6.1 Successor trustee. In the event of the death, resignation, refusal, or inability for any reason of the original trustee to serve as trustee hereunder, a successor trustee shall be appointed by the Court, whereupon such original trustee shall convey, transfer, and set over to the named successor trustee in trust by appropriate instrument or instruments all of the trust assets then unconveyed or otherwise undisposed of and all other trust assets then in the original trustees' possession and held hereunder. Upon the death, resignation, refusal, or inability for any reason of a successor trustee to continue to serve as successor trustee hereunder, the Court shall fill the vacancy of trustee in the same manner as set forth for a replacement of the original trustee and any such vacating trustee shall make the same conveyances and transfers to the named successor trustee as were required of the original trustee. In no event shall Debtors have any power to remove any trustee, whether the original trustee or any successor trustee, or to appoint either or both of the Debtors as a successor trustee of this Liquidating Trust. Any and all successor trustees shall have all of the rights, powers, and authority and be subject to the same duties and restrictions as herein granted to and imposed upon the original trustee designated hereunder.

6.2 Compensation of trustee. Trustee shall be entitled to receive reasonable compensation commensurate with the services rendered hereunder, but no corporate trustee shall receive compensation in excess of its normal and customary fees for such services. Trustee's compensation shall be deemed earned from commencement of the Liquidating Trust, and shall constitute a charge against and be paid from the trust assets, and, in any event, the timing and extent of compensation of the trustee shall be approved by the court.

6.3 Liability of trustee and others. Trustee shall not be liable for any act trustee may do or omit to do as trustee hereunder when acting in good faith and in the exercise of trustee's best judgment. Trustee shall not be liable for the acts, negligence, or defaults of any agent or person employed by trustee or for the acts of any person into whose hands any trust funds may properly be deposited or come. However, nothing in this section shall relieve (a) any corporate trustee from liability by reason of any defalcation of its regular employees, (b) any trustee from liability for failure to participate in the administration of the Liquidating Trust or to attempt to prevent a breach of trust, or (c) any trustee from liability for trustee's gross negligence or willful default or misconduct. No successor trustee shall be liable for the acts of any prior trustee, nor for failing to investigate the propriety of the acts of any prior trustee. Furthermore, no recourse shall ever be had, directly or indirectly, against trustee personally,

Debtors personally, the creditors, or any employee of trustee, by legal or equitable proceedings or by virtue of any statute or otherwise, or any deed of trust, mortgage, pledge, note, or upon any promise, contract, instrument, undertaking, obligation, covenant, or agreement whatsoever executed by trustee, Debtors, the creditors, or by any person employed by trustee, or by reason of the creation of any indebtedness by trustee under this Liquidating Trust for any purpose authorized by Liquidating Trust. It is expressly understood and agreed that all such liabilities, covenants, and agreements of trustee, Debtors, the creditors, or any employee of trustee, whether in writing or otherwise, under this Liquidating Trust shall only be enforceable against and be satisfied out of the trust assets or such part thereof as shall under the terms of any such agreement be liable therefor. Every undertaking, contract, covenant, or agreement entered into in writing by trustee or the others mentioned above shall provide expressly against the personal liability of trustee or the others mentioned above.

6.4 Resignation of trustee. Any trustee may resign upon thirty (30) days' written notice to the Court and such resignation shall be effective upon the date provided in such notice. Upon resignation, trustee shall determine the amount of unpaid compensation owing to trustee.

ARTICLE VII
REVOCATION AND AMENDMENT

7.1 Liquidating Trust may be revoked or amended only by the court. This Liquidating Trust may not be revoked or in any manner amended by Debtors or any other person. Only the Court shall have the authority to revoke or amend the terms and provisions of this Liquidating Trust.

ARTICLE VIII
LAWS OF [STATE] TO GOVERN LIQUIDATING TRUST

8.1 Laws of [state] to govern Liquidating Trust. The terms of this Liquidating Trust shall be construed and the operations of this Liquidating Trust shall be carried on in accordance with the laws of the state of [name].

IN WITNESS WHEREOF, trustee has accepted this Liquidating Trust on the day and year first above written.

____

[Name of Trustee]

Trustee

(Notarization of signature)

CHAPTER 15

CONFIRMATION OF THE PLAN

Mark A. Shaiken

§ 15.1 Plan Confirmation Generally

Title 11 U.S.C. § 1129 contains the requirements for a Chapter 11 plan to be confirmed for all sizes of cases, including small business cases. Generally, the confirmation process in Chapter 11 involves a type of congressionally mandated democracy in which creditors vote on a proposed plan, and the court makes certain factual findings and legal conclusions about the propriety of the plan under 11 U.S.C. § 1129(a). If creditors in sufficient numbers dissent and vote to reject the plan, in certain situations, the plan proponent can seek to force the plan on the dissenting creditors in a process called *cram down* under 11 U.S.C. § 1129(b).

The plan proponent must fully satisfy every applicable requirement of § 1129(a) and (b) before confirmation can be ordered,[1] and the court has an independent duty to determine that the plan complies with the provisions of § 1129.[2] This chapter discusses five general categories of confirmation requirements: voting, feasibility, best interests of creditors, miscellaneous findings, and cram down.

§ 15.2 Who May Propose a Plan

During the first 120 days of the bankruptcy case, unless the court orders otherwise, only the debtor can propose a plan.[3] If a plan is proposed during this time period, the debtor is provided an additional 60 days to obtain confirmation of the plan.[4] After the expiration of these "exclusive" time periods, unless they are extended by the court, any party in interest can propose a plan.[5] The confirmation requirements apply regardless of whether the debtor or a party-in-interest is the plan proponent.

§ 15.3 Voting

After approval of a disclosure statement,[6] the votes of holders of claims and interests are solicited in support of the plan. A *claim* is a:

> (A) right to payment, whether or not such right is reduced to judgment, liquidated, unliquidated, fixed, contingent, matured, unmatured, disputed, undisputed, legal, equitable, secured, or unsecured; or

---

1 *In re* Martin, 66 B.R. 921 (Bankr. D. Mont. 1986).

2 *In re* Valley Park Group, Inc., 96 B.R. 16 (Bankr. N.D.N.Y. 1989); *In re* Friese, 103 B.R. 90 (Bankr. S.D.N.Y. 1989); *In re* Moore, 81 B.R. 513 (Bankr. S.D. Iowa 1988).

3 11 U.S.C. § 1121(b).

4 *Id.* § 1121(c)(3).

5 *Id.* § 1121(c).

6 "An acceptance or rejection of a plan may not be solicited after the commencement of the case under this title . . . unless, at the time of or before such solicitation, there is transmitted to such holder the plan or a summary of the plan, and a written disclosure statement approved, after notice and hearing, by the court as containing adequate information." 11 U.S.C. § 1125(b). See **Ch. 13** for detailed discussion of disclosure statements.

(B) right to an equitable remedy for breach of performance if such breach gives rise to a right to payment, whether or not such right to an equitable remedy is reduced to judgment, fixed, contingent, matured, unmatured, disputed, undisputed, secured or unsecured.[7]

An equity security holder may also file a proof of interest.[8] An *equity security* includes stock and a limited partnership interest.[9]

§ 15.4 —Classification of Claims

Under the plan, holders of claims and interests are grouped in classes.[10] Classification is based on the nature of the claims or interests classified; claims or interests can be included in a particular class only if they are substantially similar to the other claims or interests of the class.[11] A *class* is the grouping together of claims or interests to be treated under a Chapter 11 plan. "Classification is simply a method of recognizing difference in rights of creditors which calls for difference in treatment."[12] Generally,

> all creditors with equal rank and with claims against the same property are usually placed in the same class, which is a natural, logical, and simple basis for division. Conversely, creditors of different ranks or creditors of the same rank but with claims against different properties, are usually placed in different classes. Finally, any classification process should not do substantial violence to any claimant's interest, nor should it uselessly increase the number of classifications, unless there exist differences in the nature of claims . . . [C]reditors should not be arbitrarily classified or discriminated against in the classification process.[13]

§ 15.5 —Voting Solicitation

Voting solicitation requires serving 25 days' notice by mail to parties-in-interest of the time fixed for filing objections and the hearing to consider confirmation of a plan.[14] The 25-day time period may be shortened by the court pursuant to Bankruptcy Rule 9006(c). *Parties-in-interest* include the debtor, the trustee, a creditors'

---

[7] *Id.* § 101(5).

[8] *Id.* § 501(a).

[9] *Id.* § 101(16).

[10] 11 U.S.C. § 1122.

[11] H.R. Rep. No. 595, 95th Cong., 1st Sess. 406 (1979), *reprinted in* 1978 U.S.C.C.A.N. 5963.

[12] Scherk v. Newton (*In re* Rocky Mountain Fuel Co.), 152 F.2d 747, 750 (10th Cir. 1945).

[13] J. Anderson, *Classification of Claims and Interests in Reorganization Cases Under the New Bankruptcy* Code, 58 Am. Bankr. L.J. 99, 101–02 (1984).

[14] Fed. R. Bankr. P. 2002(b).

committee, an equity security holders' committee, a creditor, an equity security holder, an indenture trustee, and the Securities and Exchange Commission.[15]

In conjunction with approval of the disclosure statement, the court fixes a date by which holders of claims and interests may vote to accept or reject the plan,[16] and notice is sent to parties-in-interest. In this notice, creditors and equity security holders must receive:

(1) The plan, or a court-approved summary of the plan
(2) The disclosure statement approved by the court
(3) Notice of the time within which acceptances and rejections of such plan may be filed
(4) Notice of any date fixed for the hearing on confirmation
(5) Such other information as the court may direct, including any opinion of the court approving the disclosure statement or a court-approved summary of the opinion.

In addition, a ballot conforming to Official Bankruptcy Form No. 14[17] must be mailed to creditors and equity security holders entitled to vote on the plan. If a summary of the plan is transmitted, a copy of the plan must be made available to parties-in-interest at the expense of the plan proponent.[18]

§ 15.6 —Official Bankruptcy Form: Ballot for Accepting or Rejecting Plan

FORM 15-1
OFFICIAL BANKRUPTCY FORMS

Form 14

BALLOT FOR ACCEPTING OR REJECTING PLAN

[Caption as in Form 16A]

BALLOT FOR ACCEPTING OR REJECTING PLAN

Filed By ____
on [date] ____.

The plan referred to in this ballot can be confirmed by the court and thereby made binding on you if it is accepted by the holders of two-thirds in amount

15 11 U.S.C. § 1109; Fed. R. Bankr. P. 2018.

16 Fed. R. Bankr. P. 3017(c).

17 A copy of Official Bankr. Form No. 14 is included in § **15.6.**

18 Fed. R. Bankr. P. 3017(d).

and more than one-half in number of claims in each class and the holders of two-thirds in amount of equity security interests in each class voting on the plan. In the event the requisite acceptances are not obtained, the court may nevertheless confirm the plan if the court finds that the plan accords fair and equitable treatment to the class or classes rejecting it and otherwise satisfies the requirements of § 1129(b) of the Code. To have your vote count you must complete and return this ballot.

[If holder of general claim] The undersigned, a creditor of the above-named debtor in the unpaid principal amount of $__________________,

[If bondholder, debenture holder, or other debt security holder] The undersigned, the holder of [state unpaid principal amount] $________________ of [describe security] ____________________________ of the above-named debtor, with a stated maturity date of __________________, [if applicable] registered in the name of ____________________________________, [if applicable] bearing serial number(s) __________________________,

[If equity security holder] The undersigned, the holder of [state number] __________ shares of [describe type] ____________________________stock of the above named debtor, represented by Certificate(s) No. ________________, [or held in my/our brokerage Account No. _________ at [name of broker-dealer] _________________________,

[Check One Box]

[ ] Accepts

[ ] Rejects

the plan for the reorganization of the above-named debtor proposed by [name of proponent] ____________________________,

and [if more than one plan is to be voted on]

[ ] Accepts

[ ] Rejects

the plan for the reorganization of the above-named debtor proposed by [name of proponent] ____________________________.

[If more than one plan is accepted, the following may but need not be completed.] The undersigned prefers the plans accepted in the following order.

[Identify plans]

1. ____.

2. ____.

Dated: ______________________

Print or type name :______________________

Signed :______________________

[If appropriate] By :______________________

as :______________________

Address :______________________

Return this ballot on or before ____________ to : ______________________
(date) (name)

Address : ______________________

____

§ 15.7 —Voting Requirements and Acceptance

The following entities are permitted to vote:

1. Creditors with allowed claims[19]
2. Creditors that are security holders of record as of the date of the order approving the disclosure statement whose claims have not been disallowed[20]
3. Equity security holders of record as of the date of the order approving the disclosure statement whose interest has not been disallowed.[21]

Moreover, even if an objection to a claim or interest is pending, the court may still permit the holder of such a claim or interest to vote.[22] The court can disallow the vote of any entity whose vote was not solicited, procured, or cast in good faith.[23]

---

19 11 U.S.C. § 1126(a); Fed. R. Bankr. P. 3018(a). A claim may be deemed allowed pursuant to 11 U.S.C. § 502 if the creditor files a proof of claim to which no objection has been filed, or if the court has entered an order specifically allowing the claim.

20 Fed. R. Bankr. P. 3018(a).

21 *Id.*

22 "Notwithstanding objection to a claim or interest, the court after notice and hearing may temporarily allow the claim or interest in an amount which the court deems proper for the purpose of accepting or rejecting a plan." Fed. R. Bankr. P. 3018(a).

23 11 U.S.C. § 1126(e). *See, e.g.,* Insinger Mach. Co. v. Federal Support Co. (*In re* Federal Support Co.), 859 F.2d 17, 19 (4th Cir. 1988) (good faith in casting a vote does not require a selfless disinterest; each creditor is expected to cast its vote in accordance

A class of claims accepts the plan if at least two-thirds in amount and more than one-half in number of the allowed claims in the class that have voted have accepted the plan.[24] Unimpaired classes are deemed to have accepted the plan.[25] Generally, a class is *impaired* if its legal, equitable, or contract rights are altered in any fashion.[26] Classes whose claimants or interest holders receive or retain no property under the plan are deemed to have rejected the plan.[27]

§ 15.8 —Manipulation of Classification and Impairment Requirements

One of the cornerstone requirements of confirmation is that at least one impaired, non-insider class must accept the plan, if there are any impaired classes.[28] Thus, the plan proponent cannot confirm a plan absent the acceptance of at least one impaired class. An insider of an individual debtor includes a relative of the debtor, a relative of a general partner of the debtor, a partnership in which the debtor is a general partner, a general partner of the debtor and any corporation in which the debtor is an officer, director, or person in control. An insider of a debtor corporation includes the director, officer, or person in control of the debtor, a partnership in which the debtor is a general partner, the general partner of the debtor, or a relative of the general partner, director, officer, or person in control of the debtor. An insider of a debtor partnership includes the general partner of the debtor, relative of a general partner in, general partner of, or person in control of the debtor, partnership in which the debtor is a general partner, general partner of the debtor, or person in control of the debtor. In addition, an insider includes an affiliate or insider of an affiliate of the debtor, and a managing agent of the debtor.[29]

Because of the "one accepting, non-insider, impaired class" requirement of § 1129(a)(10), some debtors have attempted to use the classification process to manipulate and create such an accepting class. One common debtor strategy is to classify impaired trade creditors holding unsecured claims separately from impaired undersecured creditors holding an unsecured claim to the extent the debt exceeds the

---

with its perception of its own self-interest, but it may not act with an ulterior or coercive purpose.); *In re* MacLeod Co., 63 B.R. 654, 656 (Bankr. S.D. Ohio 1986) (vote invalidated because it "was for the ulterior purpose of destroying or injuring debtor in its business so that the interests of the competing business with which the named individuals were associated, could be furthered.") *See also In re* Wiston XXIV, L.P., 153 B.R. 322 (Bankr. D. Kan. 1993).

24 11 U.S.C. § 1126(c).

25 *Id.* § 1126(f). Solicitation of acceptances from holders of claimants or interests in a "deemed accepted" class is not required. *Id.*

26 *See also* 641 Assocs., Ltd. v. Balcor Real Estate Fin., Inc. (*In re* 641 Assocs., Ltd.), 140 B.R. 619 (Bankr. E.D. Pa. 1992).

27 11 U.S.C. § 1126(g).

28 11 U.S.C. § 1129(a)(10). *See In re* Smith, 123 B.R. 863, 866 (Bankr. C.D. Cal. 1991) ("impairment" interpreted very broadly to include alteration of any of a claimant's rights in any respect).

29 *See* 11 U.S.C. § 101(31). For the definition of *affiliate, see id.* § 101(2).

value of the collateral. Pursuant to 11 U.S.C. § 506(a), the allowed amount of a secured claim is equal to the value of a creditor's interest in collateral. To the extent the creditor is owed more than the value of the collateral, the creditor has an unsecured claim. For example, under § 506(a), a creditor that is owed $300,000 and has a security interest in property worth $100,000 has an allowed secured claim of $100,000 and an unsecured claim of $200,000. This strategy of separating impaired trade creditors from undersecured creditors in the hopes that one class will accept has met with varying degrees of success.[30]

For example, in *In re Lumber Exchange Limited Partnership,*[31] the debtor owed $207,300 to unsecured trade creditors and in excess of $20 million to a secured creditor whose collateral was worth $7 million. The debtor proposed more favorable treatment to the secured creditor than to the unsecured trade creditors and separately classified the two groups. The secured creditor did not accept the plan, while the unsecured trade creditors did. The debtor argued that at least one impaired class had accepted the plan pursuant to 11 U.S.C. § 1129(a)(10), based "on the distinction between unsecured trade creditors and unsecured creditors who are also partially secured."[32] The court held against the debtor, saying:

> The separate classification of [the secured creditor's] undersecured claim is a thinly veiled attempt to manipulate the vote to assure acceptance of the plan by an impaired class and meet the requirement of 11 U.S.C. § 1129(a)(10).[33]

In *Windsor on the River Associates, Ltd. v. Balcor Real Estate Finance, Inc. (In re Windsor on the River Associates, Ltd.),*[34] the Eighth Circuit Court of Appeals did not permit artificial classification of claims "in order to achieve literal compliance with section 1129(a)(10)," noting,

> to achieve cram down under section 1129(a)(10) . . . many debtors have attempted to classify the often large unsecured portion of the principal creditor's claim separately from small unsecured trade claims. This is done to prevent the principal creditor from blocking approval of the debtor's plan, which a slightly impaired class of trade claimants might be persuaded to give, in light of the alternative specter of liquidation.[35]

In *Phoenix Mutual Life Insurance Co. v. Greystone III Joint Venture (In re Greystone III Joint Venture),*[36] a lender's $3.5 million deficiency claim was separately classified from the debtor's trade debt of $10,000. The Fifth Circuit Court of Appeals, reversing both the bankruptcy and the district courts, did not approve of this classification.[37]

---

30 *See* P. Meltzer, *Disenfranchising the Dissenting Creditor Through Artificial Classification or Artificial Impairment,* 66 Am. Bankr. L.J. 281 (1992).

31 125 B.R. 1000 (Bankr. D. Minn. 1991).

32 *Id.* at 1006.

33 *Id.*

34 7 F.3d 127 (8th Cir. 1993).

35 *Id.* at 129.

36 948 F.2d 134 (5th Cir.), *amended on petition for reh'g,* 948 F.2d 142 (5th Cir. 1991).

37 *Id.* at 141.

On the other hand, in *Teamsters National Freight Industry Negotiating Committee v. U.S. Truck Co. (In re U.S. Truck Co.),*[38] the Sixth Circuit Court of Appeals permitted separate classification of unsecured creditors even though the debtor admitted that the purpose of the separate classification was to line up votes in favor of the plan, because the claims in question were uniquely different.[39]

Debtors have also attempted to "artificially impair" classes to comply with 11 U.S.C. § 1129(a)(10), by paying slightly less than the full claims. In *In re Lettick Typografic, Inc.,*[40] the debtor proposed to defer payment to a secured claimant by only 15 days. The court refused to confirm the plan, stating that the debtor's proposal was a "transparent attempt to stage compliance with section [1129](a)(10), [and] . . . create . . . an artificially impaired class."[41] On the other hand, in *B.M. Brite v. Sun Country Development, Inc. (In re Sun Country Development, Inc.),*[42] the court approved artificial impairment, analyzing the issue under the good faith standard of § 1129(a)(3).

The issue of artificial classification and impairment is important in small business cases. Often, it is a struggle for a small business to reach agreement with its principal undersecured creditor in the plan process. Moreover, the undersecured creditor's unsecured claim can be so substantial that it holds a sufficient amount of the total unsecured debt to cause the unsecured class to dissent solely by its negative vote. For example, if a debtor has $100,000 of trade creditors, and an undersecured creditor whose collateral is worth $500,000 less than the total debt, the undersecured creditor's unsecured claim is $500,000[43] and constitutes over 80 percent of the total unsecured claims.

Several courts have addressed the propriety of separately classifying an undersecured creditor's unsecured claim from general unsecured claims. Title 11 U.S.C. § 1111(b) provides a deficiency claim to an undersecured, nonrecourse creditor that would otherwise have no deficiency claim under state law because the loan is nonrecourse. Courts have struggled with the issue of whether a debtor may separately classify a nonrecourse creditor's unsecured § 1111(b) deficiency claim. In *In re Greystone III Joint Venture,*[44] the court held that an unsecured deficiency claim created by § 1111(b) was substantially similar to general unsecured claims and therefore could not be separately classified from such unsecured claims. More recently, some courts have split as to whether it is proper, if not required, to separately classify the undersecured creditor's unsecured claim from general unsecured claims. In *In re D&W Realty Corp.,*[45] the district court, in a single-asset real estate case, rejected the bankruptcy court's ruling that separate classification of a nonrecourse undersecured mortgagee's unsecured claim was statutorily mandated by § 1111(b).

---

[38] 800 F.2d 581 (6th Cir. 1986).

[39] *Id.* at 586–87 n.9.

[40] 103 B.R. 32 (Bankr. D. Conn. 1989).

[41] *Id.* at 38.

[42] 764 F.2d 406 (5th Cir. 1985).

[43] *See* 11 U.S.C. § 506(a).

[44] 995 F.2d 1274, 1279–80 (5th Cir. 1991).

[45] 165 B.R. 127 (S.D.N.Y. 1994) *rev'g* 156 B.R. 140 (Bankr. S.D.N.Y. 1993).

Under § 1111(b), the bankruptcy court had reasoned that a "class of secured creditors" may elect to have their claims treated as fully secured.[46] The court held § 1111(b) was irrelevant to the unsecured claim classification issue. It disagreed with the bankruptcy court's reasoning that because the § 1111(b) election decision is a class decision, all of the rights of the secured creditor, including its unsecured rights, must be separately classified from general unsecured creditors.[47] In *In re SM 104 Ltd.*,[48] the court held that separate classification of a mortgagee's deficiency claim was permissible,[49] reasoning that outside of a bankruptcy case, a nonrecourse creditor has no unsecured claim rights against the debtor, and, further, that if the § 1111(b) nonrecourse unsecured claim was classified in the same class as general unsecured creditors, the general unsecured creditors would have the opportunity to vote on whether the § 1111(b)(2) election could be made.[50]

Therefore, if the undersecured creditor rejects the plan, a single class consisting of both the trade creditors and the undersecured creditor will be a dissenting class because less than two-thirds in amount of voting class members will have accepted the plan.[51] In order to comply with the accepting class requirement of 11 U.S.C. § 1129(a)(10), artificial classification and impairment, or a § 1111(b) classification, if permitted, may be the debtor's only hope.

§ 15.9 —Creditor Voting Manipulation

Not to be outdone, creditors have also taken steps to affect the outcome of voting by purchasing claims to control more of a class vote. In such a case, the motive and intent of the claim-purchasing creditor will be examined by the court.[52]

Thus, although the voting requirements are easy enough to state, significant jockeying can occur between the debtor's attempts to comply with § 1129(a)(10) by obtaining an accepting, non-insider class, and the creditors' attempts to block such acceptance.

§ 15.10 Feasibility

The court must find that "confirmation of the plan is not likely to be followed by the liquidation, or the need for further financial reorganization, of the debtor or any

---

46 11 U.S.C. § 1111(b)(2).

47 *Compare* 165 B.R. 127 at 128–29 *with* 156 B.R. 140 at 144.

48 160 B.R. 202 (Bankr. S.D. Fla. 1993).

49 *Id.* at 221.

50 *Id.* at 220 (citing *In re* D&W Realty Corp., 156 B.R. 140 (Bankr. S.D.N.Y. 1993)).

51 11 U.S.C. § 1126(c).

52 *See In re* Gilbert, 104 B.R. 206, 217 (Bankr. W.D. Mo. 1989) ("As long as a creditor acts to preserve what he reasonably perceives as his fair share of the debtor's estate, bad faith will not be attributed to his purchase of claims to control a class vote."). *See generally* R. Lieb, *Vultures Beware: Risks of Purchasing Claims Against a Chapter 11 Debtor,* 48 Bus. Law. 915 (1993).

successor to the debtor under the plan."[53] This so-called *feasibility requirement* is a fact determination by the court as to whether the debtor will likely be able to do what it proposes in the plan.[54] Typically, to show that a plan is feasible, the debtor's projections of future income may be higher than current and historical cash flows, and the payout under the plan may be over a long period of time. Courts have been troubled both by unrealistic income and cash flow projections, based on conjecture rather than fact,[55] and by extremely long-term payouts.[56]

To deal with a lack of current cash flow, debtors have proposed plans that defer principal payments until a time in the future, calling for interest-only payments followed by a balloon payment at which time all outstanding principal owing will be paid, usually either through a future refinancing or a future sale of assets. Debtors have faced feasibility issues in attempting to confirm plans calling for balloon payments at the end of a specified period of time,[57] based on the lack of factual proof of the ability to obtain financing or sell assets in the future.

Additionally, debtors have attempted to confirm negative amortization plans, with mixed results. Negative amortization occurs when a plan attempts to defer all or part of interest due on a secured claim, requiring such deferred interest to accrue, to be added to the principal, and to be paid later when income is higher or when the collateral is sold.[58] Courts often hold that such plans are not feasible because of the speculative nature of the debtor's ability to service an increased principal debt amount in the future.[59] Other courts have permitted such plans when the collateral securing the claim was worth more than the debt[60] or the collateral was likely to increase in value.[61] In addition, the courts have generally applied the following 10-part test to determine if such plans are feasible:

---

[53] 11 U.S.C. § 1129(a)(11).

[54] Historically,

> "'feasibility' has been synonymous with 'practicability.' The requirement of feasibility simply means will the plan work? . . . It was not the intention of Congress to place crutches under corporate cripples and send them out into the business world to be a menace to all who might purchase their securities or deal with them on credit. The word 'feasible' does not connote absolute assurance of success. It means reasonable assurance of success." 11 H. Remington, A Treatise on the Bankruptcy Law of the United States § 4583, at 348–49 (1961).

[55] *See In re* Stuart Motel, Inc., 8 B.R. 48 (Bankr. S.D. Fla. 1980); *In re* Great Northern Protective Service, Inc., 19 B.R. 802 (Bankr. W.D. Wash. 1982).

[56] *In re* White, 36 B.R. 199 (Bankr. D. Kan. 1983).

[57] *See, e.g., In re* James Wilson Assocs., 965 F.2d 160 (7th Cir. 1992); *In re* Hollanger, 15 B.R. 35 (Bankr. W.D. La. 1981); *In re* Crotty, 11 B.R. 507 (Bankr. N.D. Tex. 1981).

[58] *See In re* Club Assocs., 107 B.R. 385, 398 (Bankr. N.D. Ga. 1989).

[59] *See In re* M&S Assocs., Ltd., 138 B.R. 845 (Bankr. W.D. Tex. 1992); *In re* Edgewater Motel, Inc., 85 B.R. 989 (Bankr. E.D. Tenn. 1988); *In re* Anderson Oaks (Phase I), Ltd., 77 B.R. 108 (Bankr. W.D. Tex. 1987).

[60] *See, e.g.,* Travelers Ins. Co. v. Pikes Peak Water Co. (*In re* Pikes Peak Water Co.), 779 F.2d 1456 (10th Cir. 1985); *In re* Club Assocs., 107 B.R. 385 (Bankr. N.D. Ga. 1989).

[61] 641 Assocs., Ltd. v. Balcor Real Estate Fin., Inc. (*In re* 641 Assocs., Ltd.), 140 B.R. 619, 630–632 (Bankr. E.D. Pa. 1992).

1. Does the plan offer a market rate of interest and present value of the deferred payments as required by § 1129(b)(2)(A)?
2. Is the amount and length of the proposed deferral of interest reasonable?
3. Is the ratio of debt to value of the property satisfactory throughout the plan?
4. Are the debtors' financial projections reasonable and sufficiently proven, or is the plan feasible?
5. What is the nature of the collateral, and is the value of the collateral appreciating, depreciating, or stable?
6. Are the risks unduly shifted to the creditor?
7. Are the risks borne by one secured creditor or class of secured creditors?
8. Does the plan preclude the secured creditor's foreclosure?
9. Did the original loan terms provide for negative amortization?
10. Are there adequate safeguards to protect the secured creditor against plan failure?[62]

Although numerous courts recognize that negative amortization plans are not per se improper or infeasible,[63] the courts also recognize that such plans are "suspect" and are not often confirmed.[64] The decision of whether a negative amortization plan is feasible is fact-intensive and is subject to the clearly erroneous standard of appellate review.[65]

§ 15.11 Best Interests of Creditors

To confirm a plan, the court must find that the holders of claims either accept the plan or

> will receive or retain under the plan on account of such claim or interest property of a value, as of the effective date of the plan, that is not less than the amount that such holder would so receive or retain if the debtor were liquidated under Chapter 7 of this title on such date.[66]

---

62 *See In re* Apple Tree Partners, 131 B.R. 380 (Bankr. W.D. Tenn. 1991); Great W. Bank v. Sierra Woods Group, 953 F.2d 1174, 1178 (9th Cir. 1992).

63 Only one court to date has held that negative amortization plans are per se improper. *In re* McCombs Properties VIII, Ltd., 91 B.R. 907 (Bankr. C.D. Cal. 1988). In Great W. Bank v. Sierra Woods Group, 953 F.2d 1174 (9th Cir. 1992), however, the circuit court disapproved of the per se prohibition against negative amortization plans, and therefore, *McCombs* is no longer viable.

64 *See In re* M&S Assocs., Ltd., 138 B.R. 845, 850 (Bankr. W.D. Tex. 1992); 641 Assocs., Ltd. v. Balcor Real Estate Fin., Inc. (*In re* 641 Assocs., Ltd.), 140 B.R. 619, 630 (Bankr. E.D. Pa. 1992).

65 Great W. Bank v. Sierra Woods Group, 953 F.2d 1174, 1176 (9th Cir. 1992).

66 11 U.S.C. § 1129(a)(7)(A)(ii).

This requirement is known as the *best interest test.* The best interest test requires the plan proponent to show the distribution that creditors would receive in a Chapter 7 liquidation as compared to what the creditors will receive or retain under the proposed plan. It requires the plan proponent to perform an analysis valuing the debtor's assets that would be distributed in a Chapter 7 liquidation case, and, if the debtor is a partnership, the assets of any general partners must also be valued.[67] Then the plan proponent must determine the extent of claims against the debtor, calculate the amount that would be paid to such claimants in the hypothetical liquidation, including general partners' assets,[68] and compare it to the amount proposed to be paid to claimants under the plan.

§ 15.12 Miscellaneous Findings

The court must also find that the plan was proposed in good faith,[69] that the plan and its proponent comply with the applicable provisions of the Bankruptcy Code,[70] that all professional fees are approved or subject to approval by the court,[71] that the engagement or appointment of all postconfirmation officers, directors, paid insiders, and voting trustees are disclosed and proper,[72] that all administrative and tax claims are properly treated,[73] and that all United States Trustee fees are paid or provided for in the plan.[74] Generally, actual and necessary costs and expenses of the estate[75] and other administrative expenses must be paid in full on the effective date of the plan, absent agreement of the claim holders to the contrary. Certain employee, consumer, and agricultural claims under §§ 507 (a)(3), (4), (5), and (6) must be paid in full on the effective date of the plan unless such claimants agree to deferred payments. Finally, tax claims may be paid over a maximum of six years.[76]

§ 15.13 Cram Down

Subject to the voting requirements discussed in §§ **15.7** through **15.8,** a proposed Chapter 11 plan can be confirmed over a dissenting class under the cram down provision of 11 U.S.C. § 1129(b):

---

67 *Id.* § 723(a).

68 *Id.*

69 11 U.S.C. § 1129(a)(3).

70 *Id.* §§ 1129(a)(1) and (2).

71 *Id.* § 1129(a)(4).

72 *Id.* § 1129(a)(5).

73 *Id.* § 1129(a)(9).

74 *Id.* § 1129(a)(12).

75 11 U.S.C. § 503(b)(1).

76 *Id.* § 1129(a)(9)(C).

> Notwithstanding section 510(a) of this title, if all of the applicable requirements of subsection (a) of this section other than paragraph (8) [requiring acceptance by each impaired class] are met with respect to a plan, the court, on request of the proponent of the plan, shall confirm the plan notwithstanding the requirements of such paragraph if the plan does not discriminate unfairly, and is fair and equitable, with respect to each class of claims or interests that is impaired under, and has not accepted, the plan.[77]

The plan may be crammed down if it does not discriminate unfairly against the dissenting class and if the plan's treatment of the dissenting class is fair and equitable. The *unfair discrimination requirement* of confirmation is not defined in the statute, but

> is intended . . . to permit the court to evaluate the complex relationship inherent in the relative priority of classes caused by partial subordination. . . . [I]f the plan protects the legal rights of a dissenting class in a manner consistent with the treatment of other classes whose legal rights are intertwined with those of the dissenting class, then the plan does not discriminate unfairly with respect to the dissenting class.[78]

"A plan that does discriminate unfairly gives unequal treatment to creditors who are similarly situated regarding legal rights and priority."[79] As discussed in **§ 15.15,** the Bankruptcy Code sets out specific fair and equitable requirements for secured creditor cram down in 11 U.S.C. § 1129(b)(2). Additionally, *fair and equitable* requires that a class senior to a dissenting class cannot receive in excess of 100 percent of its claims.[80]

§ 15.14 —Unfair Discrimination Against Secured Claims

Often, a debtor will attempt to alter the interest rate paid to a secured creditor under a plan.[81] Some courts have had to decide an unfair discrimination issue when a plan proposed to pay a reduced interest rate to a senior secured creditor while paying a higher interest rate to a junior mortgagee,[82] and at least one court justified a higher rate of interest for a junior lienholder because the junior lienholder had a greater risk of nonpayment than the senior lienholder.[83] Another discrimination issue arises when debtors seek to pay secured creditors over different lengths of time, depending on the nature of the collateral at issue (land versus equipment) and the rate of

---

77 11 U.S.C. § 1129(b)(1).

78 K. Klee, *All You Ever Wanted To Know About Cram Down Under The New Bankruptcy Code,* 53 Am. Bankr. L.J. 133, 141–42 (1979).

79 J. Friedman, *What Courts Do To Secured Creditors In Chapter 11 Cram Down,* 14 Cardozo L. Rev. 1495, 1502 (1993).

80 *See* 124 Cong. Rec. H. 11,104 (daily ed. Sept. 28, 1978) (statement of Rep. Edwards).

81 *See* 11 U.S.C. §§ 1123(a) and (b).

82 *E.g., In re* Dilts, 100 B.R. 759, 762–63 (Bankr. W.D. Pa. 1989).

83 *See In re* Buttonwood Partners, Ltd., 111 B.R. 57, 63 (Bankr. S.D.N.Y. 1990).

depreciation.[84] Additionally, as discussed in § **15.8,** courts have struggled with the discriminatory nature of separate classification and disparate treatment of unsecured claims.

§ 15.15 —Fair and Equitable Treatment of Secured Claims

A plan's treatment of a dissenting secured class is fair and equitable if it provides:

> (i)(I) that the holders of such claims retain the liens securing such claims . . . ; and
> (II) that each holder of a claim of such class receive on account of such claim deferred cash payments totalling at least the allowed amount of such claim, of a value, as of the effective date of the plan, of at least the value of such holder's interest in the estate's interest in such property;
> (ii) for the sale, subject to section 363(k) of this title, of any property that is subject to the liens securing such claims, free and clear of such liens, with such liens to attach to the proceeds of such sale, and the treatment of such liens or proceeds under clause (i) or (iii) of this subparagraph; or
> (iii) for the realization by such holders of the indubitable equivalent of such claims.[85]

Under these provisions, the debtor has three basic options: (a) sell the asset with the secured creditor's lien attaching to the proceeds;[86] (b) offer the "indubitable equivalent," including abandonment of the collateral to the creditor[87] or a replacement lien on similar collateral;[88] or (c) pay periodic cash payments over time.

---

[84] *See In re* Martin, 66 B.R. 921, 929–30 (Bankr. D. Mont. 1986) (largest secured creditor with lien on real estate paid out in 20 years, while other secured creditors with security interests in personal property were paid in full over three years); Prudential Ins. Co. of Am. v. Monnier (*In re* Monnier Bros.), 755 F.2d 1336, 1342 (8th Cir. 1985) (not unfair or discriminatory for one oversecured creditor with equity cushion protection to receive full compensation later than all other unsecured creditors).

[85] 11 U.S.C. § 1129(b)(2)(A).

[86] In such a sale, the creditor has the right to "credit-bid" to the extent of its debt at the asset sale and to purchase the asset. 11 U.S.C. § 363(k).

[87] *See* 11 U.S.C. §§ 554, 1107. *See also* Sandy Ridge Dev. Corp. v. Louisiana Nat'l Bank (*In re* Sandy Ridge Dev. Corp.), 881 F.2d 1346, 1350 (5th Cir. 1989) ("[P]roperty is the indubitable equivalent of itself.").

[88] B.M. Brite v. Sun Country Dev., Inc. (*In re* Sun Country Dev., Inc.), 764 F.2d 406 (5th Cir. 1985) (first lien on 200 acres released in exchange for 21 specified notes secured by 21 separate lots sold to various individual purchasers); Metropolitan Life Ins. Co. v. San Felipe & Voss, Ltd. (*In re* San Felipe & Voss, Ltd.), 115 B.R. 526 (S.D. Tex. 1990) (combination of equity securities of a third-party purchaser of an office building pledged to secured creditor and partial cash payment and a limited guarantee constitutes indubitable equivalent of first priority mortgage lien). Some courts, however, have not approved collateral substitutions. *See, e.g., In re* Hoff, 54 B.R. 746, 753–54 (Bankr. D.N.D. 1985) (substitution of a security interest in livestock for future crops was not the indubitable equivalent); *In re* Griffiths, 27 B.R. 873 (Bankr. D. Kan. 1983) (return

Under the cash payment plan, three conditions must be met. First, the creditor must receive payments over time with a present value equal to the creditor's interest in the property.[89] *Present value* or the *time value of money* "means a dollar received today is usually worth more than a dollar to be received in one year, so that interest must be paid as compensation for delay in payment."[90] Second, the creditor must receive payments totalling the allowed amount of the creditor's secured claim.[91] A secured creditor has the option of electing to have its undersecured claim treated as fully secured pursuant to 11 U.S.C. § 1111(b)(2). If the "election" is made, the creditor waives the unsecured portion of its claim and has a secured claim for the full extent of the debt owing.[92] The last condition for a cash payment plan is that the creditor must retain a lien on collateral to secure the allowed amount of the secured claim. If the election is made, the secured creditor must still receive payments with a present value equal to the creditor's interest in the property, but the total payments received must be equal to the total amount owed to the secured creditor, and not just the extent of the value of collateral. Moreover, the creditor must retain a lien on the collateral to secure the entire claim, not just the value of the collateral.[93] An election under § 1111(b) can be used to protect the creditor from being cashed out in a depressed market in which the collateral nevertheless has the potential to appreciate in the future.[94]

Typically, in a cash payout cram down of a secured creditor, the debtor attempts to adjust the interest rate[95] and to stretch out the payment of principal and interest.[96] Additionally, the value of the collateral becomes crucial, with the debtor often attempting to assign a low value to the asset in order to establish a small secured claim that must be paid over time and thereby reduce the amount of each periodic payment.[97]

---

of a portion of collateral plus a lump sum payment equal to the value of the remaining collateral, notwithstanding an election by secured creditor under § 1111(b)(2) held not the indubitable equivalent).

89 11 U.S.C. § 1129(b)(2)(A)(i)(II).

90 *See* J. Pusateri, L. Swartz, & M. Shaiken, *Section 1111(b) of the Bankruptcy Code: How Much Does the Debtor Have to Pay and When Should the Creditor Elect?*, 58 Am. Bankr. L.J. 129, 137 (1984).

91 11 U.S.C. § 1129(b)(2)(A)(i)(II).

92 *See generally* J. Pusateri, L. Swartz, & M. Shaiken, *Section 1111(b) of the Bankruptcy Code: How Much Does the Debtor Have to Pay and When Should The Creditor Elect?*, 58 Am. Bankr. L.J. 129 (1984).

93 *Id.*

94 *See In re* Water Gap Village, 99 B.R. 226 (Bankr. D.N.J. 1989); J. Stein, *Providing Undersecured Creditors with Postconfirmation Appreciation in the Value of the Collateral,* 56 Am. Bankr. L.J. 195 (1982).

95 For a discussion of the interest rate adjustment cases, see J. Friedman, *What Courts Do to Secured Creditors in Chapter 11 Cram Down,* 14 Cardozo L. Rev. 1495, 1512–21 (1993).

96 For a discussion of the stretch-out periods, see *id.* at 1522–23.

97 For a discussion of valuation issues, see P. Fitzgerald, *Bankruptcy Code Section 506(A) and Undersecured Creditors: What Date for Valuation?*, 34 UCLA L. Rev. 1953 (1987); J. Queenan, Jr., *Valuation of Security Interests in Chapter 11,* 92 Com. L.J. 18 (1987); 5 Collier on Bankruptcy ¶ 1129.03 [f], at 1129-96 to -111 (15th Ed. 1993). See also **Ch. 11.**

§ 15.16 —Cram Down over Objection of Unsecured Class

A plan is fair and equitable to a dissenting class of unsecured creditors if:

(i) the plan provides that each holder of a claim of such class receive or retain on account of such claim property of a value, as of the effective date of the plan, equal to the allowed amount of such claim; or

(ii) the holder of any claim or interest that is junior to the claims of such class will not receive or retain under the plan on account of such junior claim or interest any property.[98]

Under § 1129(b)(2)(B), either the claims of unsecured creditors must be paid in full with interest, or no junior class may receive or retain any property. The latter requirement is known as the *absolute priority rule,* discussed in detail in **Chapter 16.**

§ 15.17 —Cram Down over Objection of Interest Holders

The requirements for cram down over the objection of dissenting interest holders is almost identical to the unsecured class cram down requirements: interest holders must be paid in full or no junior interest holders may retain or receive anything under the plan.[99]

§ 15.18 —Cram Down Observations

Cram down can be viewed as the ultimate battle between debtor and creditor. The debtor, perhaps with nothing to lose and facing only the alternative of liquidation and demise, proposes significant alterations of the treatment of the creditors' claims, such as interest rate adjustment, stretch-out, and negative amortization. The stakes are high. The court has very broad powers, and, very often, cases that begin with the prospect of a contested cram down end in settlement and a consensual plan.[100]

§ 15.19 Confirmation Order

Upon satisfying the requirements of §§ 1129(a) and, if a class dissents, (b), the court enters an order confirming the plan. A sample confirmation order appears in

---

98 11 U.S.C. § 1129(b)(2)(B).

99 11 U.S.C. § 1129(b)(2)(C).

100 *See* R. Broude, *Cram Down and Chapter 11 of the Bankruptcy Code: The Settlement Imperative,* 39 Bus. Law. 441 (1984); *see also* J. Friedman, *What Courts Do to Secured Creditors in Chapter 11 Cram Down,* 14 Cardozo L. Rev. 1495, 1497 (1993).

§ 15.20. The court is only permitted to confirm one plan. If more than one confirmable plan has been proposed, the court must consider the preferences of creditors and equity security holders in determining which plan to confirm.[101] Additionally, if requested by a governmental unit, the court may not confirm a plan if the principal purpose of the plan is the avoidance of taxes or the avoidance of any application of § 5 of the Securities Act of 1933.[102]

§ 15.20 —Form: Confirmation Order

FORM 15–2
CONFIRMATION ORDER

IN THE UNITED STATES BANKRUPTCY COURT
FOR THE [EASTERN DISTRICT OF PENNSYLVANIA]

IN RE: CHAPTER 11
[JOHN Q. SMITH,]
Debtor CASE NO.

ORDER CONFIRMING PLAN OF REORGANIZATION

[John Q. Smith] (the Debtor), Debtor-In-Possession in the above-captioned Chapter 11 case, has proposed and filed a Plan of Reorganization (including all exhibits thereto, the Plan) under Chapter 11 of Title 11 of the United States Code (the Code) on [May 27, 1993].

A copy of the Plan and of the Disclosure Statement approved by the Court on [May 23, 1993] (the Disclosure Statement) was transmitted to all holders of claims and interests, and a hearing on confirmation of the Plan was held by the Court on June 20, 1993. The Debtor, the official unsecured creditors' committee (the Committee), and [United National Bank (United)] appeared through their respective attorneys of record. After consideration of the Plan and the objections filed thereto and based on the record of the confirmation hearing held before the Court in this case, and after due deliberation, and sufficient cause appearing therefor, this Court hereby makes the following findings of fact and conclusions of law and, based thereon, issues the following order.

I. FINDINGS AND CONCLUSIONS

A. Notice. Any person or entity required to receive notice of the hearing on the adequacy of the Disclosure Statement and confirmation of the Plan has received due, proper, and adequate notice thereof.

---

101 11 U.S.C. § 1129(c).

102 *Id.* § 1129(d).

B. Code Compliance - § 1129(a)(1). The Plan complies with the applicable provisions of the Code.

C. Proponent Compliance - § 1129(a)(2). The Debtor has complied with the applicable provisions of the Code.

D. Proposed in Good Faith - § 1129(a)(3).

(i) The Plan has been proposed in good faith and not by any means forbidden by law.

(ii) The Debtor has been advised by counsel of his own choosing in the formulation of the Plan and the negotiation, execution, and delivery of the Plan, the Disclosure Statement, and all other documents related to the Plan to which the Debtor is a party.

(iii) The Debtor has made an independent decision to enter into the documents related to the Plan to which he is a party and to propose the Plan.

E. Payments - § 1129(a)(4). Any payment made or to be made by the Debtor in connection with this case, or in connection with the Plan, has been approved by the Court as reasonable, or will be subject to such approval by the Court.

F. Best Interest of Creditors - § 1129(a)(7). With respect to each impaired class of claims, each holder of a claim of such class has accepted the Plan, or will receive or retain under the Plan on account of such claim property of a value, as of the effective date of the Plan, that is not less than the amount that such holder would so receive or retain if the Debtor was liquidated under Chapter 7 of the Code. No holder of a secured claim has made an election under § 1111(b)(2) of the Code.

G. Opportunity to Vote; Acceptance by Impaired Classes - § 1129(a)(8). All holders of claims and interests impaired under the Plan have been given adequate opportunity to vote to accept or reject the Plan. Holders of allowed claims or interests in classes [class designations] have accepted the Plan within the meaning of § 1126(c) of the Code. Classes [unimpaired class designations] are unimpaired within the meaning of § 1124 and are conclusively presumed to have accepted the Plan under § 1126(f) of the Code.

H. Treatment of Priority Claims - § 1129(a)(9). Except to the extent that the holder of a particular claim has agreed otherwise, the Plan provides that: (i) with respect to a claim of a kind specified in § 507 (a)(1) or (a)(2) of the Code, on the effective date of the Plan the holder of each such claim will receive on account of such claim cash equal to the allowed amount of such claim; and (ii) with respect to claims of a kind specified in § 507(a)(7) of the

Code, the holder of each such claim will receive on account of such claim either (a) cash equal to the allowed amount of such claim on or before the effective date of the Plan, or (b) deferred cash payments, over a period not exceeding six (6) years after the date of assessment of such claim, of a value, as of the effective date of the Plan, equal to the allowed amount of such claim.

I. Acceptance by Impaired Class - § 1129(a)(10). At least one class of claims of the Debtor that is impaired under the Plan has accepted the Plan, determined without including the acceptance of the Plan by any insider of the Debtor holding a claim of such class. The classes of impaired claims that have accepted the Plan are classes [accepting class designations].

J. Feasibility - § 1129(a)(11). Confirmation of the Plan is not likely to be followed by the liquidation or need for further financial reorganization of the Debtor.

K. Payment of Fees - § 1129(a)(12). All fees payable under 28 U.S.C. § 1930, as determined by the Court at the hearings confirming the Plan, have been paid or the Plan provides for the payment of all such fees as required by § 1129(a)(12) of the Code.

L. Disclosure Statement. The Disclosure Statement meets the requirements of § 1125 of the Code. The Debtor has filed the Disclosure Statement in good faith with reasonable care and diligence, and has not knowingly or negligently included in such Disclosure Statement any materially misleading or erroneous statements or representations.

M. Good Faith Solicitation. The solicitation of acceptances of the Plan by the Debtor was in good faith.

N. Binding on Proponent and Holders. The Debtor and all holders of claims and interests are bound by the Plan within the meaning of § 1141 of the Code.

O. Fair and Equitable. The Plan (including without limitation all documents executed in conjunction therewith) is fair and equitable to all parties-in-interest, including without limitation the Debtor, all unsecured creditors, and all secured creditors.

P. Documents: Valid, Binding, and Enforceable. The documents referenced in the Plan to be executed by the Debtor pursuant to the Plan are each valid, binding, and enforceable against the Debtor, in accordance with their terms, and are entered into for good and valuable consideration, including the benefits of the Plan, and the acceptance of the Plan by [United].

Q. Agreement to Order. The Debtor, the Committee, and [United] have agreed to the provisions of this Order.

BASED ON THE FOREGOING FINDINGS OF FACT AND CONCLUSIONS OF LAW, IT IS HEREBY ORDERED THAT:

1. Confirmation. The Plan, a copy of which is annexed hereto as Exhibit A, be, and the same hereby is, confirmed.

2. Discharge. Subject to Paragraph 3 hereof, the Debtor is hereby discharged from each debt (as the term "debt" is defined in the Code) or claim that arose against him before the date of entry of this Order whether or not (a) a proof of claim based upon such debt or claim is filed or deemed to be filed under § 501 of the Code, (b) such Claim is allowed under § 502 of the Code, or (c) the holder of such claim has accepted the Plan.

3. Plan Obligations. Nothing in this Order or the Plan shall operate as a discharge of the Debtor from claims, obligations, or liabilities to be paid or performed under the Plan or any agreement executed in conjunction with the Plan and described in Paragraph P of this Order.

4. Binding Order. The provisions of the Plan, and all documents executed in conjunction with the Plan, and this confirmation Order be, and they hereby are now and forever afterwards binding on the Debtor, all creditors of the Debtor, and any other parties-in-interest, as well as their respective heirs, successors, assigns, trustees, subsidiaries, affiliates, officers, directors, agents, employees, representatives, attorneys, beneficiaries, guardians, and similar officers, or any person claiming through or in the right of any such persons.

5. Carrying-out of Plan. The Debtor and his respective agents and attorneys be, and they hereby are, authorized, empowered, and directed to carry out all of the provisions of the Plan and to perform such acts and execute and deliver such documents as are necessary or appropriate in connection with the Plan and this Order.

6. Effectiveness. On the effective date, the Plan, and all documents to be executed in conjunction therewith, including but not limited to the [United] documents, shall become effective and binding immediately.

7. Executory Contracts. The rejection of executory contracts and unexpired leases as provided in the Plan be, and hereby is, approved.

8. Making of Distributions. Except as otherwise expressly provided in the Plan, all payments and other distributions to be made under the Plan shall be timely and proper if mailed by first class mail on or before the date of distribution provided for in the Plan to the address listed in such creditor's proof of claim filed in this case, or, if no proof of claim is filed, the last known address of the creditor entitled thereto.

9. Stay Terminated. The stay in effect in the instant case pursuant to § 362(a) of the Code is hereby dissolved and is of no force or effect as of the effective date.

10. Jurisdiction. The Court shall retain jurisdiction over this case to the extent provided for in the Plan.

Dated:

[Philadelphia, Pennsylvania]

____

United States Bankruptcy Judge

§ 15.21 Treatment of Particular Claims under Plans

Disputed claims. In almost every Chapter 11 case, there are claims filed against the debtor that the debtor disputes. The debtor normally objects to the disputed claim[103] but often does not resolve the objection prior to confirmation of the plan. The usual method of dealing with disputed claims in a plan is to set up a *disputed claims reserve,* depositing funds into the reserve that the claimant would otherwise have received under the plan if the claim was allowed as filed. In this manner, the debtor can show the plan is feasible, does not discriminate unfairly, and is fair and equitable. A sample disputed claim reserve provision of a plan appears in **§ 15.22.**

Contingent, unliquidated claims. The debtor may be involved as a defendant in a lawsuit at the time it commences its Chapter 11 case. The claim of the plaintiff against the debtor is both contingent and unliquidated. The Bankruptcy Code requires the court to estimate contingent and unliquidated claims against the debtor if "the fixing or liquidation of [such claim] . . . would unduly delay the administration of the case."[104] If estimation would not unduly delay administration of the case, the contingent, unliquidated claim, which is presumably disputed by the debtor, could be treated in the disputed claims reserve. In some plans, certain types of contingent, unliquidated claims that are in litigation in nonbankruptcy forums are permitted to proceed to judgment. In essence, the nonbankruptcy forum is used to fix the claim. In this situation, if the plan proposes to treat the claim as fixed, the entire asserted claim must be reserved for in the disputed reserve account. Alternatively, some plans treat the claim by permitting it to be paid by the postconfirmation debtor from cash flow, just as any judgment debt might be paid. This alternative could raise issues of feasibility to pay such a claim in the future, and unfair discrimination if the unliquidated claimant was afforded the opportunity to recover a greater percentage of its claim after the claim is fixed than creditors paid through the plan.

---

[103] *See* 11 U.S.C. § 502 (a); Fed. R. Bankr. P. 3007.

[104] 11 U.S.C. § 502(c)(1).

Administrative convenience class. The Code contemplates that the plan can "designate a separate class of claims consisting only of every unsecured claim that is less than or reduced to an amount that the court approves as reasonable and necessary for administrative convenience."[105] In enacting the Bankruptcy Code, Congress noted that "[p]ayments in cash of small claims in full is common practice in reorganization."[106] Some courts, however, have been wary of the administrative convenience class that offers full payment of a reduced amount in an attempt to satisfy the "one accepting impaired class" requirement of 11 U.S.C. § 1129(a)(10).[107] See **§ 15.8.**

§ 15.22 —Sample Provisions Covering Disputed Claims

Following are sample clauses concerning disputed claims that can be used in a reorganization plan.

FORM 15–3
DISPUTED CLAIMS CLAUSES

Allowed claim: shall mean any claim for which an allowed amount has been determined.

Class One claims reserve: shall have the meaning set forth in Section [number].

Disputed amount: shall mean, with respect to a particular disputed claim, that amount which is equal to the difference, if any, between the face amount of the claim and the amount of the claim which the Debtor concedes.

Disputed claim: shall mean any claim for which an allowed amount has not yet been determined, and with respect to which an objection has been interposed on or prior to the confirmation date or such other date as may be fixed by the Court.

Disputed interest: shall mean any interest that has not yet been allowed and with respect to which an objection has been interposed on or prior to the confirmation date or such other date fixed by the Bankruptcy Court. An application, motion, complaint, or any other legal pleading seeking to subordinate an interest shall be deemed an objection thereto.

Estate representative: shall mean the person or persons appointed under the Plan, in accordance with § 1123(b)(3)(B) of the Code, as the party with the duties outlined in the Plan.

---

105 *Id.* § 1122(b).

106 S. Rep. 989, 95th Cong., 2d Sess. 118 n.26 (1978).

107 *In re* S&W Enter., 37 B.R. 153, 162 (Bankr. N.D. Ill. 1984).

Face amount: shall mean, with respect to a particular claim, (a) if the holder of that claim has not filed a proof of claim with the Court within the applicable period of limitation fixed by the Court pursuant to Rule 3003(c)(3) of the Bankruptcy Rules, the amount of that claim that is listed in the Debtor's schedules as not disputed, contingent, or unliquidated; or (b) if the holder of that claim has filed a proof of claim with the Court within the applicable period of limitation fixed by the Court pursuant to Rule 3003(c)(3) of the Bankruptcy Rules, the amount stated in the proof of claim; or (c) with respect to a fee request, the net amount to which the applicant would be entitled if its application were to be granted in full. **Face amount** shall mean, with respect to a particular interest, the number of shares represented by that interest if that interest were not disputed.

Pro Rata: means proportionately so that the ratio of the amount of consideration distributed on account of a particular claim to the allowed amount of that claim is the same as the ratio of the amount of consideration distributed on account of all allowed claims of the class in which the particular claim is included to the amount of all allowed claims of that class.

Class One. Creditors shall be paid in the aggregate [$600,000], as follows:

(a) On the effective date, the estate representative shall determine each Class One creditor's pro rata share of $250,000 to determine the amount of distribution due the holders of allowed claims and to be reserved for disputed claims. The pro rata calculations shall be made as if all disputed claims were allowed claims in the amounts claimed by the holders thereof in any proof of claim filed or deemed to have been filed in a timely manner. Upon such determination, each Class One creditor with an allowed claim shall receive its pro rata share of $250,000. The remaining portion of this $250,000 distribution shall be deposited in a separate account (the Class One claims reserve).

(b) On [April 16, 1991], the estate representative shall determine each Class One creditor's pro rata share of $250,000.00 to determine the amount of distribution due the holders of allowed claims, and to be reserved for disputed claims. The pro rata calculations shall be made as if all disputed claims were allowed claims in the amounts claimed by the holders thereof in any proof of claim filed or deemed to have been filed in a timely manner. Upon such determination, each Class One creditor with an allowed claim shall receive its pro rata share of $250,000.00. The remaining portion of this $250,000.00 distribution shall be deposited in the Class One claims reserve.

(c) On [April 16, 1992], the estate representative shall determine each Class One creditor's pro rata share of $100,000.00 to determine the amount of distribution due the holders of allowed claims, and to be reserved for disputed claims. The pro rata calculations shall be made as if all disputed claims were allowed claims in the amounts claimed by the holders thereof in any proof of claim filed or deemed to have been filed in a timely manner. Upon such determination, each Class One creditor with an allowed claim shall receive its pro rata share of $100,000.00. The remaining portion of this $100,000.00 distribution shall be deposited in the Class One claims reserve.

(d) At such time as a disputed claim becomes an allowed claim, the distributions reserved for that allowed claim shall be released from the Class One claims reserve for distribution to the holder of that allowed claim.

(e) At such time as all or a part of a disputed claim is disallowed pursuant to a final order, the portion of the funds in the Class One claim reserve on account of the disallowed disputed claim shall be distributed to each Class One creditor with an allowed claim after recalculating each Class One creditor's pro rata share as set forth in Section (a) above.

(f) All cash held in the Class One claims reserve shall be invested by the estate representative in accordance with § 345 of the Code, or as otherwise permitted by the Court.

(g) The estate representative shall not be obligated to distribute any amount due to Class One creditors that does not exceed One ($1.00) Dollar.

§ 15.23 Effect of Confirmation

Confirmation of the plan binds the debtor and all parties to the terms of the plan,[108] and the creditor's only rights are those set forth in the plan and confirmation order.[109] Also, except as otherwise provided in the plan, confirmation vests all property in the debtor[110] free of claims and interests of creditors, shareholders, and general partners.[111] Furthermore, confirmation discharges the debtor of all debts except as provided in the plan and the confirmation order.[112] At least two courts have held that the confirmation order had res judicata effect and barred the debtor from bringing post-confirmation litigation against third parties when the debtor did not disclose the litigation prior to confirmation.[113] It should be noted that only an individual is entitled to a discharge under Chapter 7.[114] Thus, a corporate debtor that liquidates under Chapter 11 and ceases doing business does not receive a discharge.

---

108 11 U.S.C. § 1141(a).

109 Board of County Comm'rs v. Coleman Am. Properties, Inc. (*In re* Coleman Am. Properties, Inc.), 30 B.R. 239 (Bankr. D. Kan. 1983).

110 11 U.S.C. § 1141(b).

111 *Id.* § 1141(c).

112 *Id.* § 1141(d).

113 *See* Westland Oil Dev. Corp. v. MCorp Mgmt. Solutions, Inc. 157 B.R. 100 (S.D. Tex. 1993); Heritage Hotel Partnership I v. Valley Bank (*In re* Heritage Hotel Partnership I), 160 B.R. 374 (Bankr. 9th Cir. 1993).

114 *See* 11 U.S.C. § 727(a)(1).

CHAPTER 16

ABSOLUTE PRIORITY AND NEW VALUE

Honorable James A. Pusateri and James J. O'Malley

§ 16.1 Absolute Priority Rule

A plan of reorganization may be confirmed despite rejection by one or more classes of claims if the plan satisfies the requirements of 11 U.S.C. § 1129(b). See **Chapter 15.** One of these requirements is the *absolute priority rule* set out in 11 U.S.C. § 1129(b)(2)(B), which requires full payment of all allowed claims of a dissenting class of unsecured claims if the holders of junior claims or interests, such as owners of the debtor, are to receive or retain any property on account of such junior claims or interests. In general, the absolute priority rule requires full payment of unsecured claims if the owners of a debtor are to retain their ownership interests in the reorganized business.

The absolute priority rule applies to all forms of business organizations. Arguments that the absolute priority rule is inapplicable to individual debtors because they are not holders of interests in a separate entity have been rejected by a number of courts.[1] The

[1] Unruh v. Rushville State Bank, 987 F.2d 1506 (10th Cir. 1993); Kham & Nate's Shoes No. 2, Inc. v. First Bank, 908 F.2d 1351 (7th Cir. 1990); *In re* Witt, 60 B.R. 556 (Bankr. N.D. Iowa 1986). *See* Norwest Bank Worthington v. Ahlers, 485 U.S. 197 (1988).

rule is a major obstacle to cram down reorganization under § 1129(b), especially for small, closely held businesses, in which the owners, whether sole proprietors, partners, or stockholders, are also the management. In many cases, the participation of owner-managers is essential to continuation of the business. When a small business cannot pay the claims of the dissenting class in full, its owners may well have no incentive to continue to operate the business because the absolute priority rule results in loss of ownership.[2]

A large corporation, on the other hand, may be able to reorganize despite a complete change of ownership because ownership is not synonymous with management. Moreover, it can be easier for corporations with publicly traded stock to pay claims, because they can issue stock in satisfaction of claims. That option, however, is not open to individual debtors, partnerships, and, as a practical matter, to smaller, closely held corporations whose stock is not publicly traded.[3]

The absolute priority rule existed long before the enactment of the present Bankruptcy Code,[4] but an exception or corollary[5] to it has also been recognized since at least 1939, when the United States Supreme Court decided *Case v. Los Angeles Lumber Products Co.*[6] Under the new value exception recognized in *Los Angeles Lumber,* by contributing new capital necessary for an effective reorganization in an amount reasonably equivalent to the value of the retained ownership interest, owners of a reorganizing debtor could retain their ownership interests despite the debtor's inability to make full payment to creditors.[7] See §§ **16.4** through **16.8.**

---

2 *See* Kham & Nate's Shoes No. 2, Inc. v. First Bank, 908 F.2d 1351 (7th Cir. 1990); *In re* SLC Ltd. V, 137 B.R. 847 (Bankr. D. Utah 1992); *In re* Mortgage Inv. Co., 111 B.R. 604 (Bankr. W.D. Tex. 1990); *In re* Pullman Constr. Indus., Inc., 107 B.R. 909 (Bankr. N.D. Ill. 1989). *See also In re* Yasparro, 100 B.R. 91 (Bankr. M.D. Fla. 1989) (absolute priority operates most harshly on individual debtors).

3 *See* 11 U.S.C. § 1123(a)(5)(J); *In re* Future Energy Corp., 83 B.R. 470 (Bankr. S.D. Ohio 1988); R. Peeples, *Staying In: Chapter 11, Close Corporations and the Absolute Priority Rule,* 63 Am. Bankr. L.J. 65, 74–78, 107 (1989).

4 Kansas City Terminal Ry. v. Central Union Trust Co., 271 U.S. 445 (1926); Northern Pac. Ry. v. Boyd, 228 U.S. 482 (1913).

5 There is a debate over whether retention of ownership by contributing new value is an exception to the absolute priority rule, or a corollary rule consistent with absolute priority. *See, e.g.,* Bonner Mall Partnership v. U.S. Bancorp Mortgage Co. (*In re* Bonner Mall Partnership), 2 F.3d 899 (9th Cir. 1993), *cert. granted,* ___ U.S. ___, 126 L. Ed. 2d 648, *removed from argument calendar,* ___ U.S. ___, 114 S. Ct. 1367 (1994); Travelers Ins. Co. v. Bryson Properties, XVIII (*In re* Bryson Properties, XVIII), 961 F.2d 496 (4th Cir.), *cert. denied,* ___ U.S. ___, 113 S. Ct. 191 (1992); *In re* Snyder, 967 F.2d 1126 (7th Cir. 1992); *In re* SM 104 Ltd., 160 B.R. 202 (Bankr. S.D. Fla. 1993), *In re* Bjolmes Realty Trust, 134 B.R. 1000 (Bankr. D. Mass. 1991). The authors of this chapter have used the more common term, *exception,* for convenience, but do not intend this as a comment on the merits of the debate.

6 308 U.S. 106 (1939). *See also* Kansas City Terminal Ry. v. Central Union Trust Co., 271 U.S. 445 (1926).

7 Case v. Los Angeles Lumber Prods. Co., 308 U.S. 106 (1939).

The exception proved difficult for debtors to satisfy, for confirmed new value plans are rare in the reported cases.[8] It is especially difficult for small businesses to satisfy the exception.[9] Individual business debtors have no investors to turn to for new capital, although relatives and employees may be a source of funds. And, except for exempt property, individual debtors have no personal funds to contribute that are not already property of the estate.[10] Other closely held business organizations may well have similar problems, because their owners often have little personal wealth that is not already invested in the business.[11]

In 1988, the Supreme Court called the existence of the exception into question in *Norwest Bank Worthington v. Ahlers,*[12] but did not decide the issue. Since then, a split of authority has developed over whether the new value exception continues under the Bankruptcy Code. The majority view is that the exception continues under the Code,[13] but a substantial minority of courts has expressed the opposite view.[14] In 1994, the Supreme Court granted certiorari on the issue in *In re Bonner Mall Partnership,*[15] but the case was subsequently settled, so that, apparently, the answer to the issue must wait until another term of the Court.

---

[8] *See* Ayer, *Rethinking Absolute Priority After Ahlers,* 87 Mich. L. Rev. 963, 1009–10, 1016–19 (1989); J. White, *Absolute Priority and New Value,* 8 Cooley L. Rev. 1, 13 (1991).

[9] R. Nimmer, *Negotiated Bankruptcy Reorganization Plans: Absolute Priority and New Value Contributions,* 36 Emory L.J. 1009, 1013 (1987); R. Peeples, *Staying In: Chapter 11, Close Corporations and the Absolute Priority Rule,* 63 Am. Bankr. L.J. 65, 78 (1989). *See In re* Capital Ctr. Equities, 144 B.R. 262 (Bankr. E.D. Pa. 1992); *In re* Yasparro, 100 B.R. 91 (Bankr. M.D. Fla. 1989).

[10] *See In re* Harman, 141 B.R. 878 (Bankr. E.D. Pa. 1992); *In re* Hendrix, 131 B.R. 751 (Bankr. M.D. Fla. 1991); *In re* Yasparro, 100 B.R. 91 (Bankr. M.D. Fla. 1989); *In re* Dowden, 143 B.R. 388 (Bankr. W.D. La. 1989); *In re* East, 57 B.R. 14 (Bankr. M.D. La. 1985).

[11] *See* R. Nimmer, *Negotiated Bankruptcy Reorganization Plans: Absolute Priority and New Value Contributions,* 36 Emory L.J. 1009, 1013 (1987).

[12] 485 U.S. 197 (1988).

[13] *E.g.,* Bonner Mall Partnership v. U.S. Bancorp Mortgage Co. (*In re* Bonner Mall Partnership), 2 F.3d 899 (9th Cir. 1993), *cert. granted,* ___ U.S. ___, 126 L. Ed. 2d 648, *removed from argument calendar,* ___ U.S. ___, 114 S. Ct. 1367 (1994); *In re* Snyder, 967 F.2d 1126 (7th Cir. 1992); *In re* F.A.B. Indus., 147 B.R. 763 (C.D. Cal. 1992); *In re* SM 104 Ltd., 160 B.R. 202 (Bankr. S.D. Fla. 1993); *In re* Pullman Constr. Indus., Inc., 107 B.R. 909 (Bankr. N.D. Ill. 1989).

[14] *E.g.,* Travelers Ins. Co. v. Bryson Properties, XVIII (*In re* Bryson Properties, XVIII), 961 F.2d 496 (4th Cir.), *cert. denied,* ___ U.S. ___, 113 S. Ct. 191 (1992); Kham & Nate's Shoes No. 2, Inc. v. First Bank, 908 F.2d 1351 (7th Cir. 1990); Piedmont Assocs. v. CIGNA Property & Casualty Ins. Co., 132 B.R. 75 (N.D. Ga. 1991); Pennbank v. Winters (*In re* Winters), 99 B.R. 658 (Bankr. W.D. Pa. 1989). The minority includes one of the authors of this chapter. *See In re* Drimmel, 108 B.R. 284 (Bankr. D. Kan. 1989), *aff'd,* 135 B.R. 410 (D. Kan. 1991), *aff'd,* 987 F.2d 1506 (10th Cir. 1993).

[15] Bonner Mall Partnership v. U.S. Bancorp Mortgage Co. (*In re* Bonner Mall Partnership), 2 F.3d 899 (9th Cir. 1993), *cert. granted,* ___ U.S. ___, 126 L. Ed. 2d 648, *removed from argument calendar,* ___ U.S. ___, 114 S. Ct. 1367 (1994).

Although the new value exception may be of limited direct practical utility for small businesses, its elimination would nonetheless substantially affect debtors' ability to reorganize by reducing their bargaining power in plan negotiations with creditors. If the new value exception were unavailable, debtors would have nothing with which to counter the assertion of the absolute priority rule by unsecured creditors to require payment of their claims in full. In 1992 and 1993, Congress considered establishing a separate small business reorganization chapter that would have eliminated the absolute priority rule as a requirement for confirmation for small businesses, thereby making the new value exception irrelevant for qualifying debtors.[16] However, the small business chapter was dropped from the bill in the spring of 1994. See § **16.10** and **Chapter 24.**

§ 16.2 Debate over the Existence of the New Value Exception

The language of 11 U.S.C. § 1129(b)(2)(B)(ii) is the starting place for any analysis of whether the new value exception continues under the Bankruptcy Code. Title 11 U.S.C. § 1129(b)(1) provides that a plan that satisfies all of the requirements for confirmation in § 1129(a), except for the requirement of paragraph (8) that all impaired classes accept, shall be confirmed if it "does not discriminate unfairly, and is fair and equitable, with respect to each class of claims or interests that is impaired under, and has not accepted the plan."[17] Subsection (b)(2) provides in part:

> For the purpose of this subsection, the condition that a plan be fair and equitable with respect to a class includes the following requirements: . . .
>
> (B) With respect to a class of unsecured claims—
>
> (i) the plan provides that each holder of a claim of such class receive or retain on account of such claim property of a value, as of the effective date of the plan, equal to the allowed amount of such claim; or
>
> (ii) the holder of any claim or interest that is junior to the claims of such class will not receive or retain under the plan on account of such junior claim or interest any property.[18]

The statutory language does not expressly incorporate the new value exception and expressly prohibits owners from receiving or retaining any property "on account of" their ownership interests unless objecting classes of creditors are paid in full. The crucial language is the phrase "on account of."

Courts taking the view that the new value exception is consistent with the language of § 1129(b)(2)(B)(ii) have reasoned that owners who satisfy the new value exception by contributing new capital receive ownership interests on account of the new capital, and do not retain ownership on account of their original ownership

---

[16] *See* S. 540, 103d Cong., 1st Sess. § 201 (1993); S. 540, 103d Cong., 2d Sess. § 201 (1994).

[17] 11 U.S.C. § 1129(b)(1).

[18] *Id.* § 1129(b)(2).

interests.[19] In their view, neither the pre-Code absolute priority rule nor the language of § 1129(b)(2)(B) are inconsistent with the new value exception, and the label, "exception" is misleading.[20]

Courts taking the view that the new value exception was eliminated by the Code have reasoned that plans under which owners would retain ownership of a debtor by contributing new capital would give the owners property "on account of" their prior ownership interests in violation of 11 U.S.C. § 1129(b)(2)(B)(ii).[21] In their view, such plans give owners a special opportunity or right to retain ownership of a reorganized debtor in exchange for new capital without competition from other potential buyers. Their prior ownership is the only reason they have the exclusive right, and they therefore receive or retain their ownership "on account of" their prior ownership interests.[22] One court noted that the exclusivity period of 11 U.S.C. § 1121(b), during which the debtor has the exclusive right to propose a plan, can effectively prevent any competition from other parties interested in acquiring ownership of the debtor.[23] Under this construction of the statutory language, § 1129(b)(2)(B)(ii) expressly prohibits application of the new value exception.

A variety of statutory construction, legislative history, and policy arguments have been advanced to support either view on whether the new value exception is consistent with § 1129(b)(2)(B)(ii).[24] Ultimately, the construction given the statutory

---

19 *See, e.g.*, Bonner Mall Partnership v. U.S. Bancorp Mortgage Co. (*In re* Bonner Mall Partnership), 2 F.3d 899 (9th Cir. 1993); *In re* Snyder, 967 F.2d 1126 (7th Cir. 1992); *In re* SM 104 Ltd., 160 B.R. 202 (Bankr. S.D. Fla. 1993); *In re* Pullman Constr. Indus., Inc., 107 B.R. 909 (Bankr. N.D. Ill. 1989).

20 *See, e.g.*, Bonner Mall Partnership v. U.S. Bancorp Mortgage Co. (*In re* Bonner Mall Partnership), 2 F.3d 899 (9th Cir. 1993) *cert. granted*, ___ U.S. ___, 126 L .Ed. 2d 648, *removed from argument calendar*, ___ U.S. ___, 141 S. Ct. 1367 (1994); *In re* Snyder, 967 F.2d 1126 (7th Cir. 1992); *In re* SM 104 Ltd., 160 B.R. 202 (Bankr. S.D. Fla. 1993).

21 *See* Travelers Ins. Co. v. Bryson Properties, XVIII (*In re* Bryson Properties, XVIII), 961 F.2d 496 (4th Cir.), *cert. denied*, ___ U.S. ___, 113 S. Ct. 191 (1992); Piedmont Assocs. v. CIGNA Property & Casualty Ins. Co., 132 B.R. 75 (N.D. Ga. 1991); *In re* Lumber Exch., Ltd., 125 B.R. 1000 (Bankr. D. Minn 1991), *aff'd*, 134 B.R. 354 (D. Minn. 1991), *aff'd*, 968 F.2d 647 (8th Cir. 1992).

22 *See* Travelers Ins. Co. v. Bryson Properties, XVIII (*In re* Bryson Properties, XVIII), 961 F.2d 496 (4th Cir.), *cert. denied*, ___ U.S. ___, 113 S. Ct. 191 (1992); *In re* Drimmel, 135 B.R. 410 (D. Kan. 1991), *aff'd on other grounds*, 987 F.2d 1506 (10th Cir. 1993); *In re* Lumber Exch., Ltd., 125 B.R. 1000 (Bankr. D. Minn 1991), *aff'd*, 134 B.R. 354 (D. Minn. 1991), *aff'd*, 968 F.2d 647 (8th Cir. 1992).

23 Travelers Ins. Co. v. Bryson Properties, XVIII (*In re* Bryson Properties, XVIII), 961 F.2d 496 (4th Cir.), *cert. denied*, ___ U.S. ___, 113 S. Ct. 191, 121 L. Ed. 2d 648 (1992). *But see In re* SM 104 Ltd., 160 B.R. 202 (Bankr. S.D. Fla. 1993) (disclosure and confirmation provisions of Chapter 11 permit competing bids by creditors during exclusivity period).

24 *E.g.*, Bonner Mall Partnership v. U.S. Bancorp Mortgage Co. (*In re* Bonner Mall Partnership), 2 F.3d 899 (9th Cir. 1993) *cert. granted*, ___ U.S. ___, 126 L .Ed. 2d 648, *removed from argument calendar*, ___ U.S. ___, 141 S. Ct. 1367 (1994); Travelers Ins. Co. v. Bryson Properties, XVIII (*In re* Bryson Properties, XVIII), 961 F.2d 496 (4th Cir.), *cert. denied*, ___ U.S. ___, 113 S. Ct. 191 (1992); Kham & Nate's Shoes No. 2,

language may depend on the courts' views on how difficult it should be to cram down a plan over the rejecting vote of a class of creditors.[25]

§ 16.3 Application of the New Value Exception

The scarcity of confirmed new value plans in the reported cases suggests that it is a difficult task to obtain confirmation of a new value plan. The task is made more difficult by uncertainty over what will satisfy the exception. This uncertainty leaves considerable room for counsel to use creative approaches in proposing new value reorganization plans. The uncertain state of the law, however, also provides many arguments useful in opposing new value plans. See §§ **16.4** through **16.8.**

The basis of the new value exception to absolute priority was set out in *Case v. Los Angeles Lumber Products Co.,*[26] in which the Supreme Court stated that there are circumstances under which stockholders may participate in a plan of reorganization of a debtor that is unable to pay claims of senior creditors in full. The Court stated that it recognized

> the necessity, at times, of seeking new money "essential to the success of the undertaking" from the old stockholders. Where that necessity exists and the old stockholders make a fresh contribution and receive in return a participation reasonably equivalent to their contribution, no objection can be made. . . . If . . . those conditions . . . are satisfied, the creditor cannot complain that he is not accorded "his full right of priority against the corporate assets." . . .
>
> In view of these considerations we believe that to accord "the creditor his full right of priority against the corporate assets" where the debtor is insolvent, the stockholder's participation must be based on a contribution in money or in money's worth, reasonably equivalent in view of all the circumstances to the participation of the stockholder.[27]

Inc. v. First Bank, 908 F.2d 1351 (7th Cir. 1990); *In re* SM 104 Ltd., 160 B.R. 202 (Bankr. S.D. Fla. 1993); *In re* Bjolmes Realty Trust, 134 B.R. 1000 (Bankr. D. Mass. 1991); *In re* Lumber Exch., Ltd., 125 B.R. 1000 (Bankr. D. Minn 1991), *aff'd,* 134 B.R. 354 (D. Minn. 1991), *aff'd,* 968 F.2d 647 (8th Cir. 1992); *In re* Pullman Constr. Indus., Inc., 107 B.R. 909 (Bankr. N.D. Ill. 1989); Pennbank v. Winters (*In re* Winters), 99 B.R. 658 (Bankr. W.D. Pa. 1989).

25 *Compare* Bonner Mall Partnership v. U.S. Bancorp Mortgage Co. (*In re* Bonner Mall Partnership), 2 F.3d 899 (9th Cir. 1993) *cert. granted,* ___ U.S. ___, 126 L. Ed. 2d 648, *removed from argument calendar,* ___ U.S. ___, 141 S. Ct. 1367 (1994); *In re* Greystone III Joint Venture, 102 B.R. 560 (Bankr. W.D. Tex. 1989), *aff'd,* 127 B.R. 138 (W.D. Tex. 1990), *rev'd on other grounds,* 995 F.2d 1274 (5th Cir. 1991), *petition for reh'g granted in part, opinion withdrawn in part,* 995 F.2d 1284 (5th Cir.), *cert. denied,* ___ U.S. ___, 113 S. Ct. 72 (1992); *with* Travelers Ins. Co. v. Bryson Properties, XVIII (*In re* Bryson Properties, XVIII), 961 F.2d 496 (4th Cir.), *cert. denied,* ___ U.S. ___, 113 S. Ct. 191 (1992); Kham & Nate's Shoes No. 2, Inc. v. First Bank, 908 F.2d 1351 (7th Cir. 1990).

26 308 U.S. 106 (1939).

27 *Id.* at 121 (quoting Kansas City Terminal Ry. v. Central Union Trust Co., 271 U.S. 445 (1926)) (citations omitted).

From *Los Angeles Lumber*[28] the courts have derived several requirements that must be satisfied before a new value plan can be confirmed. See §§ **16.4** through **16.8.** Some courts have stated that the requirements must be rigorously applied to ensure that the creditors' rights to absolute priority against the debtor's assets are not infringed.[29]

§ 16.4 Necessity

The basis for the new value exception is the necessity of seeking new capital from shareholders. The exception applies "where the former stockholders are the only or most feasible source of the new capital."[30] In many cases, the debtor's financial condition will be such that unavailability of capital from other sources can be easily proven.[31] In such cases, it may be self-evident that there is no other source of capital[32] because "no sane outside investor" would put new money into a business under those circumstances.[33] Unavailability of outside capital may be shown by evidence that the business was marketed without drawing interest from outside investors.[34] The purpose of the requirement is to ensure that the new value exception serves the narrow purpose of providing the debtor with capital needed for survival rather than simply permitting owners to preserve their ownership.[35] Accordingly, some courts

---

28 *Id.*

29 *See, e.g.,* Bonner Mall Partnership v. U.S. Bancorp Mortgage Co. (*In re* Bonner Mall Partnership), 2 F.3d 899 (9th Cir. 1993), *cert. granted,* ___ U.S. ___, 126 L. Ed. 2d 648, *removed from argument calendar,* ___U.S. ___, 114 S. Ct. 1367 (1994); *In re* S.A.B.T.C. Townhouse Ass'n, Inc., 152 B.R. 1005 (Bankr. M.D. Fla. 1993); *In re* 222 Liberty Assocs., 108 B.R. 971 (Bankr. E.D. Pa. 1990).

30 Case v. Los Angeles Lumber Prods. Co., 308 U.S. 106, 122 n.15 (1939) (quoting *In re* Dutch Woodcraft Shops, 14 F. Supp. 467, 471 (D. Mich. 1935)). *See* Official Creditors' Comm. on Behalf of Class 8 Unsecured Creditors v. Potter Material Serv., Inc. (*In re* Potter Material Serv., Inc.), 781 F.2d 99 (7th Cir. 1986); *In re* SABTC Townhouse Ass'n, Inc., 152 B.R. 1005 (Bankr. M.D. Fla. 1993); *In re* Creekside Landing, Ltd., 140 B.R. 713 (Bankr. M.D. Tenn. 1992); *In re* Bjolmes Realty Trust, 134 B.R. 1000 (Bankr. D. Mass. 1991); *In re* Mortgage Inv. Co., 111 B.R. 604 (Bankr. W.D. Tex. 1990).

31 *See In re* Greystone III Joint Venture, 102 B.R. 560 (Bankr. W.D. Tex. 1989), *aff'd,* 127 B.R. 138 (W.D. Tex. 1990), *rev'd on other grounds,* 995 F.2d 1274 (5th Cir. 1991), *petition for reh'g granted in part, opinion withdrawn in part,* 995 F.2d 1284 (5th Cir.), *cert. denied,* ___ U.S. ___, 113 S. Ct. 72 (1992) (necessity established by testimony of unavailability of financing for commercial real estate ventures in current economic climate).

32 *See In re* Eaton Hose & Fitting Co., 73 B.R. 139 (Bankr. S.D. Ohio 1987).

33 *In re* Aztec Co., 107 B.R. 585 (Bankr. M.D. Tenn. 1989).

34 *See In re* Resorts Int'l, Inc., 145 B.R. 412 (Bankr. D.N.J. 1990); *In re* Jartran, Inc., 44 B.R. 331 (Bankr. N.D. Ill. 1984).

35 *In re* Talahassee Assocs., 132 B.R. 712 (Bankr. W.D. Pa. 1991); *In re* Mortgage Inv. Co., 111 B.R. 604 (Bankr. W.D. Tex. 1990); *In re* Drimmel, 108 B.R. 284 (Bankr. D. Kan. 1989), *aff'd,* 135 B.R. 410 (D. Kan. 1991), *aff'd,* 987 F.2d 1506 (10th Cir. 1993); *In re* Dowden, 143 B.R. 388 (Bankr. W.D. La. 1989).

have concluded that the contribution must be necessary to fund future operations of the debtor, rather than as payment of a portion of the unsecured debt. In their view, a contribution to be used solely or largely to pay unsecured claims, therefore, may not be necessary for the survival of the business.[36] A contribution immediately used to pay creditors may weaken the debtor's financial structure over the life of the plan.[37] A contribution to pay trade debt, purchase capital, or pay labor, on the other hand, may help the debtor continue operations and, at least in theory, may pay more of the creditors' claims over time.[38]

Other courts, however, have concluded that new value plans under which contributions are not paid to creditors cannot be confirmed. In single-asset real estate cases, it may not be fair and equitable to use the owners' capital contributions to repair buildings because it may benefit only the owners at the expense of undersecured creditors, who bear the risk of any decline in value without sharing in any potential increase in value.[39]

§ 16.5 New Value

One obvious requirement of the new value exception is that the contribution by the owners must be new. The contribution must add value to the business. For example, in *In re S.A.B.T.C. Townhouse Association, Inc.*,[40] contributions from members of the debtor homeowner's association were not new value because the members owed the money for past-due assessments. The proposed contribution was merely the collection of some of the debtor's receivables. In *In re Yasparro*,[41] the bankruptcy court concluded that promissory notes executed by an individual debtor were not a contribution of new value because the debtor would owe the underlying debt to his unsecured creditors whether or not it was deemed a contribution of new value. Similarly,

---

36 *See In re* Sovereign Group 1985-27, Ltd., 142 B.R. 702 (E.D. Pa. 1992); *In re* Albrechts Ohio Inns, Inc., 152 B.R. 496 (Bankr. S.D. Ohio 1993); *In re* Mortgage Inv. Co., 111 B.R. 604 (Bankr. W.D. Tex. 1990); *In re* Snyder, 105 B.R. 898 (Bankr. C.D. Ill. 1989), *aff'd*, 967 F.2d 1126 (7th Cir. 1992); *In re* Dowden, 143 B.R. 388 (Bankr. W.D. La. 1989); *In re* Aztec Co., 107 B.R. 585 (Bankr. M.D. Tenn. 1989). *See also In re* Montgomery Court Apartments, 141 B.R. 324 (Bankr. S.D. Ohio 1992) (contribution necessary to establish operating reserve and meet current obligations); *In re* Aztec Co., 107 B.R. 585 (Bankr. M.D. Tenn. 1989) (contribution necessary for repairs).

37 *In re* Snyder, 105 B.R. 898 (Bankr. C.D. Ill. 1989), *aff'd*, 967 F.2d 1126 (7th Cir. 1992).

38 *See In re* Sovereign Group 1985-27, Ltd., 142 B.R. 702 (E.D. Pa. 1992); *In re* Albrechts Ohio Inns, Inc., 152 B.R. 496 (Bankr. S.D. Ohio 1993); *In re* Mortgage Inv. Co., 111 B.R. 604 (Bankr. W.D. Tex. 1990); *In re* Dowden, 143 B.R. 388 (Bankr. W.D. La. 1989).

39 *See In re* One Times Square Assocs., 159 B.R. 695 (Bankr. S.D. N.Y. 1993); *In re* Miami Ctr. Assocs., 144 B.R. 937 (Bankr. S.D. Fla. 1992); *In re* Talahassee Assocs., 132 B.R. 712 (Bankr. W.D. Pa. 1991).

40 152 B.R. 1005 (Bankr. M.D. Fla. 1993).

41 100 B.R. 91 (Bankr. M.D. Fla. 1989).

contribution of preconfirmation earnings of a business generally cannot be a new value contribution because they are already property of the estate.[42] Earnings from postpetition services personally performed by an individual debtor, however, are exempted from the estate.[43] A new value contribution must be over and above the business's future earnings, because it is assumed that the business's future earnings will be contributed to the plan.[44]

To the extent that the risk assumed by the contributing owner is still a factor under the new value exception,[45] it may be necessary that the contributor assume a new economic risk by making the contribution to satisfy the new value exception. A continuation of, or change in the form of an existing risk to owners does not add value to the business.[46]

Creditors may be able challenge a new value plan proposed by a closely held business on the ground that the contribution is not new capital if circumstances indicate that the owners are simply returning money withdrawn from the debtor before filing in the guise of salary increases or payments on loans to the debtor.[47] The nature of closely held businesses makes this possible. One commentator has pointed out "the ease with which close corporation shareholders can draw money out of a struggling business in anticipation of a 'purchase'" under the new value exception, and the possibility that the requirement that the owners' contribution be new could encourage "owners to delay any pre-bankruptcy contributions of capital that might well be desperately needed" until after filing in order to retain ownership.[48]

§ 16.6 Money or Money's Worth

To satisfy the new value exception, the owners' capital contribution must be in "money or money's worth."[49] In rejecting the debtors' argument in *Norwest Bank Worthington v. Ahlers*[50] that a contribution of labor, experience, and expertise satisfied the new value exception, the Supreme Court stated that a

42 *See In re* Stegall, 865 F.2d 140 (7th Cir. 1989).

43 *See In re* Pecht, 57 B.R. 137 (Bankr. E.D. Va. 1986).

44 *See In re* Harman, 141 B.R. 878 (Bankr. E.D. Pa. 1992); *In re* Pecht, 57 B.R. 137 (Bankr. E.D. Va. 1986).

45 *Compare* Official Creditors' Comm. on Behalf of Class 8 Unsecured Creditors v. Potter Material Serv., Inc. (*In re* Potter Material Serv., Inc.), 781 F.2d 99 (7th Cir. 1986), *with In re* 47th & Belleview Partners, 95 B.R. 117 (Bankr. W.D. Mo. 1988).

46 *In re* Creekside Landing, Ltd., 140 B.R. 713 (Bankr. M.D. Tenn. 1992). *But see* Official Creditors' Comm. on Behalf of Class 8 Unsecured Creditors v. Potter Material Serv., Inc. (*In re* Potter Material Serv., Inc.), 781 F.2d 99 (7th Cir. 1986) (owner's continuation of guaranty in addition to cash contribution satisfied new value exception).

47 R. Peeples, *Staying In: Chapter 11, Close Corporations and the Absolute Priority Rule,* 63 Am. Bankr. L.J. 65, 79–80 (1989).

48 *Id.* at 80.

49 Norwest Bank Worthington v. Ahlers, 485 U.S. 197 (1988); Case v. Los Angeles Lumber Prods. Co., 308 U.S. 106 (1939).

50 485 U.S. 197 (1988).

> promise of future services is intangible, inalienable, and, in all likelihood, unenforceable. It "has no place in the asset column of the balance sheet of the new [entity]." . . . Unlike "money or money's worth," a promise of future services cannot be exchanged in any market for something of value to the creditor *today.*[51]

Accordingly, after *Ahlers,* courts have required that a contribution in money or money's worth must be in cash or other tangible property that is freely tradeable in the economy, that it be a present contribution rather than a promise to pay in the future, and that it be an asset in the accounting sense.[52]

An owner's contribution of cash directly to the business, of course, satisfies the money or money's worth requirement. An owner's payment of the debtor's attorney's fees or other administrative expenses may also be a contribution in money or its worth.[53] This can, of course, be difficult for small business owners to provide. Sole proprietors have particular difficulty, because they have no investors to turn to for new cash, and their only sources of cash may be relatives[54] and exempt property.[55]

Promises of future labor cannot qualify as money or its worth after *Ahlers.*[56] Consequently, the money or money's worth requirement of the new value exception is a major obstacle to confirmation for owners of a financially strapped small business who have most of their wealth tied up in the business. However, some courts have noted that the owners' postpetition, preconfirmation labor may be the source of a capital contribution, if the labor produces an asset, such as crops, or the owner is paid wages, which are then contributed to the business.[57]

Post-*Ahlers* case law generally requires that the property must be contributed at or before confirmation. Promises to contribute capital after confirmation are not a contribution of money or its worth.[58] Accordingly, a promised payment from money to

---

51 *Id.* at 204 (emphasis in original).

52 *In re* Miami Ctr. Assocs., Ltd., 144 B.R. 937 (Bankr. S.D. Fla. 1992); *In re* Creekside Landing, Ltd., 140 B.R. 713 (Bankr. M.D. Tenn. 1992); *In re* Batten, 141 B.R. 899 (Bankr. W.D. La. 1992); *In re* 222 Liberty Assocs., 108 B.R. 971 (Bankr. E.D. Pa. 1990); *In re* Yasparro, 100 B.R. 91 (Bankr. M.D. Fla. 1989).

53 *In re* VIP Motor Lodge, Inc., 133 B.R. 41 (Bankr. D. Del. 1991); *In re* Yasparro, 100 B.R. 91 (Bankr. M.D. Fla. 1989); *In re* Future Energy Corp., 83 B.R. 470 (Bankr. S.D. Ohio 1988).

54 *See In re* Yasparro, 100 B.R. 91 (Bankr. M.D. Fla. 1989); *In re* Dowden, 143 B.R. 388 (Bankr. W.D. La. 1989); *In re* East, 57 B.R. 14 (Bankr. M.D. La. 1985).

55 *See In re* Harman, 141 B.R. 878 (Bankr. E.D. Pa. 1992).

56 *See, e.g.,* Unruh v. Rushville State Bank, 987 F.2d 1506 (10th Cir. 1993); *In re* Stegall, 865 F.2d 140 (7th Cir. 1989); Carson Nuggett, Inc. v. Green (*In re* Green), 98 B.R. 981 (Bankr. 9th Cir. 1989).

57 *In re* Stegall, 865 F.2d 140 (7th Cir. 1989); *In re* CPM Constr., 124 B.R. 335 (Bankr. D.N.M. 1991); *In re* Yasparro, 100 B.R. 91 (Bankr. M.D. Fla. 1989).

58 *E.g., In re* Snyder, 967 F.2d 1126 (7th Cir. 1992); *In re* Creekside Landing, Ltd., 140 B.R. 713 (Bankr. M.D. Tenn. 1992); *In re* Yasparro, 100 B.R. 91 (Bankr. M.D. Fla. 1989). *But see In re* Henke, 90 B.R. 451 (Bankr. D. Mont. 1988) (contribution of future patent income that averaged $40,000 per year to farm operation supported confirmation of new value plan).

be generated from future operations of the business is not a contribution of money or its worth.[59]

After *Ahlers,* most courts have held that contingent promises to pay in the future are not money or its worth.[60] Accordingly, in their view, an owner's guaranty of the business's debt cannot be money or its worth.[61] Guaranties are contingent because there is no certainty the owners will ever pay anything, and they are "intangible, inalienable, and, in all likelihood, unenforceable."[62] Some courts have noted that a guaranty is not a balance sheet asset that could be liquidated if the business failed.[63]

Other courts, however, have concluded that an owner's guaranty can be a new value contribution if the owner assumes an economic risk by making the guaranty.[64] Evidence that the debtor's assets may be insufficient to cover the loan and that owners have personal assets that could be applied against the guaranty can establish that economic risk.[65] This approach has been criticized as contrary to *Ahlers.* In *In re 47th and Bellview Partners,*[66] the bankruptcy court concluded that *Ahlers* eliminated assumption of an economic risk by the owner as a factor in determining whether a proposed contribution satisfies the new value exception. To the extent that any future contribution can be money or its worth, it should, of course, be reduced to present value.[67]

Some courts have concluded that an owner's forgiveness of debt or release of claims against the debtor may be a contribution of money or its worth.[68] It can be viewed as the functional equivalent of a cash contribution used to pay the same claim.[69] However, that conclusion can be criticized as contrary to *Ahlers.* One bankruptcy court

---

59 *In re* Olson, 80 B.R. 935 (Bankr. C.D. Ill. 1987); *In re* Pecht, 57 B.R. 137 (Bankr. E.D. Va. 1986).

60 *See, e.g.,* Kham & Nate's Shoes No. 2, Inc. v. First Bank, 908 F.2d 1351 (7th Cir. 1990); *In re* Sovereign Group 1985-27, Ltd., 142 B.R. 702 (E.D. Pa. 1992); *In re* Waldengreen Assocs., 150 B.R. 468 (Bankr. M.D. Fla. 1993).

61 Kham & Nate's Shoes No. 2, Inc. v. First Bank, 908 F.2d 1351 (7th Cir. 1990); *In re* Sovereign Group 1985-27, Ltd., 142 B.R. 702 (E.D. Pa. 1992); *In re* 47th & Belleview Partners, 95 B.R. 117 (Bankr. W.D. Mo. 1988).

62 Kham & Nate's Shoes No. 2, Inc. v. First Bank, 908 F.2d 1351 (7th Cir. 1990); *In re* 47th & Belleview Partners, 95 B.R. 117 (Bankr. W.D. Mo. 1988).

63 Kham & Nate's Shoes No. 2, Inc. v. First Bank, 908 F.2d 1351 (7th Cir. 1990); *In re* Sovereign Group 1985-27, Ltd., 142 B.R. 702 (E.D. Pa. 1992).

64 *In re* Yasparro, 100 B.R. 91 (Bankr. M.D. Fla. 1989); *In re* Snyder, 99 B.R. 885 (Bankr. C.D. Ill. 1989), *aff'd,* 144 B.R. 393 (C.D. Ill. 1990).

65 *See* Official Creditors' Comm. on Behalf of Class 8 Unsecured Creditors v. Potter Material Serv., Inc. (*In re* Potter Material Serv., Inc.), 781 F.2d 99 (7th Cir. 1986); *In re* Sawmill Hydraulics, Inc., 72 B.R. 454 (Bankr. C.D. Ill. 1987).

66 95 B.R. 117 (Bankr. W.D. Mo. 1988).

67 *See In re* Creekside Landing, Ltd., 140 B.R. 713 (Bankr. M.D. Tenn. 1992); *In re* Dowden, 143 B.R. 388 (Bankr. W.D. La. 1989).

68 *In re* VIP Motor Lodge, Inc., 133 B.R. 41 (Bankr. D. Del. 1991); *In re* River Capital Corp., 155 B.R. 382 (Bankr. E.D. Va. 1991); *In re* Sherwood Square Assocs., 107 B.R. 872 (Bankr. D. Md. 1989); *In re* Future Energy Corp., 83 B.R. 470 (Bankr. S.D. Ohio 1988).

69 *In re* Sherwood Square Assocs., 107 B.R. 872 (Bankr. D. Md. 1989).

has concluded that forgiveness of debt is not a contribution of money or its worth because it is not a balance sheet asset but is merely an accounting entry that reduces the amount of liabilities.[70]

Satisfying the money or money's worth requirement of the new value exception is a difficult task for a small business because the owners may well have no significant amount of cash that is not already invested in the business. As a practical matter, the rejection in *Ahlers* of the debtors' argument that an owner's contribution of future labor, experience, and expertise could satisfy the new value exception prevents many small businesses from using the exception.

§ 16.7 Substantial Contribution

Some courts include among the elements of the new value exception a requirement that the owners' contribution must be substantial.[71] What is meant by *substantial,* however, is uncertain. Some courts regard it as part of the reasonable equivalence requirement, discussed in § **16.8.**[72] Others regard it as part of the money or money's worth requirement discussed in § **16.6.**[73] Still others regard it as part of the necessity requirement discussed in § **16.4.**[74]

However, a substantial number of courts treat the requirement as a separate element, requiring that an owner's capital contribution must be substantial in relation to the amount of unsecured debt.[75] Under this approach, a contribution that equals only a small percentage of unsecured debt is not substantial.[76] Some courts also weigh the

---

[70] *In re* Snyder, 99 B.R. 885 (Bankr. C.D. Ill. 1989), *aff'd,* 144 B.R. 393 (C.D. Ill. 1990).

[71] *See, e.g.,* Unruh v. Rushville State Bank, 987 F.2d 1506 (10th Cir. 1993); *In re* Snyder, 967 F.2d 1126 (7th Cir. 1992); Official Creditors' Comm. on Behalf of Class 8 Unsecured Creditors v. Potter Material Serv., Inc. (*In re* Potter Material Serv., Inc.), 781 F.2d 99 (7th Cir. 1986). *But see, e.g., In re* Sovereign Group 1985-27, Ltd., 142 B.R. 702 (E.D. Pa. 1992); *In re* SABTC Townhouse Ass'n, Inc., 152 B.R. 1005 (Bankr. M.D. Fla. 1993); *In re* Montgomery Court Apartments, 141 B.R. 324 (Bankr. S.D. Ohio 1992).

[72] *E.g., In re* CPM Constr., 124 B.R. 335 (Bankr. D.N.M. 1991).

[73] *See, e.g., In re* Creekside Landing, Ltd., 140 B.R. 713 (Bankr. M.D. Tenn. 1992).

[74] *See In re* SM 104 Ltd., 160 B.R. 202 (Bankr. S.D. Fla. 1993).

[75] *See, e.g., In re* Snyder, 967 F.2d 1126 (7th Cir. 1992); *In re* Sovereign Group 1985-27, Ltd., 142 B.R. 702 (E.D. Pa. 1992); *In re* Creekside Landing, Ltd., 140 B.R. 713 (Bankr. M.D. Tenn. 1992).

[76] *See In re* Snyder, 967 F.2d 1126 (7th Cir. 1992) ($30,000 contribution not substantial in relation to $1.1 million unsecured debt); *In re* Sovereign Group 1985-27, Ltd., 142 B.R. 702 (E.D. Pa. 1992) ($135,000 not substantial in relation to unsecured debt of $3.8 million); *In re* Creekside Landing, Ltd., 140 B.R. 713 (Bankr. M.D. Tenn. 1992) ($150,000 not a substantial contribution when noninsider debt totalled over $1.5 million); *In re* Pullman Constr. Indus., Inc., 107 B.R. 909 (Bankr. N.D. Ill. 1989) ($450,000 contribution not substantial because it represented less than 2 percent of prepetition debt); *In re* Dowden, 143 B.R. 388 (Bankr. W.D. La. 1989) ($2,000 not substantial in relation to unsecured debt of $1.3 million); *In re* Rudy DeBruycker Ranch, Inc., 84 B.R. 187 (Bankr. D. Mont. 1988) ($50,000 contribution is de minimis in relation to unsecured

amount of the contribution against the amount of unsecured debt to be paid or discharged under the plan, which can work to the debtor's advantage when the plan will pay a substantial portion of the unsecured debt.[77] When defined in this manner, the substantiality requirement prevents owners from retaining ownership and control of insolvent businesses with minimal going-concern value by making nominal or token capital contributions that could otherwise be sufficient under the reasonable equivalence standard.[78]

In *In re Capital Center Equities,*[79] the bankruptcy court adapted the substantiality requirement for determining the adequacy of a contribution of new capital to small businesses. The court reasoned that the new value exception should not be strictly applied to small businesses because it was designed for large corporations with publicly traded stock. The court concluded that to determine the adequacy of a owner's contribution of new capital to a small business, the focus should be on whether the contribution represented the owners' best efforts, rather than strictly on the amount contributed in relation to the amount to be paid to creditors. The court found the initially proposed contribution of $50,000 to be too small compared to the proposed 10 percent payment of unsecured claims, but it stated that a $125,000 contribution resulting in a 30 percent payment of unsecured claims would be sufficient, given the limited means of the debtor's partners. This kind of approach to measuring the adequacy of a proposed capital contribution avoids the difficulties of valuation but may depart from the requirements for the new value exception set out in *Los Angeles Lumber.*

---

debt of $1.26 million); *In re* Kendavis Indus. Int'l, Inc., 91 B.R. 742 (Bankr. N.D. Tex. 1988) ($5 million cash and $20 million in subordinated debt "a drop in the bucket" in relation to debt of over $500 million); *In re* Olson, 80 B.R. 935 (Bankr. C.D. Ill. 1987) ($5,000 contribution represented only 1.56 percent of unsecured debt). *But see In re* SLC Ltd. V, 137 B.R. 847 (Bankr. D. Utah 1992) ($62,500 contribution not too small as a matter of law although amount was only 3 percent of total debt and 5 percent of unsecured debt); *In re* Yasparro, 100 B.R. 91 (Bankr. M.D. Fla. 1989) (amount of unsecured claims not relevant in determining adequacy of contribution by individual debtor).

[77] *See, e.g., In re* Sovereign Group 1985-27, Ltd., 142 B.R. 702 (E.D. Pa. 1992); *In re* Creekside Landing, Ltd., 140 B.R. 713 (Bankr. M.D. Tenn. 1992); *In re* Pullman Constr. Indus., Inc., 107 B.R. 909 (Bankr. N.D. Ill. 1989). *Compare In re* U.S. Truck Co., 47 B.R. 932 (E.D. Mich. 1985), *aff'd sub nom.* Teamsters Nat'l Freight Indus. Negotiating Comm. v. U.S. Truck Co., 800 F.2d 581 (6th Cir. 1986) ($100,000 contribution held sufficient in plan that proposed to pay 70 percent of unsecured claims), *with In re* Snyder, 105 B.R. 898 (Bankr. C.D. Ill. 1989), *aff'd,* 967 F.2d 1126 (7th Cir. 1992) ($30,000 contribution not substantial in plan that proposed to pay less than 10 percent of unsecured claims).

[78] *See In re* Snyder, 967 F.2d 1126 (7th Cir. 1992); *In re* Talahassee Assocs., L.P., 132 B.R. 712 (Bankr. W.D. Pa. 1991); *In re* 222 Liberty Assocs., 108 B.R. 971 (Bankr. E.D. Pa. 1990); *In re* Dowden, 143 B.R. 388 (Bankr. W.D. La. 1989).

[79] 144 B.R. 262 (Bankr. E.D. Pa. 1992).

§ 16.8 Reasonable Equivalence

The requirement that the owners' contribution be reasonably equivalent to the value of the interest retained is perhaps the most problematic of the elements of the new value exception. In *Case v. Los Angeles Lumber Products Co.,*[80] the Supreme Court stated that an owners' contribution of new capital must be reasonably equivalent to the value of the interest retained, and courts have continued to apply that standard.[81] A number of courts state the requirement somewhat differently, requiring that the contribution must be equal to or greater than the value of the retained interest.[82] This has been criticized for requiring an unrealistic degree of precision in valuation,[83] but there is probably little if any difference in result between the two standards. However the requirement is stated, its application requires a valuation of the retained ownership interest in the reorganized debtor, which is an inherently difficult and speculative task.[84] See **Chapter 11** for a discussion of methods of valuation.

An owner's retained interest must be measured in terms other than the debtor's net worth.[85] Debtors have frequently argued that an ownership interest in an insolvent business has no value, so that their proposed capital contributions are sufficient. These arguments, however, have been almost universally rejected,[86] and are untenable after *Norwest Bank Worthington v. Ahlers,* in which the Supreme Court stated:

> We join with the consensus of authority which has rejected this "no value" theory. Even where debts far exceed the current value of assets, a debtor who retains his equity interest in the enterprise retains "property." Whether the value is "present or prospective, for dividends or only for purposes of control" a retained equity interest is a property interest to "which the creditors [are] entitled . . . before the stockholders [can] retain it for any purpose whatever." . . . Indeed, even in a sole proprietorship, where "going concern" value may be minimal, there may still be some value in the control of the enterprise; obviously, also at issue is the interest in potential profits of a now-insolvent business. . . .

---

80 308 U.S. 106 (1939).

81 *E.g., In re* SM 104 Ltd., 160 B.R. 202 (Bankr. S.D. Fla. 1993).

82 *E.g.,* Official Creditors' Comm. on Behalf of Class 8 Unsecured Creditors v. Potter Material Serv., Inc. (*In re* Potter Material Serv., Inc.), 781 F.2d 99 (7th Cir. 1986); *In re* CPM Constr., 124 B.R. 335 (Bankr. D.N.M. 1991).

83 *In re* SM 104 Ltd., 160 B.R. 202 (Bankr. S.D. Fla. 1993); R. Peeples, *Staying In: Chapter 11, Close Corporations and the Absolute Priority Rule,* 63 Am. Bankr. L.J. 65, 83–84 (1989).

84 *In re* SM 104, Ltd., 160 B.R. 202 (Bankr. S.D. Fla. 1993); *In re* Bjolmes Realty Trust, 134 B.R. 1000 (Bankr. D. Mass. 1991); *In re* Pullman Constr. Indus., Inc., 107 B.R. 909 (Bankr. N.D. Ill. 1989). *In re* Future Energy Corp., 83 B.R. 470 (Bankr. S.D. Ohio 1988).

85 *In re* Resorts Int'l, Inc., 145 B.R. 412 (Bankr. D. N.J. 1990); *In re* Pullman Constr. Indus., Inc., 107 B.R. 909 (Bankr. N.D. Ill. 1989); *In re* Ag Consultants Grain Div., Inc., 77 B.R. 665 (Bankr. N.D. Ind. 1987).

86 *E.g.,* Unruh v. Rushville State Bank, 987 F.2d 1506 (10th Cir. 1993); Kham & Nate's Shoes No. 2, Inc. v. First Bank, 908 F.2d 1351 (7th Cir. 1990); *In re* Stegall, 865 F.2d 140 (7th Cir. 1989).

> "[O]bviously, there is some going concern value here, or the parties would not have been litigating over it for the last three years."[87]

If the "no value" argument were valid, any contribution by an owner of an insolvent business, no matter how small, would satisfy the reasonable equivalence requirement.[88] Although an insolvent business may well have minimal value as a going concern,[89] permitting owners to retain their interests for insignificant contributions would not serve the purpose of the new value exception, which is to provide capital necessary for survival of the business. If the business has little or no value as a going concern, an insignificant capital contribution could not significantly contribute to its survival. See **§ 16.4.** Under *Ahlers,* the value of an owner's retained interest is more than going-concern value, and includes the value of control of the business and of potential future profits.[90]

Although a reorganizing business has a value beyond its going-concern value, that has been at least a starting point for determining the value of a retained ownership interest under the new value exception.[91] Going-concern value is generally determined by capitalization of prospective earnings.[92] The determination can be extremely complex, and the result, representing the present value of projected future earnings, can vary greatly depending on the assumptions that must be made.[93] For a discussion of valuation methods, see **Chapter 11.**

The value of an owner's interest in a reorganizing business may be affected by a variety of factors. The effect of the reduction of debt under the plan on the value of the business should be considered. It is the postconfirmation value of the business that is relevant.[94] Competing offers by third parties to purchase the debtor also affect

---

87 485 U.S. 197, 207–09 (1988).

88 *In re* Stegall, 865 F.2d 140 (7th Cir. 1989); *In re* SM 104, Ltd., 160 B.R. 202 (Bankr. S.D. Fla. 1993); *In re* CPM Constr., 124 B.R. 335 (Bankr. D.N.M. 1991).

89 *See* Norwest Bank Worthington v. Ahlers, 485 U.S. 197 (1988); Unruh v. Rushville State Bank, 987 F.2d 1506 (10th Cir. 1993).

90 Norwest Bank Worthington v. Ahlers, 485 U.S. 197 (1988). *See, e.g., In re* SM 104, Ltd., 160 B.R. 202 (Bankr. S.D. Fla. 1993); *In re* Creekside Landing, Ltd., 140 B.R. 713 (Bankr. M.D. Tenn. 1992); *In re* Pullman Constr. Indus., Inc., 107 B.R. 909 (Bankr. N.D. Ill. 1989).

91 *See, e.g.,* Official Creditors' Comm. on Behalf of Class 8 Unsecured Creditors v. Potter Material Serv., Inc. (*In re* Potter Material Serv., Inc.), 781 F.2d 99 (7th Cir. 1986); *In re* Creekside Landing, Ltd., 140 B.R. 713 (Bankr. M.D. Tenn. 1992); *In re* Future Energy Corp., 83 B.R. 470 (Bankr. S.D. Ohio 1988).

92 *See, e.g., In re* SM 104, Ltd., 160 B.R. 202 (Bankr. S.D. Fla. 1993); *In re* Creekside Landing, Ltd., 140 B.R. 713 (Bankr. M.D. Tenn. 1992); *In re* SLC Ltd. V, 137 B.R. 847 (Bankr. D. Utah 1992); *In re* Future Energy Corp., 83 B.R. 470 (Bankr. S.D. Ohio 1988).

93 *E.g., In re* Pullman Constr. Indus., Inc., 107 B.R. 909 (Bankr. N.D. Ill. 1989); *In re* Future Energy Corp., 83 B.R. 470 (Bankr. S.D. Ohio 1988).

94 *In re* Future Energy Corp., 83 B.R. 470 (Bankr. S.D. Ohio 1988).

valuation.[95] Lack of interest in purchasing the debtor when placed on the market may also be relevant.[96]

Any special value of the business to the owners that is beyond market value should be considered. For example, in *In re S.A.B.T.C. Townhouse Association, Inc.*,[97] the debtor homeowners' association owned the common areas of a townhouse development. Although the common areas had no market value, they enhanced the value of each owner's unit by almost $6,000, for a total value in use of $724,000. The bankruptcy court denied confirmation in part because the owners' contribution was less than that value.

Ownership of a small business may have special value to owners because it provides employment and salary for the owner and perhaps family members.[98] This value may be substantial. For example, in *In re Pullman Construction Industries, Inc.*,[99] the value of the business to the owners was enhanced by the $225,000 in annual salaries paid to the owners and their family members. Retention of ownership may also provide tax benefits to owners that may be considered in determining the adequacy of a proposed capital contribution.[100] Other aspects of the plan that benefit the owners may also be considered in determining the value of the ownership interest retained. Payment of a debtor's claims under a plan may relieve the owners of personal liability for taxes[101] or on guaranties.[102] Owners may also benefit from payment of their claims against the debtor under a plan.[103] Finally, owners may have noneconomic reasons for valuing the ownership of a business, such as sentiment or prestige of ownership.[104] These factors all increase the value of the ownership and may require a larger contribution to satisfy the reasonable equivalence requirement.

The allocation of risks and benefits to the parties under a new value plan may affect the valuation of the retained ownership interest. In farm and single-asset real estate cases in which the debtors' principal assets consist of fully encumbered land and the principal lenders are undersecured, reorganization of the debtor may be essentially a speculative venture whose success depends on a change in real estate

---

95 *See In re* Creekside Landing, Ltd., 140 B.R. 713 (Bankr. M.D. Tenn. 1992); *In re* Kendavis Indus. Int'l, Inc., 91 B.R. 742 (Bankr. N.D. Tex. 1988).

96 *See In re* Jartran, Inc., 44 B.R. 331 (Bankr. N.D. Ill. 1984).

97 152 B.R. 1005 (Bankr. M.D. Fla. 1993).

98 *See In re* Creekside Landing, Ltd., 140 B.R. 713 (Bankr. M.D. Tenn. 1992); *In re* Pullman Constr. Indus., Inc., 107 B.R. 909 (Bankr. N.D. Ill. 1989). *See also In re* Stegall, 865 F.2d 140 (7th Cir. 1989).

99 107 B.R. 909 (Bankr. N.D. Ill. 1989).

100 *In re* Creekside Landing, Ltd., 140 B.R. 713 (Bankr. M.D. Tenn. 1992); *In re* Pullman Constr. Indus., Inc., 107 B.R. 909 (Bankr. N.D. Ill. 1989). *See In re* Aztec Co., 107 B.R. 585 (Bankr. M.D. Tenn. 1989). *But see In re* Sherwood Square Assocs., 107 B.R. 872 (Bankr. D. Md. 1989) (tax benefits to owners are not an interest in property of the debtor but rather are benefits personal to the owners).

101 *In re* Pullman Constr. Indus., Inc., 107 B.R. 909 (Bankr. N.D. Ill. 1989).

102 *In re* Creekside Landing, Ltd., 140 B.R. 713 (Bankr. M.D. Tenn. 1992).

103 *Id.*

104 *In re* Stegall, 865 F.2d 140 (7th Cir. 1989); *In re* SM 104, Ltd., 160 B.R. 202 (Bankr. S.D. Fla. 1993); *In re* Witt, 60 B.R. 556 (Bankr. N.D. Iowa 1986).

values. Some courts have found owners' proposed capital contributions in this type of case to be inadequate when the undersecured creditors will not receive any benefit if property values increase but stand to lose if property values decline.[105] However, although owners will be the principal beneficiaries of an increase in value, they also run the risk of losing their new contribution.[106] And, at least in theory, the contribution benefits creditors.[107] Moreover, because a creditor can ensure that it benefits from any increase in value by electing to waive its unsecured deficiency claim and be treated as fully secured under 11 U.S.C. § 1111(b)(2),[108] the debtor can argue that it is not the new value plan that prevents the undersecured creditor from sharing in any increase, but rather the creditor's choice to assert the deficiency claim and in all likelihood prevent confirmation of a consensual plan by controlling the vote of an unsecured class.

Some courts suggest that it may be necessary to compensate creditors for the loss of rights they would have had absent the owners' contribution.[109] What unsecured creditors lose in a new value plan is control: the right to exclude the current owners from the business unless paid in full.[110] In *In re Greystone III Joint Venture V*,[111] the court suggested that in some cases, it may be necessary for the debtors to compensate creditors for their loss of rights by conferring "offsetting rights, such as ownership participation, an option to purchase, or some other such device."[112] Other devices might include a provision that any cash flow in excess of plan projections be paid to unsecured creditors until they are paid in full,[113] or a provision for refinancing at the end of the plan period to pay any remaining debt.[114] Even if not required by the

---

105 *See In re* One Times Square Assocs., 159 B.R. 695 (Bankr. S.D.N.Y. 1993); *In re* Miami Ctr. Assocs., 144 B.R. 937 (Bankr. S.D. Fla. 1992); *In re* Talahassee Assocs., 132 B.R. 712 (Bankr. W.D. Pa. 1991); *In re* Olson, 80 B.R. 935 (Bankr. C.D. Ill. 1987).

106 *In re* 222 Liberty Assocs., 108 B.R. 971 (Bankr. E.D. Pa. 1990). *See also In re* Landau Boat Co., 13 B.R. 788 (W.D. Mo. 1981).

107 *See* Penn Mut. Life Ins. Co. v. Woodscape, Ltd. (*In re* Woodscape, Ltd.), 134 B.R. 165 (Bankr. D. Md. 1991); *In re* Sherwood Square Assocs., 107 B.R. 872 (Bankr. D. Md. 1989).

108 *See* James A. Pusateri, Lloyd C. Swartz, and Mark A. Shaiken, *Section 1111(b) of the Bankruptcy Code: How Much Does the Debtor have to Pay and When Should the Creditor Elect?,* 58 Am. Bankr. L.J. 129 (1984).

109 *See, e.g., In re* Stegall, 865 F.2d 140 (7th Cir. 1989).

110 *See id.; In re* Batten, 141 B.R. 899 (Bankr. W.D. La. 1992); *In re* Dowden, 143 B.R. 388 (Bankr. W.D. La. 1989).

111 102 B.R. 560 (Bankr. W.D. Tex. 1989), *aff'd,* 127 B.R. 138 (W.D. Tex. 1990), *rev'd on other grounds,* 995 F.2d 1274 (5th Cir. 1991), *petition for reh'g granted in part, opinion withdrawn in part,* 995 F.2d 1284 (5th Cir.), *cert. denied,* ___ U.S. ___, 113 S. Ct. 72 (1992).

112 102 B.R. at 580. *See also In re* E.I. Parks No. 1, Ltd., 122 B.R. 549 (Bankr. W.D. Ark. 1990) (plan proposed that unsecured creditors receive 15% limited partnership interest in reorganized debtor). *Cf. In re* SLC Ltd. V, 137 B.R. 847 (Bankr. D. Utah 1992) (not fair and equitable for owners to receive 18% return on their capital contribution before unsecured claims are paid).

113 *In re* Pullman Constr. Indus., Inc., 107 B.R. 909 (Bankr. N.D. Ill. 1989).

114 *In re* Henke, 90 B.R. 451 (Bankr. D. Mont. 1988).

new value exception, these kinds of provisions may alleviate some of the unfairness to creditors perceived in plans that give all the benefit of any possible future increase in value to the owners without paying unsecured claims in full.

§ 16.9 Auction Approach to New Value Contribution

In the view of many courts, retention of ownership in exchange for a contribution of new capital is essentially a purchase of the business by the owners.[115] Plans providing for sale of a business to outside investors are not improper, and some courts have concluded that it is likewise proper to sell a business to its owners under a new value plan.[116] However, as discussed above in **§ 16.2,** new value plans giving the owners the exclusive right to buy the business without competition and without following the sale requirements of §§ 363, 1123(a)(5)(d), and 1129(a)(11) may give the owners property on account of their prior ownership interests in violation of the absolute priority rule of § 1129(b)(2)(B)(ii).[117] It should be noted that in at least two of the few reported confirmed new value plans, the owners did not have an exclusive opportunity to purchase the business because the stock in the reorganized debtor was made available to creditors as well as existing shareholders.[118]

One bankruptcy court has addressed this problem by adopting an auction procedure for applying the new value exception in which creditors are given the opportunity to purchase the ownership interests.[119] In *In re Bjolmes Realty Trust,*[120] the court required as a condition of confirmation that the debtor's shares be auctioned among the shareholders and creditors. The winning bidder would receive a 100 percent equity interest in the debtor, represented by the issuance of new shares in replacement of existing shares, and would be required to cause the debtor to consummate the plan, with an increase in plan payments to the extent that the bid exceeded the

---

115 *See, e.g.,* Bonner Mall Partnership v. U.S. Bancorp Mortgage Co. (*In re* Bonner Mall Partnership), 2 F.3d 899 (9th Cir. 1993), *cert. granted,* ___ U.S. ___, 126 L. Ed. 2d 648, *removed from argument calendar,* ___ U.S. ___, 114 S. Ct. 1367 (1994); Travelers Ins. Co. v. Bryson Properties, XVIII (*In re* Bryson Properties, XVIII), 961 F.2d 496 (4th Cir.), *cert. denied,* ___ U.S. ___, 113 S. Ct. 191 (1992); Kham & Nate's Shoes No. 2, Inc. v. First Bank, 908 F.2d 1351 (7th Cir. 1990); *In re* SM 104, Ltd., 160 B.R. 202 (Bankr. S.D. Fla. 1993); *In re* Bjolmes Realty Trust, 134 B.R. 1000 (Bankr. D. Mass. 1991).

116 *E.g., In re* Snyder, 967 F.2d 1126 (7th Cir. 1992); *In re* Pullman Constr. Indus., Inc., 107 B.R. 909 (Bankr. N.D. Ill. 1989); *In re* East, 57 B.R. 14 (Bankr. M.D. La. 1985).

117 Travelers Ins. Co. v. Bryson Properties, XVIII (*In re* Bryson Properties, XVIII), 961 F.2d 496 (4th Cir.), *cert. denied,* ___ U.S. ___, 113 S. Ct. 191 (1992); Piedmont Assocs. v. CIGNA Property & Casualty Ins. Co., 132 B.R. 75 (N.D. Ga. 1991); *In re* Drimmel, 108 B.R. 284 (Bankr. D. Kan. 1989), *aff'd,* 135 B.R. 410 (D. Kan. 1991), *aff'd,* 987 F.2d 1506 (10th Cir. 1993).

118 *In re* River Capital Corp., 155 B.R. 382 (Bankr. E.D. Va. 1991); *In re* Landau Boat Co., 13 B.R. 788 (W.D. Mo. 1981).

119 *In re* Bjolmes Realty Trust, 134 B.R. 1000 (Bankr. D. Mass. 1991).

120 *Id.*

new value offered by the shareholders. The court noted that creditors would not be permitted to offset their claims against the purchase price because setoff would deprive other unsecured creditors of their share of the purchase price.[121]

In *In re SM 104, Ltd.*,[122] the court concluded it was unnecessary for the court to conduct an auction because the disclosure and confirmation procedures of Chapter 11 already afford creditors the opportunity to make counteroffers for the purchase of ownership interests in the debtor. The court stated that the information contained in a disclosure statement complying with 11 U.S.C. § 1125 "is adequate to promote an informed bidding process among the parties" and concluded that:

> Such a bidding process can take place regardless of whether the debtor's exclusive right to propose a plan has been terminated or has expired. *See* 11 U.S.C. § 1121(b), (c). If the debtor's exclusivity period has ended or been terminated, any creditor can propose a competing plan incorporating an attempt to outbid old equity for the equity in the reorganized debtor. 11 U.S.C. § 1121(c). Moreover, even if the debtor's exclusivity period has not ended, any creditor can move to lift exclusivity and then propose its own plan incorporating a competing bid. 11 U.S.C. 1121(d).[123]

An auction approach could also avoid the inherent difficulty and uncertainty of valuation, which would otherwise be required in applying the new value exception to determine if the owners' contributions are reasonably equivalent to the value of the retained ownership interest.[124] See § **16.8.** Under this approach, the market rather than the court would determine the value of the ownership interest. However, it would only do so when there are competing bids from creditors. When there are none, *Bjolmes*[125] suggests that the business would have to be placed on the market to encourage outside buyers. However, it is unlikely that a general public auction would draw bidders because "[t]he market for equity participation for failing business is thin, and the market for failing small business is even thinner."[126] Even under the auction approach, application of the new value exception may require valuation of the business by the court, which is a difficult and uncertain process. See § **16.8.**

§ 16.10 Future of the Absolute Priority Rule

The absolute priority rule and the new value exception were developed in cases involving the reorganization of large public corporations.[127] The rules make sense in

---

121 *Id.* at 1010 n.22.

122 160 B.R. 202 (Bankr. S.D. Fla. 1993).

123 *Id.* at 227.

124 *See In re* Bjolmes Realty Trust, 134 B.R. 1000 (Bankr. D. Mass. 1991).

125 *Id.*

126 *In re* SM 104, Ltd., 160 B.R. 202 (Bankr. S.D. Fla. 1993).

127 *See* Consolidated Rock Prods. Co. v. Du Bois, 312 U.S. 510 (1941); Case v. Los Angeles Lumber Prods. Co., 308 U.S. 106 (1939); Kansas City Terminal Ry. v. Central Union Trust Co., 271 U.S. 445 (1926); Northern Pac. Ry. v. Boyd, 228 U.S. 482 (1913).

that context. The absolute priority rule is not an insurmountable obstacle to reorganization of a large corporation because a large corporation with publicly traded stock that is unable to pay unsecured claims in full can nonetheless reorganize and continue to operate with entirely different ownership. The stockholders are generally passive investors whose continued participation is not essential to the business. The new value exception also may be a realistic alternative for a large public corporation. Because shareholders who are passive investors are unlikely to have most of their personal wealth tied up in the debtor, they are a possible source of new capital for the business.

For small businesses, however, the absolute priority rule can be an insurmountable obstacle to reorganization. Financially troubled small businesses are unlikely to be able to pay unsecured claims in full, and their owners have no incentive to reorganize if they will lose their ownership interests. Because in many cases the owners *are* the business, reorganization is impossible without their participation. And it is very difficult for owners of a small business to satisfy the new value exception to the absolute priority rule because the money or money's worth standard requires them to contribute cash they are very unlikely to have available.

Congress recognized the harsh effect of the absolute priority rule on small businesses in 1952, when it eliminated it as a requirement for confirmation of a plan under Chapters XI, XII, and XIII of the Bankruptcy Act but left it as a requirement for reorganization of large public corporations under Chapter X.[128] The 1952 amendment also specifically provided that confirmation of a Chapter XI arrangement could not be denied "solely because the interest of a debtor, or if the debtor is a corporation, the interests of its stockholders or members will be preserved under the arrangement."[129]

When Congress enacted the Code, it consolidated the three former business reorganization chapters of the Bankruptcy Act into a single chapter, Chapter 11, thereby applying the same confirmation standards to large public corporations and small businesses. Although the absolute priority rule has less significance now than under former Chapter X of the Bankruptcy Act because it now applies only when an impaired class of unsecured claims rejects the plan,[130] it still has a disproportionately adverse effect on small businesses. Also, the new value exception is not a realistic way for small business owners to retain ownership.

Currently, individuals who qualify for Chapter 13 relief and family farmers, whether sole proprietorships, partnerships, or close corporations, that qualify for Chapter 12 relief may reorganize their businesses without satisfying the absolute priority rule by paying unsecured claims in full if they apply all of their disposable

---

[128] *See* S. Rep. No. 1395, 82d Cong., 2d Sess. 11 (1952).

[129] Act of July 7, 1952, ch. 579, § 35, 66 Stat. 420, 433 (1952) (amending § 366 of the Bankruptcy Act of 1898) (repealed 1978). At the same time, Congress added similar provisions to § 472 of Chapter XII (governing real estate arrangements) and § 656 of Chapter XIII (governing wage earners' plans).

[130] *See* Kham & Nate's Shoes No. 2, Inc. v. First Bank, 908 F.2d 1351 (7th Cir. 1990); *In re* Lumber Exch., Ltd., 125 B.R. 1000 (Bankr. D. Minn 1991), *aff'd,* 134 B.R. 354 (D. Minn. 1991), *aff'd,* 968 F.2d 647 (8th Cir. 1992); Pennbank v. Winters (*In re* Winters), 99 B.R. 658 (Bankr. W.D. Pa. 1989).

income to the plan.[131] This *best efforts standard* is a much more realistic one for small businesses than the new value exception, which requires up-front contributions of cash beyond the means of most small business debtors. There is no reason why this standard should apply to individuals and farms but not to smaller partnerships and close corporations in other businesses, at least if those businesses are not passive investment vehicles such as real estate limited partnerships. The same kinds of policy and sentimental reasons that support special bankruptcy provisions for farmers also support them for small "mom and pop" operations in other businesses. Whether these provisions should be available at all to any debtors can be debated on economic, philosophic and moral grounds, but as long as they are available to some smaller businesses, they should be available to others.

Proposed legislation considered by Congress in 1992 and 1993 (see **Chapter 24**) would have extended those provisions to other small businesses. The bill would have established a small business chapter that would have replaced the absolute priority rule with the disposable income "best efforts" confirmation standards of Chapters 12 and 13 for businesses whose total debts did not exceed $2,500,000.[132] The proposal was controversial, however, and in the spring of 1994, the Senate dropped the small business chapter from the bill.[133]

Small businesses in Chapter 11, therefore, remain subject to the absolute priority rule. Small business owners must continue to rely on the tenuous new value exception to attempt to preserve their ownership interests.

---

131 11 U.S.C. §§ 101(18), 1225(b), 1325(b).

132 *See* S. 540, 103d Cong., 1st Sess. (1993).

133 *See* Additional Views of Senator Hatch and Detailed Statement of Position of the National Bankruptcy Conference, *printed in* S. Rep. No. 168, 103d Cong., 1st Sess. 60–63 (1993); S. 540, 103d Cong., 2d Sess. § 201 (1994). See **Ch. 24.**

CHAPTER 17

POSTCONFIRMATION ISSUES IN SMALL BUSINESS BANKRUPTCIES

F. Stannard Lentz, Carl R. Clark, Mark A. Goucher, and John J. Cruciani

§ 17.1 The Effect of Plan Confirmation

The confirmation of a plan of reorganization is an important milestone in the progress of a case, and it has significance in several areas. This chapter discusses the effect of confirmation on the debtor, the property of the estate, the automatic stay, and the discharge of the debtor.

Once a plan has been confirmed, the debtor is no longer a debtor-in-possession but rather is a reorganized debtor.[1] Debtor-in-possession status terminates at confirmation.[2]

The Bankruptcy Code states that confirmation of a plan vests all of the property of the estate in the reorganized debtor unless the plan itself provides otherwise.[3]

---

1 *In re* NTG Indus., Inc., 118 B.R. 606, 610 (Bankr. N.D. Ill. 1990).

2 *In re* Grinstead, 75 B.R. 2, 3 (Bankr. D. Minn. 1985).

3 11 U.S.C. § 1141(b); *see* United States v. Redmond, 36 B.R. 932, 934 (D. Kan. 1984); *In re* HRP Auto Ctr., Inc., 130 B.R. 247, 256 (Bankr. N.D. Ohio 1991); *In re* TSP Indus., Inc., 120 B.R. 107, 109 (Bankr. N.D. Ill. 1990); *In re* NTG Indus., Inc., 118 B.R. 606, 610 (Bankr. N.D. Ill. 1990); *In re* TSP Indus., Inc., 117 B.R. 375, 377 (Bankr. N.D. Ill. 1990); *In re* WRMJ Johnson Fruit Farm, Inc., 107 B.R. 18, 19 (Bankr. W.D.N.Y.

Once a plan has been confirmed, in "the absence of any contrary provisions in [the] plan, title to property revests in the [reorganized] debtor along with normal ownership rights."[4]

In a 1982 case,[5] a debtor, Westholt Manufacturing, filed a voluntary petition under Chapter 11 of the Bankruptcy Code. After confirmation of the debtor's plan, the case was converted to Chapter 7 on motion by the debtor. The issue before the Court in the *Westholt Manufacturing* case was the priority to be given to a tax liability that was incurred by the debtor subsequent to the commencement of the Chapter 11 case but prior to its conversion to Chapter 7. As a preliminary issue, the court held that once a plan has been confirmed, the bankruptcy estate is terminated and all property revests in the debtor.[6] On appeal, the district court affirmed, stating, "[i]t is clear that upon confirmation of a plan of reorganization, property of the bankruptcy estate vests in the reorganized debtor, a new entity, and administration of the estate ceases."[7] As another court put it, "Once a plan has been confirmed, there is no longer a trustee and no longer an estate."[8]

Confirmation also affects the automatic stay. Section 362(c) controls termination of the automatic stay in a confirmed Chapter 11 case. It states in relevant part, "the stay of any other act under subsection (a) of this section continues until . . . the time a discharge is granted or denied."[9] This section was interpreted in *In re Herron,*[10] a case in which a reorganized debtor under a confirmed plan and a secured creditor argued over whether or not the automatic stay provision of § 362 applied following confirmation. The court held that because confirmation of the plan both revests the debtor with title to its property and discharges the debtor from all of its dischargeable debts, the automatic stay of § 362 cannot apply postconfirmation.[11] Other courts agree,[12] and one has said, "[t]he automatic stay of section 362 remains in effect while a chapter 11 plan is pending confirmation. Upon the plan's confirmation, . . . however, the automatic stay terminates pursuant to section 362(c) and creditors may proceed to collect post-confirmation debts from the debtor."[13]

In spite of the termination of the automatic stay, creditors are not free to pursue the debtor postconfirmation on prepetition debts because confirmation serves as a discharge of the debtor's obligations. Section 1141(d)(1) states, "Except as otherwise

---

1989); *In re* Grinstead, 75 B.R. 2, 3 (Bankr. D. Minn. 1985); *In re* Ford, 61 B.R. 913, 917 (Bankr. W.D. Wis. 1986).

4 *In re* Ford, 61 B.R. 913, 917 (Bankr. W.D. Wis. 1986).

5 *In re* Westholt Mfg., Inc., 20 B.R. 368 (Bankr. D. Kan. 1982), *aff'd sub nom.,* United States v. Redmond, 36 B.R. 932 (D. Kan. 1984).

6 *In re* Westholt Mfg., Inc., 20 B.R. at 372.

7 United States v. Redmond, 36 B.R. at 934.

8 *In re* WRMJ Johnson Fruit Farm, Inc., 107 B.R. 18, 19 (Bankr. W.D.N.Y. 1989).

9 11 U.S.C. § 362(c)(2).

10 60 B.R. 82 (Bankr. W.D. La. 1986).

11 *Id.* at 83–84.

12 *E.g., In re* Draggoo Elec. Co., 57 B.R. 916, 919 (Bankr. N.D. Ind. 1986); *In re* Paradise Valley Country Club, 31 B.R. 613 (Bankr. D. Colo. 1983).

13 *In re* Westholt Mfg., Inc., 20 B.R. 368, 372 (Bankr. D. Kan. 1982).

provided in this subsection, in the plan, or in the order confirming the plan, the confirmation of a plan . . . discharges the debtor from any debt that arose before the date of such confirmation."[14] This section of the Bankruptcy Code applies to all debtors, individual, partnership, and corporate. Although creditors may not like this rule, one court has explained it in these words:

> The discharge provided by Section 1141(d) presumes that, in the process of formulating and voting on a reorganization plan, all classes of claimants will be able to use whatever leverage they may have, such as priority status, to effect the best treatment they can obtain for their particular claims.[15]

Because it functions as a discharge, an order of confirmation enjoins creditors from "the commencement or continuation of any action, the employment of process, or an act, to collect, recover, or offset" any dischargeable debts against the debtor or its property.[16]

In summary, the entry of an order of confirmation has four significant effects on the bankruptcy proceeding:

1. Debtor-in-possession status terminates
2. All property of the bankruptcy estate reverts back to the debtor, thereby terminating the estate
3. The automatic stay is no longer in effect
4. The debtor is discharged of all dischargeable debts.

§ 17.2 Postconfirmation Jurisdiction of the Court

Even if a plan of reorganization does not provide specifically for the retention of jurisdiction by the bankruptcy court, the general rule of the case law and the Code is that at least limited postconfirmation jurisdiction exists.

Section 1142(b) authorizes the exercise of postconfirmation jurisdiction. It states:

> The court may direct the debtor and any other necessary party to execute or deliver or to join in the execution or delivery of any instrument required to effect the transfer of property dealt with by a confirmed plan, and to perform any other act, including the satisfaction of any lien, that is necessary for the consummation of the plan.[17]

Additionally, § 105(a) can be read to grant postconfirmation jurisdiction to the bankruptcy courts. It is entitled "Power of court" and states:

> The court may issue any order, process, or judgment that is necessary or appropriate to carry out the provisions of this title. No provision of this title providing for the raising

[14] 11 U.S.C. § 1141(d)(1)(A).

[15] *In re* Benjamin Coal Co., 978 F.2d 823, 827 (3d Cir. 1992).

[16] 11 U.S.C. § 524(a)(2) and (3).

[17] 11 U.S.C. § 1142(b).

> of an issue by a party in interest shall be construed to preclude the court from, sua sponte, taking any action or making any determination necessary or appropriate to enforce or implement court orders or rules, or to prevent an abuse of process.[18]

This section opens the possibility of discretionary assumption of postconfirmation jurisdiction, at the very least on the basis of the last clause, "or to prevent an abuse of process."

A leading case in this area is *In re Johns-Manville Corp.*[19] In that case, after confirmation, several parties named the debtor as the defendant in certain lawsuits. These lawsuits were in clear violation of the plan of reorganization.

As a preliminary matter, the court addressed the issue of postconfirmation jurisdiction. First it noted, "[t]o the extent provided for in a plan of reorganization, a bankruptcy court retains post-confirmation jurisdiction to determine certain disputes, especially those that arise under the plan."[20] Then it stated, "Even without a specific retention provision in the plan, this Court has previously held that jurisdiction of the bankruptcy court continues post-confirmation as to fundamental questions of interpretation and administration of a plan . . . [Jurisdiction] continues whether future consideration of them was expressly reserved or not."[21]

The *Johns-Manville* court took a broad view of postconfirmation jurisdiction. Other courts, however, have held that the Bankruptcy Code provides for more limited jurisdiction postconfirmation. In *Goodman v. Phillip R. Curtis Enterprises, Inc.,*[22] the Fourth Circuit Court of Appeals stated, "[the § 1142] grant of post-confirmation authority thus undoubtedly limits the authority of the court to matters concerning the implementation or execution of a confirmed plan."[23]

Although the *Goodman* court held that postconfirmation jurisdiction is not as expansive as preconfirmation jurisdiction, it conceded that postconfirmation jurisdiction exists: "Whatever the technical effect of confirmation on the court's authority under the new Code, it obviously does not divest the bankruptcy court of all jurisdiction in the case."[24] Therefore, even under the view of the *Goodman* court, a court retains postconfirmation jurisdiction for certain matters related to the plan and other similar issues.[25]

It is not settled whether the bankruptcy courts have jurisdiction after a plan is confirmed to deal with a debtor's default under the plan. One court stated, "The [reorganized] debtor's property is not subject to trustee or court control. If the debtor fails to carry out the confirmed plan, this court may or may not even have jurisdiction to grant relief."[26] Similarly, in *In re Ernst,*[27] the court stated:

---

18 *Id.* § 105(a).

19 97 B.R. 174 (Bankr. S.D.N.Y. 1989).

20 *Id.* at 180.

21 *Id.* (citing *In re* Johns-Manville Corp., 91 B.R. 225, 228 (Bankr. S.D.N.Y. 1988)).

22 809 F.2d 228 (4th Cir. 1987).

23 *Id.* at 232.

24 *Id.*

25 *See In re* NTG Indus., Inc. 118 B.R. 606, 611 (Bankr. N.D. Ill. 1990).

26 *In re* Barker Medical Co., 55 B.R. 435, 436 (Bankr. M.D. Ala. 1985).

27 45 B.R. 700 (Bankr. D. Minn. 1985).

> Retention by the Bankruptcy Court of jurisdiction in the case post-confirmation merely continues availability of the Court as a forum for resolution of questions regarding administration of the plan and disputes that might arise under it. But it is not in all instances the only forum available to interested parties . . . [T]he mere reservation of jurisdiction in the case by the Bankruptcy Court post-confirmation does not foreclose the right of a party to seek his remedy upon default under the plan in a state court having jurisdiction over the subject matter of the dispute.[28]

The district court in *In re Paradise Valley Country Club*[29] held similarly, stating that "[t]he retained [post-confirmation] jurisdiction of [the] court to aid in the completion of the plan is not exclusive of the state courts' jurisdiction to remedy violation of contracts entered into by the reorganized debtor."[30]

§ 17.3 Effect of Plan Confirmation on Guarantors

Whether a confirmed plan operates as a discharge of the debtor's guarantors or sureties is an important issue for small businesses. This is because the principals of small businesses, and, in many cases, their relatives, are frequently required to sign personal guaranties of business loans.

As noted in **§ 17.2,** confirmation generally serves as a discharge of the debtor's obligations. Section 524(e) of the Bankruptcy Code deals with how discharge of a debtor affects the obligations of others outside the scope of the plan of reorganization. It states, in relevant part, that "discharge of a debt of the debtor does not affect the liability of any other entity on, or the property of any other entity for, such debt."[31]

Union Carbide Corp. v. Newboles[32] is a leading case dealing with the effect a plan has on guarantors. In that case, Union Carbide loaned $225,000 to New-Kro Oil Company. The president of New-Kro and his wife, Allen and Mary Newboles, personally guaranteed the loan. New-Kro defaulted on the loan and subsequently filed for protection under Chapter 11 of the Bankruptcy Code. The plan of reorganization provided that the corporate debtor, as well as all guarantors of the debtor, would be discharged at the time of confirmation of the plan. The plan was approved by a majority of creditors, including Union Carbide, and was confirmed by the bankruptcy court. Subsequent to confirmation, Union Carbide brought an action against the Newboles, and summary judgment was granted in favor of Union Carbide for the remaining balance due on the note.[33]

On appeal, the Circuit Court of Appeals affirmed the lower court's decision, reasoning that the language in the plan discharging the Newboles of liability was not effective against Union Carbide. "A creditor's approval of the bankruptcy plan does

---

28 *Id.* at 702.

29 31 B.R. 613 (D. Colo. 1983).

30 *Id.* at 615.

31 11 U.S.C. § 524(e).

32 686 F.2d 593 (7th Cir. 1982).

33 *Id.* at 594–95.

not discharge the bankrupt's guarantors . . . [It] cannot be deemed an act of assent having significance beyond the confines of the bankruptcy proceedings."[34]

Some other cases also hold that guarantors or sureties are not discharged of their liabilities in a bankruptcy as debtors are.[35] However, *In re Monroe Well Service, Inc.*[36] held that if creditors consent to the discharge of a guarantor or surety (for example, by releasing a nondebtor obligor of an obligation in return for payment by a nondebtor pursuant to the plan), then that guarantor or surety is discharged in the same manner as the debtor-principal obligor.[37] *Monroe Well Service* is not really in conflict with *Union Carbide* because a distinction can be drawn between merely voting in favor of a plan that provides for guarantor discharge and expressly consenting to a guarantor's discharge. Also, if a plan of reorganization provides for the discharge of a guarantor or surety, and a creditor objects to that discharge, the guarantor or surety would not be discharged.[38]

§ 17.4 Modification of the Plan

A confirmed plan of reorganization may be modified, in certain situations, to allow a reorganized debtor or another plan proponent to effectuate a meaningful reorganization of the business. Section 1127(b) controls plan modification postconfirmation. It states:

> The proponent of a plan or the reorganized debtor may modify such plan at any time after confirmation of such plan and before substantial consummation of such plan, but may not modify such plan so that such plan as modified fails to meet the requirements of sections 1122 and 1123 of this title. Such plan as modified under this subsection becomes the plan only if circumstances warrant such modification and the court, after notice and a hearing, confirms such plan as modified, under section 1129 of this title.[39]

Substantial consummation is defined in § 1101(2) of the Bankruptcy Code as a:

> (A) transfer of all or substantially all of the property proposed by the plan to be transferred;
> (B) assumption by the debtor or by the successor to the debtor under the plan of the business or of the management of all or substantially all of the property dealt with by the plan; and
> (C) commencement of distribution under the plan.[40]

---

34 *Id.* at 595.

35 *E.g., In re* Western Real Estate Fund, Inc., 922 F.2d 592 (10th Cir. 1990); Underhill v. Royal, 769 F.2d 1426 (9th Cir. 1985); United States v. Stribling Flying Serv., 734 F.2d 221 (5th Cir. 1984).

36 80 B.R. 324 (Bankr. E.D. Pa. 1987).

37 *Id.* at 334.

38 *See In re* Consolidated Motor Inns, 666 F.2d 189 (5th Cir. 1982).

39 11 U.S.C. § 1127(b).

40 *Id.* § 1101(2).

All three criteria of [§ 1101(2)] must be satisfied before a plan may be considered substantially consummated.[41]

Substantial consummation of a plan of reorganization is a question of fact and is determined on a case-by-case basis.[42] The proponent of the modification has the burden of proof that the plan has not been substantially consummated.[43] If a plan of reorganization has been substantially consummated, it may not be modified by anyone.[44]

An early case dealing with substantial consummation is *In re Heatron, Inc.*[45] In that case, the reorganized debtor sought to amend its plan of reorganization to add an unsecured creditor who was suing the debtor for breach of warranty concerning items purchased from the debtor. The creditor objected, contending that the plan was substantially consummated and, therefore, modification was precluded by § 1127(b). At the time of this dispute, approximately 53 percent of the total amount due under the plan had been paid to creditors.[46] The court held that, "53% of the property transferred . . . does not constitute 'substantially all' of the property under the plan."[47] Further, it said, "The word 'substantial' suggests more than halfway, more than a mere preponderance. When used with the word 'all' . . . there is a suggestion of completeness."[48]

The court in *In re Hayball Trucking, Inc.*[49] was troubled by the portion of the *Heatron* decision that seemed, by the interpretation of § 1101(2)(A), not to give effect to § 1101(2)(C) of the Code. The *Hayball* court emphasized that

> subsections (A) and (C) [of § 1101(2)] appear to distinguish between transfers of property to or from the debtor at or near the time the plan is confirmed undertaken to shape the new financial structure of the debtor and distributions of dividends to creditors made over a period of time from operating revenues. "Substantial Consummation" requires completion or near completion of the former, but only commencement of the latter.[50]

The *Hayball* rationale was adopted by the court in *United States v. Novak*[51] and by *In re Bedford Springs Hotel, Inc.*,[52] which held that distributions to creditors which are

---

41 United States v. Novak, 86 B.R. 625, 628 (D.S.D. 1988) (citing *In re* Heatron, Inc., 34 B.R. 526 (Bankr. W.D. Mo. 1983)). *See also In re* Fansal Shoe Corp., 119 B.R. 28, 30 (Bankr. S.D.N.Y. 1990).

42 *In re* Jorgenson, 66 B.R. 104, 106 (Bankr. 9th Cir. 1986).

43 *In re* Modern Steel Treating Co., 130 B.R. 60, 64 (Bankr. N.D. Ill. 1991); *In re* Fansal Shoe Corp., 119 B.R. 28, 30 (Bankr. S.D.N.Y. 1990).

44 *In re* Northampton Corp., 37 B.R. 110, 113 (Bankr. E.D. Pa. 1984).

45 34 B.R. 526 (Bankr. W.D. Mo. 1983).

46 *Id.* at 527.

47 *Id.*

48 *Id.* at 529. *Accord In re* Bedford Springs Hotel, Inc., 99 B.R. 302, 303 (Bankr. W.D. Pa. 1989).

49 67 B.R. 681 (Bankr. E.D. Mich. 1986).

50 *Id.* at 684.

51 86 B.R. 625 (D.S.D. 1988).

52 99 B.R. 302 (Bankr. W.D. Pa. 1989).

to occur over time need only to be commenced to meet the requirements of § 1101(2)(C).[53]

Another aspect of plan modification postconfirmation is who may modify the plan. Only the reorganized debtor or the proponent of the plan may propose a modification of the plan under § 1127(b) of the Bankruptcy Code.[54]

In re Charterhouse, Inc.[55] lends guidance on this subject. In that case, the court noted:

> The term "proponent of a plan" is not defined in 11 U.S.C. § 101, but it is clear from a contextual reading of the provisions of Chapter 11 that the "proponent" contemplated by § 1127 is the party in interest who negotiates, formulates, disseminates, makes disclosure in connection with, and seeks acceptances of, a reorganization plan.[56]

In *Charterhouse,* the official bondholders' committee moved to have the plan of reorganization modified under § 1127(b) to obtain authority to use accrued interest to pay a professional fee retainer. The court did not allow the committee to modify the plan because it was not the proponent of the plan, and, therefore, it lacked standing to modify. The court stated that the committee was not the proponent because "[t]he committee did not engage in the initial process of plan formulation or preparation; neither was it responsible for, nor did it undertake, the process of pre-solicitation disclosure, plan dissemination, monitoring of acceptances, or presentation of evidence at the confirmation hearing."[57]

It appears that a party cannot gain standing to propose modifications to a confirmed plan as a proponent merely by voting in favor of the plan of reorganization. This is true even if the party took a very active role in the bankruptcy proceeding that benefitted all parties-in-interest in the case.[58]

The final issue regarding modification of a confirmed plan is how a plan may be modified. A plan of reorganization, as modified, must still meet the requirements of § 1122 of the Bankruptcy Code dealing with classification of claims or interests.[59] That is to say, a modified plan may not propose to group together claims or interests that are not substantially similar to other claims or interests in that class.[60] A plan of reorganization, as modified, must also contain all the information that § 1123 required the original plan to contain. Finally, the plan, as modified, can only become the plan if the court, "after notice and a hearing, confirms [the] plan, as modified, under section 1129 of [Title 11]."[61]

---

53 United States v. Novak, 86 B.R. 625, 628 (D.S.D. 1988); *In re* Bedford Springs Hotel, Inc., 99 B.R. 302, 303 (Bankr. W.D. Pa. 1989).

54 11 U.S.C. § 1127(b); *In re* Charterhouse, Inc., 84 B.R. 147, 151 (Bankr. D. Minn. 1988); *In re* Auto Dealers Servs., Inc., 89 B.R. 233, 236 (Bankr. M.D. Fla. 1988).

55 84 B.R. 147 (Bankr. D. Minn. 1988).

56 *Id.* at 151.

57 *Id.*

58 *See In re* Charterhouse, Inc., 84 B.R. 147 (Bankr. D. Minn. 1988); *see also In re* Temple Zion, 125 B.R. 910 (Bankr. E.D. Pa. 1991).

59 11 U.S.C. § 1127(b).

60 *See id.* § 1122(a).

61 *Id.* § 1127(b). *See id.* § 1129.

§ 17.5 Converting or Dismissing a Confirmed Case

A creditor or other party-in-interest may seek to have the confirmed case converted to Chapter 7 or dismissed.[62] Section 1112(b) states that a court may convert a case to Chapter 7 or it may dismiss a case,

> whichever is in the best interest of the creditors and the estate, for cause, including— . . .
>
> (6) revocation of an order of confirmation under section 1144 of this title, and denial of confirmation of another plan or a modified plan under section 1129 of this title;
>
> (7) inability to effectuate substantial consummation of a confirmed plan;
>
> (8) material default by the debtor with respect to a confirmed plan;
>
> (9) termination of a plan by reason of the occurrence of a condition specified in the plan; or
>
> (10) nonpayment of any fees or charges required under chapter 123 of title 28.[63]

There is nothing in § 1112(b) that requires a court to convert or dismiss a case.[64] The court in *In re Jartran, Inc.,* stated:

> By no means does § 1112(b) require a court to convert a case when the post-confirmation entity is unable to fulfill the obligations contained in a confirmed plan. Rather, this court *may* convert or dismiss such a case for cause if it is in the best interest of the creditors and the estate. The court must balance equities and consider the interests of creditors and the estate in determining whether conversion is appropriate.[65]

The choice to convert or dismiss (or to do neither) is based on a best interest of creditors and the estate test.[66] *Best interest of the creditors and the estate* is not defined in the Code. Courts determine what is in the best interest of the creditors and the estate on a case-by-case basis, looking primarily at what effects each option will have on those involved in the case.[67]

As a practical matter, conversion or dismissal after confirmation is almost never beneficial to the creditors and the estate. This is because confirmation vests property of the estate in the reorganized debtor. See **§ 17.1.** Therefore, when a confirmed Chapter 11 case is converted to Chapter 7, the Chapter 7 estate is essentially an

---

62 *See generally* 11 U.S.C. § 1112(b).

63 *Id.* § 1112(b)(6)–(10).

64 *In re* HRP Auto Ctr., Inc., 130 B.R. 247, 256 (Bankr. N.D. Ohio 1991).

65 *In re* Jartran, Inc., 71 B.R. 938, 943 (Bankr. N.D. Ill. 1987) (emphasis added).

66 *In re* Page, 118 B.R. 456, 459 (Bankr. N.D. Tex. 1990); *In re* TSP Indus., Inc., 117 B.R. 375, 377 (Bankr. N.D. Ill. 1990).

67 *See, e.g., In re* Geiger Enters., Inc., 635 F.2d 106, 109 (2d Cir. 1980), *rev'd on other grounds sub nom.* Central Trust Co. v. Official Creditors' Comm., 454 U.S. 354 (1982) (best interests meant to include not only the estate but creditors and debtor); *In re* HRP Auto Ctr., Inc., 130 B.R. 247, 256 (Bankr. N.D. Ohio 1991) (relative benefit depends on resulting effect in a given case); *In re* Michael S. Starbuck, Inc., 14 B.R. 134 (Bankr. S.D.N.Y. 1981) (efficiency and economy of administration are primary concerns); *In re* TSP Indus., Inc., 117 B.R. 375, 376 (Bankr. N.D. Ill. 1990) (ramifications of conversion and dismissal must be explored).

empty shell of the previous Chapter 11 estate containing no assets for a Chapter 7 trustee to administer.[68]

Dismissal after conversion has little purpose. Dismissal revests the property of the estate in the entity which owned the property at the commencement of the bankruptcy case.[69] Dismissal reinstates custodianships, avoided transfers, and avoided liens.[70] Dismissal does not affect the finality of the confirmation order or the discharge that is granted in the case.[71] Situations in which the effect of postconfirmation dismissal would be in the best interests of the creditors and the estate are rare.

§ 17.6 Revocation of an Order of Confirmation

In the limited context of fraud, a party-in-interest can file a complaint to revoke an order of confirmation. An order of confirmation can only be revoked; it cannot be voided or stricken.[72] The statutory provision of the Bankruptcy Code detailing the requirements for revocation of an order of confirmation is § 1144, which states:

> On request of a party in interest at any time before 180 days after the date of the entry of the order of confirmation, and after notice and a hearing, the court may revoke such order if and only if such order was procured by fraud. An order under this section revoking an order of confirmation shall—
>
> (1) contain such provisions as are necessary to protect any entity acquiring rights in good faith reliance on the order of confirmation; and
>
> (2) revoke the discharge of the debtor.[73]

As a threshold requirement, the petitioner must have standing to request that the court revoke an order of confirmation. To have standing, the petitioner must be a party-in-interest.[74] The term *party in interest* is not defined in § 101 of the Bankruptcy Code; however, § 1109(b) states that party-in-interest includes, "the debtor, the trustee, a creditors' committee, an equity security holders committee, a creditor, an equity security holder, or any indenture trustee."[75]

---

68 *In re* TSP Indus., Inc., 120 B.R. 107 (Bankr. N.D. Ill. 1990) (if there are preferences or fraudulent transfers to pursue under §§ 547 and 548, or there is for some reason unadministered property still in the hands of the debtor-in-possession, conversion might make sense; *In re* TSP Indus., Inc., 117 B.R. 375 (Bankr. N.D. Ill. 1990); *see In re* T.S. Note Co., 140 B.R. 812 (Bankr. D. Kan. 1992).

69 *In re* Page, 118 B.R. 456, 459 (Bankr. N.D. Tex. 1990).

70 *Id.*

71 *In re* Depew, 115 B.R. 965, 967 (Bankr. N.D. Ind. 1989); *In re* Bishop, 74 B.R. 677, 681 (Bankr. M.D. Ga. 1987).

72 *In re* Modern Steel Treating Co., 130 B.R. 60, 66 (Bankr. N.D. Ill. 1991).

73 11 U.S.C. § 1144.

74 11 U.S.C. § 1144.

75 11 U.S.C. § 1109(b). *See also In re* TM Carlton House Partners, Ltd., 110 B.R. 185, 189 (Bankr. E.D. Pa. 1990) (§ 1109 should be construed broadly).

The 180-day limit of § 1144(a) is self-explanatory. If the plan has been modified, however, the confirmation date of the modified plan is the date from which the 180-day time limit begins to run pursuant to § 1144.[76]

The last requirement of § 1144 is that the petitioner show that the confirmation order was procured by fraud. *Fraud* is not defined in the Bankruptcy Code.

A proceeding to revoke an order of confirmation must be brought as an adversary proceeding.[77] Federal Rule of Civil Procedure 9 governs;[78] therefore, "[i]n all averments of fraud or mistake, the circumstances constituting fraud or mistake shall be stated with particularity."[79]

One court has held that misrepresentations made to the court concerning the value of certain pieces of property in the bankruptcy estate constituted fraud for purposes of § 1144 of the Code. In reasoning through its decision, that court said:

> As a matter of law, we think that [fraud] encompasses any action in a bankruptcy proceeding by which a party obtains confirmation of a Plan by deceptive practices with a deceptive intent . . . [I]t [is] sufficient that a showing be made that the court relied thereon and that a creditor or other party was damaged thereby.[80]

Additionally, should a debtor request that confirmation of its own plan be revoked, the debtor would be held to the same requirements that any other party in interest must meet under § 1144 of the Code.[81]

§ 17.7 Successive or Serial Filings

After a case has been confirmed, the reorganized debtor might want to file again. The Code places some limits on such successive or serial filings.

Section 109 states:

> [N]o individual or family farmer may be a debtor under this title who has been a debtor in a case pending under this title at any time in the preceding 180 days if—
>
> (1) the case was dismissed by the court for willful failure of the debtor to abide by orders of the court, or to appear before the court in proper prosecution of the case, or
>
> (2) the debtor requested and obtained the voluntary dismissal of the case following the filing of a request for relief from the automatic stay provided by section 362 of this title.[82]

---

76 *In re* TM Carlton House Partners, Ltd., 110 B.R. at 188–89.

77 Fed. R. Bankr. P. 7001(5).

78 Fed. R. Bankr. P. 7009; *In re* Grossman, 46 B.R. 319, 320 (Bankr. E.D. Pa. 1985).

79 Fed. R. Civ. P. 9(b). *In re* Longardner & Assocs., Inc., 855 F.2d 455, 461–62 (7th Cir. 1988); *In re* Crusader Oil Refining Corp., 47 F. Supp. 873, 874 (D.N.J. 1942); *In re* Grossman, 46 B.R. 319, 320 (Bankr. E.D. Pa. 1985); *In re* Hertz, 38 B.R. 215, 220 (Bankr. S.D.N.Y. 1984).

80 *In re* Kostoglou, 73 B.R. 596, 599 (Bankr. N.D. Ohio 1987).

81 *In re* Errington, 39 B.R. 968 (Bankr. D. Minn. 1984).

82 11 U.S.C. § 109(g).

This statutory prohibition does not apply to corporate or partnership businesses.[83] However, a successive Chapter 11 case should be filed in good faith. "The determination of whether a Chapter 11 filing is made in good faith demands the objective consideration of 'the collective impact of facts and circumstances, not a single feature in a particular case' to ascertain a valid reorganization purpose consistent with the debtor's economic reality."[84]

A successive Chapter 11 case that is really a disguised plan modification is not allowed.[85] If there is a bona fide change in the debtor's circumstances from the time of the first Chapter 11 filing to the time of the second Chapter 11 filing, the successive filing of two Chapter 11 cases may be warranted.[86] The court in the case known as *Jartran II*[87] allowed the debtor to file a successive Chapter 11 case, because new assets and liabilities were involved and the debtor had different objectives than it did in the first case. The court found it important that the agreements made with the creditors in the plan of reorganization of the first case were not being modified by the second case.[88] Another court has stated that "[t]he real test that still remains is the presence of honest intention of the Debtor and some real need and real ability to effectuate the aim of the reorganization even if it involves the total liquidation of the assets."[89]

There is a question of how unpaid claims from the first Chapter 11 case are dealt with in the subsequent Chapter 11 case. In *Jartran II,* a creditor with an administrative expense claim from the first *Jartran* Chapter 11 case was only partially paid, so it sought administrative expense treatment in the second Chapter 11 case for the remainder of its unpaid claim.[90] The court allowed the creditor's claim in the second bankruptcy, but as only a general unsecured claim. The *Jartran II* court stated, "when . . . substantial operations under a confirmed plan are followed by a second case, the entity's unpaid liabilities under the first case plan become general unsecured claims in the second case."[91]

The Seventh Circuit reached a different conclusion in a case[92] dealing with whether "a priority claim for trust fund taxes [owed to the IRS] retains its priority in a second Chapter 11 petition."[93] The court held that "[u]nlike other sorts of tax claims, which are given priority under § 507(a)(7) for only a limited time, trust fund taxes are, moreover, granted priority under § 507(a)(7) regardless of their age."[94] The

---

83 *See id.*

84 *In re* Garsal Realty, Inc., 98 B.R. 140, 151 (Bankr. N.D.N.Y. 1989).

85 *See In re* AT of Me., Inc., 56 B.R. 55 (Bankr. D. Me. 1985); *In re* Northampton Corp., 37 B.R. 110 (Bankr. E.D. Pa. 1984).

86 *In re* Garsal Realty, Inc., 98 B.R. 140, 150 (Bankr. N.D.N.Y. 1989). *See also In re* Casa Loma Assoc., 122 B.R. 814 (Bankr. N.D. Ga. 1991).

87 *In re* Jartran, Inc., 71 B.R. 938 (Bankr. N.D. Ill. 1987).

88 *Id.* at 942.

89 *In re* North Redington Beach Assoc., Ltd., 91 B.R. 166, 169 (Bankr. M.D. Fla. 1988).

90 *In re* Jartran, 76 B.R. 123, 124 (Bankr. N.D. Ill. 1987).

91 *Id.* at 125.

92 Official Comm. of Unsecured Creditors of White Farm Equip. Co. v. United States, 943 F.2d 752 (7th Cir. 1991).

93 *Id.* at 753.

94 *Id.* at 756.

court noted that *Jartran II* held only that "administrative claims arising from expenses incurred solely to preserve the first estate were not entitled to administrative priority in a second bankruptcy proceeding . . . [A]dministrative claims are intimately tied to a single bankruptcy estate in a manner that is completely different from the trust fund tax claims at issue here."[95]

---

[95] *Id.* at 757.

CHAPTER 18

OUT-OF-COURT WORKOUTS

R. Greg Wright

§ 18.1 Introduction

Businesses that depend on external financing are often hit hard in difficult economic times by the tightening of credit and the down-sizing of banks' commercial loan portfolios. Although many businesses attempt to reorganize under Chapter 11, a large number of small businesses attempt to negotiate out-of-court settlement agreements with their creditors. This chapter discusses out-of-court workout strategies and specific settlement vehicles as initial alternatives to businesses seeking relief in the bankruptcy arena.

§ 18.2 Identifying the Problem

Depending on the nature of the debtor's business, the debtor or the debtor's bookkeeper-accountant is usually the first to know of impending financial difficulty. Hopefully, the situation will be recognized and acted on before a lender cuts off credit, accelerates loans, calls personal guaranties, or files foreclosure notices against either real or personal property. If the problem is identified in time, the debtor may be able to negotiate a favorable settlement of its financial affairs. If, however, the debtor has either waited too long or its creditors are unwilling to negotiate, a Chapter 11 or 7 bankruptcy proceeding may be inevitable.

§ 18.3 The Workout Team

Once a debtor has identified the problem and a decision to pursue a workout has been made, the debtor should take steps to put in place a workout team. Depending on the size and sophistication of the debtor and its business, this team may include the debtor, legal counsel, accounting personnel, a business consultant, and, if the debtor's assets consist of real property, possibly a qualified appraiser. Each member of the team plays a valuable role in the workout.

The team should commence the process by taking the following steps:

1. Set a goal for the debtor, for example, to stay in business or to obtain maximum value for its assets through an orderly liquidation
2. Address areas needing immediate attention, such as lawsuits, either threatened or pending, or the debtor's nearing or exceeding its credit limit, or lost customer confidence in the debtor's ability to provide goods or services
3. Analyze the debtor's current financial status and project how long the debtor can maintain current operations
4. Formulate a "plan" by which the debtor can reach its identified goal.

In connection with these actions, the debtor should provide the following information to the workout team:

1. Debtor's full name, address, Social Security number, or employer identification number
2. List of assets, including copies of deeds to real property, titles to vehicles, stock certificates, bonds, and documents regarding the debtor's interest in general and limited partnerships
3. Current accounts payable list, including each creditor's name, address, brief description of debt, and description, location, and value of any collateral
4. Copies of the debtor's federal tax returns for the past three years
5. List of any assets sold or transferred outside of the normal course of business within the past three years
6. List of all judgments or pledges of property as collateral within the past year
7. Copies of all mortgages, deeds of trust, security agreements, promissory notes, guaranties, financing statements, and any other documents creating a liability, either present or contingent
8. Copy of current and aged accounts receivable
9. Copies of any and all documents pertaining to pending or threatened lawsuits, judgments, and other legal proceedings
10. Copies of the debtor's bank statements for the prior six months.

§ 18.4 Disclosure to the Creditor

As a prerequisite to a creditor's agreeing to meet with a debtor and its workout team, the loan officer conducting the negotiations usually requires the debtor to provide updated financial information. The type and amount of information requested depends on the status of the loan default, if there is one, the amount of the loan, the nature of the debtor's business, the sophistication of the loan officer, and the size of the financial institution. The requested information is usually determined on a case-by-case basis, but most institutions, at a minimum, require the following:

1. Updated financial statements from all obligors and guarantors signed under penalty of perjury
2. Current income statement and balance sheet
3. Copies of the debtor's federal and state income tax returns for the past three years
4. Current listing of inventory, if applicable
5. If real property is involved, the most recent appraisal on the property
6. Aged accounts receivable, if applicable, for the prior 180 days.

In addition, the creditor usually performs a lien/judgment search in the county where the debtor maintains its principal place of business, conducts a credit check of the individual debtor, and may contact a commercial credit service such as Dunn & Bradstreet for additional information.

If the creditor subsequently finds that the debtor provided false information upon which the creditor reasonably relied in entering into an agreement, and the debtor thereafter defaults and files a bankruptcy proceeding, the creditor may seek to have the debt determined to be nondischargeable under Bankruptcy Code § 523(a)(2) or have the debtor's discharge denied under § 727. Even if the debtor does not file bankruptcy, the creditor may be able to declare a default under the terms of the settlement agreement and accelerate the balance due.

When a creditor requests updated financial information, the debtor should take all steps to ensure the accuracy of the information provided. This may be accomplished by using an accountant or other financial advisor to assist the debtor in compiling the requested information.

§ 18.5 Settlement Agreements

The primary objective of an out-of-court workout is to create a settlement agreement (extension or composition) between the debtor and creditor. An *extension agreement,* sometimes termed a forbearance or standstill agreement, provides for an extension of payment of the debtor's obligation without altering the amount of the creditor's claims. A *composition agreement* reduces the amount to be paid to the creditor by providing for payment either in cash or other property over a period of time. These two types of agreements form a binding contract only between the debtor and the creditor who consents to it.

When attempting to reach an agreement, the debtor should first meet with its major creditors, disclose its financial condition, inform them of its intentions for the future, and seek their participation in developing a global workout. If there is a very large number of creditors, the creditors might elect a creditors' committee designed to represent all of the creditors with whom the debtor will negotiate an agreement.

Although such a workout committee would ideally represent all creditors, secured and unsecured, the guidelines in the Bankruptcy Code relating to the election and formation of an unsecured creditors' committee can be used as a model.[1] There is also a possibility that a committee formed for workout negotiations can continue as an unsecured creditors' committee if negotiations are unsuccessful and a Chapter 11 bankruptcy proceeding is filed. The Bankruptcy Code authorizes the continuation of a committee selected prior to filing the petition if it is representative of the different kinds of claims to be represented and was fairly chosen.[2]

The advantages of entering into a settlement agreement for the debtor and the creditor are as follows:

Advantages to Debtor

1. Avoids stigma of bankruptcy and damage to credit
2. Avoids expense of bankruptcy, that is, attorney's and accountant's fees, bankruptcy filing fee, and monthly U.S. Trustee fee (if Chapter 11)
3. Avoids public disclosure of assets and liabilities
4. Avoids dealing with bankruptcy court and U.S. Trustee
5. Bankruptcy option remains available in the event of a default under the settlement agreement.

Advantages to Creditor

1. Allows creditor to shore up its position by correcting and/or reaffirming loan documents, obtaining additional collateral and personal guaranties, and perfecting security interests
2. Avoids costs associated with bankruptcy litigation
3. Gives time to obtain updated financial information
4. Buys time to render preference and/or fraudulent conveyance issues moot
5. Possibly removes loan from "classified" status for federal reporting purposes and frees up capital previously placed in reserve.

A settlement agreement may modify the parties' loan documents by:

1. Extending the maturity of a loan
2. Reducing monthly payments in an agreement known as a *cash flow mortgage*
3. Modifying the annual interest rate

---

[1] 11 U.S.C. § 1102.

[2] *Id.* § 1102(b)(1); Fed. R. Bankr. P. 2007.

4. Providing for the accrual of interest
5. Providing for the creditor's forbearance from foreclosing or executing on judgments
6. Pledging additional collateral or cross-collateralizing existing loans
7. Providing for placement of an executed deed in escrow
8. Providing for personal guaranties
9. Adding any other lawful provision to which the debtor and creditor may agree.

From the debtor's point of view, a settlement agreement would ideally contain the following provisions:

1. Extension of loan term
2. Reduced monthly payments
3. Reduced interest rate
4. Payment grace period
5. Release of personal guaranties (if applicable)
7. Cap deficiency amount (if applicable)
8. Additional extension period in consideration of principal payment
9. Forbearance by the creditor from executing on judgments (if applicable)
10. Reduction of principal.

From a creditor's perspective, the ideal settlement agreement should address the following issues:

1. Provide for finality
2. Reaffirm the validity of loan documents
3. Provide for the payment of real/personal property taxes (if applicable)
4. Provide for interest to be brought current
5. Allow recordation of consent judgments, if applicable in jurisdiction
6. Obtain additional collateral or additional guaranties
7. Require monthly or weekly financial reporting
8. Establish payment benchmarks, such as lump sum payments of accrued but unpaid interest or principal which must be paid by a date certain
9. Waive defenses, redemption periods, exemptions, and counterclaims
10. Release the creditor, its employees, agents, and attorneys from liability stemming from the original loan or workout process
11. Limit the debtor's use of cash to an agreed upon budget.

An example of a settlement agreement appears in **§ 18.6.**

§ 18.6 Form: Settlement Agreement

FORM 18–1
SETTLEMENT AGREEMENT

THIS SETTLEMENT AGREEMENT (the Agreement) is made and entered into this [date] between [Debtors] (the debtors) and [Bank] (the Bank), all of whom may collectively hereinafter be referred to as the parties.

RECITALS

1. The debtors have defaulted under the terms of a promissory note payable to the order of the Bank, dated [note date], for the sum of [note amount].

2. The Bank filed suit against the debtors in the case captioned [case name] in the District Court for [county], [state] (the underlying Litigation).

3. On or about [judgment date], judgment was entered in favor of the Bank against the debtors, jointly and severally, in the amount of [judgment amount], with interest at [interest amount] per day from [date] to the date of judgment and then at the statutory rate thereafter (the judgment).

4. Pursuant to the terms and covenants set forth herein, the parties desire to settle this matter.

NOW, THEREFORE, in consideration of the promises contained herein and for other good and valuable consideration, the receipt and sufficiency of which is acknowledged by the parties hereto, the parties agree as follows:

1. **Recitals.** The recitals are incorporated herein by this reference.

2. **Initial Payment.** On or before [payment date], the debtors will pay to the Bank the sum of [payment amount] in immediately available funds, time being of the essence.

3. **Additional Collateral.** On or before [date], the debtors shall deliver to and in favor of the Bank an executed and acknowledged mortgage in the amount of [mortgage amount] encumbering their entire fee simple interest in certain real property commonly known as [property description] (the property), in a form and substance satisfactory to the Bank, together with evidence that the Bank's lien is not inferior to that of any mortgage, judgment, tax, assessment, or other lien, encumbrance, or charge, except those mortgages held by [mortgagee], having a combined outstanding principal balance (as evidenced by proof in the form of a full title search and judgment report performed at the debtors' expense to be concurrently provided by the debtors to the Bank) not exceeding [mortgage interest amount], with interest not more than thirty (30) days in arrears.

4. **Insurance.** The debtors shall maintain satisfactory hazard insurance on the property, with the policy naming the Bank as mortgagee.

5. **Installment Payments.** Beginning on [date] and continuing every [number] day thereafter until the [number] anniversary date of this Agreement, the debtors shall unconditionally pay to the Bank in immediately available funds the amount of [installment payment amount].

6. **No Prepayment Penalty.** This Agreement shall not be construed to prohibit the debtors, at any time, from prepaying all or any part of the debt of [debt amount] referred to herein, with any such payments to be applied first to accrued but unpaid interest and then to principal.

7. **Further Undertakings and Representations**

a. The debtors represent and acknowledge that their joint, signed personal financial statements, dated [financial statement date] and transmitted to the Bank, is the basis of this Agreement. The debtors warrant and represent that said statements were and remain accurate in all material respects as of the date of this Agreement.

b. The debtors further warrant and represent that:

(i) All cash, checks, drafts, or other negotiable instruments payable to either of them, bearer bonds, bank accounts, rights to fees and commissions, contract rights, accounts receivable, rights to insurance, partnership interests, stocks and bonds, interests in trusts (whether vested or contingent and whether or not subject to a spendthrift clause), real and leasehold property interests, and all other tangible and intangible property interests owned directly or indirectly by either of them are disclosed on the financial statement.

(ii) The debtors, jointly or individually, have no contingent or undisclosed liabilities exceeding [liability amount] in the aggregate, other than those disclosed on the financial statement.

(iii) No transfers have been made since [date], other than payments of bona fide obligations to unrelated parties or payments made for the support and maintenance of the members of the debtors' immediate family.

(iv) The debtors, jointly or individually, are not the owners or beneficiaries of any bank account or investment account or other source of funds located outside of the United States; and

(v) Neither of the debtors has been the subject of a voluntary or involuntary bankruptcy filing as of the date of this Agreement.

c. The debtors acknowledge and agree that, upon discovery of any assets existing prior to [date] but not disclosed on the financial statement, the debtors shall, at the Bank's sole option, immediately assign such assets or transfer the proceeds from the sale thereof to the Bank. The debtors agree that they shall promptly notify the Bank if they discover any cash, checks, drafts, or other negotiable instruments payable to or to the benefit of either of them, bearer bonds, bank accounts, rights to fees or commissions, contract rights, accounts receivable, rights to insurance, partnership interests, stocks and bonds, interests in trusts, real and leasehold property interests, intangible property interests, transfers without consideration, or transfers not disclosed in the financial statement.

d. The debtors, jointly and individually, hereby release, relinquish, and extinguish all claims of any kind or nature, liquidated or unliquidated, absolute or contingent, which they or either of them may have against the Bank, its attorneys, officers, directors or employees.

8. **Remedies upon Breach of Warranty.** In the event of a material default in the terms of this Agreement or breach of warranty by the debtors, which default has not been cured within 15 days following written notice thereof to the debtors by the Bank, the Bank shall be permitted to execute on the judgment and enforce it to the maximum extent permitted by law. The debtors agree to waive any applicable state or federal statute of limitations or any other affirmative defense to permit the Bank or its assigns to reopen the case upon proof of their breach of the warranties set forth in this Agreement. The issue of whether or not the debtors have breached any of the warranties in this Agreement shall be decided by a court of appropriate jurisdiction, and the Bank shall have the burden to show the debtors' breach of any warranty by a preponderance of the evidence. In the event of such adjudication, the debtors shall, on demand, pay the Bank reasonable counsel fees and expenses.

9. **Undertakings and Representations**

a. If and so long as there is no uncured default of the terms of this Agreement or uncured material breach of warranty by the debtors, the Bank will forbear from proceeding on a writ of execution or otherwise enforcing the judgment.

b. Immediately upon the execution of this Agreement, counsel for the debtors shall prepare and execute, along with counsel for the Bank, a satisfaction of judgment (the satisfaction) of the underlying litigation. The Bank shall deliver the satisfaction to a mutually satisfactory escrow agent (escrow agent). The satisfaction shall never become operative, be filed with the Clerk of the Court, or be delivered to the escrow agent until such time as the debtors have completely performed all the terms of this Agreement.

c. Upon the complete performance of all the terms of this Agreement, the judgment will be discharged by stipulation as an accord and satisfaction. There will be no forgiveness of indebtedness unless there is final performance of all of the terms of this Agreement by the debtors.

d. If each of the terms and conditions of this Agreement is fully performed, and if each of the payments provided for in this Agreement is fully and timely made, and there is no other uncured default under this Agreement, including without limitation the commencement of federal or state bankruptcy or insolvency proceedings for either of the debtors or their making of an assignment for the benefit of creditors, then and only then shall the Bank cause to be delivered to the debtors from escrow the stipulation, which shall serve as an accord and satisfaction agreement, discharging the debtors from any and all liabilities to the Bank related to the above-referenced money judgment or the indebtedness thereby represented, whereupon satisfaction of such judgment shall be entered.

10. **Miscellaneous.**

a. If, for any reason, any provision herein is determined to be invalid, such invalidity shall not impair or otherwise affect the validity of the other provisions of this Agreement. Moreover, the parties agree to replace such invalid provision(s) with a substitute provision that will satisfy the intent of the parties.

b. Paragraph titles herein are for descriptive purposes only and shall not control or alter the meaning of the provisions of this Agreement as set forth in the text.

c. All exhibits and schedules attached hereto shall be deemed a part hereof to the same extent as if fully set forth herein.

d. The parties shall do all such further actions and execute all such further documents as are necessary and proper to effectuate the intents and purposes of this Agreement.

e. This Agreement shall be governed by and construed in accordance with the laws of the state of [state]. The debtors irrevocably consent to the nonexclusive jurisdiction of the courts of the state of [state] (including federal courts sitting there) concerning all matters relating to the terms of this Agreement.

f. Both parties acknowledge that they have been represented by counsel. Each party will bear its own costs and expenses, including attorney's fees, concerning the performance of this Agreement.

g. This Agreement shall be binding upon and inure to the benefit of the parties and their respective successors and permitted assigns. Nothing in this Agreement shall create or be deemed to create any third-party beneficiary rights in any person or entity not a party to this Agreement.

h. This Agreement contains and is intended as a complete statement of all the terms of the arrangements and agreements between the parties with respect to the matters provided for herein. This Agreement supersedes any previous agreements and understandings between the parties with respect to those matters and can be amended or modified only by a written document executed by all of the parties hereto. Any other attempted modification shall be void.

i. This Agreement shall be interpreted and construed without regard to the identity of the party selecting the language of this Agreement.

j. Any party may waive compliance by another with any of the provisions of this Agreement. No waiver of any one provision shall be construed as a waiver of any other provision. Any waiver must be in writing and signed in order to be effective.

k. Except as otherwise specifically set forth herein, this Agreement and the various rights and obligations of the parties contained herein shall survive all payments and obligations to be made hereunder indefinitely.

l. This Agreement may be executed in any number of counterparts, each of which shall be an original, but all of which taken together shall constitute one and the same instrument.

IN WITNESS WHEREOF, the parties have set their hands on the date first above written.

[Signatures]

§ 18.7 Settlement Agreements Utilizing the Sale of Property

Depending on the specific facts and circumstances, a settlement agreement may include a provision requiring the sale or surrender of property. Settlement vehicles commonly used in this scenario are bulk sales, friendly foreclosures, and deeds in lieu of foreclosure.

§ 18.8 —Bulk Sale

If, as part of a settlement agreement, the debtor sells the majority of its inventory, supplies, and so forth, the debtor should be aware of and comply with the jurisdiction's bulk sale or bulk transfer act, if there is one.

A *bulk sale* is a transfer, not in the ordinary course of the transferor's business, of a major part of the transferor's materials, supplies, merchandise, or inventory. The sale is usually made to one buyer in one transaction. The typical scenario is a sale in which a merchant transfers all of the stock in trade to one buyer, sometimes followed by the merchant-debtor's disappearance. The purpose of the bulk sale act is to prevent such a sale of goods until the seller's creditors have been paid in full. Bulk sale acts typically require that creditors be given notice so that they may take appropriate action. Also, an affirmative obligation is usually imposed on the buyer to ensure, to the extent possible, that the money paid to the seller is applied to pay the seller's obligations.

§ 18.9 —Friendly Foreclosure

When the debtor and creditor cooperate in reaching a mutually acceptable agreement regarding the debtor's peaceful surrender of the creditor's collateral, it is said to be a *friendly foreclosure.* In return, the creditor may agree either to release a personal guaranty or cap a deficiency, if any, upon the resale of the collateral.

A typical friendly foreclosure scenario occurs when the debtor allows a secured creditor to foreclose, and then the debtor, through another entity or a successor, purchases the collateral from the creditor at either a public or private sale for the amount of the creditor's claim. Once the transaction has been completed, the original debtor either dissolves under state law or files a Chapter 7 bankruptcy proceeding. The intent is to transfer assets free and clear of liens to a financially healthy successor person or entity, without the assets' being subject to the claims of the debtor's unsecured creditors. The advantages of a friendly foreclosure include:

1. The transaction may entice the foreclosing creditor to release personal guaranties or cap any deficiency claim upon resale of the collateral
2. The buyer acquires assets free and clear of liens and claims
3. The transaction is relatively inexpensive and, subject to applicable Uniform Commercial Code notice requirements, may be completed in a timely manner
4. No public disclosure of assets and liabilities occurs.

The disadvantages include:

1. Depending on the ownership of the acquiring entity, creditors may allege liability for pretransfer debts under a successor liability theory[3]
2. If the transfer is for arguably less than fair market value, and the debtor thereafter liquidates under Chapter 7, the trustee may attempt to avoid the transaction as a fraudulent conveyance under Bankruptcy Code § 544 or § 548. See **Chapter 12** for discussion of these avoiding powers.

§ 18.10 —Deed in Lieu of Foreclosure

To avoid the expense of a foreclosure and to sell the collateral under better conditions than a distress sale, a debtor and creditor may agree upon a deed in lieu of foreclosure as opposed to a foreclosure sale. One major prerequisite for a deed in lieu of

---

[3] R. Taylor, *Corporate Successor Liability Comes to Maryland*, 4 Md. B.J. XXII (1990).

foreclosure is, however, that the property being surrendered be held free and clear of junior liens.

The advantages of a deed in lieu of foreclosure include:

1. Maximization of the sale price of the asset
2. Avoidance of the expense of a foreclosure sale
3. Possible release of guaranty or a cap of any deficiency
4. Avoidance of public disclosure of sale normally required by foreclosure proceedings.

The main disadvantage is that, unless negotiated, the debtor may lose control of the method and manner by which the property is sold. Because of the control issue, if the creditor has not released the debtor from any deficiency following the sale, the debtor should insist on certain written guidelines pertaining to the sale of the collateral, and should attempt to make the best deal possible, because the provisions of the Uniform Commercial Code may not offer adequate protection after the sale.[4] Another disadvantage is that transfer of low basis property might result in adverse tax consequences to the debtor. See **Chapter 10.** A nonexhaustive list of conditions which a debtor and its counsel should propose includes:

1. A written agreement between the debtor and creditor clearly spelling out the terms of the parties' understanding regarding the sale of the collateral
2. No future release of the creditor because that would presumably preclude the debtor from later asserting that the collateral was not sold in a commercially reasonable manner
3. If the asset is personal property, sale of the property in a "commercially reasonable" manner, and pursuant to applicable provisions of the Uniform Commercial Code
4. If the asset is real property, sale of the property according to standards specified in the agreement
5. Ample written notice to debtor prior to the sale
6. Input of debtor regarding appraisal matters. Often, a creditor will insist that if the collateral is not sold by a certain date, the debtor will receive only a credit equal to a percentage of the appraised value of the property. The debtor should insist that the agreement provide that the creditor will give the debtor a copy of the appraisal, and possibly also insist that the debtor have the right to have a say in the selection of the appraiser or to have a second appraisal prepared.

---

[4] Ford & Vlahos v. ITT Commercial Fin., 23 Cal. Rptr. 2d 175 (Cal. Ct. App. 1993) (pursuant to Cal. Com. Code § 9504(3), secured creditor gave sufficient notice of sale of repossessed C-130 aircraft by publishing notice of time and place of sale at least five days before the sale date in newspaper of general circulation in county where sale was to be held, without regard to whether newspaper was read by potential buyers of cargo plane or whether publication in trade journal might have attracted additional buyers).

§ 18.11 Selecting Workout or Chapter 11

When a debtor is considering whether to pursue a workout or Chapter 11 or to cease operations, the debtor should contact an attorney familiar with the bankruptcy process. If, within the prior 90 days, substantial cash was paid or other property was transferred or pledged to a creditor, which enabled it to improve its financial position, the debtor may be better off filing a Chapter 11 in order to make full use of the trustee's (that is, the debtor's) avoiding powers under § 547 and § 548. In any event, a small business should consult competent counsel in deciding whether to attempt an out-of-court workout or to file a Chapter 11 reorganization proceeding.

CHAPTER 19

CHAPTER 13 AS AN ALTERNATIVE FOR SOLE PROPRIETORSHIPS

Lloyd C. Swartz

§ 19.1 Introduction

Many small businesses are sole proprietorships. They are the coffee shops, florists, bookstores, and hair stylists on Main Street and in the mall. Small plumbing and air conditioning contractors, auto body shops, and food stores are also sometimes sole proprietorships. Often husband and wife work together in these enterprises, sharing office management, record keeping, and provision of the primary service between them, neither one receiving compensation other than periodic draws for personal and family expenses. These are "mom and pop" enterprises, the typical small business in the minds of many. Unfortunately, despite the efforts of their owners, from time to time these businesses fail, just like any others, and their owners seek bankruptcy protection.

In many cases, Chapter 13 is an effective alternative for these small businesses that can give debtors more leverage against creditors than Chapter 11, with fewer creditor roadblocks. Chapter 13 does not involve disclosure statements, plan acceptance by voting, or competing plans. Also, the absolute priority rule (see **Chapter 16**) is not applied, so owners may retain an interest in the business after bankruptcy.

This chapter reviews Chapter 13 as a tool for small businesses in financial difficulty. The limitations on who may file, the requirements for plan confirmation, and the roles of debtor, standing trustee, debtor's attorney, and creditor's attorney are examined.

§ 19.2 Who May Be a Debtor in Chapter 13

To begin with, the debtor must be an "individual," a living, breathing person, not a corporation or partnership.[1] Stockbrokers and commodity brokers, however, may not file under Chapter 13.[2] A married debtor and spouse may file a joint petition.[3] The filing of a joint petition by a husband and wife does not result in the automatic substantive consolidation of the two debtors' estates. It has been held that the court may consolidate the cases as provided in § 302(b), but in the absence of consolidation, the two estates are separate.[4]

The debtor must have a regular source of income.[5] A tax refund has been found to be income for Chapter 13 purposes,[6] as well as child support payments.[7] Gratuitous assistance from the debtor's church and relatives has been held not to qualify as regular income.[8]

The noncontingent, liquidated, unsecured debts must be less than $100,000 and the noncontingent, liquidated secured debts must be less than $350,000.[9]

Because corporations and partnerships are not allowed to file for relief under Chapter 13, it is very important to review closely the nature of the relationship that husband and wife have had in the conduct of their business. The finding that they are in partnership may defeat their attempts to use Chapter 13. The legislative history of the Bankruptcy Code states,

> Whether a small business operated by a husband and wife, the so-called "mom and pop grocery store," will be a partnership and thus excluded from chapter 13, or a business owned by an individual, will have to be determined on the facts of each case. Even if partnership papers have not been filed, for example, the issue will be whether the assets of the grocery store are for the benefit of all creditors of the debtor or only for business creditors, and whether such assets may be the subject of a chapter 13 proceeding.[10]

State law determines the nature of the relationship.[11] Not surprisingly, decisions applying state law vary widely. In a New York case, a mom and pop retail store

---

1 11 U.S.C. § 109(c).

2 *See id.* §§ 101(30), 109(e).

3 *Id.* § 109(c).

4 *In re* Chandler, 148 B.R. 13 (Bankr. E.D.N.C. 1992).

5 *See* 11 U.S.C. § 109(e).

6 *In re* Cochran, 141 B.R. 270 (M.D. Ga. 1992).

7 *In re* Taylor, 15 B.R. 596 (Bankr. D. Ariz. 1981).

8 *In re* Ward, 129 B.R. 664 (Bankr. W.D. Okla. 1991).

9 11 U.S.C. § 109(e).

10 H.R. Rep. No. 595, 95th Cong., 1st Sess. 319–20 (1977).

11 William L. Norton, Jr., *Norton Bankruptcy Law and Practice 2d* § 115.1 (1993).

operating as a business partnership was held to be ineligible for Chapter 13,[12] but in a Florida case, a mom and pop business was held not to be an ineligible partnership.[13]

A corporation with a single shareholder is ineligible for Chapter 13 relief.[14] In one case, however, an incorporated husband and wife dairy was granted confirmation of a Chapter 13 plan. One of the debtors was personally obligated for the corporation's truck, and the plan proposed to pay for the truck. The court found that it would be unreasonable "to require a debtor to file both a Chapter 11 and a Chapter 13 as a result of a single corporate debt that the court finds is also the personal obligation of the individual."[15]

§ 19.3 How Chapter 13 Works

A Chapter 13 case proceeds much more rapidly than a Chapter 11 case. The debtor is allowed 15 days after filing in which to propose a plan of reorganization.[16] After proposing a plan, the debtor is allowed 30 days in which to make the first payment toward the fulfillment of the plan.[17] Generally, the confirmation hearing is held within the first 40 days following the filing of the case. Bankruptcy Rule 2002(b) provides:

> Except as provided in subdivision (1) of this rule, the clerk, or some other person as the court may direct, shall give the debtor, the trustee, all creditors and indenture trustees not less than 25 days notice by mail of . . . the time fixed for filing objections and the hearing to consider confirmation of a . . . Chapter 13 plan.

Thus, the notice for the first meeting of creditors under § 341 is combined with the notice for confirmation, resulting in a 25- to 45-day notice. This is a far cry from the 120-day exclusive time to file a plan allowed to a debtor-in-possession in a case under Chapter 11.[18] Also in contrast to Chapter 11, in Chapter 13, the debtor is the only party who may propose a plan.[19]

Unless the debtor can pay all claims in full earlier, a Chapter 13 plan must extend three years and no longer than five years. Section § 1322(c) states, "The plan may not provide for payments over a period that is longer than three years, unless the court, for cause, approves a longer period, but the court may not approve a period that is longer than five years."

---

12 *In re* Krokos, 13 B.R. 520 (Bankr. S.D.N.Y. 1981).

13 *In re* Ward, 6 B.R. 93 (Bankr. M.D. Fla. 1980).

14 *In re* La Cache Land Co., 54 B.R. 629 (E.D. La. 1985); Forestry Prods., Inc. v. Hope, 34 B.R. 753 (M.D. Ga. 1983).

15 *In re* Stevenson, 28 B.R. 37 (Bankr. S.D. Miss. 1982), *aff'd,* 28 B.R. 39 (S.D. Miss. 1983).

16 Fed. R. Bankr. P. 3015(b). In *In re* Novak, 143 B.R. 154 (Bankr. N.D. Ill. 1992), the court concluded that the failure to file a plan within 15 days of the petition is a ground for dismissal under § 1307(c)(3).

17 11 U.S.C. § 1326(a)(1).

18 *See* 11 U.S.C. § 1121(b).

19 *See id.* § 1321.

This five-year outside limit requires the repayment of debt in a fairly short period of time. This is important when counsel reviews the amount of debt to be repaid and the cash flow available to repay it. If the cash flow will not support payments large enough to pay off the plan in five years, the plan cannot be confirmed. The length of the plan is calculated from the date that the debtor is first obligated to begin making payments to the Chapter 13 trustee.[20] Some debts survive the completion of the plan. If the last payment on a debt is due after the due date of the last payment under the plan, the plan may provide for curing of default and maintenance of payments while the case is pending.[21] Most creditors, however, are dealt with by the plan within the five-year time limit.

The debtor is generally allowed to continue the operation of the business.[22] The debtor may do so in substantially the same manner as a Chapter 11 debtor-in-possession; however, there is an additional requirement of filing periodic reports of the operation of the business.[23]

The standing trustee has a very specific role.[24] That role is to move the case forward to confirmation and be the disbursing agent for plan payments during the pendency of the plan. Except for requiring regular reports regarding the operation of the business, the standing trustee does not step between the debtor and the operation of the business.[25]

§ 19.4 Plan and Standards for Confirmation

Under 11 U.S.C. § 1322(a), a Chapter 13 plan must:

> (1) provide for the submission of all or such portion of future earnings or other future income of the debtor to the supervision and control of the trustee as is necessary for the execution of the plan;

---

20 *In re* Duckett, 139 B.R. 6 (Bankr. E.D. Tex. 1992).

21 11 U.S.C. § 1322(b)(5). *See also* Homebanc v. Chappell (*In re* Chappell), 984 F.2d 775 (7th Cir. 1993) (A Chapter 13 debtor has discretion whether to use § 1322(b)(5) to cure defaults and maintain payments on a long term obligation.)

22 *See* 11 U.S.C. § 1304(b).

23 *Id.* §§ 704(8), 1304(c).

24 *See generally id* § 1302. In deciding *In re* Foulk, 134 B.R. 929 (Bankr. D. Neb. 1991), the court examined the role of the standing trustee and found the requirement that the standing Chapter 13 trustee "appear and be heard" at any hearing regarding confirmation of a plan, and required the trustee to make a recommendation for or against confirmation.

25 *In re* Walls, 17 B.R. 701 (Bankr. S.D. W. Va. 1982) (debtor engaged in business has, exclusive of trustee, powers enumerated in §§ 363(c), 364). *See also* Spicer v. Woodhouse, 17 B.R. 275 (Bankr. S.D. Ohio 1982); *In re* Ballard, 4 B.R. 271 (Bankr. E.D. Va. 1980). *But see In re* Clark, 91 B.R. 324 (Bankr. E.D. Pa. 1988) (Chapter 13 debtor engaged in business as a landlord was ordered to make payments to the Chapter 13 trustee to fund repairs of apartments. The trustee was directed to make the repairs and given limited authority under §1304(b) to operate the debtor's business. If the debtor failed to comply with prior orders requiring repairs, the court said it would replace the debtor with the Chapter 13 trustee and give the trustee total charge of the debtor's business).

(2) provide for the full payment, in deferred cash payments, of all claims entitled to priority under section 507 of this title, unless the holder of a particular claim agrees to a different treatment of such claim; and

(3) if the plan classifies claims, provide the same treatment for each claim within a particular class.

Section 1322(a)(1) is often interpreted as a requirement that the payments made to the creditors go through the standing trustee. In at least one case, however, the court stated that § 1322(a)(1) does not prohibit a Chapter 13 debtor from making payments directly to a mortgage holder.[26]

Payment in full of priority claims, as defined in § 507, generally includes administrative expenses such as filing fees, attorney's fees, and trustee's expenses and fees. It also includes taxes having priority status and other claims that fall within § 507. The plan may provide for less than full payment of priority claims if the holder of the claim agrees.[27] What constitutes assent by the creditor is not settled in the case law. Some cases require an express affirmation, not merely failure to object to confirmation.[28] At least one case, however, has held that the failure of the Internal Revenue Service to object to a plan that proposed to pay a tax claim in full but without interest constituted an "agreement" to such treatment.[29]

Paragraph (b) of 11 U.S.C. § 1322 sets out the provisions that a Chapter 13 plan may contain. Paying secured creditors only the value of the supporting collateral is generally allowed. The rights of a holder of a secured claim that is secured by the debtor's principal residence, however, cannot be modified.[30] The rights of other creditors may be modified in several ways. The plan may alter the amount and frequency of contract payments, reduce interest to a court-approved rate, or return some property while retaining other property and providing for payment only for the retained property.

The plan may provide for curing or waiving a default.[31] This includes curing a default on the principal residence of the debtor and continuing the regular payments. Claims may be paid in any order selected by the debtor.[32] However, the plan should not propose payment terms that will draw an objection on the ground that the plan

---

26 *In re* Aberegg, 121 B.R. 553 (N.D. Ind. 1990).

27 11 U.S.C. § 1322(a)(2).

28 *In re* Northrup, 141 B.R. 171 (N.D. Iowa 1991) (finding Internal Revenue Service's failure to object to plan that proposed to pay tax claim in full but without interest constituted an "agreement" to such treatment).

29 *In re* Hebert, 61 B.R. 44 (Bankr. W.D. La. 1986).

30 11 U.S.C. § 1322(b)(2). Nobleman v. American Sav. Bank (*In re* Nobleman), 968 F.2d 483 (5th Cir.), *aff'd,* 508 U.S. ___, 124 L. Ed. 2d 228 (1993) ("We hold that . . . the bifurcation of an undersecured home mortgage runs afoul of the specific protection afforded under Section 1322(b)(2) to home mortgage creditors whose claims are secured only by a debtor's principal residence. Section 506(a) cannot be used to bifurcate the claim and vitiate the protection of Section 1322(b)(2).").

31 11 U.S.C. § 1322(b)(3).

32 *Id.* 1322(b)(4). A Chapter 13 debtor may pay unsecured claim holders concurrently with other claim holders, but § 1322(b)(4) does not require any particular order. *See generally In re* Bradley, 705 F.2d 1409 (5th Cir. 1983).

does not pay secured claims in a manner that provides adequate protection against depreciation. The plan may provide for the payment of claims that arise postpetition[33] and may also assume or reject executory contracts or unexpired leases.[34]

Section 1325 governs the standards for confirmation. Unlike Chapter 11, Chapter 13 does not require acceptance by a vote of the creditors for confirmation. The trustee or unsecured creditors may object to confirmation, however, under § 1325(b). In the absence of objections, the court must confirm a Chapter 13 plan that complies with paragraph (a) of § 1325. The general requirements of § 1325(a) are compliance of the plan with the Bankruptcy Code, payment of court fees and court costs, good faith, and feasibility.[35]

Subparagraph (5) of § 1325(a) governs the treatment of secured claims. A plan must either: (1) be accepted by the secured creditor; (2) provide that the creditor retain the lien on the secured property and receive its value under the plan; or (3) provide for the surrender of the secured property to the creditor.

Subparagraph (4) of § 1325(a) governs the treatment of unsecured claims. It requires that the plan must provide for payment on each unsecured claim of at least as much as would be received in a liquidation of the debtor's estate under Chapter 7.[36]

If the trustee or an unsecured creditor objects, however, the plan must also either pay the claim in full under § 1325(b)(1)(A), or satisfy what is referred to as the *best efforts test.* That test is set out in § 1325(b)(1)(B):

> If the trustee or the holder of an allowed unsecured claim objects to the confirmation of the plan, then the court may not approve the plan unless, as of the effective date of the plan . . . the plan provides that all of the debtor's projected disposable income to be received in the three-year period beginning on the date that the first payment is due under the plan will be applied to make payments under the plan.

Disposable income is defined in § 1325(c) as income beyond that reasonably necessary for maintenance and support of the debtor or a dependent, and, for debtors engaged in business, "for the payment of expenditures necessary for the continuation, preservation, and operation" of the business.

The best efforts test permits debtors to continue their business without paying unsecured claims in full. This stands in sharp contrast to the absolute priority rule applicable in Chapter 11, which requires full payment of claims of a rejecting unsecured class before a debtor or its owners can retain ownership of a business. See **Chapter 16.**

---

33 11 U.S.C. § 1322(b)(6).

34 *Id.* § 1322(b)(7).

35 *Id.* § 1325(a)(1), (2), (3), (6).

36 11 U.S.C. § 1325(a)(4). *See generally In re* Santa Maria, 128 B.R. 32 (Bankr. N.D.N.Y. 1991) (failure to provide for interest on unsecured claims resulted in failure to provide the creditor what it should receive on liquidation and sale of unencumbered real property). *Accord In re* Coonrod, 135 B.R. 375 (Bankr. D. Neb. 1991); *In re* Foulk, 134 B.R. 929 (Bankr. D. Neb. 1991); *In re* Pinkston, 134 B.R. 932 (Bankr. D. Neb. 1991).

§ 19.5 Role of the Debtor

The debtor is responsible for performing several duties generally attributed to the trustee in Chapter 7 cases.[37] Observance of the notice and hearing requirement for certain sales, lease, and other actions not in the ordinary course of business[38] is particularly important.

Section 1304 gives the debtor in Chapter 13 who is operating a business considerable leeway, requiring only periodic reports and payment of appropriate taxes.

§ 19.6 Creditor's Perspective

In Chapter 13, there is no vote on the plan; there are no disclosure statements to debate and no absolute priority rule to require that creditors are paid in full before the owners receive anything. The only leverage that creditors have in Chapter 13 is their right to object to the plan on the basis of §§ 1322 and 1325.

Creditors need to spend their time preconfirmation reviewing the proposed plan. Feasibility of the proposed plan needs to be considered. When mom and pop file for Chapter 13, the budget needs to reflect an ability to keep up not only with plan payments but also with payments for ongoing expenses. A creditor should review not only the value attributed to the collateral supporting its claim but also the value of the other assets, including nonexempt, unencumbered assets. This is necessary for evaluation of the plan under the liquidation test.

The proper filing of claims is often overlooked by creditors in Chapter 13 cases. In the experience of this author as a former Chapter 13 standing trustee, a great majority of unsecured creditors fail to file claims, even when there is a proposed distribution for the class that they fall into. Rarely do even a majority of unsecured creditors file claims.

Secured creditors must provide legible copies of the appropriate documents supporting their claims. Also, the proof of claim must properly state the balance that was due on the date the case was filed.[39]

Debts are not discharged until the debtor completes the plan.[40] A large number of cases fail prior to discharge, so a vigilant creditor that monitors the progress of a plan may reap great rewards.

§ 19.7 Practice Tips for Debtor's Counsel

Because Chapter 13 relief is limited to individuals, debtor's counsel needs to ask penetrating questions regarding the structure of the business. Asking, "Are you a

---

37 *See generally* 11 U.S.C. §§ 1303, 1304.

38 *See id.* § 363(b)(1).

39 *See* 11 U.S.C. § 502(b).

40 *See id.* § 1328(a).

sole proprietor?" may not be enough.[41] Counsel needs to look at the tax reporting statements and check into the tax identification numbers and see to whom they are assigned. It is too late to fold up a corporation after the case has been filed.

Prefiling is also the time to look closely at the debt levels of the business. A debtor may be able to get in under the Chapter 13 limits by repaying specific debts or by returning some collateral to the secured party.[42]

It is very likely in a mom and pop or other sole proprietorship case that the business habits of the debtors will need to be reviewed and adjusted. Counsel might be able to obtain some professional advice or training for the debtors. This might help the debtors adjust their habits in order to avoid repeating the same mistakes while under the protection of a Chapter 13.

Good communication among all parties is a must. Default in payments to the standing trustee, lapse in insurance, and failure to report periodically to the standing trustee or taxing authorities are bound to occur from time to time. Effective communication with the debtor allows counsel an opportunity to forestall problems that might otherwise lead to involvement of the court.

The phone call to a secured creditor or its attorney returns more benefit than any other call that can be made. A meeting between the debtor's attorney and a creditor and its attorney can educate the creditor about the purpose of the proposed plan. The debtor's attorney may also discover a concern of the creditor that can be addressed without impairing the proposed reorganization.

Counsel should also communicate with the standing trustee and staff of the standing trustee's office. The standing trustee's duties focus on supervision and overview; therefore, counsel should allow the trustee to function as effectively as possible by communicating with the trustee on a regular basis.

Chapter 13 is often looked upon as a model for new bankruptcy legislation because it is perceived as a system that works. It has already been used as a basis for Chapter 12 (family farm reorganization) and has recently been used as a model for proposed small business amendments to the Bankruptcy Code. See **Chapter 24.** Mom and pop businesses and other sole proprietorships that meet the threshold requirements certainly should at least consider filing under Chapter 13.

---

41 *See generally In re* Norman, 32 B.R. 562 (Bankr. W.D. Mo. 1983).

42 There has been some effort to amend the debt limits of Chapter 13. It is proposed that the limit be raised to $1 million, without regard to the classification of the debt. S. 540, § 109(a), 103d Cong., 1st Sess. (1993). See **Ch. 24.**

CHAPTER 20

PERSONAL EXEMPTIONS FOR SOLE PROPRIETORS

R. Greg Wright

§ 20.1 Introduction

In times of economic uncertainty, many people operating small businesses as sole proprietors find themselves in financial difficulty. Most people would prefer to satisfy their creditors' claims through an out-of-court workout, but in many instances personal bankruptcy may be the only option. When an individual is deciding whether to file a bankruptcy proceeding, questions commonly asked are "What assets, if any, may I retain?" and "What, if anything, can I do to maximize the retention of those assets?"

Because the intent of Congress in enacting the Bankruptcy Code was to give individuals a fresh start, an individual debtor may, despite a bankruptcy filing, retain both possession and uninterrupted use of property that is successfully claimed exempt. This chapter explores some issues surrounding exemptions and how to claim them successfully.

§ 20.2 Property of the Bankruptcy Estate

Upon the filing of a bankruptcy petition, an estate is created which is comprised of virtually all the property owned by the debtor. Pursuant to 11 U.S.C. § 541 and subject to few restrictions, the estate specifically consists of:

1. All legal and equitable interests of the debtor in property as of the date of filing[1]
2. Any interest the debtor acquires within 180 days following the date of filing through inheritance, property settlement or divorce decree, or as beneficiary under a life insurance policy[2]
3. Proceeds, product, offspring, rents, or profits of property of the estate.[3]

Section 541 does not define *property of the estate* to include wages or earnings from services performed by an individual debtor after the date of filing. Chapters 13 and 12, however, have provisions that include postpetition earnings as property of the estate.[4] The estate does not include any interest of the debtor in property that contains a "restriction on the transfer of a beneficial interest of the debtor in a trust that is enforceable under applicable non-bankruptcy law."[5] Consequently, the estate would not include a debtor's interest in a spendthrift trust[6] that is valid under the law of the state in which the petition is filed.

Although issues concerning what constitutes property of the estate have remained somewhat static in recent years, in the 1992 case of *Patterson v. Shumate*,[7] the United States Supreme Court held that a debtor's interest in an ERISA[8] qualified pension plan is not property of the estate. To be an ERISA qualified plan, the pension plan must meet the following three criteria:

1. It must be subject to ERISA
2. It must be "qualified" under Internal Revenue Code § 401(a)
3. It must contain an anti-alienation provision stating that it cannot be assigned.

The Supreme Court reasoned that the plain language of 11 U.S.C. § 541(c)(2) mandates that an anti-alienation provision in an ERISA qualified pension plan constitutes a restriction on transfer that is enforceable under nonbankruptcy law and, therefore, the pension plan is not property of the estate. This decision is good news

---

[1] 11 U.S.C. § 541(a)(1).

[2] *Id.* § 541(a)(5).

[3] *Id.* § 541(a)(6).

[4] *Id.* §§ 1305(a)(2) and 1207(a)(2), respectively.

[5] 11 U.S.C. § 541(c)(2).

[6] A *spendthrift trust* is a trust created to provide a fund for the maintenance of a beneficiary and at the same time to secure it against the beneficiary's improvidence or incapacity. Black's Law Dictionary 1256 (5th ed. 1979).

[7] ___ U.S. ___, 112 S. Ct. 2242 (1992).

[8] Employee Retirement Income Security Act of 1974, 29 U.S.C. §§ 1000–1461.

for debtors, especially in jurisdictions that do not exempt a debtor's interest in a qualified retirement plan.

Despite the *Patterson v. Shumate* decision, this issue continues in some jurisdictions to be the subject of much litigation. In Michigan,[9] New York,[10] and California,[11] property of a qualified retirement plan has been judicially determined to be an asset of the estate, particularly when the debtor is a sole proprietor who owns a single-person pension plan.[12] ERISA plans are discussed in more detail in **Chapter 21.**

§ 20.3 Exempt Property

One of the goals of the Bankruptcy Code is to give debtors a fresh start. Allowing the debtor to exempt certain property from the reach of creditors furthers this goal in one or more of the following ways:

1. By providing the debtor with property necessary for physical survival
2. By protecting the dignity and cultural and religious identity of the debtor
3. By enabling the debtor to be rehabilitated financially and earn income in the future
4. By protecting the debtor's family from the adverse consequences of impoverishment
5. By minimizing the likelihood that the debtor and the debtor's family will need public financial assistance.[13]

Depending on the jurisdiction in which the case is filed, an individual may choose between the exemptions available under the Bankruptcy Code[14] or those permitted under nonbankruptcy federal law and the law of the state in which the petition is filed.[15] A majority of states, however, have enacted legislation to opt out of the exemptions under the Bankruptcy Code, so that only state and nonbankruptcy federal exemptions[16] are available to debtors in those states.[17]

---

[9] *In re* Hall, 151 B.R. 412 (Bankr. W.D. Mich. 1993).

[10] *In re* Lane, 149 B.R. 760 (Bankr. E.D.N.Y. 1993).

[11] *In re* Witwer, 148 B.R. 930 (Bankr. C.D. Cal. 1992).

[12] For a more in-depth discussion of this issue, see Christy & Skeldon, *Shumate and Pension Benefits in Bankruptcy,* 2 J. Bankr. L. & Proc. 719 (1992).

[13] Norwest Bank Neb., N.A. v. Tveten, 848 F.2d 871, 876 (8th Cir. 1988); *see also* Resnick, *Prudent Planning or Fraudulent Transfer: The Use of Nonexempt Assets to Purchase or Improve Exempt Property on the Eve of Bankruptcy,* 31 Rutgers L. Rev. 615, 621 (1978).

[14] 11 U.S.C. § 522(b)(1).

[15] *Id.* § 522(b)(2).

[16] For a thorough list of available nonbankruptcy federal exemptions, see 3 Collier on Bankruptcy 2d § 522.25 (15th ed. 1993).

[17] The following states have opted out of exemptions available to a debtor under 11 U.S.C. § 522(b)(1): Alabama, Arizona, Arkansas, California, Colorado, Delaware, Florida, Georgia, Idaho, Illinois, Indiana, Iowa, Kansas, Kentucky, Louisiana, Maine, Maryland,

Exemptions available under state law are a creation of each respective legislature, and the nature and dollar amount of property capable of being claimed exempt vary greatly. **Table 20–1,** which reflects selected exemptions available in Kansas and Maryland, contrasts the difference in available exemptions that depend on a person's residence.[18]

Table 20–1

Selected Exemptions under Kansas and Maryland Law

Category	What Is Exempt	Statutory Provision
	Kansas Law	
Homestead	A residence containing one acre within city limits or 160 acres outside of city limits. Such property, however, shall not be exempt from sale for taxes or payment of obligations contracted for the purchase of the premises, or for the erection of improvements thereon.	Kan. Stat. Ann. § 60-2301(e) (1993)
Life insurance	The cash value of a life insurance policy provided, however, that the policy was purchased more than one year prior to the bankruptcy filing.	Kan. Stat. Ann. § 40-414
Retirement plan	A retirement plan qualified under I.R.C. 401(a), 403(a), 403(b), 408 or 409.	Kan. Stat. Ann. § 60-2308 (1993)
Tools of the trade	Tools of the trade up to a value of $7,500.	Kan. Stat. Ann. § 60-2304(e) (1993)

Mississippi, Missouri, Montana, Nebraska, Nevada, New Hampshire, New York, North Carolina, North Dakota, Ohio, Oklahoma, Oregon, South Dakota, Tennessee, Utah, Virginia, West Virginia, and Wyoming.

18 These tables contain only a selected list of exemptions available in Kansas and Maryland. For an exhaustive list of available exemptions, the reader should consult pertinent state statutes.

Table 20–1 (*continued*)

Category	What Is Exempt	Statutory Provision
Household goods & personal property	Reasonably necessary household goods and personal property in the debtor's possession	Kan. Stat. Ann. § 60-2304(a) (1993)
Vehicle	One vehicle up to the amount of $20,000. However, the dollar limit does not apply to a vehicle equipped for handicapped operation.	Kan. Stat. Ann. § 60-2304(c) (1993)
Jewelry	Ornaments of the debtor's person, including jewelry, having a value not to exceed $1,000.	Kan. Stat. Ann. § 60-2304(b) (1993)
Burial plot or crypt	A burial plot, crypt, or cemetery lot.	Kan. Stat. Ann. § 60-2340(d) (1993)
	Maryland Law	
Homestead	No specific exemption; a debtor may exempt up to $5,500 of equity in a residence.	Md. Cts. & Jud. Proc. Code Ann. §§ 11-504, -507
Insurance	Proceeds of life insurance and annuity contracts generally exempt unless pledged as collateral.	Md. Ann. Code arts. 48A & 385 (1973)
Retirement plan	Interest in ERISA-qualified plan and IRA.	Md. Ann. Code art. 73B, § 17; Md. Cts. & Jud. Proc. Code Ann. § 11-504(h)
Tools of trade	Generally, $2,500 of personalty necessary for trade or profession.	Md. Cts. & Jud. Proc. Code Ann. § 11-504(b)(1)

Table 20–1 (*continued*)

Category	What Is Exempt	Statutory Provision
Household goods	$500 worth of household goods.	Md. Cts. & Jud. Proc. Code Ann. § 11-504
Personal property	In conjunction with a debtor's homestead exemption, a debtor may exempt up to $5,500 in personal property.	Md. Cts. & Jud. Proc. Code Ann. § 11-504

Assets successfully claimed exempt may generally not be sold or otherwise disposed of to satisfy claims of creditors.[19] Exemptions also may not be waived. A prepetition waiver of an exemption in favor of an unsecured creditor is unenforceable in a bankruptcy proceeding.[20] In addition, a waiver of exemptions has been held void as against public policy.[21]

§ 20.4 How to Claim an Exemption

As part of the filing process, a debtor is required to file with the Bankruptcy Court schedules of assets and liabilities (schedules). The schedules must be filed with the petition or within 15 days thereafter, unless the time is extended by the court for good cause shown.[22] The schedules contain a section in which a debtor may claim various assets exempt under 11 U.S.C. § 522. If a debtor fails either to claim exemptions or file the schedules within the time period allowed, a dependent of the debtor may file the list within 30 days thereafter.[23]

To successfully claim an asset exempt, a debtor must identify the asset, disclose the authority (state or federal) that is the basis for the claimed exemption, and indicate its value. In addition, and depending on the local practice in the court in which the petition is filed, the debtor may be required to itemize each pot and pan, instead of lumping such items into a catch-all category such as "household goods."

Prior to filing the case, counsel should not only discuss available exemptions with the client but also should review various documents that pertain to assets that may be claimed exempt. For example, many states have a homestead exemption whereby a certain amount of real property may be exempt as the debtor's homestead. The acreage of property exempt under the homestead exemption usually depends on

[19] 11 U.S.C. § 522(c).

[20] *Id.* § 522(e).

[21] *See, e.g.*, Celco, Inc. v. Davis Van Lines, Inc., 226 Kan. 366, 598 P.2d 188 (1979) (waiver of homestead and personal exemptions by executory contract is contrary to public policy); Iowa Mut. Ins. Co. v. Parr, 189 Kan. 475, 370 P.2d 400 (1962).

[22] Fed. R. Bankr. P. 1007(c).

[23] Fed. R. Bankr. P. 4003(a).

whether the property is located within city limits. In addition, some states, such as Maryland and Florida, do not permit creditors to levy on property held between husband and wife as tenants by the entireties[24] to satisfy the debt of an individual spouse. A Chapter 7 trustee in those jurisdictions would not be able to sell a debtors' residence held by tenants by the entireties, regardless of the amount of equity in the property if, other than a current mortgage, the debtors have no joint creditors.[25]

To avoid the harsh surprise sometimes encountered when a Chapter 7 trustee requests copies of documents regarding claimed exemptions such as deeds, retirement plans, vehicle titles, and stock certificates, prudent counsel should review such documents prior to filing the petition in order to ensure, as best as possible, that the exemption cannot be successfully challenged. Such review may also permit the prepetition correction of title to property to maximize available exemptions.

§ 20.5 Objections to Claimed Exemptions

Despite a debtor's claimed exemption, a bankruptcy trustee, creditor, or other party-in-interest may object to the debtor's claim that the asset is exempt. If the objection is based on an exemption claimed by the debtor under § 522(b)(2), state law governs the proceeding.[26] Pursuant to Bankruptcy Rule 4003, objections to an exemption must be filed within 30 days following the conclusion of the meeting of creditors,[27] unless the court extends the time for good cause shown. The entity filing the objection has the burden of proving that the exemption is not properly claimed.[28] If the objection is not consensually resolved, the bankruptcy court holds a hearing on the objection and ultimately renders a decision in the matter.

In the 1992 case of *Taylor v. Freeland & Kronz,*[29] the United States Supreme Court held that unless an objection to a claimed exemption is filed within the period prescribed by Rule 4003(b), the asset is exempt, even if the debtor had no good faith reason for the claimed exemption. The Court reasoned that the plain language of § 522(l) and Rule 4003(b) is controlling and rejected the argument that a good faith requirement should be implied to discourage meritless claims. Despite its decision not to limit the application of § 522(e) to exemptions claimed in good faith, the Court, though in dicta, provided a clear warning that debtors and their counsel may face severe penalties for engaging in improper conduct in bankruptcy proceedings,

---

24 11 U.S.C. § 522(b)(2)(B); *see also* United States v. One Single Family Residence, 894 F.2d 1511, 1514 (11th Cir. 1990); Pepenalla v. Life Ins. Co., 103 B.R. 299 (Bankr. N.D. Fla. 1988); Sumy v. Schlossberg, 777 F.2d 921 (4th Cir. 1985).

25 Sumy v. Schlossberg, 777 F.2d 921 (4th Cir. 1985) (to extent that debtor and spouse are not jointly indebted, bankruptcy trustee may not administer property held as tenants by the entireties for the benefit of non-joint creditors).

26 Norwest Bank Neb., N.A. v. Tveten, 848 F.2d 871 (8th Cir. 1988).

27 Fed. R. Bankr. P. 4003(b).

28 Fed. R. Bankr. P. 4003(c). *See also In re* Meckfessel, 67 B.R. 277 (Bankr. D. Kan. 1986).

29 ___ U.S. ___, 112 S. Ct. 1644 (1992).

such as claiming an asset exempt with no legal basis for its exemption.[30] In addition, the Tenth Circuit has held that pursuant to Rule 4003(b), a motion seeking additional time to object to a claimed exemption must not only be filed within the 30-day period, but also it must be ruled upon prior to the expiration of such period, because that is the plain meaning of the rule.[31]

§ 20.6 Avoidance of Liens

Consistent with the intent of Congress to give a debtor a fresh start, a debtor may avoid a judicial lien to the extent that the lien impairs an exemption to which the debtor would have been entitled under § 522(b).[32] A *judicial lien* is a lien obtained by judgment, levy, sequestration, or other legal or equitable process or proceeding.[33] Likewise, a nonpossessory, nonpurchase-money lien may be avoided in any of the following described property:

1. Household furnishings, household goods, wearing apparel, appliances, books, animals, crops, musical instruments, or jewelry that are held primarily for the personal, family, or household use of the debtor or a dependent of the debtor
2. Implements, professional books, or tools, of the trade of the debtor or the trade of a dependent of the debtor
3. Professionally prescribed health aids for the debtor or a dependent of the debtor.[34]

Therefore, even if a creditor obtains a judicial lien attaching to property that would otherwise be exempt, or obtains a consensual, nonpurchase-money lien on any of the above-described property, a debtor may avoid the lien.

Pursuant to Rule 4003(d), a debtor seeking to avoid a lien under § 522(f) must do so by motion. Under Rule 9013, the motion must state with particularity the grounds and the specific relief sought. In addition, and pursuant to Rules 4003(b) and 9014, the motion is considered a contested matter and the Federal Rules of Civil Procedure apply to the use of discovery. Although the Bankruptcy Code and Rules provide no time limit within which a debtor must act to avoid a lien under § 522(f), counsel should review applicable case law reported in the jurisdiction and applicable local rules. For example, District of Kansas Bankruptcy Rule 4003.1 requires that a

---

30 *See, e.g.,* 11 U.S.C. § 727(a)(4)(B) (authorizing denial of discharge for presenting fraudulent claims); Rule 1008 (requiring filings to be verified or to contain an unsworn declaration of truthfulness under penalty of perjury); Rule 9011 (authorizing sanctions for signing certain documents not well grounded in fact, warranted by existing law, or supportable by a good faith argument for the extension, modification, or reversal of existing law); 18 U.S.C. § 152 (imposing criminal penalties for fraud in bankruptcy cases).

31 *In re* Bradshaw, 912 F.2d 1255 (10th Cir. 1990).

32 11 U.S.C. § 522(f)(1).

33 *Id.* § 101(36).

34 *Id.* § 522(f)(2)(A), (B) & (C).

motion in a case under Chapter 7 to avoid nonpossessory, nonpurchase-money security interests or judicial liens on exempt property must be filed at least five business days before the date initially set for the debtor's discharge.[35] Similarly, reopening a case under 11 U.S.C. § 350 to file a motion under § 522(f) is discretionary.[36] In considering whether to act on a debtor's motion under § 522(f) after discharge, at least one court suggests that the following factors should be examined:

1. The good faith of the creditor
2. The resulting prejudice
3. The length of time
4. The diligence of the creditor prior to bankruptcy.[37]

An example of a motion to avoid a judicial lien and order avoiding judicial lien appear at §§ **20.7** and **20.8,** respectively.

§ 20.7 Form: Motion to Avoid Judicial Lien

FORM 20–1
MOTION TO AVOID JUDICIAL LIEN

IN THE UNITED STATES BANKRUPTCY COURT
FOR THE DISTRICT OF [state]

In re:	)	
	)	
BRADLEY C. DEBTOR,	)	Case No. ________
	)	Chapter 7
Debtor.	)	
______________________	)	

MOTION TO AVOID JUDICIAL LIEN

COMES NOW, Bradley C. Debtor, debtor herein, by and through undersigned counsel, and, in support of his Motion, states as follows:

1. The debtor filed a voluntary petition for relief under Chapter 7 of Title 11 U.S.C. on or about [filing date].

---

35 In the case of *In re* McDonald, 161 B.R. 697 (D. Kan. 1993), however, the district court reversed the bankruptcy court's denial of a debtor's motion to avoid a lien as untimely, reasoning that each case must be determined under principles of equity and on a case-by-case basis.

36 *In re* Serafini, 41 B.R. 880 (Bankr. W.D. Pa. 1984); *In re* Terrat, 19 B.R. 360 (Bankr. D. Alaska 1982).

37 Nobel v. Ungling, 8 Collier Bankr. Cas. 2d (MB) 1188, 1194–95 (D. Del. 1983).

2. The debtor owns certain real property located at [property description/address] comprising approximately [number] acres, more or less, which is the debtor's homestead.

3. Pursuant to 11 U.S.C. § 522(b) and [state statute], the debtor's homestead is exempt.

4. On or about [judgment date], [creditor name] obtained a judgment against the debtor for approximately [lien amount], in [county name] County District Court, Case No. __________.

5. Pursuant to applicable [state] law, the lien discussed in ¶ 4 above attached to all real property owned by the debtor in [county, state].

6. Pursuant to 11 U.S.C. § 522(f)(1), the debtor may "avoid the fixing of a lien on an interest of the debtor in property to the extent that such lien impairs an exemption to which the debtor would have been entitled to under subsection (b) of this section if such lien is a judicial lien."

7. Pursuant to 11 U.S.C. § 101(36), a judicial lien is a lien obtained by judgment, levy, sequestration, or other legal or equitable process or proceeding.

8. Pursuant to the authority contained in 11 U.S.C. § 522(f)(1), the debtor requests that this Court enter an order avoiding the judgment lien of [creditor name] because it constitutes a judicial lien that impairs an exemption to which the debtor is entitled.

WHEREFORE, Bradley C. Debtor respectfully requests that this Honorable Court enter an order:

(1) Avoiding the judgment lien of [creditor name] filed on or about [judgment date], in the approximate amount of [lien amount], because it constitutes a judicial lien on the debtor's homestead; and

(2) For such other and further relief that this Court deems just and proper.

Respectfully submitted,

[Attorney Signature]

§ 20.8 Form: Order Avoiding Judicial Lien

FORM 20–2
ORDER AVOIDING JUDICIAL LIEN

IN THE UNITED STATES BANKRUPTCY COURT
FOR THE DISTRICT OF [state]

In re:	)	
	)	
BRADLEY C. DEBTOR,	)	Case No. __________
	)	Chapter 7
Debtor.	)	
______________________________	)	

ORDER AVOIDING JUDICIAL LIEN

AT [location of court] this ____ day of ________, [year]:

Upon consideration of the debtor's Motion to Avoid Judicial Lien filed herein, the Court finding that the judgment lien of [creditor name] recorded on or about [recording information], in the approximate amount of $ [lien amount] which, by operation of law, attached to the debtor's homestead located at [address], constitutes a judicial lien within the meaning of Bankruptcy Code § 522(f)(1), it is

ORDERED, that the judgment lien of [creditor name] against Bradley C. Debtor, debtor herein, in the approximate amount of [lien amount] should be and is hereby avoided against as to the debtor's homestead, located at [address], pursuant to Bankruptcy Code § 522(f)(1).

____
UNITED STATES BANKRUPTCY JUDGE

§ 20.9 Prebankruptcy Planning: Let the Debtor Beware

Depending on the nature of the debtor's assets and available exemptions, a debtor may, on the advice of counsel, seek to shelter nonexempt assets from the reach of creditors through prebankruptcy planning. Although a debtor's ability to take full advantage of available exemptions is generally permissible, a debtor must be extremely careful that such planning does not rise to the level of attempting to defraud creditors. This chapter does not discuss specific prebankruptcy planning methods, but §§ **20.10** through **20.12** present an overview of the risks associated with the conversion of nonexempt assets to exempt assets under the guise of prebankruptcy planning.

§ 20.10 Congressional Intent to Favor Exemptions

It is well settled that a debtor's conversion of nonexempt property to exempt property on the eve of bankruptcy for the purpose of placing that property beyond the reach of creditors, without more, will not deprive the debtor of the exemption to which the debtor would otherwise be entitled.[38] Both the House of Representatives and the Senate affirmed this policy when debating the enactment of the Bankruptcy Code. The House Report states:

> As under current law, the debtor will be permitted to convert non-exempt property into exempt property before filing a bankruptcy petition. The practice is not fraudulent as to creditors, and permits the debtor to make full use of the exemptions to which he is entitled under the law.[39]

The rationale behind the intent of Congress is that if debtors were not allowed to convert nonexempt property into exempt property, the result would be extremely harsh, especially in those states that have opted out under Bankruptcy Code § 522(d)(2) and have a minimal exemption allowance. See **§ 20.3.** This liberal policy regarding the prepetition conversion of exempt property, however, is not absolute. If the debtor's actual intent in converting or transferring property prefiling is determined to be to defraud creditors, the transfer may be avoided as a fraudulent conveyance (see **§ 20.11**) and/or the debtor's discharge may be denied (see **§ 20.12**).

§ 20.11 Avoidance of Transfer as Fraudulent Conveyance

Depending on the specific facts, a creditor or the bankruptcy trustee, as the case may be, may seek to avoid a prepetition transfer of property into exempt assets as a fraudulent conveyance. If the debtor has not filed bankruptcy, a creditor may file suit in state court to avoid the transfer as a fraudulent conveyance under applicable state law.[40]

If, after the transfer, the debtor files a bankruptcy proceeding, a creditor or the trustee may attack a transfer of nonexempt assets into exempt assets as a fraudulent conveyance if the transfer occurred within one year prior to filing, and if the court finds that the debtor:

1. Made the transfer with actual intent to hinder, delay, or defraud a creditor
2. Received less than reasonably equivalent value in exchange for such transfer

---

[38] Norwest Bank Neb., N.A. v. Tveten, 848 F.2d 871 (8th Cir. 1988); Ford v. Poston, 773 F.2d 52 (4th Cir. 1984); *In re* Reed, 700 F.2d 986 (5th Cir. 1983).

[39] H.R. Rep. No. 595, 95th Cong., 1st Sess. 361 (1977), *reprinted in* 1978 U.S.C.C.A.N. 5963, 6317; S. Rep. No. 989, 95th Cong., 2d Sess. 76 (1978), *reprinted in* 1978 U.S.C.C.A.N. 5787, 5862.

[40] Nine jurisdictions, including New York, have adopted and codified the Uniform Fraudulent Conveyance Act (UFCA), first promulgated in 1918. However, 29 states have adopted the Uniform Fraudulent Transfer Act to replace the UFCA.

3. Was insolvent on the date that the transfer was made, or became insolvent as a result of the transfer.[41]

In *Hanson v. First National Bank in Brookings,*[42] the Eighth Circuit affirmed the bankruptcy court and district court, allowing the debtor's prefiling conversion of nonexempt assets into exempt assets. In *Hanson,* the debtors sold a car, two vans, and a motor home to their son for the appraised value of $27,115. The debtors further sold various household goods to the debtor's brother for the appraised value of $7,300. Approximately two weeks prior to filing, the debtors used the proceeds to purchase two life insurance policies having respective cash surrender values of $9,977 and $9,978, and paid $11,033 on their homestead mortgage. Under South Dakota law, both the insurance policies and the homestead were exempt.

When an objection to the exemptions as an allegedly fraudulent conveyance was filed, the bankruptcy court overruled the objection and permitted the debtors their claimed exemptions. In denying the objection, the bankruptcy court accepted the debtors' reasoning for paying off their homestead, namely that they desired not only to protect their homestead but also to reduce their monthly living expenses because they believed they would have difficulty finding employment after they terminated their farming business.

With regard to the sale of assets to family members, the bankruptcy court found that the items transferred were sold for fair market value. Further, the bankruptcy court reasoned that no money was borrowed and placed into exempt property, the debtors accounted for the cash received, and they had a pre-existing homestead. In affirming the district court, the Eighth Circuit found that the bankruptcy court was not clearly in error in finding no fraudulent intent by the debtors and permitting them to claim their full exemptions.

The trustee's powers to avoid fraudulent transfers in contexts other than conversion to exempt property are discussed in more detail in **Chapter 12.**

§ 20.12 Denial of Discharge

One of the main reasons for an individual to file a bankruptcy proceeding is to obtain a discharge.[43] If the debtor is successful and a discharge is granted, the debtor is under no legal obligation to pay any prepetition, dischargeable debt. If, however, a debtor is denied a discharge, creditors may pursue the debtor on prepetition liabilities as if the bankruptcy never occurred.

When there has been a suspect transfer of nonexempt property into exempt property, a creditor or trustee may file an adversary complaint, asking the court to deny the debtor's discharge under 11 U.S.C. § 727(a)(2). The statute provides in pertinent part:

---

41 11 U.S.C. § 548.

42 848 F.2d 866 (8th Cir. 1988).

43 11 U.S.C. §§ 727, 1328, 1141, 1228.

> The court shall grant the debtor a discharge, unless . . .
>
> (2) the debtor, with intent to hinder, delay, or defraud a creditor or an officer of the estate charged with custody of property under this title, has transferred, removed, destroyed, mutilated, or concealed
>
> (A) property of the debtor within one year before the date of the filing of the petition.

To determine whether a debtor's conversion of assets was with the intent to hinder, delay, or defraud creditors, the bankruptcy court, using federal law,[44] must ascertain the debtor's actual intent in converting such property prior to filing. Fraudulent intent is a question of fact, and extrinsic evidence of such intent is required if the court is to deny the debtor's discharge.[45]

In deciding denial of discharge claims under § 727, many courts rely on so-called badges or indicia of fraud.[46] Although not every one must be shown, there must be sufficient indicia to reach the level of a preponderance of the evidence showing the debtor's intent to hinder, delay, or defraud creditors.[47]

Although the final outcome of a § 727 complaint to deny discharge because of a debtor's conversion of nonexempt property to exempt property depends upon the specific facts of the case, the following decisions suggest that this area is less than well settled, as decisions rest on both sides of the fence.

In *Norwest Bank Nebraska, N.A., v. Tveten,*[48] the physician debtor owed approximately $19 million in personal guaranties. Once the investments he had guaranteed went sour, the debtor filed a Chapter 11. Prior to filing the proceeding, however, the debtor, through 17 separate transfers, used approximately $700,000 in cash and other nonexempt assets to purchase various life insurance and annuity policies, which were exempt under Minnesota law. In ruling on a complaint to deny discharge under § 727, the bankruptcy court denied the debtor's discharge, finding that the debtor had actual intent to defraud creditors.[49] In affirming the district court's decision that upheld the bankruptcy court's decision,[50] the Eighth Circuit reasoned that to permit the debtor to "convert all of his major non-exempt assets into sheltered property on the eve of bankruptcy with actual intent to defraud creditors, would constitute a perversion of the purposes of the Bankruptcy Code."[51]

---

44 A debtor's discharge is determined by federal law. *See,* Norwest Bank Neb., N.A. v. Tveten, 848 F.2d 871, 873–74 (8th Cir. 1988).

45 Hanson v. First Nat'l Bank in Brookings, 848 F.2d 866, 868 (8th Cir. 1988); Ford v. Poston, 773 F.2d 52 (4th Cir. 1985); *In re* Reed, 700 F.2d 986, 991 (5th Cir. 1983).

46 *See, e.g.,* Uniform Fraudulent Transfer Act, § 4(b); 37 Am. Jur 2d, *Fraudulent Conveyances; In re* Fine, 89 B.R. 167, 174 (Bankr. D. Kan. 1988). *See also In re* Davis, 124 B.R. 831, 835 (Bankr. D. Kan. 1991).

47 In *Grogan v. Garner,* 498 U.S. 279 (1991), the United States Supreme Court changed the evidentiary standard in a bankruptcy denial of discharge proceeding from "clear and convincing evidence" to a "preponderance of the evidence."

48 848 F.2d 871 (8th Cir. 1988).

49 *In re* Tveten, 70 B.R. 529 (Bankr. D. Minn. 1987).

50 *In re* Tveten, 82 B.R. 95 (D. Minn. 1987).

51 848 F.2d at 876.

In *Ford v. Poston,*[52] the Fourth Circuit reached a similar result. In *Ford,* a creditor obtained a judgment against the debtor in the amount of $20,288. One day after the entry of the judgment, the debtor recorded a "Deed of Correction" in the land records, thereby transferring a tract of land adjacent to his homestead to himself and his wife as tenants by the entireties. Approximately one year later, the debtor set aside the same tract of land in a homestead deed, indicating his intention to exempt this property from his creditors under applicable West Virginia law. The next day, the debtor filed a Chapter 7 proceeding.

The judgment creditor filed a denial of discharge complaint under § 727(a)(2)(H), and the bankruptcy court denied the debtor's discharge, finding that the initial transfer was not an attempt to correct a then six-month old mistake, but rather was intended to defraud creditors. Thereafter, the Fourth Circuit affirmed the district court's finding that its decision upholding the bankruptcy court was not clearly erroneous.

In contrast to the *Tveten* and *Ford* decisions, in *In re Johnson,*[53] the physician debtor converted approximately $434,000 of nonexempt assets into assets exempt under Minnesota law within one year preceding filing bankruptcy. In a lengthy opinion, the bankruptcy court denied a creditor's § 727 denial of discharge complaint, finding that the debtor did not have the intent to hinder, delay, or defraud creditors under § 727(a)(2). Rather, the court found that the debtor made a conscious, albeit selfish, decision to fully avail himself of the full range of exemptions allowed by the Minnesota state legislature, and in a fashion which had been explicitly condoned by decisions of both state and federal courts. The *Johnson* court, however, noted that its decision was "diametrically opposed" to that of *In re Tveten.*[54] Not surprisingly, the Eighth Circuit reversed and remanded the case for the court to consider *Tveten.*[55]

If a debtor desires to convert nonexempt property into exempt property prior to filing bankruptcy, the potentially harsh consequences of § 727 should be kept in mind. If the court finds that the debtor has violated § 727, the debtor's discharge may be denied, and that is a very high price to pay.

---

[52] 773 F.2d 52 (4th Cir. 1985).

[53] 80 B.R. 953 (Bankr. D. Minn. 1987), *aff'd,* 101 B.R. 997 (D. Minn. 1988), *rev'd and remanded* (to consider *Tveten*), 880 F.2d 78 (8th Cir. 1989).

[54] 70 B.R. 529 (Bankr. D. Minn. 1987).

[55] *In re* Johnson, 880 F.2d 78 (8th Cir. 1989).

CHAPTER 21

RETIREMENT, PENSION, AND PROFIT SHARING PLANS

Gary D. Barnes

§ 21.1 Introduction

A retirement, pension, or profit sharing plan may often be the most valuable asset of a small business owner. Preserving such plans from the claims of creditors can be of great importance to individual debtors.

Plans may be preserved from creditors' claims in three ways. First, ERISA qualified plans are excluded from the property of the estate under 11 U.S.C. § 541. Second, plans might also be excluded from the estate under state spendthrift trust laws. See **§ 21.5.** Third, plans that are property of the estate may be exempt under state law. See **§ 21.6.**

The effect bankruptcy will have on the retirement, pension, or profit sharing plan of a small business owner can be an important factor in the decision on whether to file a bankruptcy case. Consequently, counsel for a small business owner must carefully review the facts of the case, the specifics of the plan, the structure and actual operations of the plan, and the evolving law in order to adequately advise the owner on whether the plan can be preserved from the claims of creditors.

§ 21.2 Property Excluded from the Estate under § 541(c)(2)

The basis for excluding ERISA qualified plans from the property of the estate is 11 U.S.C. § 541(c)(2). Section 541(a)(1) defines *property of the estate* generally to include "all legal or equitable interests of the debtor in property as of the commencement of the case." Under § 541(c)(1), a debtor's interest in property is property of the estate even though it is subject to an agreement, transfer instrument, or nonbankruptcy law restricting transfer of the property by the debtor, unless the interest falls within subparagraph (c)(2), which provides that: "[a] restriction on the transfer of a beneficial interest of the debtor in a trust that is enforceable under applicable nonbankruptcy law is enforceable under this title." ERISA qualified plans must contain an anti-alienation clause and may be excluded from the property of the estate under this provision. A plan that is a valid spendthrift trust under state law is excluded from the bankruptcy estate because of the restriction on transfer of the beneficial interests of the debtor pursuant to applicable nonbankruptcy law.[1]

In *Patterson v. Shumate,*[2] the Supreme Court resolved a split among the circuits by holding that ERISA qualified plans are excluded from the bankruptcy estate under § 541(c)(2). In that case, Shumate, the president and chairman of the board of directors of Coleman Furniture Corporation, filed a Chapter 11 bankruptcy proceeding, which was converted to a Chapter 7 proceeding. Coleman Furniture also filed a Chapter 11 bankruptcy proceeding, and that case was also converted to a Chapter 7 liquidation case. Coleman Furniture had a pension plan that satisfied the requirements of ERISA, including the requirement that the plan have an anti-alienation provision. The plan also qualified for favorable tax treatment pursuant to the Internal Revenue Code. The Coleman Furniture pension plan participants included Shumate and approximately 400 other employees.

The trustee in bankruptcy for Coleman Furniture terminated the plan and paid all participants except Shumate. Patterson, the trustee for Shumate, filed an adversary proceeding in the bankruptcy court to obtain Shumate's interest in the plan for the benefit of the creditors of Shumate's bankruptcy estate. A related proceeding was pending in the district court, and Shumate asked the district court to require Coleman Furniture's trustee to pay the plan distributions to Shumate.

The district court held that Shumate's distribution from the plan was an asset of his bankruptcy estate that was not excluded under § 541(c)(2) of the Bankruptcy Code and, further, that it was not exempt. The Fourth Circuit Court of Appeals reversed, holding that ERISA qualified plans with an anti-alienation provision meet the requirement of having a restriction on transfer applicable under nonbankruptcy law. Therefore, the Fourth Circuit held that Shumate's plan was excluded from the bankruptcy estate.

The Supreme Court held that "applicable non-bankruptcy law" in § 541(c)(2) of the Bankruptcy Code is not limited exclusively to state law.[3] The Supreme Court then went on to hold that the anti-alienation provision contained in the Coleman Furniture plan, which is required of an ERISA qualified plan, constituted an enforceable restriction on the beneficial interest of the debtor.[4] Therefore, the Court held that Shumate's plan was excluded from his bankruptcy estate.

---

[1] 11 U.S.C. § 541(c)(2).

[2] ___ U.S. ___, 119 L. Ed. 2d 519 (1992).

[3] *Id.*, 119 L. Ed. 2d at 527.

[4] *Id.* at 528.

Pension, profit sharing, and retirement plans continue to generate bankruptcy litigation after *Shumate,* especially in cases involving small business owners or professionals. The typical issues that arise in these cases are:

1. Whether a plan is ERISA qualified
2. Whether a plan must also qualify for special tax treatment under the Internal Revenue Code
3. Whether a plan is excluded from the estate under state spendthrift trust laws
4. Whether a plan is exempt under state law or § 522(d)(10)(E) of the Bankruptcy Code.

§ 21.3 Requirements of an ERISA Qualified Plan

To be excluded from the bankruptcy estate under *Patterson v. Shumate,* the plan must of course be ERISA qualified. ERISA is the acronym for the Employee Retirement Income Security Act; it is a part of the labor laws. Courts have held that the intent of Congress in passing ERISA was to develop "a body of Federal substantive law . . . to deal with issues involving rights and obligations under private welfare and pension plans."[5] With certain exceptions, ERISA covers employee benefit plans

> established or maintained
>
> (1) by any employer engaged in commerce or in any industry or activity affecting commerce; or
>
> (2) by any employee organization or organizations representing employees engaged in commerce or in any industry or activity affecting commerce; or
>
> (3) by both.[6]

ERISA does not cover governmental plans, church plans (unless the church plan elects to be covered under ERISA), plans maintained solely to comply with workers' compensation or disability insurance laws, or plans maintained outside the United States and which are primarily for the benefit of persons, substantially all of whom are nonresident aliens, or unfunded excess benefit plans.[7] Individual retirement arrangements (IRAs) established and funded by an individual who is not an employer or an employee organization are not covered by ERISA.[8]

The secretary of labor has promulgated regulations that state, "[a]n individual and his or her spouse shall not be deemed to be employees with respect to a trade or business, whether incorporated or unincorporated, which is wholly owned by the individual and his or her spouse."[9] Therefore, a plan that covers only a sole

---

[5] Amato v. Bernard, 618 F.2d 559, 567 (9th Cir. 1980) (citing 120 Cong. Rec. 29942 (1974)).

[6] 29 U.S.C. § 1003(a).

[7] *Id.* § 1003(b).

[8] *In re* Bharucha, 115 B.R. 671, 673 (Bankr. D. Ariz. 1990).

[9] 29 C.F.R. § 2510.3-3(b), (c)(1) (1988).

proprietor or sole stockholder and spouse is not covered by ERISA because the plan has no employees.[10]

It has been held that an anti-alienation clause by itself in a plan is not sufficient to exclude the plan from the estate. In *In re Witwer,*[11] a medical doctor filed a Chapter 7 bankruptcy and claimed as exempt his profit sharing plan corpus with a present net value of $1.8 million. Certain creditors objected to the claimed exemption. The doctor-debtor was the sole stockholder and president of James J. Witwer, M.D., Inc. He was the only employee of the corporation and only beneficiary of the corporate profit sharing plan. The plan contemplated extending coverage to future employees, but the debtor was and always had been the sole participant in the plan. The plan was established and was amended to remain consistent with the Internal Revenue Service regulations for tax-favored status, and the plan contained an anti-alienation provision.

The court found that "[p]lainly read, the regulation [promulgated by the Secretary of Labor] specifically excludes an individual from ERISA qualification when the corporation is wholly owned by the individual."[12] The court then held that the debtor was not a plan participant and a plan without eligible participants cannot be an ERISA qualified employee pension benefit plan. Therefore, the plan was not excluded from the debtor's bankruptcy estate.

In another case, *In re Lane,*[13] a self-employed dentist filed a Chapter 7 petition and scheduled among his assets an individual retirement arrangement, a checking account, and two Keogh plan accounts. The Keogh plan documents required that the employees receive a contribution for each plan year based on a percentage of their compensation. The debtor's tax returns for 1989 through 1991 reflected wages paid to employees; however, no contributions were made on behalf of the employees to the Keogh plans during those years. The court found that the debtor's Keogh plans were "top heavy" plans that failed to meet the minimum contribution requirements for non-key employees and were not qualified pension plans pursuant to the Internal Revenue Code and the provisions of the plans. Therefore, this debtor's Keogh plans were not excluded from the estate because they were not subject to the anti-alienation provision of ERISA. ERISA applies only if there is an employee benefit plan that would be subject to ERISA. Because the debtor was and always had been the only participant in the Keogh plans, the plans could not be subject to ERISA. The court noted if the debtor had made contributions for even one employee, the Keogh plans might have been subject to ERISA.

In a third case, *In re Hall,*[14] a debtor filed a Chapter 13, which was converted to a Chapter 7 proceeding. The debtor claimed as exempt his interest in a pension plan and an IRA. The debtor was the president and the sole shareholder of a company named Middle Earth Graphics. The debtor's spouse was the secretary of Middle Earth Graphics. The pension plan was for the exclusive benefit of the debtor and his wife. The debtor and his wife were the trustees, sole beneficiaries, and only participants of the pension plan. The pension plan was qualified under the Internal

---

[10] *In re* Witwer, 148 B.R. 930, 936 (Bankr. C.D. Cal. 1992).

[11] 148 B.R. 930 (Bankr. C.D. Cal. 1992).

[12] *Id.* at 936.

[13] 149 B.R. 760 (Bankr. E.D.N.Y. 1993).

[14] 151 B.R. 412 (Bankr. W.D. Mich. 1993).

Revenue Code and ERISA at the time of its inception and it contained anti-alienation language. The pension plan had terminated effective October 1, 1986, but the debtor and his wife had not requested distribution of the funds in the pension plan. The bankruptcy court noted that the *Shumate* court may have intended any of three interpretations for the term "*ERISA qualified plan:*"

1. A plan subject to ERISA
2. A plan subject to ERISA that contains an anti-alienation provision
3. A plan that is tax qualified under IRC § 401(a), is subject to ERISA, and has an anti-alienation provision.

The bankruptcy court reviewed *Patterson v. Shumate* and Sixth Circuit decisions and went on to hold that there is a very strong indication that the Sixth Circuit requires an "ERISA qualified" plan (1) to be tax qualified under I.R.C. § 401(a); (2) to be subject to ERISA; and (3) to include an anti-alienation provision. If even one requirement is not satisfied, a plan is not ERISA qualified, under the Sixth Circuit's analysis.

The court applied this test to the pension plan in the case. The court found that for a plan to be subject to ERISA it must exclusively provide benefits to employees and former employees. The debtor and his spouse, however, were the only persons eligible to be participants in the pension plan; therefore, the court concluded that the pension plan was without employees. The debtor and his spouse were employers, not employees, of the company for ERISA purposes. The court held that the pension plan was not subject to ERISA and not ERISA qualified. Therefore, the pension plan was not excluded from the bankruptcy estate.

In the subsequent case of *In re Hanes,*[15] a bankruptcy court declined to follow the definition of an "ERISA qualified plan" set out in the *Hall* case. The *Hanes* court held that a plan is "ERISA qualified" for purposes of exclusion from the bankruptcy estate if:

1. The plan is governed by ERISA
2. The plan includes an anti-alienation provision
3. The anti-alienation provision is enforceable under ERISA.

The court applied this test and held that one of the debtor's three retirement plans satisfied the test and was excluded from the bankruptcy estate on that ground.

§ 21.4 Qualification of ERISA Plan for Special Tax Treatment under the IRC

There is a split of authority on whether *Patterson v. Shumate*[16] requires qualification for special tax treatment in order for an ERISA plan to be excluded from the estate.

---

[15] 162 B.R. 733 (Bankr. E.D. Va. 1994).

[16] ___ U.S. ___, 119 L. Ed. 2d 519 (1992).

The bankruptcy court in *In re Hall*[17] found that, based on a reasonable reading of certain language in *Shumate* citing the tax code and tax regulations, one would conclude that the *Shumate* court intended an "ERISA qualified" plan to satisfy both the Internal Revenue Code and ERISA. The court in *Hall* also reviewed Sixth Circuit cases and found that the Sixth Circuit had indicated in a decision prior to *Shumate* that it would require an "ERISA qualified" plan to be qualified under the IRC.[18]

The court in *In re Hanes*[19] reached a different result on this issue. The *Hanes* court held that the requirement that a plan be qualified under the IRC in order to be an "ERISA qualified" plan placed too much emphasis on the technical requirements of the IRC and not enough emphasis on § 541(c)(2) of the Bankruptcy Code. The *Hanes* court stated that the references in *Shumate* to the tax code are only to acknowledge that the IRC, in conjunction with ERISA, requires pension plans to have an anti-alienation provision.[20]

§ 21.5 State Spendthrift Trust Law

A plan that is a valid spendthrift trust under state law may be excluded from the estate under Bankruptcy Code § 541(c)(2). However, plans that are not valid spendthrift trusts are not excluded.[21]

Even if a trust contains spendthrift provisions, however, the court can declare them unenforceable if:

1. The settlor of the trust is also the beneficiary of the trust, that is, the plan is self-settled
2. The beneficiary of the trust has dominion or control over the trust
3. The beneficiary may revoke the trust
4. The beneficiary has power in the trust.[22]

Spendthrift trust provisions also will not be upheld if the court finds that enforcement violates public policy.[23]

It has been held that even a very limited right of control or dominion by a beneficiary over the proceeds of a trust may negate the spendthrift nature of the trust.[24] Evidence of control by the debtor-plan participant may include:

---

17 151 B.R. 412 (Bankr. W.D. Mich. 1993).

18 *Id.* at 419.

19 162 B.R. 733 (Bankr. E.D. Va. 1994).

20 *Id.* at 740.

21 *In re* Schmitt, 113 B.R. 1007, 1010 (Bankr. W.D. Mo. 1990).

22 *Id.* at 1011.

23 *Id.*

24 *In re* Swanson, 873 F.2d 1121, 1124 (8th Cir. 1989). *See In re* Schmitt, 113 B.R. at 1012–13.

1. The right of the debtor-participant to make investment decisions regarding funds of the plan
2. The right of the debtor-participant to determine the time or method of distributions from the plan
3. The right of the debtor-participant to elect to participate in the plan or to make contributions to the plan
4. The right of the debtor-participant to make withdrawals or borrow from the plan.

In *In re Witwer,*[25] the court noted that a key factor in determining whether or not a plan meets the state spendthrift requirements is the debtor's degree of control over the trust. The court found that the debtor's degree of control over the plan in that case made the restriction on alienation unenforceable. Therefore, the plan was not excluded from the bankruptcy estate under § 541(c)(2) of the Code.

§ 21.6 Exemption under § 522(d)(10)(E) or State Law

Even if a plan is not excluded from the estate under § 541(c)(2), it may be exempt under § 522(d)(10)(E) of the Bankruptcy Code or state law. In *In re Hall,*[26] the court addressed the issue of whether a pension plan or IRA could be claimed as exempt pursuant to § 522(d)(10)(e) of the Bankruptcy Code. The court found that the pension plan was not exempt because it was established by an insider, any payment under the plan was on account of age or length of service, and the pension plan was not tax qualified pursuant to the Internal Revenue Code sections cited in § 522(d)(10)(e).

As for the IRA, the court noted that there is a split of authority as to whether an IRA is exempt under § 522(d)(10)(E) of the Bankruptcy Code. One issue is whether the IRA is a "similar plan or contract" as required by § 522(d)(10)(E). Some cases have ignored the similar plan or contract issue and have held that the IRA is exempt if the debtor has a present right to payment, that is, the debtor is more than 59 and one-half years old. In *Hall,* the court held that the IRA was exempt to the extent reasonably necessary for support.

To decide whether the IRA was reasonably necessary for support, the court used the eight factors from *In re Rector:*[27]

1. Debtor's present and anticipated living expenses
2. Debtor's present and anticipated income from all sources
3. Age of debtor and dependents
4. Health of debtor and dependents
5. Debtor's ability to work and earn a living

---

25 148 B.R. 930 (Bankr. C.D. Cal. 1992).

26 151 B.R. 412 (Bankr. W.D. Mich. 1993).

27 134 B.R. 611 (Bankr. W.D. Mich. 1991).

6. Debtor's job skills, training, and education
7. Debtor's other assets, including exempt assets
8. Funds available from liquidating other assets.[28]

The court also noted in that case that no contributions had been made to the IRA within a year prior to the filing of the bankruptcy case. This note is a caveat for all bankruptcy lawyers. It may be argued that payments to a retirement, pension, or profit sharing plan can be the targets of transfer avoidance actions under the Code or under applicable state law as provided by § 544 of the Code.

A plan may also be exempt if state law rather than § 522(d)(10)(E) governs and the relevant state law exempts such plans. For example, the application of state law exemptions allowed the plan in the *Witwer*[29] case to be fully exempted while the court held the Keogh plans in *In re Lane*[30] were not exempt under applicable state law.

---

[28] *In re* Hall, 151 B.R. 412, 427 (Bankr. W.D. Mich. 1993) (citing *In re* Rector, 134 B.R. 611, 617 (Bankr. W.D. Mich. 1991)).

[29] *In re* Witwer, 148 B.R. 930 (Bankr. C.D. Cal. 1992).

[30] 149 B.R. 760 (Bankr. E.D.N.Y. 1993).

CHAPTER 22

REORGANIZING A PARTNERSHIP

Kathleen V. Yurchak

§ 22.1 Introduction

A *partnership* is defined as "the association of two or more persons to carry on as co-owners a business for profit."[1] Partners, therefore, by definition aspire to form a profitable enterprise. Reality dictates, however, that not all partnerships will survive or escape business failure. Consequently, as in any business relationship, it is essential to consider the effect of bankruptcy laws on individual partners and on both general and limited partnerships. The bankruptcy treatment of partnerships may influence the extent to which creditors are willing to finance the entity and may be influential in shaping the partnership's capital structure. To the extent the bankruptcy law treats partnerships differently from a corporation or other entity, these differences should be taken into account when making an initial organizational choice so that the interests of prospective partners may be protected.

Provisions of the Bankruptcy Code relating to partnerships, partners, and their creditors have resulted in difficulties in administering the bankruptcy estates of partnership and partner debtors. Dissolution of partnerships and assignability of partnership

[1] Uniform Partnership Act § 202(a) (1992). This Act is commonly referred to as the Revised Uniform Partnership Act [hereinafter RUPA].

agreements present special problems under the Bankruptcy Code. The interrelationship between the statutes governing partnerships and the Bankruptcy Code has resulted in inconsistent decisions and few clear-cut guidelines.

This chapter briefly overviews the treatment of partnerships under the Bankruptcy Code, focusing on rehabilitation and reorganization of a partnership.[2] The areas addressed in this chapter are not by any means the only issues relevant to partnerships in bankruptcy, but they are fundamental issues concerning the bankruptcy process in the partnership context.

§ 22.2 Sources of Partnership Law

Familiarity with state partnership law is essential to appreciating the ramifications of a bankruptcy filing and guiding a partnership through a bankruptcy case. Like many areas of law, the law of partnership has been codified. Partnership statutes typically are based on the Uniform Partnership Act.[3] The Uniform Partnership Act (UPA) was promulgated by the National Conference of Commissioners on Uniform Laws (the Conference) in 1914. Since 1988, a committee of the Conference had been working on a revision of the Uniform Partnership Act, and the Revised Uniform Partnership Act (RUPA) was approved on August 5, 1992. Applicable to limited partnerships is the Uniform Limited Partnership Act (ULPA), as revised by the Revised Uniform Limited Partnership Act (RULPA) in 1976 and further amended in 1985, with further refinements in several states.[4] In addition to statutory law, court cases analyzing the statutes provide guidance on a wide variety of issues.[5]

Although large, complex partnerships exist, general partnerships with few members and informal organizations are the most basic form of business enterprise. Although corporations and even limited partnerships take some affirmative steps to organize, state partnership laws are typically designed to cover even informal associations.[6]

---

[2] Because most partnerships (particularly real estate partnerships) are likely, at least initially, to attempt reorganization under Chapter 11 of the Bankruptcy Code rather than liquidation under Chapter 7, this article will focus on Chapter 11 cases, although much of what is said is applicable to Chapter 7 cases.

[3] *See* H. Rueschlein & W. Gregory, The Law of Agency & Partnership 287 (2d ed. 1990).

[4] The most notable refinement is the Delaware Revised Uniform Limited Partnership Act, 6 Del. Code Ann. §§ 17-101 to -1108 (Supp. 1993). Also, Texas has adopted its own revision of the Uniform Partnership Act, called the Texas Revised Partnership Act, Tex. Rev. Civ. Stat. art. 61325-1 (West 1993).

[5] Many courts have continued to rely on pre-UPA precedents for concepts clearly spelled out in the UPA. Professors Bromberg and Ribstein attribute such cases to the premise that the UPA merely codified the common law. I. Bromberg and L. Ribstein, Bromberg and Ribstein on Partnership § 1.02 (1988).

[6] Under RUPA § 202(a), the association of two or more persons to carry on as co-owners a business for profit creates a partnership, whether or not the persons intend to create a partnership.

§ 22.3 Law of Partnerships Generally

A partnership's assets are the partnership property, for example, real estate, cash, equipment, and the partnership agreement itself. The partnership holds legal and equitable title to these partnership assets.[7] Property initially contributed to a partnership or subsequently acquired by the partnership by purchase or otherwise is partnership property and not property of the partners individually.[8] Real property may be held directly in the name of a partnership.[9] A partner's interest may also be assigned, but the assignee does not thereby become a partner. The assignee is simply entitled to receive the profits to which the assignor would be entitled.[10]

Under the UPA, in a general partnership, a partner is jointly liable for all obligations of the partnership incurred while the person is a partner, and severally liable as well for wrongful acts and omissions and breaches of trust.[11] In many states and under the RUPA,[12] partners are jointly and severally liable for all partnership obligations. Some states, such as Arizona, Colorado, Mississippi, and North Carolina, have provided for joint and several liability in all situations under the UPA.[13] A partner's individual interest in a partnership is personal property.[14]

Historically, the limited partnership represented a compromise in which an investing party gave up rights to participate in management of the business in exchange for insulation from liability while keeping the flexibility and the tax advantages of the partnership form.[15] A limited partner is not liable for the obligations of the limited partnership unless the limited partner is also the general partner or takes part in the control of the business.[16]

Because limited partnerships did not exist at common law, the statutes providing for them define the rights and duties of the partners in more specific terms than statutes dealing with general partnerships. The limited partnership statutes call for a more formalized formation process[17] and more clearly delineated liability of the limited partners.[18] Further, distinctions are drawn between the powers and duties of general partners on the one hand and those of the limited partners on the other hand. The

---

[7] RUPA § 204 (1992).

[8] RUPA § 203.

[9] UPA § 8(3); RUPA § 203.

[10] UPA § 26.

[11] UPA § 15.

[12] RUPA § 306.

[13] 6 U.L.A. 55 (Supp. 1993).

[14] RUPA § 306.

[15] UPA § 27(i); RUPA § 503(d).

[16] RULPA § 303(a).

[17] *See* Uniform Limited Partnership Act § 2(1)(b) [hereinafter ULPA]; Revised Uniform Limited Partnership Act § 201(a) [hereinafter RULPA] (filing of a certificate of limited partnership, which includes required consents and signatories, with the appropriate state authority).

[18] Under ULPA, the limited partner does not become liable as a general partner unless the limited partner takes part in control of the business. ULPA § 7. RULPA has greatly

law of general partnerships applies with full force to limited partnerships except when it conflicts with the limited partnership statute.[19] The limited partnership is, in short, a subset of partnerships generally.

At least one general partner is necessary to either a general or limited partnership. A general partner has, with all other general partners, an equal duty to manage and conduct the partnership's business and must contribute to the losses of the partnership according to his or her share of profits.[20] In contrast, a limited partner's only duties to the partnership are contribution of capital and voting, if required in the partnership agreement.[21]

§ 22.4 Partnerships in Bankruptcy

The Bankruptcy Code does not define a partnership. Thus, the definition is "left to state law as construed by the bankruptcy court."[22] In applying that definition, the bankruptcy courts have generally closely tracked the definition of partnerships provided by the UPA.[23] The Bankruptcy Code treats a partnership as a separate entity which may become a debtor under the Code.[24] Of course, an individual partner may also be a debtor under the Bankruptcy Code.[25] The commencement of a bankruptcy case creates a bankruptcy estate, which is very broadly defined[26] and would include, in a partnership case, the partnership's right to contribution from the partners. Similarly, in the case of an individual partner, the estate would include the debtor-partner's interest in the partnership or partnership property.[27] Assets owned by the partnership, however, including any real property, would not themselves be treated as property of the partner's bankruptcy estate.[28]

During the last decade, the bankruptcy courts have witnessed a proliferation of what has become known as *single-asset partnership cases.*[29] The interplay of various

---

narrowed the ability of anyone to successfully hold a limited partner liable for partnership liabilities because, in addition to requiring control, the person alleging liability must have relied reasonably on the limited partner's being a general partner. RULPA § 303(a).

19 RUPA § 6(2); RULPA § 1105.

20 UPA § 17; RULPA § 403.

21 RULPA §§ 302 and 592.

22 R. Anzivino, Partner and Partnership Bankruptcy § 1.1 at 7 (1987).

23 *Id.*

24 *See* 11 U.S.C. §§ 101(30), 109(b) & (d), 301, 303.

25 *Id.*

26 11 U.S.C. § 541(a).

27 *See, e.g., In re* Minton Group, Inc., 46 B.R. 222 (S.D.N.Y. 1985).

28 *See, e.g., In re* Dreske, 25 B.R. 268 (Bankr. E.D. Wis. 1982).

29 *See In re* South County Realty, Inc. II, 69 B.R. 611, 615 (Bankr. M.D. Fla. 1987) ("The Courts are increasingly expressing serious concern and view with a jaundiced eye Chapter 11 petitions by debtors with a single asset and with no meaningful body of creditors other than those who hold a mortgage on the single asset.").

unique features of partnership law with sections of the Bankruptcy Code creates a complicated set of procedural or substantive limitations on the enforcement of partnership obligations in these cases.

§ 22.5 Dissolution of Partnership

One of the most confusing aspects of both partner and partnership bankruptcy cases is the status of the partnership after the partnership or one of its general partners files a bankruptcy petition. That confusion arises originally from § 31 of the UPA, which provides that dissolution of the partnership is caused by the bankruptcy of any partner or the partnership.[30] The RULPA addresses this issue in a different manner. Section 402 of RULPA specifies that the filing of a bankruptcy petition by a general partner constitutes an act of withdrawal from a limited partnership. Section 801 of RULPA then provides for a dissolution of the limited partnership if a partner withdraws from the partnership unless there is another general partner and the partnership agreement permits the business to be carried on or unless, within 90 days, the limited partners appoint a new general partner. These provisions must be analyzed along with § 365(e) of the Bankruptcy Code, which blocks the operation of any contract clause or applicable law that terminates an executory contract solely because of the debtor's bankruptcy, insolvency, or financial condition.

Since the decision in *In re Harms,*[31] courts have struggled with the issue of whether dissolution of the partnership results from the general partner's filing of a bankruptcy case. In *Harms,* the court determined that the various partnership agreements in which the debtor was a general partner were executory contracts within the meaning of § 365 of the Bankruptcy Code. In making this determination, the court found that there is no precise definition of what constitutes an executory contract under the Bankruptcy Code but that the legislative history of § 365 suggests that executory contracts generally include "contracts on which performance remains due to some extent on both sides."[32] The court determined that because the general partner had a multitude of services to perform and the limited partners were obligated to make future payments, that performance was not complete.[33]

A determination that the partnership agreement constitutes an executory contract could arguably render the provisions of the UPA and RULPA unenforceable by reason of Bankruptcy Code § 365(e). However, taking a different approach, the court in *Harms* found that the partnerships were dissolved because of the provisions of § 365(c), which prohibits the assumption of an executory contract if applicable law

---

30 RUPA does not require the ipso facto winding up and dissolution of a partnership of more than two persons when a partner becomes a debtor in bankruptcy. The remaining partners have 90 days to elect whether to buy out the interest of the partner who is a debtor in bankruptcy or cause a winding up of the business. RUPA § 801.

31 10 B.R. 817 (Bankr. D. Colo. 1981).

32 *Id.* at 820 (citing H.R. Rep. No. 595, 95th Cong., 1st Sess. 347 (1977), *reprinted in* 1978 U.S.C.C.A.N. 5787, 6303, S. Rep. No 989, 95th Cong., 2nd. Sess. 58 (1978), *reprinted in* 1978 U.S.CC.A.N. 5844).

33 *Id.* at 821.

excuses the other parties to the contract from accepting performance from an entity other than the debtor. The court reasoned that upon the filing of the Chapter 11 petition, the debtor-general partner became a separate legal entity, the debtor-in-possession, and the limited partners could not be forced against their will to continue in a contractual relationship with this new entity. Accordingly, the court ruled that the limited partnerships were without a general partner, and this constituted a separate ground for dissolution under RULPA.[34] The *Harms* analysis has come into question because the notion that a debtor-in-possession is a separate legal entity has been rejected by the Supreme Court.[35]

Most courts currently addressing the issue adopt the position that the mere filing of a Chapter 11 petition does not dissolve the partnership either by virtue of an ipso facto clause in the partnership agreement or applicable nonbankruptcy law.[36] For example, in *In re Safren,*[37] the court considered whether the filing of a Chapter 11 case or the subsequent filing of the partners' Chapter 11 cases dissolved the partnership. The court examined § 31(5) of UPA, which provides for dissolution of a partnership upon the bankruptcy of any partner or the partnership. The court reasoned that because liquidation was the only bankruptcy option available when the UPA was promulgated, the UPA does not speak to reorganization under Chapter 11. It found sound policy reasons for refusing to apply UPA to dissolve a partnership upon the Chapter 11 filing by the partnership or the general partners. It could discern no benefit under partnership law from the automatic dissolution of a partnership and determined that the dissolution of a partnership upon filing a Chapter 11 would render its reorganization difficult or impossible because of administrative and tax consequences.[38] Thus, the court found that sound policy supports refusing to use the provisions of UPA to dissolve a partnership that is a debtor in Chapter 11.

Surprisingly, over 10 years after the *Harms* decision, the issue remains controversial, due to a Fifth Circuit case which sent a clear signal that state partnership law should not be engulfed by the Bankruptcy Code. In *In re Phillips,*[39] Harry Phillips, who previously had filed his own Chapter 11 petition, proceeded to file a Chapter 11 petition on behalf of Phillips & Phillips, a limited partnership in which he was the sole general partner. The limited partner moved to dismiss the partnership's Chapter 11 petition, arguing that the prior bankruptcy of the general partner divested him of authority to file a bankruptcy on the partnership's behalf. The circuit court held that under Texas partnership law, the partnership is not bound by any act of a partner "after dissolution" by which the partner has become bankrupt.[40] Rejecting the general partner's contention that he had not become "bankrupt" within the meaning of the Texas statute because he filed his voluntary petition under Chapter 11, which facilitates debtor reorganizations, the court held that *bankrupt* included any debtor under the Bankruptcy Code.

---

[34] *Id.* at 822.

[35] NLRB v. Bildisco & Bildisco, 465 U.S. 513 (1984).

[36] *See, e.g., In re* Cardinal Indus. Inc., 116 B.R. 964 (Bankr. S.D. Ohio 1990).

[37] 65 B.R. 566 (Bankr. C.D. Cal. 1986).

[38] *Id.* at 570.

[39] 966 F.2d 926 (5th Cir. 1992).

[40] *Id.* at 931.

Although the effect of a filing of a Chapter 11 petition on a partnership may still be unsettled, most bankruptcy courts have agreed on one issue: that the partnership agreement is an executory contract, and that bears on the issues discussed in **§ 22.6.**

§ 22.6 Control and Governance

Control and governance of the debtor can present a problem in any Chapter 11 case, but the problems are magnified in a partnership case. Questions arise relating to ongoing management, continuation and enforceability of contract provisions that affect the management, and the economic interest of the general partner. Attempts have been made by limited partners to remove or replace a general partner.[41] These issues are especially important in a Chapter 11 case, because the goals of asset preservation and reorganization may be interfered with by provisions in the partnership agreement. Surprisingly few cases have dealt with this issue.

If partnership agreements are determined to be executory contracts, as most courts have held, then a partner who files bankruptcy may reject, assume, or assign his or her partnership interest. Assignment of a partnership interest includes assigning management, voting, and distribution rights.[42] Obviously, without transferability of management and voting rights, the value of a partnership interest would be lower.

Typically, partnership agreements prohibit transfer of at least the general partner's interest unless there is consent of a majority of the other partners.[43] Section 365 of the Bankruptcy Code appears to negate such provisions, because it provides that, despite a provision in an agreement or in applicable law prohibiting assignment, a trustee or debtor-in-possession may assign a contract like a partnership agreement. Section 365, however, contains further restrictions that can be read to prohibit assumption or assignment of a partnership agreement if applicable law excuses a nondebtor party to the partnership agreement (a partner) from accepting performance from or rendering performance to an entity other than the debtor or the debtor-in-possession.[44] This is usually referred to as the *personal service test.*[45]

Using this analysis, assumption and assignment of a partnership interest can arguably be blocked if the contract could be characterized as a personal service contract. For example, in *In re Sunset Developers, Inc.*,[46] the general partner filed an involuntary petition for the partnership, and the nonpetitioning general partner objected, asserting that the general partner had no authority to file an involuntary petition because he had previously filed a bankruptcy petition. The court found that by filing his individual bankruptcy petition, the petitioning general partner had transferred his partnership interest to the bankruptcy estate. However, state law excuses a partner from accepting performance from an entity other than the partner.[47]

---

41 *See, e.g.*, *In re* Priestly, 93 B.R. 253 (Bankr. D.N.M. 1988).

42 *Id.*

43 This is also the rule under UPA § 27 and RULPA § 401.

44 11 U.S.C. § 365(c).

45 *In re* Braniff Airways, Inc., 700 F.2d 935, 943 (5th Cir. 1983).

46 69 B.R. 710 (Bankr. D. Idaho 1987).

47 *Id.* at 713.

Consequently, the court found that § 365(c) prevented the petitioning partner from filing the involuntary case.[48] The court held that except for the right to receive profits, no contract rights under a partnership agreement and no interest arising thereunder may be assumed or assigned.

However, in *In re Mays 1978 Drilling Partnership,*[49] in interpreting a Texas limited partnership statute, the court found that the Bankruptcy Code, and not the partnership agreement, determined the manner in which limited partners would be counted for acceptance or rejection of the plan. The court held that a new partnership could be imposed on the partners even though the partners had not approved the change under the partnership agreement.

In drafting partnership agreements, a carefully created agreement can attempt to guard against such results in the event of bankruptcy. For example, the agreement can state that the partnership rights cannot be assigned, or it can set forth voting rights in the event of a bankruptcy. With the current state of the law, however, there is no certainty that these provisions will be upheld.

§ 22.7 Automatic Stay and Injunctions

Upon the filing of a bankruptcy petition, § 362(a)(3) automatically stays "any act to obtain possession of property of the estate or of property from the estate or to exercise control over property of the estate." In addition, § 105(a) provides:

> The court may issue any order, process, or judgment that is necessary or appropriate to carry out the provisions of this title. No provision of this title providing for the raising of an issue by a party in interest shall be construed to preclude the court from, sua sponte, taking any action or making any determination necessary or appropriate to enforce or implement court orders or rules, or to prevent an abuse of process.

The applicability of the automatic stay to an act against a particular interest depends on whether the interest is property of the estate under § 541. It is clear that a partner's economic rights, for example to surplus and profits, are property of the estate under § 541.[50] However, bankruptcy courts have traditionally held that the bankruptcy of a partnership does not automatically stay actions against the general partners individually because property of the estate is not affected.[51] In fact, most courts have declined to hold that the automatic stay in a partnership case applies to actions against a partner or partner's property.[52] Likewise, when the debtor is a partner, actions of a creditor of the partnership against partnership property are not subject to the automatic stay.[53]

---

48 *Id.*

49 95 B.R. 432 (Bankr. N.D. Tex. 1989).

50 *See* **§ 22.4.**

51 *In re* Minton Group, Inc., 46 B.R. 222, 225–26 (S.D.N.Y. 1985).

52 However, in Litchfield Co. of S.C., Ltd., 135 B.R. 797 (W.D.N.C. 1992), Judge Mullen ruled that an action against a general partner to recover on a partnership debt was stayed by § 362(a)(3).

53 *See, e.g., In re* Myerson & Kuhn, 121 B.R. 145 (Bankr. S.D.N.Y. 1990).

However, there is less agreement about the application of § 105 of the Bankruptcy Code to enjoin acts against persons or property of persons other than the debtor. Recently, courts have used their injunctive powers in creative ways to facilitate a reorganization and have done so also in the partnership arena. In the leading case, *In re Cardinal Industries, Inc.*,[54] the court determined that the automatic stay did not prevent foreclosure against the nondebtor's real property but considered whether an injunction should be issued pursuant to § 105(a). The court refused to issue an injunction against all foreclosures, as requested by the debtor, but agreed to consider injunctions on a case-by-case basis. It determined that future requests for injunctions would be granted when a foreclosure sale was imminent and would result in a surplus of value over encumbrances. Several courts have used this § 105 analysis to protect a partner's property against dissipation when necessary to assure equitable distributions to the partnership creditors.[55]

§ 22.8 Avoidance Actions

Although the Bankruptcy Code contains few provisions that specifically address partnerships, there are some in the provisions regarding avoidance actions. The Bankruptcy Code includes special partnership rules relating to fraudulent conveyances and preferences. Section 548, which grants to the trustee or the debtor-in-possession the power to avoid fraudulent conveyances, ordinarily requires either some form of fraudulent intent or insolvency, insufficient capitalization, or intent to incur debts beyond the ability to pay. In addition to these basic provisions, § 548(b) makes avoidable any and all transfers to a general partner within one year of the filing of the petition by or against the partnership if the partnership was insolvent at the time or rendered insolvent by the transfer, regardless of the intent or fairness of consideration requirements for nonpartnership entities.[56]

A *preference*, under § 547, generally is a transfer of the debtor's property, to or for the benefit of a creditor on account of an antecedent debt, made while the debtor is insolvent and within 90 days of the filing of the petition, and which enables the creditor to obtain a greater percentage of its claim than other members of its class. In the definition of *insolvent*, § 101(32) of the Bankruptcy Code indicates that a partnership is insolvent when the sum of the partnership's debts is greater than the aggregate of all of such partnership's property (exclusive of property fraudulently transferred) and the sum of the excess of the value of each general partner's nonpartnership property (again exclusive of fraudulently transferred property) over the partner's nonpartnership debts. An implication of this definition is that, at least when the partnership's property is worth less than the partnership's debts, the portion of the property of a general partner constituting an excess over the partner's nonpartnership debts is an asset of the partnership. If the excess value in the property of the general

---

[54] 116 B.R. 964 (Bankr. S.D. Ohio 1990).

[55] *See, e.g.*, MacArthur Co. v. Johns Manville Corp., 837 F.2d 89, 92–93 (2d Cir. 1988).

[56] 11 U.S.C. § 548(a) requires actual intent or that the debtor received less than "reasonably equivalent value" for the transfer.

partner suffices to make the partnership solvent, it would be incongruous to state that the partner may dispose of that excess as he or she pleases without any recourse available to the partnership's creditors. Consequently, the trustee of a partner's bankruptcy estate should be able to recover such a transfer made by the debtor-partner to partnership's creditors because those creditors are also creditors of the partner. Some courts have held that the trustee of a partnership's bankruptcy estate may recover a transfer made by a partnership to a partner's separate creditor, on the theory that the partner's individual creditors have a claim on the partnership estate to the extent that it contains a surplus to be distributed to the individual partners.[57]

§ 22.9 Plan Confirmation Standard

A partnership case is subject to all of the same requirements for a plan of reorganization as any corporate or individual Chapter 11 case. An interesting question, however, is whether a partnership's plan of reorganization may or should include assets of the partners as well as assets of the partnership. Central to this issue is the applicability of § 723 of the Bankruptcy Code. A standard for confirmation of any Chapter 11 plan is that each creditor must receive or retain under the plan property not less in value than it would have received or retained in a liquidation under the Code.[58] Section 723(b) entitles the creditors of a partnership to distribution not only from the partnership assets but also from the assets of the general partners if there is a deficiency of partnership assets.

The Bankruptcy Code does not impose on the trustee or the debtor-in-possession the duty of collecting assets of the partners or the partnership estate in a Chapter 11 or Chapter 12 case. Each holder of a claim or interest, however, is entitled to object to the confirmation of a plan that does not give the holder at least as much value as would have been obtainable in a liquidation under Chapter 7 on the effective date of the plan. This is commonly referred to as the *best interest of creditors test* of § 1129(a)(7).

Consequently, courts have suggested that in certain circumstances the general partner's assets must be included in the debtor's disclosure statement, to enable the court to make the best interest of creditors determination.[59] However, later cases addressing the same issue make the distinction that such disclosure is meaningful when the plan provides for less than 100 percent payment to all creditors.[60] Bankruptcy Rule 1007(g) also authorizes the court to "order any general partner to file a statement of personal assets and liabilities with the court," which serves to assist the court in determining the confirmability of a partnership's plan of reorganization. At a minimum, the Bankruptcy Code affords the creditors of a partnership leverage to obtain contributions from the partners when a partnership's assets are not sufficient to meet its obligations.

---

[57] *See In re* Jercyn Dress Shop, 516 F.2d (2d Cir. 1975).

[58] 11 U.S.C. § 1129(a)(7)(A)(ii).

[59] *See In re* M. Long Arabians, 103 B.R. 211 (Bankr. 9th Cir. 1989).

[60] *See In re* Diversified Investors Fund XVII, 91 B.R. 559 (Bankr. C.D. Cal. 1988); *In re* 222 Liberty Assocs., 108 B.R. 971 (Bankr. E.D. Pa. 1990).

CHAPTER 23

JURISDICTION, VENUE, AND APPEALS

John Lewis, Jr.

§ 23.1 Introduction

One of the most disconcerting aspects of bankruptcy practice is coping with and understanding the maze of rules and foreign terminology that comprise bankruptcy procedure. The purpose of this chapter is to examine, in survey fashion: (1) the evolution of bankruptcy jurisdiction; (2) procedural oddities that have resulted from early jurisdictional disputes; (3) the core/noncore dichotomy; (4) abstention and removal; and (5) the issue of the right to trial by jury, (6) venue of bankruptcy matters; and (7) bankruptcy appeals. Although not exhaustive, this overview is intended to help the small business bankruptcy practitioner and the client understand certain aspects of procedure and practice that may not be self-evident.

JURISDICTION

§ 23.2 History of Bankruptcy Jurisdiction

The Bankruptcy Reform Act of 1978[1] (the Bankruptcy Code) was a major overhaul and restructuring of the bankruptcy system which had existed in this country for eighty years. Its predecessor, the Bankruptcy Act of 1898[2] (the Bankruptcy Act), was viewed by many as a confusing and unpredictable hodge-podge of often conflicting rules and conflicting interests presided over by an individual who was, in terms of duties and powers, somewhere between an administrative law judge and a trustee. Under prior law, these presiding officers, known as *referees,* were selected by the district court judges and had administrative duties, such as preparing and filing schedules of property and declaring and accounting for dividends paid in asset cases.[3] Although they sometimes functioned in a quasi-judicial capacity, referees were always subject to de novo review by the district court.[4]

---

[1] Pub. L. No. 95–598, 92 Stat. 2549 (codified at 11 U.S.C. §§ 101–1330) [hereinafter Bankruptcy Reform Act or Bankruptcy Code].

[2] Ch. 541, 30 Stat. 544 (repealed 1979) [hereinafter Bankruptcy Act].

[3] Bankruptcy Act § 39(a) (repealed 1979) (formerly codified at 11 U.S.C. § 67(a)).

[4] The referee's jurisdiction was specifically limited under the Bankruptcy Act to "consider all petitions" referred; administer oaths; examine witnesses and require production of documents; exercise certain powers of the district judge in the event of absence, sickness or inability to act of the latter; to grant, deny or revoke discharges; determine

The Bankruptcy Act also distinguished between "controversies at law and in equity."[5] Although the law/equity distinction was consistent with federal practice in the district courts at the time the Bankruptcy Act was enacted, its subsequent elimination in the modernized Federal Rules of Civil Procedure also led to its elimination in the 1978 Code.[6]

Another problematic aspect of practice under the Bankruptcy Act was the question of whether the bankruptcy court was exercising summary or plenary jurisdiction in a particular proceeding. Bankruptcy courts were only allowed to exercise jurisdiction over summary matters, such as claims objections, plan confirmations, and the granting, denying, or revoking of discharge.[7] Further, consent of the adverse party was required before referees could determine disputes over property that was not in the possession of the court.[8] Absent consent, only the district court had the power to settle such disputes. These procedural and jurisdictional hurdles, along with many other factors, imposed tremendous obstacles and costs on the average bankruptcy reorganization and served as the impetus for the radical legislative reform of the Bankruptcy Code.

One of the principal goals of the new Code was pervasive jurisdiction. Under its provisions, a single forum was to be created for the adjudication of bankruptcy and related issues. The resulting new court, as a separate department of the district court, would no longer be headed by a referee but rather by a United States Bankruptcy Judge.[9] The powers of the bankruptcy judge under the Bankruptcy Code were not specifically limited by statute as they had been under the Bankruptcy Act. The Bankruptcy Code specifically vested bankruptcy judges with equitable powers, the power to issue writs of habeas corpus,[10] and the power to conduct jury trials.[11] Most notably, the Bankruptcy Code conferred virtually unfettered power on the judge to hear and decide any issue "arising under," "arising in," or "related to" a bankruptcy case, as well as the power to "issue any order, process, or judgment that is necessary or appropriate to carry out the provisions [of Title 11]."[12] Appellate review of bankruptcy court decisions under the Code was to be taken directly to the federal appellate courts and would be reversible only if found clearly erroneous.[13] The Code

---

dischargeability; to confirm or refuse arrangements; set aside confirmations; reinstate proceedings or cases; and authorize the employment of stenographers. Bankruptcy Act § 38 (repealed 1978) (formerly codified at 11 U.S.C. § 66).

[5] Bankruptcy Act §§ 2, 23 (repealed 1978) (formerly codified at 11 U.S.C. §§ 11, 46).

[6] Prior to the enactment of the Federal Rules of Civil Procedure in 1938, separate procedures existed in federal courts for actions at law and suits in equity. *See* 2 Moore's Federal Practice ¶ 2.03 (2d ed. 1993).

[7] Bankruptcy Act § 38 (repealed 1979) (formerly codified at U.S.C. § 66).

[8] *Id.*

[9] Bankruptcy Reform Act § 201, 92 Stat. 2549, 2657 (repealed 1984) (formerly codified at 28 U.S.C. § 151(b)).

[10] *Id.* § 2256, 92 Stat. 2672 (repealed 1984) (formerly codified 28 U.S.C. § 2256).

[11] *See* Bankruptcy Reform Act § 241(a), 92 Stat. 2549, 2668–71 (originally intended to be codified at 11 U.S.C. §§ 1480, 1481, but it never went in force because of later enactments).

[12] *Id.* § 105, 92 Stat. 2549, 2555 (repealed 1984) (formerly codified at 11 U.S.C. § 105.

[13] *See* Northern Pipeline Constr. Co. v. Marathon Pipe Line Co., 458 U.S. 50, 55 n.5 (1982).

imposed a number of other sweeping changes, which have fundamentally impacted the conduct of business in bankruptcy court.[14] Despite contentious debate in Congress over the constitutionality of the broad jurisdictional grant to bankruptcy courts and judges in the new legislation, the Code was enacted and took effect on October 2, 1979. It was not long thereafter that the United States Supreme Court considered those same jurisdictional provisions and rendered a decision that temporarily placed the entire bankruptcy system in chaos.

In *Northern Pipeline Construction Co. v. Marathon Pipeline Co.,*[15] a Chapter 11 debtor brought an adversary proceeding in bankruptcy court against one of its creditors seeking damages for breach of contract and warranty, misrepresentation, coercion, and duress. The creditor moved to dismiss the suit, alleging, among other things, that the Code impermissibly conferred Article III judicial power upon the bankruptcy court.[16] In a plurality decision, the Supreme Court held that: (1) the Code removed "essential attributes of the judicial power" typically reserved for Article III courts (the district courts)[17] and vested them in non-Article III courts (the bankruptcy courts) in contravention of the Constitution; and (2) because the unconstitutional grant of authority was not "readily separable" from the remaining otherwise permissible provisions, the entire jurisdictional provision should be struck down as unconstitutional.[18]

Recognizing that the practical import of its decision was to effectively dismantle the bankruptcy system created by the Code, the Supreme Court stayed execution of its decision in *Marathon* until October 4, 1982, to "afford Congress an opportunity to reconstitute the bankruptcy courts or to adopt other valid means of adjudication, without impairing the interim administration of the bankruptcy laws."[19]

As Congress toiled in vain to enact jurisdictional provisions that would pass the constitutional test set forth in *Marathon,* the Judicial Conference of the United States, in an effort to keep bankruptcy courts around the country open for business, took the unprecedented step of proposing an emergency model rule to be adopted as a local rule by each of the district courts in the country. The Emergency Rule, as it has come to be known, provided that the district court would have original and

---

[14] One question that concerned the drafters was who would take over the administrative duties once performed by the referee. In the end, the United States Trustee Pilot Program was created under the Department of Justice, as the result of an eleventh hour compromise between the House and Senate. The program, modeled after the United States Attorney program, made the United States Trustee the administrative watchdog in bankruptcy cases and relieved the bankruptcy judge from the role of interested party in a proceeding. *See* 28 U.S.C. §§ 581–589a.

[15] 458 U.S. 50 (1982).

[16] *Id.* at 56–57.

[17] *Id.* at 84–85. Article III of the Constitution provides that the Supreme Court, the only constitutionally mandated court, may create such other lower courts as it deems appropriate. Because bankruptcy courts, as separate departments of the district courts, were created by Congress in the Code, bankruptcy courts are not Article III courts.

[18] *Id.* at 91–92. The Court declined to rewrite the single provision granting jurisdiction by paring out offending portions and leaving permissible portions intact, reasoning that, as a court, its place was to construe the statute as drafted.

[19] *Id.* at 92.

exclusive jurisdiction over all bankruptcy proceedings with automatic referral to the bankruptcy court, rendering the bankruptcy court's jurisdiction derivative in nature.[20] The automatic reference could be withdrawn by the district court at any time and for any reason. Although the bankruptcy court could issue orders in matters "arising in" a proceeding, which became effective upon entry, orders in related matters (for example a claim based on state law against an entity that had not filed a claim against the estate, like the defendant in *Marathon*) would be subject to de novo review by the district court.

The stated purpose of the Emergency Rule was to "supplement existing law and rules in respect to the authority of bankruptcy judges . . . until Congress enacts appropriate remedial legislation in response to [the *Marathon* decision] . . . or until March 31, 1984, whichever comes first."[21] The Rule, which took effect on December 25, 1982, over two months after the expiration of stay imposed in the *Marathon* decision, was adopted as a local rule by all of the district courts in the country. Though the Emergency Rule reduced much of the confusion concerning bankruptcy court jurisdiction during its effective period, Congress was still unable to enact remedial legislation prior to expiration of the Rule in March 1984. During the months between the expiration of the Emergency Rule and the enactment of the bankruptcy amendments by Congress on July 10, 1984, considerable confusion abounded in bankruptcy courts throughout the country because the invalidation of bankruptcy court jurisdiction by *Marathon* negated the existence of bankruptcy courts. After strenuous debate over whether to grant bankruptcy judges Article III status or to revert to the adjunct status favored by the pre-*Marathon* Code, Congress enacted the Bankruptcy Amendments and Federal Judgeship Act of 1984,[22] commonly known as BAFJA.

Instead of vesting bankruptcy courts with Article III powers, BAFJA took a less direct (and politically less controversial) approach to jurisdiction. Under BAFJA, the district court has original jurisdiction over bankruptcy "cases" and proceedings.[23] It shares with the state courts jurisdiction over "all civil proceedings arising under title 11, or arising in or related to cases under title 11."

The bankruptcy court was transformed by BAFJA into a "unit" of the district court.[24] The district court may refer "any or all cases under title 11 and any or all proceedings arising under title 11 or arising in or related to a case under title 11"[25] to the bankruptcy court. The bankruptcy court may "hear and determine all cases under title 11 and all core proceedings arising under title 11, or arising in a case under title 11"[26] that are referred by the district court. The power to hear and determine cases and core proceedings includes the power to enter orders and judgments.[27]

---

20 This was a departure from the granting language of the Bankruptcy Code which vested original and exclusive jurisdiction in the bankruptcy court.

21 Emergency Rule (a).

22 Pub. L. No. 98-353, 98 Stat. 333 (1979). BAFJA became effective immediately upon enactment on July 10, 1984.

23 28 U.S.C. § 1334(a), (b).

24 *Id.* § 151.

25 *Id.* § 157(a).

26 *Id.* § 157(b)(1).

27 *Id.*

Except for personal injury tort and wrongful death claims, which must be tried in district court, noncore proceedings that are "otherwise related to a case under title 11" may be heard but not determined by the bankruptcy court.[28] Instead, the bankruptcy court must submit proposed findings of fact and conclusions of law to the district court, which enters any orders or judgments.[29] However, proceedings "related to a case under title 11" may be heard and determined by the bankruptcy court with the consent of the parties upon referral by the district court.[30]

§ 23.3 Cases and Proceedings

Case under BAFJA refers to the matter begun by the filing of the bankruptcy petition and all proceedings predicated upon filing of the petition.[31] A *proceeding* under BAFJA may be any one of a multitude of subparts within a case, including but not limited to dischargeability complaints;[32] priority disputes;[33] and any other core or noncore proceedings consistent with 28 U.S.C. § 157. The term *proceeding* covers everything ranging from matters clearly and directly related to the bankruptcy case (that is, "arising under" or core), such as a motion for relief from stay, to matters only tangentially related to the bankruptcy (that is, "related to" or noncore), such as a state law claim relating to postpetition conduct of a corporate debtor's principal.[34]

BAFJA further divides proceedings into three subcategories. The jurisdiction of the bankruptcy court is determined by the extent to which issues raised in the proceeding require interpretation of bankruptcy law or nonbankruptcy law.

§ 23.4 Categories of Proceedings

The pervasive jurisdiction/single forum model favored by the pre-*Marathon* Code changed into a subject-matter-driven analysis under BAFJA. Under BAFJA, the jurisdictional weight afforded a bankruptcy court's ruling or its ability to hear a certain issue hinges on whether the issue involves or materially affects a party to the bankruptcy or whether the issue turns on some aspect of bankruptcy law. In fact, the type of proceeding also determines the standard of review on appeal (see **§ 23.24**), whether a jury trial is available (see **§ 23.15**), and whether removal or abstention is proper (see **§§ 23.8** through **23.14**). These subcategories of proceedings created by BAFJA are "arising under," "arising in," and "related to."[35]

---

28 28 U.S.C. § 157(c)(1).

29 *Id.*

30 *Id.* § 157(c)(2).

31 *See In re* Hudson Oil Co., 68 B.R. 735 (Bankr. D. Kan. 1986).

32 *In re* Hohenberg, 143 B.R. 183 (Bankr. W.D. Tenn. 1992).

33 *In re* Zachman Homes, Inc., 83 B.R. 633 (Bankr. D. Minn. 1985).

34 *In re* Cinematronics, Inc., 916 F.2d 1444 (9th Cir. 1990).

35 *See* 28 U.S.C. §§ 157(a), 1334(b).

§ 23.5 —Arising under and Arising in

The strongest jurisdiction of the bankruptcy court is found in proceedings "arising under title 11" or "arising in a case under title 11" of the Code. At least one group of commentators is of the opinion that the terms *arising under* and *arising in* are generally synonymous with the term *core* in 28 U.S.C. § 157.[36] "Arising under" and "arising in" proceedings encompass matters that are at the core of bankruptcy court jurisdiction and depend on application or construction of pure bankruptcy law, as delineated in Title 11.[37] Traditionally construed broadly by courts, a proceeding arises in or under Title 11 practically any time a provision of Title 11 is invoked as a basis for a claim or request for relief.[38]

§ 23.6 —Related to

In order to comply with the mandate of *Marathon,* Congress felt that a line had to be drawn somewhere on the bankruptcy court's pervasive jurisdiction. Congress drew such a line in BAFJA by reverting to a hybrid version of derivative jurisdiction that existed under prior law for the genre of proceedings that do not arise in but still bear some relationship to the bankruptcy case. In "related to" or noncore proceedings, the power of the bankruptcy court is, as a technical matter, substantially curtailed.

Section 157(c)(1) imposes a significant limitation on the bankruptcy judge's power in a "related to" proceeding, which is not present in an "arising under" proceeding. Specifically, the bankruptcy court's decision is subject to de novo review by the district court if the bankruptcy court's jurisdiction is not specifically consented to by the adverse party.[39] Stated differently, a bankruptcy judge may hear and decide a matter tangentially related to the bankruptcy case, such as an action by a debtor based on a state law tort theory, only if the nondebtor, nonparty-defendant consents.[40] In the absence of consent, the bankruptcy court may still hear the case,

---

36 D. Epstein, S. Nickels, & J. White, 3 Bankruptcy 197 (1992). *See also* Plaza at Latham Assoc. v. Citicorp N. Am. Inc., 150 B.R. 507 (Bankr. N.D.N.Y. 1993); *In re* Cossett, 75 B.R. 766 (Bankr. S.D. Ohio 1987).

37 *See In re* Leco Enters. Inc., 144 B.R. 244 (Bankr. S.D.N.Y. 1992); *In re* Chambers, 125 B.R. 788 (Bankr. W.D. Mo. 1991).

38 *In re* Harlon Properties, Inc., 56 B.R. 794 (Bankr. 9th Cir. 1985).

39 Recall that the notion of consent to jurisdiction was one of the characteristics of the referee system.

40 Courts considering the question of consent have rejected the notion of implied consent by the adverse party's filing a proof of claim, *In re* Castlerock Properties, 781 F.2d 159 (Bankr. 9th Cir. 1986), or moving to dismiss and conducting discovery, Interconnect Tel. Servs., Inc. v. Farren, 59 B.R. 397 (Bankr. S.D.N.Y. 1986). An admission that a proceeding is core, however, even if the proceeding is not core, is binding and empowers the bankruptcy court to issue a final judgment. *In re* St. Mary Hosp., 117 B.R. 759 (Bankr. E.D. Pa. 1990). Further, an allegation in a pleading that a matter is core, if not specifically denied, constitutes consent. *See, e.g., In re* Johnson, 124 B.R. 648 (Bankr. E.D. Pa. 1991).

but, rather than rendering a final judgment, the bankruptcy judge is required to submit proposed findings of fact and conclusions of law to the district court. The district court may either adopt such findings and conclusions or totally disregard them.

§ 23.7 Withdrawal of Reference

Recall that, as a procedural matter, all cases and proceedings are referred from the district court to the bankruptcy court for final disposition in some instances and less than final disposition in others. As a function of the district court's original jurisdiction over both cases and proceedings, 28 U.S.C. § 157(d) authorizes the district court to "withdraw, in whole or in part, any case or proceeding referred . . . , on its own motion or on timely motion of any party, for cause shown."[41] In addition to discretionary withdrawal for cause, § 157(d) also imposes mandatory withdrawal on timely motion of a party, if the case or proceeding requires consideration of bankruptcy law and other federal law regulating organizations or activities affecting interstate commerce."[42]

Section 157(d) thus raises two principal questions regarding withdrawal, namely, what constitutes cause for discretionary withdrawal, and when is mandatory withdrawal appropriate? Although the answers to these questions have varied widely among the courts, a few constants have emerged.

For instance, with regard to discretionary withdrawal, courts have concluded that the mere fact that a proceeding is not core does not constitute cause for discretionary withdrawal.[43] On the other hand, a demand for a jury trial in a "related to" proceeding generally suffices as cause for withdrawal, because BAFJA has been construed to prohibit the bankruptcy court from conducting jury trials in "related to" (noncore) proceedings.[44]

Effect on interstate commerce is grounds for withdrawal. Sufficient impact on interstate commerce has been found in bankruptcy matters involving federal labor law,[45] federal securities law,[46] the RICO statute,[47] ERISA,[48] federal environmental laws,[49] and federal antitrust law.[50]

---

41 28 U.S.C. § 157(d). Fed. R. Bankr. P. 5011 requires that a motion requesting withdrawal of reference be heard by the district court.

42 28 U.S.C. § 157(d).

43 *In re* Wedtech Corp., 81 B.R. 237 (Bankr. S.D.N.Y. 1987).

44 *See, e.g., In re* Smith-Douglass, Inc., 43 B.R. 616, 618 (Bankr. E.D.N.C. 1984); UNR Indus., Inc. v. Continental Ins. Co., 46 B.R. 727 (Bankr. M.D. Ga. 1984).

45 NLRB v. Bildisco & Bildisco, 456 U.S. 513 (1984) (concerning rejection of a collective bargaining agreement under 11 U.S.C. § 365(a)).

46 *In re* Contemporary Lithographers, Inc., 127 B.R. 122 (Bankr. M.D.N.C. 1991).

47 *In re* Rubin Bros. Footwear, Inc., 73 B.R. 346 (Bankr. S.D.N.Y. 1987).

48 Martin v. Friedman, 133 B.R. 609 (Bankr. N.D. Ohio 1991).

49 *In re* National Gypsum Co., 134 B.R. 188 (Bankr. N.D. Tex. 1991).

50 Boricua Motor Corp. v. Tamachi, Inc., 76 B.R. 891 (Bankr. D.P.R. 1987).

§ 23.8 Abstention

Many of the procedural mechanisms created by BAFJA, such as withdrawal of reference and the core/noncore distinction, were implemented to ensure that bankruptcy and nonbankruptcy issues in bankruptcy cases would be heard in the most appropriate forum, consistent with considerations of judicial economy, the relative complexity of the issues, and consistency (thus discouraging forum shopping). The withdrawal of reference rules offer guidance on the choice of forum as between bankruptcy court and district court. The doctrine of *abstention* identifies the most appropriate forum as between federal court (bankruptcy or district) and state court.[51] Under the abstention rules, the district court must abstain in certain instances (mandatory abstention) and may abstain in others (permissive abstention). A form motion for abstention is presented in § **23.11.**

§ 23.9 —Mandatory Abstention

Title 28 § 1334(c)(2) requires abstention by the district court, and therefore also the bankruptcy court, "upon timely motion of a party" if a "state law claim" or "cause of action" that is "related to" a bankruptcy "is commenced" and can be "timely adjudicated" in state court. Thus, at least seven criteria must be met before mandatory abstention applies:

1. There must be a timely motion by a party
2. There must be a purely state law claim or cause of action
3. The claim or cause of action must be of the "related to" variety (see § **23.6**)
4. The claim or cause of action must have been commenced in state court prepetition
5. The claim or cause of action must be capable of timely adjudication in state court
6. There must be no basis for federal jurisdiction absent the bankruptcy petition
7. There must be a state forum with jurisdiction over the claim.[52]

Probably the most litigated aspect of mandatory abstention is what constitutes timely adjudication by a state court. In a Chapter 11 reorganization, for example, all claims must be liquidated (or at least quantifiable) before a plan of reorganization can be formulated and filed. Hence, the timeliness of a related state court action must be considered in the context of the overall reorganization. For this reason, courts have defined *timely* on a case-by-case basis. One court found no mandatory abstention when the earliest trial date available on the state court's docket was nearly three years away.[53] Another court declined to mandatorily abstain based solely on the

---

[51] *See* 28 U.S.C. § 1334(c).

[52] Bowen Corp. v. Security Pac. Bank Idaho, FSB, 150 B.R. 777 (Bankr. D. Idaho 1993).

[53] *In re* DeLorean Motor Co., 49 B.R. 900 (Bankr. E.D. Mich. 1985).

unsubstantiated representations of a party that the matter could be timely adjudicated in state court.[54]

§ 23.10 —Permissive Abstention

Section 1334(c)(1) allows for permissive abstention by the district court to allow the appropriate state court to decide a particular issue when "the interest of justice" or "the interest of comity with State Courts" is best served or "in respect for State law." Although the mere presence of state law issues is insufficient to warrant discretionary abstention,[55] courts have exercised discretionary abstention when the proceeding turned on an unsettled question of state law.[56] Bankruptcy courts also abstain if adjudication of certain state law issues in state court would simplify the bankruptcy case.[57] In determining whether to abstain, the court also considers such factors as judicial economy,[58] the stage of the proceedings,[59] and in some instances, the preference of a party.[60]

§ 23.11 Form: Motion for Abstention

FORM 23-1
MOTION FOR ABSTENTION

IN THE UNITED STATES BANKRUPTCY COURT
FOR THE ____ DISTRICT OF _____

In Re:	)	
	)	
____________________,	)	Case No. _______
	)	Chapter ___
Debtor.	)	
	)	
____________________,	)	
	)	
Plaintiff,	)	
	)	
v.	)	
	)	

[54] *In re* Burgess, 51 B.R. 300 (Bankr. S.D. Ohio 1985).

[55] *In re* Republic Reader's Serv., Inc., 81 B.R. 422 (Bankr. S.D. Tex. 1987).

[56] *In re* Earle Indus., Inc., 72 B.R. 131 (Bankr. E.D. Pa. 1987); *In re* Double TRL, Inc., 65 B.R. 993 (Bankr. E.D.N.Y. 1986).

[57] *In re* J.F. Naylor & Co., 67 B.R. 184 (Bankr. M.D. La. 1986).

[58] *In re* Verazano Holding Corp., 86 B.R. 755 (Bankr. E.D.N.Y. 1988).

[59] *In re* Chapman, 132 B.R. 153 (Bankr. N.D. Ill. 1991).

[60] *In re* Counts, 54 B.R. 730 (Bankr. D. Colo. 1985).

______________________,)
)
Defendant.)

MOTION FOR ABSTENTION

COMES NOW [party name], a party herein, pursuant to 28 U.S.C. § 1334(c)(2), and respectfully requests that the court enter an order abstaining from further action in the matter captioned [state case caption], which is currently pending in [state] court and, in support thereof, states as follows:

1. On [date] a civil action captioned [state case caption], [case number], was filed in [state] court.

2. The above-referenced action involves [briefly describe state law claim or cause of action].

3. The claim/cause of action arising in the above-captioned lawsuit is related to the matter captioned In re [bankruptcy caption], a case commenced under Chapter 11 of the Bankruptcy Code in the [District court]. [Briefly describe the relationship to the bankruptcy case, for example, debtor is plaintiff.]

4. [The state court civil action] was filed on [date], which was prior to the commencement of the bankruptcy case.

5. The [state court action] is capable of timely adjudication in state court [include factors which support statement, such as, a trial date has already been set, discovery is underway, a jury has been impanelled].

6. There is no basis for federal jurisdiction absent the bankruptcy petition, and the issues involved are purely state court issues.

7. Abstention by the bankruptcy court is in the best interests of the estate because it will expedite disposition of the litigation that is currently pending in state court.

8. No party will be unfairly prejudiced by abstention.

WHEREFORE, movant respectfully requests that an order abstaining from the [state case caption] civil action be entered and for such further relief as the court deems appropriate.

____
[Attorney for Applicant]

[Certificate of Service]

§ 23.12 Removal

In the nonbankruptcy context, 28 U.S.C. § 1441 provides the procedural mechanism whereby "any civil action brought in a State court" over which a federal district court has original jurisdiction may be removed "by the defendant or defendants" to the federal district court in the jurisdiction in which the action is pending. Similarly, BAFJA affords federal courts a vehicle for removal of claims related to bankruptcy cases to the district court.

The bankruptcy removal provisions are found at 28 U.S.C. § 1452. That section provides that a party may remove "any claim or cause of action" to the district court for the district in which the civil action is pending if the district court has jurisdiction under 28 U.S.C. § 1334. The two exceptions to removal of bankruptcy cases are: (1) a proceeding before the United States Tax Court, and (2) a civil action by a governmental unit to enforce its regulatory or police power.[61]

Although the bankruptcy and nonbankruptcy civil removal provisions are similar in most respects, there are at least two major distinctions between the statutes which are noteworthy.

First, nonbankruptcy civil removal may only be requested by a defendant.[62] The rationale for this rule is obvious. Because the plaintiff chose the state court forum in which the suit was filed, the plaintiff should have no complaints about the forum. Because bankruptcy cases rarely, if ever, involve only two parties, § 1452 allows any party to seek removal of a claim or cause of action. In fact, the term *party* has been construed liberally by some courts to allow removal by entities not directly related to the removed state court action. In *In re Wesco Products Co.,*[63] a corporate debtor was allowed to remove to bankruptcy court a state court cause of action between a creditor and the debtor's corporate secretary. Further, although nonbankruptcy civil removal is only effective if requested by all co-defendants in an action, bankruptcy removal only requires one party, who may be either plaintiff or defendant in the removed action.

The second major difference between nonbankruptcy civil removal and bankruptcy removal are the limitations imposed upon the latter. The two exceptions to bankruptcy removal, claims or causes of action pending before the United States Tax Court and civil actions brought by a governmental unit to enforce its "police or regulatory power," do not appear in 28 U.S.C. § 1441.[64]

Courts have found removal to be appropriate in a variety of circumstances, but they generally consider the following factors in deciding whether to allow removal of the claim or cause of action or to remand to the prior forum:

---

61 28 U.S.C. § 1452.

62 *Id.* § 1441.

63 19 B.R. 908 (Bankr. N.D. Ill. 1982).

64 Hence, an enforcement action brought by the National Labor Relations Board, the Environmental Protection Agency, Department of Labor, or any other regulatory body against a debtor could not be removed to federal district court. *See, e.g., In re* Adams Delivery Serv., Inc., 24 B.R. 589, 592 (Bankr. 9th Cir. 1982) (enforcement action by NLRB not removable); *In re* Rabzak, 79 B.R. 966, 967–68 (Bankr. E.D. Pa. 1987) (denying removal of a state court prosecution of a debtor for violation of local rubbish ordinance).

1. The effect of remand on administration of the bankruptcy case
2. The prospect of duplicative or inefficient utilization of judicial resources
3. Whether questions of nonbankruptcy law predominate
4. The likelihood of prejudice to unremoved parties
5. Whether remand will minimize the chance of inconsistent results
6. Comity concerns
7. The relative expertise of the court in which the action originated.[65]

The mechanics of bankruptcy removal are set out in Bankruptcy Rule 9027. Under Rule 9027, a notice of removal is filed with the clerk for the district court and division within which is located the state or federal court in which the removed civil action is pending. The notice is subject to the following requirements:

1. It must be signed pursuant to Bankruptcy Rule 9011
2. It must contain a brief recitation of the facts entitling the applicant to removal
3. It must designate the removed proceeding as core or noncore
4. If the removed proceeding is noncore, there must be a statement whether the noticing party consents to entry of final orders or judgment by the bankruptcy judge
5. It must be accompanied by a copy of all pleadings filed in the removed action.[66]

Generally, a party has 90 days from the bankruptcy petition date to seek removal.[67] The removing party must serve a copy of the notice on all parties to the removed action.[68] With the exception of debtors and trustees, a bond must be posted with a notice of removal to ensure against improper removal.[69]

The proper procedural vehicle to challenge removal is a motion for remand.[70] The grounds for remand are generally limited as discussed earlier in this section. By statute, remand orders by bankruptcy judges are nonappealable.[71] Forms for an application for removal and motion for remand appear in §§ **23.13** and **23.14**, respectively.

---

[65] *See, e.g.*, Baxter Healthcare Corp. v. Hemex Liquidation Trust, 132 B.R. 863, 868 (Bankr. N.D. Ill. 1991); Drexel Burnham Lambert Group, Inc. v. Vigilant Ins. Co., 130 B.R. 405, 407 (Bankr. S.D.N.Y. 1991).

[66] Fed. R. Bankr. P. 9027(a)(1).

[67] Fed. R. Bankr. P. 9027(a)(2), (3). But note special times in the case of stay of civil action and action filed after bankruptcy case has commenced.

[68] Fed. R. Bankr. P. 9027(b).

[69] Fed. R. Bankr. P. 9027(b). Counsel should consult district court local rules for determination of bond amount.

[70] Fed. R. Bankr. P. 9027(d).

[71] 28 U.S.C. § 1478(b).

§ 23.13 Form: Application for Removal

FORM 23–2
APPLICATION FOR REMOVAL

IN THE UNITED STATES BANKRUPTCY COURT
FOR THE ____ DISTRICT OF _____

In Re:	)	
	)	
____________________,	)	Case No. _______
	)	Chapter ___
Debtor.	)	
	)	
____________________,	)	
	)	
Plaintiff,	)	
	)	
v.	)	
	)	
____________________,	)	
	)	
Defendant.	)	

APPLICATION FOR REMOVAL

COMES NOW [party name], a party in interest herein, by and through undersigned counsel and pursuant to 28 U.S.C. §§ 1334, 1452, and 157, and removes the above-captioned matter, currently pending in state court, and in support thereof states as follows:

1. On [date], a civil action was brought in the [state court], which is captioned [state court caption], [case number].

2. [Bankruptcy caption] relates to the above-referenced case which was commenced under Chapter 11 of the Bankruptcy Code and is now pending before this court.

3. [Party name], a party to the above-referenced civil action, is also a party in this case under Chapter 11.

4. The summons, complaint, and all other pleadings filed in the state court action are attached to this application.

5. The removed action, as an adversary proceeding under Federal Bankruptcy Rule 7001, is a [core proceeding or noncore proceeding].

6. Applicant [consents/does not consent] to entry of final orders/judgments/decrees by the bankruptcy court in this matter.

DATED ____________, 19__.

____
[Attorney for Applicant]

[Certificate of Service]

§ 23.14 Form: Motion for Remand

FORM 23–3
MOTION FOR REMAND

IN THE UNITED STATES BANKRUPTCY COURT
FOR THE ____ DISTRICT OF _____

In Re:)
)
________________________,) Case No. _______
) Chapter ___
Debtor.)

MOTION FOR REMAND

COMES NOW [party name], a party in interest, by and through its undersigned counsel, and moves to remand the above-captioned civil action, which was removed to this court by notice dated [date], to the [state court]. In support thereof, movant respectfully states:

1. On [date], a civil action was filed in the [state court] captioned [caption of the case].

2. On [date], the above-referenced action was removed by [removing party] to this court pursuant to 28 U.S.C. § 1452.

3. Removal is not appropriate because [state reasons; for example, notice of removal was not timely made; parties in the civil action bear no relation to the bankruptcy case; the case has progressed to a stage at which it will be more expeditiously disposed of in state court; no legal issues involving bankruptcy law are implicated; the case involves issues of state law which are unsettled; absent the bankruptcy no basis for federal jurisdiction exists].

WHEREFORE, movant respectfully requests that the above-referenced civil action previously removed to this court be remanded to state court for disposition, and for other relief as the court deems appropriate.

____

[Attorney for Applicant]

[Certificate of Service]

§ 23.15 Jury Trials in Bankruptcy

In the post-*Marathon* era, perhaps no other jurisdictional topic has been the source of more confusion by courts and practitioners alike than the question of when a bankruptcy court may, consistent with its less-than-pervasive jurisdiction, conduct a jury trial. The importance of this question was underscored by the *Marathon* court's specific reference to pre-*Marathon* Code provisions allowing Article I judges to conduct jury trials.[72] Jury trial issues in the context of a bankruptcy may be distilled to two questions: (1) Is a party entitled to a jury in a particular bankruptcy proceeding; and (2) If so, is a bankruptcy court legally competent to hear the proceeding, or must it be conducted by the district court?

Although the Seventh Amendment provides for jury trials for actions "at law," the only bankruptcy proceedings for which a clear right to a jury trial is set out in the statute are personal injury actions and wrongful death actions.[73] The appropriateness of a jury trial with respect to all other actions has been left to the courts.

Under the Bankruptcy Act[74] and later the pre- and post-*Marathon* Code, three schools of thought developed concerning how to determine which cases qualified for jury trial. Some courts reasoned that the right to a jury trial in bankruptcy courts turned on whether the proceeding was summary or plenary.[75] Other courts denied parties any right to jury trial except when it was specifically authorized by statute.[76] Still other courts adhered to a Seventh Amendment-oriented view that a right to jury trial exists when the underlying issues are deemed to be legal as opposed to equitable. This analysis focused primarily upon the remedy sought by the requesting party.[77]

---

[72] Northern Pipeline Constr. Co. v. Marathon Pipeline Co., 458 U.S. 50, 85, (1982).

[73] 28 U.S.C. § 1411.

[74] Ch. 541, 30 Stat. 544 (repealed 1979).

[75] Under the Bankruptcy Act, plenary actions were the more complex actions and were not within the jurisdiction of the referee. This analysis survived enactment of the Code because of an oft-cited, pre-Code Supreme Court decision which held that if resolution of a summary proceeding (an objection to claim) was necessary for the court to get to a plenary proceeding (a preference action), no right to a jury existed. Katchen v. Landy, 382 U.S. 323 (1966).

[76] *In re* Franz, 82 B.R. 835, 836–37 (Bankr. S.D. Tex. 1988).

[77] American Universal Ins. Co. v. Pugh, 821 F.2d 1352 (9th Cir. 1987).

Although it did not conclusively resolve all of the uncertainties relating to jury trials in bankruptcy, the Supreme Court's 1989 decision in *Granfinanciera, S.A. v. Nordberg*[78] is widely considered to be the Court's most authoritative (and helpful) discussion on this issue. In *Granfinanciera,* Nordberg, the trustee, brought a fraudulent transfer action in bankruptcy court against Granfinanciera and another defendant.[79] Granfinanciera, which had not submitted a proof of claim in the bankruptcy, responded to the trustee's suit with a request for a jury trial. The bankruptcy court denied Granfinanciera's request for a jury trial and was affirmed by the district court and by the Eleventh Circuit.[80]

The Court, finding that the petitioners were entitled to a jury trial, reversed and remanded. Justice Brennan, writing for the majority, chided Congress for its failure to clearly articulate its intention regarding the statutory right to a jury in §§ 1411 and 1480. Absent clear guidance from Congress on the question, the Court concluded that the right to a jury in bankruptcy "must necessarily be predicated on the Seventh Amendment."[81] Under the Court's reasoning, because of the Seventh Amendment, a right to jury trial must exist in bankruptcy except when:

1. The claim is "equitable" as opposed to "legal"[82]
2. The statutory remedy is in a tribunal that does not have the power to conduct jury trials (that is, in administrative proceedings)
3. The parties voluntarily submit to the jurisdiction of the bankruptcy court (such as a creditor's filing a proof of claim).[83]

Once it has been determined with some degree of confidence that there exists a right to a jury trial in bankruptcy, the more difficult question to be answered is whether the jury trial may be conducted by the bankruptcy court. The *Granfinanciera* decision provided no guidance on this point, specifically declining to address the question at all.[84] The failure of the Supreme Court or Congress to resolve this question has predictably led to confusion among practitioners and a split in the circuits.

On the one hand, a line of cases following a Second Circuit case[85] have concluded that bankruptcy judges may, consistent with Article III and the Seventh Amendment,

---

78 492 U.S. 33 (1989).

79 *Id.* at 36.

80 *Id.* The Eleventh Circuit adopted the view that 28 U.S.C. § 1411 provided the only basis for a jury trial in bankruptcy. *In re* Chase & Sanborn Corp., 835 F.2d 1341 (11th Cir.), *cert. granted sub nom.* Granfinanciera, S.A. v. Nordberg, 486 U.S. 1054 (1988).

81 492 U.S. at 41 n.3.

82 *Id.* at 47–48. Although the distinction between actions at law and actions at equity was abolished under the modern rules of civil procedure, the *Granfinanciera* Court's holding requires a court to consider whether, under English common law, the action at bar would be considered to be at law or in equity.

83 *Id.* at 58.

84 *Id.* at 64.

85 *In re* Ben Cooper, Inc., 896 F.2d 1394 (2d Cir.), *vacated & remanded,* 498 U.S. 964, (1990), *reinstated,* 924 F.2d 36 (2d Cir.); *cert. denied,* ___ U.S. ___; 111 S. Ct. 2041 (1991) (holding that bankruptcy court has statutory and constitutional authority to conduct jury trials).

conduct jury trials in core proceedings. These cases reason that statutory authority for jury trials in bankruptcy may be found in 28 U.S.C. §§ 151 and 157(b). Section 151 establishes the bankruptcy court as "a unit" of the district court and the bankruptcy judge as its judicial officer. It empowers the bankruptcy judge to "exercise the authority conferred under this chapter with respect to any action, suit, or proceeding."

Section 157(b) allows bankruptcy judges to "hear and determine *all* cases under Title 11 and *all* core proceedings arising under Title 11, or arising in a case under Title 11" (emphasis added). Under the reasoning of this line of cases, by empowering the bankruptcy court to decide all Title 11 cases, Congress impliedly authorized jury trials in bankruptcy.[86]

Other cases, following the lead of an Eighth Circuit decision,[87] take the opposite view, that the bankruptcy court may never conduct jury trials because Congress neither expressly nor impliedly granted statutory authority to do so. Under these cases, only the district court may conduct a jury trial in bankruptcy. This latter view appears to be the majority view.[88]

It is apparent that the split in the circuits on this issue will only be resolved by a definitive statement from the Supreme Court. Until that happens, counsel should review the status of the law in the applicable jurisdiction to determine whether a right to jury trial before a bankruptcy judge exists.

§ 23.16 Jurisdiction under 11 U.S.C. § 105

It should be apparent to one reviewing the jurisdictional provisions under the Code, the Bankruptcy Rules, and Title 28 that clear and unqualified answers concerning jurisdiction are extremely few and far between. To add to this confusion, creative counsel have urged another possible basis for bankruptcy jurisdiction: 11 U.S.C. § 105. Section 105 grants a bankruptcy court what appears to be virtually unfettered power to "issue any order, process, or judgment that is necessary or appropriate to carry out the provision of [Title 11]" and reinforces the power of the court to take "any action or mak[e] any determination necessary or appropriate to enforce or implement court orders or rules." Although this chapter does not extensively treat the § 105 approach to jurisdiction, counsel should be aware of it as a possible alternative argument favoring jurisdiction.

Given the sweeping grant of power to bankruptcy judges by § 105, it would seem that § 105 might, in at least some circumstances, impact the bounds of bankruptcy court jurisdiction. But to what extent, if any, does § 105 broaden the jurisdiction of bankruptcy courts? Is § 105 an attempt to bridge some legislative gap not adequately addressed by the post-*Marathon* Code? Is § 105 merely a codification of the

---

86 The only circuit case that seems to follow *Ben Cooper* is Travellers Int'l AG v. Robinson, 982 F.2d 96, 100 n.5 (3d Cir. 1992) (citing *Ben Cooper* with approval in dicta).

87 *In re* United Mo. Bank, 901 F.2d 1449 (8th Cir. 1990).

88 Three other circuits have followed *United Missouri Bank.* Rafoth v. National Union Fire Ins. Co., 954 F.2d 1169, 1173 (6th Cir. 1992); *In re* Grabill Corp., 967 F.2d 1152, 1158 (7th Cir. 1992); Kaiser Steel Corp. v. Frates, 911 F.2d 380, 388 (10th Cir. 1990).

equitable powers possessed by bankruptcy courts prior to enactment of the Code? Courts which have considered these and related questions have reached little in the way of consensus.

The Fifth Circuit held in *NLRB v. Evans Plumbing Co.*[89] that § 105 does not provide an independent statutory basis for jurisdiction if none existed previously. Hence, the bankruptcy court could not rely on § 105 as a basis for enjoining an administrative proceeding involving the debtor merely because the debtor and property of the estate are implicated. However, § 105 does empower the court, when appropriate, to enjoin suits by creditors against a debtor's directors, officers, insurer, attorneys, and other third parties who are not, themselves, in bankruptcy.[90]

VENUE

§ 23.17 Venue of Cases

Title 28 U.S.C. § 1408 establishes proper venue for bankruptcy *cases.* Generally, it provides that venue is proper in a particular judicial district if, for the 180 days immediately preceding the petition date or for a majority of the 180 days preceding the petition date: 1) the debtor is domiciled in the district, 2) the debtor resides in the district, 3) the debtor has its principal place of business within the district, or 4) the debtor has its principal assets within the district. Under § 1408(2), venue is also proper in a district in which a bankruptcy case involving the debtor's affiliate, general partner, or partnership is pending. The statute does not indicate that venue predicated on affiliate status is subject to the 180-day requirement.

Fortunately, proper venue for the bankruptcy petition of the typical small business client is not difficult to identify because the district in which the client's income is generated, the client's home office is located, the client's books are kept, and the client's bank accounts are located is usually one and the same.

§ 23.18 Venue of Proceedings

Venue of *proceedings* arising under Title 11 or arising in or related to cases under Title 11 is governed by 28 U.S.C. § 1409, which imposes four basic rules regarding venue for proceedings in bankruptcy cases. First, the trustee in bankruptcy is required to bring a lawsuit to recover money or property worth less than $1,000 (if a consumer debt, $5,000) in the federal court for the judicial district in which the defendant resides.[91] Second, a trustee suing in furtherance of statutory avoidance powers conferred by the Code may bring the cause of action in any court, whether

---

[89] 639 F.2d 291 (5th Cir. 1981).

[90] *In re* A.H. Robins Co., 880 F.2d 694, 700–02 (4th Cir.), *cert. denied,* 493 U.S. 959 (1989).

[91] 28 U.S.C. § 1409(b).

state or federal, in which a creditor or the debtor could have sued, absent the bankruptcy.[92] Third, with regard to a business debtor, causes of action arising as a consequence of postpetition business operations may be brought by the trustee anywhere the action lawfully could have been brought under nonbankruptcy law.[93] Finally, a party wishing to bring a suit against the representative of the bankruptcy estate may choose either of two available venues: the district in which the bankruptcy case is pending, or in the district court for the district in which the state or federal court sits in which the party could have brought the proceeding under nonbankruptcy rules.[94]

§ 23.19 Transfer of Venue

Transfer of venue (if venue is otherwise technically proper) is governed by 28 U.S.C. § 1412. Section 1412 provides for venue transfer by the district court "in the interest of justice" or "for the convenience of the parties." Courts generally analyze requests for transfer of venue by reviewing six factors:

1. The proximity of creditors to the court
2. The proximity of the debtor to the court
3. The proximity of witnesses whose participation will be required for case administration
4. The location of the debtor's assets
5. The possibility that ancillary administration of the case will be required in the event of liquidation of the estate
6. The economical administration of the estate.[95]

The mechanics of venue transfer are set out in Bankruptcy Rule 1014. Under Rule 1014, if a case is filed in a proper yet less-than-optimal forum, any party may file a motion requesting transfer to a more suitable forum. As is typical, the party requesting the venue change bears the burden of proving that transfer is warranted.[96] Further, the court in which the petition is first filed must hear the motion, even when another forum may be a more logical choice.[97] A form for a motion to transfer venue appears in **§ 23.20.**

Although § 1412 clearly authorizes venue transfer if it would have otherwise been proper, courts have been hesitant to rely on § 1412 as a basis for dismissal of cases when venue is not proper.[98] This matter was clarified by amendments to

---

[92] *Id.* § 1409(c).

[93] *Id.* § 1409(d).

[94] *Id.* § 1409(e).

[95] *See In re* Industrial Pollution Control, Inc., 137 B.R. 176 (Bankr. W.D. Pa. 1992); *In re* Thomasson, 60 B.R. 629 (Bankr. M.D. Tenn. 1986).

[96] *In re* Manville Forest Prods. Corp., 896 F.2d 1384 (2d Cir. 1990).

[97] *In re* Reddington Invs., 90 B.R. 429 (Bankr. 9th Cir. 1988).

[98] *See e.g., In re* Dew Mortgage Co., 10 B.R. 242 (Bankr. M.D. Fla. 1981).

Bankruptcy Rule 1014(a)(2) which prescribe the process for disposing of cases where venue is improper. Under Rule 1014, if a case is filed in the wrong venue, upon "timely" motion of a party in interest, the case may, in the court's discretion, be dismissed or transferred if transfer is in the interest of justice or for the convenience of the parties.[99] Hence, otherwise legitimate challenges to venue may be waived if not promptly brought before the court.

§ 23.20 Form: Motion to Transfer Venue

FORM 23–4
MOTION TO TRANSFER VENUE

IN THE UNITED STATES BANKRUPTCY COURT
FOR THE ____ DISTRICT OF _____

In Re:	)	
	)	
________________________,	)	Case No. _______
	)	Chapter ___
Debtor.	)	

MOTION TO TRANSFER VENUE

COMES NOW [name], a party herein, by and through counsel of record and pursuant to 28 U.S.C. § 1412 and Federal Rule of Bankruptcy Procedure 1014, and moves for a transfer of venue from [original venue] to [requested venue], and, in support thereof, respectfully states as follows:

1. On [date], the debtor filed a voluntary petition under Chapter 11 with the U. S. Bankruptcy Court for the [district].

2. A transfer of venue to the U.S. Bankruptcy Court for the [requested district], [Division], is appropriate because [state reasons, such as it is geographically closer for witnesses whose participation will be required for case administration; it is the location of a majority of the debtor's assets; it is the venue of cases that are related to the instant case; the case may be administered more economically if transferred.]

3. Transferring venue would serve the interest of justice and would be more convenient for the parties involved.

4. No party would be unfairly prejudiced by transfer of this case.

---

[99] Fed. R. Bankr. P. 1014(b).

WHEREFORE, movant respectfully requests that this case be transferred to the U. S. Bankruptcy Court for the [requested district], and for such other relief as the court deems appropriate.

____

[Attorney for Applicant]

[Certificate of Service]

APPEALS

§ 23.21 Bankruptcy Appeals

Sections 23.22 through **23.29** introduce the practitioner to the unusual path that a bankruptcy case takes on appellate review. It is not intended to be an exhaustive discourse on appellate procedure but instead serves as a survey of the major points.

§ 23.22 Appealable Orders

Appellate review of a bankruptcy court's decision is generally available under the same circumstances and is subject to many of the same limitations as appellate review of federal civil matters. Thus, federal appellate concepts, such as finality and interlocutory orders, are also important in bankruptcy. In addition, bankruptcy appeals present a number of unique issues because of the bankruptcy court's unique relationship with the district court.

Appeals from decisions of a bankruptcy court are governed by 28 U.S.C. § 158, which grants to the district court jurisdiction to "hear appeals from final judgments, orders, and decrees, and, with leave of court, from interlocutory orders and decrees, of bankruptcy judges entered in cases and proceedings referred to the bankruptcy judges."[100]

Section 158 also authorizes the creation of bankruptcy appellate panels (BAPs) comprised of bankruptcy judges to hear and determine appeals from the bankruptcy court within its district. The jurisdiction of the BAP is predicated on the consent of the parties and is not binding on the district court, because the panel is composed of non-Article III judges.[101] Only the Ninth Circuit has an operating bankruptcy appellate panel.

Appeals from either the district court or a BAP are to the circuit court of appeals and are governed by the Federal Rules of Appellate Procedure. The district court, or BAP when acting as an appellate court in a bankruptcy proceeding, is bound by the

[100] 28 U.S.C. § 158(a).

[101] Bank of Maui v. Estate Analysis, Inc., 904 F.2d 470 (9th Cir. 1990).

same limitations imposed upon courts of appeal.[102] Practice and procedure under the Federal Rules of Appellate Procedure are beyond the scope of this chapter.

With regard to finality, courts that have considered whether a particular order is final for purposes of appeal have considered factors like:

1. Whether the order directly affects disposition of the estate's assets
2. Whether the order will determine the outcome of a particular proceeding
3. Whether the order will irrevocably decide or dispose of property rights of a party
4. Whether the order conclusively determines a discrete issue
5. Whether the order requires any further action by the court with regard to the issue decided.[103]

Applying these principles, an order denying confirmation of the debtor's Chapter 11 plan is not final.[104] Similarly, an order granting interim attorney's fees is not appealable.[105] Courts have, however, found the following orders to be final for appeal purposes: order determining a debt to be nondischargeable;[106] order dismissing an adversary complaint;[107] order authorizing employment of professionals;[108] and an order denying a creditor's relief from stay motion, under certain circumstances.[109]

If an order is not final for purposes of appeal, it may nonetheless be appealable with leave of court, as provided under § 158(a) or under exceptions to the final order doctrine developed through case law. The most well-known of these judicially carved exceptions is the *collateral order doctrine* first announced by the Supreme Court in *Cohen v. Beneficial Industrial Loan Corp.*[110] Under the collateral order doctrine, an otherwise nonfinal order is eligible for appellate review if:

1. The order conclusively determines a disputed question
2. The disputed question is collateral to the merits of the overall action
3. The disputed question is effectively unreviewable on appeal.[111]

---

102 *See* Dallas v. S.A.G., Inc., 836 F.2d 1307 (11th Cir. 1988) (holding that district court could not consider an issue relating to a default judgment that was not properly raised before bankruptcy court).

103 *See* Kubicik v. Apex Oil Co., 884 F.2d 343 (8th Cir. 1989); *In re* Medomak Canning Co., 123 B.R. 671 (Bankr. D. Me. 1991); *In re* Murray, 116 B.R. 6 (Bankr. D. Mass. 1990).

104 *In re* MCorp Fin., Inc., 139 B.R. 820 (Bankr. S.D. Tex. 1992).

105 *In re* W.J. Serv., Inc., 139 B.R. 824 (Bankr. S.D. Tex. 1992).

106 *In re* Bathlater, 123 B.R. 568 (Bankr. S.D. Ohio 1990), *aff'd,* 951 F.2d 349 (6th Cir. 1991).

107 Southerland v. Smith, 136 B.R. 565 (Bankr. M.D. Fla. 1992).

108 *In re* Middleton Arms, Ltd., 119 B.R. 131 (Bankr. M.D. Tenn. 1990), *aff'd,* 934 F.2d 723 (6th Cir. 1991).

109 *See In re* Chateaugay Corp., 880 F.2d 1509 (2d Cir. 1989).

110 337 U.S. 541 (1949).

111 337 U.S. at 546–47.

In other words, a debtor/appellant would have to show that denial of leave to appeal would result in irreparable harm to its reorganization effort. There is some disagreement as to whether federal case law exceptions to the final order doctrine apply to bankruptcy appeals or whether § 158 was intended to provide the exclusive basis for appellate jurisdiction in bankruptcy cases. A form motion for leave to appeal an interlocutory order appears in § **23.23.**

§ 23.23 Form: Motion for Leave to Appeal Interlocutory Order

FORM 23-5
MOTION FOR LEAVE TO APPEAL INTERLOCUTORY ORDER

IN THE UNITED STATES BANKRUPTCY COURT
FOR THE ____ DISTRICT OF _____

In Re:)
)
______________________,) Case No. _______
) Chapter ___
Debtor.)

MOTION FOR LEAVE TO APPEAL INTERLOCUTORY ORDER
[TO THE UNITED STATES DISTRICT COURT FOR THE [DISTRICT]/
TO THE BANKRUPTCY APPELLATE PANEL

COMES NOW [party name], a party-in-interest in the above-referenced proceeding under Title 11, by and through its undersigned counsel of record, and pursuant to 28 U.S.C. § 158(a), and moves for leave to appeal from an order [state nature of order, such as transferring venue] of the United States Bankruptcy Court [briefly describe relief afforded by order], and in support thereof respectfully states as follows:

1. On [date], the United States Bankruptcy Court for the [District] entered an order [briefly describe relief granted, for example, transferring venue of the case within the circuit].

2. [Recite facts that tend to show error by the bankruptcy court.]

3. If leave for appeal is granted, the questions to be presented for review are as follows: [state questions, for example, whether the bankruptcy court erred in transferring venue and whether its findings of fact were clearly erroneous].

4. The movant seeks the following relief: [state requested relief, for example, reconsideration of the order transferring venue].

5. Interlocutory appeal is appropriate under these circumstances because [indicate reason, for example, the new venue is inconvenient for a majority of the estate's creditors; the instant order qualifies for interlocutory appellate review under the collateral order doctrine].

WHEREFORE, movant respectfully requests that leave to appeal be granted and for such other relief as the court deems appropriate.

____

[Attorney for Applicant]

[Certificate of Service]

§ 23.24 Standard of Review on Appeal

As discussed in Chapter § **23.2,** under prior law, bankruptcy court findings of fact and conclusions of law were always subject to de novo review by the district court. As part of the expansion of bankruptcy court jurisdiction under the 1978 Code, a *clearly erroneous* standard was adopted for district court appellate review of all bankruptcy court findings. The invalidation of this standard by the *Marathon* decision resulted in a standard under the Emergency Rule by which district courts were to give no deference to findings of the bankruptcy judge. The 1984 BAFJA amendments to the Bankruptcy Code ultimately resolved the issue by creating different standards of review for a bankruptcy court's factual findings in core proceedings and related proceedings.

Under BAFJA, when a proceeding is core, a finding of fact by the bankruptcy court is subject to a clearly erroneous standard of review. Thus, the district court, sitting as an appellate court, may only disregard the bankruptcy court's findings of fact if it determines that the findings are clearly erroneous.[112]

With regard to related proceedings, however, 28 U.S.C. § 157 provides that findings by a bankruptcy court are subject to de novo review by the district court if a party has "timely and specifically objected" to final disposition by the bankruptcy court. Stated differently, if the proceeding is noncore, the bankruptcy court may hear the matter but must submit proposed findings of fact and conclusions of law to the district court. The district court reviews the findings utilizing the clearly erroneous standard unless the matter appealed was specifically and timely objected to before the bankruptcy court.

Although the district court is, in most cases, required to accept the findings of fact of the bankruptcy court in core proceedings, the district court may always conduct a de novo review of conclusions of law reached by the bankruptcy court in both core and noncore proceedings.[113]

---

[112] *See, e.g., In re* Reid, 757 F.2d 230 (10th Cir. 1985).

[113] Richmond Leasing Co. v. Capital Bank, 762 F. 2d 1303 (5th Cir. 1985).

§ 23.25 Stay Pending Appeal

Under bankruptcy appellate rules, as under the Federal Rules of Civil Procedure, a party may request a stay pending appeal of a bankruptcy court order to be reviewed by the district court sitting as an appellate court. In many instances, a stay is necessary to preserve the interests of the parties (particularly the aggrieved party), until the appellate court has had an opportunity to review the matter. For example, a stay of an order granting relief from stay would probably be justified when, in the absence of a stay pending appeal, the relief would destroy the debtor's prospects of reorganization such that a favorable disposition on appeal would be meaningless.

Bankruptcy Rule 8005, which governs stays pending appeal, provides that a motion for a stay pending appeal, for approval of a supersedeas bond, or for other relief pending appeal must first be brought before the bankruptcy court. The court's objective in fashioning the stay is to minimize the effect of the stay on the appellee while adequately reserving the rights of the appellant. Rule 8005 also allows the district court to review an order by the bankruptcy court denying a stay. The bankruptcy court also has discretionary power to condition any stay on the posting of a supersedeas bond. The United States is specifically exempted from the bond requirement under Rule 8005. See **§ 23.26** for a form motion for a stay pending an appeal.

§ 23.26 Form: Motion for Stay Pending Appeal

FORM 23-6
MOTION FOR STAY PENDING APPEAL

IN THE UNITED STATES BANKRUPTCY COURT
FOR THE ____ DISTRICT OF _____

In Re:)
)
______________________,) Case No. _______
) Chapter ___
Debtor.)

MOTION FOR STAY PENDING APPEAL

COMES NOW Appellant [appellant name], by and through its undersigned attorney of record, and pursuant to Bankruptcy Rule 8005, and moves for an order staying this court's prior order entered on [date], pending appeal, and in support thereof respectfully states as follows:

1. On [date] this court entered an order/judgment/decree providing [state relief granted from which appeal is taken].

2. Appellant filed a proper and timely notice of appeal on [filing date], which was within ten (10) days of the entry of the court's order.

3. Irreparable harm will be suffered by the appellant if the court's order dated [date] is not stayed pending disposition of appellant's appeal. [State the irreparable harm to be suffered.]

4. Appellant has a reasonable likelihood of success on the merits of the appeal because [state reasons].

5. [If stay is ordered, appellant will post a supersedeas bond in the amount of [bond amount], which will preserve the interests of appellee during the pendency of the appeal/or Appellant is not required to post a bond because appellant is the United States of America/the debtor/the trustee].

6. Imposing a stay is consistent with public policy because it favors and aids in the rehabilitation of the debtor rather than its liquidation.

WHEREFORE Appellant respectfully moves that this court's order dated [date] be stayed pending appeal and for such other relief as the court deems appropriate.

____

[Attorney for Applicant]

[Certificate of Service]

§ 23.27 Bankruptcy Appellate Procedure

Part VIII of the Bankruptcy Rules sets out the mechanics of appeal of a bankruptcy order or judgment from the bankruptcy court to the district court. The Federal Rules of Appellate Procedure govern bankruptcy appeals to the circuit court of appeals.[114] Upon entry of an adverse judgment, order, or decree, the aggrieved party has 10 days within which to file a timely notice of appeal. Upon receipt of a notice of appeal, the other party has the longer of 10 days from the date of the appellant's notice or any longer period allowed in the Rules to file its own notice of cross-appeal.[115] Notices of appeal are to be filed with the bankruptcy court but will be forwarded to the clerk of the bankruptcy court if filed in error with the clerk of the district court or bankruptcy appellate panel.[116] A form notice of appeal appears in **§ 23.28.**

Generally, postjudgment motions do not toll the 10-day period within which a party is required to file a notice of appeal. Bankruptcy Rule 8002(b) provides the only exceptions to this general rule. Under Rule 8002(b), the following will toll the 10-day appeals period:

---

[114] Rosner v. Worcester, 811 F.2d 589 (9th Cir. 1987).

[115] Fed. R. Bankr. P. 8002(a).

[116] *Id.*

1. A motion to amend or make additional findings of fact under Rule 7052(b)
2. A motion to alter or amend the judgment under Rule 9023
3. A motion for a new trial under Rule 9023.

A notice of appeal filed prior to the disposition of any of these motions shall have no effect, and a new notice must be filed upon their disposition.[117] It should also be noted that all of the above motions pertain to judgments rendered in adversary proceedings. Hence, a postjudgment or post-order motion filed in a contested matter (such as a motion for reconsideration) does not toll the applicable appeals period.

Upon filing the notice of appeal, the appellant has 10 days to designate the record and the appellee has 10 days from the service of the statement of issues to designate any additional items deemed necessary. The record, as designated, must establish that the issues presented on appeal were properly raised and preserved at the bankruptcy court.[118] The parties are then required to assist the clerk by requesting any transcripts or other items designated as part of the appeal record.[119] See **§ 23.29** for a form designation of record and statement of issues on appeal.

Once the appeals record on appeal is complete, the bankruptcy court clerk transmits the record to the district court clerk or bankruptcy appellate panel clerk who, in turn, enters the appeal on the district court docket.[120] From the date that the appeal is docketed by the district court clerk, the appellant has 15 days to file and serve an appellant's brief. After service of the appellant's brief, the appellee has 15 days to file and serve a brief.[121]

After briefs have been filed by the parties, each party is entitled to an oral argument before the district court, unless the district judge determines that oral argument is unnecessary.[122] A timeline for the steps to an appeal to the district court appears in **Figure 23–1.**

Bankruptcy Rule 8010 sets out the minimum requirements for an appellate brief in a bankruptcy matter. Under Rule 8010, the appellant's brief should consist of the following in this order:

1. A table of contents, with page references and a table of cases alphabetically arranged, statutes and other authorities cited, with references to the page of the brief on which they are cited
2. A statement of the basis for appellate jurisdiction
3. A statement of the issues presented and the applicable standard of review
4. A statement of the case, including relevant facts and procedural history, with appropriate references to the record

---

117 Fed. R. Bankr. P. 8002(b).

118 Hofer v. Merchants State Bank, 823 F.2d 271 (8th Cir. 1987).

119 Fed. R. Bankr. P. 8006.

120 Fed. R. Bankr. P. 8007.

121 Fed. R. Bankr. P. 8009.

122 Fed. R. Bankr. P. 8012.

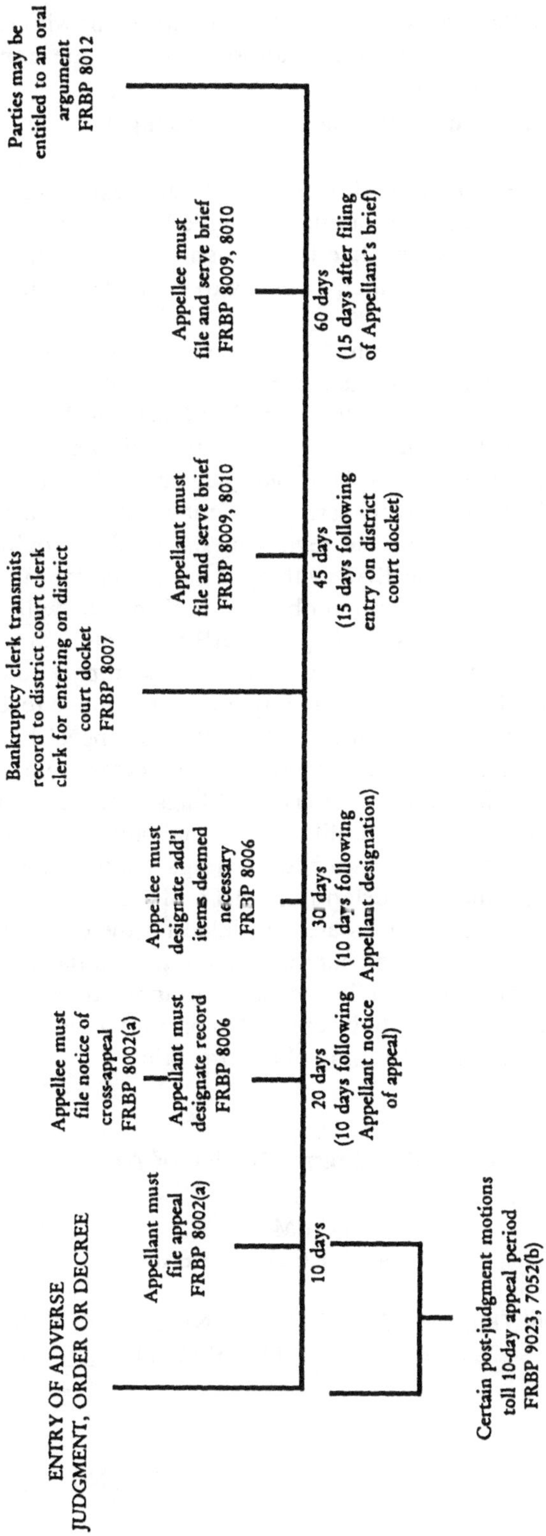

Figure 23–1. Timeline for appeal to district court under Federal Rules of Bankruptcy Procedure (FRBP).

5. An argument containing the contentions of appellant with respect to the issues presented, including any legal authority which the appellant wishes the reviewing court to consider
6. A conclusion, which briefly states the relief sought.

The appellee's brief should be similarly constituted, except that the appellee is not required to restate the facts, the issues presented, or the jurisdictional statement except to the extent that the appellee is dissatisfied with the appellant's statements. Generally, Rule 8010 limits principal briefs to 50 pages in length and any reply briefs to 25 pages.

Practitioners in the Ninth Circuit should note that appellate practice before the Ninth Circuit BAP differs somewhat from appeals to the district court. Under the Rules of the United States Bankruptcy Appellate Panels of the Ninth Circuit (hereinafter the Ninth Circuit BAP Rules), as amended through May 1, 1993, when a notice of appeal is filed with the clerk of the bankruptcy court, the appeal is referred immediately to the BAP. All interested parties are immediately noticed of the reference, and any party objecting to appellate review by the BAP is required to file a written objection with the clerk of the BAP within 20 days from the filing of the notice of appeal. In the absence of any written objections, all parties will be deemed to have consented to disposition of the appeal by the BAP pursuant to 28 U.S.C. § 158.

Generally, Ninth Circuit BAP Rule 5 mirrors Bankruptcy rule 8010 except that main briefs are limited to 30 pages and reply briefs are limited to 20 pages.

Ninth Circuit BAP Rule 6 requires that a notice of appeal be accompanied by a file-stamped copy of the bankruptcy court order or decree from which the appeal is being taken. Because all communications and filings to the BAP are to be addressed to its principal office in Pasadena, California, special provisions are made in the Rules for the scheduling of the time and place for hearings and oral arguments. Under Ninth Circuit BAP Rule 3, if the BAP determines that oral argument is needed in a particular case, time and place of hearings are scheduled for the convenience of the parties and the panel. Rule 6 encourages counsel to participate in the scheduling process by suggesting to the panel clerk possible venues for hearing an appeal. Further, any party who believes a particular matter to be entitled to priority in setting a hearing date is to inform the BAP clerk prior to the filing of the first brief.

§ 23.28 Form: Notice of Appeal

FORM 23-7
NOTICE OF APPEAL

IN THE UNITED STATES BANKRUPTCY COURT
FOR THE ____ DISTRICT OF ____

In Re:	)	
	)	
________________,	)	Case No. ______

) Chapter ___
Debtor.)

NOTICE OF APPEAL TO
UNITED STATES DISTRICT COURT

COMES NOW the Debtor [or defendant, or movant, or applicant, or other party], by and through the undersigned counsel of record and pursuant to Federal Rule of Bankruptcy Procedure 8001, and appeals to the United States District Court for the [District] [or the Bankruptcy Appellant Panel], from the final [order/judgment/decree] of the United States Bankruptcy Court for the [District] concerning [describe proceeding] entered on [date].

In conformity with Rule 8001(a), below are the names, addresses, and telephone numbers of all of the parties and their respective attorneys of record:

[List names of parties to appeal and counsel of record.]

____
[Attorney for Applicant]

[Certificate of Service]

§ 23.29 Form: Designation of Record and Statement of Issues on Appeal

FORM 23-8
DESIGNATION OF RECORD AND STATEMENT OF ISSUES ON APPEAL

IN THE UNITED STATES BANKRUPTCY COURT
FOR THE ____ DISTRICT OF _____

In Re:)
)
________________________,) Case No. _______
) Chapter ___
Debtor.)

DESIGNATION OF RECORD AND
STATEMENT OF ISSUES ON APPEAL

COMES NOW Appellant, by and through its undersigned counsel of record, pursuant to Federal Rule of Bankruptcy Procedure 8006, and hereby designates the following documents for inclusion in the record on appeal along with the document number and title given it by the Bankruptcy Court's docket entry:

Document 1: Debtor's petition for relief under chapter 11.

Document 2: Motion/petition/application for [requested relief], along with brief(s) in support of motion, affidavits of [affiant], and exhibits [numbers].

Document 3: Reply, with supplemental briefs and affidavits.

Document 4: Transcript of hearing held on [date].

Document 5: Movant/Petitioner/Debtor's exhibits [numbers] introduced into evidence at hearing held on [date].

Document 6: The bankruptcy court's findings of fact, conclusions of law, or memorandum order and opinion.

Document 7: Notice of appeal.

Document 8: This designation of record and statement of issues on appeal.

STATEMENT OF ISSUES

The issues to be presented on appeal are:

1. Whether the court erred in [granting relief from stay, sustaining an objection, confirming plan, etc.]

____

[Attorney for Applicant]

[Certificate of Service]

CHAPTER 24

PROPOSED AMENDMENTS TO THE BANKRUPTCY CODE

Karen S. Kressin

§ 24.1 Introduction

The Bankruptcy Code has been law since 1979, and, although amendments have been made from time to time, the basic original scheme of the Code has become an established and, on the whole, successful system for handling liquidations and reorganizations of all sorts of entities, from individuals to corporations. In recent years, however, there has been a growing feeling that Chapter 11 is too cumbersome and expensive for small business cases and that the Bankruptcy Code should be amended to streamline small business bankruptcies. This chapter outlines the progress to date of small business bankruptcy reform legislation.

§ 24.2 History of Small Business Bankruptcy Legislation

Congress began to respond to the perceived need for special treatment of small business bankruptcies by holding hearings in the spring and summer of 1991. On November 19, 1991, Senator Heflin, joined by Senator Grassley, introduced Senate Bill 1985. That bill included a proposed new Chapter 10 for small business bankruptcies.[1] In general, the proposal was patterned after Chapters 12 and 13 of the

[1] *See* S. Rep. No. 168, 103d Cong., 1st Sess. 38 (1993) [hereinafter S. Rep. No. 168].

Bankruptcy Code and provided for accelerated time schedules, the appointment of a trustee, and nonapplicability of the absolute priority rule.[2]

Senate Bill 1985 was passed by the full Senate on two separate occasions, but the final version was not considered by the House of Representatives before adjournment of the 102d Congress.[3] The proposal was reintroduced by Senators Heflin and Grassley in March 1993 as Senate Bill 540. The content was largely the same as that of Senate Bill 1985. Senate Bill 540 as further amended was favorably reported to the full Senate on September 15, 1993,[4] but was not passed before adjournment of the first session of the 103d Congress.

In April 1994, consideration of the bill was resumed. During consideration, a number of substantive amendments were made, most notably one by Senator Heflin[5] that completely changed the proposed scheme by deleting proposed Chapter 10 for small businesses. A definition of *small business,* some expedited time schedules, and other minor alterations of the reorganization process were all that remained as special provisions for small business bankruptcies.[6] Senate Bill 540 as amended was passed by the full Senate on April 21, 1994, by a 94–0 vote[7] and sent to the House of Representatives. The legislation now before Congress contains one other provision that could affect small business bankruptcies. The current version of Senate Bill 540, like the earlier versions, proposes to raise the debt limits for Chapter 13. Under the proposal, the "unsecured debts of less than $100,000 and noncontingent, liquidated, secured debts of less than $350,000" of current 11 U.S.C. § 109(e) would be changed to "debts of less than $1,000,000." This change would increase the number of sole proprietorships that would qualify for Chapter 13. See **Chapter 19** for a discussion of the advantages and disadvantages of Chapter 13 for small businesses.

It is, of course, impossible to know in advance what the House of Representatives will do regarding small business bankruptcies. Chapter 10 may or may not be dead but the fact remains that it was the centerpiece of small business bankruptcy reform proposals for several years. The major elements of the Chapter 10 proposal are set out in this chapter in the interest of broader understanding of the current legislation as it progresses.

§ 24.3 Features of Chapter 10

The three most important features of Chapter 10 were an accelerated timetable, Chapter 10 trustees, and the nonapplicability of the absolute priority rule.

---

2 *See generally* S. 1985, 102d Cong., 2d Sess. (1992).

3 S. Rep. No. 168 at 38.

4 *Id.* at 39.

5 Heflin Amendment No. 1638, 140 Cong. Rec. § 4543 (Apr. 20, 1994) (*cited in* Bill Tracking Report, S. 540 (Mead Data Central, Inc. 1994) [hereinafter Bill Tracking Report, S. 540]).

6 *See generally* S. 540 §§ 201, 223, 103d Cong., 2d Sess. (1994) [hereinafter S. 540 (1994)].

7 Bill Tracking Report, S. 540.

Accelerated timetable. The Senate Report to the original form of Senate Bill 540 stated,

> [T]his chapter attempts to expedite the bankruptcy process by establishing an accelerated time table. Full participation in the reorganization process by creditors is to be encouraged; however, on an historical basis, there is often creditor apathy in small business reorganization cases. In this chapter, apathy is addressed by expediting the process.[8]

"Expediting the process" was manifested at several points along the way in Chapter 10. The time for filing the plan was set at 90 days after filing, except that the court might extend or shorten the period for cause shown, after notice and hearing.[9] By contrast, in Chapter 11, the debtor has exclusive right to file a plan for 120 days after filing unless extended or shortened by the court. After that, however, any party-in-interest, including the debtor, may file a plan.[10] From the debtor's point of view, Chapter 10 balanced the early plan filing deadline by not providing that other parties may file a plan; the right to file a plan belonged exclusively to the debtor.

Chapter 10 took some steps toward simplifying the plan and disclosure statement process. As in Chapter 11, acceptance or rejection of a Chapter 10 plan could not have been solicited from creditors unless, at the time of or before the solicitation, there was transmitted to the creditor "a summary of the plan and a written disclosure statement that include[d] information sufficient to show whether or not the plan [met the statutory plan confirmation standards]."[11] In contrast to § 1125(b), Chapter 10 had no requirement of a separate hearing on the adequacy of the disclosure statement. It did, however, provide that a party-in-interest, the trustee, or the U.S. Trustee could object to the disclosure statement at the confirmation hearing.[12]

Like Chapters 11, 12, and 13, proposed Chapter 10 would have required that, after notice, the court would hold a hearing on confirmation of the plan and that a party-in-interest could object to confirmation of the plan. However, Chapter 10 would have required "expedited notice" and, "except for cause, the hearing [would have to] be concluded not later than 45 days after the filing of the plan."[13] These latter two provisions were modeled after Chapter 12.

Chapter 10 trustee. The report accompanying Senate Bill 1985 had the following to say about the proposed Chapter 10 trustee:

> [The proposal] provides for the appointment of a trustee to oversee the business of a debtor during the pendency of a case brought under this chapter. Such a trustee shall have very broad duties and authorities, and shall not only consider the desirability of

---

8 S. Rep. No. 168 at 43.

9 S. 540 § 201(c), 103d Cong., 1st Sess. (1993) (proposed § 1021) [hereinafter S. 540 (1993)].

10 11 U.S.C. § 1121(b), (c).

11 S. 540 (1993), § 201(c) (proposed § 1023(a)).

12 S. 540 (1993), § 201(c) (proposed § 1025(c)).

13 *Id.* (proposed § 1025(a), (d)).

> having a business successfully reorganize, but also must protect the rights of creditors of such debtors to ensure than debts are paid to the maximum extent feasible while maintaining the viability of the debtor.[14]

The duties assigned to the trustee by proposed Chapter 10 were modeled after the provisions of §§ 1202 and 1302, which deal with appointment and duties of trustees in Chapters 12 and 13, respectively. In addition, some new duties were enumerated, some necessitated by the fact that a debtor in Chapter 10 would be in business and some implementing other specific aspects of Chapter 10.[15]

Absolute priority rule. The most noteworthy difference between business reorganization under Chapter 11 and under proposed Chapter 10 would have been the non-applicability of the absolute priority rule to Chapter 10. The absolute priority rule does not apply to Chapters 12 and 13, either. Under Chapter 10, owners of a small business would not have been required to give up their ownership interests, even if unsecured creditors were not paid in full, so long as the owners completed a plan that complied with the confirmation requirements of the statute. Specifically, a plan could have been confirmed over the objection of an unsecured creditor that was to receive less than 100 percent of its claim so long as the plan provided that the owners would apply toward the plan all of their projected disposable income during the life of the plan.[16] This is what is known as the *best efforts test.* After completion of the plan, the owners would still be owners.

The absolute priority rule has been the subject of much scholarly and judicial attention, particularly in the small business context. See **Chapter 16.** Given the understandable reluctance of owners to reorganize unless they can retain ownership, relief from the absolute priority rule was perhaps the greatest benefit to small businesses offered by the original version of Senate Bill 540.

§ 24.4 Opposition to Chapter 10

Voices in opposition to proposed Chapter 10 for small businesses included the National Bankruptcy Conference and Senator Hatch. A statement by Senator Hatch appears in *Senate Report No. 168.*[17] He appends to his remarks the *Detailed Statement of Position of the National Bankruptcy Conference on S. 540.* The reservations of Senator Hatch and the National Bankruptcy Conference fall into four categories: (1) lack of uniformity of application, (2) increased complexity of the bankruptcy laws, (3) relaxation of creditor protections (including the absolute priority rule), and (4) Chapter 10 trustee.

---

14 S. Rep. No. 279, 103d Cong., 2d Sess. 32 (1992).

15 S. 540 (1993) § 201(c) (proposed § 1003).

16 *Id.* (proposed § 1026(b)(2)). Compare this proposed section with 11 U.S.C. §§ 1225(b)(1)(B) and 1325 (b)(1)(B).

17 It should be noted that Senator Hatch began his remarks by stating that he supported Senate Bill 540. S. Rep. No. 168 at 60.

Lack of uniformity of bankruptcy laws. Article 1, Section 8, Clause 4 of the United States Constitution requires Congress to enact uniform laws on the subject of bankruptcies. Chapter 10 was proposed to be implemented on a temporary basis in eight pilot districts.[18] Although the U.S. Trustee program was originally implemented on a pilot basis, its provisions were administrative; Chapter 10 was substantive. Opponents of proposed Chapter 10 felt that because it would not apply uniformly to the entire country, it was constitutionally infirm.

Increased complexity of bankruptcy laws. The passage of the Bankruptcy Code in 1978 unified the various reorganization chapters of the former Bankruptcy Act into a single Chapter 11. Senator Hatch stated, "While I support small business and believe [small businesses] should have a fair opportunity to reorganize, creating a separate bankruptcy chapter is not the most effective way to protect them. In my view it is unwise to experiment, especially when so much progress has been made since 1978."[19] The National Bankruptcy Conference *Statement of Position* states,

> [U]nder the Bankruptcy Act of 1898, debtors could reorganize under four reorganization chapters, section 77, chapter X, chapter XI, or chapter XII. One of the significant reforms of the 1978 Bankruptcy Code was to consolidate business reorganizations into a single chapter 11. In the collective experience of the 65 members of the National Bankruptcy Conference, chapter 11 has worked well.[20]

Relaxation of creditor protections. Several aspects of proposed Chapter 10 that would have relaxed creditor protections troubled Senator Hatch and the National Bankruptcy Conference. The Conference specifically objected to Chapter 10's lack of a disclosure statement hearing. Its *Statement of Position* pointed out disapprovingly that requiring that the determination of adequacy of disclosure be made at the confirmation hearing would permit solicitation even though disclosure might be inadequate and would permit false or misleading information to be circulated to parties-in-interest.[21]

The Conference also disapproved of the proposal's granting to the debtor the exclusive right to file a plan. It notes that "[i]t is anomalous (to say the least) for Congress . . . to be tightening exclusivity against family farmers and others while simultaneously creating exclusivity with no limits in proposed new chapter 10."[22] The tightening of exclusivity referred to was the provisions then contained in Senate Bill 540 (1993) §§ 102 and 103, which would have limited the time periods and availability of extensions in Chapters 11 and 12. Amended Senate Bill 540 contains only the provision applicable to Chapter 11.[23] The Conference further disapproved of

---

[18] S. 540 (1993) § 201(e).

[19] S. Rep. No. 168 at 60.

[20] *Id.* at 62 (citation omitted).

[21] *Id.*

[22] *Id.*

[23] S. 540 (1994) § 102 (proposed amendment to § 1121(d)).

the debtor's ability to request and obtain modifications of the plan without a vote of creditors and without complying with the protections governing confirmation of the plan.[24]

The most fundamental objection of the National Bankruptcy Conference and Senator Hatch had to do with the absolute priority rule. Both objected to the debtor's ability under proposed Chapter 10 to obtain confirmation, without a vote by unsecured creditors, of a plan proposing to pay unsecured creditors less than their claims but at the same time proposing that the debtor keep its ownership interest.[25]

Chapter 10 trustee. Senator Hatch was concerned about the fees that a Chapter 10 trustee could be awarded, in the form of a percentage of the distribution made to creditors under the plan. He stated,

> While this provision might work in a chapter 12 or 13 case respecting individuals or family farmers, it is unwise to impose this procedure on business creditors who have claims that might total $2.5 million. In addition, upon conversion of the case, the compensation of the trustee is not limited by reference to a percentage of the estate's assets. Thus, a court could award "reasonable" compensation that could deprive creditors from receiving any distribution.[26]

Senator Hatch and the National Bankruptcy Conference apparently were joined by others opposing the proposal because, as noted in **§ 24.2,** Chapter 10 was deleted from the version of Senate Bill 540 that was passed. The few remaining provisions regarding small business bankruptcies do not much resemble the provisions that were proposed as Chapter 10.

§ 24.5 Small Business Provisions in Amended Senate Bill 540

Amended Senate Bill 540 still contains Chapter 10's original definition of *small business* as "a person engaged in commercial or business activities (but . . . not includ[ing] a person whose primary activity is the business of owning or operating real property and activities incidental thereto) whose aggregate liquidated secured and unsecured debts as of the date of the petition do not exceed $2,500,000."[27]

---

24 S. Rep. No. 168 at 63. The statement of the National Bankruptcy Conference also complains of the lack of creditor voting on the plan and states that the court "may confirm a 'cram down' plan over the objection of unsecured creditors even if the plan pays creditors less than they would receive in chapter 7, so long as the debtor turns over all its projected disposal [sic] income for the next 3 to 5 years." This statement appears to have been incorrect; proposed § 1026(a)(4) required that to be confirmed, the plan had to provide for the payment on each unsecured claim of at least the amount that would be paid on the claim under Chapter 7. S. 540 (1993) § 201(c) (proposed § 1026(a)(4)).

25 S. Rep. No. 168 at 60, 62.

26 *Id.* at 60.

27 S. 540 (1994) § 201(a). The exclusion of ownership and operation of real property from the definition of small businss may have originally had the purpose of avoiding any

The provisions applicable to debtors who are small businesses are few. First, in cases in which the debtor is a small business, the committees of creditors would be appointed less frequently than § 1102(a) currently contemplates.[28] Second, in a small business case, the debtor has the exclusive right to file a plan for 90 days after filing, and all plans must be filed within 150 days after filing the case.[29] The court may, on request of a party-in-interest and after notice and a hearing, reduce the time period for cause or increase the 90-day exclusive time to file a plan if "the debtor shows that the need for an increase is caused by circumstances for which the debtor should not be held accountable." The bill does not indicate that the court has any discretion to increase the 150-day period, however.[30]

Another new provision for small business cases has to do with the disclosure statement and plan. In that provision, the court "may conditionally approve a disclosure statement subject to final approval after notice and a hearing." The conditionally approved disclosure statement may be used for soliciting acceptances and rejections of the plan, "so long as the debtor provides adequate information to each holder of a claim or interest that is solicited." A conditionally approved disclosure statement must be mailed at least 10 days before the plan confirmation hearing. Also, the hearing on the disclosure statement may be combined with the plan confirmation hearing.[31]

The only other provision that pertains to small businesses provides:

> [A plan may,] in a case in which the debtor is a small business, modify the rights of holders of secured claims, other than a claim secured only by a security interest in real property that is the debtor's principal residence . . . , but the plan may not modify a claim pursuant to section 506 of a person holding a primary or a junior security interest in real property or a manufactured home . . . that is the debtor's principal residence,

---

injustice that might have resulted from permitting real estate limited partnerships to escape the absolute priority rule currently codified at 11 U.S.C. § 1129(b) but not contained in proposed Chapter 10. See **§ 24.3.** Real estate limited partnerships account for a large number of the recent cases in which the debtor has sought to avoid the absolute priority rule by invoking the new value exception. See **Ch. 16.** In real estate limited partnerships, the owners are passive investors, much like owners of mutual fund shares, and this definition in proposed Chapter 10 would have prevented them from avoiding the operation of the absoulute priority rule. The retention of this exception to the definition of small businesses, in light of the deletion of Chapter 10, is an anomaly that may be eliminated in future revision. It serves little or no purpose; indeed it may conflict with § 202 of amended Senate Bill 540 (1994), which sets out an expedited procedure for relief from the automatic stay in single-asset real estate cases. S. 540 (1994) § 202(b) (proposed amendment to § 362). It is not clear why single-asset real estate businesses should be exempted from the small business provisions in general (which contain significant acceleration of time limits), when those businesses are subject to accelerated relief-from-stay procedures.

28 S. 540 (1994) § 201(b) (proposed amendment to § 1102(a)).

29 *Id.* § 201(d) (proposed amendment to § 1121). Currently the debtor has the exclusive right to file a plan for 120 days, and, after that, any party-in-interest may file a plan until 180 days after filing. 11 U.S.C. § 1121(b), (c).

30 *Id.* Bankruptcy Code § 1121(d) gives the court the power to reduce or increase the 120-day period or the 180-day period.

31 S. 540 (1994) § 201(e) (proposed amendment to § 1125). Currently in Chapter 11, the disclosure statement and plan confirmation processes are considerably more complicated than this. See **Chs. 13** and **16.**

except that the plan may modify the claim of a person holding such a junior security interest that was undersecured at the time the interest attached to the extent that the interest remains undersecured.[32]

§ 24.6 Observations on the Small Business Provisions

Whatever balance there was in proposed Chapter 10 between the interests of the debtor and the interests of creditors has been removed from the small business provisions in amended Senate Bill 540. Chapter 10 was originally conceived as a way to make it easier for small businesses in trouble to reorganize and benefit the economy by their continued existence. Ironically, however, a small business going into bankruptcy under the bill as it now stands would be worse off than a large business filing under Chapter 11. Small businesses would be required to file a plan in a much shorter time than large businesses. This might be more of a hardship than a benefit to the debtor small business.

Also, under this bill, a small business owner whose residence is encumbered would not be able to bifurcate the lien and pay only the fair market value of the residence to the secured creditor. This leaves the individual small business Chapter 11 debtor in a less favorable position than an individual, wealthy enough to have higher debts, who files a consumer or business Chapter 11 proceeding, in which there is no such restriction.

Chapters 12 and 13 have restrictions similar to these, but under those chapters, the debtor receives something very valuable to balance the relative disadvantages. In Chapters 12 and 13 cases, debtors are exempt from the absolute priority rule. Small businesses would not be eligible for that benefit now that Chapter 10 has been dropped from amended Senate Bill 540. Without exemption from the absolute priority rule, the fast-track scheduling and other provisions would place burdens on small business debtors that are not placed on similar debtors in Chapter 12 or 13 or even on debtors in larger individual Chapter 11 reorganizations.

The small business provisions are mandatory as currently written.[33] They probably need to be mandatory because, in light of the imbalance of detriments and benefits, it is unlikely that many debtors would elect to file as a small business under this bill.

---

32 *Id.* § 223 (proposed amendment to § 1123(b). The bill also amends Chapter 13 in this manner. S. 540 (1994) § 307 (proposed § 1322(b)(2)). When this section was originally included in Senate Bill 1985, the case law was unsettled regarding the ability of the debtor to bifurcate a home mortgage into a secured portion and an unsecured portion, paying the secured creditor only the value of the secured portion. Since then, in June 1993, the Supreme Court resolved the matter, at least for Chapter 13 cases, in *Nobleman v. American Sav. Bank (In re Nobleman),* 508 U.S. ___, 124 L. Ed. 2d 228, 113 S. Ct. ___ (1993), which held that § 1322(b)(2) prohibits the use of § 506(a) to bifurcate a home mortgage.

33 The Bill Digest from the Congressional Research Service (*available in* LEXIS, Legis Library, appended to Bill Tracking Report, S. 540 (1994)) says, "[Section 201] establishes the legal parameters under which a business debtor (or a party in interest) may elect to convert the case to expedited bankruptcy proceedings customized to small businesses." This is not accurate, at least regarding the bill as it was passed by the Senate. In amended Senate Bill 540, simply by virtue of fitting the definition of small business, the debtor is subject to the provisions that are applicable to "a debtor that is a small business," whether he likes it or not.

TABLE OF CASES

Case	*Book §*
Abbotts Dairies of Pa., Inc., *In re,* 788 F.2d 143 (3d Cir. 1986)	§§ 9.5, 9.8
Aberegg, *In re,* 121 B.R. 553 (N.D. Ind. 1990)	§ 19.4
ABN Amro Bank N.V. v. Carmania Corp. N.V. (*In re* Carmania Corp. N.V.), 154 B.R. 160 (S.D.N.Y. 1993)	§ 3.8
Adams, *In re,* 2 B.R. 313 (Bankr. M.D. Fla. 1980)	§ 3.10
Adams Apple, Inc., *In re,* 829 F.2d 1484 (9th Cir. 1987)	§§ 6.12, 6.26
Adams Delivery Serv., Inc., *In re,* 24 B.R. 589 (Bankr. 9th Cir. 1982)	§ 23.12
Advanced Elecs., Inc., *In re,* 108 B.R. 53 (Bankr. M.D. Pa. 1989)	§ 7.8
Advanced Ribbons & Office Prods., Inc., *In re,* 125 B.R. 259 (Bankr. 9th Cir. 1991)	§ 5.3
Advisory Info. & Management Sys., Inc., *In re,* 50 B.R. 627 (Bankr. M.D. Tenn. 1985)	§ 3.10
Aerco Metals, Inc., *In re,* 60 B.R. 77 (Bankr. N.D. Tex. 1985)	§ 12.21
After Six, Inc., *In re,* 154 B.R. 876 (Bankr. E.D. Pa. 1993)	§ 9.4
Ag Consultants Grain Div., Inc., *In re,* 77 B.R. 665 (Bankr. N.D. Ind. 1987)	§ 16.8
Agricultural Research & Technology Group, Inc., *In re,* 916 F.2d 528 (9th Cir. 1990)	§ 12.7
A.H. Robins Co., *In re,* 880 F.2d 694 (4th Cir.), *cert. denied,* 493 U.S. 959 (1989)	§ 23.16
A.H. Robins Co. v. Piccinin, 788 F.2d 994 (4th Cir.), *cert. denied,* 479 U.S. 876 (1986)	§ 5.3
Ahlers v. Norwest Bank (*In re* Ahlers), 794 F.2d 388 (8th Cir. 1986), *cert. granted in part sub nom.* Norwest Bank Worthington v. Ahlers, 483 U.S. 1004 (1987), *rev'd on other grounds,* 485 U.S. 197 (1988)	§§ 3.10, 5.8, 14.4
Airlift Int'l, Inc., *In re,* 761 F.2d 1503 (11th Cir. 1985)	§§ 7.1, 7.17
Airlines Reporting v. Charrington, 922 F.2d 847 (11th Cir. 1990)	§ 7.13
Airport Inn Assocs. v. Travelers Ins. Co. (*In re* Airport Inn Assocs.), 132 B.R. 951 (Bankr. D. Colo. 1990)	§ 4.6
A.J. Lane & Co., *In re,* 133 B.R. 264 (Bankr. D. Mass. 1991)	§§ 10.7, 10.8, 10.9, 10.10
Albany Partners, Ltd., *In re,* 749 F.2d 670 (11th Cir. 1984)	§§ 5.6, 8.6
Albrechts Ohio Inns, Inc., *In re,* 152 B.R. 496 (Bankr. S.D. Ohio 1993)	§ 16.4
Allegheny Int'l, Inc., *In re,* 93 B.R. 903 (Bankr. W.D. Pa. 1988)	§ 12.30

Case	*Book §*
Alpco, Inc., *In re,* 62 B.R. 184 (Bankr. S.D. Ohio 1986)	§ 12.29
Alten, *In re,* 108 B.R. 16 (Bankr. D.R.I. 1989)	§ 5.3
Alyucan Interstate Corp., *In re,* 12 B.R. 803 (Bankr. D. Utah 1981)	§ 11.5
Amato v. Bernard, 618 F.2d 559 (9th Cir. 1980)	§ 21.3
American Continental Corp., *In re,* 105 B.R. 564 (Bankr. D. Ariz. 1989)	§ 3.8
American Nat'l Bank v. MortgageAmerica Corp. (*In re* MortgageAmerica Corp.), 714 F.2d 1266 (5th Cir. 1983)	§ 12.8
American Sav. & Loan Ass'n v. Weber (*In re* Weber), 99 B.R. 1001 (Bankr. D. Utah 1989)	§ 3.13
American Universal Ins. Co. v. Pugh, 821 F.2d 1352 (9th Cir. 1987)	§ 23.15
Ames Dep't Stores, Inc., *In re,* 150 B.R. 107 (Bankr. S.D.N.Y. 1993)	§ 7.5
Ames Dep't Stores, Inc., *In re,* 115 B.R. 34 (Bankr. S.D.N.Y. 1990)	§§ 6.4, 6.19, 6.20, 6.23, 6.25
AMT Inv. Corp., *In re,* 53 B.R. 274 (Bankr. E.D. Va. 1985)	§ 3.10
Anchor Sav. Bank FSB v. Sky Valley, Inc., 99 B.R. 117 (N.D. Ga. 1989)	§ 6.7
Anchorage Boat Sales, *In re,* 4 B.R. 635 (Bankr. E.D.N.Y. 1980)	§ 3.13
Ancor Exploration Co., *In re,* 30 B.R. 802 (N.D. Okla. 1983)	§ 9.5
Anderson, *In re,* 913 F.2d 530 (8th Cir. 1990)	§ 5.9
Anderson v. Bessemer City, 470 U.S. 564 (1985)	§ 6.6
Anderson Oaks (Phase I), Ltd. Partnership, *In re,* 77 B.R. 108 (Bankr. W.D. Tex. 1987)	§ 15.10
A-1 Hydro Mechanics Corp., *In re,* 92 B.R. 451 (Bankr. D. Haw. 1988)	§ 12.29
AOV Indus., Inc., *In re,* 792 F.2d 1140 (D.C. Cir. 1986)	§ 9.6
APC Constr., Inc., *In re,* 112 B.R. 89 (Bankr. D. Vt. 1990), *aff'd,* 132 B.R. 690 (D. Vt. 1991)	§ 12.10
Apple Tree Partners, *In re,* 131 B.R. 380 (Bankr. W.D. Tenn. 1991)	§ 15.10
Aqua Assocs., *In re,* 123 B.R. 192 (Bankr. E.D. Pa. 1991)	§§ 6.10, 6.19
Arizona Appetito's Stores, Inc., *In re,* 893 F.2d 216 (9th Cir. 1990)	§ 7.6
Arnette, *In re,* 156 B.R. 366 (Bankr. D. Conn. 1993)	§ 11.25
Arriens, *In re,* 25 B.R. 79 (Bankr. D. Or. 1982)	§ 4.10
Art Shirt Ltd., *In re,* 93 B.R. 333 (E.D. Pa. 1988)	§§ 11.13, 11.34
Ascher, *In re,* 146 B.R. 764 (Bankr. N.D. Ill. 1992)	§§ 11.6, 11.24
Ashkenazy Enter., *In re,* 94 B.R. 645 (Bankr. C.D. Cal. 1986)	§§ 4.6, 4.7
Ashland Oil, Inc. v. Arnett, 875 F.2d 1271 (7th Cir. 1989)	§ 12.8
Association of St. Croix Condominium Owners v. St. Croix Hotel Corp., 682 F.2d 446 (3d Cir. 1982)	§ 5.1
AT of Me., Inc., *In re,* 56 B.R. 55 (Bankr. D. Me. 1985)	§ 17.7

Case	*Book §*
Atlantic Business & Community Corp., *In re,* 901 F.2d 325 (3d Cir. 1990)	§ 5.3
Auto Dealers Servs., Inc., *In re,* 89 B.R. 233 (Bankr. M.D. Fla. 1988)	§ 17.4
Aztec Co., *In re,* 107 B.R. 585 (Bankr. M.D. Tenn. 1989)	§§ 16.4, 16.8
Backhus v. Central Trust Co., N.A. (*In re* Duccilli Formal Wear, Inc.), 8 Bankr. Ct. Dec. (CRR) 1180 (Bankr. S.D. Ohio 1982)	§ 12.21
Bakst v. Schilling (*In re* Cove Patio Corp.), 19 B.R. 843 (Bankr. S.D. Fla. 1982)	§ 12.21
Balbus, *In re,* 933 F.2d 246 (4th Cir. 1991)	§ 11.18
Ballard, *In re,* 4 B.R. 271 (Bankr. E.D. Va. 1980)	§ 19.3
Bank Hapoalim B.M. v. E.L.I., Ltd., *In re,* 42 B.R. 376 (N.D. Ill. 1984)	§ 3.10
Bank of Edwardsville v. J.D. Monarch Dev. Co. (*In re* J.D. Monarch Dev. Co.), 153 B.R. 829 (Bankr. S.D. Ill. 1993)	§ 3.8
Bank of Maui v. Estate Analysis, Inc., 904 F.2d 470 (9th Cir. 1990)	§ 23.22
Bank of New England v. SWL, Inc., 121 B.R. 413, (D. Me. 1990)	§ 6.6
Barker Medical Co., *In re,* 55 B.R. 435 (Bankr. M.D. Ala. 1985)	§ 17.2
Barnhill v. Johnson, 112 S. Ct. 1386 (1992)	§ 12.15
Bartley Lindsay Co., *In re,* 120 B.R. 507 (Bankr. D. Minn. 1990), *aff'd,* 137 B.R. 305 (D. Minn. 1991)	§ 2.2
Bass Mechanical Contractors, Inc., *In re,* 84 B.R. 1009 (Bankr. W.D. Ark. 1988)	§ 12.28
Bathlater, *In re,* 123 B.R. 568 (Bankr. S.D. Ohio 1990), *aff'd,* 951 F.2d 349 (6th Cir. 1991)	§ 23.22
Batten, *In re,* 141 B.R. 899 (Bankr. W.D. La. 1992)	§§ 16.6, 16.8
Baxter Healthcare Corp. v. Hemex Liquidation Trust, 132 B.R. 863 (Bankr. N.D. Ill. 1991)	§ 23.12
Beacon Hill Apartments, Ltd., *In re,* 118 B.R. 148 (N.D. Ga. 1990)	§ 11.18
Bedford Springs Hotel, Inc., *In re,* 99 B.R. 302 (Bankr. W.D. Pa. 1989)	§ 17.4
Begier v. IRS, 496 U.S. 53 (1990)	§ 12.15
Beker Indus. Corp., *In re,* 58 B.R. 725 (Bankr. S.D.N.Y. 1986)	§§ 6.6, 6.9, 6.11, 6.19
Belisle v. Plunkett, 876 F.2d 512 (7th Cir. 1989)	§ 12.8
Bellanca Aircraft Corp., *In re,* 56 B.R. 339 (Bankr. D. Minn. 1985), *aff'd in part, remanded in part,* 850 F.2d 1275 (8th Cir. 1988)	§§ 11.13, 11.19, 11.28, 11.30, 12.5
Ben Cooper, Inc., *In re,* 896 F.2d 1394 (2d Cir.), *vacated & remanded,* 498 U.S. 964 (1990), *reinstated,* 924 F.2d 36 (2d Cir.), *cert. denied,* ____ U.S. ____, 111 S. Ct. 2041 (1991)	§ 23.15

Case	*Book §*
Benjamin Coal Co., *In re,* 978 F.2d 823 (3d Cir. 1992)	§ 17.1
Bentley, *In re,* 916 F.2d 431 (8th Cir. 1990), *aff'g* 89 U.S. Tax Cas. (CCH) ¶ 9597 (N.D. Iowa 1989), *rev'g* 79 B.R. 413 (Bankr. S.D. Iowa 1987)	§ 10.5
Bergquist v. Anderson-Greenwood Aviation Corp. (*In re* Bellanca Aircraft Corp.), 850 F.2d 1275 (8th Cir. 1988)	§ 12.5
Bernhardy, *In re,* 103 B.R. 198 (Bankr. N.D. Ill. 1989)	§ 2.25
Best Prods. Co., Inc., *In re,* 138 B.R. 155 (Bankr. S.D.N.Y. 1992)	§ 3.10
Bethesda Air Rights Ltd., *In re,* 117 B.R. 202 (Bankr. D. Md. 1990)	§ 4.5
BFP v. Imperial Sav. & Loan Ass'n (*In re* BFP), 974 F.2d 1144 (9th Cir. 1992)	§ 12.25
BGNX, Inc., *In re,* 75 B.R. 44 (Bankr. S.D. Fla. 1987)	§ 12.24
Bird v. Plains State Bank, 86 B.R. 660 (D. Kan. 1988)	§ 4.2
Bishop, *In re,* 74 B.R. 677 (Bankr. M.D. Ga. 1987)	§ 17.5
Bittner v. Borne Chem. Co., 691 F.2d 134 (3d Cir. 1982)	§ 11.35
Bjolmes Realty Trust, *In re,* 134 B.R. 1000 (Bankr. D. Mass. 1991)	§ 16.1, 16.2, 16.4, 16.8, 16.9
B-K of Kan., Inc., *In re,* 69 B.R. 812 (Bankr. D. Kan. 1987)	§ 5.8
B&L Oil Co., *In re,* 782 F.2d 155 (10th Cir. 1986)	§ 12.29
Blackford Farms, Inc., *In re,* 68 B.R. 639 (Bankr. N.D. Iowa 1986)	§ 3.10
Bloom, *In re,* 875 F.2d 224 (9th Cir. 1989)	§ 5.5
B.M. Brite v. Sun Country Dev., Inc. (*In re* Sun Country Dev., Inc.), 764 F.2d 406 (5th Cir. 1985)	§§ 15.8, 15.15
Board of County Comm'rs v. Coleman Am. Properties, Inc. (*In re* Coleman Am. Properties, Inc.), 30 B.R. 239 (Bankr. D. Kan. 1983)	§ 15.23
Bonner Mall Partnership v. U.S. Bancorp Mortgage Co. (*In re* Bonner Mall Partnership), 2 F.3d 899 (9th Cir. 1993), *cert. granted,* ____ U.S. ____, 126 L. Ed. 2d 648, *removed from argument calendar,* ____ U.S. ____, 114 S. Ct. 1367 (1994)	§§ 11.31, 14.4, 16.1, 16.2, 16.3, 16.9
Borg-Warner Acceptance Corp. v. Hall, 685 F.2d 1306 (11th Cir. 1982)	§ 5.2
Boricua Motor Corp. v. Tamachi, Inc., 76 B.R. 891 (Bankr. D.P.R. 1987)	§ 23.7
Borman v. Raymark Indus., Inc., 946 F.2d 1031 (3d Cir. 1991)	§ 5.1
Bowen Corp. v. Security Pac. Bank Idaho, FSB, 150 B.R. 777 (Bankr. D. Idaho 1993)	§ 23.9
Bradley, *In re,* 705 F.2d 1409 (5th Cir. 1983)	§ 19.4
Bradshaw, *In re,* 912 F.2d 1255 (10th Cir. 1990)	§ 20.5
Brady Mun. Gas Corp., *In re,* 936 F.2d 212 (5th Cir.), *cert. denied sub nom.* Sanders v. City of Brady, ____ U.S. ____, 112 S. Ct. 657 (1991)	§ 5.4

Case	*Book §*
Braniff Airways, Inc., *In re,* 700 F.2d 935 (5th Cir. 1983)	§§ 9.5, 22.6
Braniff, Inc., *In re,* 113 B.R. 745 (Bankr. M.D. Fla. 1990)	§ 8.3
Braniff, Inc., *In re,* 118 B.R. 819 (Bankr. M.D. Fla. 1989)	§§ 7.7, 7.15
Brantz, *In re,* 106 B.R. 62 (Bankr. E.D. Pa. 1989)	§ 12.24
Briggs v. Kent (*In re* Professional Inv. Properties of Am.), 955 F.2d 623 (9th Cir. 1992)	§ 12.7
Briggs Transp. Co., *In re,* 780 F.2d 1339 (8th Cir. 1985)	§ 5.8
Briggs Transp. Co., *In re,* 47 B.R. 6 (Bankr. D. Minn. 1984)	§ 3.10
Brints Cotton Mktg., Inc., *In re,* 737 F.2d 1338 (5th Cir. 1984)	§ 11.35
Briscoe Enters., *In re,* 994 F.2d 1160 (5th Cir. 1993)	§ 11.8
Broadmoor Place Inv., *In re,* 994 F.2d 744 (10th Cir. 1993)	§ 9.4
Brock v. Rusco Indus., Inc., 842 F.2d 270 (11th Cir.), *cert. denied,* 488 U.S. 889 (1988)	§ 5.3
Brookfield Clothes, Inc., *In re,* 31 B.R. 978 (S.D.N.Y. 1983)	§ 9.3
Brookfield Prod. Credit Ass'n v. Borron, 36 B.R. 445 (E.D. Mo. 1983), *aff'd,* 738 F.2d 951 (8th Cir. 1984)	§ 3.10
Broomall Printing Corp., *In re,* 131 B.R. 32 (Bankr. D. Md. 1991)	§ 3.10
Brown v. Armstrong, 949 F.2d 1007 (8th Cir. 1991)	§ 5.3
Brown v. O'Keefe, 300 U.S. 598 (1937)	§§ 10.5, 10.6
Browning v. Navarro, 743 F.2d 1069 (5th Cir. 1984), *reh'g denied,* 830 F.2d 1126 (5th Cir. 1987)	§ 5.4
Browning Seed, Inc. v. Bayles, 812 F.2d 999 (5th Cir. 1987)	§ 5.3
Bumper Sales, Inc., *In re,* 907 F.2d 1430 (4th Cir. 1990)	§ 3.10
Bundles, *In re,* 856 F.2d 815 (7th Cir. 1988)	§ 12.25
Burden v. United States, 917 F.2d 115 (3d Cir. 1990)	§ 12.6
Burgess, *In re,* 51 B.R. 300 (Bankr. S.D. Ohio 1985)	§ 23.9
Burns, *In re,* 894 F.2d 361 (10th Cir. 1990)	§ 2.25
Burpo, *In re,* 148 B.R. 918 (Bankr. W.D. Mo. 1993)	§§ 10.7, 10.10
Busy Beaver Bldg. Ctrs., Inc., *In re,* 133 B.R. 753 (Bankr. W.D. Pa. 1992)	§ 2.20
Butler, *In re,* 51 B.R. 261 (Bankr. D.D.C. 1984)	§ 10.6
Butler Aviation Int'l, Inc. v. Whyte (*In re* Fairchild Aircraft Corp.), 6 F.3d 1119 (5th Cir. 1993)	§ 12.27
Butner v. United States, 440 U.S. 48 (1979)	§§ 3.6, 4.4
Butterfield, Ltd. Partnership, *In re,* 131 B.R. 67 (Bankr. E.D. Mich. 1990)	§ 2.3
Buttonwood Partners, Ltd., *In re,* 111 B.R. 57 (Bankr. S.D.N.Y. 1990)	§ 15.14
By-Rite Distribution, Inc., *In re,* 55 B.R. 740 (D. Utah 1985)	§ 7.8
Calder, *In re,* 907 F.2d 953 (10th Cir. 1990)	§ 5.2
Callister, *In re,* 15 B.R. 521 (Bankr. D. Utah 1981)	§ 3.10
Canal Place, Ltd., *In re,* 921 F.2d 569 (5th Cir. 1991)	§ 5.9
Capital Ctr. Equities, *In re,* 144 B.R. 262 (Bankr. E.D. Pa. 1992)	§§ 16.1, 16.7
Capitol Bank & Trust Co. v. 604 Columbus Ave. Realty Trust (*In re* 604 Columbus Ave. Realty Trust), 968 F.2d 1332 (1st Cir. 1992)	§ 12.5

Case	*Book §*
Cardinal Export Corp., *In re,* 30 B.R. 682 (Bankr. E.D.N.Y. 1983)	§ 7.5
Cardinal Indus., Inc., *In re,* 116 B.R. 964 (Bankr. S.D. Ohio 1990)	§§ 5.7, 7.15, 22.5, 22.7
Cardinal Indus., Inc., *In re,* 109 B.R. 748 (Bankr. S.D. Ohio 1989)	§ 5.1
Carley Capital Group v. Fireman's Fund Ins. Co., 889 F.2d 1126 (D.C. Cir. 1989)	§ 5.3
Carlisle Homes, Inc., *In re,* 103 B.R. 524 (Bankr. D.N.J. 1988)	§§ 7.13, 7.15
Carlson v. W.J. Menefree Constr. Co. (*In re* Grassridge Indus.), 78 B.R. 978 (Bankr. W.D. Mo. 1987)	§ 4.13
Carolina Parachute Corp., *In re,* 108 B.R. 100 (N.D.N.C. 1989), *aff'd in part, vacated in part sub nom.* Department of Air Force v. Carolina Parachute Corp., 907 F.2d 1469 (4th Cir. 1990)	§§ 5.4, 7.15
Carpenter, *In re,* 14 B.R. 405 (Bankr. M.D. Tenn. 1981)	§ 3.7
Carron, *In re,* 50 B.R. 27 (Bankr. N.D. Ga. 1984)	§§ 10.4, 10.6
Carson Nuggett, Inc. v. Green (*In re* Green), 98 B.R. 981 (Bankr. 9th Cir. 1989)	§ 16.6
Carver v. Carver, 954 F.2d 1573 (11th Cir.), *cert. denied,* ____ U.S. ____, 113 S. Ct. 496 (1992)	§ 5.3
Casa Loma Assoc., *In re,* 122 B.R. 814 (Bankr. N.D. Ga. 1991)	§ 17.7
Casbeer v. State Fed. Sav. & Loan Ass'n (*In re* Casbeer), 793 F.2d 1436 (5th Cir. 1986)	§§ 3.8, 12.7
Cascade Oil Co., *In re,* 126 B.R. 99 (D. Kan. 1991)	§ 2.21
Case v. Los Angeles Lumber Prods. Co., 308 U.S. 106 (1939)	§§ 14.4, 16.1, 16.3, 16.4, 16.6, 16.8, 16.10
Castlerock Properties, *In re,* 781 F.2d 159 (Bankr. 9th Cir. 1986)	§ 23.6
Cavalieri, *In re,* 142 B.R. 710 (Bankr. E.D. Pa. 1992)	§ 9.6
CCDC Fin. Corp., *In re,* 143 B.R. 946 (D. Kan. 1992)	§ 5.3
Celco, Inc. v. Davis Van Lines, Inc., 226 Kan. 366, 598 P.2d 188 (1979)	§ 20.3
Cena's Fine Furniture, *In re,* 109 B.R. 575 (E.D.N.Y. 1990)	§ 2.20
Center Wholesale, Inc., *In re,* 759 F.2d 1440 (9th Cir. 1985)	§ 12.7
Centerre Bank Nat'l Ass'n v. Continental Marine Corp. (*In re* Continental Marine Corp.), 35 B.R. 990 (Bankr. E.D. Mo. 1984)	§ 3.13
Central Trust Co. v. Official Creditors' Comm., 454 U.S. 354 (1982)	§ 17.5
Centre of Mo., Ltd., *In re,* 116 B.R. 138 (Bankr. E.D. Mo. 1990)	§ 4.5
Century Brass Prod., Inc., *In re,* 127 B.R. 720 (Bankr. D. Conn. 1991)	§ 12.33
Century Steel, Inc., *In re,* 56 B.R. 268 (Bankr. M.D. La. 1985)	§ 9.6
CGR, Ltd., *In re,* 56 B.R. 305 (Bankr. S.D. Tex. 1985)	§ 5.7

Case	*Book §*
Chambers, *In re,* 125 B.R. 788 (Bankr. W.D. Mo. 1991)	§ 23.5
Chandler, *In re,* 148 B.R. 13 (Bankr. E.D.N.C. 1992)	§ 19.2
Channel One Communications, Inc., *In re,* 125 B.R. 234 (Bankr. E.D. Mo. 1991)	§ 12.6
Chapman, *In re,* 132 B.R. 153 (Bankr. N.D. Ill. 1991)	§ 23.10
Chapman, *In re,* 135 B.R. 11 (Bankr. M.D. Pa. 1990)	§ 11.25
Chapman Inv. Assocs. v. American Healthcare Management, Inc. (*In re* American Healthcare Management, Inc.), 900 F.2d 827 (5th Cir. 1990)	§ 7.8
Charrington Worldwide Enter., Inc., *In re,* 110 B.R. 973 (M.D. Fla.), *remanded sub nom.* Airlines Reporting v. Charrington, 922 F.2d 847 (11th Cir. 1990)	§ 7.13
Charterhouse, Inc., *In re,* 84 B.R. 147 (Bankr. D. Minn. 1988)	§ 17.4
Chase & Sanborn Corp., *In re,* 835 F.2d 1341 (11th Cir.), *cert. granted sub nom.* Granfinanciera, S.A. v. Nordberg, 486 U.S. 1054 (1988), *rev'd,* 492 U.S. 33 (1989)	§ 23.15
Chateaugay Corp., *In re,* 920 F.2d 183 (2d Cir. 1990)	§ 5.5
Chateaugay Corp., *In re,* 880 F.2d 1509 (2d Cir. 1989)	§ 23.22
Chateaugay Corp., *In re,* 112 B.R. 335 (Bankr. S.D.N.Y. 1989)	§ 7.3
Chattanooga Wholesale Antiques, Inc., *In re,* 930 F.2d 458 (6th Cir. 1991)	§ 12.34
Chbat v. Tleel (*In re* Tleel), 876 F.2d 769 (9th Cir. 1989)	§ 12.8
Chevy Devco, *In re,* 78 B.R. 585 (Bankr. C.D. Cal. 1987)	§ 6.8
Chicago Florsheim Shoe Co. v. Cluett, Peabody & Co., 826 F.2d 725 (7th Cir. 1987)	§ 12.8
Chicago, Milwaukee, St. P. & Pac. R.R., *In re,* 799 F.2d 317 (7th Cir. 1986), *cert. denied,* 481 U.S. 1068 (1987)	§ 6.12
Chicago, Mo. & W. Ry., *In re,* 124 B.R. 769 (Bankr. N.D. Ill. 1991)	§ 12.27
Child World, Inc., *In re,* 161 B.R. 571 (S.D.N.Y. 1993)	§ 7.5
Childworld, *In re,* 142 B.R. 87 (Bankr. S.D.N.Y. 1992)	§ 6.4
Chipwich, Inc., *In re,* 54 B.R. 427 (Bankr. S.D.N.Y. 1985)	§ 6.4
Chorus Data Sys., Inc., *In re,* 122 B.R. 845 (Bankr. D.N.H. 1990)	§ 7.16
Cinematronics, Inc., *In re,* 916 F.2d 1444 (9th Cir. 1990)	§ 23.3
Cissell v. First Nat'l Bank, 476 F. Supp. 474 (S.D. Ohio 1979)	§ 11.2, 11.11, 11.12
Citibank, N.A. v. Phoenix Resources Co., 454 U.S. 881 (1981)	§ 2.1
City Nat'l Bank v. General Coffee Corp., 828 F.2d 699 (11th Cir. 1987)	§ 12.8
Clark, *In re,* 91 B.R. 324 (Bankr. E.D. Pa. 1988)	§ 19.3
CLC of Am., Inc., *In re,* 68 B.R. 512 (Bankr. E.D. Mo. 1986)	§ 8.9
Club Assocs., *In re,* 107 B.R. 385 (Bankr. N.D. Ga. 1989)	§ 15.10
Club Dev. & Management Corp., *In re,* 27 B.R. 610 (Bankr. 9th Cir. 1982)	§ 6.3
Coastal Dry Dock & Repair Corp., *In re,* 62 B.R. 879 (Bankr. E.D.N.Y. 1986)	§ 7.5

Case	*Book §*
Coastal Equities, Inc., *In re,* 39 B.R. 304 (Bankr. S.D. Cal. 1984)	§ 2.20
Coastal Indus., Inc., *In re,* 58 B.R. 48 (Bankr. D.N.J. 1986)	§ 7.8
Coastal Petroleum Corp. v. Union Bank & Trust Co. (*In re* Coastal Petroleum Corp.), 91 B.R. 35 (Bankr. N.D. Ohio 1988)	§ 12.21
Coated Sales, Inc., *In re,* 144 B.R. 663 (Bankr. S.D.N.Y. 1992)	§ 11.12, 11.13, 11.24, 11.30, 11.32
Coby, *In re,* 109 B.R. 963 (Bankr. D. Nev. 1990)	§ 11.25
Cochran, *In re,* 141 B.R. 270 (M.D. Ga. 1992)	§ 19.2
Coffman, *In re,* 104 B.R. 958 (Bankr. S.D. Ind. 1988)	§ 7.2
Cohen v. Beneficial Indus. Loan Corp., 337 U.S. 541 (1949)	§ 23.22
Cokkinias, *In re,* 28 B.R. 304 (Bankr. D. Mass. 1983)	§ 2.25
Collins v. Environmental Sys. Co., No. 92-3519, 1993 WL 302863 (8th Cir. 1993)	§ 12.24
Columbus One Parcel Serv., Inc., *In re,* 138 B.R. 194 (Bankr. S.D. Ohio 1992)	§ 7.8
Commerce Bank of K.C., N.A. v. Achtenberg, No. 90-0950-CV-W-6, 1993 WL 476510 (W.D. Mo. Nov. 10, 1993)	§ 12.27
Commercial Consortium, *In re,* 135 B.R. 120 (Bankr. C.D. Cal. 1991)	§ 2.18
Commissioner v. Tufts, 461 U.S. 300 (1983)	§ 10.5
Commonwealth Cos., *In re,* 913 F.2d 518 (8th Cir. 1990)	§ 5.3
Commonwealth Mortgage Co., *In re,* 149 B.R. 4 (Bankr. D. Mass. 1992)	§ 7.15
Conroe Forge & Mfg. Corp., *In re,* 82 B.R. 781 (Bankr. W.D. Pa. 1988)	§ 9.5
Consolidated Motor Inns, *In re,* 666 F.2d 189 (5th Cir. 1982)	§ 17.3
Consolidated Rock Prods. Co. v. DuBois, 312 U.S. 510 (1941)	§§ 11.31, 16.10
Conston Corp., *In re,* 130 B.R. 449 (Bankr. E.D. Pa. 1991)	§ 7.18
Contemporary Lithographers, Inc., *In re,* 127 B.R. 122 (Bankr. M.D.N.C. 1991)	§ 23.7
Continental Airlines, Inc., *In re,* 780 F.2d 1223 (5th Cir. 1986)	§§ 7.7, 9.8
Continental Country Club, Inc., *In re,* 114 B.R. 73 (Bankr. M.D. Fla. 1970)	§ 7.11
Coonrod, *In re,* 135 B.R. 375 (Bankr. D. Neb. 1991)	§ 19.4
Cooper-Jarrett, Inc. v. Central Transp., Inc., 726 F.2d 93 (3d Cir. 1984)	§ 12.28
Coors of N. Miss., Inc., *In re,* 27 B.R. 918 (Bankr. N.D. Miss. 1983)	§ 7.13
Corey, *In re,* 892 F.2d 829 (9th Cir. 1989)	§ 11.35
Corland Corp., *In re,* 967 F.2d 1069 (5th Cir. 1992)	§ 5.2
Corpus Christi Hotel Partners, *In re,* 133 B.R. 850 (Bankr. S.D. Tex. 1991)	§§ 4.6, 4.8
Cossett, *In re,* 75 B.R. 766 (Bankr. S.D. Ohio 1987)	§ 23.5
Counts, *In re,* 54 B.R. 730 (Bankr. D. Colo. 1985)	§ 23.10
CPM Constr., *In re,* 124 B.R. 335 (Bankr. D.N.M. 1991)	§§ 16.6, 16.7, 16.8

Case	*Book §*
Craddock-Terry Shoe Corp., *In re,* 91 B.R. 392 (Bankr. W.D. Va. 1988)	§ 12.28
Credit Alliance Corp. v. Williams, 851 F.2d 119 (4th Cir. 1988)	§ 5.3
Creekside Landing, Ltd., *In re,* 140 B.R. 713 (Bankr. M.D. Tenn. 1992)	§§ 16.5, 16.6, 16.7, 16.8
Crescent Beach, Inc., *In re,* 22 B.R. 155 (Bankr. D. Me. 1982)	§ 8.17
Crispell, *In re,* 73 B.R. 375 (Bankr. E.D. Mo. 1987)	§ 12.28
Critical Fork Coal Corp., *In re,* 18 B.R. 422 (Bankr. W.D. Va. 1982)	§ 5.4
Crotty, *In re,* 11 B.R. 507 (Bankr. N.D. Tex. 1981)	§ 15.10
Crouse Group, Inc., *In re,* 71 B.R. 544 (Bankr. E.D. Pa. 1987)	§ 6.4
Crowthers McCall Pattern, Inc., *In re,* 24 Collier Bankr. Cas. 2d (MB) 611 (Bankr. S.D.N.Y. 1990)	§ 11.19
Crowthers McCall Pattern, Inc. v. Lewis, 129 B.R. 992 (S.D.N.Y. 1991)	§ 12.26
Crusader Oil Ref. Corp., *In re,* 47 F. Supp. 873 (D.N.J. 1942)	§ 17.6
Cruseturner, *In re,* 8 B.R. 581 (Bankr. D. Utah 1981)	§§ 10.5, 10.6
Crysen/Montenay Energy Co., *In re,* 902 F.2d 1098 (2d Cir. 1990)	§ 5.5
C-T of Va., Inc. v. Euroshoe Assoc., 762 F. Supp. 675 (W.D. Va. 1991), *aff'd,* 953 F.2d 637 (4th Cir. 1992)	§ 12.26
C-T of Va., *In re,* 124 B.R. 700 (W.D. Va. 1990)	§ 12.27
Currivan's Chapel of the Sunset, *In re,* 51 B.R. 217 (C.D. Cal. 1985)	§ 7.12
Curtis, *In re,* 40 B.R. 795 (Bankr. D. Utah 1984)	§§ 8.7, 8.9
Cusanno v. Fidelity Bank, 29 B.R. 810 (E.D. Pa.), *aff'g In re* Cusanno, 17 B.R. 879 (Bankr. E.D. Pa. 1983)	§ 3.7
Dallas v. S.A.G., Inc., 836 F.2d 1307 (11th Cir. 1988)	§ 12.10, 23.22
Damron, *In re,* 8 B.R. 323 (Bankr. S.D. Ohio 1980)	§ 11.13
Dant & Russell, Inc., *In re,* 853 F.2d 700 (9th Cir. 1988)	§ 9.2
Datair Sys. Corp., *In re,* 42 B.R. 241 (Bankr. N.D. Ill. 1984)	§§ 3.10, 11.7
Data-Link Sys., Inc. v. Whitcomb & Keller Mortgage Co., (*In re* Whitcomb & Keller Mortgage Co.), 715 F.2d 375 (7th Cir. 1983)	§§ 7.4, 7.7
David Jones Builder, Inc., *In re,* 129 B.R. 682 (Bankr. S.D. Fla. 1991)	§ 11.24
Davidovich, *In re,* 901 F.2d 1533 (10th Cir. 1990)	§ 12.29
Davis, *In re,* 124 B.R. 831 (Bankr. D. Kan. 1991)	§ 20.12
Davis, *In re,* 120 B.R. 823 (Bankr. W.D. Pa. 1990)	§§ 11.13, 11.14, 11.30, 11.35
Dean v. Davis, 242 U.S. 438 (1917)	§§ 12.17, 12.24
Defender Drug Stores, Inc., *In re,* 145 B.R. 312 (Bankr. 9th Cir. 1992)	§ 6.28
Deico Elecs., *In re,* 139 B.R. 945 (Bankr. 9th Cir. 1992)	§ 5.8
Deihl, *In re,* 80 B.R. 1 (Bankr. D. Me. 1987)	§ 2.20
Delaware & Hudson Ry., *In re,* 124 B.R. 169 (D. Del. 1991)	§ 9.5

Case	*Book §*
DeLorean Motor Co., *In re,* 49 B.R. 900 (Bankr. E.D. Mich. 1985)	§ 23.9
Dembo, *In re,* 126 B.R. 195 (Bankr. E.D. Pa. 1991)	§ 11.7
Department of Air Force v. Carolina Parachute Corp., 907 F.2d 1469 (4th Cir. 1990)	§§ 5.4, 7.15
Depew, *In re,* 115 B.R. 965 (Bankr. N.D. Ind. 1989)	§ 17.5
Dew Mortgage Co., *In re,* 10 B.R. 242 (Bankr. M.D. Fla. 1981)	§ 23.19
Dewsnup, *In re,* 87 B.R. 676 (Bankr. D. Utah 1988), *aff'd on other grounds,* 908 F.2d 588 (10th Cir. 1990), *aff'd sub nom.* Dewsnup v. Timm, ____ U.S. ____, 112 S. Ct. 773 (1992)	§ 10.6
Dilts, *In re,* 100 B.R. 759 (Bankr. W.D. Pa. 1989)	§ 15.14
Diversified Investors Fund XVII, *In re,* 91 B.R. 559 (Bankr. C.D. Cal. 1988)	§ 22.9
Dobbins, *In re,* 120 B.R. 120 (Bankr. W.D. Mo. 1990), *aff'd,* 151 B.R. 509 (W.D. Mo. 1991)	§ 2.25
Docktor Pet Ctr., Inc., *In re,* 144 B.R. 14 (Bankr. D. Mass. 1992)	§§ 7.11, 7.13
Don & Lin Trucking Co., *In re,* 110 B.R. 562 (Bankr. N.D. Ala. 1990)	§ 7.18
Doors & More, Inc., *In re,* 127 B.R. 1001 (Bankr. E.D. Mich. 1991)	§ 2.18
Double TRL, Inc., *In re,* 65 B.R. 993 (Bankr. E.D.N.Y. 1986)	§ 23.10
Dowden, *In re,* 143 B.R. 388 (Bankr. W.D. La. 1989)	§§ 16.1, 16.4, 16.6, 16.7, 16.8
Draggoo Elec. Co., *In re,* 57 B.R. 916 (Bankr. N.D. Ind. 1986)	§ 17.1
Dreske, *In re,* 25 B.R. 268 (Bankr. E.D. Wis. 1982)	§ 22.4
Drexel Burnham Lambert Group, Inc. v. Vigilant Ins. Co., 130 B.R. 405 (Bankr. S.D.N.Y. 1991)	§ 23.12
Drimmel, *In re,* 108 B.R. 284 (Bankr. D. Kan. 1989), *aff'd,* 135 B.R. 410 (D. Kan. 1991), *aff'd,* 987 F.2d 1506 (10th Cir. 1993)	§§ 16.1, 16.2, 16.4, 16.9
Duckett, *In re,* 139 B.R. 6 (Bankr. E.D. Tex. 1992)	§ 19.3
Duckwall-Alco Stores, Inc., *In re,* 150 B.R. 965 (D. Kan. 1993)	§§ 7.5, 7.6
Dunes Casino Hotel, *In re,* 69 B.R. 784 (Bankr. D.N.J. 1986)	§§ 6.6, 6.7
Dunes Casino Hotel, *In re,* 63 B.R. 939 (D.N.J. 1986)	§ 7.7
Durrett v. Washington Nat'l Ins. Co., 621 F.2d 201 (5th Cir. 1980)	§ 12.25
Dutch Woodcraft Shops, *In re,* 14 F. Supp. 467 (D. Mich. 1935)	§ 16.4
D&W Realty Corp., *In re,* 156 B.R. 140 (Bankr. S.D.N.Y. 1993)	§ 15.8

Case	*Book §*
Everett Home Town, Ltd., *In re,* 146 B.R. 453 (Bankr. D. Ariz. 1992)	§ 4.10
Ewing, *In re,* 147 B.R. 970 (Bankr. D.N.M. 1992)	§ 7.15
Executive Assocs., *In re,* 24 B.R. 171 (Bankr. S.D. Tex. 1982)	§ 3.7
Eye Contact, Inc., *In re,* 97 B.R. 990 (Bankr. W.D. Wis. 1989)	§ 12.33
F.A.B. Indus., *In re,* 147 B.R. 763 (C.D. Cal. 1992)	§ 16.1
Fabricators, Inc. v. Technical Fabricators, Inc. (*In re* Fabricators, Inc.), 926 F.2d 1458 (5th Cir. 1991)	§ 12.5
Fairchild, *In re,* 31 B.R. 789 (Bankr. S.D. Ohio 1983)	§ 11.7
Faires, *In re,* 34 B.R. 549 (Bankr. W.D. Wash. 1983)	§ 11.6
Fansal Shoe Corp., *In re,* 119 B.R. 28 (Bankr. S.D.N.Y. 1990)	§ 17.4
Farley, *In re,* 146 B.R. 748 (Bankr. N.D. Ill. 1992)	§ 11.35
Farmers & Merchants Bank & Trust v. Trail W., Inc., 28 B.R. 389 (D.S.D. 1983)	§ 5.7
Farrell, *In re,* 79 B.R. 300 (Bankr. S.D. Ohio 1987)	§ 7.15
Fastrans, Inc., *In re,* 142 B.R. 241 (Bankr. E.D. Tenn. 1992)	§ 12.21
Fastrax, Inc., *In re,* 129 B.R. 274 (Bankr. M.D. Fla. 1991)	§ 7.15
FCX, Inc., *In re,* 54 B.R. 833 (Bankr. E.D.N.C. 1985)	§ 6.20
Federal Press Co., *In re,* 116 B.R. 650 (Bankr. N.D. Ind. 1989)	§ 11.35
Fernwood Mkts., *In re,* 73 B.R. 616 (Bankr. E.D. Pa. 1987)	§ 9.6
Financial News Network, Inc., *In re,* 980 F.2d 165 (2d Cir. 1992)	§ 9.4
Fine, *In re,* 89 B.R. 167 (Bankr. D. Kan. 1988)	§ 20.12
First Alliance Corp., *In re,* 126 B.R. 589 (Bankr. S.D. Cal. 1991)	§ 7.18
First Int'l Serv. Corp., *In re,* 25 B.R. 66 (Bankr. D. Conn. 1982)	§ 9.6
First Nat'l Bank v. Rafoth (*In re* Baker & Getty Fin. Serv., Inc.), 974 F.2d 712 (6th Cir. 1992)	§ 12.5
First Nat'l Bank v. Texas Tri-Collar (*In re* Texas Tri-Collar), 29 B.R. 724 (Bankr. W.D. La. 1983)	§ 4.2
First RepublicBank Corp., *In re,* 95 B.R. 58 (Bankr. N.D. Tex. 1988)	§ 8.5
First S. Sav. Ass'n, *In re,* 820 F.2d 700 (5th Cir. 1987)	§§ 6.6, 6.8, 7.7
First State Bank v. W.E. Tucker Oil Co. (*In re* W.E. Tucker Oil Co.), 64 B.R. 183 (W.D. Ark. 1986)	§ 12.21
Fisher, Hecht & Fisher v. D.H. Overmyer Telecasting Co. (*In re* D.H. Overmyer Telecasting Co.), 56 B.R. 657 (Bankr. N.D. Ohio 1986)	§ 12.8
Fitzsimmons Trucking, Inc., *In re,* 124 B.R. 556 (Bankr. D. Minn. 1991)	§ 2.11
Florida Airlines, Inc., *In re,* 110 B.R. 570 (M.D. Fla. 1990)	§ 2.2
F&N Acquisition Corp., *In re,* 152 B.R. 304 (Bankr. W.D. Wash. 1993)	§ 7.13
Ford, *In re,* 61 B.R. 913 (Bankr. W.D. Wis. 1986)	§ 17.1
Ford v. Poston, 773 F.2d 52 (4th Cir. 1984)	§§ 20.10, 20.12
Ford & Vlahos v. ITT Commercial Fin., 23 Cal. Rptr. 2d 175 (Ct. App. 1993)	§ 18.11
Forestry Prods., Inc. v. Hope, 34 B.R. 753 (M.D. Ga. 1983)	§ 19.2

Case	*Book §*
George Worthington Co., *In re,* 921 F.2d 626 (6th Cir. 1990)	§ 8.5
GHR Energy Corp., *In re,* 41 B.R. 668 (Bankr. D. Mass. 1984)	§ 7.7
Giant Mkts., Inc., *In re,* 28 B.R. 335 (Bankr. M.D. Pa. 1983)	§ 7.7
Gibraltar Sav. v. LD Brinkman Corp., 860 F.2d 1275 (5th Cir. 1988), *cert. denied,* 490 U.S. 1091 (1989)	§ 12.8
Giesing, *In re,* 96 B.R. 229 (Bankr. W.D. Mo. 1989)	§ 7.16
Gilbert, *In re,* 104 B.R. 206 (Bankr. W.D. Mo. 1989)	§ 15.9
Gilchrist, *In re,* 891 F.2d 559 (5th Cir. 1990)	§ 9.3
Gilmore, *In re,* 127 B.R. 406 (Bankr. M.D. Tenn. 1991)	§ 2.4
Glasply Marine Indus., Inc., *In re,* 971 F.2d 391 (9th Cir. 1992)	§ 5.3
Glenn, *In re,* 760 F.2d 1428 (6th Cir.), *cert. denied sub nom.* Miller v. First Fed., 474 U.S. 849 (1985)	§ 5.3
GMAC v. Bell, 700 F.2d 1053 (6th Cir. 1983)	§ 10.6
GMAC v. Busenlahner (*In re* Busenlahner), 918 F.2d 928 (11th Cir. 1990)	§ 12.10
Goodman v. Phillip R. Curtis Enters., Inc., 809 F.2d 228 (4th Cir. 1987)	§ 17.2
Gourmet Serv., Inc., *In re,* 142 B.R. 216 (Bankr. S.D. Ohio 1992)	§ 7.2
Grabill Corp., *In re,* 967 F.2d 1152 (7th Cir. 1992)	§ 23.15
Grambling, *In re,* 85 B.R. 675 (Bankr. D. Conn. 1988)	§ 12.28
Grant Broadcasting of Phila., Inc., *In re,* 71 B.R. 891 (Bankr. E.D. Pa. 1987)	§ 7.7
Great Nat'l Life Ins. Co. v. Pine Gate Assocs., 2 Bankr. Ct. Dec. (CRR) 1478 (Bankr. N.D. Ga. 1976)	§ 8.18
Great N. Protective Serv., Inc., *In re,* 19 B.R. 802 (Bankr. W.D. Wash. 1982)	§ 15.10
Great W. Bank v. Sierra Woods Group, 953 F.2d 1174 (9th Cir. 1992)	§ 15.10
Green, *In re,* 986 F.2d 145 (6th Cir. 1993)	§ 12.7
Green, *In re,* 151 B.R. 501 (Bankr. D. Minn. 1993)	§ 11.25
Green v. Bates Records, Inc. (*In re* 10th Ave. Record Distribs., Inc.), 97 B.R. 163 (S.D.N.Y. 1989)	§ 12.8
Green St., *In re,* 132 B.R. 460 (Bankr. D. Utah 1991)	§ 2.3
Greives, *In re,* 81 B.R. 912 (Bankr. N.D. Ind. 1987)	§ 3.10
Greyhall Resources, Inc., *In re,* 63 B.R. 382 (Bankr. D. Colo. 1986)	§ 7.13
Greyhound Real Estate Fin. Co. v. Official Unsecured Creditors' Comm. (*In re* Northview Corp.), 130 B.R. 543 (Bankr. 9th Cir. 1991)	§ 4.6
Greystone III Joint Venture, *In re,* 102 B.R. 560 (Bankr. W.D. Tex. 1989), *aff'd,* 127 B.R. 138 (W.D. Tex. 1990), *rev'd,* 948 F.2d 134 (5th Cir.), *rev'd & remanded,* 995 F.2d 1274 (5th Cir. 1991)	§§ 8.18, 15.8, 16.2, 16.4, 16.8
Griffin Retreading Co., *In re,* 795 F.2d 676 (8th Cir. 1986)	§ 8.3
Griffiths, *In re,* 27 B.R. 873 (Bankr. D. Kan. 1983)	§ 15.15

Case	*Book §*
Grinstead, *In re,* 75 B.R. 2 (Bankr. D. Minn. 1985)	§ 17.1
Grogan v. Garner, 498 U.S. 279 (1991)	§§ 5.1, 20.12
Grossman, *In re,* 46 B.R. 319 (Bankr. E.D. Pa. 1985)	§ 17.6
Grubb v. General Contract Purchase Corp., 94 F.2d 70 (2d Cir. 1938)	§ 12.20
Grundy Nat'l Bank v. Rife, 876 F.2d 361 (4th Cir. 1989)	§ 3.10
Hall, *In re,* 151 B.R. 412 (Bankr. W.D. Mich. 1993)	§§ 20.2, 21.3, 21.4, 21.6
Halle, *In re,* 132 B.R. 186 (Bankr. D. Colo. 1991)	§ 10.13
Hanes, *In re,* 1994 WL 14536 (Bankr. E.D. Va. 1994)	§§ 21.3, 21.4
Hanson v. First Nat'l Bank in Brookings, 848 F.2d 866 (8th Cir. 1988)	§§ 20.11, 20.12
Hardzog v. Federal Land Bank, 901 F.2d 858 (10th Cir. 1990)	§ 14.4
Harlon Properties, Inc., *In re,* 56 B.R. 794 (Bankr. 9th Cir. 1985)	§ 23.5
Harman, *In re,* 141 B.R. 878 (Bankr. E.D. Pa. 1992)	§§ 16.1, 16.5, 16.6
Harms, *In re,* 10 B.R. 817 (Bankr. D. Colo. 1981)	§ 22.5
Harrell, *In re,* 14 Collier Bankr. Cas. 2d (MB) 212 (Bankr. E.D.N.C. 1985)	§ 6.3
Harrison, *In re,* 117 B.R. 570 (Bankr. C.D. Cal. 1990)	§ 7.16
Hayball Trucking, Inc., *In re,* 67 B.R. 681 (Bankr. E.D. Mich. 1986)	§ 17.4
Hazen First State Bank v. Speight, 888 F.2d 574 (8th Cir. 1989)	§ 5.3
Heatron, Inc., *In re,* 34 B.R. 526 (Bankr. W.D. Mo. 1983)	§ 17.4
Hebert, *In re,* 61 B.R. 44 (Bankr. W.D. La. 1986)	§ 19.4
Helvering v. Hammel, 311 U.S. 504 (1941)	§§ 10.2, 10.6, 10.12
Helvering v. Nebraska Bridge Supply & Lumber Co., 312 U.S. 666 (1941)	§ 10.8
Hendrix, *In re,* 131 B.R. 751 (Bankr. M.D. Fla. 1991)	§ 16.1
Henke, *In re,* 90 B.R. 451 (Bankr. D. Mont. 1988)	§§ 16.6, 16.8
Heritage Hotel Partnership I v. Valley Bank (*In re* Heritage Hotel Partnership I), 160 B.R. 374 (Bankr. 9th Cir. 1993)	§§ 12.29, 15.23
Herron, *In re,* 60 B.R. 82 (Bankr. W.D. La. 1986)	§ 17.1
Hertz, *In re,* 38 B.R. 215 (Bankr. S.D.N.Y. 1984)	§ 17.6
Hester v . NCNB Tex. Nat'l Bank (*In re* Hester), 899 F.2d 361 (5th Cir. 1990)	§ 3.13
Hewett, *In re,* 32 B.R. 605 (Bankr. W.D. Wash. 1983)	§ 3.13
Hickson v. Home Fed., 805 F. Supp. 1567 (N.D. Ga. 1992)	§ 5.3
Hill, *In re,* 981 F.2d 1474 (5th Cir. 1993)	§ 12.7
Hillsborough Holdings Corp., *In re,* 126 B.R. 895 (Bankr. M.D. Fla. 1991)	§ 7.13
Hinckley, *In re,* 40 B.R. 679 (Bankr. D. Utah 1984)	§ 3.10
Hirschorn, *In re,* 156 B.R. 379 (Bankr. E.D.N.Y. 1993)	§ 7.16
Hofer v. Merchants State Bank, 823 F.2d 271 (8th Cir. 1987)	§ 23.27
Hoff, *In re,* 54 B.R. 746 (Bankr. D.N.D. 1985)	§ 15.15

Case	*Book §*
Hoffman, *In re,* 51 B.R. 42 (Bankr. W.D. Ark. 1985)	§ 3.7
Hoffman v. Connecticut Dep't of Income Maintenance, 492 U.S. 96 (1989)	§ 12.31
Hohenberg, *In re,* 143 B.R. 183 (Bankr. W.D. Tenn. 1992)	§ 23.3
Holford, *In re,* 896 F.2d 165 (5th Cir. 1990)	§ 5.2
Hollanger, *In re,* 15 B.R. 35 (Bankr. W.D. La. 1981)	§ 15.10
Holly's, *In re,* 140 B.R. 643 (Bankr. W.D. Mich. 1992)	§§ 5.6, 5.7, 7.16
Holywell v. Smith, ____ U.S. ____, 112 S. Ct. 1021 (1992)	§ 10.13
Home Sav. Ass'n of Kan. City v. Woodstock Assocs. I (*In re* Woodstock Assocs. I), 120 B.R. 436 (Bankr. N.D. Ill. 1990)	§ 3.8
Homebanc v. Chappell (*In re* Chappell), 984 F.2d 775 (7th Cir. 1993)	§ 19.3
Homeowner's Outlet Mall Exch., Inc., *In re,* 89 B.R. 965 (Bankr. S.D. Fla. 1988)	§ 7.5
Hooker Invs., Inc., *In re,* 145 B.R. 138 (Bankr. S.D.N.Y. 1992)	§ 7.7
Hotel Assocs., Inc., *In re,* 1 Collier Bankr. Cas. 2d (MB) 819 (Bankr. E.D. Pa. 1980)	§ 11.7
House of Deals of Broward, Inc., *In re,* 67 B.R. 23 (Bankr. E.D.N.Y. 1986)	§ 7.8
House of Emeralds, Inc., *In re,* 57 B.R. 31 (Bankr. D. Haw. 1985)	§ 7.8
Howe, *In re,* 913 F.2d 1138 (5th Cir. 1990)	§ 12.29
H.R.P. Auto Ctr., Inc., *In re,* 130 B.R. 247 (Bankr. N.D. Ohio 1991)	§§ 17.1, 17.5
Hub of Military Circle, Inc., *In re,* 19 B.R. 460 (Bankr. E.D. Va. 1982)	§ 7.13
Hub of Military Circle, Inc., *In re,* 13 B.R. 288 (Bankr. E.D. Va. 1981)	§ 7.6
Hudson Oil Co., *In re,* 68 B.R. 735 (Bankr. D. Kan. 1986)	§ 23.3
Huff, *In re,* 159 B.R. 262 (Bankr. W.D. Mo. 1993)	§ 11.18
Hugo v. United States *ex rel.* Farmers Home Admin. (*In re* Hugo), 50 B.R. 963 (Bankr. E.D. Mich. 1985)	§ 4.2
Huntmar Beaumeade I Ltd. Partnership, *In re,* 127 B.R. 363 (Bankr. E.D. Va. 1991)	§ 2.4
Hutter Constr. Co., *In re,* 126 B.R. 1005 (Bankr. E.D. Wis. 1991)	§§ 2.15, 2.18, 2.20, 2.21
I.C.C. v. Holmes Transp., Inc., 931 F.2d 984 (1st Cir. 1991)	§ 5.4
Impulsora del Territorio Sur, S.A. v. Cecchini (*In re* Cecchini), 780 F.2d 1440 (9th Cir. 1986)	§ 3.13
Industrial Pollution Control, Inc., *In re,* 137 B.R. 176 (Bankr. W.D. Pa. 1992)	§ 23.19
Industrial Valley Refrigeration & Air Conditioning Supplies, Inc., *In re,* 77 B.R. 15 (Bankr. E.D. Pa. 1987)	§ 9.5
Ingersoll-Rand Fin. Corp. v. Miller Mining Co., 817 F.2d 1424 (9th Cir. 1987)	§ 5.3

Case	*Book §*
Johnson, *In re,* 880 F.2d 78 (8th Cir. 1989)	§ 20.12
Johnson, *In re,* 145 B.R. 108 (Bankr. S.D. Ga. 1992)	§ 11.25
Johnson, *In re,* 124 B.R. 648 (Bankr. E.D. Pa. 1991)	§ 23.6
Johnson, *In re,* 117 B.R. 577 (Bankr. D. Idaho 1990)	§ 11.25
Johnson, *In re,* 80 B.R. 953 (Bankr. D. Minn. 1987), *aff'd,* 101 B.R. 997 (D. Minn. 1988), *rev'd and remanded,* 880 F.2d 78 (8th Cir. 1989)	§ 20.12
Johnson v. First Nat'l Bank, 719 F.2d 270 (8th Cir. 1983), *cert. denied,* 465 U.S. 1012 (1984)	§ 5.3
Johnson v. Georgia Highway Express, Inc., 488 F.2d 714 (5th Cir. 1974)	§ 2.15
Jolly, *In re,* 574 F.2d 349 (6th Cir.), *cert. denied,* 439 U.S. 929 (1978)	§ 7.2
Jones v. United Sav. & Loan Ass'n, 9 F.3d 680 (8th Cir. 1993)	§ 12.18
Jorgenson, *In re,* 66 B.R. 104 (Bankr. 9th Cir. 1986)	§ 17.4
Joseph C. Spiess Co., *In re,* 145 B.R. 497 (Bankr. N.D. Ill. 1992)	§ 7.6
Joshua Slocum, Ltd., *In re,* 922 F.2d 1081 (3d Cir. 1990)	§§ 7.13, 7.14
Joshua Slocum, Inc., *In re,* 103 B.R. 601 (Bankr. E.D. Pa. 1989)	§ 7.13
Joshua Slocum, Ltd., *In re,* 99 B.R. 261 (Bankr. E.D. Pa. 1989), *aff'd,* 914 F.2d 243 (3d Cir. 1990)	§ 9.4
J.P. Fufe, Inc. v. Bradco Supply Corp., 891 F.2d 66 (3d Cir. 1989)	§ 12.18
Kahihikolo, *In re,* 807 F.2d 1540 (11th Cir. 1987)	§ 8.6
Kahl Iron Foundry, *In re,* 21 B.R. 372 (Bankr. E.D. Mich. 1982)	§ 4.2
Kain, *In re,* 86 B.R. 506 (Bankr. W.D. Mich. 1988)	§ 3.10
Kaiser Steel Corp. v. Frates, 911 F.2d 380 (10th Cir. 1990)	§ 23.15
Karl A. Neise, Inc., *In re,* 31 B.R. 409 (Bankr. S.D. Fla. 1983)	§ 10.6
Kansas City Terminal Ry. v. Central Union Trust Co., 271 U.S. 445 (1926)	§§ 16.1, 16.10
Katchen v. Landy, 382 U.S. 323 (1966)	§ 23.15
Kearney Hotel Partners v. Richardson (*In re* Kearney Hotel Partners), 92 B.R. 95 (Bankr. S.D.N.Y. 1988)	§§ 4.6, 4.7
Kehn Ranch, Inc., *In re,* 41 B.R. 832 (Bankr. D.S.D. 1984)	§ 13.19
Kendavis Indus. Int'l, Inc., *In re,* 91 B.R. 742 (Bankr. N.D. Tex. 1988)	§§ 2.17, 16.7, 16.8
Kenney's Franchise Corp. v. Central Fidelity Bank, 22 B.R. 747 (W.D. Va. 1982), *rev'g In re* Kenney's Franchise Corp., 12 B.R. 390 (Bankr. W.D. Va. 1981)	§ 3.7
Kham & Nate's Shoes No. 2, Inc. v. First Bank of Whiting, 908 F.2d 1351 (7th Cir. 1990)	§§ 6.25, 12.5, 16.1, 16.2, 16.6, 16.8, 16.9, 16.10
King Resources Co., *In re,* 651 F.2d 1349 (10th Cir.), *cert. denied sub nom.* Citibank, N.A. v. Phoenix Resources Co., 454 U.S. 881 (1981)	§ 2.1

Case	*Book §*
Lilliston, *In re,* 127 B.R. 119 (Bankr. D. Md. 1991)	§ 2.17
Lindbergh Plaza Assoc., *In re,* 115 B.R. 202 (Bankr. E.D. Mo. 1990)	§ 8.6
Lionel Corp., *In re,* 722 F.2d 1063 (2d Cir. 1983)	§§ 9.5, 9.8
Lionel Corp., *In re,* 23 B.R. 224 (Bankr. S.D.N.Y. 1982)	§ 7.7
Lippi v. City Bank, 955 F.2d 599 (9th Cir. 1992)	§ 12.7
Lister, *In re,* 846 F.2d 55 (10th Cir. 1988)	§ 2.25
Litchfield Co. of S.C., Ltd., 135 B.R. 797 (W.D.N.C. 1992)	§ 22.7
Little Creek Dev. Co., *In re,* 779 F.2d 1068 (5th Cir. 1986)	§§ 5.7, 8.6
Local Loan Co. v. Hunt, 292 U.S. 234 (1934)	§§ 5.1, 10.10
Lockhard, *In re,* 884 F.2d 1171 (9th Cir. 1989)	§ 5.3
Logan v. Basic Distrib. Corp. (*In re* Fred Hawes Org., Inc.), 957 F.2d 239 (6th Cir. 1992)	§ 12.18
Longardner & Assocs., Inc., *In re,* 855 F.2d 455 (7th Cir. 1988)	§ 17.6
Lopez-Soto, *In re,* 764 F.2d 23 (1st Cir. 1985)	§ 5.8
Loretto Winery, Ltd., *In re,* 898 F.2d 715 (9th Cir. 1990)	§ 12.13
Louden, *In re,* 69 B.R. 723 (Bankr. E.D. Mo. 1987)	§ 8.10
Louisville Joint Stock Land Bank v. Radford, 295 U.S. 555 (1935)	§ 5.8
Lovett v. St. Johnsburg Trucking, 931 F.2d 494 (8th Cir. 1991)	§ 12.18
Lumber Exch. Ltd. Partnership, *In re,* 125 B.R. 1000 (Bankr. D. Minn.), *aff'd,* 134 B.R. 354 (D. Minn. 1991), *aff'd,* 968 F.2d 647 (8th Cir. 1992)	§§ 15.8, 16.2, 16.10
Lyons Transp. Lines, Inc., *In re,* 123 B.R. 526 (Bankr. W.D. Pa. 1991)	§ 9.1
M. Long Arabians, *In re,* 103 B.R. 211 (Bankr. 9th Cir. 1989)	§ 22.9
Maanum, *In re,* 828 F.2d 459 (8th Cir. 1987), *reh'g denied,* 838 F.2d 991 (8th Cir. 1988)	§ 5.3
MacArthur Co. v. Johns Manville Corp., 837 F.2d 89 (2d Cir. 1988)	§ 22.7
MacDonald, *In re,* 755 F.2d 715 (9th Cir. 1985)	§ 5.7
MacLeod Co., *In re,* 63 B.R. 654 (Bankr. S.D. Ohio 1986)	§ 15.7
Madrid, *In re,* 21 B.R. 424 (Bankr. 9th Cir.), *aff'd on other grounds,* 725 F.2d 1197 (9th Cir. 1982), *cert. denied,* 469 U.S. 833 (1984)	§ 12.25
Majestic Motel Assocs., *In re,* 131 B.R. 523 (Bankr. D. Me. 1991)	§§ 4.4, 4.6, 4.7, 4.9
Mako, Inc., *In re,* 102 B.R. 818 (Bankr. E.D. Okla. 1988)	§ 7.13
Mako, Inc., *In re,* 102 B.R. 814 (Bankr. E.D. Okla. 1988)	§ 7.2
Malek, *In re,* 35 B.R. 443 (Bankr. E.D. Mich. 1983)	§§ 13.2, 13.22
Malody, *In re,* 102 B.R. 745 (Bankr. 9th Cir. 1989)	§ 11.25
Manufacturers Hanover Leasing Corp. v. Lowrey (*In re* Robinson Bros. Drilling, Inc.), 892 F.2d 850 (10th Cir. 1989)	§ 12.21

Case	*Book §*
Manville Forest Prods. Corp., *In re,* 896 F.2d 1384 (2d Cir. 1990)	§ 23.19
Maralak, Ltd., *In re,* 104 B.R. 446 (Bankr. M.D. Fla. 1989)	§ 7.2
Marathon Oil Co. v. Flatau (*In re* Craig Oil Co.), 785 F.2d 1563 (11th Cir. 1986)	§ 12.18
Marcus Hook Dev. Park, Inc., *In re,* 143 B.R. 648 (Bankr. W.D. Pa. 1992)	§ 9.6
Mares v. Credit Bureau, 801 F.2d 1197 (10th Cir. 1986)	§ 2.20
Marin Motor Oil, Inc., *In re,* 740 F.2d 220 (3d Cir. 1984)	§ 8.3
Marine Optical, Inc., *In re,* 10 B.R. 893 (Bankr. D. Mass. 1981)	§ 3.10
Marion St. Partnership, *In re,* 108 B.R. 218 (Bankr. D. Minn. 1989)	§ 5.8
Maritime Elec. Co. v. United Jersey Bank, 959 F.2d 1194 (3d Cir. 1991)	§§ 5.1, 5.3
Markim, *In re,* 15 B.R. 56 (Bankr. E.D. Pa. 1981)	§ 3.10
Marko Elecs., Inc., *In re,* 145 B.R. 25 (Bankr. N.D. Ohio 1992)	§ 8.3
Martin, *In re,* 817 F.2d 175 (1st Cir. 1987)	§ 2.4
Martin, *In re,* 761 F.2d 1163 (6th Cir. 1985)	§ 2.25
Martin, *In re,* 66 B.R. 921 (Bankr. D. Mont. 1986)	§§ 15.1, 15.14
Martin v. Friedman, 133 B.R. 609 (Bankr. N.D. Ohio 1991)	§ 23.7
Martin v. United States (*In re* Martin), 761 F.2d 472 (8th Cir. 1985)	§ 3.10
Martin Bros. Toolmakers, Inc., *In re,* 796 F.2d 1435 (11th Cir. 1987)	§ 7.2
Martin Exploration Co., *In re,* 731 F.2d 1210 (5th Cir. 1984)	§ 12.13
Martin-Trigona v. Champion Fed. Sav. & Loan Ass'n, 892 F.2d 575 (7th Cir. 1989)	§§ 5.1, 5.3
Mason v. Commissioner, 646 F.2d 1309 (9th Cir. 1980)	§ 10.5
Matson, *In re,* No. 90-42308-7 (Bankr. D. Kan. Dec. 13, 1991)	§§ 10.10, 10.12
Matthews v. Rosene, 739 F.2d 249 (7th Cir. 1984)	§ 5.2
Maui 14K, Ltd., *In re,* 133 B.R. 657 (Bankr. D. Haw. 1991)	§ 2.3
Mays 1978 Drilling Partnership, *In re,* 95 B.R. 432 (Bankr. N.D. Tex. 1989)	§ 22.6
McCombs Properties VIII, Ltd., *In re,* 91 B.R. 907 (Bankr. C.D. Cal. 1988)	§ 15.10
McCuskey v. National Bank of Waterloo (*In re* Bohlen Enter.), 859 F.2d 561 (8th Cir. 1988)	§ 12.20
McDonald, *In re,* 161 B.R. 697 (D. Kan. 1993)	§ 20.6
McDonald, *In re,* 128 B.R. 161 (Bankr. W.D. Tex. 1991)	§ 10.13
McGowan, *In re,* 95 B.R. 104 (Bankr. N.D. Iowa 1988)	§§ 10.5, 10.8, 10.9
McGowan, *In re,* 19 B.R. 952 (Bankr. E.D. Pa. 1982)	§ 9.6
McKillips, *In re,* 81 B.R. 454 (Bankr. N.D. Ill. 1987)	§ 5.8
McKinney Ranch Assocs., *In re,* 62 B.R. 249 (Bankr. C.D. Cal. 1986)	§ 2.3
McLean v. City of Phila., 891 F.2d 474 (3d Cir. 1989)	§ 12.7
McLean Enter., *In re,* 105 B.R. 928 (Bankr. W.D. Mo. 1989)	§ 2.25
McLean Indus., *In re,* 132 B.R. 247 (Bankr. S.D.N.Y. 1991)	§§ 11.2, 11.12

Case	*Book §*
McMartin Indus., Inc., *In re,* 62 B.R. 718 (Bankr. D. Neb. 1986)	§ 5.7
MCorp Fin., Inc., *In re,* 139 B.R. 820 (Bankr. S.D. Tex. 1992)	§ 23.22
Meckfessel, *In re,* 67 B.R. 277 (Bankr. D. Kan. 1986)	§ 20.5
Medomak Canning Co., *In re,* 123 B.R. 671 (Bankr. D. Me. 1991)	§ 23.22
Mellon Bank, N.A. v. Metro Communications, Inc., 945 F.2d 635 (3d Cir. 1991)	§ 12.26
Mercon Indus., *In re,* 37 B.R. 549 (Bankr. E.D. Pa. 1984)	§ 12.21
Meredith Manor, Inc., *In re,* 902 F.2d 257 (4th Cir. 1990)	§ 12.19
Merritt Dredging Co., *In re,* 839 F.2d 203 (4th Cir. 1988)	§ 12.7
Met-L-Wood Corp., *In re,* 861 F.2d 1012 (7th Cir. 1988), *cert. denied sub nom.* Gekas v. Pipin, 490 U.S. 1006 (1989)	§ 9.6
Metro Air N.E., Inc., *In re,* 131 B.R. 555 (Bankr. W.D.N.Y. 1989)	§ 7.2
Metro Communications, Inc., *In re,* 95 B.R. 921 (Bankr. W.D. Pa.), *amended,* 135 B.R. 17 (Bankr. W.D. Pa. 1989)	§ 12.27
Metropolitan Life Ins. Co. v. Monroe, 17 B.R. 934 (D. Del. 1982)	§ 3.10
Metropolitan Life Ins. Co. v. San Felipe @ Voss, Ltd. (*In re* San Felipe @ Voss, Ltd.), 115 B.R. 526 (S.D. Tex. 1990)	§§ 11.19, 15.15
MGN Co., III, *In re,* 116 B.R. 654 (Bankr. S.D. Ind. 1989)	§§ 5.7, 8.6
Miami Ctr. v. Bank of N.Y., 838 F.2d 1547 (11th Cir.), *cert. denied,* 488 U.S. 823 (1988)	§ 9.6
Miami Ctr. Assocs., *In re,* 144 B.R. 937 (Bankr. S.D. Fla. 1992)	§§ 16.4, 16.6, 16.8
Mid Atl. Fund, Inc., *In re,* 60 B.R. 604 (Bankr. S.D.N.Y. 1986)	§ 12.33
Mid-City Hotel Assocs. v. Prudential Ins. Co. (*In re* Mid-City Hotel Assocs.), 114 B.R. 634 (Bankr. D. Minn. 1990)	§ 4.10
Middleton Arms, Ltd., *In re,* 119 B.R. 131 (Bankr. M.D. Tenn. 1990), *aff'd,* 934 F.2d 723 (6th Cir. 1991)	§ 23.22
Midlantic Nat'l Bank v. New Jersey Dep't of Envtl. Protection, 474 U.S. 494, *reh'g denied,* 475 U.S. 1090 (1986)	§ 5.3
Midlantic Nat'l Bank v. Sourlis, 141 B.R. 826 (D.N.J. 1992)	§§ 3.6, 3.8
Midtown Skating Corp., *In re,* 3 B.R. 194 (Bankr. S.D.N.Y. 1980)	§ 7.7
Midwest Serv. & Supply Co., *In re,* 44 B.R. 262 (D. Utah 1983)	§ 12.29
Midwestern Cos., *In re,* 47 B.R. 16 (Bankr. W.D. Mo. 1984)	§ 6.18
Miller v. First Fed., 474 U.S. 849 (1985)	§ 5.3
Minges, *In re,* 602 F.2d 38 (2d Cir. 1979)	§ 7.18
Minichello, *In re,* 120 B.R. 17 (Bankr. N.D. Pa. 1990)	§ 12.33
Minton Group, Inc., *In re,* 46 B.R. 222 (S.D.N.Y. 1985)	§§ 22.4, 22.7
Missionary Baptist Found. of Am., Inc., 796 F.2d 752 (5th Cir. 1986)	§ 12.7
Mitchell, *In re,* 954 F.2d 557 (9th Cir. 1992)	§ 11.25

Case	*Book §*
National Gypsum Co., *In re,* 134 B.R. 188 (Bankr. N.D. Tex. 1991)	§ 23.7
National Real Estate Ltd. Partnership-II, *In re,* 104 B.R. 968 (Bankr. E.D. Wis. 1989)	§ 3.8
National Serv., *In re,* 742 F.2d 859 (5th Cir. 1984)	§ 5.2
National Sugar Ref. Co., *In re,* 21 B.R. 196 (Bankr. S.D.N.Y. 1982)	§ 7.11
Nelson, *In re,* 6 B.R. 248 (Bankr. D. Kan. 1980)	§ 3.7
Nendels-Medford Joint Venture, *In re,* 127 B.R. 658 (Bankr. D. Or. 1991)	§§ 4.6, 4.7
New Concept Realty & Dev., Inc., 753 F.2d 804 (9th Cir. 1985)	§ 12.7
New Hampshire Bus. Dev. Corp. v. Cross Baking Co., (*In re* Cross Baking Co.), 818 F.2d 1027 (1st Cir. 1987)	§ 3.10
New York City Shoes, Inc., *In re,* 78 B.R. 426 (Bankr. E.D. Pa. 1987)	§§ 3.7, 12.28
Newberry Elec., Inc. v. MCI Constructors, Inc. (*In re* Newberry Corp.), 145 B.R. 998 (Bankr. 9th Cir. 1992)	§ 12.29
Newman, *In re,* 993 F.2d 90 (5th Cir. 1993)	§ 12.7
Nielsen, *In re,* 48 B.R. 274 (D.N.D. 1984)	§ 4.2
Nitec Paper Corp., *In re,* 43 B.R. 492 (S.D.N.Y. 1984)	§ 7.15
NLRB v. Bildisco & Bildisco, 465 U.S. 513 (1984)	§§ 7.11, 7.12, 22.5, 23.7
NLRB v. Edward Cooper Painting, Inc., 804 F.2d 934 (6th Cir. 1986)	§ 5.3
NLRB v. Evans Plumbing Co., 639 F.2d 291 (5th Cir. 1981)	§ 23.16
NLT Computer Servs. Corp. v. Capital Computer Sys., Inc., 755 F.2d 1253 (6th Cir. 1985)	§ 5.2
Nobel v. Ungling, 8 Collier Bankr. Cas. 2d (MB) 1188 (D. Del. 1983)	§ 20.6
Nobleman v. American Sav. Bank (*In re* Nobleman), 968 F.2d 483 (5th Cir.), *aff'd,* 508 U.S. ____, 113 S. Ct.____, 124 L. Ed. 2d 228 (1993)	§§ 19.4, 24.5
Noli v. Commissioner, 860 F.2d 1521 (9th Cir. 1988)	§ 5.6
Norman, *In re,* 32 B.R. 562 (Bankr. W.D. Mo. 1983)	§ 19.7
North Redington Beach Assoc., Ltd., *In re,* 91 B.R. 166 (Bankr. M.D. Fla. 1988)	§ 17.7
Northampton Corp., *In re,* 37 B.R. 110 (Bankr. E.D. Pa. 1984)	§§ 17.4, 17.7
Northeast Chick Servs., *In re,* 43 B.R. 326 (Bankr. D. Mass. 1984)	§ 3.10
Northern Pac. Ry. v. Boyd, 228 U.S. 482 (1913)	§§ 16.1, 16.10
Northern Pipeline Constr. Co. v. Marathon Pipe Line Co., 458 U.S. 50 (1982)	§§ 23.2, 23.15
Northrup, *In re,* 141 B.R. 171 (N.D. Iowa 1991)	§ 19.4
Northwestern Nat'l Life Ins. Co. v. Metro Square (*In re* Metro Square), 106 B.R. 584 (Bankr. D. Minn. 1989)	§ 4.5
Norwest Bank Neb., N.A. v. Tveten, 848 F.2d 871 (8th Cir. 1988)	§§ 20.3, 20.5, 20.10, 20.12

Case	*Book §*
Norwest Bank Worthington v. Ahlers, 483 U.S. 1004 (1987), *rev'd on other grounds,* 485 U.S. 197 (1988)	§§ 3.10, 5.8, 14.4, 16.1, 16.6, 16.8
Nova Real Estate Inv. Trust, *In re,* 23 B.R. 62 (Bankr. E.D. Va. 1982)	§ 11.35
Novak, *In re,* 143 B.R. 154 (Bankr. N.D. Ill. 1992)	§ 19.3
N&T Assocs., Inc., *In re,* 134 B.R. 17 (D. Nev. 1991)	§ 2.21
NTG Indus., Inc., *In re,* 118 B.R. 606 (Bankr. N.D. Ill. 1990)	§§ 17.1, 17.2
Nucorp Energy, Inc., *In re,* 902 F.2d 729 (9th Cir. 1990)	§ 12.11
Oceanview/Va. Beach Real Estate Assocs., *In re,* 116 B.R. 57 (Bankr. E.D. Va. 1990)	§ 4.6
O'Connor, *In re,* 808 F.2d 1393 (10th Cir. 1987)	§ 5.8
Octagon Roofing, *In re,* 156 B.R. 214 (Bankr. N.D. Ill. 1993)	§ 12.33
O'Day Corp., *In re,* 126 B.R. 370 (Bankr. D. Mass. 1991)	§ 12.26
Offices & Servs. of White Plains Plaza, Inc., *In re,* 58 B.R. 441 (Bankr. S.D.N.Y. 1986)	§ 7.13
Official Comm. of Unsecured Creditors of White Farm Equip. Co. v. United States, 943 F.2d 752 (7th Cir. 1991)	§ 17.7
Official Creditors' Comm. on Behalf of Class 8 Unsecured Creditors v. Potter Material Serv., Inc. (*In re* Potter Material Serv., Inc.), 781 F.2d 99 (7th Cir. 1986)	§§ 16.4, 16.5, 16.6, 16.7, 16.8
Offield, *In re,* 128 B.R. 548 (Bankr. W.D. Mo. 1991)	§ 2.9
Ohio Corrugating Co., *In re,* 70 B.R. 920 (Bankr. N.D. Ohio 1987)	§ 12.26
Oklahoma P.A.C. First, Ltd., *In re,* 122 B.R. 394 (Bankr. D. Ariz. 1990)	§ 5.7
Olive St. Inv., Inc. v. Howard Sav. Bank, 972 F.2d 214 (8th Cir. 1992)	§ 5.4
Oliver, *In re,* 819 F.2d 550 (5th Cir. 1987)	§ 12.24
Oliver v. MBank Dallas (*In re* Oliver), 66 B.R. 426 (Bankr. N.D. Tex. 1986)	§ 4.5
Olsen, *In re,* 87 B.R. 148 (Bankr. D. Colo. 1988)	§ 4.2
Olson, *In re,* 930 F.2d 6 (8th Cir. 1991), *aff'g per curiam* 121 B.R. 346 (N.D. Iowa 1990), *aff'g* 100 B.R. 458 (Bankr. N.D. Iowa 1989)	§§ 10.5, 10.8, 10.9, 10.10
Olson, *In re,* 80 B.R. 935 (Bankr. C.D. Ill. 1987)	§§ 16.6, 16.7, 16.8
1 Potato 2, Inc., *In re,* 58 B.R. 752 (Bankr. D. Minn. 1986)	§ 7.6
One Times Square Assocs., *In re,* 159 B.R. 695 (Bankr. S.D.N.Y. 1993)	§§ 16.4, 16.8
Orfa Corp. of Phila., *In re,* 22 Bankr. Ct. Dec. (CRR) 427, 1991 WL 225985 (Bankr. E.D. Pa. Oct. 30, 1991)	§ 9.6
Orion Pictures Corp. v. Showtime Networks, Inc. (*In re* Orion Pictures Corp.), 4 F.3d 1095 (2d Cir. 1993)	§ 7.11
Ostano Commerzanstalt v. Telewide Sys., Inc., 790 F.2d 206 (2d Cir. 1986)	§ 5.1
Otoe County Nat'l Bank v. W&P Trucking, Inc., 754 F.2d 1324 (10th Cir. 1984)	§ 5.3

Case	*Book §*
Owens, *In re,* 120 B.R. 487 (Bankr. E.D. Ark. 1990)	§ 11.25
Pacesetter Designs, Inc., *In re,* 114 B.R. 731 (Bankr. D. Colo. 1990)	§ 6.3
Pacific Express, Inc., *In re,* 780 F.2d 1482 (9th Cir. 1986)	§ 12.7
Pacific Sea Farms, Inc., *In re,* 134 B.R. 11 (Bankr. D. Haw. 1991)	§ 2.25
Page, *In re,* 118 B.R. 456 (Bankr. N.D. Tex. 1990)	§ 17.5
Paradise Valley Country Club, *In re,* 31 B.R. 613 (Bankr. D. Colo. 1983)	§§ 17.1, 17.2
Park at Dash Point, Ltd., *In re,* 121 B.R. 850 (Bankr. W.D. Wash. 1990)	§ 3.8
Parker Steel Co., *In re,* 149 B.R. 834 (Bankr. N.D. Ohio 1992)	§ 11.12, 11.14
Parr Meadows Racing Ass'n, Inc., *In re,* 880 F.2d 1540 (2d Cir. 1989), *cert. denied sub nom.* Suffolk County Treasurer v. Barr, 493 U.S. 1058 (1990)	§ 5.1
Patella Constr. Corp., *In re,* 114 B.R. 53 (Bankr. D.N.J. 1990)	§ 7.16
Patterson, *In re,* 967 F.2d 505 (11th Cir. 1992)	§ 5.2
Patterson v. Shumate, ____ U.S. ____, 112 S. Ct. 2242 (1992)	§§ 20.2, 21.2, 21.3, 21.4
Paul Harris Stores, Inc., *In re,* 148 B.R. 307 (S.D. Ind. 1992)	§ 7.5
Paul Potts Builders, Inc., *In re,* 608 B.R. 1279 (9th Cir. 1979)	§ 12.10
Pearson, *In re,* 917 F.2d 1215 (9th Cir. 1990), *cert. denied,* ____ U.S. ____, 112 S. Ct. 1291 (1992)	§ 12.31
Pearson v. Salina Office Coffee House, Inc., 831 F.2d 1531 (10th Cir. 1987)	§ 12.7
Pecht, *In re,* 57 B.R. 137 (Bankr. E.D. Va. 1986)	§§ 8.17, 16.5, 16.6
Pecht, *In re,* 53 B.R. 768 (Bankr. E.D. Va. 1985)	§ 13.19
Pelika Mfg. Corp., *In re,* 66 B.R. 444 (Bankr. N.D. Ill. 1986)	§ 5.7
Pembroke Dev. Corp., *In re,* 122 B.R. 610 (Bankr. S.D. Fla. 1991)	§ 11.19
Penn Mut. Life Ins. Co. v. Woodscape, Ltd. (*In re* Woodscape, Ltd.), 134 B.R. 165 (Bankr. D. Md. 1991)	§ 16.8
Pennbank v. Winters (*In re* Winters), 99 B.R. 658 (Bankr. W.D. Pa. 1989)	§§ 16.1, 16.2, 16.10
Pennsylvania Dep't of Pub. Welfare v. Davenport, 495 U.S. 552 (1990)	§ 5.2
Pension Benefit Guar. Corp. v. Sharon Steel Corp. (*In re* Sharon Steel Corp.), 159 B.R. 730 (Bankr. W.D. Pa. 1993)	§ 3.10
Peoples Gas Sys., Inc. v. Thatcher Glass Corp. (*In re* Thatcher Glass Corp.), 59 B.R. 797 (Bankr. D. Conn. 1986)	§ 7.5
Pepenalla v. Life Ins. Co., 103 B.R. 299 (Bankr. N.D. Fla. 1988)	§ 20.4
Pepper v. Litton, 308 U.S. 295 (1939)	§ 12.5
Perry, *In re,* 29 B.R. 787 (D. Md. 1983), *aff'd sub nom.* Riggs Nat'l Bank v. Perry, 729 F.2d 982 (4th Cir. 1984)	§ 10.6
Pester Ref. Co., *In re,* 964 F.2d 842 (8th Cir. 1992)	§ 8.3
Peterson, *In re,* 116 B.R. 247 (D. Colo. 1990)	§ 5.7
Philadelphia Athletic Club, Inc., *In re,* 17 B.R. 345 (Bankr. E.D. Pa. 1982)	§ 6.25

Case	*Book §*
Philadelphia Light Supply Co., *In re,* 39 B.R. 51 (Bankr. E.D. Pa.1984)	§ 12.30
Philip Morris Capital Corp. v. Bering Trader, Inc. (*In re* Bering Trader, Inc.), 944 F.2d 500 (9th Cir. 1991)	§§ 4.2, 4.3
Phillips, *In re,* 966 F.2d 926 (5th Cir. 1992)	§ 22.5
PHM Credit Corp., *In re,* 110 B.R. 284 (E.D. Mich. 1990)	§ 2.3
Phoenix Mut. Life Ins. Co. v. Greystone III Joint Venture (*In re* Greystone III Joint Venture), 948 F.2d 134 (5th Cir.), *rev'd & remanded,* 995 F.2d 1274 (5th Cir. 1991)	§ 15.8
Phoenix Steel Corp., *In re,* 39 B.R. 218 (D. Del. 1984)	§§ 6.7, 6.11, 11.4, 11.13
Piedmont Assocs. v. CIGNA Property & Casualty Ins. Co., 132 B.R. 75 (N.D. Ga. 1991)	§§ 16.1, 16.2, 16.9
Pierce, *In re,* 809 F.2d 1356 (8th Cir. 1987)	§ 2.4
Pierce v. Underwood, 487 U.S. 552 490 (1988)	§ 2.25
Pinkston, *In re,* 134 B.R. 932 (Bankr. D. Neb. 1991)	§ 19.4
Pinto Trucking Serv., Inc., *In re,* 93 B.R. 379 (Bankr. E.D. Pa. 1988)	§ 12.24
Pioneer Inv. Servs. v. Brunswick Assocs., ____U.S. ____, 113 S. Ct. 1489 (1993)	§§ 2.9, 8.4
Pizza of Haw., Inc., *In re,* 761 F.2d 1374 (9th Cir. 1985)	§ 10.13
Plabell Rubber Prods., Inc., *In re,* 137 B.R. 897 (Bankr. N.D. Ohio 1992)	§§ 6.10, 6.19
Planned Sys., Inc., *In re,* 78 B.R. 852 (Bankr. S.D. Ohio 1987)	§ 3.10
Plant Specialties, Inc., *In re,* 59 B.R. 1 (Bankr. W.D. La. 1986)	§ 8.5
Plihal, *In re,* 97 B.R. 554 (Bankr. D. Neb. 1989)	§ 11.29
Polo Club Apartments Assocs., *In re,* 150 B.R. 840 (Bankr. N.D. Ga. 1993)	§ 3.8
Porter v. Yukon Nat'l Bank, 866 F.2d 355 (10th Cir. 1989)	§§ 11.14, 11.29
Potts, *In re,* 142 F.2d 883 (6th Cir. 1944), *cert. denied,* 324 U.S. 868 (1945)	§ 5.2
Practical Inv. Corp., *In re,* 95 B.R. 935 (Bankr. E.D. Va. 1989)	§ 12.10
Price v. Rochford, 947 F.2d 829 (7th Cir. 1991)	§ 5.5
Priestly, *In re,* 93 B.R. 253 (Bankr. D.N.M. 1988)	§ 22.6
Prime, Inc., *In re,* 15 B.R. 216 (Bankr. W.D. Mo. 1981)	§ 7.15
Prime, Inc., *In re,* 8 Bankr. Ct. Dec. (CRR) 389 (Bankr. W.D. Mo. 1981)	§ 6.2
Princeton Overlook Joint Venture, *In re,* 143 B.R. 625 (Bankr. D.N.J. 1992)	§ 3.8
Professional Dev. Corp., *In re,* 129 B.R. 522 (Bankr. W.D. Tenn. 1991)	§ 2.3
Professional Sales Corp., *In re,* 56 B.R. 753 (N.D. Ill. 1985)	§ 12.31
Prospero, *In re,* 107 B.R. 732 (Bankr. C.D. Cal. 1989)	§ 10.11
Providence Television, Ltd., *In re,* 113 B.R. 446 (Bankr. N.D. Ill. 1990)	§ 7.4
Prudential Ins. Co. of Am. v. Monnier (*In re* Monnier Bros.), 755 F.2d 1336 (8th Cir. 1985)	§ 15.14

Case	*Book §*
Public Serv., *In re,* 884 F.2d 11 (1st Cir. 1989)	§ 7.4
Public Serv. Co., *In re,* 107 B.R. 441 (Bankr. D.N.H. 1989)	§ 12.29
Public Serv. Co., *In re,* 88 B.R. 521 (Bankr. D.N.H. 1988)	§ 8.17
Puhlman Constr. Indus., *In re,* 27 Collier Bankr. Cas. 2d (MB) 707 (Bankr. N.D. Ill. 1992)	§ 12.31
Pullman Constr. Indus., *In re,* 107 B.R. 909 (Bankr. N.D. Ill. 1989)	§§ 16.1, 16.2, 16.7, 16.8, 16.9
Pursifull v. Eakin, 814 F.2d 1501 (10th Cir. 1987)	§ 5.7
Rabzak, *In re,* 79 B.R. 966 (Bankr. E.D. Pa. 1987)	§ 23.12
Rafoth v. National Union Fire Ins. Co., 954 F.2d 1169 (6th Cir. 1992)	§ 23.15
Raleigh/Spring Forest Apartment Assocs., *In re,* 118 B.R. 42 (Bankr. E.D.N.C. 1990)	§ 3.8
Ram Constr. Co. v. American States Ins. Co., 749 F.2d 1049 (3d Cir. 1984)	§ 12.28
Randall Enters., Inc., *In re,* 115 B.R. 292 (Bankr. D. Colo. 1990)	§ 5.6
Ray v. City Bank & Trust Co. (*In re* C-L Cartage Co.), 899 F.2d 1490 (6th Cir. 1990)	§ 12.21
Ray v. Norseworthy, 90 U.S. (23 Wall.) 128 (1874)	§ 9.6
Raymark Indus., Inc. v. Lai, 973 F.2d 1125 (3d Cir. 1992)	§ 5.2
Raymond, *In re,* 99 B.R. 819 (Bankr. S.D. Ohio 1989)	§ 3.10
R-B Co., *In re,* 59 B.R. 43 (Bankr. W.D. La. 1986)	§ 10.6
RB Furniture, Inc., *In re,* 141 B.R. 706 (Bankr. C.D. Cal. 1992)	§ 7.5
Reading Tube Indus., *In re,* 72 B.R. 329 (Bankr. E.D. Pa. 1987)	§§ 6.6, 6.9, 6.19
Realty S.W. Assocs., *In re,* 140 B.R. 360 (Bankr. S.D.N.Y. 1992)	§§ 3.4, 3.10
Rector, *In re,* 134 B.R. 611 (Bankr. W.D. Mich. 1991)	§ 21.6
Reddington Invs., *In re,* 90 B.R. 429 (Bankr. 9th Cir. 1988)	§ 23.19
Reed, *In re,* 890 F.2d 104 (8th Cir. 1989)	§ 2.20
Reed, *In re,* 700 F.2d 986 (5th Cir. 1983)	§§ 20.10, 20.12
Register, *In re,* 95 B.R. 73 (Bankr. M.D. Tenn.), *aff'd,* 100 B.R. 360 (M.D. Tenn. 1989)	§ 7.1
Reid, *In re,* 757 F.2d 230 (10th Cir. 1985)	§ 23.24
Republic Reader's Serv., Inc., *In re,* 81 B.R. 422 (Bankr. S.D. Tex. 1987)	§ 23.10
Resorts Int'l, Inc., *In re,* 145 B.R. 412 (Bankr. D.N.J. 1990)	§§ 16.4, 16.8
Ressler, *In re,* 61 B.R. 403 (Bankr. E.D. Tenn. 1986)	§ 12.10
Revco D.S., Inc., *In re,* 111 B.R. 626 (Bankr. N.D. Ohio 1989)	§ 7.5
Revco D.S., Inc., *In re,* 109 B.R. 264 (Bankr. N.D. Ohio 1989)	§ 7.6
Reynolds, *In re,* 17 B.R. 489 (Bankr. N.D. Ga. 1981)	§ 11.25
R.H. Williams, *In re,* 61 B.R. 567 (Bankr. N.D. Tex. 1986)	§ 3.13
Richard v. City of Chicago, 80 B.R. 451 (N.D. Ill. 1987)	§ 5.2

Case	*Book §*
Richmond Leasing v. Capital Bank, 762 F.2d 1303 (5th Cir. 1985)	§§ 7.13, 23.24
Ridgemont Apartment Assocs., Ltd. v. Atlanta English Village, Ltd., 110 B.R. 77 (N.D. Ga.), *aff'd,* 890 F.2d 1166 (11th Cir. 1989)	§ 5.8
Riggs Nat'l Bank v. Perry, 729 F.2d 982 (4th Cir. 1984)	§ 10.6
Rio, *In re,* 55 B.R. 814 (Bankr. M.D. Ala. 1985)	§ 3.7
River Capital Corp., *In re,* 155 B.R. 382 (Bankr. E.D. Va. 1991)	§§ 16.6, 16.9
R&O Elevator Co., v. Harmon, 93 B.R. 667 (D. Minn. 1988)	§ 7.17
Robbins, *In re,* 964 F.2d 342 (4th Cir. 1992)	§ 5.7
Roberts, *In re,* 46 B.R. 815 (Bankr. D. Utah 1985), *modified,* 75 B.R. 402 (D. Utah 1987)	§ 2.3
Rodriguez, *In re,* 895 F.2d 725 (11th Cir. 1990)	§ 12.27
Rooster, Inc., *In re,* 127 B.R. 560 (Bankr. E.D. Pa. 1991)	§ 12.29
Rosner v. Worcester, 811 F.2d 589 (9th Cir. 1987)	§ 23.27
Royster Co., *In re,* 137 B.R. 530 (Bankr. M.D. Fla. 1992)	§ 7.16
R/P Int'l Technologies, Inc., *In re,* 57 B.R. 869 (Bankr. S.D. Ohio 1985)	§ 7.13
Rubin, *In re,* 154 B.R. 897 (Bankr. D. Md. 1992)	§§ 10.8, 10.10
Rubin v. Manufacturers Hanover Trust Co., 661 F.2d 979 (2d Cir. 1981)	§ 12.27
Rubin Bros. Footwear, Inc., *In re,* 73 B.R. 346 (Bankr. S.D.N.Y. 1987)	§ 23.7
Rudy DeBruycker Ranch, Inc., *In re,* 84 B.R. 187 (Bankr. D. Mont. 1988)	§ 16.7
Rusty Jones, Inc., *In re,* 134 B.R. 321 (Bankr. N.D. Ill. 1991)	§ 2.8
Rusty Jones, Inc., *In re,* 110 B.R. 362 (Bankr. N.D. Ill. 1990)	§ 11.19
SAAB Cars USA, Inc. v. Wills Motors, Inc., 134 B.R. 124 (S.D.N.Y. 1991)	§ 7.15
S.A.B.T.C. Townhouse Ass'n, Inc., *In re,* 152 B.R. 1005 (Bankr. M.D. Fla. 1993)	§§ 16.3, 16.4, 16.5, 16.7, 16.8
Sacramento Mansion v. Sacramento Sav. & Loan Ass'n (In re Sacramento Mansion), 117 B.R. 592 (Bankr. D. Colo. 1990)	§§ 4.4, 4.6, 4.7
Safren, *In re,* 65 B.R. 566 (Bankr. C.D. Cal. 1986)	§ 22.5
St. Louis Globe-Democrat, Inc., *In re,* 63 B.R. 131 (Bankr. E.D. Mo. 1985)	§ 8.20
St. Mary Hosp., *In re,* 117 B.R. 759 (Bankr. E.D. Pa. 1990)	§ 23.6
St. Mary Hosp., *In re,* 86 B.R. 393 (Bankr. E.D. Pa. 1988)	§ 6.4
St. Paul Fire & Marine Ins. Co. v. Pepsico, Inc., 884 F.2d 688 (2d Cir. 1989)	§ 12.8
St. Petersburg Hotel Assocs., *In re,* 44 B.R. 944 (Bankr. M.D. Fla. 1984)	§ 6.8
Salem Plaza Assocs., *In re,* 135 B.R. 753 (Bankr. S.D.N.Y. 1992)	§ 3.10
Saline State Bank v. Mahloch, 834 F.2d 690 (8th Cir. 1987)	§ 3.8

Case	*Book §*
San Felipe @ Voss, Ltd., *In re,* 115 B.R. 526 (S.D. Tex. 1990)	§ 11.19, 15.15
Sanders v. City of Brady, ____ U.S. ____, 112 S. Ct. 657 (1991)	§ 5.4
Sanders Confectionery Prod., Inc. v. Heller Fin., Inc. 973 F.2d 474 (6th Cir. 1992), *cert. denied,* ____ U.S. ____, 113 S. Ct. 1046 (1993)	§ 12.34
Sandy Ridge Dev. Corp. v. Louisiana Nat'l Bank (*In re* Sandy Ridge Dev. Corp.), 881 F.2d 1346 (5th Cir. 1989)	§§ 11.8, 15.15
Santa Maria, *In re,* 128 B.R. 32 (Bankr. N.D.N.Y. 1991)	§ 19.4
Sanyo Elec., Inc. v. Howard's Appliance Corp. (*In re* Howard's Appliance Corp.), 874 F.2d 88 (2d Cir. 1989)	§ 12.8
Saturley, *In re,* 131 B.R. 509 (Bankr. D. Me. 1991)	§§ 2.8, 2.17
Savannah Gardens-Oaktree, *In re,* 146 B.R. 306 (Bankr. S.D. Ga. 1992)	§§ 11.7, 11.13, 11.15, 11.16, 11.20, 11.21
Sawmill Hydraulics, Inc., *In re,* 72 B.R. 454 (Bankr. C.D. Ill. 1987)	§§ 11.31, 16.6
Saybrook Mfg. Co., *In re,* 963 F.2d 1490 (11th Cir. 1992)	§§ 6.12, 6.26
Scherk v. Newton (*In re* Rocky Mountain Fuel Co.), 152 F.2d 747 (10th Cir. 1945)	§ 15.4
Schmitt, *In re,* 113 B.R. 1007 (Bankr. W.D. Mo. 1990)	§ 21.5
Schmitt v. Equibank (*In re* R.A. Beck Builder, Inc.), 34 B.R. 888 (Bankr. W.D. Pa. 1983)	§ 12.21
Schultz Broadway Inn v. United States, 912 F.2d 230 (8th Cir. 1990)	§ 12.6
Schulz v. Homes Transp., Inc., 149 B.R. 251 (D. Mass. 1993)	§ 5.6
Schwartz, *In re,* 954 F.2d 569 (9th Cir. 1992)	§§ 5.2, 5.3, 5.6
Scottsdale Medical Pavilion v. Mutual Benefit Life Ins. Co. (*In re* Scottsdale Medical Pavilion), 159 B.R. 295 (Bankr. 9th Cir. 1993)	§ 3.8
Sears Sav. Bank v. Tucson Indus. Partners (*In re* Tucson Indus. Partners), 129 B.R. 614 (Bankr. 9th Cir. 1991), *vacated as moot,* 990 F.2d 1099 (9th Cir. 1993)	§ 3.8
Seaway Express Corp., *In re,* 912 F.2d 1125 (9th Cir. 1990)	§§ 12.7, 12.8
Sechuan City, Inc., *In re,* 96 B.R. 37 (Bankr. E.D. Pa. 1989)	§ 5.3
Sedona San Carlos Dev. Co., *In re,* 59 B.R. 113 (Bankr. D. Ariz. 1986)	§ 9.5
Selgar Realty Corp., *In re,* 85 B.R. 235 (Bankr. E.D.N.Y. 1988)	§ 9.2
Serafini, *In re,* 41 B.R. 880 (Bankr. W.D. Pa. 1984)	§ 20.6
S.F. Drake Hotel Assocs., *In re,* 131 B.R. 156 (Bankr. N.D. Cal. 1991)	§ 4.10
Shattuc Cable Corp., *In re,* 138 B.R. 557 (Bankr. N.D. Ill. 1992)	§ 8.3
Sherwood Square Assocs., *In re,* 107 B.R. 872 (Bankr. D. Md. 1989)	§ 16.6, 16.8
Shore Haven Motor Inn, *In re,* 124 B.R. 617 (Bankr. S.D. Fla. 1991)	§§ 4.6, 4.7
S.I. Acquisition, Inc. v. Eastway Delivery Serv. (*In re* S.I. Acquisition, Inc.), 817 F.2d 1142 (5th Cir. 1987)	§ 12.8
Sierra Steel, Inc., *In re,* 96 B.R. 275 (Bankr. 9th Cir. 1989)	§§ 11.14, 11.33

Case	*Book §*
Sikes v. Global Marine, 881 F.2d 176 (5th Cir. 1989)	§ 5.2
Simco Mechanical, *In re,* 151 B.R. 978 (Bankr. S.D. Fla. 1993)	§ 11.14, 11.20
Sir Julian, Inc., *In re,* 95 B.R. 851 (Bankr. S.D. Fla. 1989)	§ 9.3
641 Assocs., Ltd. v. Balcor Real Estate Fin., Inc. (*In re* 641 Assocs., Ltd.), 140 B.R. 619 (Bankr. E.D. Pa. 1992)	§§ 15.7, 15.10
Skinner, *In re,* 90 B.R. 470 (D. Utah 1988), *aff'd,* 917 F.2d 444 (10th Cir. 1990)	§ 5.2
Sky Valley, Inc., *In re,* 100 B.R. 107 (Bankr. N.D. Ga. 1988)	§ 6.19
SLC Ltd. V, *In re,* 137 B.R. 847 (Bankr. D. Utah 1992)	§§ 16.1, 16.7, 16.8
SLC Ltd. V v. Bradford Group W. (*In re* SLC Ltd. V), 152 B.R. 755 (Bankr. D. Utah 1993)	§ 4.5
Sloan v. Zions First Nat'l Bank (*In re* Castletons, Inc.), 990 F.2d 551 (10th Cir. 1993)	§ 12.5
SM 104, Ltd., *In re,* 160 B.R. 202 (Bankr. S.D. Fla. 1993)	§§ 11.17, 11.20, 11.21, 15.8, 16.1, 16.2, 16.7, 16.8, 16.9
Small Business Admin. v. Rinehart, 887 F.2d 165 (8th Cir. 1989)	§§ 5.1, 5.2, 12.26
Smith, *In re,* 123 B.R. 863 (Bankr. C.D. Cal. 1991)	§ 15.8
Smith, *In re,* 876 F.2d 524 (6th Cir. 1989)	§ 5.2
Smith Corset Shops, Inc., *In re,* 696 F.2d 971 (1st Cir. 1982)	§ 5.2
Smith-Douglass, Inc., *In re,* 43 B.R. 616 (Bankr. E.D.N.C. 1984)	§ 23.7
SMS, Inc., *In re,* 15 B.R. 496 (Bankr. D. Kan. 1981)	§ 2.16
S.N. Brown Elec. Corp., *In re,* 136 B.R. 598 (Bankr. D. Mass. 1992)	§ 11.33
Snowshoe Co., *In re,* 789 F.2d 1085 (4th Cir. 1986)	§§ 6.6, 6.7, 6.8, 6.16, 6.19
Snyder, *In re,* 105 B.R. 898 (Bankr. C.D. Ill. 1989), *aff'd,* 967 F.2d 1126 (7th Cir. 1992)	§§ 16.1, 16.2, 16.4, 16.6, 16.7, 16.9
Snyder, *In re,* 99 B.R. 885 (Bankr. C.D. Ill. 1989), *aff'd,* 144 B.R. 393 (C.D. Ill. 1990)	§ 16.6
Software Centre Int'l, Inc., *In re,* 994 F.2d 682 (9th Cir. 1993)	§ 12.33
Solar Mfg. Corp., *In re,* 176 F.2d 493 (3d Cir. 1949)	§ 9.5
Somero, *In re,* 122 B.R. 634 (Bankr. D. Me. 1991)	§ 3.8
Sonnax Indus., Inc., *In re,* 99 B.R. 591 (D. Vt. 1989), *aff'd,* 907 F.2d 1280 (2d Cir. 1990)	§§ 5.6, 5.7
Sonora Convalescent Hosp., Inc., *In re,* 69 B.R. 134 (Bankr. E.D. Cal. 1986)	§ 7.8
South County Realty, Inc. II, *In re,* 69 B.R. 611 (Bankr. M.D. Fla. 1987)	§ 22.4
Southerland v. Smith, 136 B.R. 565 (Bankr. M.D. Fla. 1992)	§ 23.22
Southerton Corp., *In re,* 46 B.R. 391 (D. Pa. 1982)	§ 5.8
Southmark Corp. v. Southmark Personal Storage, Inc. (*In re* Southmark Corp.), 993 F.2d 117 (5th Cir. 1993)	§ 12.21
Southwest Aircraft Servs., Inc., *In re,* 831 F.2d 848 (9th Cir. 1987), *cert. denied,* 487 U.S. 1206 (1988)	§ 7.8

Case	*Book §*
Southwest Oil Co., *In re,* 84 B.R. 448 (Bankr. W.D. Tex. 1987)	§ 8.17
Sovereign Group 1985-27, Ltd., *In re,* 142 B.R. 702 (E.D. Pa. 1992)	§§ 16.4, 16.6, 16.7
Spacek v. Thomen (*In re* Universal Farming Indus.), 873 F.2d 1334 (9th Cir. 1989)	§ 12.5
Spanish Lake Assocs., *In re,* 92 B.R. 875 (Bankr. E.D. Mo. 1988)	§ 8.17
Spanish River Plaza Realty Co., *In re,* 155 B.R. 249 (Bankr. S.D. Fla. 1993)	§ 3.13
Sparmal Enters., Inc. v. Moffit Realty Corp., 126 B.R. 559 (S.D. Ind. 1991)	§ 12.33
Specialty Equip. Cos., *In re,* 3 F.3d 1043 (7th Cir. 1993)	§ 9.6
Spencer, *In re,* 115 B.R. 471 (D. Del. 1990)	§ 5.7
Spicer v. Woodhouse, 17 B.R. 275 (Bankr. S.D. Ohio 1982)	§ 19.3
Stadium Management Corp., *In re,* 895 F.2d 845 (1st Cir. 1990)	§ 7.14
Stanley Hotel, Inc., *In re,* 15 B.R. 660 (D. Colo. 1981)	§§ 6.7, 6.19
Stanley Station Assocs., *In re,* 139 B.R. 990 (Bankr. D. Kan. 1992)	§ 3.8
Stann, *In re,* 39 B.R. 246 (D. Kan. 1984)	§ 3.7
Stanolind Oil & Gas Co. v. Logan, 92 F.2d 28 (5th Cir.), *cert. denied,* 302 U.S. 763 (1938)	§ 10.5
Starbuck, *In re,* 14 B.R. 134 (Bankr. S.D.N.Y. 1981)	§ 17.5
Statewide Oilfield Constr., Inc., *In re,* 134 B.R. 399 (Bankr. E.D. Cal. 1991)	§ 7.18
Stauffer, *In re,* 141 B.R. 612 (Bankr. N.D. Ohio 1992)	§ 11.25
Stegall, *In re,* 865 F.2d 140 (7th Cir. 1989)	§§ 16.5, 16.6, 16.8
Stephens Indus., Inc. v. McClung, 789 F.2d 386 (6th Cir. 1986)	§ 9.5
Stern v. Continental Assurance Co. (*In re* Ryan), 851 F.2d 502 (1st Cir. 1988)	§ 12.7
Stevenson, *In re,* 28 B.R. 37 (Bankr. S.D. Miss. 1982), *aff'd,* 28 B.R. 39 (S.D. Miss. 1983)	§ 19.2
Stewart v. Gurley, 745 F.2d 1194 (9th Cir. 1984)	§§ 5.9, 8.10, 11.6
Steyr-Daimler-Puch of Am. Corp. v. Pappas, 852 F.2d 132 (4th Cir. 1988)	§ 12.8
STN Enters., *In re,* 779 F.2d 901 (2d Cir. 1985)	§ 12.25
Stockbridge Properties I, Ltd., *In re,* 141 B.R. 469 (Bankr. N.D. Ga. 1992)	§ 11.21
Stone Ridge Assocs., *In re,* 142 B.R. 967 (Bankr. D. Kan. 1992)	§§ 3.6, 3.8
Stonegate Sec. Servs., Ltd., *In re,* 56 B.R. 1014 (N.D. Ill. 1986)	§ 5.2
Stoumbos v. Kiliminik, 988 F.2d 949 (9th Cir. 1993)	§ 12.5
Stratford Ass'n, *In re,* 145 B.R. 689 (Bankr. D. Kan. 1992)	§§ 10.13, 14.4
Streets & Beard Farm Partnership, *In re,* 882 F.2d 233 (7th Cir. 1989)	§ 7.2
Stringer, *In re,* 847 F.2d 549 (9th Cir. 1988)	§ 5.3

Case	*Book §*
Stuart Motel, Inc., *In re,* 8 B.R. 48 (Bankr. S.D. Fla. 1980)	§ 15.10
Suffolk County Treasurer v. Barr, 493 U.S. 1058 (1990)	§ 5.1
Sufolla, Inc., *In re,* 2 F.3d 977 (9th Cir. 1993)	§ 12.21
Sumitomo Trust & Banking Co., v. Holly's, Inc. (*In re* Holly's, Inc.), 140 B.R. 643 (Bankr. W.D. Mich. 1992)	§ 3.10
Summit Coffee Co. v. Herby's Foods, Inc. (*In re* Herby's Foods, Inc.), 2 F.3d 128 (5th Cir. 1993)	§ 12.5
Sumy v. Schlossberg, 777 F.2d 921 (4th Cir. 1985)	§ 20.4
Sun Island Foods, *In re,* 125 B.R. 615 (Bankr. D. Haw. 1991)	§ 12.30
Sun Runner Marine, Inc., *In re,* 116 B.R. 712, *vacated in part, aff'd in part,* 945 F.2d 1089 (Bankr. 9th Cir. 1991)	§§ 6.2, 7.2, 7.14
Sundial Asphalt Co., *In re,* 147 B.R. 72 (E.D.N.Y. 1992)	§ 7.11
Sunset Developers, Inc., *In re,* 69 B.R. 710 (Bankr. D. Idaho 1987)	§ 22.6
Super 8 Motels v. M. Vickers, Ltd. (*In re* M. Vickers, Ltd.), 111 B.R. 332 (D. Colo. 1990)	§§ 4.4, 4.6, 4.7
Sure-Snap Corp. v. State St. Bank & Trust Co., 948 F.2d 869 (2d Cir. 1991)	§ 12.34
Sutton, *In re,* 904 F.2d 327 (5th Cir.), *reh'g denied,* (5th Cir. 1991)	§ 5.9
S&W Enter., *In re,* 37 B.R. 153 (Bankr. N.D. Ill. 1984)	§ 15.21
Swanson, *In re,* 873 F.2d 1121 (8th Cir. 1989)	§ 21.5
Tallahassee Assocs., *In re,* 132 B.R. 712 (Bankr. W.D. Pa. 1991)	§§ 16.4, 16.7, 16.8
Tape City, U.S.A., Inc., *In re,* 677 F.2d 401 (5th Cir. 1982)	§ 12.13
Tavern Motor Inn, *In re,* 80 B.R. 659 (D. Vt. 1987)	§ 4.10
Taxman Clothing Co., *In re,* 134 B.R. 286 (N.D. Ill. 1991)	§ 2.18
Taxman Clothing Co., *In re,* 905 F.2d 166 (7th Cir. 1990)	§§ 11.9, 11.10, 11.13, 11.23
Taylor, *In re,* 130 B.R. 849 (Bankr. E.D. Ark. 1991)	§ 7.17
Taylor, *In re,* 884 F.2d 478 (9th Cir. 1989)	§ 5.5
Taylor, *In re,* 15 B.R. 596 (Bankr. D. Ariz. 1981)	§ 19.2
Taylor v. Freeland & Kronz, ____ U.S. ____, 112 S. Ct. 1644 (1992)	§ 20.5
T.B. Westex Foods, Inc. v. Alaska Continental Bank (*In re* T.B. Westex Foods, Inc.), 96 B.R. 77 (Bankr. W.D. Tex. 1989)	§ 12.21
Teamsters Nat'l Freight Indus. Negotiating Comm. v. U.S. Truck Co. (*In re* U.S. Truck Co.), 800 F.2d 581 (6th Cir. 1986)	§§ 15.8, 16.7
Tek-Aids Indus., Inc., *In re,* 145 B.R. 253 (Bankr. N.D. Ill. 1992)	§ 12.30
Temple Zion, *In re,* 125 B.R. 910 (Bankr. E.D. Pa. 1991)	§ 17.4
Tennessee Chem. Co., *In re,* 143 B.R. 468 (Bankr. E.D. Tenn. 1992)	§§ 11.2, 11.9, 11.13, 11.14, 11.24, 11.27, 11.33, 11.34, 11.36
Tenney Village Co., *In re,* 104 B.R. 562 (Bankr. D.N.H. 1989)	§§ 6.10, 6.11

Case	*Book §*
Terjen, *In re,* 154 B.R. 456 (Bankr. E.D. Va. 1993)	§ 10.7
Terrace Apartments, Ltd., *In re,* 107 B.R. 382 (Bankr. N.D. Ga. 1989)	§ 7.15
Terrat, *In re,* 19 B.R. 360 (Bankr. D. Alaska 1982)	§ 20.6
Terrell, *In re,* 892 F.2d 469 (6th Cir. 1989)	§ 7.2
T-H New Orleans, Ltd., *In re,* 148 B.R. 456 (E.D. La. 1992)	§ 5.9
T-H New Orleans, Ltd. v. Financial Sec. Assurance (*In re* T-H New Orleans, Ltd.), 5 F.3d 86 (5th Cir. 1993)	§ 4.10
Theatre Holding Corp. v. Mauro, 681 F.2d 102 (2d Cir. 1982)	§ 7.7
Thirtieth Place, *In re,* 30 B.R. 503 (Bankr. 9th Cir. 1983)	§ 8.6
Thomas B. Hamilton Co., *In re,* 115 B.R. 384 (Bankr. N.D. Ga. 1990)	§ 7.15
Thomasson, *In re,* 60 B.R. 629 (Bankr. M.D. Tenn. 1986)	§ 23.19
Thompson, *In re,* 788 F.2d 560 (9th Cir. 1986)	§ 7.4
Three Star Telecast, Inc., *In re,* 93 B.R. 310 (D.P.R. 1988)	§ 7.16
Three Star Telecast, Inc., *In re,* 73 B.R. 270 (Bankr. D.P.R. 1987)	§ 7.4
Thunderbird Inn, *In re,* 151 B.R. 224 (Bankr. D. Ariz. 1993)	§§ 4.6, 4.7, 4.13
Tidwell v. Amsouth Bank, N.A. (*In re* Cavalier Homes, Inc.), 102 B.R. 878 (M.D. Ga. 1989)	§ 12.21
Tilco, Inc., *In re,* 558 F.2d 1369 (10th Cir. 1977)	§ 7.11
Timber Prods., Inc., *In re,* 125 B.R. 433 (Bankr. W.D. Pa. 1990)	§§ 6.7, 6.8, 6.18
Timbers of Inwood Forest Assocs., *In re,* 808 F.2d 363 (5th Cir. 1987), *aff'd,* 484 U.S. 365 (1988)	§§ 5.8, 5.9, 6.7, 8.10, 11.5
Titusville Country Club, Inc., *In re,* 128 B.R. 396 (Bankr. W.D. Pa. 1991)	§ 9.5
TM Carlton House Partners, Ltd., *In re,* 110 B.R. 185 (Bankr. E.D. Pa. 1990)	§ 17.6
TM Carlton House Partners, Ltd., *In re,* 91 B.R. 349 (Bankr. E.D. Pa. 1988)	§ 3.8
TMA Assocs., Ltd., *In re,* 129 B.R. 643 (Bankr. D. Colo. 1991)	§ 2.3
Tolona Pizza Prod. Corp., *In re,* 2 F.3d 1029 (7th Cir. 1993)	§ 12.18
Tom Stimus Chrysler-Plymouth, Inc., *In re,* 134 B.R. 676 (Bankr. M.D. Fla. 1991)	§ 7.15
Torgerson Co., *In re,* 114 B.R. 899 (Bankr. S.D. Tex. 1990)	§ 7.3
Total Technical Servs., Inc., *In re,* 150 B.R. 893 (Bankr. D. Del. 1993)	§§ 11.11, 11.12, 11.22, 11.23
Travelers Ins. Co. v. American Agcredit Corp. (*In re* Blehm Land & Cattle Co.), 859 F.2d 137 (10th Cir. 1988)	§ 3.10
Travelers Ins. Co. v. Bryson Properties, XVIII (*In re* Bryson Properties, XVIII), 961 F.2d 496 (4th Cir.), *cert. denied,* ____ U.S. ____, 113 S. Ct. 191 (1992)	§§ 16.1, 16.2, 16.9
Travelers Ins. Co. v. Cambridge Meridian Group, Inc. (*In re* Erin Food Serv., Inc.), 980 F.2d 792 (1st Cir. 1992)	§ 12.21

Case	*Book §*
United States v. Mansfield Tire & Rubber Co. (*In re* Mansfield Tire & Rubber Co.), 942 F.2d 1055 (6th Cir. 1991)	§ 12.6
United States v. McPeck, 910 F.2d 509 (8th Cir. 1990)	§ 12.26
United States v. Nordic Village, Inc., 503 U.S. ____, 112 S. Ct. 1011 (1992)	§§ 5.5, 12.31
United States v. Novak, 86 B.R. 625 (D.S.D. 1988)	§ 17.4
United States v. One Single Family Residence, 894 F.2d 1511 (11th Cir. 1990)	§ 20.4
United States v. Redmond, 36 B.R. 932 (D. Kan. 1984)	§ 17.1
United States v. Stribling Flying Serv., 734 F.2d 221 (5th Cir. 1984)	§ 17.3
United States v. 10,031.98 Acres of Land, 850 F.2d 634 (10th Cir. 1988)	§ 11.20
United States v. Whiting Pools, Inc., 462 U.S. 198 2309 (1983)	§ 3.2
University Medical Ctr., *In re,* 973 F.2d 1065 (3d Cir. 1992)	§ 7.4
UNR Indus., Inc. v. Continental Ins. Co., 46 B.R. 727 (Bankr. M.D. Ga. 1984)	§ 23.7
Unruh v. Rushville State Bank, 987 F.2d 1506 (10th Cir. 1993)	§§ 16.1, 16.6, 16.7, 16.8
Unsecured Creditors Comm. v. Marepcon Fin. Corp. (*In re* Bumper Sales), 907 F.2d 1430 (4th Cir. 1990)	§§ 4.2, 4.8
U.S. Fax, Inc., *In re,* 114 B.R. 70 (E.D. Pa. 1990)	§ 7.18
U.S. Truck Co., 47 B.R. 932 (E.D. Mich. 1985), *aff'd sub nom.* Teamsters Nat'l Freight Indus. Negotiating Comm. v. U.S. Truck Co., 800 F.2d 581 (6th Cir. 1986)	§ 16.7
Usry, *In re,* 106 B.R. 759 (Bankr. M.D. Ga. 1989)	§§ 11.7, 11.18
Utility Stationery Stores, *In re,* 12 B.R. 170 (Bankr. N.D. Ill. 1981)	§ 11.2
Utrecht Coal Co., *In re,* 63 F.2d 745 (2d Cir. 1933)	§ 11.2
Valrico Square Ltd. Partnership, *In re,* 113 B.R. 794 (Bankr. S.D. Fla. 1990)	§ 13.19
Valley Park Group, Inc., *In re,* 96 B.R. 16 (Bankr. N.D.N.Y. 1989)	§ 15.1
Vaughter, *In re,* 109 B.R. 229 (Bankr. W.D. Tex. 1989)	§ 12.29
Verazano Holding Corp., *In re,* 86 B.R. 755 (Bankr. E.D.N.Y. 1988)	§ 23.10
Vescovo, *In re,* 125 B.R. 468 (Bankr. W.D. Tex. 1990)	§ 12.10
Victor Sav. & Loan Ass'n v. Grimm (*In re* Greater Atl. & Pac. Inv. Group), 88 B.R. 356 (Bankr. N.D. Okla. 1988)	§§ 4.6, 4.7
Victoria Station, Inc., *In re,* 875 F.2d 1380 (Bankr. 9th Cir. 1989)	§ 7.8
Victoria Station, Inc., *In re,* 88 B.R. 231 (Bankr. 9th Cir. 1988)	§ 7.8
Vienna Park Properties, *In re,* 136 B.R. 43 (S.D.N.Y. 1992)	§ 3.8
Village Properties, Ltd., *In re,* 723 F.2d 441 (5th Cir.), *cert. denied sub nom.* Wolters Village, Ltd. v. Village Properties, Ltd., 466 U.S. 974 (1984)	§§ 3.6, 3.8

Case	*Book §*
Vineyard v. McKenzie (*In re* Quality Holsteen Leasing), 752 F.2d 1009 (5th Cir. 1985)	§ 12.8
VIP Motor Lodge, Inc., *In re,* 133 B.R. 41 (Bankr. D. Del. 1991)	§ 16.6
Virginia Beach Fed. Sav. & Loan Ass'n v. Wood, 97 B.R. 71 (N.D. Okla. 1988), *aff'd,* 901 F.2d 849 (10th Cir. 1990)	§ 3.8
Virtual Network Serv. Corp., *In re,* 902 F.2d 1246 (7th Cir. 1990)	§ 12.6
Viscount Furniture Corp., *In re,* 133 B.R. 360 (Bankr. N.D. Miss. 1991)	§ 2.11
Voest-Alpine Trading USA Corp. v. Vantage Steel Corp., 919 F.2d 206 (3d Cir. 1990)	§ 12.26
Wadsworth, Inc., *In re,* 711 F.2d 122 (9th Cir. 1983)	§ 12.19
Wainer v. A.J. Equities, Ltd., 984 F.2d 679 (5th Cir. 1993)	§ 7.17
Waldengreen Assocs., *In re,* 150 B.R. 468 (Bankr. M.D. Fla. 1993)	§ 16.6
Wallace v. Lawrence Warehouse Co., 338 F.2d 392 (9th Cir. 1964)	§ 10.5
Walls, *In re,* 17 B.R. 701 (Bankr. S.D. W. Va. 1982)	§ 19.3
Ward, *In re,* 129 B.R. 664 (Bankr. W.D. Okla. 1991)	§ 19.2
Ward, *In re,* 6 B.R. 93 (Bankr. M.D. Fla. 1980)	§ 19.2
Washburn & Roberts, Inc., *In re,* 795 F.2d 870 (9th Cir. 1986)	§ 12.7
Water Gap Village, *In re,* 99 B.R. 226 (Bankr. D.N.J. 1989)	§ 15.15
Waterfront Cos., *In re,* 56 B.R. 31 (Bankr. D. Minn. 1985)	§ 6.3
Watson, *In re,* 148 B.R. 930 (Bankr. C.D. Cal. 1992)	§ 21.3
Wedtech Corp., *In re,* 81 B.R. 237 (Bankr. S.D.N.Y. 1987)	§ 23.7
Wedtech Corp., *In re,* 72 B.R. 464 (Bankr. S.D.N.Y. 1987)	§ 7.8
Weiboldt Stores, Inc. v. Schottenstein, 845 F.2d 842 (9th Cir. 1988)	§ 12.26
Weisman, *In re,* 5 F.3d 417 (9th Cir. 1993)	§ 12.7
Wesco Prods. Co., *In re,* 19 B.R. 908 (Bankr. N.D. Ill. 1982)	§ 23.12
West Elecs., Inc., *In re,* 852 F.2d 79 (3d Cir. 1988)	§ 7.15
Western Monetary Consultants, *In re,* 100 B.R. 545 (Bankr. D. Colo. 1989)	§ 7.5
Western Real Estate Fund, Inc., *In re,* 922 F.2d 592 (10th Cir. 1990)	§ 17.3
Westholt Mfg., Inc., *In re,* 20 B.R. 368 (Bankr. D. Kan. 1982), *aff'd sub nom.* United States v. Redmond, 36 B.R. 932 (D. Kan. 1984)	§ 17.1
Westland Oil Dev. Corp. v. MCorp Mgmt. Solutions, Inc., 157 B.R. 100 (S.D. Tex. 1993)	§ 15.23
Westview 74th St. Drug Corp., *In re,* 59 B.R. 747 (Bankr. S.D.N.Y. 1986)	§§ 7.13, 8.13
Westworld Community Healthcare, Inc., *In re,* 95 B.R. 730 (Bankr. C.D. Cal. 1989)	§ 7.13
Whitcomb & Keller Mortgage Co., *In re,* 715 F.2d 375 (7th Cir. 1983)	§ 7.7

Case	*Book §*
White, *In re,* 36 B.R. 199 (Bankr. D. Kan. 1983)	§ 15.10
White Motor Credit Corp., *In re,* 14 B.R. 584 (Bankr. N.D. Ohio 1981)	§ 9.5
White Plains Dev. Corp., *In re,* 136 B.R. 93 (Bankr. S.D.N.Y. 1992)	§ 3.4
Wieseler, *In re,* 934 F.2d 965 (8th Cir.), *reh'g denied,* 1991 U.S. App. LEXIS 15273 (8th Cir. July 8, 1991)	§ 5.6
Wildcat Constr. Co., *In re,* 57 B.R. 981 (Bankr. D. Vt. 1986)	§ 3.7
Wilde, *In re,* 85 B.R. 147 (Bankr. D.N.M. 1988)	§ 12.28
Willemain v. Kivitz, 764 F.2d 1019 (4th Cir. 1985)	§ 9.3
William Brittingham, Inc., *In re,* 39 B.R. 575 (Bankr. D. Del. 1984)	§ 7.18
Williams, *In re,* 61 B.R. 567 (Bankr. N.D. Tex. 1986)	§§ 3.7, 12.28
Williams v. California 1st Bank, 859 F.2d 664 (9th Cir. 1988)	§ 12.8
Wills Motors, Inc., *In re,* 133 B.R. 303 (S.D.N.Y.), *aff'd sub nom.* SAAB Cars USA, Inc. v. Wills Motors, Inc., 134 B.R. 124 (S.D.N.Y. 1991)	§ 7.15
Wilson, *In re,* 94 B.R. 886 (Bankr. E.D. Va. 1989)	§ 10.5
Wilson, *In re,* 70 B.R. 46 (Bankr. N.D. Ill. 1987)	§ 3.10
Wilson v. Huffman, (*In re* Missionary Baptist Found. of Am., Inc.), 712 F.2d 206 (5th Cir. 1983)	§ 12.5
Wilson Foods Corp., *In re,* 36 B.R. 317 (Bankr. W.D. Okla. 1984)	§ 2.18
Wilson Foods Corp., *In re,* 31 B.R. 272 (Bankr. W.D. Okla. 1983)	§ 8.5
Windmill Farms, Inc., *In re,* 841 F.2d 1467 (9th Cir. 1988)	§ 7.2
Windsor on the River Assocs., Ltd. v. Balcor Real Estate Fin., Inc. (*In re* Windsor on the River Assocs., Ltd.), 7 F.3d 127 (8th Cir. 1993)	§ 15.8
Winslow, *In re,* 39 B.R. 869 (Bankr. M.D. Ga. 1984)	§ 8.6
Wise Transp., Inc., *In re,* 148 B.R. 52 (Bankr. N.D. Okla. 1992)	§ 3.10
Wiston XXIV, L.P., *In re,* 153 B.R. 322 (Bankr. D. Kan. 1993)	§ 15.7
Witwer, *In re,* 148 B.R. 930 (Bankr. C.D. Cal. 1992)	§§ 20.2, 21.3, 21.5, 21.6
Witt, *In re,* 60 B.R. 556 (Bankr. N.D. Iowa 1986)	§§ 16.1, 16.8
W.J. Serv., Inc., *In re,* 139 B.R. 824 (Bankr. S.D. Tex. 1992)	§ 23.22
WJM, Inc. v. Massachusetts Dep't of Pub. Welfare, 840 F.2d 996 (1st Cir. 1988)	§ 12.18
Wolters Village, Ltd. v. Village Properties, Ltd. (*In re* Village Properties, Ltd.), 723 F.2d 441 (5th Cir.), *cert. denied,* 466 U.S. 974 (1984)	§§ 3.6, 4.4
Wood, *In re,* 113 B.R. 253 (S.D. Miss. 1990)	§ 12.33
Woods Farmers Co-op Elevator Co., *In re,* 946 F.2d 1411 (8th Cir. 1991)	§ 12.12
Woodward v. White Satin Mills Corp., 42 F.2d 987 (8th Cir. 1930)	§ 11.30
World Skating Ctr., Inc., *In re,* 100 B.R. 147 (Bankr. D. Conn. 1989)	§ 7.13

TABLE OF UNITED STATES CODE CITATIONS

U.S.C. §	*Book §*
11 U.S.C. § 11	§ 23.2
11 U.S.C. § 46	§ 23.2
11 U.S.C. § 66	§ 23.2
11 U.S.C. § 67(a)	§ 23.2
11 U.S.C. §§ 101 *et seq.*	§§ 6.30, 9.7, 14.9, 14.11
11 U.S.C. §§ 101–151326	§ 14.10
11 U.S.C. §§ 101–1330	§ 23.2
11 U.S.C. § 101	§§ 12.30, 13.20, 13.21, 17.4, 17.6
11 U.S.C. § 101(2)	§ 15.8
11 U.S.C. § 101(5)	§ 15.3
11 U.S.C. § 101(14)(A)–(D)	§ 2.4
11 U.S.C. § 101(14)(E)	§ 2.4
11 U.S.C. § 101(16)	§ 15.3
11 U.S.C. § 101(18)	§ 16.10
11 U.S.C. § 101(30)	§§ 19.2, 22.4
11 U.S.C. § 101(31)	§ 15.8
11 U.S.C. § 101(32)	§§ 11.2, 22.8
11 U.S.C. § 101(32)(A)(i)	§ 11.2
11 U.S.C. § 101(32)(B)	§ 11.2
11 U.S.C. § 101(36)	§§ 12.10, 20.6, 20.7
11 U.S.C. § 101(37)	§ 12.10
11 U.S.C. § 101(49)	§ 12.4
11 U.S.C. § 101(50)	§ 10.5
11 U.S.C. § 101(53)	§ 12.10
11 U.S.C. § 101(58)	§ 10.5
11 U.S.C. § 102	§ 6.29
11 U.S.C. § 102(1)	§§ 2.10, 3.14, 3.17, 3.18, 9.3
11 U.S.C. § 105	§§ 6.29, 9.7, 22.7, 23.2, 23.16
11 U.S.C. § 105(a)	§§ 17.2, 22.7
11 U.S.C. § 106	§ 12.31
11 U.S.C. § 106(a)	§ 12.31
11 U.S.C. § 106(b)	§ 12.31
11 U.S.C. § 106(c)	§ 12.31
11 U.S.C. § 108(a)	§ 12.33
11 U.S.C. § 108(b)(2)	§ 10.13
11 U.S.C. § 109	§ 17.7
11 U.S.C. § 109(b)	§ 22.4

U.S.C. §	*Book §*
11 U.S.C. § 109(c)	§ 19.2
11 U.S.C. § 109(d)	§ 22.4
11 U.S.C. § 109(e)	§§ 19.2, 24.2
11 U.S.C. § 109(g)	§ 17.7
11 U.S.C. § 151(b)	§ 23.2
11 U.S.C. § 157	§ 23.3
11 U.S.C. §§ 301–303	§ 12.33
11 U.S.C. § 301	§ 22.4
11 U.S.C. § 302(b)	§ 19.2
11 U.S.C. § 303	§ 22.4
11 U.S.C. § 303(h)	§ 11.3
11 U.S.C. § 303(i)	§ 2.25
11 U.S.C. § 303(i)(1)	§ 2.25
11 U.S.C. § 326	§ 14.11
11 U.S.C. § 327	§§ 1.8, 2.1, 2.2, 2.3, 2.4, 2.8, 2.10, 2.14, 2.16, 2.25, 14.11
11 U.S.C. § 327(a)	§§ 2.2, 2.3, 2.4, 2.8, 2.10, 2.12, 2.14
11 U.S.C. § 327(b)	§§ 2.2, 2.4
11 U.S.C. § 327(c)	§ 2.3
11 U.S.C. § 327(d)	§ 2.2
11 U.S.C. § 327(e)	§§ 2.2, 2.4, 2.7
11 U.S.C. § 328	§§ 2.11, 2.14, 14.11
11 U.S.C. § 328(a)	§§ 2.16, 2.17
11 U.S.C. § 328(b)	§§ 2.16, 2.17
11 U.S.C. § 329	§§ 2.8, 2.11, 2.14, 2.17
11 U.S.C. § 329(a)	§ 2.17
11 U.S.C. § 330	§§ 1.8, 2.1, 2.14, 2.18, 2.22, 13.10, 14.11, 24.8
11 U.S.C. § 330(a)	§§ 2.14, 2.18, 2.20, 2.23, 2.24
11 U.S.C. § 331	§§ 2.14, 2.18, 14.11
11 U.S.C. § 341	§§ 10.4, 19.3
11 U.S.C. § 345	§§ 14.11, 15.22
11 U.S.C. § 346	§ 10.10
11 U.S.C. § 346(g)(1)(B)	§ 10.9
11 U.S.C. § 350	§§ 10.4, 20.6
11 U.S.C. § 361	§§ 3.16, 5.6, 6.6, 6.29, 11.1, 11.5
11 U.S.C. § 361(1)	§ 5.8
11 U.S.C. § 361(2)	§§ 3.16, 4.12, 5.8
11 U.S.C. § 361(3)	§§ 5.8, 6.7
11 U.S.C. § 362	§§ 3.7, 3.14, 3.16, 5.1, 5.2, 6.29, 11.1, 11.5, 17.1
11 U.S.C. § 362(a)	§§ 8.1, 15.20
11 U.S.C. § 362(a)(1)–(8)	§ 5.2
11 U.S.C. § 362(a)(3)	§ 22.7

U.S.C. §	Book §
11 U.S.C. § 362(a)(6)	§ 5.2
11 U.S.C. § 362(b)	§ 8.1
11 U.S.C. § 362(b)(1)–(6)	§ 5.3
11 U.S.C. § 362(b)(1)	§§ 2.10, 5.3
11 U.S.C. § 362(b)(2)	§ 5.3
11 U.S.C. § 362(b)(4)	§ 5.3
11 U.S.C. § 362(c)	§§ 5.2, 17.1
11 U.S.C. § 362(c)(1)	§ 5.4
11 U.S.C. § 362(c)(2)	§§ 5.4, 17.1
11 U.S.C. § 362(d)	§§ 3.14, 5.2, 5.4, 5.6, 8.8, 8.10
11 U.S.C. § 362(d)(1)	§§ 3.13, 5.6, 5.8, 8.7, 8.8
11 U.S.C. § 362(d)(2)	§§ 5.4, 5.9, 8.8, 8.10, 11.6
11 U.S.C. § 362(e)	§ 8.11
11 U.S.C. § 362(f)	§§ 3.14, 8.11
11 U.S.C. § 362(g)	§§ 5.4, 8.10
11 U.S.C. § 362(g)(1)	§ 5.6
11 U.S.C. § 362(g)(2)	§ 5.6
11 U.S.C. § 362(h)	§§ 2.25, 5.5, 8.1, 12.31
11 U.S.C. § 363	§§ 2.2, 2.11, 3.4, 3.8, 3.9, 3.10, 3.14, 3.16, 4.10, 4.12, 6.1, 6.3, 6.29, 9.2, 9.7, 9.8, 11.1, 11.5, 12.28, 13.20, 16.9
11 U.S.C. § 363(a)	§§ 3.5, 3.7, 3.8, 3.9, 3.10, 4.12, 8.12
11 U.S.C. § 363(b)	§§ 3.4, 7.14, 9.2, 9.4, 9.5, 9.6, 9.7, 9.8
11 U.S.C. § 363(b)(1)	§§ 9.2, 9.3, 9.6, 19.5
11 U.S.C. § 363(c)	§§ 3.7, 3.10, 7.14, 11.4, 19.3
11 U.S.C. § 363(c)(1)	§§ 3.3, 3.4, 8.2, 9.2
11 U.S.C. § 363(c)(2)	§§ 3.4, 3.13, 3.14, 4.12, 8.12
11 U.S.C. § 363(c)(2)(A)	§ 3.12
11 U.S.C. § 363(c)(2)(B)	§ 3.12
11 U.S.C. § 363(c)(3)	§ 3.12
11 U.S.C. § 363(c)(4)	§§ 3.4, 3.10, 3.13
11 U.S.C. § 363(d)	§ 9.2
11 U.S.C. § 363(d)(3)	§ 7.9
11 U.S.C. § 363(e)	§§ 3.4, 3.10, 3.14, 3.16, 8.12, 9.2
11 U.S.C. § 363(f)–(k)	§ 9.2
11 U.S.C. § 363(f)	§§ 9.7, 9.8
11 U.S.C. § 363(k)	§§ 9.6, 15.15
11 U.S.C. § 363(m)	§§ 7.14, 9.2, 9.3, 9.6, 9.7, 9.8

U.S.C. §	*Book §*
11 U.S.C. § 363(n)	§§ 2.25, 9.2
11 U.S.C. § 363(o)	§ 3.10
11 U.S.C. § 364	§§ 2.25, 6.2, 6.4, 6.19, 6.29, 11.5, 13.20, 19.3
11 U.S.C. § 364(a)	§§ 6.2, 6.3, 6.30, 8.2
11 U.S.C. § 364(b)	§§ 6.2, 6.3, 6.4, 6.29, 6.30
11 U.S.C. § 364(c)	§§ 6.4, 6.5, 6.29, 6.30
11 U.S.C. § 364(c)(1)	§§ 6.2, 6.4, 6.29, 6.30
11 U.S.C. § 364(c)(2)	§§ 6.2, 6.4, 6.29
11 U.S.C. § 364(c)(3)	§§ 6.2, 6.4, 6.29
11 U.S.C. § 364(d)	§§ 3.16, 6.2, 6.5, 6.6, 6.7, 6.10, 6.29, 6.30, 11.4
11 U.S.C. § 364(d)(1)(A)	§ 6.5
11 U.S.C. § 364(d)(1)(B)	§§ 6.5, 6.10
11 U.S.C. § 364(d)(2)	§ 6.5
11 U.S.C. § 364(e)	§§ 6.12, 6.30, 7.14
11 U.S.C. § 365	§§ 2.2, 6.2, 7.1, 7.2, 7.3, 7.10, 7.14, 8.13, 8.15, 9.7, 9.8, 22.6
11 U.S.C. § 365(a)	§§ 7.11, 23.7
11 U.S.C. § 365(a)(4)	§ 7.8
11 U.S.C. § 365(b)	§ 2.25
11 U.S.C. § 365(b)(1)	§§ 7.10, 7.13, 8.13, 8.16
11 U.S.C. § 365(b)(1)(A)	§ 7.13
11 U.S.C. § 365(b)(1)(B)	§ 7.13
11 U.S.C. § 365(b)(1)(C)	§ 7.13
11 U.S.C. § 365(b)(2)	§§ 7.12, 7.15, 8.13
11 U.S.C. § 365(b)(3)	§§ 7.13, 8.16
11 U.S.C. § 365(c)	§§ 22.5, 22.6
11 U.S.C. § 365(c)(1)	§ 7.15
11 U.S.C. § 365(c)(2)	§§ 6.2, 7.15
11 U.S.C. § 365(d)	§ 2.25
11 U.S.C. § 365(d)(2)	§§ 7.2, 7.6, 7.7
11 U.S.C. § 365(d)(3)	§§ 2.25, 7.5, 7.18
11 U.S.C. § 365(d)(4)	§§ 7.7, 7.8, 7.18
11 U.S.C. § 365(e)	§ 22.5
11 U.S.C. § 365(e)(1)	§§ 7.12, 7.15
11 U.S.C. § 365(f)	§ 9.8
11 U.S.C. § 365(f)(2)(A)	§ 7.14
11 U.S.C. § 365(f)(2)(B)	§ 7.14
11 U.S.C. § 365(g)	§ 8.13
11 U.S.C. § 365(g)(1)	§ 7.18
11 U.S.C. § 365(h)	§ 7.2
11 U.S.C. § 365(i)	§ 7.2
11 U.S.C. § 365(k)	§§ 7.14, 8.14, 9.8
11 U.S.C. § 365*(l)*	§ 8.16

U.S.C. §	*Book §*
11 U.S.C. § 442	§ 10.14
11 U.S.C. § 443(a)(1)	§ 10.14
11 U.S.C. § 443(b)–(d)	§ 10.14
11 U.S.C. § 501	§§ 14.11, 15.20
11 U.S.C. § 501(a)	§ 15.3
11 U.S.C. § 502	§§ 8.13, 14.11, 15.7, 15.20
11 U.S.C. § 502(a)	§§ 8.4, 15.21
11 U.S.C. § 502(b)	§ 19.6
11 U.S.C. § 502(b)(3)	§ 3.7
11 U.S.C. § 502(b)(4)	§ 2.23
11 U.S.C. § 502(b)(6)	§§ 2.25, 7.18, 8.13
11 U.S.C. § 502(c)	§ 11.35
11 U.S.C. § 502(c)(1)	§ 15.21
11 U.S.C. § 502(d)	§ 12.33
11 U.S.C. § 502(e)	§ 11.35
11 U.S.C. § 502(g)–(i)	§ 14.11
11 U.S.C. § 502(h)	§ 12.14
11 U.S.C. § 503	§§ 7.5, 13.3, 14.9, 14.10, 14.11
11 U.S.C. § 503(b)	§§ 6.4, 6.30, 8.2, 10.5, 14.11, 24.8
11 U.S.C. § 503(b)(1)	§§ 2.18, 2.23, 6.30, 7.5, 7.9, 15.12
11 U.S.C. § 503(b)(1)(A)	§§ 6.3, 7.5
11 U.S.C. § 503(b)(2)	§§ 2.23, 2.24
11 U.S.C. § 503(b)(4)	§§ 2.23, 2.25
11 U.S.C. § 504	§ 2.16
11 U.S.C. § 504(a)	§ 2.23
11 U.S.C. § 504(b)(1)	§ 2.23
11 U.S.C. § 504(b)(2)	§ 2.23
11 U.S.C. § 506	§§ 3.7, 13.10, 13.20, 13.21
11 U.S.C. § 506(a)	§§ 3.7, 8.10, 11.1, 11.7, 11.18, 11.25, 12.28, 15.8
11 U.S.C. § 506(b)	§§ 2.23, 2.25
11 U.S.C. § 506(c)	§ 3.9
11 U.S.C. § 507	§§ 2.18, 2.23, 2.24, 12.2, 13.3, 19.4
11 U.S.C. § 507(a)(1)	§§ 2.24, 12.12, 13.20, 13.21, 14.9, 14.10, 14.11, 15.20
11 U.S.C. § 507(a)(2)	§§ 12.12, 15.20
11 U.S.C. § 507(a)(3)	§§ 12.12, 13.20, 13.21, 15.12
11 U.S.C. § 507(a)(4)	§§ 12.12, 15.12
11 U.S.C. § 507(a)(5)	§§ 13.20, 13.21, 15.12

U.S.C. §	*Book §*
11 U.S.C. § 507(a)(6)	§§ 12.12, 13.20, 13.21, 15.12
11 U.S.C. § 507(a)(7)	§§ 13.20, 13.21, 14.9, 14.10, 14.11, 15.20, 17.7
11 U.S.C. § 507(b)	§§ 3.10, 3.16, 6.4, 6.30
11 U.S.C. § 510	§§ 12.1, 12.2, 12.3, 12.28
11 U.S.C. § 510(a)	§§ 12.3, 12.35
11 U.S.C. § 510(b)	§§ 12.4, 12.35
11 U.S.C. § 510(c)	§§ 8.9, 12.5, 12.35
11 U.S.C. § 521(1)	§§ 10.4, 10.5, 14.9, 14.10, 14.11
11 U.S.C. § 522	§§ 10.14, 20.4
11 U.S.C. § 522(b)	§§ 20.6, 20.7
11 U.S.C. § 522(b)(1)	§ 20.3
11 U.S.C. § 522(b)(2)	§§ 20.3, 20.5
11 U.S.C. § 522(b)(2)(B)	§ 20.4
11 U.S.C. § 522(c)	§ 20.3
11 U.S.C. § 522(d)(2)	§ 20.10
11 U.S.C. § 522(d)(10)(E)	§§ 21.2, 21.6
11 U.S.C. § 522(e)	§§ 20.3, 20.5
11 U.S.C. § 522(f)	§§ 12.1, 20.6
11 U.S.C. § 522(f)(1)	§§ 20.6, 20.7, 20.8
11 U.S.C. § 522(f)(2)(A)–(C)	§ 20.6
11 U.S.C. § 522(k)	§ 10.5
11 U.S.C. § 522*(l)*	§ 20.5
11 U.S.C. § 523	§§ 1.12, 10.10
11 U.S.C. § 523(a)(1)(A)	§ 10.13
11 U.S.C. § 523(a)(2)	§§ 2.25, 18.4
11 U.S.C. § 523(a)(2)(B)	§ 2.25
11 U.S.C. § 523(a)(4)	§ 3.13
11 U.S.C. § 523(d)	§ 2.25
11 U.S.C. § 524(a)(2)	§ 17.1
11 U.S.C. § 524(a)(3)	§ 17.1
11 U.S.C. § 524(e)	§ 17.3
11 U.S.C. § 541	§§ 3.2, 20.2, 21.1, 22.7
11 U.S.C. § 541(a)	§§ 10.3, 22.4
11 U.S.C. § 541(a)(1)	§§ 20.2, 21.2
11 U.S.C. § 541(a)(5)	§ 20.2
11 U.S.C. § 541(a)(6)	§§ 14.11, 20.2
11 U.S.C. § 541(c)(1)	§§ 10.6, 21.2
11 U.S.C. § 541(c)(2)	§§ 20.2, 21.2, 21.4, 21.5, 21.6
11 U.S.C. § 541(d)	§ 12.8
11 U.S.C. § 542	§ 3.7
11 U.S.C. § 542(b)	§ 3.7
11 U.S.C. § 543	§ 2.25
11 U.S.C. §§ 544–550	§ 14.11

U.S.C. §	*Book §*
11 U.S.C. § 544	§§ 3.8, 3.9, 3.11, 12.1, 12.7, 12.8, 12.9, 12.23, 12.33, 12.35, 13.11, 18.10, 21.6
11 U.S.C. § 544(a)	§§ 3.9, 12.7, 12.8
11 U.S.C. § 544(a)(3)	§ 12.12
11 U.S.C. § 544(b)	§ 12.7
11 U.S.C. § 545	§§ 3.8, 3.9, 12.1, 12.9, 12.10, 12.11, 12.12, 12.35
11 U.S.C. § 545(1)	§ 12.11
11 U.S.C. § 545(2)	§ 12.12
11 U.S.C. § 546	§ 12.33
11 U.S.C. § 546(a)	§ 12.33
11 U.S.C. § 546(b)	§§ 3.8, 12.12
11 U.S.C. § 546(c)	§§ 3.4, 8.3
11 U.S.C. § 546(c)(1)	§ 8.3
11 U.S.C. § 547	§§ 3.9, 11.1, 12.1, 12.11, 12.14, 12.16, 12.21, 12.24, 12.28, 12.33, 13.11, 18.12, 22.8
11 U.S.C. § 547(a)(2)	§ 12.17
11 U.S.C. § 547(b)	§§ 2.4, 11.1, 11.19, 12.15, 12.21, 12.35
11 U.S.C. § 547(b)(2)	§ 12.17
11 U.S.C. § 547(b)(3)	§ 11.9
11 U.S.C. § 547(b)(4)(B)	§ 2.4
11 U.S.C. § 547(c)	§§ 12.15, 12.16, 12.20, 12.21
11 U.S.C. § 547(c)(1)	§ 12.17
11 U.S.C. § 547(c)(1)(A)	§ 12.17
11 U.S.C. § 547(c)(1)(B)	§ 12.17
11 U.S.C. § 547(c)(2)	§ 12.18
11 U.S.C. § 547(c)(5)	§ 11.1
11 U.S.C. § 547(c)(6)	§ 12.11, 12.19
11 U.S.C. § 547(e)	§ 12.15
11 U.S.C. § 547(e)(2)	§ 12.15
11 U.S.C. § 547(f)	§§ 11.19, 12.15, 12.24
11 U.S.C. § 548	§§ 3.9, 10.6, 12.1, 12.7, 12.21, 12.23, 12.24, 12.26, 12.33, 12.35, 13.11, 18.10, 18.12, 20.11, 22.8
11 U.S.C. § 548(a)	§ 22.8
11 U.S.C. § 548(a)(1)	§§ 12.24, 12.35
11 U.S.C. § 548(a)(2)	§§ 12.24, 12.25, 12.35
11 U.S.C. § 548(a)(2)(B)(i)	§ 11.9
11 U.S.C. § 548(b)	§ 22.8

U.S.C. §	*Book §*
11 U.S.C. § 727(a)(2)	§§ 3.13, 12.24, 20.12
11 U.S.C. § 727(a)(2)(H)	§ 20.12
11 U.S.C. § 727(a)(4)(B)	§ 20.5
11 U.S.C. § 727(a)(7)	§ 3.13
11 U.S.C. § 941	§ 13.20
11 U.S.C. § 1101(1)	§§ 7.1, 10.3
11 U.S.C. § 1101(2)	§ 17.4
11 U.S.C. § 1101(2)(A)	§ 17.4
11 U.S.C. § 1101(2)(C)	§ 17.4
11 U.S.C. § 1102	§§ 2.5, 18.5
11 U.S.C. § 1102(a)	§ 24.5
11 U.S.C. § 1102(a)(1)	§ 8.5
11 U.S.C. § 1102(b)(1)	§ 18.5
11 U.S.C. § 1103	§§ 2.2, 2.4, 2.8, 2.10, 2.14, 2.16, 14.11
11 U.S.C. § 1103(a)	§§ 2.5, 8.5
11 U.S.C. § 1103(b)	§ 2.5
11 U.S.C. § 1103(c)(1)	§ 8.5
11 U.S.C. § 1103(c)(2)	§ 8.5
11 U.S.C. § 1103(c)(3)	§ 8.5
11 U.S.C. § 1104	§§ 2.7, 3.13
11 U.S.C. § 1104(a)	§ 8.20
11 U.S.C. § 1104(a)(1)	§ 9.3
11 U.S.C. § 1104(b)	§ 8.20
11 U.S.C. § 1106(a)(1)	§ 13.6
11 U.S.C. § 1107	§§ 2.12, 8.2, 9.7, 9.8, 12.30, 15.15
11 U.S.C. § 1107(a)	§§ 3.3, 7.1, 13.6
11 U.S.C. § 1107(b)	§ 2.4
11 U.S.C. § 1108	§§ 2.12, 3.3, 7.1, 8.2, 9.7, 9.8
11 U.S.C. § 1109	§ 15.5
11 U.S.C. § 1109(b)	§§ 8.5, 17.6
11 U.S.C. § 1110	§ 7.2
11 U.S.C. § 1111(a)	§ 8.4
11 U.S.C. § 1111(b)	§§ 8.18, 15.8, 16.8
11 U.S.C. § 1111(b)(2)	§§ 14.11, 15.8, 15.15, 16.8
11 U.S.C. § 1112	§ 3.13
11 U.S.C. § 1112(b)	§§ 8.19, 17.5
11 U.S.C. § 1112(b)(2)	§ 8.19
11 U.S.C. § 1112(b)(6)–(10)	§ 17.5
11 U.S.C. § 1113	§ 7.2
11 U.S.C. § 1121	§§ 8.19, 24.5
11 U.S.C. § 1121(b)	§§ 8.17, 15.2, 16.2, 16.9, 19.3, 24.3, 24.5
11 U.S.C. § 1121(c)	§§ 8.17, 15.1, 16.9, 24.3, 24.5
11 U.S.C. § 1121(c)(1)	§ 8.20

U.S.C. §	*Book §*
11 U.S.C. § 1121(c)(3)	§ 15.1
11 U.S.C. § 1121(d)	§§ 8.17, 16.9, 24.4
11 U.S.C. § 1122	§§ 15.4, 17.4
11 U.S.C. § 1122(a)	§ 17.4
11 U.S.C. § 1122(b)	§ 15.21
11 U.S.C. § 1123	§§ 7.10, 17.4
11 U.S.C. § 1123(a)	§§ 14.2, 15.14
11 U.S.C. § 1123(a)(1)	§ 14.2
11 U.S.C. § 1123(a)(2)	§ 14.2
11 U.S.C. § 1123(a)(3)	§ 14.2
11 U.S.C. § 1123(a)(4)	§ 14.2
11 U.S.C. § 1123(a)(5)	§ 14.2
11 U.S.C. § 1123(a)(5)(B)	§ 9.1
11 U.S.C. § 1123(a)(5)(D)	§§ 9.1, 9.5, 16.9
11 U.S.C. § 1123(a)(5)(J)	§ 16.1
11 U.S.C. § 1123(b)	§§ 14.2, 15.14, 24.5
11 U.S.C. § 1123(b)(2)	§ 7.10
11 U.S.C. § 1123(b)(3)(B)	§ 15.22
11 U.S.C. § 1123(b)(4)	§ 9.1
11 U.S.C. § 1124	§§ 14.11, 15.20
11 U.S.C. § 1124(1)	§ 14.2
11 U.S.C. § 1125	§§ 13.1, 13.3, 13.16, 13.20, 13.21, 15.20, 16.9, 24.5
11 U.S.C. § 1125(a)	§ 8.17
11 U.S.C. § 1125(b)	§§ 8.17, 13.14, 15.3, 24.3
11 U.S.C. § 1126	§§ 12.3, 14.6
11 U.S.C. § 1126(a)	§ 15.7
11 U.S.C. § 1126(c)	§§ 15.7, 15.8, 15.20
11 U.S.C. § 1126(e)	§ 15.7
11 U.S.C. § 1126(f)	§§ 8.17, 15.7, 15.20
11 U.S.C. § 1126(g)	§§ 8.17, 15.7
11 U.S.C. § 1127	§§ 14.9, 14.10, 17.4
11 U.S.C. § 1127(b)	§§ 14.9, 14.10, 17.4
11 U.S.C. § 1129	§§ 5.6, 8.18, 8.19, 13.3, 13.20, 13.21, 15.1, 17.4, 17.5
11 U.S.C. § 1129(a)	§§ 8.17, 14.11, 15.1, 15.19, 16.2
11 U.S.C. § 1129(a)(1)	§§ 15.12, 15.20
11 U.S.C. § 1129(a)(2)	§§ 9.3, 15.12, 15.20
11 U.S.C. § 1129(a)(3)	§§ 10.13, 15.8, 15.12, 15.20
11 U.S.C. § 1129(a)(4)	§§ 2.11, 2.24, 15.12, 15.20
11 U.S.C. § 1129(a)(4)(A)	§§ 13.20, 13.21
11 U.S.C. § 1129(a)(5)	§ 15.12
11 U.S.C. § 1129(a)(7)	§§ 8.17, 12.12, 15.20, 22.9

U.S.C. §	*Book §*
11 U.S.C. § 1129(a)(7)(A)(ii)	§§ 15.11, 22.9
11 U.S.C. § 1129(a)(7)(B)	§ 14.6
11 U.S.C. § 1129(a)(8)	§§ 14.11, 15.20, 16.2
11 U.S.C. § 1129(a)(9)	§§ 13.4, 15.12, 15.20
11 U.S.C. § 1129(a)(9)(A)	§§ 2.24, 10.13
11 U.S.C. § 1129(a)(9)(C)	§ 13.3
11 U.S.C. § 1129(a)(10)	§§ 15.8, 15.20, 15.21
11 U.S.C. § 1129(a)(11)	§§ 8.17, 15.10, 15.20, 16.9
11 U.S.C. § 1129(a)(12)	§§ 15.12, 15.20
11 U.S.C. § 1129(b)	§§ 11.19, 11.31, 13.20, 15.1, 15.6, 15.13, 15.19, 16.1, 24.5
11 U.S.C. § 1129(b)(1)	§§ 14.3, 14.4, 15.13, 16.2
11 U.S.C. § 1129(b)(2)	§§ 14.3, 15.3, 15.15, 16.2
11 U.S.C. § 1129(b)(2)(A)	§§ 8.10, 13.3, 14.3, 15.10, 15.15
11 U.S.C. § 1129(b)(2)(A)(i)	§§ 11.8, 14.3, 14.4
11 U.S.C. § 1129(b)(2)(A)(i)(II)	§ 15.15
11 U.S.C. § 1129(b)(2)(A)(ii)	§ 14.3
11 U.S.C. § 1129(b)(2)(A)(iii)	§ 14.3
11 U.S.C. § 1129(b)(2)(B)	§§ 13.3, 14.6, 15.16, 16.1, 16.2
11 U.S.C. § 1129(b)(2)(B)(i)	§ 16.2
11 U.S.C. § 1129(b)(2)(B)(ii)	§§ 16.2, 16.9
11 U.S.C. § 1129(b)(2)(C)	§§ 13.3, 15.17
11 U.S.C. § 1129(c)	§ 15.19
11 U.S.C. § 1129(d)	§§ 10.13, 15.19
11 U.S.C. § 1141	§§ 2.19, 14.11, 15.20, 20.12
11 U.S.C. § 1141(a)	§ 15.23
11 U.S.C. § 1141(b)	§§ 10.13, 15.23, 17.1
11 U.S.C. § 1141(c)	§ 15.23
11 U.S.C. § 1141(d)	§ 15.23
11 U.S.C. § 1141(d)(1)	§ 17.1
11 U.S.C. § 1141(d)(1)(A)	§ 17.1
11 U.S.C. § 1142(b)	§ 17.2
11 U.S.C. § 1144	§§ 8.19, 9.6, 17.5, 17.6
11 U.S.C. § 1144(a)	§ 17.6
11 U.S.C. § 1201	§ 5.3
11 U.S.C. § 1203	§ 3.3
11 U.S.C. § 1204	§ 3.3
11 U.S.C. § 1207(a)(2)	§ 20.2
11 U.S.C. § 1222(a)(2)	§ 2.24
11 U.S.C. § 1225(b)	§ 16.10
11 U.S.C. § 1228	§ 20.12
11 U.S.C. § 1301	§ 5.3

U.S.C. §	*Book §*
11 U.S.C. § 1302	§ 19.3
11 U.S.C. § 1303	§ 19.5
11 U.S.C. § 1304	§§ 3.3, 19.5
11 U.S.C. § 1304(b)	§ 19.3
11 U.S.C. § 1304(c)	§ 19.3
11 U.S.C. § 1305(a)(2)	§ 20.2
11 U.S.C. § 1321	§ 19.3
11 U.S.C. § 1322	§§ 19.4, 19.6
11 U.S.C. § 1322(a)	§ 19.4
11 U.S.C. § 1322(a)(1)	§ 19.4
11 U.S.C. § 1322(a)(2)	§§ 2.24, 19.4
11 U.S.C. § 1322(b)(2)	§ 19.4
11 U.S.C. § 1322(b)(3)	§ 19.4
11 U.S.C. § 1322(b)(4)	§ 19.4
11 U.S.C. § 1322(b)(5)	§ 19.3
11 U.S.C. § 1322(b)(6)	§ 19.4
11 U.S.C. § 1322(b)(7)	§ 19.4
11 U.S.C. § 1322(c)	§ 19.3
11 U.S.C. § 1325	§§ 19.4, 19.6
11 U.S.C. § 1325(a)(1)–(6)	§ 19.4
11 U.S.C. § 1325(b)	§§ 16.10, 19.4
11 U.S.C. § 1325(b)(1)(A)	§ 19.4
11 U.S.C. § 1325(b)(1)(B)	§§ 19.4, 24.3
11 U.S.C. § 1325(c)	§ 19.4
11 U.S.C. § 1326(a)(1)	§ 19.3
11 U.S.C. § 1328	§ 20.12
11 U.S.C. § 1328(a)	§ 19.6
11 U.S.C. § 1478(b)	§ 5.4
18 U.S.C. § 152	§ 20.5
26 U.S.C. § 61(a)(3)	§ 10.6
26 U.S.C. § 61(a)(12)	§ 10.2
26 U.S.C. § 108	§ 10.13
26 U.S.C. § 108(a)(1)	§ 10.2
26 U.S.C. § 108(b)(1)	§ 10.13
26 U.S.C. § 108(b)(2)(A)	§ 10.13
26 U.S.C. § 108(b)(5)(A)	§ 10.13
26 U.S.C. § 108(b)(5)(B)	§ 10.13
26 U.S.C. § 111	§ 10.14
26 U.S.C. § 170(d)(1)	§ 10.14
26 U.S.C. § 172	§ 10.14
26 U.S.C. § 172(b)(1)(A)	§ 10.13
26 U.S.C. § 172(c)	§ 10.13
26 U.S.C. § 401(a)	§§ 20.3, 21.3
26 U.S.C. § 403(a)	§ 20.3
26 U.S.C. § 403(b)	§ 20.3
26 U.S.C. § 408	§ 20.3
26 U.S.C. § 409	§ 20.3

U.S.C. §	*Book §*
26 U.S.C. § 465	§ 14.11
26 U.S.C. §§ 671–678	§ 14.11
26 U.S.C. § 1001(a)	§ 10.2
26 U.S.C. § 1001(b)	§ 10.2
26 U.S.C. § 1011(a)	§ 10.2
26 U.S.C. § 1012	§ 10.2
26 U.S.C. § 1016	§ 10.2
26 U.S.C. § 1212	§ 10.14
26 U.S.C. § 1398	§§ 10.3, 10.5, 10.13, 10.14, 14.11
26 U.S.C. § 1398(a)	§ 10.3
26 U.S.C. § 1398(c)	§ 10.3
26 U.S.C. § 1398(d)(2)(A)	§ 10.13
26 U.S.C. § 1398(f)(1)	§§ 10.3, 10.9
26 U.S.C. § 1398(f)(2)	§§ 10.3, 10.5, 10.9, 10.11
26 U.S.C. § 1398(g)	§§ 10.9, 10.13
26 U.S.C. § 1398(g)(6)	§ 10.3
26 U.S.C. § 1398(i)	§ 10.9
26 U.S.C. § 6323(a)	§ 12.12
26 U.S.C. § 6323(b)(1)	§ 12.12
26 U.S.C. § 6323(b)(2)	§ 12.12
26 U.S.C. § 6323(b)(3)	§ 12.12
26 U.S.C. § 7703	§ 10.14
28 U.S.C. § 123	§ 17.5
28 U.S.C. § 151	§§ 23.2, 23.15
28 U.S.C. § 157	§§ 6.29, 6.30, 8.8, 8.9, 9.8, 23.5, 23.13, 23.24
28 U.S.C. § 157(a)	§§ 23.2, 23.3
28 U.S.C. § 157(b)	§ 23.15
28 U.S.C. § 157(b)(1)	§ 23.2
28 U.S.C. § 157(b)(2)	§§ 6.29, 9.8
28 U.S.C. § 157(b)(2)(A)	§ 9.7
28 U.S.C. § 157(b)(2)(G)	§§ 8.8, 8.9
28 U.S.C. § 157(b)(2)(N)	§ 9.7
28 U.S.C. § 157(b)(2)(O)	§ 9.7
28 U.S.C. § 157(c)(1)	§§ 23.2, 23.6
28 U.S.C. § 157(c)(2)	§ 23.2
28 U.S.C. § 157(d)	§ 23.7
28 U.S.C. § 158	§§ 23.22, 23.27
28 U.S.C. § 158(a)	§§ 23.22, 23.23
28 U.S.C. §§ 581–589(a)	§ 23.2
28 U.S.C. § 586(a)(3)(H)	§ 2.10
28 U.S.C. § 1334	§§ 6.29, 8.8, 8.9, 9.7, 9.8, 23.12, 23.13
28 U.S.C. § 1334(a)	§ 23.2
28 U.S.C. § 1334(b)	§§ 23.2, 23.3
28 U.S.C. § 1334(c)	§ 23.8

U.S.C. §	*Book §*
28 U.S.C. § 1334(c)(1)	§ 23.10
28 U.S.C. § 1334(c)(2)	§§ 23.9, 23.11
28 U.S.C. § 1408	§§ 6.29, 9.8, 23.17
28 U.S.C. § 1408(2)	§ 23.17
28 U.S.C. § 1409	§§ 6.29, 9.7, 9.8, 23.18
28 U.S.C. § 1409(b)–(e)	§ 23.18
28 U.S.C. § 1411	§ 23.15
28 U.S.C. § 1412	§§ 23.19, 23.20
28 U.S.C. § 1441	§ 23.12
28 U.S.C. § 1452	§§ 23.12, 23.13, 23.14
28 U.S.C. § 1478(b)	§ 23.12
28 U.S.C. § 1480	§ 23.15
28 U.S.C. § 1927	§ 2.26
28 U.S.C. § 1930	§§ 14.9, 14.10, 15.20
28 U.S.C. § 1930(a)	§ 6.30
28 U.S.C. § 1930(a)(6)	§§ 6.23, 6.29
28 U.S.C. § 1930(b)	§ 6.30
28 U.S.C. § 2256	§ 23.2
28 U.S.C. § 2412(d)	§ 2.25
29 U.S.C. §§ 1000–1461	§ 20.2
29 U.S.C. § 1003(a)	§ 21.3
29 U.S.C. § 1003(b)	§ 21.3

INDEX

www.ingramcontent.com/pod-product-compliance
Lightning Source LLC
LaVergne TN
LVHW082007200926
848481LV00010B/2819